Treat this book with care and re[...]

*It should become part of your personal
and professional library. It will
serve you well at any number
of points during your
professional career.*

Business
Its Nature and Environment
An Introduction

Eighth Edition

RAYMOND E. GLOS, Ph.D., C.P.A.

Dean Emeritus
School of Business Administration
Miami University
Oxford, Ohio

RICHARD D. STEADE, Ph.D.

Professor of Management
College of Business
Colorado State University
Fort Collins, Colorado

JAMES R. LOWRY, Ph.D.

Head, Department of Marketing
Ball State University
Muncie, Indiana

Published by

G72   **SOUTH-WESTERN PUBLISHING CO.**

CINCINNATI   WEST CHICAGO, ILL.   DALLAS   PELHAM MANOR, N.Y.   PALO ALTO, CALIF.   BRIGHTON, ENGLAND

Preface

This 8th edition of *Business: Its Nature and Environment — An Introduction* is more than a routine revision. Two of the three of us who have written this text are new authors, which is the first change in authorship since the 1st edition appeared in 1947. Despite the similarity in many chapter titles to those in the 7th edition, we believe that each reflects new thoughts, new ideas, and new emphasis.

In addition to a fresh look at materials covered in previous editions, the change in emphasis to reflect social and environmental concerns, which was stressed in the last edition, has been expanded. Two new chapters have been added. One of these, Marketing and Consumer Issues, examines the growing influence of the buying public and the effect consumerism is having on business practices. The last chapter in the text, Futurism and Business, gives consideration to foreseeable changes that in some instances will take place even before today's freshmen become college graduates.

Despite the addition of two new chapters, the total number has remained at the 7th edition level of 29. The chapters formerly devoted to short-term and long-term financing have been combined, and the chapter on budgeting and forecasting has been eliminated although a portion of its content appears in other chapters. The comprehensive case in Appendix B is new with this edition. Another change has been the addition at the beginning of each chapter of a brief narrative describing an actual or fictitious situation relevant to the chapter topic. We believe this device will enhance the student's interest in the copy that follows.

For the first time this text recognizes that business activities in this country are carried on by businesspersons rather than by businessmen. The growing importance of women in the business world, aided by their own efforts as well as legislation, is reflected in the text copy. It is hoped that in the interest of fairness to both sexes the former male bias has been eliminated.

A major change has been made in the organization of supplementary materials that accompany this text. The manual for teachers, in addition to its former coverage, now includes answers to incidents and problems contained in the student supplement and suggested examination questions and answers. We believe instructors will welcome this reduction in the number of separate items. Also, the manual includes the listing of suggested readings that formerly appeared in the text.

The authors are enthusiastic about the value of a beginning business course designed primarily for freshmen at the collegiate level. In our opinion such a course can achieve the following objectives:

1. For both nonbusiness and business majors, it provides a knowledge of what business is all about. For the students enrolled in other majors, it is a general education course that should eliminate illiteracy about an area vital to every person's day-to-day living. For fledgling business majors, it provides an overview of all areas of business that will prove invaluable when he or she subsequently enrolls in courses in such specific areas as marketing, finance, management, etc. These segments are more meaningful when they can be fitted into the unified framework provided by an introductory business course.
2. Students acquire a business vocabulary. As a result, reading newspapers and magazines or listening to radio or television becomes more meaningful. The course provides a first exposure to many new terms, some of which will be remembered and, by the end of the course, will become a part of the student's vocabulary. Other terms will require the reinforcement that business majors will receive in subsequent courses.
3. It explains capitalism and how it functions, which apparently is not very well understood by a large segment of our population. Students will become informed citizens who can do much to prevent the erosion of a system that has brought to this country the highest standard of living the world has ever known.
4. It brings into focus the conflicting demands made on business by such diverse groups as owners, employees, suppliers, customers, government, and the general public. The student has an opportunity to appreciate the conflict with profit-seeking activities brought about by the desire or requirement that business discharge its social and environmental responsibilities.
5. Students can gain an understanding of the decision-making process in business. Furthermore, after studying the descriptive material, they can acquire some meaningful experience in making decisions using the questions, problems, and cases provided.
6. A first course provides a great deal of information about employment opportunities in business. By direction and indirection, many types of jobs are described or suggested throughout the text. This objective can be reinforced by instructors who wish to emphasize vocational information by the use of Appendix A.
7. Finally, but not the least among the objectives, an introductory business course can be interesting and fascinating to students. Compared to many areas of knowledge, business is more dynamic and more relevant.

The authors believe that these objectives can be achieved within the confines of a college course, and that they can best be accomplished by the use of a text that surveys all of the major functions of business with a description of each. Although we are vitally interested in the ability of students to apply knowledge to specific problems, we believe that at the freshmen level a fundamental knowledge about business is a basic necessity. Consequently, we do not apologize for the application of such terms as descriptive and encyclopedic to this text. We do not believe our objectives can be accomplished as efficiently by any other approach.

Our thanks go to the many instructors who have used previous editions and have taken the time and interest to write their suggestions for changes and improvements. A number of businesses have provided illustrative materials and their permission to reproduce these is appreciated. We wish, particularly, to take this opportunity to express our heartfelt gratitude to Dr. Harold A. Baker, a coauthor of the first seven editions, for his valuable contributions, and to wish him well in his retirement years. Our thanks also go to Mr. Joel J. Lerner, Chairman of the Division of Business, Sullivan County Community College, Loch Sheldrake, New York, who provided the manuscript for the transparency masters.

R. E. G.
R. D. S.
J. R. L.

Contents

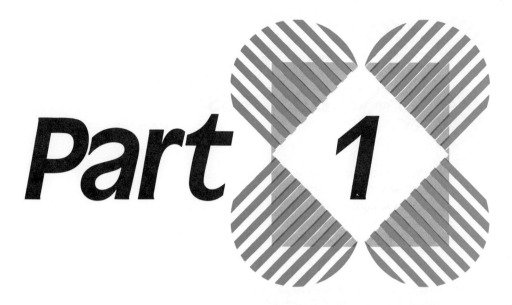

Part 1

Business and Society

Business is a key institution in our society. It is the activating element in our capitalistic enterprise system — the means through which the United States has achieved great economic progress in its relatively short history. In fulfilling this role, business performs in accordance with the expectations of the larger society of which it is a part. Thus, today's manager is faced with the exciting and challenging demands of anticipating and providing the needs of people while remaining responsive to the goals and expectations of other elements in the society.

Chapter 1 examines the three elements comprising the enterprise system: our capitalistic economic system, constitutional democracy, and the social institution of business itself. Profit and competition are recognized as necessary and justifiable phenomena in a capitalistic economy. A brief discussion of socialism and communism helps students to identify the major points of difference between those systems and capitalism.

In Chapter 2 the relationship between business and its environment is noted as one of mutuality; business influences its environment and, in turn, forces in the environment exert pressures on business. In particular, this chapter deals with the social, economic, political, physical, and technical factors that are vital forces in the changing business scene.

The pluralistic nature of our society and the resulting feeling that corporations must accept the responsibility that goes with their position of leadership and power in society are discussed in Chapter 3. It is suggested that business demonstrates its fitness to be the trustee of our nation's resources by the way it responds to at least two major elements in its environment: the social and the physical.

The Nature of Business

Kim Collin's social science teacher took every opportunity to characterize businesspersons as second-class citizens engaged in the single-minded pursuit of money and material self-interest. After one such discourse, Kim got her courage up and stated that her father worked long hours in his farm supply business; performed a needed function in the community; and had a reputation for fair dealing. "You're confusing the basic issue," the teacher retorted. "Any businessperson is motivated by only one factor — profit! Businesspersons can make profits only when they pursue self-seeking goals." Kim resented this. She felt, instead, that her father earned profits because he worked hard and was honest in his dealings.

Business is a primary social institution in our society. It is defined as the sum total of the organized efforts by which the people engaged in commerce and industry provide the goods and services needed to maintain and improve the standard of living and quality of life to which each of us may aspire.

The purpose of this book is to consider systematically how business combines human, material, and capital resources as it strives to earn a profit by anticipating and satisfying the needs and wants of the people in our society and throughout the world.

In a complex economy such as ours, someone must accept the challenge and the risk to bring labor, materials, and capital together before a single gallon of milk can be marketed or a single automobile produced. In our society that function rests with the businessperson. The owner of a lumber mill has to make various types of lumber as efficiently as possible in the amounts and varieties needed. A trucker is supposed to move goods quickly from places where they are not needed to where they are needed. When a businessperson operates a retail store, the function of the store is to make a variety of goods available at a price the consumer is willing to pay. And these are only a few examples of the almost limitless business activities in our complex market enterprises.

OUR ENTERPRISE SYSTEM

At this point an expansion of the definition of business is in order, for business does not stand alone as a clearly defined entity in our society. Business is the activating element in our enterprise system. But the **enterprise system** also results from a combination of (1) the nature of our capitalistic economic system, (2) constitutional democracy, and (3) the social institution of business itself. Figure 1-1 illustrates this relationship. Each of these major elements will be considered in order to appreciate the basic factors that help to shape our enterprise system into the dynamic force that it is today.

The Nature of Capitalism

Capitalism is an economic system in which individuals with comparative freedom from external restraint produce goods and services for public consumption under conditions of competition and with private profit or gain as the principal motivating force. These goods and services move from producers to consumers by means of an exchange (or sales) procedure in which the

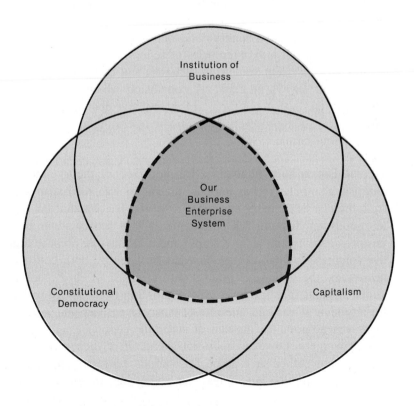

Figure 1-1 **Elements in Our Business Enterprise System**

common medium of payment is usually money or some acceptable substitute for it, such as credit.

ECONOMIC CONCEPTS OF CAPITALISM

For many years economists, who study the operation of economic systems, have developed various theories designed to explain the operation of capitalism. These theories have ranged from explanations of the functioning of capitalism as an organic whole (**macroeconomics**) to a consideration of the decisions to be made by individual firms with regard to prices and profits (**microeconomics**). Many theories exist, but only two basic economic models that have influenced the fiscal policies of the federal government will be briefly discussed here: (1) the classical theory of capitalism, and (2) the income-expenditure or "Neo-Keynesian" model.

The Classical Theory. The older of the two, the **classical theory of capitalism,** makes the following assumptions: (a) normally there is full employment of labor, and if this condition does not exist, it is only a temporary deviation; (b) all income from the production of goods and services will be spent immediately to buy the current goods and services required, or invested in capital goods such as materials, machinery, and buildings, and consumer goods that are destined to be put into inventories of sellers; and (c) the production of goods creates an equivalent amount of demand, and therefore aggregate supply and demand will always be equal. A conclusion which the classical theory propounds, then, is that the forces of supply and demand, together with investment, are adequate to keep the economy operating at its highest level and in a state of equilibrium.

Income-Expenditure Analysis. The more recent theory, **income-expenditure analysis,** also is known as **national income** or **Neo-Keynesian theory.** It differs from the classical theory in several respects. It holds that the economy can be in equilibrium without full employment. This theory states that the level of business activity and also of employment at any one point in time is based on the volume of demand for goods and services by both consumers and businesses and the volume of investment by businesses in economic goods of all kinds. Inasmuch as the level of consumption is presumed to be fairly steady for any level of income, the rate of business activity and the level of employment depend upon the amount of investment.

Consumers, however, may not spend all of their incomes for goods and services but rather save some for various reasons. This tends not only to reduce consumption but, unless the savings are invested in economic goods, also tends to lower the investment rate. Therefore, it is held that if the rate of consumption, and particularly the rate of investment, is not great enough to insure relatively full employment, government spending must provide the additional expenditures necessary to raise the level of employment.

Income-expenditure analysis follows the reasoning of a famous English economist, John Maynard Keynes, who proposed that the federal government should embark on a program of spending to stimulate the recovery of an economy. Since the end of World War II, the theories of Keynes have achieved even greater attention. The persistently high level of business activity, with a few minor deviations, is largely credited to the fact that the federal government, guided to a considerable extent by economists, has adopted policies that have permitted businesses and consumers to take those steps likely to keep the economy in high gear.

For example, the Employment Act of 1946, a federal law sometimes referred to as the **full employment act,** placed upon the federal government the responsibility for taking such measures as seem advisable to maintain the economic health of the nation. It established a Federal Council of Economic Advisers to "develop and recommend to the President national economic policies to foster and promote free competitive enterprise, to avoid economic fluctuations or to diminish the effects thereof, and to maintain maximum employment, production, and purchasing power." The Council prepares an Annual Economic Review for the President, who transmits an Economic Report to the Congress.

In the present period of combined inflation and recession, neither the classical view of the "monetarists" nor the "new economics" of Keynesian theorists seems to have the needed answers. To the classical economist recession is a natural cure for inflation in a free market system. Any attempt to check the recession will interfere with the market mechanisms and prolong the agony of readjustment. Likewise, Keynesian economics are seen as depression-oriented and thus unsuitable for dealing with today's problems of inflation, recession, and shortages. And both schools of thinking are not able to divorce "pure" economic reasoning from the politics and emotions of unemployment and general social unrest.

MODIFIED CAPITALISM

Capitalism in its purest form is what emerges in a situation of freedom in decision and action. This type of capitalism is often called **laissez-faire,** a French term that signifies noninterference by government in the conduct of business by individual businesspersons and firms. American business in the earlier years of its existence probably typified laissez-faire capitalism to a considerable extent. In recent years, however, the increase in restraints by government upon business has been such that our economy is frequently referred to as a "modified capitalism." In fact, since the early 1930s the trend toward the abridgment of freedom in many phases of business has been a notable aspect of the twentieth century. There is reason to believe that this trend will continue particularly with regard to the federal government. Vigorous enforcement of antitrust laws, pollution laws, the Civil Rights Act of 1964, minimum-wage laws, and the growing power of governmental agencies, such as the Federal Trade Commission, support this trend.

Regardless of the growing impact of governmental policies and practices on our enterprise system, capitalism still offers to a large degree the opportunity for freedom, participation, and progress. Capitalism is based on relationships of a mutually supportive nature, and these provide the foundation for productive, innovative business activity in our society. There are three major groups of factors that underpin capitalism: the basic freedoms of capitalism, the role of individuals in capitalism, and the key functions in a capitalistic economy.

THE BASIC FREEDOMS OF CAPITALISM

The basic freedoms of capitalism are: (1) private property, (2) private enterprise, and (3) freedom of choice.

Private Property. Capitalism can operate only where the institution of **private property** prevails. This means that individuals and business firms have the right to purchase, own, and sell property of all kinds, including land, buildings, machinery, and equipment. It also implies that businesspersons have the right to ownership of the goods which they produce and to any profits which may come about through the sale of these goods.

Private Enterprise. The second important freedom of capitalism is **private enterprise,** which means that most business ventures in this country are owned by individuals who have invested their own funds in businesses of their own choosing, from which they hope to realize gains (or profits). This is true regardless of the size of the companies. Large enterprises, such as General Motors Corporation, Exxon Corporation, and the General Electric Company, as well as such small businesses as a hardware store or a barbershop, are all private enterprises. In no sense are they public or government projects such as the United States Postal Service, police and fire departments, county homes, and the Tennessee Valley Authority.

Even though a corporation must go through certain routine formalities to secure a charter to conduct its business, it is still a private enterprise. In granting a charter the state does not enter into partnership with the corporation, does not supply any of the capital, and does not agree to share in any of the losses that may be suffered. The state ordinarily cannot require that the concern applying for a charter show that there is any need for its being brought into existence, or refuse a charter if such proof is not forthcoming.

Thus, this characteristic of capitalism, private enterprise, pertains to ownership and indicates that business is owned by private individuals rather than by public bodies such as federal, state, or local governments.

Freedom of Choice. An outstanding feature of capitalism, especially in a country with a democratic form of government, is **freedom of choice** in economic actions. In our country businesspersons are free to choose the field of business in which they will engage and to combine the factors of land, labor, capital, and management to generate profits as they see fit, so long as they conform to the laws and goals of society. Businesspersons may also choose their customers with almost complete freedom. Workers are at liberty to choose the jobs that they wish, in the trades they prefer, and with the companies that offer them the best deal for their efforts. Consumers are free to buy the goods and services they wish because there is no compulsion for them either to purchase or not. This freedom of choice is found at all economic levels; the chief limiting factor, as a general rule, is that of the financial resources of the individuals themselves, and sometimes it is racial or ethnic discrimination.

A variant of the concept of freedom of choice is **freedom of contract.** This means that individuals or firms are free to enter into contracts that call for the performance of services or the delivery of goods in accordance with their own best judgments, provided that there is no violation of law involved. Likewise, they may decline to enter such contracts on the same basis.

THE ROLE OF INDIVIDUALS IN CAPITALISM

Four groups of individuals play essential roles in capitalism: (1) entrepreneurs, (2) managers, (3) workers, and (4) consumers.

Entrepreneurs. The term applied to the individual or group who engages in business under the capitalistic system is entrepreneur. This is a French word for which no completely accurate or satisfactory counterpart exists in the English language. The word "enterpriser," a fairly literal translation, is seldom used.

An **entrepreneur** may be regarded as the one who, having the necessary capital or being able to secure it, enters some area of business in which he or she believes that there is an opportunity for profit. Subject to certain outside influences, such as competition, laws, government action, and chance, entrepreneurs manage their businesses as they wish and are willing, at least tacitly, to accept the risk of loss. They know that the more efficiently they can operate their businesses, the larger will be their profits and the better their chances of surviving competitively. The entrepreneur thus is seen as the prime initiator of all economic activity in a capitalistic system.

The entrepreneurial functions may be performed by a single individual in the form of a sole proprietorship or by several individuals, either as a partnership, corporation, or some other form of business ownership.

Among the critics of our economic system are those who would substitute some measure of governmental ownership and operation of certain types of business enterprise for private entrepreneurship. This is particularly true in the field of public utilities, notably the generation and distribution of electric power. However, the government is neither equipped nor intended to assume the risks of enterprise; nor are the incentives to more efficient operation present when the government runs a business.

Managers. The individuals charged with the responsibility of operating business enterprises profitably are commonly referred to as **managers.** The total managerial staff is referred to as the **management.** In the earlier days of business in this country, the owners were also the management, a circumstance that is still found in small-scale firms. In most of the larger companies, however, particularly those with great numbers of stockholders (or owners), the managers are individuals who may not own any stock in the companies that they operate. Managers in these instances are salaried persons whose incentives for the efficient direction of the enterprises with which they are connected come from the expectation of higher salaries and possibly job security, rather than from profits.

The importance of professional managers in the setting of American capitalism can scarcely be overemphasized. The decisions made by managers acting either as owners or as top-ranking employees are vital to the successful functioning of our economic system. This has become increasingly apparent in recent years as many business firms have grown markedly in sales, number of employees, variety of products, physical plants, and financial requirements. Indeed, some students of American business believe the further growth of many of these companies will be limited by their ability to discover and develop managers capable of successfully directing these enterprises.

Despite the complexity of our enterprise system, the role of business managers is relatively clear. They occupy formal positions of responsibility and must behave according to the expectations of society to justify these positions of trust. Regardless of other demands on business, the primary expectation of society is that business managers will effectively and efficiently operate the complex business mechanism by which a person's needs are met. This provides the business manager with great challenge, opportunity, and potential satisfaction.

Workers. Capitalism depends upon a large group of individual workers who must perform the actual physical and mental labor necessary to produce all the many and varied goods and services available. The worker group includes the skilled, semiskilled, and unskilled. **Workers** may be defined as those who have no formal authority over other workers; as soon as an individual achieves control over other workers, that individual ceases to be a worker and becomes part of management.

Workers, however, are not helpless pawns in the capitalistic system. They are free to move from one company to another if they believe the move may better their situation. Their right to form unions to protect their interests and improve their economic status is established by law.

Consumers. The role of the consumer in a capitalistic economy is a dual one. In the first place, every individual is a consumer. Each one of us needs the basic necessities of life. Upward from this lowest point of consumption are various levels of consumption. Any modern economic system such as capitalism exists for the primary purpose of providing goods and services required by the consumers who are a part of it. Consumer demand for the products of the system determines the success or the failure of the individual firms that comprise the economic organization of the country and, to a considerable degree, the level of business activity in the nation. **Consumer demand** may be defined as the desire for goods and services coupled with the requisite purchasing power.

The critics of capitalism today often charge that a few people benefit at the expense of the masses — that for one group to gain, the others must lose. Figure 1-2 refutes this belief; it reveals that each group of individuals in our society is involved in this meaningful economic activity and benefits from this involvement.

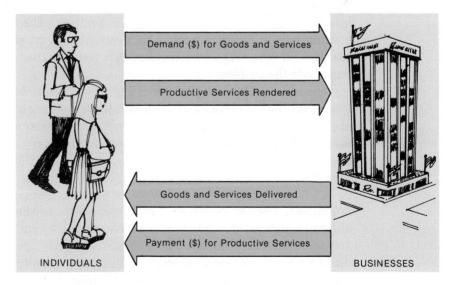

Figure 1-2 **The Circular Flow of Economic Activity**

In order that people may consume goods in our economic system, they must possess purchasing power. In most instances this purchasing power is gained when the person is paid for doing something (producing, in the broad sense of the term), whether the payment is in the form of wages, rent, profits, or other types of income. The consumer thus emerges in a second role — that of a producer. For various reasons, some historic and some psychological, consumers have generally thought of themselves as producers first and consumers second. In their attempts to better their economic status (either singly or in groups such as labor unions), consumers have customarily sought greater rewards in their roles as producers, such as higher wages, rather than striving to achieve the same objectives through the improvement of their positions as consumers through more prudent purchasing. Business and government are also end purchasers of goods and services, absorbing about one third of the total, but they are customarily placed in a separate category from that of consumers.

OTHER KEY FACTORS IN A CAPITALISTIC ECONOMY

A number of additional factors are essential to understanding the operation of our capitalistic enterprise system: (1) capital, (2) production, (3) distribution, (4) price, (5) competition, (6) risk, and (7) profit.

Capital. Capital can best be understood in terms of its two forms — capital goods and capital funds. **Capital goods** consist of such things as tools, equipment, buildings, fixtures, patents, and land, as well as raw materials in the process of manufacture and merchandise for sale. **Capital funds** refer to money that is available from individual savers or from groups through savings institutions for investment in business enterprises. The capital needed by a business may be obtained through the investment of the entrepreneur, by borrowing from others, and by using the funds resulting from business profits and retained in the business.

The owners of capital, known as capitalists, contribute their resources to a business either as owners or creditors. If they assume the risks of entrepreneurship, they are interested in profits; if as creditors, in interest on their investment. It is probable that the term "capitalism" owes its origin and meaning to its dependence upon the decisions and actions of the owners of capital.

Production. Used in its broadest economic sense, **production** means the furnishing by the entrepreneur of some economically valuable goods or services that are to be sold to others. Economists commonly speak of production as the creation of utilities. Production in this sense includes not only the manufacture of such products as automobiles, food, radios, and so on, but also their transportation and their distribution at wholesale and retail.

10

In its narrower and more common business usage, production refers to the physical manufacture of goods, whether this be a simple extractive process, such as lumbering or mining, or the highly complex types necessary to produce rubber tires, washing machines, and electrical appliances. It is in this latter sense that production will be used in this text.

Distribution of Goods. The ways by which the output of production is made available to its users, the consumers, are regarded as **distribution.** From the standpoint of the capitalistic system, the entrepreneur in distribution is one who seeks profit by providing the facilities whereby products may reach their destination. Similar to the entrepreneur in production, the entrepreneur in distribution will use the factors of land, labor, capital, and management in combinations that will best meet society's needs and produce a profit.

Price. Under capitalism the movement of goods from the producer to the consumer takes place on an exchange basis; or to use the customary phrase, a sale takes place. The buyer gives something of value to the seller in exchange for the goods that the seller has available for sale. In our economy this "something of value" is usually money, our medium of exchange; and the amount of money for which a good or service is exchanged is the **price.**

Over a period of time the prices that sellers receive presumably will be high enough to cover their costs of doing business and yield them desired profits. If prices are too low, the sellers will supposedly withdraw from their present business and enter more profitable fields. On the other hand, it is presumed that the prices that the buyers will pay over a period of time must at least equal the satisfaction or usefulness that they will receive from the purchase of the goods. If prices are too high, buyers will withhold their purchases or transfer them to other, lower-priced goods.

Competition. Under capitalism the entrepreneurs in each line of business compete with each other in the sale of their products or services. Thus, **competition** is basic to the capitalistic system. The institution of free private enterprise implies freedom on the part of any entrepreneur to enter business and to compete for the customers of the established firms. However, a range of competitive models, discussed in the following paragraphs, exists in theory and practice.

Pure Competition. Early economists pursued the concept of **pure competition.** Four criteria were assumed under this concept: (a) a large number of sellers are in the market, all selling an identical product; (b) all buyers and sellers are completely informed about all markets and prices; (c) buyers and sellers move freely in and out of the market; and (d) no individual buyer or seller is able to influence the price, which is determined by supply and demand, or the total actions of all buyers and sellers. Under these assumptions competition was based solely on price. Over a period of time it became evident that, except for a few farm products such as wheat, corn, and soybeans, pure competition simply did not exist. Eventually supplanting it was the theory of **imperfect competition** which can be classified into oligopoly and monopolistic competition.

Oligopoly and Monopolistic Competition. A market situation in which comparatively few firms produce identical or similar products and where individual firms have the ability to influence price is known as an **oligopoly.** Major steel companies form an oligopoly. **Monopolistic competition** assumes that there are many makers of goods with identical end usage who brand their products to differentiate them from those of their competitors. The producers of these branded goods, such as motor oils, hope to convince consumers that their products are different from and presumably better than those of their competitors in some important aspect to prevent comparison of their goods with similar wares of other manufacturers. Through this practice producers endeavor to create a "brand loyalty" among consumers, so that they may avoid the rigors of strict price competition. The large number of different brands to be found among consumer goods supports this theory.

Innovistic Competition. To some extent, **innovistic competition** deemphasizes the role of price and stresses instead customer convenience and novelty, both in goods and the places where they may be purchased. It is a dynamic type of competition that threatens the status quo of many historic competitive practices in the area of consumer goods. "Hobie Cat" catamaran sailboats are an example of innovistic competition. Many observers believe that innovistic competition will be the rule in the foreseeable future.

There is, however, a strong conviction that price will continue to retain its preeminence as a base for competition, despite the inroads of innovation, service, convenience, prestige, and reputation. But it should be recognized that despite the lip service that is paid to competition by businesspersons, the fact of the matter is that many of them like it only when it applies to other individuals and businesses. They want the sellers from whom they buy to compete in order that the prices which they have to pay may be as low as possible; and they likewise desire competition among their buyers in order that they may sell at higher prices. But they do not care for a competitive situation into which they themselves must fit.

Risk. Risk is always present in private enterprise. Of greatest importance is the risk of complete failure — of bankruptcy — in which case the entrepreneur stands to lose all that has been invested. A sole proprietor or partner also may lose personal property and savings. This risk is apt to be greater with a new business than with a well-established one. A similar danger exists, however, when an old concern fails to keep abreast of the times and loses customers to newer, more alert competitors.

At all times a firm must be aware of the risks that are inherent in competition: chances of loss through shifts in the price level; changes in style and fashion; the appearance of substitutes on the market that sometimes render present models obsolete; and changes in the desirability of business locations, distribution methods, and public demand. All these must be accepted by entrepreneurs as integral parts of capitalism. Their success or failure in business will depend on their ability to meet the situations surrounding and creating these hazards.

Profit. Profit comes last in the discussion of key factors in capitalism because it relates importantly to each of the other factors. For all practical purposes business **profit** is defined as the earnings that remain in a firm after the costs of its operations have been deducted. But this definition does not capture the real importance of profit; if the key factors developed here are primary building blocks in capitalism, profit is the mortar that holds these blocks together.

The anticipation of profit provides the motivation to owners or creditors to invest in private enterprise. Production and distribution could not continue to grow without the reinvestment of earnings or profit in plant, equipment, and human resources. Low profits stifle plant expansion in three ways: (a) by making it harder for business to borrow money and sell equity shares, (b) by cutting back on the money directly available for expansion, and (c) by inhibiting decisions to invest in new plant and equipment because the expected returns will not justify the cost. Without the possibility of gain the business owner or manager would not be willing to face the rigors of competition that, in fact, benefit society. In summation, the expectation of profit and the fear of loss provide incentives for effective management.

Constitutional Democracy

Capitalism is an economic, not a political, system. Capitalism flourishes best, however, in a country with a democratic rather than a totalitarian form of government. **Totalitarianism** is distinguished by its use of state power to impose an official ideology on its citizens; and nonconformity of opinion is treated as resistance or opposition to the government. The political party thus becomes the vehicle of social control.

Constitutional democracy, on the other hand, provides for periodic elections with a free choice of candidates, decision by majority vote with protection of minority rights, constitutional safeguards for basic civil liberties, and provisions for fixed limitations on the exercise of power.

ECONOMIC GROWTH AND THE CONSTITUTION

After the Revolutionary War, interstate trade and foreign trade were hindered by state-imposed tariff duties on goods. These duties were a key source of revenue for some states and penalized merchants while benefiting "back-country" farming interests by holding down their taxes. These tariffs also stood in the way of a Continental revenue duty needed to pay off public debt and as a bargaining tool for foreign trade concessions.

The Constitution of the United States drawn up in Philadelphia in 1787 was a victory for businesspersons and lawyers, such as Alexander Hamilton, James Madison, and Robert and Gouverneur Morris, who wanted to provide a stable and supportive environment for the ownership of private property and the building of trade and manufacturing.

CONSTITUTIONAL SUPPORT OF BUSINESS

The Constitution was written with provisions to restrain tariffs and taxes on interstate trade, state issuance of currency, and any federal taxation on bases other than population. Also, uniform bankruptcy laws were established, and the rights of authors and inventors to copyrights and patents were recognized. Perhaps the most basic and necessary clause is Amendment V to the Constitution which states, in part, that the federal government shall not deprive any person of life, liberty, or property without due process of law.

These Constitutional provisions helped set the stage for American business growth. Federal trade tariffs provided revenue and the means to protect our infant industries. The federal issuance of money allowed the starting of a strong central banking system and the governmental backing of public debt. Both provisions served to reinvite foreign investment in America.

A BALANCED RELATIONSHIP

Clearly, business enterprise in our capitalistic system has never experienced a true laissez-faire, "hands-off" stance from government. Equally clear, however, is the point that a capitalistic enterprise system requires a balanced working relationship with a strong, stable government. This is true with regard to the enforcement of contracts and the protection of property rights by a stable and vigorous government. Also, saving, investment, and risk-taking are encouraged when the power of government is not imposed arbitrarily or capriciously on the system, as is often the case in autocratic, totalitarian countries.

Business as a Social Institution

Business is a major **institution** in our society; its values and consequences are accepted as an important and fundamental part of our culture. Business is, moreover, a **social institution** as it is comprised of human groups working toward goals compatible with the overall goals of society. Although the totality of the industries and firms that comprise the institution of business exerts great influence over our way of life, it nevertheless exists within a framework provided by other social institutions such as religion, politics and law, the military, agriculture, family life, and culture and education. This is a dynamic, interactive relationship, as business and the other institutions in our complex social system face pressures to change from each other and from other organizations, associations, and groups.

SIZES AND TYPES OF BUSINESS FIRMS

American business is carried on by firms that range in size from the small enterprise in which a single person conducts business, such as a shoe repair or an upholstering shop; through medium-sized firms, such as grocery wholesalers or paper box manufacturers; to such industrial and commercial giants as the International Business Machines Corporation and the S. S. Kresge Company, whose sales volumes amount to billions of dollars annually and who employ many thousands of workers. In later chapters attention will be given to companies of all sizes.

Table 1-1   **The 20 Largest Industrial Corporations Ranked by Sales, 1974**

Rank	Company	Sales (Thousands of Dollars)	Assets	Employees	Net Income as Percentage of Sales
1	Exxon	42,061,336	31,332,440	133,000	7.5
2	General Motors	31,549,546	20,468,100	734,000	3.0
3	Ford Motor	23,620,600	14,173,600	464,731	1.5
4	Texaco	23,255,497	17,176,121	76,420	6.8
5	Mobil Oil	18,929,033	14,074,290	73,100	5.5
6	Standard Oil of California	17,191,186	11,639,996	39,540	5.6
7	Gulf Oil	16,458,000	12,503,000	52,700	6.5
8	General Electric	13,413,100	9,369,100	404,000	4.5
9	International Business Machines	12,675,292	14,027,108	292,350	14.5
10	International Tel. & Tel.	11,154,401	10,696,544	409,000	4.0
11	Chrysler	10,971,416	6,732,756	255,929	—
12	U.S. Steel	9,186,403	7,717,493	187,503	6.9
13	Standard Oil (Ind.)	9,085,415	8,915,190	47,217	10.7
14	Shell Oil	7,633,455	6,128,884	32,287	8.1
15	Western Electric	7,381,728	5,239,551	189,972	4.2
16	Continental Oil	7,041,423	4,673,434	41,174	4.7
17	E.I. du Pont de Nemours	6,910,100	5,980,300	136,866	5.8
18	Atlantic Richfield	6,739,682	6,151,608	28,771	7.0
19	Westinghouse Electric	6,466,112	4,301,804	199,248	0.4
20	Occidental Petroleum	5,719,369	3,325,471	34,400	4.9

SOURCE: Reprinted from the 1975 *Fortune Directory* by special permission; © 1975 Time, Inc., pp. 210–211.

Small and Large Businesses

Over 98 percent of all enterprises in the United States can be classified as small businesses according to Congressional definition. A retail store or a dealer in services whose annual sales do not exceed $2 million is classified as a small business. A wholesaler whose annual sales do not exceed $9.5 million is a small businessperson. A manufacturing company that does not have more than 250 employees is ordinarily classified as a small business; and under some circumstances it retains that classification even though it employs up to 1,000 workers. Thus, small businesses are very important in our economy.

Table 1-1 on page 15 presents certain pertinent data for the 20 largest industrial corporations in the United States for 1974. Particularly notable are the wide variations among different firms in assets, employees, and especially in net income as a percentage of sales.

Industrial and Commercial Businesses

Two basic types of business firms are industrial and commercial. **Industrial businesses** include all businesses that are engaged in producing things — by extraction from the earth, by fabrication in the factory, or by construction on a building site. **Commercial businesses** include firms engaged in marketing, such as wholesalers and retailers; in finance, such as banks and investment concerns; and in services, which include advertising, repair services, laundries, hotels, and theaters. Table 1-2 presents selected data on manufacturing, selected services, retail trade, and wholesale trade.

Table 1-2 **Number of Units, Dollar Volume of Sales, and Number of Employees for Selected Types of Business**

Type of Business	Number of Units	Sales (Millions of Dollars)	Number of Employees
Manufacturing	320,710	756,534	19,028,700
Selected services	1,590,248	112,970	5,305,181
Retail trade	1,934,466	470,806	11,359,605
Wholesale trade	348,168	683,659	3,878,181

SOURCE: U.S. Bureau of the Census, *1972 Census of Business*, Washington, D.C., 1972.

CAPITALISM VERSUS OTHER ECONOMIC SYSTEMS

Every society follows a certain system of ideas, called an **ideology,** that embodies the society's concepts of fundamental values and human relationships. There is a great difference between the ideology of a capitalistic enterprise system and various forms of socialism and communism.

Key Economic Questions

Regardless of a nation's political and economic ideologies, its managers will face the same basic economic problems. All economic systems must respond to three basic questions or demands: (a) What consumption and capital goods will be produced from the limited supply of available resources? (b) How will these goods be produced? (c) On what basis and to whom should the goods be distributed? The decisions concerning these questions will vary depending on the ideological framework of a nation.

Capitalistic Ideology

Various key aspects of capitalism have already been covered. The ideology of capitalism embraces the concept that the greatest good of the largest number of people should be the goal of society. To implement the ideology, the individual citizen should enjoy the greatest amount of freedom, hence the acceptance of laissez-faire as an underlying principle in capitalism. Over the years the tendency has developed for the government to impose an ever-increasing number of restraints on the freedom of our citizens, but with the fundamental idea that their well-being would be advanced through this trend. However, our people have not moved too far away from the basic concept of the primacy of individuals in our society.

Capitalism, nevertheless, is often rejected by large and small nations that have adopted other economic systems — usually some form of socialism or communism. In fact, the United States stands alone in the world today in terms of the degree of freedom from government involvement in our economy. It is important, then, to note how we differ from other systems in order to understand the reasons for the success of our dynamic capitalistic enterprise system.

Socialism

Socialism generally is devoted extensively to promotion of the welfare of its individuals. Further, the major factors of production and distribution in a socialistic economy — factories, mines, banks, stores, transportation systems, and farms — are owned and controlled by the government for the benefit of society as a whole. A basic level of welfare is guaranteed, taxes are high, and incomes are equalized.

Both capitalism and socialism are market-oriented, but in much different ways. In socialism, profit and efficiency often yield to government-dictated employment levels and bureaucratic overlays. Competition is regarded as wasteful, and it is replaced by a government-monitored market in which the state exercises considerable control over major industries and the smaller businesses of individuals.

Communism

Communism is a doctrine based on the writings of Karl Marx in which the concept of a classless society and the absence of the state as an instrument of social control were advocated. The Union of Soviet Socialist Republics is the leading exponent of communism. As yet there is little evidence of the disappearance of government. Rather the state is the ruling power over the entire economic system. A more correct term for the Russian economy might be that of **state capitalism** with all of the instruments of production owned and controlled by the government. In this instance, economic planners establish the nation's basic economic objectives — both military and civilian — and this total program is translated into national production objectives and imposed on the industries and plants in the system. The citizens' well-being may be sacrificed to industrial growth, and a misallocation of resources often occurs.

Perhaps one of the most outstanding differences is that of incentives. In our capitalistic economy a number of built-in incentives play a significant role in inducing workers at all levels to exert their best efforts at their jobs and in persuading those who have saved funds to invest in business enterprise. These inducements are both monetary and social. They include not only profits for entrepreneurs, wage incentives, and opportunities for promotion for employees, but also the prestige that attaches to success in almost all lines of economic endeavor. Under socialism and communism workers are supposed to do their best for the state without personal incentives. If extra effort is required, it is presumed to be forthcoming because the government has ordered it and not because of any personal gain that may be achieved by the workers.

Summary of Differences among Economic Systems

Figure 1-3 summarizes some of the differences among capitalism, socialism, and communism in five important dimensions: (a) ownership of means of production, (b) degree of central control, (c) pervasiveness of managerial decision making, (d) occupational choice, and (e) incentives.

Our profit-oriented capitalistic enterprise system has received a great deal of criticism recently. The critics often dwell on any flaws that inevitably will emerge from time to time without recognizing the giant role it has played in productively combining our resources, building and defending our nation, and allowing us to achieve great abundance and prosperity in our relatively short history. It has achieved an almost miraculous balance in the production of consumption and capital goods in a complex economic system involving thousands of independent processes and activities.

The form of our enterprise system undoubtedly will change over time as the needs of society change; but it should continue to live up to these changing expectations effectively and efficiently and serve us well.

CHARACTERISTIC	CAPITALISM	SOCIALISM	COMMUNISM
1. OWNERSHIP OF MEANS OF PRODUCTION	Private ownership of business and industry with right to freedom of economic choice sanctioned by the Constitution and protected by law.	Public ownership of basic industries.	Public (state) ownership of virtually all industrial and agricultural productive capacity.
2. DEGREE OF CENTRAL CONTROL	None; product and pricing goals established by consumers and managers in the competitive marketplace.	Major goals of economy set by government; personal freedom exists to vary occupation and consumption within this broad governmental framework.	Central determination of prices, investments, and all major resource values and proportions in production, distribution, and consumption.
3. PERVASIVENESS OF MANAGERIAL DECISION MAKING	Private managerial initiative supported by governmental actions to promote private enterprise.	Managers of major firms must obey the central control plans, thus precluding major independent business decisions.	Managers selected through state political party; highly bureaucratized, with managerial decisions imposed through state administrative hierarchy.
4. OCCUPATIONAL CHOICE	Individual freedom to choose and bargain for jobs, employers, fields of business, and locations.	Individuals may own small businesses and land and choose occupations within the state-controlled economy.	State government owns all business and is the only employer. Individual's work prescribed by state.
5. INCENTIVES	Monetary and social in the form of profit and prestige, and self-control.	"To each according to one's need, from each according to one's ability."	Nationalistic appeals, peer pressure, public recognition, threats of punitive action, and work standards.

Figure 1-3 *Comparisons of Representative Economic Systems*

BUSINESS TERMS

QUESTIONS FOR DISCUSSION AND ANALYSIS

1. "The role of business is to produce profit." Do you agree with this statement? Explain.
2. What are some factors that may be used to reduce the importance of price as a base for competition?
3. Some critics of business regard product differentiation as a wasteful practice. Do you agree? Give reasons.
4. Why is private property vital to capitalism?
5. Do you regard the tendency toward the separation of ownership and management in many large companies as a favorable or unfavorable trend from the standpoint of the public good? Explain.
6. Do you see any drawbacks in categorizing a service station with ten employees as a "small business"?
7. What effect may high interest rates, or cost of capital, have on a person's decision to be an entrepreneur or a professional manager?
8. What suggestions do you have for measures that might help small businesses to compete against large, strong companies?
9. A basic tenet of socialism is "to each according to his need, from each according to his ability." Why would this not be workable in a capitalistic economy?
10. Some critics of our capitalistic enterprise system argue that profit is generated by a few "fat cats" at the expense and exploitation of the masses. Do you agree? Explain.

PROBLEMS AND SHORT CASES

1. Prepare a brief report in which you compare and contrast how you think the following businesspersons might respond to the question, "How do you see profit and community service as business objectives?": (a) a banker, (b) a supermarket manager, (c) an owner or manager of a retail clothing store, (d) an owner of a bicycle or motorcycle shop.
2. Refer to Table 1-1 on page 15, which presents the 20 largest industrial corporations, and compute: (a) the ratio of sales to employees and (b) the ratio of assets to employees for (1) Standard Oil of California, Shell Oil, and Standard Oil (Ind.) and for (2) International Business Machines, U.S. Steel, and Westinghouse Electric. What do you infer from your figures?
3. William C. Durant was the entrepreneur who started the company that later became General Motors. He was replaced by Alfred P. Sloan, Jr., a professional manager. Look up Durant, Sloan, and General Motors in an encyclopedia and determine: (a) Durant's contributions and weaknesses, and (b) how the role of an entrepreneur may differ from that of a professional manager.

2 The Changing Environment of Business

With the advent of rising incomes, shorter workweeks, and earlier retirements, numerous companies have ventured into leisure markets. AMF, Inc., formerly American Machine & Foundry Co., is one of these companies. Since the late 1960s, it has spent millions of dollars to acquire leisure-oriented firms, such as Harley-Davidson motorcycles and snowmobiles; Head skis, tennis rackets, and sportswear; Skamper trailers; and Sunfish sailboats. The proportion of its sales in leisure products moved from 38 percent in 1967 to 63 percent in 1973.

Then came the energy crisis. Boaters were stranded on shore, campers garaged, and snowmobilers and skiers stayed home and watched television. As AMF's earnings slid, the company's chief executive stated that the firm would move away from a concentration on leisure products while continuing to stress their long-term importance.[1]

When this country was young and businesses were small, the profit motive was readily accepted as the only reason for a business's existence. Since the 1930s, however, some moralists and managerial philosophers have taken the position that corporations should assume important social responsibilities. This feeling was openly expressed very early by several influential management leaders, such as Henry Ford I, who asserted that the only worthwhile goal of business was the elimination of poverty. In the mid-1970s this philosophy is generally accepted, for many business leaders feel that the job of management is to conduct its business in such a manner as to maintain an equitable balance among the claims of its various publics. This chapter will introduce a variety of forces that may affect the goals and operation of the business system over a period of time.

[1]Reprinted with permission of *The Wall Street Journal*, © Dow Jones & Company, Inc. (1974). All Rights Reserved.

HISTORICAL SETTING

As the last quarter of this century begins, the major managerial challenges are directed more to social, political, and physical environmental problems than solely to economic and technological considerations. An understanding of these factors that make up the business environment will be aided by a brief consideration of the following historical references: (1) the land and the people and (2) the industrial revolution.

The Land and the People

The United States comprises a very large territory with a widely varied climate and vast natural resources of timber, metal ores, waterways, water power sources, and fertile farmland. When the first settlers began arriving, these resources were almost completely undeveloped. This was virgin land admirably adapted to support an agricultural and industrial population.

With few exceptions the people who migrated to this country in the early days of its history were strong, courageous, adventurous, and self-reliant. In many instances they came here to be free from oppression — political, economic, or religious. Deeply ingrained in many of them was an intense suspicion of and dislike for a strong central government, coupled with a belief in the dignity of hard work. While they naturally brought with them from Great Britain and continental Europe many native customs and traditions, they were confronted with new problems in strange surroundings that demanded different approaches to survival and making a satisfactory living. The attitude of the ruling groups in England and elsewhere that the settlements in America were to have the status of colonies, contributing needed materials to the mother countries and at the same time remaining always dependent upon and subservient to them, aroused a deep resentment among the colonists. It stimulated them to become more completely self-sustaining and politically independent of the countries from which they and their parents had come.

Thus was the attitude of self-reliance and independence developed here. It was expressed in the belief that a person's success in life was, in a large measure, due to one's own energy, courage, and resourcefulness. It spawned the concept of "going into business for one's self" that was a dominant characteristic of our economic thinking for many years, and which survives even today.

An important by-product of this type of thinking was the general attitude that private business enterprise was important. Success in business was highly regarded, and successful businesspersons were honored and respected as leaders in their communities. Even though the doctrine of **caveat emptor**, let the buyer beware, was generally accepted by the people, they accorded honor and prestige to the leading entrepreneurs of the times.

The Industrial Revolution

The middle of the 18th century has been commonly, if somewhat inaccurately, accepted as the time of the onset of the **industrial revolution**. Stated briefly, this revolution consisted of the application of mechanical power to productive processes hitherto derived from human or animal sources; the extensive development of machinery to which the new power sources could be applied; and the establishment of the **factory system,** under which production workers were assembled in a central location as opposed to the precedent **domestic system,** under which the workers performed their productive tasks in their own homes. The effect of the industrial revolution was to bring about a far-reaching change in business organization. Whereas production formerly was carried on in small family groups with minimal capital requirements, now the advent of mechanical power, complicated machinery, and extensive factory buildings called for large amounts of capital and, to an increasing extent, for more competent managerial personnel.

The industrial revolution developed principally in England but moved within a relatively short time to America, where it had a profound impact on the industrial development of the country. Prior to this time business had been conducted to a large extent on a local basis, with most firms being of relatively small size. Furthermore, the philosophy of laissez-faire was predominant here as it was abroad. The industrial revolution brought about a gradual increase in the size and scope of manufacturing establishments that was accelerated by the demands for war matériel generated by the Civil War. After the war, with the progressive opening-up of the western parts of the country to a growing population, with a consequent broadening of markets and of business activity, large companies began to appear and the dominance of the corporation began to emerge. Along with this trend there came a gradual weakening of the laissez-faire idea, brought about by the competitive practices of some of the large concerns, which were believed to be harmful to the best interest of the country. This development was the source of many business environmental factors of the present time.

CHANGING ENVIRONMENTAL FACTORS

The environmental factors which affect business can be categorized as: (1) social, (2) economic, (3) political, (4) physical, and (5) technological. Since one factor may affect another factor, there is an interrelationship among them. In varying degrees all businesses are influenced by the changes in one or more of the environmental factors. Some of the more important changes affecting managerial decision making are discussed in this section.

Social Changes

Over the past several decades there have been several significant social developments that have influenced the function and structure of American society. Successful businesses have responded to these changed social conditions by altering their company policies and product offerings. Businesses that have failed to recognize and adapt to the social trends have experienced sales and profit declines.

MIGRATION OF POPULATION

Since 1950, there have been significant population shifts between states and between central cities and the suburbs. The Southwest, Mountain, and Pacific states have grown faster than the national average while some upper Midwest and Southern states have grown slower. One of the greatest growth periods for the suburbs was between 1950 and 1963 when development was three times greater than in the central cities. Companies that have followed their markets have prospered, while others who did not have faltered.

MEGALOPOLIS

In some sections of the United States, formerly separate metropolitan areas have grown to the point where their boundaries join each other. Each such region of dense population is known as a **megalopolis** or an **interurbia**. For example, a 600-mile stretch along the East coast from Boston to Washington containing 20 percent of the U.S. population and 6 percent of the land is rapidly becoming a megalopolis. The concentration of population in a megalopolis presents a challenge to urban planners and an opportunity for marketing personnel.

INCREASED EDUCATION

A renewed emphasis on educational achievement has resulted in a higher average level of education for the population. From 1940 to 1970, the median years of education completed by individuals 25 years or older increased from 8.6 to 11.6 years. As a result, there is a greater mass market for more sophisticated goods and services.

In the 1970s, however, many high school graduates who seek additional education are shifting from strictly academic programs to vocational ones. This trend may be attributed to the fact that in some fields the supply of college graduates is greater than the demand for their services. Hence, there are schoolteachers who work in factories and physicists who drive taxis.

Nevertheless, such individuals with higher levels of education are potentially able to attain larger incomes, increased social status, and greater personal achievements than those with less education.

INFLUENCE OF CULTURE

During President John F. Kennedy's administration in the early 1960s, a strong cultural influence developed in this country. As material wants were satisfied, individuals turned to cultural pursuits. Support for the arts, theater, and other scholarly endeavors were funded by numerous business foundations and other civic groups. Stores added paintings, sculptures, and other works of art to their inventories. Sears, Roebuck and Co., the mass retailer, employed Vincent Price, actor and art expert, to select paintings which could be sold in Sears' stores.

CHANGED VALUES

Over the last several decades the value system of American society has changed. In the wake of Watergate the desire for individual honesty and untarnished credibility has increased. Any false or misleading promotion or deceptive practice by business is viewed as an immoral act.

Furthermore, a permissive society has replaced an authoritarian one. Because younger workers frequently hold values which are quite different from those of their older managers, employers are confronted with employees who do not accept the so-called **puritan ethic** of self-sacrifice and hard work. The resistance of workers to strict authority and discipline has resulted in a trend to participatory management which provides the worker with a voice in decision making.

Another result of these changing social values has been the increase of all types of crimes throughout the nation. Business management has discovered that losses from employee theft are usually greater than losses from shoplifting and other forms of theft. In addition, some workers have brought the drug problem from the streets into the factories. The threat of industrial spying and the loss of company secrets have forced many firms to employ greater plant security measures. Various antibusiness and antiestablishment groups have committed bombings and other crimes against business. The Bank of America in California has been a frequent target of these organizations.

INCREASED LEISURE TIME

Reduced workweeks, longer vacations, early retirements, and the scheduling of several national holidays to create three-day weekends have increased people's leisure time. Several industries — such as recreational vehicles, skiing, and motorcycling — have benefited greatly from the way in which individuals spend their free time. In some instances the desire by workers for additional leisure time has created managerial problems. For example, as workers seek to extend their weekend, the Monday absentee rate in some factories is frequently higher than for the other days of the week.

MINORITY GROUP RIGHTS

The Civil Rights Act of 1964 and its enforcement by the Equal Employment Opportunity Commission (EEOC) dramatically increased employment opportunities for blacks, Spanish-speaking Americans, and American Indians. These groups were previously the subject of job and pay discrimination. By the early 1970s, most enlightened business firms had taken affirmative actions to employ more minorities. In some organizations, such as the Ford Motor Company, managers are evaluated on their ability to recruit and develop promotable individuals from minority groups.

WOMEN'S RIGHTS

Fueled by the passage of the Equal Pay Act in 1963 and the Civil Rights Act in 1964, the **women's liberation movement** has demonstrated the changing status of women in society. The Equal Rights Amendment to the Constitution, which will become law after ratification by 38 states, practically eliminates all social, economic, and legal distinctions between the sexes. As a result of all this, job and promotional opportunities which were closed to women a few years ago are now open to them. Female managers are no longer uncommon. Men and women college graduates are vigorously competing for the same engineering, accounting, and sales positions. As indicated in Table 2-1, in the early 1970s, 38 percent of the work force were women and 63 percent of this group were married.

Table 2-1 **Growth of Women Workers in the Civilian Labor Force**

Year	Number of Women Workers (Millions)	Women as Percentage of All Workers	Percentage of Working Women Who Are Married
1940	13.8	24.9	36.4
1950	17.8	28.6	52.1
1960	22.5	32.3	59.9
1970	31.2	37.8	63.4
1973	33.9	38.2	63.0

SOURCE: U.S. Bureau of the Census, *Statistical Abstract of the United States: 1974.* (95th edition.) Washington, D.C., 1974. Pages 336 and 340.

SOCIAL WELFARE PROGRAMS

Public social consciousness indicating a concern for the welfare of less fortunate segments of society was first expressed by the passage of the federal Social Security Act in 1935. Since then the coverage of the act has been broadened and new programs, such as the Medicare plan of 1965, have been added. Medicare, which assists retirees in paying medical and hospital costs, has contributed to the growth of geriatric centers and nursing homes. Vocational rehabilitation for the handicapped, job training for the hard-core unemployed, remedial education for poverty children, and food stamps for the economically disadvantaged are other federal programs which show the willingness of society to accept responsibility for the less fortunate. If the present growth in local, state, and federal programs continues, government spending — which is now nearly 33 percent of the total output of all goods and services — could reach the 50 percent level in 20 years.

ADVERSE OPINION OF BUSINESS

Public confidence in business has been eroding. Business has been blamed for many of our economic, social, and environmental problems. The proportion of the public who had great confidence in corporate management dropped from 55 percent in 1966 to 21 percent in 1974. To numerous individuals a big company is a bad company and profit is a dirty word. In one survey the public expressed the belief that after-tax corporate profits were 33 percent of sales, rather than the actual 5 to 6 percent. Unfortunately many persons, particularly those who do not own or manage businesses, are unaware of the economics of a business operation. They know little about accounting and finance, and they are unable to grasp the relationships between capital investment and the need for an adequate return to investors. They do not understand that free enterprise, capitalism, responsible government, and individual freedom are all delicately interlocked.

Many businesspersons and educators are aware of the lack of public confidence in business and are trying, with minor success, to correct the situation. For example, executives in the Eaton Corporation, a Midwest producer of auto parts and other industrial products, have received training in how to explain the Eaton story and the operation of the American business system to the public. Some companies and colleges have joined forces to present economic education workshops to high school social studies teachers. With so many groups expressing opposition to business, businesspersons need to expend additional time and effort to present their story to the public.

CONSUMERISM

The consumer protection movement was originally directed against those few areas of business that discredit all business by their questionable acts. All businesspersons, however, need to work to maintain the confidence of consumers. Chapter 12 provides a thorough discussion of this movement.

DESIRE FOR INDIVIDUAL RECOGNITION

In the early part of this century, managers often considered their workers as just another tool of production. The worker's emotions and desires were frequently subordinate to the goal of increased production. Today the desire for expression of individuality is a reaction to our mass-production, assembly-line operations. In this quest for individuality, factory workers have discarded their blue-collar work clothes and corporate executives have laid aside their gray flannel suits for more personalized wardrobes.

To cope with this desire for individual recognition, various companies have restructured their jobs to provide workers with more responsibility and recognition. Different goods and services are made available to satisfy the diversified wants of each sector of our society.

INFLUENCE OF LABOR

With the passage of the National Labor Relations Act of 1935, organized labor, which had hitherto played a somewhat minor role in the business environment, grew in size and importance. Employers were required to bargain with the unions that represented their employees, and such vast industrial areas as steel and automobile production were thoroughly unionized. As a result, the traditional freedom of action and decision in the area of labor relations, which businesspersons had long enjoyed, was greatly curtailed; and the owners and managers of business firms discovered in the new-found strength of labor a difficult opponent in bargaining and in politics.

Economic Changes

Businesspersons are making decisions in an economic environment which is more complex than ever before in history. Factors outside the control of a firm, such as international economic developments, are exerting a greater impact upon American business. The policies of government and business have a strong influence upon our economic environment; and, in turn, the economic environment affects the policies devised by government and business.

EQUALIZATION OF INCOME

Since 1950, there has been a greater equalization of income among families. In 1971, for the first time in history, over half of American families recorded incomes over $10,000 a year. The trend toward more than one worker in a family and **moonlighting,** which is the employment of an individual at more than one job, have contributed to this equalization. In 1972 families with more than one worker accounted for almost 55 percent of all families headed by married men in the labor force, compared with only 45 percent a decade earlier. Estimates have been made that about five percent of the labor force moonlights.

Several other factors have a leveling effect on take-home incomes. One is the progressive federal income tax which penalizes the high-income earners and favors the low-income workers. Another factor is the larger retirement incomes which have been provided through increases in both company and government benefit programs. By the mid-1970s company pension plans covered nearly 30 million workers and government plans included another 14 million. This constituted a 50 percent increase in coverage since 1960.

DECLINE OF SMALL BUSINESS

Small firms in many lines of business must follow the lead of the large firms in order to compete successfully. However, it is apparent that small firms find it extremely difficult to survive in the presence of very large firms with huge resources, well-trained managerial and operative personnel, and extensive research facilities. As a result, over the last several decades small businesses in many industries have shown a steady erosion in their proportion of sales and employment. Moreover, the rate of failure among small companies has been relatively high.

For big business, competition is rugged; for small business, it has become a life-or-death matter. In an attempt to help the small business entrepreneurs meet the rigors of competition, the Small Business Administration was established by Congress in 1953. Other legislation passed at the urging of small businesses has been designed to equalize the competitive advantages that the large firms would otherwise enjoy. Faced with mounting costs, vigorous competition, and increased government red tape known as **federal form pollution,** small businesses continue their struggle to survive.

REDUCED PROFITS

Since the post-World War II years, there has been an overall reduction in profits as a percentage of sales. In the late 1940s manufacturers' profits averaged 6 to 7 percent of sales; by 1974, as shown in Figure 2-1 on page 30, the profit ratio had decreased to 5.0 percent. Several factors which have caused profit margins to narrow are listed at the top of page 31.

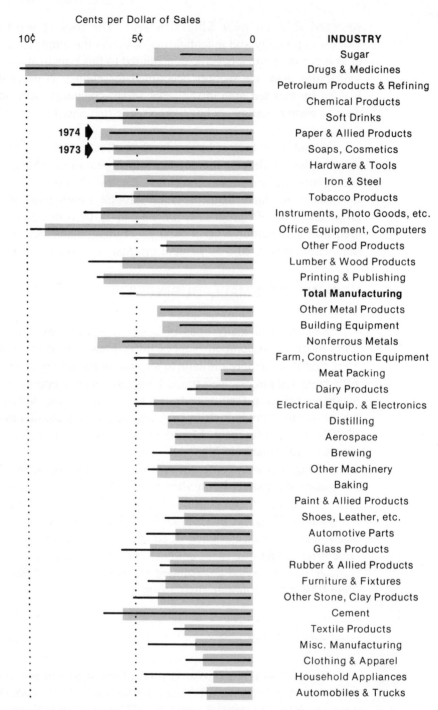

Cents per Dollar of Sales

			INDUSTRY
10¢	5¢	0	

Sugar
Drugs & Medicines
Petroleum Products & Refining
Chemical Products
Soft Drinks
1974 Paper & Allied Products
1973 Soaps, Cosmetics
Hardware & Tools
Iron & Steel
Tobacco Products
Instruments, Photo Goods, etc.
Office Equipment, Computers
Other Food Products
Lumber & Wood Products
Printing & Publishing
Total Manufacturing
Other Metal Products
Building Equipment
Nonferrous Metals
Farm, Construction Equipment
Meat Packing
Dairy Products
Electrical Equip. & Electronics
Distilling
Aerospace
Brewing
Other Machinery
Baking
Paint & Allied Products
Shoes, Leather, etc.
Automotive Parts
Glass Products
Rubber & Allied Products
Furniture & Fixtures
Other Stone, Clay Products
Cement
Textile Products
Misc. Manufacturing
Clothing & Apparel
Household Appliances
Automobiles & Trucks

SOURCE: "Corporate Profits: Manufacturing," *Road Maps of Industry*, No. 1761, The Conference Board (May 1, 1975).

Figure 2-1 **Profits After Taxes of Leading Manufacturing Corporations**

1. More effective competition.
2. Government price restraints.
3. Higher wage costs.
4. Rising raw material costs.
5. Increased Social Security contributions.
6. Additional expenditures in order to meet the requirements of government agencies.

TIGHT MONEY

As business expanded in the late 1960s the demand for loanable funds from banks and other institutions reduced the available supply of funds. Major corporations were forced to pay interest of 10 percent or more on borrowed money. This **tight money** condition prevailed in the early 1970s and caused financial managers to appraise carefully their need for funds. In some cases the cost of financing a new business investment was more than the anticipated profits which would be generated from the new expenditure.

INFLATION

Since the mid-1960s, the United States has entered into a period of **inflation,** causing prices at various times to rise over 10 percent a year.

In the early 1970s a basic cause of inflation was a strong demand which increased the prices of both raw materials and finished goods. Other causes of inflation are discussed in Chapter 14. Inflation has the unfortunate following features:

1. Shrinking personal savings.
2. Reducing the expected return on new investments.
3. Distorting the national economy.
4. Perpetuating a price-wage spiral.

BUSINESS CYCLES

The history of business activity in this country has been one of alternate prosperity and depression. The movement has been termed the **business cycle**. Production, employment, profits, and prices rise during periods of **prosperity** and decrease in times of **depression**. When the downward movement of the business cycle is slight and of short duration, the term **recession** is applied.

For many years the belief prevailed in business and governmental circles that these cyclical movements were inevitable and that there was little anyone could do about them. However, the Great Depression of the 1930s — which was one of extreme severity following the post-World War I era of prosperity — changed the thinking of governmental officials and many businesspersons. Instead of merely waiting for the downward trend of the cycle to run its course, attempts were made through a number of legislative enactments to induce a recovery.

Since World War II, several recessions of relatively brief duration have occurred, each followed by a recovery period. Unemployment, which had historically increased during depressions and decreased during prosperity, failed to improve during the recovery periods of these years. This situation led to widespread discussion of the emerging effect of business cycles on employment and of the part that government is able to play in decreasing unemployment. The actions taken by government to stabilize the economy are discussed later in this chapter.

GROWTH OF CONSUMER CREDIT

In recent years all forms of consumer credit have grown sharply. One form of consumer credit which has received prominent attention is the credit card movement. Even merchants who are too small to administer their own credit plan may offer credit service through a **bank credit card plan,** a system by which banks associated with the plan collect from card-holding consumers and remit to the merchants, less a commission. BankAmericard and Master Charge are the two most popular bank credit card plans. American Express, Diners' Club, and Carte Blanche are three widely accepted travel and entertainment cards.

One of the major results of the credit card movement has been a notable increase in the amount of consumer credit. Another has been a sizable increase in the cash reserves required of the sellers who need funds to pay their own bills and meet their payrolls. The growth of consumer credit is dramatically illustrated in Table 2-2 which shows that total consumer credit recently reached $190 billion, a level over twice that of 1965.

SERVICE ECONOMY

Historically the economy of the United States has been regarded as devoted principally to the production of goods rather than services. This concept has been based on the impact of the industrial revolution on the manufacture of and demand for goods. It has also been affected by the historically larger employment in production as contrasted to services. Because of the growth of automation and other technological developments, which reduced the need for production workers in the early 1950s, the United States became the first nation in the world to employ the majority of its labor force in production of services such as education, health, government, and distribution.

Since that time, six out of seven new jobs added in the country have been service jobs.

INTERNATIONAL ECONOMIC DEVELOPMENTS

Rising levels of economic activity abroad and improved communication and transportation have caused numerous companies to seek new markets in other countries. Factors which relate to the international economic environment, such as rising nationalism in developing countries, operations of multinational corporations, and the complexities of the balance of trade and payments problems, are more than ever exerting a greater impact upon American business. These developments are more thoroughly discussed in Chapter 28.

Political Changes

In the third quarter of this century the East-West cold war, the Korean conflict, and the Vietnam conflict produced high levels of government spending and regulation. Federal actions contributed to greater employment, some shortages, and inflation. Although it is difficult to separate political factors from social and economic factors, this section will attempt to indicate governmental actions which affect managerial decision making.

Table 2-2   *Total Consumer Credit Outstanding, 1965–1973 (In Millions of Dollars)*

End of Period	Total	Installment					Noninstallment				
		Total	Auto-mobile Paper	Other Consumer Goods Paper	Home Improve-ment Loans[1]	Personal Loans	Total	Single-Payment Loans	Charge Accounts		Service Credit
									Retail Outlets	Credit Cards[2]	
1965	89,883	70,893	28,437	18,483	3,736	20,237	18,990	7,671	5,724	706	4,889
1966	96,239	76,245	30,010	20,732	3,841	21,662	19,994	7,972	5,812	874	5,336
1967	100,783	79,428	29,796	22,389	4,008	23,235	21,355	8,558	6,041	1,029	5,727
1968	110,770	87,745	32,948	24,626	4,239	25,932	23,025	9,532	5,966	1,227	6,300
1969	121,146	97,105	35,527	28,313	4,613	28,652	24,041	9,747	5,936	1,437	6,921
1970	127,163	102,064	35,184	31,465	5,070	30,345	25,099	9,675	6,163	1,805	7,456
1971	138,394	111,295	38,664	34,353	5,413	32,865	27,099	10,585	6,397	1,953	8,164
1972	157,564	127,332	44,129	40,080	6,201	36,922	30,232	12,256	7,055	1,947	8,974
1973	180,486	147,437	51,130	47,530	7,352	41,425	33,049	13,241	7,783	2,046	9,979
1974	190,121	156,124	51,689	52,009	8,162	44,264	33,997	12,979	8,012	2,122	10,884

SOURCE: *Federal Reserve Bulletin* (August, 1975), p. A45.

[1]Holdings of financial institutions; holdings of retail outlets are included in "Other Consumer Goods Paper."

[2]Service station and miscellaneous credit-card accounts and home heating oil accounts.

ECONOMIC STABILIZATION

In recent years full employment and economic stabilization have become important goals of the government. The Employment Act of 1946 decreed that the federal government should exercise all of its resources to maintain a high level of employment. Although the government cannot directly legislate a particular level of employment, it can determine the level of unemployment benefits. Thus, employers are taxed to provide unemployment benefits which are paid by each state to its unemployed. Some unemployed workers also receive supplemental unemployment benefits (SUB) which are drawn from an employer-financed trust fund.

As indicated in Chapter 1, since the Depression of the 1930s the government has accepted Keynesian economic policy. This means that in times of recession and high unemployment the government uses various methods to stabilize the economy. One method is to adjust the timing of government contracts to meet the changing supply and demand conditions in our economy. This action is possible since the money earmarked by Congress for federal expenditures does not have to be spent in the fiscal year for which it is appropriated. Another method is to permit larger depreciation allowances and special investment credit for business. These actions stimulate corporate expenditures for new plants and equipment. In an effort to encourage consumer expenditures during a recession, Congress usually acts to reduce personal income taxes, particularly for low- and middle-income families. Spending is also encouraged by government actions which enlarge the supply of money and lower interest rates. Other methods used to stabilize the economy include the creation of public service jobs and the construction of public works.

MERGERS AND ANTITRUST LEGISLATION

Since the enactment of the Sherman Antitrust Act in 1890, a goal of public policy has been to maintain competition and to restrain the concentration of corporate power. This goal was disturbed in the mid-1960s when many companies were purchased by or merged into other businesses to help these businesses grow rapidly, acquire new facilities cheaply, and obtain tax and competitive advantages. A high point for the merger movement occurred in 1969 when 4,550 firms were acquired by other organizations. Stricter enforcement of the antitrust laws has been a factor in reducing the number of mergers during the 1970s.

PRICE AND WAGE CONTROLS

The 1970 series of **price and wage controls** (known as Phase 1, Phase 2, Phase 3, and Phase 4) restricted price increases on most manufactured goods and limited wage increases in order to combat inflation. Each successive phase reduced the categories of goods under price controls until nearly all goods and wages were decontrolled in April, 1974. The government, however, continues to monitor prices and wages and to focus public attention on inflationary actions. Through its many regulatory agencies, it has additional leverage which may be used to persuade companies to adopt what it feels to be realistic pricing policies.

INCREASED BUSINESS REGULATIONS

In recent years Presidential orders and Congressional actions have increased government regulation of business. For example, the Occupational Safety and Health Act of 1970 (OSHA) requires business to conform to stringent new safety and health regulations. By some estimates the act contains as many as 20,000 specific rules which apply to any single work establishment. Another example is the establishment by Congress of the Consumer Product Safety Commission (CPSC) which exerts authority over an estimated 10,000 to 100,000 consumer products. The CPSC can ban unsafe products and ask business to adopt product safety and performance standards.

Recently older regulatory bodies, such as the Federal Trade Commission, the Food and Drug Administration, and the Federal Communications Commission, have become more watchful of business practices. All businesses, but particularly small businesses with limited funds and personnel, frequently find that it is extremely difficult to comply with a complicated structure of federal, state, and local regulations.

Physical Changes

For years it was believed that our natural resources were free goods which, although wasted and exploited, would be replenished by nature. This nation did not recognize that it was destroying the ability of nature to maintain a balanced ecological system. Today many of our lakes and streams are too polluted to support plant and fish life. In strip-mine areas the wasted land lies barren. Energy sources that took nature thousands of years to create are consumed within minutes. As indicated by these few examples, a realistic program of environment and energy conservation should be adopted by every business. The specific responses of business to its physical environment are discussed in Chapter 3.

Technological Changes

Technology is the practical application of research and discovery which results in a higher standard of living and increased productivity. Since many of the technological advancements in production cause a greater amount of pollution and utilize a greater amount of energy than the production facilities which they replace, they have added to our pollution and energy problems. The estimate that 90 percent of all the scientists who ever lived are still alive today indicates that even greater technological achievements can be expected.

RESEARCH AND DEVELOPMENT

Expenditures for research and development have dramatically increased. Since the 1960s, research spending has been about 3 percent of the total output of goods and services in this country. In the early 1970s, 50 percent of the research was sponsored by the federal government, 40 percent by private industry, and 10 percent by other institutions. In some industries, such as chemicals and ethical drugs, research expenditures approach 7 or 8 percent of sales. For many major companies 50 percent or more of their current sales are from products which were new in the last ten years.

COMPUTERS AND QUANTIFIED DECISION MAKING

With the development of electronic data-processing equipment, great stress is being placed on the assembling and analysis of statistical and other numerical information for **quantified decision making**. While close attention has long been paid to this area of business information, the tremendous increase in the amount of quantitative data that can be processed by these machines, plus the speed with which they operate, has provided management with noteworthy assistance in decision making. As a result, managers have developed quantitative approaches to decision making by combining and interrelating knowledge from many different fields.

AUTOMATION

Automation is the controlling of the production process by electronic or mechanical means. Although the concept of automation has been present since the industrial revolution, the term became a scare word in the late 1950s. Workers were worried about a mass replacement by machines. In addition, critics of automation believed that there would be an extensive loss of job skills and job satisfaction for the blue-collar workers. In reality, the way for workers to raise their standard of living is by placing less human labor into the production of goods. As shown in Table 2-3, several highly automated industries, such as petroleum, tobacco, and chemicals, have made large capital expenditures in plant and equipment per production worker.

Table 2-3   *Capital Invested per Worker in Manufacturing, 1964 to 1970 (In Thousands of Dollars)*

Industry	Per Production Worker					
	1964	1966	1967	1968	1969	1970
Total Manufacturing	23.1	25.9	27.8	30.3	33.9	38.3
Food	24.8	28.9	28.6	32.6	37.4	39.4
Tobacco	46.2	65.2	50.8	51.2	69.2	77.4
Textiles	12.2	13.5	13.9	14.5	16.1	16.1
Apparel	5.9	7.3	7.3	8.7	8.6	9.1
Lumber	14.2	16.7	17.6	18.7	23.2	27.0
Furniture	8.4	10.1	9.2	9.0	10.9	10.3
Paper	21.9	25.4	27.2	28.3	30.9	33.7
Printing	17.7	20.9	20.5	21.8	25.7	25.6
Chemicals	49.0	54.5	60.0	61.5	67.7	75.5
Petroleum[1]	152.6	179.0	204.3	226.0	247.7	269.1
Rubber	17.3	18.7	20.0	20.3	22.8	24.7
Leather	7.0	8.1	8.2	9.0	9.9	11.6
Stone, clay, glass	20.7	23.1	24.3	24.0	26.7	27.4
Fabricated metals	15.7	17.5	18.5	21.3	21.4	23.7
Non-electrical machinery	21.2	23.6	25.3	27.6	31.2	40.6
Electrical machinery	16.5	18.0	21.5	24.3	28.9	33.9
Motor vehicles	39.6	47.8	52.0	53.5	59.4	29.8
Other transportation	20.8	21.9	26.5	30.1	35.0	43.1
Instruments	20.8	24.8	26.5	31.2	33.6	34.1
Miscellaneous[2]	10.2	11.5	10.4	8.4	14.9	18.3

SOURCE: Adapted by The Conference Board from U.S. Bureau of the Census, *Statistical Abstract of the United States: 1974.* (95th edition.) Washington, D.C., 1974. Page 217.

[1]Petroleum extraction, refining, and pipeline transportation.

[2]Includes ordnance and accessories.

In conclusion, managerial decisions are made within a continuously changing and challenging environment. As has been noted, the relationship between business and its environment is one of mutuality; that is, business influences the various factors of its environment, and these forces, in turn, exert pressures on the business community. This interaction constantly affects the public and is reflected in the public's attitude toward the actions of businesspersons as they endeavor to provide at a profit the goods and services which this country requires.

BUSINESS TERMS

caveat emptor	22	megalopolis or interurbia	24
industrial revolution	23	puritan ethic	25
factory system	23	women's liberation movement	26
domestic system	23	moonlighting	29

QUESTIONS FOR DISCUSSION AND ANALYSIS

1. Do you believe that the desire to go into business for one's self is as dominant a characteristic today as it was in the past? Explain.
2. Discuss why the industrial revolution generated a movement by government and the public away from the philosophy of laissez-faire.
3. Cite several types of business positions which in the past were generally closed to women. Why were women formerly excluded from these positions?
4. How do you determine a satisfactory rate of profit for a company?
5. If someone should ask you, "What type of small business should I go into?" what kind of advice would you give?
6. How do we know if too much consumer credit is outstanding in our economy? What actions would you advise businesses and the government to take in order to avoid an overextension of consumer credit?
7. What are the implications for labor and business of the change from a production to a service economy in the United States?
8. Should the government play a greater, the same, or a lesser role in the stabilization of our economy? Discuss.
9. What are the factors that cause government to enact regulations for business?
10. What are the fears of labor toward automation?

PROBLEMS AND SHORT CASES

1. The Tyler Metal Company was recently awarded a government contract to produce armor plate. Tyler management estimated that the contract would require the employment of approximately 100 additional workers. Tyler, which was located in a metropolitan area in southern Illinois, was a family-owned company with nearly 1,000 workers. Many of the employees had been with Tyler for 20 years or longer, and a large number of the employees were related. In the past all levels of Tyler management from the president to the supervisors had expressed little interest in hiring and promoting members of minority races and women. Management was afraid that such employment practices would destroy the excellent esprit de corps within its labor force. With the government contract, however, came a close check by federal authorities on the employment policies of Tyler. As a result, Tyler was reprimanded by the government for its discriminatory practices. The company was told to initiate a plan of action which would ensure the recruitment and promotion of individuals from minority races and women. Develop a specific plan for Tyler which would ensure the employment and promotion of persons from all aspects of society.
2. Abel Industries is a large manufacturer with numerous factories and sales offices scattered across the country. Much of the firm's spectacular growth was obtained during the mid-1960s through mergers with smaller organizations. At one point observers of its merger activities compared the firm to television's cookie monster, calling Abel the merger monster. Abel appeared to be

gobbling up every company in sight. In the early 1970s, corporate indigestion occurred and Abel sold several unprofitable operations.

By 1975 the company was producing at a profit a line of goods which ranged from abrasives to zwieback. In order to prepare for future growth the company commissioned an independent think-tank organization to recommend future market opportunities. This research firm recommended that Abel consider the development of the following five new products:

a. For the U.S. Postal Service, the facsimile transmission of letters which would serve as a substitute for air mail service.

b. For public utility companies, computers which would provide remote readings of home and industrial utility meters and would then automatically prepare billings.

c. For human consumption, synthetic food from petrochemical protein.

d. For theater operators, holographic equipment which would permit three-dimensional movie presentation in commercial theaters.

e. For secretaries and office managers, dictation-writing units which would automatically prepare a letter from direct voice transcription.

Indicate the environmental conditions which could affect the acceptance of each product. Rank the products in order of their probable success.

3. Advancing technology has resulted in the need by industry for new types of job skills and knowledge. Check the help-wanted section of a metropolitan newspaper and list 10 positions which, because of the absence of certain technology, were probably not in existence 25 years ago. Identify the technology that led to the creation of each of these positions.

3 Business Response to Its Environment

Ken Gershen, manager of a national company's local plant, always welcomed the chance to discuss business at the high school's "Career Day." However, this was becoming more difficult each year. The students seemed to respond well to his comments about the company's "good works" — aiding education, serving the community, and its concern for employees and customers. But lately when the questions inevitably came to business and ecology, Ken found that there was considerable resistance to the idea that the social responsibility of a business is both economic and altruistic, and that even the seemingly "selfish" pursuits often benefit society.

In Chapter 1 it was noted that profits are a vital factor in our business enterprise system. Today it is further recognized that the responsible behavior of business in providing goods and services is a key contributor to its long-term profitability. Yet expectations as to how business should respond to society's problems and pressures have changed markedly over the past few years.

BUSINESS AND SOCIETY: THEN AND NOW

In January, 1925, President Calvin Coolidge made a speech to the Society of American Newspaper Editors in which he made the often-quoted remark: "The business of America is business." By and large that statement was accepted then as a reasonably accurate definition of what the United States was all about. Corporations generated a large part of the nation's wealth and growth at the time, and the government was committed to furthering the prosperity of these and other business activities. It was indeed the heyday of corporate business.

Business Dethroned

With the Depression and the emergence of the New Deal era in the 1930s, the "Captain of Industry" no longer guided the corporate ship of growth and affluence with a sure and steady hand. A combination of massive unemployment and the collapse of farm prices created a popular demand for governmental intervention and control over many aspects of our economy not previously regulated. This expansion of government involvement included control of agricultural prices, support of collective bargaining, Social Security legislation, regulation of security exchanges, and increased supervision over money and banking. No longer was the role of government to support business; it was now to regulate and moderate business behavior.

Traditional Business Responsibility

Clearly the attitudes and the expectations of society concerning business behavior changed dramatically from 1929 to 1935. But how did business view its responsibilities? Basically business saw its obligations as it had since the 1800s: (1) the pursuit of profit tempered with (2) occasional corporate and personal philanthropy.

THE PURSUIT OF PROFIT

The position taken by many entrepreneurs of the 19th century was that their exclusive obligation was to make profits. This was consistent with the economic philosophy of the times. The nation was best served, it was maintained, when each businessperson and company sought maximum gain in the competitive business scene. Consider, for example, this passage from Adam Smith's *The Wealth of Nations* (published in 1776):

> It is not from the benevolence of the butcher, the brewer, or the baker that we expect our dinner, but from their regard for their own interest. We address ourselves not to their humanity, but to their self-love, and never talk to them of our own necessities but of their own advantages.[1]

In the Smithian approach the businessperson should always operate to enhance the owner's **self-interest**. An entrepreneur had no social responsibility except to provide the best possible products and services at competitive prices. A corollary belief was that this self-interest would benefit the country as a whole in the goods and services provided, and this was the entrepreneur's sole responsibility to society.

[1]Adam Smith, *The Wealth of Nations* (London: George Routledge & Sons, n.d.), p. 11.

The assumption here is that the social needs of the country would be cared for through the private philanthropy of the dividend-receiving stockholders or through government agencies, churches, and community activities. This traditional credo of responsibility to the stockholder has carried over into the present in many companies.

CORPORATE AND PERSONAL PHILANTHROPY

As the country grew in population, a number of institutions emerged that needed financial help from outside sources in order to survive. Among these were colleges and universities, libraries, hospitals, and museums. Wealthy owners of successful businesses felt the need to make large contributions to these various institutions. In 1847 Amos Lawrence gave a grant of $50,000 to Harvard University. Andrew Carnegie established a number of libraries bearing his name. Leland Stanford created a university, also bearing his name, in California. John D. Rockefeller founded the University of Chicago in 1896 and later endowed the General Education Board with $53 million to help in the education of Southern black persons. In 1914 Henry Ford created a sensation in the industrial world by raising his worker's wages from $2.34 to $5.00 a day; two years later he established the Henry Ford Trade School where young men were taught a trade. He also changed his hiring policies to encourage the employment of various types of disadvantaged persons and instituted a profit-sharing system for the benefit of his employees. It is notable that all these men either made these benefactions from their own funds or owned the companies whose profits provided them.

In 1951 the A. P. Smith Manufacturing Company gave $1,500 to Princeton University for its use. Here was an instance of a corporation using its funds, legally the property of the stockholders, for a purpose not connected with its own business. Nevertheless, in 1953 the New Jersey court ruled that this action was not illegal, for prior to this case the revision of the Federal Revenue Act in 1935 had included a section that permitted corporations to deduct up to five percent of their net income for contributions made to nonprofit organizations. Since then many businesses regularly make such contributions with the amounts varying considerably from company to company.

Enlarging the Scope of Business Responsibilities

Ten years ago the business-society relationship was relatively clear. Government and business each had its role, and it was felt that both would only perform their roles effectively if they recognized their respective boundaries. Now social expectations that business accept a social commitment beyond profit require possible changes in the image of business and in the self-interest argument of traditional economists and moral philosophers such as Adam Smith.

Today the spotlight is focused more squarely on business, and many corporations are seeking a philosophy that will include the well-being of society as a whole. This social involvement is not regarded, however, as simply an extension of the corporation's traditional philanthropic activities. Underpinning this social awareness and responsibility is the acceptance of the pluralistic nature of our society and the feeling that corporations must accept the responsibility that goes with their position of leadership and power in our country.

SOCIAL PLURALISM AND BUSINESS POWER

Pluralism refers to institutional, organizational, and associational arrangements for distributing power. Thus, a **pluralistic society** is composed of many diverse institutions, associations, and groups with a wide dispersion of leadership that effects a power balance among these groups.

Although business is a major social institution in our society, it exists within the framework provided by other institutions such as government, religion, law and politics, the military, agriculture, family life, and education. Perhaps the more noticeable trend at the institutional level is the growing distribution of power between business and government. Yet within our institutions one finds semiautonomous groups that likewise command attention, such as professional associations, trade associations, farm organizations, and fraternal and service groups.

A POWER BALANCE

Generally the exemplary pluralistic state is one in which autonomous or semiautonomous groups will naturally complement and moderate each other, requiring a minimum of government control. The pluralistic nature of our society would be threatened if one or a few of the institutions became too powerful. Thus, the desirability of maintaining social pluralism has been a key consideration in defending the growing social involvement of business and in explaining the relatively restrained use of power by corporate business.

Beyond the Profit Motive

The motivation to economic activity in our society comes from the profit motive — from the carrot rather than the stick. Without the profit motive, some form of compulsion would have to be used; one cannot organize the economic activity of the nation based solely on altruism, good works, or volunteer public service.

The corporate manager knows that the dynamic force of the profit motive works to build a better society. But corporate managers are in charge of a social institution and have responsibilities not just to shareholders but to society at large. The expectation is that business, in addition to its traditional accountability for economic performance and results, will be concerned with the quality of life in our society. This new role requires business to respond to the challenges of two major elements in its environment: the social element and the physical element.

BUSINESS RESPONSE TO ITS SOCIAL ENVIRONMENT

In demonstrating to society its fitness to be the trustee of our nation's resources, a business earns the right to make a profit by the way it conducts itself with at least five groups: (1) its customers, (2) its stockholders, (3) its employees, (4) its suppliers and distributors, and (5) its community.

Customers

Consumerism, from food cleanliness to protection from rotary lawn mowers, indicates something fundamental is happening. Serving the customer today involves much more than a rehash of old marketing techniques. Value is provided by consistently offering the desired quality, price, packaging, and service; and these evoke some hard questions. Does one's advertising and sales techniques clearly reveal the true quality, function, and price of the product? Does the service measure up to the warranties? Are the advertising claims truthful? Generally businesspersons must assess their marketing practices not only in the business context, but also in terms of their social implications. Chapter 12 will deal far more extensively with such points.

Stockholders

Stockholders must get a proper return on their investment or they will sell their stock and dry up a company's resources through lower stock prices in the future. But this is not a mandate for corporations to pursue only profit and turn their backs on social issues. Stockholders are beginning to recognize that enlightened company managers often perform well in both arenas. Stockholders also are aware that opportunities for the future profit performance of a company often involve an awareness of and response to activities that both enhance social good and earn a profit.

Employees

Traditional economic theory, as well as actual practice at times, regarded the elements of production — land, labor, and capital — as more or less impersonal factors to be manipulated to maximize profit. Today, however, employees are being regarded instead as an important asset that does not appear on the balance sheet. These **human resources** desire not only a paycheck but a good place to work, including job security, opportunity for development, fringe benefits, and good relationships with co-workers and the company.

This more recent viewpoint often requires that business managers grapple with questions such as the relationship of pay to productivity; the responsibility to senior workers; the involvement of employees in decision-making processes; and the responsibility to hire and train disadvantaged persons such as hard-core minorities, school dropouts, and ex-convicts.

Suppliers and Distributors

It is not enough simply to avoid favoritism and discrimination in dealing with suppliers and agencies in the channel of distribution such as wholesalers, brokers, and retailers. To be fair and equitable today means recognizing that these parties have a right to make a profit — to earn a proper return on their service — rather than wringing the last dollar out of a transaction. Furthermore, a mutually honest relationship with these parties may yield new ideas for product development and distribution.

Community

A company's **community** may be local, national, or worldwide. Response to community pressures means more than paying taxes. It may require dealing with questions such as the possible involvement of the company in urban and social renewal, major contributions of funds and employee support of civic programs, whether or not to support private and public schools, and whether to encourage employees to enter politics and to take part in city councils and other agencies.

The key function and obligation of business managers is to generate long-term profits for the owners of the enterprise, as well as goods and services needed by society. What is being asked in this section, however, is whether business is being socially responsive when it makes a good product or service, pays decent wages, and yields a good profit to its owners. Or is something further required of the business community in its various relationships with customers, suppliers, human resources, the community, and society in general?

BUSINESS RESPONSE TO ITS PHYSICAL ENVIRONMENT

Progress may be defined as gradual betterment, especially the growing development of people. In this regard many view progress and growth — particularly economic growth — as nearly synonymous. The high priority that public policy assigns to the goal of economic growth suggests that it serves as a sort of proxy indicator of progress and our gradual betterment.

As the U.S. economy recently surpassed the $1 trillion GNP (gross national product) mark, Americans have made the painful discovery that bigness does not necessarily mean best. Along with the highest standard of living in the world, bigness has brought problems in the deterioration of land, air, and water that our nation has not learned to handle. Is this a necessary result of enterprise capitalism? Not really, for **pollution** is not a political phenomenon but rather a by-product of an attitude toward a commitment to growth, with the least-cost use of technological power.

Global Pollution

Pollution is an international problem. And because so much of it is caused by industry, it is rapidly becoming an international business problem. It would be hard to overestimate the scope of problems facing those who want to curb international pollution. For example, Jacques Picard, the Swiss oceanographer, has estimated that 10 million tons of petroleum products are being dumped into oceans each year. The Adriatic Sea is regarded as a cesspool by international health authorities. And Thor Heyerdahl reports that during a voyage in 1971 from Morocco to Barbados in a primitive vessel, his party encountered obvious waterborne pollution on 43 of the 57 days of the trip.

Ecology and Our Ecosystem

Years ago **ecology** was defined as the economy of animals and plants. In its present use ecology is the science of the relations between organisms and their environment. Recognizing that organisms and their environment are interacting parts of a system, an ecologist uses the term **ecosystem** to mean the community of living things and the physical environment of this system.

Unfortunately our examples of global pollution reinforce the fact that people are involved in a massive, complicated, interdependent ecosystem where everything is related to everything else. No human being, whether living in

Belgrade or Boston, can consider that he or she is living in a world apart from everyone else; everything is connected even if in ways that may neither be understood nor appreciated.

Business and Pollution

Business is clearly implicated in environmental issues, since it is the activating element — the transforming mechanism — in our enterprise system. It is the institution that combines our raw and semiprocessed resources and creates goods from them. Because it organizes and channels a high proportion of the activity in this society, there is little chance that business can emerge unscathed from discussions of pollution pressure points.

But this section is not intended as a whipping post for business. Federal, state, and municipal governments are also implicated in acts of environmental crime as are our military services. Instead the purpose is to provide an overview of three environmental areas that business faces and of the growing expectations of society that business recognize its responsibility to cease its contributions to ecological problems and to exercise its leadership and expertise in their solution.

AIR POLLUTION

Our nation is annually attacked by over 214 million tons of air pollutants, including carbon monoxide, hydrocarbons, nitrogen oxides, particulates, and sulfur oxides. The effects of this bombardment range from stunting the growth of citrus groves and cattle to interfering with the work of airline pilots, city planners, and farmers and manufacturers who need clean air to produce the goods they market.

Part of the problem lies in its complexity. The nature and seriousness of air pollution can vary from place to place, season to season, and even hour to hour. The major variables affecting the air pollution problem at any one time and place are: types of pollutants, quantity of pollutants, wind speed and direction, topography, sunlight, precipitation, and changes in air temperature with altitude.

Further insight into the overall complexity of the air problem may be acquired by realizing that just one of the dimensions — types of pollutants — is potentially composed of carbon monoxide, sulfur dioxide, photochemical smog, nitric oxide, nitrogen dioxide, hydrocarbons, and particulates such as arsenic, asbestos fibers, beryllium, cadmium, and fluorides.

Source Emissions. What causes all these pollutants? A few years ago the Office of Air Programs of the Environmental Protection Agency estimated national emissions of principal pollutants by major source category. Figure 3-1 reveals that transportation (using the internal combustion engine), commerce, and industry are major offenders. But even these data must be taken with a grain of salt, for the extent of air pollution varies widely from one city to another and within each city. A city's size, population, topography, type of industry, and amount of traffic all exert important influences on the amount and type of waste material in the air.

The Control of Air Pollution. The Clean Air Act as amended in 1970, the "Muskie Bill," is an ambitious and rigorous act directed by the administrator of the Environmental Protection Agency (EPA) that sets acceptable maximum levels for 10 major pollutants. Each state was originally required to translate federal standards into emission tolerances for local industry and to require full enforcement by 1975. It also required 1975 model cars to reduce carbon monoxide and hydrocarbons by 90 percent, and nitrogen oxides by the same amount in 1976.

The implementation of this act is receiving some resistance from utilities and smelters, the automobile industry, and the EPA's own limited human and technical resources. Nevertheless, despite the hesitations and the energy crunch, the general thrust of the 1970 Clean Air Act is still attainable before 1980.

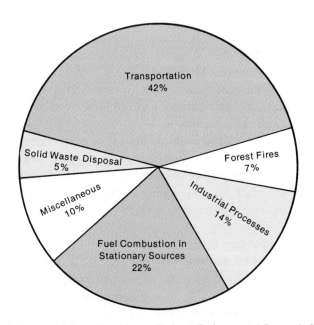

SOURCE: U.S. Environmental Protection Agency, National Environmental Research Center, February, 1973.

Figure 3-1 *Estimate of Nationwide Emissions by Source*

WATER POLLUTION

Just how bad water pollution can get was dramatically illustrated in the summer of 1969 when the Cuyahoga River in Cleveland, supersaturated with unreclaimed oils and other wastes from steel mills and other industries lining the bank, caught fire! In this instance a slick comprised of a huge accumulation of oil that apparently was dumped into the river ignited and shot flames 200 feet into the air. It floated downstream under two wooden railway trestles, which also caught fire. Both tracks curled from the heat and had to be closed. State and local laws prohibited dumping of industrial wastes into the Cuyahoga, but the laws rarely have been invoked.

Quantity of Industrial Wastes. A 21-month study performed in 1970-1971 by a Ralph Nader task force concluded that the single most important shortcoming of the federal water control program begun in 1956 has been its failure to control industrial wastes. In addition to direct industrial discharges, industries also are believed to contribute almost half of the loads handled by municipal waste-water plants, and thus are much to blame for the overloaded facilities at many such plants. Figure 3-2 presents the ranges of adequacy found in municipal sewage treatment plants.

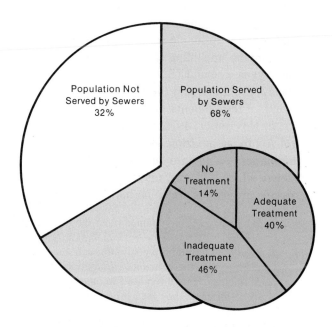

SOURCE: U.S. Department of the Interior, *Clean Water for the 1970s* (as presented in the Council on Environmental Quality's booklet, *Controlling Pollution*, p. 6).

Figure 3-2 Municipal Wastes: Adequacy of Treatment

Quality of Industrial Wastes. The quality of waste water often is measured in terms of its **biochemical oxygen demand (BOD)**, or the amount of dissolved oxygen that is needed by bacteria in decomposing the wastes. Waste water with a much higher BOD content than sewage is produced by such operations as leather tanning, beet sugar refining, and meat packing. Industry also contributes a vast amount of organic chemicals. All together, manufacturing activities, transportation, and agriculture probably account for about two thirds of all water degradation.

Control of Water Pollution. Two basic approaches to the control of water pollution are being pursued at the present time: the Refuse Act Permit Program and the Federal Water Pollution Control Act (Zero-Discharge "Muskie Bill"). In 1899 President William McKinley signed a relatively simple law known as the Refuse Act. Its basic purpose was to keep the nation's waterways free of obstacles to navigation, and it did this by barring anyone from dumping refuse into rivers or lakes without a permit from the Army Corps of Engineers.

In 1971 President Nixon updated the old law to regulate discharge from some 40,000 industrial plants across the country. Since July, 1971, companies discharging effluents into virtually any waterway must apply for a permit from the Corps of Engineers and the regional EPA administrators, who jointly run the program. In an eleven-page form the companies must disclose what they are dumping, including chemical composition, temperature, acidity, biochemical oxygen demand (BOD), and solids content. After a review by the state agency, the EPA, and the Corps of Engineers, the Corps of Engineers issues permits if the effluents meet existing state water-quality standards.

In November, 1971, the Senate passed the Federal Water Pollution Control Act by an amazing 86-0 roll-call vote. Under this law every company that discharges waste into any waterway must receive a permit from a state agency which will set emission limits under EPA guidelines. In addition three specific provisions are to be met:

1. By July, 1977, companies must employ the best practicable control technology.
2. By 1985 the ultimate goal, although not enforceable under the law, is **zero discharge** — the complete elimination of water pollution.
3. Municipalities are required to have secondary treatment plants under way by 1974. Then they face the same zero-discharge goals as industry.

Lined up against the bill were the Administration, some economists, and most business groups. Supporting the bill were the environmentalists and large sectors of the public, as indicated by the Senate vote. If Senator Muskie's bill and the EPA can successfully balance the nation's need for higher water standards with the tough problem of gearing those standards to what is both economically and ecologically acceptable, this effort deserves public support and gratitude. This is a big "if," but the country can no longer afford not to take calculated risks to resolve water pollution problems.

SOLID WASTES POLLUTION

Solid wastes are generated by many varied industrial activities. Whey from the production of cheese; iron oxides, acids, and slag from steel production; radioactive materials from nuclear power plants; ash and particulates from fossil-fueled plants; taconite tailings from mining; and junk cars are only a few of the possible offenders from industry. And industry is one offender among many.

Solid wastes total around 5 billion tons a year. Mineral wastes, mostly from mining, come to about 2 billion tons; agricultural wastes such as manure in feed lots, about 2.5 billion tons; and nonrecycled industrial wastes, about 150 million tons. Residential, commercial, and institutional wastes come to about 300 million tons, of which about 200 million tons are collected and disposed of by public agencies.

The Health, Education, and Welfare (HEW) Department's Bureau of Solid Waste Management is looking for solutions to the problem, but the choices are not wide. Most experts conclude that there are really only two practical ways to get rid of solid junk: (1) burn it or (2) recycle it.

Burning. There are about 400 municipal incinerators in America; many of them are woefully inefficient except as air polluters. Nevertheless, they continue to gain in use as an alternative to landfill because of the lack of landfill sites in metropolitan areas.

Recycling. The reprocessing of used materials and waste into a form that is salable and/or reusable is called **recycling**. Our economic system has been built on nearly cost-free use of abundant resources: air, water, and land. It has generated ingenious processes to extract raw materials and turn them into finished products. But it has done little to turn exhausted products into useful material. Industry must begin to look seriously at pollution as unused resources. The idea that waste is a raw material and that it can be converted into new and useful products by recycling is gaining support. While recycling support grows, our priorities and the means of meeting them are unclear. For the intermediate future at least, dumping and landfill will continue as prime disposal methods for the majority of American communities.

Industry, however, faces more visible internal and external constraints and pressures. The packaging industry favors more waste accumulation, along with the development of power generation using refuse as a fuel. The salvage industry tends to support better collection and separation. And environmentalists would ban many disposable goods, which would reduce collection costs as well as the loss of raw materials used in disposables. There is no single answer at this point, nor is there even a clear equation for balancing the various possibilities.

Business in the Middle

Some level of concern about the deterioration of our environment is indicated by public opinion polls; letters to the President, Congress, and newspapers; and the efforts of countless local student and citizen-action groups. This problem has many dimensions: air, water, and noise pollution; inadequate disposal of solid waste; loss of open space to development; and the effects of technology and "progress." When it comes to the design and implementation of remedial action programs, however, this momentum loses much of its steam. To manage our nation as an ecosystem would be like fighting a major war and would cost billions of dollars.

Businesspersons are caught up in all of these issues. They trust neither the government nor one another to strike a realistic balance. While conceding their responsibility, they feel they should not be singled out as the only culprits since municipalities and the military are also heavily involved. Businesspersons are also concerned that the government may respond to public pressure by dictating the rapid spending of huge sums of money by industry on pollution abatement. This would sap the financial position of their companies without really getting down to the long-term resolution of the basic causes of the environmental problems.

Furthermore, when one business commits money to better the environment, it incurs costs that will compromise its competitive position in the marketplace unless other companies in the industry follow suit. The sums are often so large that no matter how much a company may want to be a good citizen, it will be more a matter of "cannot" than "will not." It is unrealistic to expect that business leadership, however well-intentioned, can clean up the environment without guidelines from government. For an all-out attack on pollution the federal government should set the standards and regulate the involvement of all enterprises within an industry so that a legitimate balance is achieved.

BUSINESS ETHICS AND ENLIGHTENED SELF-INTEREST

Ethics is a philosophical discipline that deals with the "rightness" or the morality of human conduct — what is good and bad and what constitutes moral duty and obligation. **Business ethics** is a set or code of principles or values accepted by business and society in general as being moral guides to conduct in business situations. Ethics can be distinguished from morals. Ethics are situational and temporal; what is considered good or right varies over time and from group to group. **Morals,** on the other hand, are enduring, absolute standards or principles that guide behavior regardless of the situation. Figure 3-3 below shows the Code of Ethics for the American Marketing Association.

It is frequently quite difficult to distinguish between the concepts of ethics and social responsibility. Ethical actions are often the specific end results of a general awareness by businesspersons of the need to respond to social expectations.

Ethics in the Nineteenth Century

A century ago people in business did not find business ethics a problem. The free competitive market of the 19th century, based on the market system presented in Adam Smith's *The Wealth of Nations*, was both ethical and moral. It rewarded and penalized according to a standard that was considered righteous and just by allowing each person to follow selfish pursuits. The market guided the entrepreneur in providing goods and services, with the "invisible hand" of competition penalizing those who abused customers and rewarding those who dealt justly.

The golden rule was replaced by a belief that any action businesspersons could take to increase their profits in the competitive marketplace was moral because it would prove to be good for the public and the nation. Surprisingly, one still often hears this viewpoint expressed today in business.

As a member of the American Marketing Association, I recognize the significance of my professional conduct and my responsibilities to society and to the other members of my profession:

1. By acknowledging my accountability to society as a whole as well as to the organization for which I work.

2. By pledging my efforts to assure that all presentations of goods, services and concepts be made honestly and clearly.

3. By striving to improve marketing knowledge and practice in order to better serve society.

4. By supporting free consumer choice in circumstances that are legal and are consistent with generally accepted community standards.

5. By pledging to use the highest professional standards in my work and in competitive activity.

6. By acknowledging the right of the American Marketing Association, through established procedure, to withdraw my membership if I am found to be in violation of ethical standards of professional conduct.

Figure 3-3 **AMA Code of Ethics**

Old Ethics; New Demands

A new role of business in America — a transformation from the tough, single-minded, profit-seeking entrepreneur to the responsive manager with the vision and willingness to help right the wrongs of society — is being demanded. Businesspersons look to the old traditional business ethic and no longer find it comfortable to be told that only the market determines their decisions and ethics. Hard-hitting, aggressive practices of the past may now be considered arrogant or unconscionable. Personal standards or codes of ethics do not always face up to the realities of specific daily challenges at the business-society interface; neither do these standards account for the complexities of differing situations.

Enlightened Self-Interest

Recognizing that the old business ethic often fails to bring together business responsibilities and personal ethics in a social climate that increasingly highlights the discrepancies between the two, business decision makers often develop situational standards that allow them to adjust their firm's behavior to fit specific circumstances. That is, they hope to balance the profit expectations of stockholders with the needs and expectations of groups concerned with social and environmental issues. This approach is that of **enlightened self-interest,** defined as creating a social and physical environment that allows one to remain in business.

An example of enlightened self-interest is found in the instance where a company locates a new plant in a congested, dilapidated racial ghetto. Mixed motives of social activism, public relations, and profit are almost certain to be involved in this decision. On the one hand, ghetto production costs, especially for hiring and training, will be high. City taxes are high. Black resentment can flare at white intrusion, however altruistic management's motives may be.

On the other hand, with generous help from government orders for ghetto plants' products and federal training grants for workers, as well as possible tax incentives for ghetto-located plants, it is possible that manufacturing in the ghetto may be better business than it seems. But the chances of a ghetto plant's returning as much on the investment as a more favorably located facility seem slim.

A move into the ghetto, then, may be a good business move in terms of acceptable profit. But in most instances social activism and public relations figure in decisions to enter a ghetto. In all, the country benefits from decisions of this type.

BUSINESS TERMS

QUESTIONS FOR DISCUSSION AND ANALYSIS

1. In *The Wealth of Nations*, Adam Smith took the position that the pursuit of one's self-interest works to the benefit of society. When may this not be true?
2. What strengths does the traditional view of social responsibility have?
3. Should the quality of life of employees be a part of a firm's social commitment? Discuss.
4. "A trade-off exists between social concern and profit; executives who show concern for environmental problems do so at the expense of their stockholders." Do you agree with this statement?
5. "Controlling pollution destroys jobs. Environmentalists are anti-worker; they would make air and water pure without regard as to whether or not people have food on their tables." Defend or reject this statement.
6. What type of pollution is the most difficult to eliminate or control?
7. What might be some arguments used to support and reject recycling of solid wastes?
8. Do you think that the federal government should stay out of pollution control? Discuss.
9. Discuss whether "good" ethical practices should be enacted into law.
10. What is your opinion of an industry code of ethics?

PROBLEMS AND SHORT CASES

1. Ask three business managers what business social responsibility means to them and how they feel about it. Classify the general responses of each person into one of the three following categories: profit-maximization and self-interest, "enlarged" pluralistic responsibility, or enlightened self-interest. Before your interviews make a list of questions you may need to ask to verify that the businesspersons are responding as they really feel.
2. George Anderson saw the 1976 U.S. Bicentennial celebration as a chance of a lifetime to promote the visibility of his stationery supply company and make a substantial profit at the same time. He planned to produce desk sets, bookends, stationery, calendars, and appointment books in red, white, and blue colors, affixed with the official star-shaped bicentennial logotype. For the use of this logotype, Anderson paid a fee of 5 percent of his sales to the U.S. American Bicentennial Administration (ARBA). This licensing arrangement,

although expensive, allowed Anderson to nearly double the usual prices for such merchandise. Despite the lucrative nature of these products, Anderson was disturbed when a Revolutionary War study group in his town accused his company of lacking social responsibility with its crass, tasteless commercialism. Prepare an oral report presenting some pros and cons of this situation from the standpoint of: (a) business, and (b) government.

3. Prepare a report on the pros and cons of Senator Muskie's zero-discharge water control bill from the standpoints of: (a) a manager of an industrial plant such as a steel mill, and (b) a government environmental official.

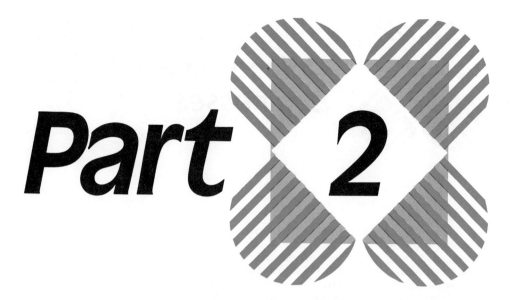

Part 2

Business Ownership, Organization, and Management

One of the outstanding characteristics of a capitalistic economic system is the ownership of the vast majority of business enterprises by one, two, or even thousands of individuals. These persons not only own but also organize their firms in such a manner that the businesses can then be managed efficiently. These important steps in creating and operating a business are the main topics of the chapters that comprise Part 2.

A sharp distinction as to ownership exists between unincorporated units and those that are incorporated. Although Chapter 4 describes several types of unincorporated businesses, it devotes major attention to sole proprietorships and partnerships as these two forms dominate this category of ownership. Chapter 5 presents a similar treatment of incorporated businesses with considerable stress on the corporation and its importance in the business world.

The last two chapters in this part take up the topics of organizing for management and the actual activities in which managers engage. Almost every business needs to have an internal organization that allows employees — from laborers to executives — to know their areas of responsibility and authority. Once these are established, as described in Chapter 6, the methods used and functions performed by managers can be explained. These, as well as the factors that motivate those who are classified as business leaders, are discussed in Chapter 7.

4

Unincorporated Businesses

Andrew Harris couldn't sleep. Business was excellent at his sporting goods store but his bank account was down to a few dollars. Several bills for merchandise were overdue and payday was next week. Unexpected family needs had exhausted all of his resources. He knew more than one individual who would be happy to invest in his business but only on a profit-sharing basis. If a change in type of ownership was a necessity, what shape should it take? Over and over he considered one option after another, but as the sun came up Harris hadn't had any sleep nor had he reached a decision.

Ownership of business units by one individual or by a group of individuals is an important characteristic of capitalism. As noted in Chapter 1, the right to own property and to use it for profit-making purposes is basic to a free enterprise system. Government ownership of business, nevertheless, also exists in a capitalistic economy. In our country most men and women are familiar with such examples as the federal postal system, state parks, liquor stores, municipal water systems, and bus lines. But they are also aware that the vast majority of businesses are privately owned. Furthermore, because the general public believes that business operations are conducted more efficiently under private ownership, a change in the current situation seems very unlikely.

Another characteristic of business ownership in the United States is that the all-important private sector can be divided into two major categories. One includes all forms of unincorporated business ownership; the other, all types that have been incorporated. The distinction between the two is simply that the one or more individuals who organized the unincorporated business did not apply for nor receive permission from any governmental body to operate, whereas the incorporated business was chartered by a state or in rare instances the federal government.

A further breakdown of the two major types discloses that sole proprietorships and partnerships dominate the unincorporated category and that a high percentage of incorporated businesses are corporations. The extensive use of these three forms of business ownership comprises a large part of the environment in which business operates in the United States. Despite the availability of optional unincorporated and incorporated forms, which will be described in this and the next chapter, an individual or group of persons starting a business will almost universally organize either a sole proprietorship, a partnership, or a corporation.

The type of ownership used can be and frequently is vital to the success of a business enterprise. A sole proprietorship, for example, may fail for want of capital that could have been provided by a partnership or corporation. Partners may disagree so violently that the success of the firm is jeopardized by internal strife which could have been avoided had there been a single owner. Since an understanding of ownership is basic to an understanding of business, two chapters will be devoted to an explanation of the various forms of business ownership and their uses. This chapter will dwell at some length on sole proprietorships, partnerships, and other forms of unincorporated business ownership. Chapter 5 will be devoted primarily to the corporation, although other forms of incorporated businesses will also be discussed.

SOLE PROPRIETORSHIPS

A **sole proprietorship** is a business owned by one person and operated for one's own profit. Such an individual who goes into business is, for certain purposes, classified as self-employed. The term "sole proprietorship" is interchangeable with single proprietorship, individual enterprise, sole ownership, and individual proprietorship.

Characteristics of a Sole Proprietorship

Although a few large proprietorships do exist, typically the sole proprietorship is the ownership form for the small-town restaurant, the neighborhood grocery store, the local TV and radio repair shop, and the bakery. The owner, aided by a few employees, conducts a small business that usually caters to the consuming public. Although the owner may employ someone to manage the business, more commonly he or she is the active manager of the firm.

The capital necessary for operating the business is normally provided by the sole proprietor from personal wealth, frequently augmented by borrowing. The owner is responsible for all decisions and usually makes them personally rather than delegating them to employees. The business may well be the owner's sole source of livelihood and, if it is, the ability to operate it at a profit is vitally important to the sole proprietor's family.

Sometimes a sole proprietorship can be identified by the name used, such as Judy Hawkins — Photographer, or Paul Palmer — Cement Contractor.

More commonly, however, the firm name does not indicate the type of owner-ship, e.g., the University Women's Shop or even the King Paint Company. In these two cases the owner must usually clear the name at the county court-house. Franchise holders, frequently operating as sole proprietors, often use the name of the parent concern, e.g., Kentucky Fried Chicken.

Table 4-1 shows that in the United States almost seven million individuals operate their own businesses. These figures, taken from income tax returns, include those who devoted full time to their establishments as well as those who operated a business as a sideline on a part-time basis. The figures do not include over three million persons who were engaged primarily in farming on their own account.

The table also shows that the largest number of sole proprietorships can be found in services, closely followed by the division of wholesale and retail trade, with retailers accounting for 82 percent of this category. Business re-ceipts, on the average, are approximately $32,000. The net profit of all sole proprietorships averages only about $4,850.

A comparison of these figures with similar data shown in Table 4-2 on page 66 and Table 5-2 on page 96 for partnerships and corporations will reveal another important characteristic of the sole proprietorship form of business ownership. Although constituting approximately 72 percent of all forms of

Table 4-1   *Sole Proprietorship Income Tax Returns*
(Number, Receipts, Net Profits, and Average Receipts by Industries[1])

Industry	Number of Returns	Business Receipts	Net Profit (Loss)	Average Business Receipts
		(Millions of Dollars)		
ALL INDUSTRIES[2]	6,966,411	$224,398	$33,884	$32,211
Mining	51,411	1,651	(13)	32,122
Construction	804,528	27,109	4,073	33,695
Manufacturing	202,776	7,916	949	39,039
Transportation, communication, electric, gas, and sanitary services	338,844	7,856	1,100	23,185
Wholesale and retail trade	2,172,991	124,207	8,300	57,159
Finance, insurance, and real estate	666,036	10,072	3,592	15,123
Services	2,693,126	44,864	15,787	16,659
Nature of business not allocable	36,699	722	96	19,684

SOURCE: United States Department of the Treasury, Internal Revenue Service, Preliminary Statistics of Income 1972, Business Income Tax Returns.

[1]Agriculture, forestry, and fisheries omitted.

[2]Due to rounding, items may not add to totals.

ownership, the volume of business done by sole proprietorships is less than 10 percent of the total volume of all three types.

Advantages of a Sole Proprietorship

Why is the sole proprietorship the most common form of business ownership? Aside from the innate urge many people have to go into business for themselves, some with the hope of high profits and others merely because they enjoy being the "boss," sole proprietorships have several advantages: (1) ease and low cost of organization, (2) ownership of all profits, (3) freedom and promptness of action, (4) personal incentive and satisfaction, (5) credit standing, (6) secrecy, and (7) ease of dissolution.

EASE AND LOW COST OF ORGANIZATION

Anyone can usually go into business without "red tape" or special legal procedures. For example, a farm hand who finishes painting a barn in the evening decides that he likes painting better than other farm chores, and the next morning he quits the farm to become a house painter. He can work by himself or, if his services are much in demand, he may hire others to work for him. In the latter case he may dignify his occupation by calling himself a painting contractor.

Restrictions on becoming a businessperson are not numerous or serious. Of course, the type of business chosen must be legal. In some instances a license is required by the state, city, or county. For example, in most localities a restaurant cannot operate without being approved by a county board of health and, if alcoholic beverages are served, it must secure a license from the appropriate state. An interesting exception to the no-restriction rule is that banks may not be organized by a single proprietor.

A sole proprietorship also costs little, if indeed anything at all, to be organized. The form is so simple and the amount of capital involved frequently is so minimal that no formal statement of ownership is required. By contrast, partnerships usually incur legal fees in drawing up a partnership agreement, and a corporation must pay an incorporation fee to the state that issues its charter.

OWNERSHIP OF ALL PROFITS

All the profits of a sole proprietorship always go to one individual. In a partnership at least one other person will receive a portion of the profits even though it might be a very small share. In the states that permit a corporation to be organized by one person, the advantage of 100 percent ownership of all profits would be comparable with a sole proprietorship. This condition would not prevail, however, in the several states that require multiple ownership of corporations.

FREEDOM AND PROMPTNESS OF ACTION

A sole proprietor has the maximum freedom of action. This individual is the "boss"; decisions made by this person are final. Sole proprietors may expand their businesses at will; they may add new products or discontinue old ones at their discretion; they may sell or close their businesses as they wish; and they may change from one kind of business to another as they please. Furthermore, these decisions can be made promptly because they need not consult others nor secure approval from any other individual or group. For the individual who does not work well with or for others, the sole proprietorship is the ideal form of business ownership.

The sole proprietorship is also free from government control to a greater extent than any other form of business ownership. A sole proprietor is usually allowed to do business in states other than the one in which the proprietor resides without special permission. Sole proprietors can work as many hours a day or week as they choose; they may pay themselves a large or a small salary. This freedom is, however, not complete. Sole proprietors must abide by state and federal labor laws as applicable to their employees. Sole proprietors must file reports if requested by authorized government agencies. Furthermore, they cannot ship certain merchandise into states that prohibit such shipments. Such government restrictions affect some sole proprietorships more than others, but for the vast majority they have little effect on the owner's freedom of action.

PERSONAL INCENTIVE AND SATISFACTION

Persons in business for themselves have everything to lose if their efforts are not successful; this makes them willing to devote a maximum amount of time, thought, and energy to the successful prosecution of the activity for which their firms were organized. Since there is no penalty for overtime, they may find themselves working 12 hours a day and 7 days a week. Nevertheless, if their businesses are successful, the individual owners enjoy a sense of accomplishment that cannot be matched when the glory must be shared with others.

CREDIT STANDING

Anyone who extends credit to a business owned by one person may look beyond the value of the firm to the owner's nonbusiness wealth. In contrast, an extension of credit to a corporation must be based entirely on the ability of the business to repay the debt. Assuming that a sole proprietorship and a corporation are identical in size and in the nature of the wealth owned, the credit standing of the sole proprietor usually will be better than that of the corporation unless the sole proprietor owns no assets beyond those invested in the business.

SECRECY

In some businesses the success of the enterprise is based on a secret process or formula. In others, general knowledge of profit margins, lease agreements, or other operative information might injure the competitive position of the firm. The sole proprietorship offers the best possibility that such information will not become known to others, particularly when the one person who knows these secrets is also the owner of the business.

EASE OF DISSOLUTION

Although it may not be as easy to dissolve a sole proprietorship as it is to form one, there are no legal complications and the procedure may be very simple. For example, a building contractor who has already completed a construction project decides that it would be better now to accept a job offer as a carpenter. Assuming that this individual has paid for the materials and labor used as a contractor, this decision is all that is needed to terminate the sole proprietorship.

Disadvantages of a Sole Proprietorship

Although the advantages of a sole proprietorship are more numerous than the disadvantages, any one of the objections may outweigh all the favorable factors. Before deciding that the sole proprietorship is the best form of business ownership, consideration should be given to the following possible disadvantages: (1) unlimited liability, (2) limitation on size, (3) difficulties of management, (4) lack of opportunities for employees, and (5) lack of continuity.

UNLIMITED LIABILITY

Unlimited liability refers to the availability of a person's wealth beyond the amount invested in a business to satisfy the claims of creditors of the business. For a sole proprietorship it means that practically everything an individual owns is subject to liquidation for the purpose of paying business debts. Every year thousands of sole proprietorships discontinue operations either voluntarily or because of failure. In each case creditors expect to collect the amounts owed them either from the business itself or from the non-business assets of the owner of the firm.

LIMITATION ON SIZE

The investment in a sole proprietorship is limited to the amount one person can raise by investing one's own estate, by borrowing, or by a combination of the two. If the business to be organized or expanded requires a substantial amount of capital, it may well be that the individual will find it necessary to choose another form of ownership.

Many of today's partnerships and corporations started out as sole proprietorships and changed because of capital requirements. For example, a sole proprietor operating a print shop determined that the volume of business and profits could be doubled by purchasing certain equipment that involved an immediate cash outlay of $36,000. Not having this amount of money on hand and not being able to raise it, the only recourse was to change the form of business ownership.

DIFFICULTIES OF MANAGEMENT

Since a sole proprietorship is ordinarily a small business, the owner often assumes the responsibility for managing such diverse tasks as purchasing, merchandising, extending credit, financing, and employing personnel. This individual may be unusually capable of handling some of these functions but unable to perform others. For example, a retail store with a large volume of business went into bankruptcy because the owner was so generous with extension of credit and was so poorly qualified to collect accounts that finally there was not sufficient money left to pay current bills.

LACK OF OPPORTUNITY FOR EMPLOYEES

If an employee of a sole proprietorship proves to be unusually able, he or she may not be content to work indefinitely for the owner. Even though an employee is well paid, including a generous bonus based on profits, this person may not be satisfied with a continuing status of being merely an employee. If the owner wishes to retain the employee's services, it may be necessary to form a partnership or a corporation in order to extend to this individual an opportunity to become a part owner of the business. Otherwise the employee may quit and, as frequently happens, start a competitive business in the same locality.

LACK OF CONTINUITY

Death, insanity, imprisonment, or bankruptcy of the owner terminates the life of a proprietorship. Furthermore, the physical inability of the owner to continue work often forces the enterprise to close its doors. A person may build up a fine business, but it is profitable only as long as this individual is able to run it. After the death of the owner, the heirs may try to continue the business, but they frequently lack the knowledge or the ability to operate it successfully.

PARTNERSHIPS

The Uniform Partnership Act[1] defines a **partnership** as "an association of two or more persons to carry on as co-owners a business for profit." Such a relationship is based on an agreement, written or oral, that is both voluntary and legal. A partnership is also referred to as a "copartnership."

Characteristics of a Partnership

Although the typical partnership is larger than the typical sole proprietorship, most partnerships are relatively small businesses. Even though the average annual total receipts for partnerships amount to approximately $111,500, the average net profits are only slightly more than $10,000, which are divided among two or more owners. Table 4-2 on page 66 shows that the finance, insurance, and real estate classification holds first place among partnerships in contrast with sole proprietorships, where this industrial division ranks fourth out of seven categories. The main reason for this number one ranking is that partnerships are a common form of business ownership for brokerage firms that sell securities, fire and casualty insurance, and real estate.

Some of the partnerships that do business in every city, town, and village can be identified by the firm name; others cannot. Names such as McGinnis, Hopkins, Wessel and Bassett, or Stanley & Son usually denote a partnership; whereas the Greenville Food Market might or might not be owned and operated as a partnership. If a fictitious partnership name is used, such as Read and Wright, some states require that a record showing the names of all partners be filed in the county office.

Of the three common forms of business ownership, partnerships are the least popular despite the sizable total of 877,586, not counting approximately 115,000 additional partnerships engaged in agriculture, forestry, and fisheries.

---

[1]The following ten states have not adopted the Uniform Partnership Act: Alabama, Florida, Georgia, Hawaii, Iowa, Kansas, Louisiana, Maine, Mississippi, and New Hampshire.

Table 4-2 **Partnership Income Tax Returns**
(Number, Receipts, Net Profits, and Average Receipts by Industries[1])

Industry	Number of Returns	Business Receipts (Millions of Dollars)	Net Profit (Loss) (Millions of Dollars)	Average Business Receipts
ALL INDUSTRIES[2]	877,586	$97,816	$8,870	$111,460
Mining	13,562	1,416	(386)	104,415
Construction	60,945	9,455	908	155,141
Manufacturing	30,176	5,689	400	188,538
Transportation, communication, electric, gas, and sanitary services	18,710	1,612	169	86,162
Wholesale and retail trade	196,486	36,656	2,221	186,560
Finance, insurance, and real estate	375,752	21,693	(949)	57,732
Services	172,864	20,991	6,463	121,429
Nature of business not allocable	9,091	303	43	33,371

SOURCE: United States Department of the Treasury, Internal Revenue Service, Preliminary Statistics of Income 1972, Business Income Tax Returns.

[1]Agriculture, forestry, and fisheries omitted.

[2]Due to rounding, items may not add to totals.

There are almost eight times as many sole proprietorships and over twice as many corporations. It is interesting that this form of ownership, which now ranks a poor third, was in second place ahead of corporations a quarter of a century ago.

THE PARTNERSHIP CONTRACT

It is most desirable, although usually not necessary, that the agreement between the parties be written and signed. Such a contract, known as **articles of partnership** or "articles of copartnership," may prevent misunderstanding and ill will among the partners at a future date. An oral contract is especially unsatisfactory if profits and losses are to be divided on any basis other than equal shares because positive proof is required to overcome the presumption of equality among partners.

The common provisions of a partnership contract cover the following:

1. The name of the firm.
2. The location and the type of business.
3. The length of life of the partnership agreement.
4. The names of the partners and the investment made by each.
5. The distribution of profits and losses.
6. A provision for salaries of partners.

7. An agreement on the amount of interest to be allowed on capital and drawing account balances.
8. A limitation on withdrawals of funds.
9. A provision for an accounting system and a fiscal year.
10. The method that will be followed in case of the withdrawal of a partner from the firm and other causes of dissolution.

Figure 4-1 on pages 68 and 69 shows how these items of information are included in formal articles of partnership.

NUMBER OF PARTNERS IN A PARTNERSHIP

Data provided by the Internal Revenue Service indicate that the vast majority — almost three fourths — of partnerships in this country consist of two partners. When the number of partnerships with three and four partners is included, the coverage increases to more than 92 percent. Most of the larger partnerships, in terms of members, are in the professions such as law and public accounting. For example, some firms of certified public accountants have over 500 partners and these large partnerships are responsibile for raising the average number of partners in all partnerships to 4.05. Retail stores, restaurants, and bowling alleys, if operated under the partnership form of business ownership, usually have two partners with the possibility of a third or fourth member. Exact percentages for each of five groupings are shown in Table 4-3.

Advantages of a Partnership

All forms of unincorporated businesses, including partnerships, share some advantages when contrasted with incorporated forms of business ownership. A partnership can be organized as easily as a sole proprietorship although an agreement based on a handshake is not as satisfactory as written articles of partnership. Freedom from governmental regulation approximates that of sole proprietorships, but it is not quite as extensive due to a variety of

Table 4-3 **Percentage Distribution of Number of Partners**

Two partners	73.1%
Three partners	13.8
Four partners	5.5
Five to nine partners	4.6
Ten or more partners	3.0
	100.0%

SOURCE: United States Department of the Treasury, Internal Revenue Service.

Articles of Partnership

THIS CONTRACT, made and entered into on the second day of January, 197-, by and between George C. Good and Arthur W. Hills, each of Columbus, Ohio.

WITNESSETH: That the said parties have this day formed a partnership for the purpose of engaging in and conducting a laundry, pressing, and dry cleaning business, and the doing of all things necessary and incident thereto, under the following stipulations which are made a part of this contract:

1. The said partnership shall commence on the second day of January, 197-, and continue from and after said date for a period of ten years at the pleasure of said partners; and shall be otherwise terminated by the death, bankruptcy, insolvency, or disability of either of the said parties thereto, or under the provisions for such act hereinafter set forth.

2. The business shall be conducted under the firm name of The Good Hills Laundromat at 987 N. High, Columbus, Ohio 43201.

3. The investments are as follows: George C. Good agrees to contribute to the capital of said partnership the sum of $30,000.00 and Arthur W. Hills the sum of $20,000.00, which shall be paid on the date of the execution of this agreement, and by the execution thereof by said partners the receipt of same is hereby acknowledged.

4. All profits and losses arising from said business are to be shared as follows: George C. Good, 60 percent; and Arthur W. Hills, 40 percent.

5. Each of said partners shall devote his entire time, skill, labor, and experience to advancing and rendering profitable the interests and business of said partnership, and neither partner shall engage in any other business or occupation whatever on his individual account during the existence of said partnership without the written consent of the other partner.

6. A systematic record of all transactions is to be kept in a double-entry set of books in which shall be promptly and properly entered an account and record of all the transactions and business of the partnership. All books of account and all contracts, letters, papers, documents, and memoranda belonging to the partnership shall be open, at all times, to the examination of either of the partners. On December 31 hereafter a statement of the business is to be made, the books closed, and each partner credited with the amount of the gain or charged with his share of the loss. A statement may be made at such other times as the partners agree upon.

7. Each partner shall furnish to the other, on request, full information and account of any and all transactions and matters relating to the business of the partnership, within his knowledge.

8. All moneys received by, or paid to, said partnership shall be daily deposited in the Ohio National Bank, Columbus, Ohio, except a small change account used in the operations of said business not to exceed $30.00, or in such other bank as said partners may mutually agree upon. All disbursements of partnership moneys in excess of $10.00 shall be made by check on said partnership bank account. Checks for amounts drawn on partnership accounts may be drawn by either of said partners.

9. No partner shall at any time sign the firm name, or his own name, or pledge the firm's credit, or his own individual credit, in any manner as surety or guarantor on any paper, bill, bond, note, or draft or other obligation whatsoever. Neither shall he assign, pledge, or mortgage any of the partnership property, or his interest therein, or do anything or permit any act whereby the firm's money, interest, or property, or his interest therein, may be liable to seizure, attachment, or execution.

10. Each partner shall promptly pay his individual debts and liabilities and shall at all times indemnify and save harmless the partnership property therefrom.

11. Each partner is to have a salary of $950.00 per month, the same to be withdrawn at such time or times as he may elect. Neither partner is to withdraw from the business an amount in excess of his salary without the written consent of the other. Interest at the rate of 6 percent per annum shall be allowed on the amount of investment each partner shall have in the business in excess of his original contribution as determined at the close of each month. Salaries and interest shall be considered expenses of doing business before arriving at net profit or net loss.

Figure 4-1 **Articles of Partnership**

12. The duties of each partner are defined as follows: George C. Good is to have general supervision of the business and have charge of the accounting records, correspondence, and credits and collections. Arthur W. Hills is to have supervision of all machinery used within and without the business and the purchase of supplies and equipment. Each partner is to attend to such other duties as are deemed necessary for the successful operation of the business.

13. One partner may, at any time, dissolve said partnership by written notice of his intention to do so, delivered or mailed to the other partner, and said partnership shall be dissolved at the expiration of sixty days after the giving of such notice.

14. At the time of giving notice of dissolution of said partnership, or any other termination thereof as set out in the first stipulation above, an inventory and appraisement of all assets and property of said partnership shall be made by three disinterested parties engaged in the same or similar business in this vicinity, to be chosen by the partners to this agreement or their legal representative, at the true value to the business thereof; and an account shall be taken of all assets and liabilities. After payment of all debts and liabilities of said partnership, the assets and property so remaining shall be divided between the partners, their heirs and assigns, in the proportion in which the capital of said partnership has been contributed by each. Provided, however, that if either of the original partners to this agreement desires to carry on the said business he shall have the first option to take over said business at the net value as calculated from the account so made and assume all operations thereunder in his own right and relieve the other partner, his heirs and assigns from all liabilities. Said option to be enforceable shall be exercised within ten days after the accounting of the partnership has been made. Each partner for himself, his heirs and assigns hereby agrees to execute all instruments necessary or proper to invest the other with the property, real, personal or mixed, so taken over by him.

15. No changes, alterations, additions, modifications, or qualifications shall be made or had in the terms of this contract unless made in writing and signed by each of the partners.

IN WITNESS WHEREOF, the parties have hereunto set their hands to duplicate copies hereof, the day and year first above written.

Signed in the presence of:

Betty Barnett   _George C. Good_

Lee N. DeVore   _Arthur W. Hills_

STATE OF OHIO, COUNTY OF FRANKLIN, SS:

Personally appeared before me, a Notary Public within and for said State and County, the above named George C. Good and Arthur W. Hills, the parties to the foregoing contract, who each acknowledged the signing thereof to be his voluntary act and deed, for the uses and purposes therein mentioned.

IN WITNESS WHEREOF, I have hereunto set my hand and seal this second day of January, 197–

Helen Thomas
Notary Public, Franklin County, Ohio

Figure 4-1   **Articles of Partnership (concluded)**

state laws covering partnerships. The tax situation can be favorable as, unlike corporations, there is no levy against unincorporated forms of business ownership. Taxes on income, however, can be favorable or unfavorable depending on the level of income of the owners, as well as other factors.

A partnership does have several distinct advantages. These include: (1) larger amount of capital, (2) credit standing, (3) combined judgment and managerial skills, (4) retention of valuable employees, (5) personal interest in business, and (6) definite legal status.

LARGER AMOUNT OF CAPITAL

In a sole proprietorship the amount of capital is limited to the personal fortune and credit of one individual. In a partnership the capital can easily be doubled, trebled, or otherwise increased by bringing in additional owners. An inventor with little capital, for example, may locate a rich person who is willing to become a partner by contributing a major portion of the total capital needed to produce and market the inventor's product.

CREDIT STANDING

Assuming three firms exactly equal in size, one a sole proprietorship, another a corporation, and the third a general partnership, the partnership would usually enjoy the highest credit standing. As in the case of the sole proprietorship, the personal wealth of the owners is available to satisfy business debts; and two or more owners should be an improvement favorable to creditors. In the case of the corporation, the owners do not risk their personal fortunes to satisfy business debts.

COMBINED JUDGMENT AND MANAGERIAL SKILLS

The old adage that two heads are better than one is true in the case of many partnerships. Partners can consult each other about proposed actions, and a wiser course of procedure may result. Sometimes two or three individuals complement each other in securing maximum operating efficiency. Adams is a genius at producing precision tools, but loses all interest in them as soon as they pass final inspection. Brown, on the other hand, is an outstanding salesperson but has no interest in the problems of manufacturing. As partners, the two individuals are very effective, but neither would be a success as a sole proprietor.

RETENTION OF VALUABLE EMPLOYEES

Changing to a partnership offers an opportunity for a sole proprietorship to retain the services of a valuable employee by making the latter a partner.

The same opportunity also applies to existing partnerships, although new articles of partnership are necessary. Legal and professional accounting firms make extensive use of the practice of admitting new partners.

PERSONAL INTEREST IN BUSINESS

Since each general partner is liable for the actions of the other partners, all are vitally concerned in every move made by the business. A sense of responsibility to those with whom each is closely associated enhances the personal interest factor. Compared to the average corporation, this advantage may be very important in the ultimate success of the firm. Only in the sole proprietorship, where little or no opportunity exists to share or delegate responsibility, does the personal interest factor have greater weight.

DEFINITE LEGAL STATUS

Partnerships are one of the oldest forms of business ownership. Over centuries a series of court decisions have established clear-cut answers to the questions of rights, powers, liabilities, and duties of partners. A partner should have no difficulty in securing a concise answer from a lawyer on any legal question concerning the partnership.

Disadvantages of a Partnership

After noting the many excellent advantages of partnerships when contrasted with sole proprietorships and corporations, the question might well be raised as to the reason or reasons for the relative lack of popularity for this form of business ownership. It appears obvious that one or more of the following disadvantages must frequently weigh heavily against selecting the partnership as the preferred type of business ownership: (1) unlimited liability of the partners, (2) lack of continuity, (3) managerial difficulties, (4) frozen investment, and (5) limitation on size.

UNLIMITED LIABILITY OF THE PARTNERS

The greatest disadvantage is that of unlimited liability of the partners. Each general partner is liable personally for the partnership debts. If one partner makes an unwise commitment, even against the wishes of the other partners, all the partners may be liable for the loss that results. If partnership A, B, and C fails with net losses totaling $100,000, and if neither A nor B has any private resources except what each had invested in the business, the entire loss would fall on C, assuming that C owns assets that, when liquidated, are adequate to cover the debts.

LACK OF CONTINUITY

If a partner dies or withdraws from the business, the partnership is dissolved. Also, if a partner becomes mentally impaired or takes out bankruptcy papers, the business is terminated. The more persons there are in a partnership, the greater are the chances that this will occur. Frequently the remaining partners find it possible to buy out the interest of the individual who withdraws or dies, and they can reorganize the business with little outward change. If it is necessary to admit a new partner to assume the interest of the old one, however, it may not always be easy to find an individual who is satisfactory to all of the old partners and who will work in reasonable harmony with them in the operation of the business.

MANAGERIAL DIFFICULTIES

Although better decisions usually result from the combined judgments of two or more partners, such divided control can also cause trouble. If some partners are not active in the business, time can be lost in making contact with them. Although any partner can take an action that is legally binding on the partnership, a partner might be reluctant to do so on important matters. Furthermore, the friendly spirit among partners that drew them together in the first place can give way in time to distrust and enmity. If the number of partners is odd, such as three or five, the minority will be outvoted by the majority. If the number of partners is even, some written agreements provide for referral to a disinterested party when the partners are equally divided on a proposed course of action.

FROZEN INVESTMENT

For an individual who wishes to invest some money in a business, the partnership form may prove to be a poor choice from the viewpoint of liquidity and transferability. It is almost axiomatic that it is easy to invest in a partnership and difficult to withdraw these funds. If a partner withdraws or dies, the existing firm is dissolved. Even if the remaining partners or outsiders are willing to purchase the vacated interest, it is often extremely difficult to arrive at a fair price.

LIMITATION ON SIZE

The advantage held by a partnership over a sole proprietorship as to availability of capital can easily become a disadvantage when contrasted with a corporation. Some businesses, such as those producing steel or making automobiles, require the investment of millions of dollars by the owners. Even if composed of several wealthy individuals, a partnership would have great difficulty in raising adequate capital for organizing a successful firm in many lines of business.

Limited Partnerships

Whenever the word partnership appears by itself, the reference is always to what might more correctly be termed a **general partnership**, that is, one in which all partners have unlimited liability. By contrast, a **limited partnership** is an ownership form in which one or several partners can have limited liability as long as at least one partner has unlimited liability. A limited partnership cannot be formed unless enabling legislation has been enacted, but most states have passed the Uniform Limited Partnership Act so that this restriction is not usually a problem.

Under the Uniform Limited Partnership Act a detailed statement concerning the limited partnership must be filed with the appropriate official at the county courthouse. Limited partners cannot be active nor appear to be active in the management of the firm; their names cannot be used in the name of the partnership. The purpose of a limited partnership is to allow one or more individuals to provide capital, on which a return is expected, without assuming liability for debts beyond the amount or amounts invested. If the firm is liquidated, the capital provided by limited partners becomes a preferred claim after all debts are paid.

Limited partnerships have been widely used in recent years as an ownership form for highly speculative undertakings such as drilling for oil or operating cattle feeding lots. Wealthy individuals who discover the federal and state governments taking healthy bites out of their incomes find that becoming a limited partner is a method of investing that may give them a tax advantage.

Kinds of Partners

The individuals who comprise a partnership are known as **partners** or **co-partners**. They are classified in several different ways, depending upon their extent of liability, participation in management, share of profits, and other factors.

GENERAL AND LIMITED PARTNERS

A member of a general or limited partnership who has unlimited liability for the debts of the firm is a **general partner**. Usually such a partner is active in the management. The vast majority of all partners fall into this category.

Members of a limited partnership who do not assume responsibility for the debts beyond the amount of their investment are **limited** or **special**

partners. As mentioned under a description of limited partnerships, certain restrictions are imposed on this type of partner.

SECRET, SILENT, DORMANT, AND NOMINAL PARTNERS

An individual who is active in the affairs of a partnership but who is not known to the public as a partner is a **secret partner**. A mother might want to give the impression that she was merely helping her daughter launch a gift shop when actually she was her daughter's partner. A person who is known to the public as a partner but does not take an active part in the management is a **silent partner**. A banker might invest in a business as a partner but not have time to become involved in its operations.

A partner who does not take an active part in the management and who is not known to the public as a partner is a **dormant** or **sleeping partner**. A contractor, for example, found it necessary to provide financial help to one of his subcontractors. He agreed to invest the necessary funds in return for a share of the profits provided that his status as a partner be kept secret. He was fearful that other subcontractors would seek a similar but unwanted arrangement, and the management of his own firm already took all of his time.

An individual who is not actually a partner but who claims to be one or allows others to make such a statement is a **nominal partner** even though this person does not share in the profits and does not have an investment in the business. When a partnership needed some money, it allowed the bookkeeper to sign a note as a partner. When the note came due, none of the partners was able to pay. The bank sued the partners including the bookkeeper who, as the only person with resources, was required to pay the debt.

SENIOR AND JUNIOR PARTNERS

A general partner who has a substantial investment in the firm, who receives a relatively larger percentage of the profits, and who, by virtue of age and years of association with the firm, assumes a major role in the management, is a **senior partner**. A **junior partner** is the opposite of a senior partner. Normally the junior partner is a young man or woman only recently admitted to a partner's status. This individual does not have very much money invested, receives only a minor share of the profits, and is not expected to assume responsibility for major decisions even though he or she has equal voting rights with other partners.

OTHER UNINCORPORATED FORMS OF BUSINESS OWNERSHIP

In addition to general and limited partnerships, there are a few other forms of ownership that do not require incorporation. Some of these can be classified as special types of partnerships while others make use of alternate approaches to creating a business entity. In specific instances each has advantages over any other unincorporated or incorporated form.

Joint Ventures

When two or more persons join together for the purpose of a single undertaking, such an association is called a **joint venture** or "joint adventure." Usually, although not necessarily, the undertaking is of short duration. For example, 20 investors may join together to buy 80 acres of farmland adjacent to a city. The land is then developed into a subdivision, the lots are sold, and the joint venture is ended.

During the relatively short life of the joint venture, each participant is in the same legal position as a general partner in a partnership. Despite this hazard of unlimited liability, the management of the undertaking is frequently delegated to one individual. This difference is in line with the basic distinction between a joint venture and a general partnership, namely, that a joint venture is not a continuing business.

Syndicates

A **syndicate** is an association of two or more individuals or companies for a particular purpose, which almost always involves a financial transaction. It differs from a joint venture in that the activity is financial, and syndicates need not be terminated after the purpose is completed. In contrast with a general partnership, members can sell their interest in the syndicate to buyers of their choice who then assume the rights and risks of the former owners.

The most common type of syndicate in use today is the **underwriting syndicate**. This is an association of investment banking companies formed for the purpose of selling a large issue of corporation bonds or stocks. Management is in the hands of the company that forms the underwriting syndicate. Because of the commodity handled by an underwriting syndicate, each member's liability is effectively, even if not legally, restricted to the agreed-upon portion of the total issue.

Mining Partnerships

Another special type of partnership that has been legalized in some states is the **mining partnership**, which is an association of two or more individuals for the specific purpose of conducting mining operations. It differs from a general partnership in that, when there are numerous members, management is delegated to one or a few partners, shares of ownership are issued and can be sold without the consent of other partners, and profits are distributed on the basis of the number of shares owned. Unlimited liability for debts of the mining partnership is effective against the owners only for necessary costs of operating the mine, and the death of a partner does not dissolve it.

Joint-Stock Companies

Joint-stock companies were important in the early development of our nation but have now been almost universally replaced by the corporation. They were formed by drawing up **articles of association**, not unlike articles of partnership, with the addition of stating the number of shares of stock to be issued and providing for an annual meeting at which the stockholders would elect a board of directors. Joint-stock companies resemble general partnerships in that all have unlimited liability. They differ in that management is delegated to a board of directors, ownership is represented by shares of stock that can be sold or transferred to others, profits are distributed on the basis of the number of shares owned, and the firm is not affected by the death of one or more stockholders.

Business Trusts

A **business trust** is a form of ownership in which investors, under a trust agreement, transfer cash or other property to a small number of trustees who manage the firm for the benefit of the owners. This is an entirely different approach to organizing and operating a business when contrasted with other types of unincorporated ownership described in this chapter. The trustees issue certificates of beneficial interest, called **trust certificates** or **trust shares**, to those who organized the trust, and these shares provide the basis for the distribution of profits.

If the trust agreement gives the investors any control over the management, such as the right to elect trustees, courts have held that each owner has unlimited liability. Since one of the reasons for using the trustee device is to secure the advantage of limited liability without incorporating, the customary procedure is to deny the owners any right to elect the trustees or to have any voice in management. The holders of trust certificates do have the right to sell them to a buyer of their choice, and the death of an owner does not affect the continuation of the trust. Business trusts are also known as **common-law trusts** or **Massachusetts trusts**.

Unincorporated Associations

An **unincorporated association** can be formed by any number of persons or companies by drawing up and signing an agreement. It differs from some other special forms of business ownership in that its purpose is always non-profit and it exists to render a service to its members. National fraternal organizations, trade associations, and the like are frequently unincorporated associations as are most security exchanges, bank clearinghouses located in large cities, and retail credit associations. In the business world there is usually a fee to join the association, and its expenses of operation are divided among its members based on their use of the services rendered. The members elect a board of governors, or directors, or trustees, who employ personnel to run the organization. Although the members probably have unlimited liability, the nonprofit and service nature of an unincorporated association are such that this risk is negligible.

BUSINESS TERMS

QUESTIONS FOR DISCUSSION AND ANALYSIS

1. In light of the operation of many businesses by governmental units, how can it be said that private ownership is a basic and important characteristic of capitalism?
2. Does the general public prefer to patronize a sole proprietorship, for example, over a large corporation assuming that prices charged are comparable?
3. The figures shown for sole proprietorships indicate that, on the average, they are not very profitable. Why doesn't this fact discourage individuals from starting and operating their own businesses?
4. Unlimited liability is the chief disadvantage of both sole proprietorships and partnerships. Why should business creditors have access to the nonbusiness wealth of these persons?

5. Twenty-five years ago there were more partnerships engaged in business than corporations. Today partnerships rank a poor third among the three major types of business ownership. What factors have caused this change?
6. Two women and one man form a partnership with each contributing a different amount of the original capital. Would it be fairer to divide profits on the basis of capital contributed rather than equally?
7. Why shouldn't partnership law require that each general partner sign all orders for merchandise, various types of contracts, and other binding documents in order for the partnership to become legally liable?
8. Why does the Uniform Limited Partnership Act provide that a limited partner

cannot be active in the management of a business?

9. Would a general partnership that dissolved by mutual consent after operating less than a year have been better off if it had been organized as a joint venture?

10. Why isn't a business trust a preferable type of ownership over a general partnership when a firm is organized by a group that includes a substantial number of individuals?

PROBLEMS AND SHORT CASES

1. For the past eight years Cynthia Roberts had been employed as a cook at a drive-in restaurant located in the suburb of a large city. On a trip to visit her parents, who lived in a city of 12,000 population, she observed that it did not have a drive-in eating facility. Convinced that her background of experience plus $8,000 she had on deposit in a savings bank should make a successful combination, she decided to quit her job and open a similar type outlet in her old hometown.

Within a few days she was able to locate two buildings that were reasonably suitable for her needs. One, situated near the center of town, was for sale at $30,000, and a local savings and loan association indicated that it would loan up to 80% of its cost. The other location was at the edge of town on a side street. It could be rented for $250 a month, but the owner would not sign a lease for more than one year. The fixtures, equipment, and supplies necessary to acquire prior to opening were carefully itemized and priced. The total came to $12,000 but Ms. Roberts was assured that her credit would be good for half of this amount.

Ms. Roberts leaned strongly in favor of the central location but realized that it would take every cent she had plus $4,000 more that she hoped a bank would loan her. If successful in obtaining the loan, she would also have a long-term commitment of $24,000 and a short-term debt of $6,000. At the alternate location, she could finance necessary purchases without borrowing and would still have a modest financial cushion left over. A realistic appraisal, however, of the two locations indicated that the volume of business available in the downtown building might easily be double that of the rental property.

On a visit back to her old job, she discussed her dilemma with Dan Southard, the night manager, whom she admired as a competent and friendly person. To her surprise Southard indicated that he has been thinking about going into business on his own, and he suggested that they join forces and take over the downtown spot. He offered to invest $6,000 and devote full time to the business. He proposed that each be paid $5.00 an hour for time worked, that interest at the rate of 6% be paid on the capital invested, and that profits, after wages and interest, be divided equally.

On the basis of these facts, should Ms. Roberts form a partnership with Southard or should she persist in her original idea of going into business for herself? Support your recommendation with a list of the advantages and disadvantages of each course of action and give reasons for your decision.

2. Refer to Problem 1 and make the assumption that Cynthia Roberts and Dan Southard form a partnership to operate the Sin-Dan Drive-in Restaurant and locate it at 201 South Main Street, Centerberg, Nebraska. In addition to the facts stated above, each partner agrees to work a minimum of 40 hours a week with no premium for overtime. The books are to be closed on December 31 of each year; the agreement is to run for ten years from January 2, 19—; and in case the firm is dissolved, the net assets are to be divided in the ratio of their capital accounts at that date. Neither partner is to withdraw cash from the firm other than wages, interest, and net profits without the written consent of the other.

Using this information, plus any additional assumptions you care to make that are not inconsistent with the stated facts, draw up articles of partnership for Cynthia Roberts and Dan Southard.

3. For the past twelve years Harry Cummins and George Ronson have operated a retail florist shop under the name of Colonial Flowers. The partnership has been profitable, providing about $15,000 a year for each man in wages and net income. It has been the sole source of support for both families so, consequently, $30,000 in cash has been regularly withdrawn from the business. Each had originally contributed $10,000 and this partnership capital has remained relatively stable. It was and is invested in delivery trucks, refrigerators, inventories of plants and flowers, supplies, fixtures, and the maintenance of a bank balance.

The firm has been renting an old one-story building that is barely adequate for its needs. Display space is limited; and on such days as Easter, Mother's Day, and Christmas, the partners have reluctantly turned away available business. They do not have a lease, but the owner seems content with receiving $350 each month and has not raised the rent in 12 years. Cummins and Ronson have been aware of the possibility of a long overdue rent increase and also that no other location is now available in their community.

They discussed this situation with Albert McDonald, their banker and personal friend, who expressed a willingness to build a combination store and greenhouse designed to fit their present and anticipated needs. He already owned a piece of land, which he valued at $10,000, and estimated that the cost of the completed structure would be $80,000. He would be willing to sign a lease for $600 a month provided that it ran for 10 years. As an alternative to a lease, he proposed that Cummins and Ronson take him into the firm as a limited partner. In return for his investment, which would be the land and building, he wished to receive one third of the net profits of the business after an allowance of $600 a month as a salary to each of the general partners. It is estimated that taxes and insurance on the new building would amount to $1,300 per year and that the building will last 40 years.

Should Cummins and Ronson admit McDonald to Colonial Flowers as a limited partner? Give reasons for your decision.

5 Incorporated Businesses

It was a sad day for Mrs. Winters. The morning mail brought an announcement that the Airwax Corporation had been declared bankrupt. Six years ago when her husband died she had, on the advice of a friend, invested the $50,000 proceeds from his life insurance in Airwax shares of stock. Originally she received dividends of $5,000 annually but her quarterly checks had stopped coming a year ago. Now it appeared that her stock certificates were valueless. Mrs. Winters, contemplating a bleak financial future, bitterly regretted that she had ever become a part owner of a corporation.

Several types of businesses require millions or even billions of dollars in order to operate efficiently. The only way that such huge sums can be assembled is to divide the ownership among thousands of investors. Unincorporated businesses, as described in Chapter 4, do not lend themselves to having many owners who do not participate in the management or even know each other. Incorporated businesses, on the other hand, provide a method by which owners who may be spread over a wide geographical area (see Figure 5-1) can delegate the responsibility of running a business to a handful of paid managers.

This chapter will describe some of these types of ownership and their uses with a considerable amount of emphasis given to the corporation. The importance of incorporated business units can hardly be overemphasized as one form or another is used by all of the private industrial, commercial, and financial giants. These large enterprises are responsible, to a great extent, for the high standard of living in the United States. Only big businesses can mass produce and mass merchandise goods and services at prices consumers can afford to pay. At the same time it would be a mistake to assume that all incorporated business units are necessarily large when, in fact, many are as small as the typical sole proprietorship or partnership.

CORPORATIONS

Incorporated businesses are dominated by one type — the corporation. Contrasted with the types of ownership described in Chapter 4, corporations

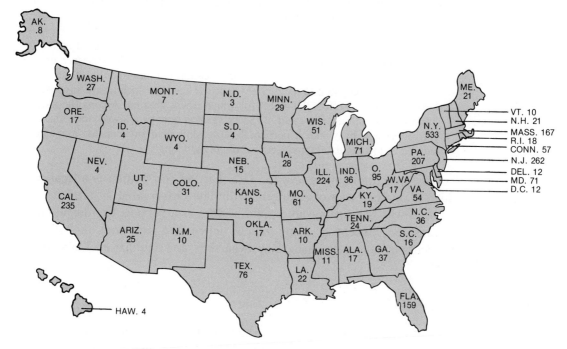

SOURCE: AT&T, *Share Owners Newsletter* (Second Quarter, 1975).

NOTE: AT&T share owners live in 50 states and 127 nations. Of the company's 565 million common shares outstanding, 31 percent are owned by women, 17 percent by men, 18 percent by a joint ownership, and 34 percent by trusts, financial institutions, and brokers. Of 2,934,000 share owners holding common stock, more than 12,500 live in foreign countries.

Figure 5-1   **Distribution of AT&T Common Share Owners (In Thousands)**

are twice as numerous as partnerships but only one fourth as common as sole proprietorships. Despite the fact that they comprise less than 20 percent of all unincorporated and incorporated types of business ownership, over 1.7 million corporations account for approximately 87 percent of total business receipts and more than 69 percent of all net profits. They employ millions of workers and are owned by millions of investors. Their activities and actions have a profound effect on the economic activity of our nation.

Corporations have an impact on the lives of every person in the United States. Despite their reputed impersonality, most people can identify such abbreviations as AT&T, A&P, GE, Sears, GM, and a host of others. This familiarity is evidence of the widespread influence corporations have achieved and of consumer dependence on these giants for goods and services.

Nature of a Corporation

What is this form of business ownership that is so important in our economy? Probably the most famous definition of a corporation was written by

Chief Justice John Marshall of the United States Supreme Court in 1819 in the case of *Dartmouth College* v. *Woodward*:

> A **corporation** is an artificial being, invisible, intangible, and existing only in contemplation of law. Being the mere creature of law, it possesses only those properties which the charter of its creation confers upon it, either expressly or as incidental to its very existence. These are such as are supposed best calculated to effect the object for which it was created. Among the most important are immortality, and, if the expression may be allowed, individuality; properties, by which a perpetual succession of many persons are considered as the same, and may act as a single individual.

This definition emphasizes the fact that the corporation is a **legal entity**, which is another way of saying that the law has created an artificial being endowed with the rights, duties, and powers of a person. The definition also includes the concept of many people united into one body that does not change its identity with changes in ownership, and one that may have perpetual life.

The Corporate Structure

The structure of a corporation sheds further light on this form of business ownership. Its status as a legal entity stems from a **charter**, which is a document issued by a state authorizing the formation of a corporation. The owners are called **stockholders**, or **shareholders**. Except in a few instances when voting rights may have been restricted on certain classes of stock, they vote the shares they own (one share = one vote) at an annual meeting called primarily to elect a **board of directors**. These individuals represent the stockholders, and they elect the high-ranking **corporate officers**, such as president, vice-president or vice-presidents, secretary, and treasurer. These officers are responsible for the day-by-day operation of the corporation and report periodically to the board of directors. Although some boards of directors may meet as seldom as once a year, monthly meetings lasting a few hours or even a full day are more common. In large corporations the board is divided into committees that meet separately and in addition to full board meetings.

Figure 5-2 pictures in a simple manner the organization of the corporate form. The stockholders may number in the thousands or even millions. The board of directors usually has between 9 and 17 members although there are numerous exceptions at both ends of the scale. It is customary to include among the members of the board at least the president of the corporation and frequently other top ranking officers.

STOCKHOLDERS

The stockholders of a corporation have purchased shares of stock in the company; hence, they are also called shareholders. In small businesses these

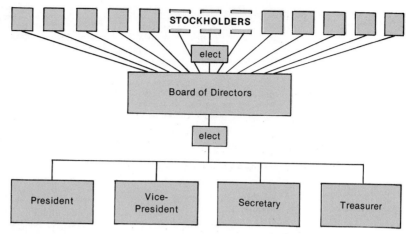

Figure 5-2   *Chart of Corporate Structure*

persons, or at least some of them, run the corporation as well as own all or most of it. In large corporations the vast majority of the stockholders own shares purchased either as an investment or speculation and have absolutely no direct connection with the management of the corporation.

Annual Meeting of Stockholders. Once each year stockholders are notified by mail concerning the time and place of the annual meeting of the corporation. If the stockholder attends in person, he or she will vote for a slate of directors, a firm of certified public accountants to audit the books, and sometimes on a few other matters. Although all stockholders are invited to attend the meeting, large corporations realize that only a relatively small percentage will appear in person. Consequently, all are urged to sign and mail a written authorization, called a **proxy**, that gives someone else the right to cast their votes. Proxies are necessary as a majority of the shares of stock outstanding must be represented at each annual meeting. Figure 5-3 on page 84 shows a simple notice of meeting and proxy form.

Voting for the Board of Directors. The solicitation of proxies is a company expense that can amount to thousands of dollars. In corporations with a large number of stockholders, the persons named in the proxy form — usually members of the board of directors — frequently cast over 90 percent of the votes. As a result, board members perpetuate themselves in office and select their own successors. Occasionally a group of dissatisfied stockholders may attempt to solicit proxies for a rival slate of board members. Because they must do this at their own expense, proxy battles are relatively rare when the corporation has thousands of stockholders. If the dissidents win the election, however, the new board will doubtless vote to reimburse those who financed the opposition.

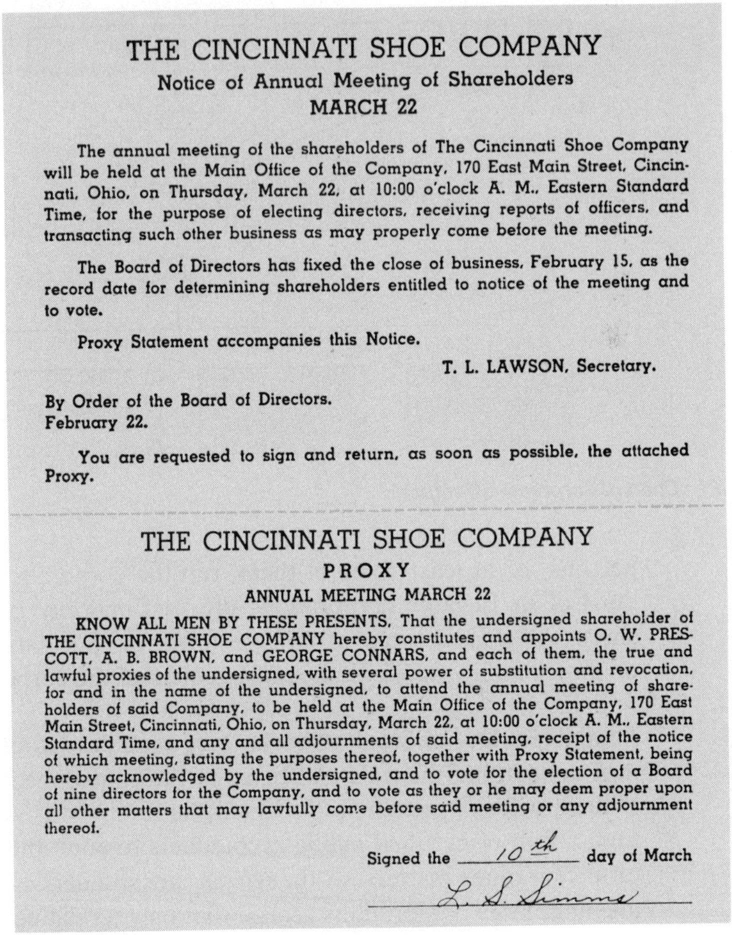

THE CINCINNATI SHOE COMPANY

Notice of Annual Meeting of Shareholders

MARCH 22

The annual meeting of the shareholders of The Cincinnati Shoe Company will be held at the Main Office of the Company, 170 East Main Street, Cincinnati, Ohio, on Thursday, March 22, at 10:00 o'clock A. M., Eastern Standard Time, for the purpose of electing directors, receiving reports of officers, and transacting such other business as may properly come before the meeting.

The Board of Directors has fixed the close of business, February 15, as the record date for determining shareholders entitled to notice of the meeting and to vote.

Proxy Statement accompanies this Notice.

T. L. LAWSON, Secretary.

By Order of the Board of Directors.
February 22.

You are requested to sign and return, as soon as possible, the attached Proxy.

THE CINCINNATI SHOE COMPANY

PROXY

ANNUAL MEETING MARCH 22

KNOW ALL MEN BY THESE PRESENTS, That the undersigned shareholder of THE CINCINNATI SHOE COMPANY hereby constitutes and appoints O. W. PRESCOTT, A. B. BROWN, and GEORGE CONNARS, and each of them, the true and lawful proxies of the undersigned, with several power of substitution and revocation, for and in the name of the undersigned, to attend the annual meeting of shareholders of said Company, to be held at the Main Office of the Company, 170 East Main Street, Cincinnati, Ohio, on Thursday, March 22, at 10:00 o'clock A. M., Eastern Standard Time, and any and all adjournments of said meeting, receipt of the notice of which meeting, stating the purposes thereof, together with Proxy Statement, being hereby acknowledged by the undersigned, and to vote for the election of a Board of nine directors for the Company, and to vote as they or he may deem proper upon all other matters that may lawfully come before said meeting or any adjournment thereof.

Signed the 10th day of March

L. S. Simms

Figure 5-3 ***Notice of Annual Meeting of Stockholders and Proxy Form***

A method of electing members of the board of directors that may allow a minority group of stockholders to secure representation is **cumulative voting**. Under this plan, if there are 15 directors to be elected, the owner of a single share of voting stock can cast 15 votes in several ways. For example, the owner can cast one vote for each of 15 nominees or 15 votes for one nominee. By concentrating their voting, the owners of a modest fraction of the entire stock issue can elect at least one individual to the board. Cumulative voting is required by law in approximately half of the states; in most other states it is permitted if a corporation wishes to include such a provision in its bylaws.

Voting on Other Matters. In addition to voting for members of the board of directors and the auditor, stockholders vote on any amendments to the charter, on bylaws (unless this authority is delegated to the board of directors), on such broad policies as retirement or pension plans for officers and employees, stock options for key personnel, the waiver of preemptive rights to subscribe to new stock issues, on dissolution of the corporation, and on any appropriate resolution a stockholder wishes to propose at the annual meeting.

Other stockholder rights include the following:

1. To receive dividends in proportion to stock owned, provided, however, that such dividends have been legally declared by the board of directors, which has sole authority to do so.
2. To hold or to sell stock certificates registered in his or her name.
3. To share pro rata in the assets that remain after the debts have been paid when a corporation is dissolved.
4. To subscribe to additional stock offerings before such stock is made available to the general public, unless this right is waived.
5. To inspect the books and records when good cause is shown.

BOARD OF DIRECTORS

As soon as stockholders have elected a board of directors, responsibility for directing the affairs of the business rests with this body. The usual term of office is one year although some corporations have longer terms, such as three years with only one third of the board members up for election at any annual meeting. The members of the board of directors of most small corporations are usually the stockholders who own all or most of the shares of stock. The stockholders of many large corporations elect to their boards outstanding businesspersons who have no other connection with the firm, as well as some officers of the company. Of 19 directors of General Electric Co., 15 are "outsiders" and only 4 are company executives. On the other hand, only 2 of the 18 directors of American Brands, Inc., provide the broader perspective associated with noncompany directors, frequently called public members; the other 16 are "insiders."

Adoption of Bylaws. Within the framework of the charter that authorized the creation of the corporation, the board of directors is usually delegated the authority by the stockholders to adopt a set of **bylaws**. These specify the rules and regulations under which the board operates. Some of the important provisions in a set of bylaws cover the time and place of the stockholders' regular meetings, methods of calling special meetings of stockholders, the number of directors and their organization and remuneration, the names of the officers to be chosen by the board of directors, the duties of these officers, provisions for filling vacancies on the board, rules for the issuance and transfer of stock, provisions for publishing an annual statement and other accounting matters, and the method by which the bylaws can be amended.

Authority and Responsibility. Final authority for the actions of a corporation rests with the board of directors; but it customarily votes on, and usually approves, recommendations coming to it from the chief executive officer or other officials of the company. In large corporations the board rarely initiates changes in policies although it may make a choice among alternate courses of action. The individual members are not liable for actions of the board except when it does something illegal, such as declaring a dividend out of nonexistent profits. A board member may serve on the board of directors of more than one company, but not if any of the corporations are in competition with each other.

CORPORATE OFFICERS

The bylaws usually specify the officers of the corporation to be elected by the board of directors. The most important position is that of chief executive officer, sometimes referred to as the **CEO**. This individual is either the chairperson of the board of directors or the president of the corporation. Other officers usually approved by the board of directors are the vice-president or vice-presidents — who frequently are further identified as Executive Vice-President or Vice-President, Marketing — and a secretary and treasurer.

The secretary, who is in possession of the corporate seal, signs or countersigns many corporation documents. This individual also attends all meetings of the stockholders and directors and keeps the minutes of these meetings. The finances of a corporation are under the supervision of a treasurer; in recent years, however, much of the responsibility for this detail has been transferred in some corporations to an elected officer called the controller.

NAME

All corporations must obviously have a name. The only restriction in choosing a name is that the one under consideration cannot be the same, or so nearly the same as to cause confusion, as that of another corporation already doing business in the state. Some states specify that the last word of the name be Corporation, Company, Incorporated, or Limited. In the United States the abbreviations Corp., Co., or Inc. are commonly used. Corporations chartered in Canada and England usually end the firm name with the abbreviation Ltd.

Separation of Ownership and Management

Another feature of corporations, particularly the industrial, commercial, and financial giants, is the distinction between ownership and management. In the small corporation one stockholder may own 100 percent of the shares outstanding or three or four individuals may each own a substantial number of shares. When the outstanding shares are closely held, the chances are good that all the owners are on the board of directors, each is an officer, and they all manage the business. Except for the ownership form, the situation is not unlike that of sole proprietors and partners working for themselves. In large corporations that have thousands of stockholders (see Table 5-1), however, the executives as a rule do not own very many shares; and even the total holdings of all management personnel are an insignificant percentage of total shares outstanding. When this condition exists, the result is a separation between ownership and management.

The effect of divorcing ownership from management is that the executives regard the stockholders as just one group who must be kept satisfied rather than as their "bosses" to whom, by way of the board of directors, they should be solely responsible. The executives' decisions take the stockholders into consideration, but only on an equal and separate basis with the rank-and-file company employees, the firm's customers, the government, and the general public. The concept of maximizing profits for the benefit of the stockholders is not as potent a factor in decision making as it is when there is no separation between management and ownership.

Advantages of a Corporation

The corporate form of business ownership, when compared with other types, has several important advantages. If this were not the case, corporations would not dominate our capitalistic system. Although there is some logic to the order in which these advantages are listed in the following paragraphs, it should be remembered that under a given set of circumstances any one of the factors might prove to be of maximum importance.

The principal advantages of a corporation are: (1) limited liability of stockholders, (2) larger size, (3) transfer of ownership, (4) length of life, (5) efficiency of management, (6) ease of expansion, and (7) legal entity.

Table 5-1   *Corporations in the United States with 250,000 or More Stockholders*

Name of Corporation	Number of Stockholders
American Telephone & Telegraph Co.	2,934,000
General Motors Corp.	1,283,000
Exxon Corp.	725,000
International Business Machines Corp.	557,000
General Electric Co.	537,000
General Telephone & Electronics Corp.	430,000
Ford Motor Co.	341,000
Gulf Oil Corp.	333,000
Texaco, Inc.	310,000
Consolidated Edison of New York	308,000
United States Steel Corp.	302,000
RCA Corp.	295,000
Sears, Roebuck & Co.	267,000
Standard Oil Co. of California	253,000

SOURCE: New York Stock Exchange, 1974.

LIMITED LIABILITY OF STOCKHOLDERS

The corporate form of business organization offers the owners the advantage of **limited liability**, which means that each stockholder risks only the amount invested in the corporation. If the company proves unprofitable and fails, creditors cannot look beyond the assets of the corporation for funds to settle their just claims. Since a corporation is a separate entity, it owes the debts in place of the owners. There is little question that this advantage is one of the major reasons why over 30 million individuals own stock of corporations. If Robert Tyler, a successful lawyer, invests $10,000 in the Stone Manufacturing Company, his total risk on this investment is exactly $10,000 even though his remaining personal wealth may be sizable.

LARGER SIZE

The original size of a sole proprietorship or a partnership is limited to the amount of capital that one or several individuals can provide by recourse to their own fortunes or by borrowing. The corporation, by dividing its ownership into shares of small denomination, can attract capital from thousands of individuals. If it is necessary to secure capital amounting to millions of dollars in order to organize a firm, a corporation is the only feasible form of ownership that can be used.

TRANSFER OF OWNERSHIP

Ownership evidenced by stock certificates gives maximum ease of transfer. If Andrews sells her interest in a corporation to Bennett, she merely endorses her stock certificate and this change of ownership is recorded in the books of the corporation. As a general rule, corporations allow their stockholders to transfer ownership to anyone at any time; some corporations that have only a few stockholders attempt to control the ownership group by restricting transfers to the corporation itself or other remaining stockholders. Through stockbrokers and organized stock exchanges, millions of shares of stock change hands daily.

Although a corporation usually has no voice in the matter of who buys its shares of stock, it is responsible for keeping an accurate record of the stockholders. Because large corporations are subject to numerous changes in owners, some hire a separate organization, usually a bank, to handle this task.

LENGTH OF LIFE

The corporation is potentially a permanent enterprise. The death or incapacity of stockholders, officers, and employees usually has little bearing on the continued existence of the business. If the firm can thrive and prosper, it can remain in business indefinitely. Corporations with over one hundred years of continuous life are not uncommon. Many well-known firms, such as the Procter and Gamble Company, are included in this group.

EFFICIENCY OF MANAGEMENT

Unlike proprietorships and partnerships, the owners of a corporation do not manage it except to the extent that directors and officers are also stockholders. In the small corporation this dual role may be quite extensive on the part of management, but it is not true for medium- and large-size corporations. The corporate structure permits delegation of authority by the stockholders to the board of directors and by it to the administrative officials. Corporations frequently seek and secure the services of outstanding individuals on their boards of directors. These persons give a continuity to management that is valuable. The board hires the top executives and, if these individuals do not perform efficiently, they can be replaced.

Another reason for the more efficient management of corporations stems from the attribute of size. In large corporations it is possible to delegate duties to specialists in various lines and to pay salaries high enough to attract the most competent individuals. On the payroll of such a firm may be found a purchasing agent, a sales manager, an advertising manager, a production superintendent, accountants, lawyers, and other specialists. In small firms, notably sole proprietorships and partnerships, one individual usually has to perform many functions and it is highly unlikely that this person will be competent enough to cover the diverse duties for which he or she is responsible.

EASE OF EXPANSION

Assuming that all resources possessed by a sole proprietorship have been exhausted, the only way the business can expand is by allowing profits to remain in the business. The partnership offers limited additional possibilities to the extent that one or more partners may be added to the firm. In contrast, the corporation has an almost unlimited opportunity for expansion as long as investors are willing to purchase additional shares of stock. Furthermore, large corporations find it much easier to borrow substantial sums of money because the amounts needed are large enough to interest appropriate financial agencies in marketing the securities. In general, large corporations have attained a high degree of confidence among the members of the investing public, who are willing to purchase securities that are issued for expansion purposes.

LEGAL ENTITY

A corporation can sue and be sued, make contracts, and secure title to property in its own name. In this respect, the corporation is in sharp contrast to the sole proprietorship and partnership, which must use individual names in legal matters even though operating under firm names not unlike those of corporations.

Disadvantages of Corporate Ownership

The corporate form of business ownership has its disadvantages as well as its advantages. Some of the more important disadvantages are: (1) taxation, (2) organization expenses, (3) government restrictions and reports, (4) lack of personal interest, (5) lack of secrecy, (6) relative lack of credit, and (7) charter restrictions.

TAXATION

In addition to an annual franchise tax in the state of incorporation, an annual payment is required by every state from corporations for the right to do business in that state. Similar fees are not exacted from sole proprietorships and partnerships. Also, some states levy taxes on the net income of corporations to the extent it was earned within the state and often they levy special taxes on certain types of corporations such as public utilities, railroads, and insurance companies.

Of even more importance, and a major disadvantage of the corporate form of business ownership, is the federal tax on income. The minimum rate on the first $25,000 of income has varied in recent years from 30 percent down to 22 percent, and the applicable rates on income in excess of $25,000 has varied from 52.8 percent down to 48 percent.[1] Then, when the corporation distributes all or a part of its earnings after taxes to its stockholders, these individuals must pay personal income taxes on dividends received in excess of $100. The only exception to this double taxation occurs when a corporation has 10 or fewer stockholders and elects to be taxed in the same manner as a proprietorship or a partnership. Subchapter S of the Internal Revenue Code permits this tax variation and is responsible for identifying these businesses as **Subchapter S corporations**.

ORGANIZATION EXPENSES

Of all the various forms of business enterprise, corporations are the most expensive to organize. An **incorporation fee** must be paid to the state in order to receive a charter. Furthermore, stock certificates and record books must be purchased. Because of the legal nature of a corporation, it is usually advisable

---

[1] In 1975, as part of a tax reduction act designed to stimulate the economy, the first $25,000 of earnings were taxed at 20 percent, the next $25,000 at 22 percent, and earnings in excess of $50,000 at 48 percent.

to engage a lawyer to assist in the organization procedures. For both large and small business these costs may prove to be a real drawback.

If, for example, the Vertiplane Corporation wishes to secure a charter from Ohio, it will be subject to the following incorporation fees charged in this state:

First 1,000 shares	10 cents a share
1,001 to 10,000 shares	5 cents a share
10,001 to 50,000 shares	2 cents a share
50,001 to 100,000 shares	1 cent a share
100,001 to 500,000 shares	½ cent a share
Over 500,000 shares	¼ cent a share

Assuming that Vertiplane wishes to have 3,000,000 shares of stock authorized, the cost of a charter will be $10,100.

1,000 shares @ 10¢	$ 100
9,000 shares @ 5¢	450
40,000 shares @ 2¢	800
50,000 shares @ 1¢	500
400,000 shares @ ½¢	2,000
2,500,000 shares @ ¼¢	6,250
3,000,000 shares	$10,100

Many states base the cost of a charter on dollar values rather than shares. If the Vertiplane Corporation states that each share is worth $5.00, the cost of a charter in Illinois would be $7,500 but California would charge only $300. In some states, New Jersey for example, $1,000 is the maximum fee charged.

GOVERNMENT RESTRICTIONS AND REPORTS

Because the corporation is a creature of the government, various departments of the state and federal governments have the right to exercise certain restrictions and to require certain reports. For example, a corporation cannot conduct business in a state in which it is not registered. This registration involves the payment of a special tax.

All types of annual and special reports, which frequently become burdensome and costly to the corporation, must be prepared. Some corporations, particularly public utilities, find it necessary to maintain report departments for the sole purpose of providing governmental bureaus and agencies with figures that must be furnished.

LACK OF PERSONAL INTEREST

A corporation has an identity of its own. All who work for a corporation, therefore, assume the role of employees. This relationship sometimes results in a lack of personal interest in the success or failure of the organization unless the employee is also a stockholder. It is probable that the efforts of many firms to sell stock to their employees have been motivated by a desire to mitigate the effects of this disadvantage. It is assumed that these employees will work harder in order to increase profits that will then flow to their pocket-books in the form of dividends.

Managers draw a salary paid by the corporations; and they take it for granted that, as long as they produce reasonable profits, they will continue to be paid. Mistakes resulting in a loss of potential profits are detrimental to the corporation, but ordinarily a reduction in profits that might have been earned does not affect executives individually as it would if their role were that of a sole proprietor or a partner.

LACK OF SECRECY

A corporation is duty bound to make an annual report to each stockholder. If it has only a few stockholders, these reports ordinarily do not become available to outsiders. When a considerable number of stockholders are involved, however, the annual reports become public property. Generally, such figures as sales volume, gross profit, net profit, total assets, and other financial matters are furnished in some detail. Furthermore, payments to each director and to each of the three highest paid officers of the corporation whose aggregate remuneration during the year exceeded $40,000 are detailed in the proxy statement. Other corporations, sometimes keen rivals, have an opportunity to examine the financial details of all companies that find it necessary to disclose this information.

RELATIVE LACK OF CREDIT

It may seem strange that corporations do not enjoy higher credit ratings than proprietorships and partnerships, but size for size this is true. Creditors of a $100,000 corporation can look only to the assets of the organization for any debts incurred whereas a $100,000 proprietorship or partnership offers the additional security of owners' private fortunes.

CHARTER RESTRICTIONS

A sole proprietor can change the business almost at will. A corporation, on the other hand, must state the business it intends to pursue at the time of applying for a charter. Unless the charter of a corporation is amended, the company may not engage in any type of business not covered by the original permit.

Some states grant charters with a wide latitude in permissible corporate activities. Nevertheless, an unanticipated opportunity may suddenly appear that cannot be seized because the type of business involved is not within the scope of the charter.

Organizing a Corporation

After weighing the advantages and the disadvantages, if the decision is to form a corporation, it will be necessary to secure a charter from one of the 50 states. The federal government charters national banks, federal credit unions and savings and loan associations, a few government corporations, and some scientific and educational organizations; but all industrial and commercial corporations are organized under state laws.

MEETING REQUIREMENTS FOR A CHARTER

Although incorporation laws in the several states vary in detail, they follow a general pattern. The first step necessary is to secure an application form, usually from the secretary of state of the state in which the corporation is to be formed. This form provides spaces for the name of the corporation, the names of the principal stockholders, the number and the types of shares of capital stock, the place of business, the type of business, and so forth.

When the application form is available, it is filled out, with special care given to fulfilling all specific requirements. Some states require only one stockholder but others specify a minimum of three owners. Also, the minimum amount of capital for a business corporation is usually specified within a range of $500 to $1,000.

After the requirements have been met the completed form with the requisite incorporation fee is forwarded to the secretary of state. As has been previously indicated, this charge varies by states and is based on either the number of shares to be authorized or on the dollar value of these shares. The minimum fee ranges from $10 to $100 throughout the states.

SELECTING THE STATE OF INCORPORATION

The selection of the state in which to file incorporation papers depends on a number of factors. Usually, if a corporation plans to concentrate its activities within one state, it will be advantageous to secure its charter from the state. If its operations will be conducted in all 50 states, the choice may hinge on the cost of the incorporation fee, the minimum of charter restrictions, and the amount of the continuing franchise tax. A **franchise tax** is an annual levy by a state on a corporation it has chartered granting permission to continue in business for another year.

Classification of Corporations

Corporations may be classified as follows: (1) private and governmental corporations, (2) profit and nonprofit corporations, (3) stock and nonstock corporations, (4) domestic, foreign, and alien corporations, (5) close and open corporations, and (6) industrial classifications.

PRIVATE AND GOVERNMENTAL CORPORATIONS

A **private corporation** is one chartered, owned, and operated by individuals either for the profit of its owners or for social, charitable, or educational purposes. The vast majority of corporations are private in nature, and by far the larger number are organized with the intent of making a profit. A **governmental corporation** is one organized by the federal government, a state, a city, or some other political subdivision. Examples of governmental corporations are incorporated cities, municipally owned water companies, state universities, and the Commodity Credit Corporation. Governmental corporations are sometimes referred to as public corporations; but unless this meaning is made clear, there may be confusion with private corporations owned by the general public.

The Communications Satellite Corporation is an interesting mixture of a private and governmental corporation. The ownership is private, but the Corporation was authorized by the Congress and three members of the board of directors are appointed by the President. Of the remaining twelve board members, six are elected by the companies owning stock and six by the individual stockholders.

PROFIT AND NONPROFIT CORPORATIONS

A **profit corporation** is one that is privately owned and operated to make profits for its stockholders. The vast majority of all corporations in the United States are of this type. A **nonprofit corporation** is somewhat of a misnomer in that its receipts may exceed its disbursements but a distribution is never made to its owners, and any income that may result from its operations is used to further the purposes for which it was organized. Governmental as well as social, charitable, religious, and educational corporations are examples of this classification.

STOCK AND NONSTOCK CORPORATIONS

Business corporations issue **stock certificates**, representing shares of ownership, which provide a basis for distributing the profits to the stockholders.

In general, governmental corporations, as well as private corporations not organized to make profits for their members, do not issue stock. Examples of such private corporations are churches, hospitals, and schools.

DOMESTIC, FOREIGN, AND ALIEN CORPORATIONS

A corporation is usually organized under the laws of one state. In that state the business is regarded as a **domestic corporation**, but in every other state in which it may operate it is considered a **foreign corporation**. For example, the U.S. Steel Corporation, which is organized under New Jersey law, is considered a domestic corporation in that state; but in Pennsylvania, where it has numerous offices and factories, it is a foreign corporation.

A company doing business within the United States that has been organized in another country, such as Canada, Mexico, England, or The Netherlands, is known in the United States as an **alien corporation**.

CLOSE AND OPEN CORPORATIONS

If the stock of a corporation is not available for purchase by outsiders, it is a **close corporation**. Typical of this classification are corporations with relatively few stockholders. These are frequently family businesses that were originally sole proprietorships or partnerships.

If the stock of a corporation is available for purchase by anyone having sufficient funds, it is an **open corporation**. Most of the large corporations are open, and shares can be purchased through a stockbroker. Within recent years many close corporations, needing funds for expansion or for other reasons, have "gone public," that is, have made shares available to investors. As previously mentioned, this has given rise to the use of the term "public corporation" for what is more accurately an open corporation.

INDUSTRIAL CLASSIFICATIONS

Private, profit-making, business corporations may be classified in several ways. *Moody's Manuals*, which include a description of almost every corporation in the United States as well as those in foreign countries, are titled Industrial, Public Utilities, Banks & Finance, and Transportation. Within each manual there is a further breakdown; for example, the Industrial volumes are subdivided into such categories as aviation, chemical, petroleum, tobacco, and many others.

The Office of Statistical Standards of the Bureau of the Budget, Executive Office of the President, is responsible for the Standard Industry Classification of Corporations. The first two digits of this four-digit detailed breakdown of types of corporations refer to the same major industry divisions used by the Internal Revenue Service. These designations were employed for income tax information on sole proprietorships and partnerships in Chapter 4, and comparable information on corporations appears in Table 5-2. The figures in this table reflect an accurate picture of the number and financial details of corporations operating in each classification because all corporations must file returns even if they did not realize any profits.

OTHER INCORPORATED BUSINESSES

Although the corporation is the dominant form of incorporated business ownership, there are a few other types that, in specific areas, are more widely used. Since in each case the business conducted is of a corporate nature, it seems obvious that there are unique advantages attached to the firms which use these different forms of incorporated business ownership. Such advantages will be pointed out in the following description and explanation of: (1) cooperatives, (2) credit unions, (3) mutual companies, and (4) savings and loan associations.

Table 5-2   *Corporation Income Tax Returns*
(Number, Receipts, Net Profits, and Average Receipts by Industries[1])

Industry	Number of Returns	Business Receipts (Millions of Dollars)	Net Profit (Loss) (Millions of Dollars)	Average Business Receipts
ALL INDUSTRIES[2]	1,781,117	$2,140,687	$96,232	$1,201,879
Mining	14,257	22,226	3,198	1,558,930
Construction	155,311	109,553	1,909	705,378
Manufacturing	203,798	861,650	48,209	4,227,961
Transportation, communication, electric, gas, and sanitary services	74,042	167,425	8,128	2,261,220
Wholesale and retail trade	571,312	663,423	14,119	1,161,227
Finance, insurance, and real estate	426,439	231,760	18,417	543,478
Services	319,191	83,822	2,259	262,608
Nature of business not allocable	16,763	828	(9)	49,404

SOURCE: United States Department of the Treasury, Internal Revenue Service, Preliminary Statistics of Income 1972, Corporation Income Tax Returns.

[1]Agriculture, forestry, and fisheries omitted.

[2]Due to rounding, items may not add to totals.

Cooperatives

Cooperatives, or **co-ops** as they are commonly called, are incorporated under the laws of a state. They are to be distinguished from corporations in the following respects:

1. Each cooperative unit is owned by the user-members of the group.
2. Each member has only one vote regardless of the number of shares of stock owned.
3. There is a limitation on the amount of stock that each member may own.
4. The capital for the enterprise is subscribed only by the members.
5. Interest is paid on the investment of each member-stockholder.
6. Dividends are paid on a patronage basis, in proportion to the amount of goods that each member has bought or sold through the co-op. These are referred to as **patronage dividends**.

ADVANTAGES AND DISADVANTAGES OF COOPERATIVES

Cooperatives have all of the advantages of corporations although the requirement of ownership by user-members limits the size and ease of expansion. They also have a tax advantage in that patronage dividends are considered a refund of overpayments rather than a distribution of profits, and the federal government provides financial assistance not available to profit-seeking corporations. In agricultural co-ops members are frequently intensely loyal to their firm and support the business with zeal and enthusiasm.

On the other hand, cooperatives lack the profit-making incentive common to other forms of ownership, which appears to be a serious handicap. Also, there is an unfortunate tendency to rely on volunteers; for example, members of the board of directors customarily are not paid for their services, and the salary scales for employees are frequently on the low side.

VARIOUS KINDS OF COOPERATIVES

The most extensive use of co-ops is in the field of agriculture. Farm products that are marketed through farmer cooperatives include citrus fruits, butter, potatoes, milk, prunes, apricots, wool, grains of all kinds, livestock, eggs, poultry, and rice. Such well-known brands as Sunkist oranges and Sun Maid raisins are the property of **producer cooperative associations** engaged in the marketing of these products grown by their many members. There are more than 5,000 producer cooperative associations in the United States with annual sales in excess of $15 billion. In addition to producer co-ops, there are approximately 3,000 farmer-owned **buying cooperatives** whose purchases of seeds, gasoline, farm machinery, etc., total about $4 billion annually.

Although **consumer co-ops**, which are user-owned retail outlets of goods and services, have long been a dominant factor in such countries as Denmark and Sweden, their influence in the United States has been relatively minor. Aided by the Rural Electrification Administration, a federal agency, the sales of electricity by consumer cooperatives has grown, and rural telephone co-ops have also increased, again with federal financial aid. Recently cooperative health plans have shown some growth, but in other retail areas the cooperative movement has failed to generate any enthusiasm among our general public. There is a possibility, however, that the recent rise in consumerism may increase interest in the cooperative retailing of consumer goods. This is a potential trend worth watching in the immediate years ahead.

Credit Unions

A **credit union** is a type of financial institution designed to assist a homogeneous group to save money and loan it to one another. For example, the group may be the employees of a firm, members of a church, or residents of a community. A credit union is an incorporated entity that can secure a charter from a state or, unlike cooperatives and corporations, it can secure one from the federal government.

Each member of a credit union purchases at least one share, which usually costs $5; in some instances members pay a membership fee of 25 cents. All members elect a board of directors from among themselves who serve without pay. The board elects officers who are likewise not paid, except that some larger credit unions may employ an office manager and the necessary clerical help. If the credit union is organized among the employees of a factory or business establishment, it is customary for the company to provide them free office space.

By using funds available from shares sold to members, on which there is no limit, loans are made to other members. Most of these loans are for amounts ranging from $100 to $1,000, although some credit unions make larger loans. Interest is usually charged at the rate of one percent a month on the unpaid balance. Net earnings provide funds to pay dividends on shares outstanding and, in some instances, to reduce the interest charge on loans to less than 12 percent a year.

There are approximately 23,000 credit unions with 27,000,000 members in the United States. Total assets owned are in excess of $24 billion. Most credit unions are relatively small with memberships ranging from 100 to 1,000. This type of incorporated business ownership is currently operating in 70 countries although approximately one half of all credit unions are located in the United States.

Mutual Companies

Mutual companies receive a charter from a state, but the owners are the users of the service rendered rather than being stockholders. There are two primary uses of mutual companies: life insurance companies and savings banks. The purchaser of a policy from a mutual life insurance company is automatically a member as is the individual who deposits money in a mutual savings bank. These owners theoretically elect a board of directors to manage the business. Actually, since it is unusual to solicit proxies from policyholders or depositors, the owners rarely bother to vote, and boards of directors tend to be self-perpetuating.

Mutual companies have most of the advantages of corporations, including limited liability. They also enjoy special federal income tax treatment. For example, dividends on life insurance policies are considered a partial refund of premiums paid by the policyholder. Mutual savings banks can insure their accounts with an agency of the federal government and can borrow funds from the federal home loan bank system.

Although only about 10 percent of all life insurance companies are organized as mutuals, the mutual life insurance companies based in this country own two thirds of the assets of all life insurance companies and have written over one half of all life insurance outstanding. For legal reasons most mutual savings banks are located in the Middle Atlantic and New England states but, despite this restriction, their total assets amount to $106 billion. These figures seem to indicate that, despite the lack of pressure from stockholders for dividends, mutual companies have been aggressive and efficiently managed.

Savings and Loan Associations

Savings and loan associations are financial institutions that accept deposits from savers and loan these funds to borrowers to build homes. In those that are mutually owned, which are the ones of concern here, both savers and borrowers are members; and they elect a board of directors who manage the association. The major difference between savings and loan associations and mutual companies is that, in the former, charters are available from the federal government as well as from a state. Usually there is also a difference in voting in that a saver has a vote for each $100 invested up to a limit of 50 votes. A borrower is normally required to become a member by buying one share which entitles the borrower to one vote.

There are approximately 5,300 savings and loan associations operating in the United States and of these about 88 percent are mutual type companies. Total assets of these associations amount to $215 billion contributed in large measure by some 40 million buyers of shares. The advantages of this type of incorporated business ownership are similar to those applying to mutual companies, and the desire of management to pay dividends to depositors has led to efficiency of operation for most savings and loan associations.

BUSINESS TERMS

QUESTIONS FOR DISCUSSION AND ANALYSIS

1. At the annual meeting of a corporation a stockholder casts as many votes as the number of shares owned. Why wouldn't it be acceptable to restrict the stockholder to one vote as is customary for practically all other elections?

2. The use of proxies by a corporation at its annual meeting practically guarantees approval of all management proposals and the defeat of all stockholder motions opposed by management. Is this situation desirable and, in any event, how could it be changed?

3. In states that do not require cumulative voting, why do boards of directors oppose granting this privilege to their stockholders?

4. Why do some corporations have a majority of so-called public members on their boards while other companies stress "insiders?"

5. What, if any, are the advantages that accrue to a corporation when its stockholders number in the hundreds of thousands?

6. Why should a stockholder owning 100 percent of the stock of a corporation have limited liability when unlimited liability would be present if the business were operated as a sole proprietorship?

7. Would a requirement that all employees become stockholders be beneficial to a corporation adopting this rule?

8. Are there any steps an open corporation can take to prevent an unwanted individual from acquiring shares of its stock?

9. Why haven't consumer co-ops been more successful in the United States?

10. What reasons can be given for the success of credit unions, mutual companies, and nonstock savings and loan associations that are in competition with investor-owned, profit-seeking corporations rendering comparable services?

PROBLEMS AND SHORT CASES

1. A group of promotors decide to incorporate the Whitehead Leasing Corporation with an authorized capital stock of 3,000,000 shares of preferred stock with a par value of $10 a share, and 6,000,000 shares of no-par common

stock. Ohio and Delaware have been suggested as logical states in which to file incorporation papers. The cost of obtaining a charter may prove to be the deciding factor in the choice between the two states. (Preferred and common stock and par and no-par stock will be discussed in Chapter 18. An understanding of these kinds of stock is not necessary for solving this problem.)

Compute: (a) the amount of the incorporation fee in Ohio (see page 91), (b) the amount of the incorporation fee in Delaware, and (c) the amount of savings one state offers over the other.

Incorporation fees for Delaware are as follows:

For each share of authorized capital stock up to 20,000 shares without par value	½ cent
For each share in excess of 20,000 shares and up to 2,000,000 shares without par value	¼ cent
For each share in excess of 2,000,000 shares without par value	⅕ cent
For each share up to 20,000 shares having par value	1 cent
For each share in excess of 20,000 shares and up to and including 200,000 shares having par value	½ cent
For each share in excess of 200,000 shares having par value	⅕ cent

In no case less than $10. Each one-hundred-dollar unit of par-value stock shall be counted as one taxable share.

2. Using the information in Table 5-2 on page 96, compute: (a) the percentage of total number of returns for each of the eight industrial divisions to the number of returns for all eight industrial divisions, and (b) the percentage of business receipts for each of the eight divisions to the total business receipts for all industrial divisions. List each set of percentages in descending order. What conclusions can be drawn from these computations?

3. Lucille Alvarez always felt that she had been brought up in her father's florist shop. As an only child she had helped out after school and during vacations. Following graduation from college in 1955, she reduced her work load considerably over a fifteen-year span that included marriage, the birth of a son and daughter, and the untimely death of her husband. In 1970 her father died and she and her mother each inherited a one-half interest in the florist business, which had always been operated as a sole proprietorship. Articles of partnership were drawn up that provided a $12,000 annual salary to compensate Lucille for managing the business, with an equal distribution of profits to the two owners.

Between 1970 and 1976 the business prospered under Lucille's experienced guidance. Greenhouses were acquired, contracts with chain stores were signed, and the original store was now twice its former size. The labor force had grown from one full-time and one part-time employee to eight full-time employees. Sales that had averaged around $50,000 before 1970 passed $300,000 in 1976. Profits had also grown and now exceeded $40,000 annually.

When seeking further possibilities for expansion, a competitor offered to sell his business, including the building in which it was located, for $100,000. Lucille's banker indicated that she could borrow this amount but suggested, as an alternative plan, that she incorporate the business and sell $100,000 in stock to employees and friends. He felt that $400,000 was a reasonable price for the partnership, which would leave control in the family by a comfortable margin. Lucille's mother was now 72 years of age and had never taken an active part in the management. Lucille's children were 18 and 15 and, so far at least, neither one had shown any great interest in the business.

On the basis of the above information: (a) what are the arguments in favor of incorporation, (b) what are the arguments against incorporation, and (c) would you advise incorporation of the partnership?

6 Organizing for Management

Sick and tired of the restrictions and hassles he felt were dumped on young people by the establishment, Bud Rodriguez realized a long-time dream with the founding of a commune called Sunbeam. Its goals were simple — togetherness and spontaneity. Bud rejected the managerial role and intended rather to act as a facilitator of the group's decisions. Problems soon developed when some of the members did not contribute to the $400 monthly rent of the sprawling house they occupied. The utilities were cut off and the house was discovered by noncontributing drifters. The group seemed uninterested in establishing any rules of operation and were generally unable to decide how to bring in money. The venture folded.

An organization is not an end in itself, but should function to achieve a particular purpose. All organizations should be goal-oriented, and the managerial process of organizing is essential in small as well as large enterprises.

The word "organization" suggests order; it is the instrument by which people get things done. People organize because they achieve more by working together than alone. This applies not only to business organizations but also to governmental, educational, and religious activities.

The organizing process is demanded by specialization and the division of labor in our society. When two or more people become involved in a joint enterprise, it is necessary to determine the contribution of each to the goals of the enterprise. This is not repressive, but instead recognizes the fact that human talents often are not interchangeable. The large organization, for example, is composed of differentiated people — many of them highly trained specialists. In providing for the effective use of individual specialties, organizations enhance, rather than reduce, the possibilities for individual self-realization.

THE ORGANIZING PROCESS: AN OVERVIEW

Organizing is the process by which management strives to achieve its objectives by combining the efforts of the people under its supervision. While the success of a company may be attributed to many factors, the skill with which management determines and implements its organizational plan is one of the major factors in the end result.

An **organization plan** is a blueprint or description of the process of coordinating the efforts of a number of people for the achievement of some goal through the division of work and through the assignment of various levels and degrees of authority and responsibility. Specifically, the process of organizing an enterprise consists of (1) departmentalization, or the rational grouping of the operating tasks to be performed, (2) establishing the authority relationships among those who will be performing the tasks, (3) decentralizing or dividing up the managerial work, and (4) determining the overall organizational structure.

The process of organization planning is a continuing challenge to management because organizations may change goals, find new ways of dividing and coordinating work activities, and modify the scope of authority and responsibility. The balance of this chapter will develop the basic elements shown in Figure 6-1, as they are highly important in the establishment and maintenance of an effective and efficient organization.

DEPARTMENTALIZATION OF OPERATING TASKS

Today's large, complex organizations are characterized by a high degree of division of labor and task specialization. Thus, the operating and managerial work of the organization must be broken up, or differentiated, to determine which departments and persons are responsible for the specialized activities. In the organizational hierarchy, **horizontal differentiation** relates to operating tasks, and **vertical differentiation** to managerial tasks.

Departmentalization deals with the horizontal dimension of organization structure and is the process of rationally grouping the work necessary to achieve the goals of the organization on a basis that permits cooperation and coordination. This process takes place at all levels in an organization, and in most cases the activities are grouped on the basis of (1) function, (2) process, (3) geographical areas, (4) products, or (5) customers.

By Function

Departmentalization by function occurs when the activities of the organization are grouped into the primary tasks to be performed such as production,

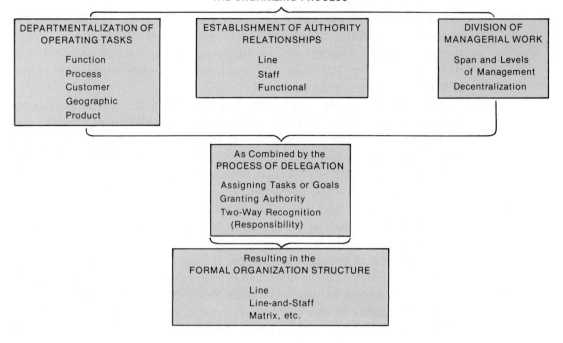

THE ORGANIZING PROCESS

DEPARTMENTALIZATION OF OPERATING TASKS	ESTABLISHMENT OF AUTHORITY RELATIONSHIPS	DIVISION OF MANAGERIAL WORK
Function Process Customer Geographic Product	Line Staff Functional	Span and Levels of Management Decentralization

As Combined by the
PROCESS OF DELEGATION

Assigning Tasks or Goals
Granting Authority
Two-Way Recognition
(Responsibility)

Resulting in the
FORMAL ORGANIZATION STRUCTURE

Line
Line-and-Staff
Matrix, etc.

Figure 6-1   The Organizing Process: An Overview

marketing, and finance. This grouping also includes any aspect of operations or management that requires technical knowledge or skill such as legal work, consumer affairs, or industrial engineering.

By Process

The basis of departmentalization by process refers to a type of functional departmentalization at the operating level of the organization where people using a specialized type of equipment or techniques are grouped into one department. An example is a manufacturing department of a job-shop operation that is divided into the grinding department, the welding department, the polishing department, the paint department, and the assembly department.

By Geographical Area

In geographical departmentalization all the organizational activities performed in a particular region or location are brought together and integrated into a single unit. Geographical divisions are common, for example, in the regional offices of chain store operations; and territories are a common way of dividing the work of salespersons. Recently the geographical basis of departmentalization has become important to multinational business corporations.

By Products

Activities directly associated with a product or service are often grouped together in product departmentalization. For example, the groups reporting to the top managers of American Machine and Foundry Company are: Electrical Products Group, Tobacco Machinery Group, Bowling Products Group, Governmental Products Group, General Products Group, and an International Products Group. On a smaller scale a food market may be divided into groups for meat, groceries, and produce.

By Customer

Departmentalization by customer is often found in sales operations, as large customers with their purchasing departments and technical requirements may have to be treated differently than smaller customers, or even military customers. Likewise, a hardware company may group its activities into wholesale and retail divisions in order to serve the different types of customers who buy from the company.

In Figure 6-2 a simplified organization chart is shown for a hypothetical business firm, the 3-W Company, which manufactures wagons, wheelbarrows, and watering tanks. This figure shows that various departmental groupings may exist simultaneously in the various levels of a business firm.

Each basis of departmentalization has its advantages and disadvantages. Therefore, management must balance the gains from one kind against the disadvantages of another and set up departments that lead to the firm's goals and facilitate the coordination of the essential efforts.

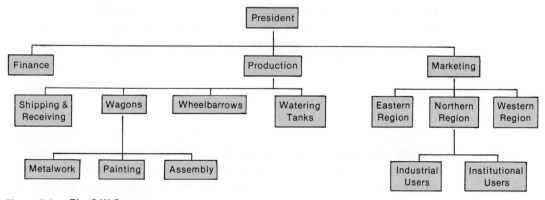

*Figure 6-2   **The 3-W Company***

AUTHORITY RELATIONSHIPS

An **organization chart** of a company shows how the work load is divided and assigned to specific individuals or departments. An equally important step that rarely appears on organization charts describes authority-responsibility relationships between the persons doing these jobs. Managers must have an understanding of who is supposed to do what before a managerial team is effectively organized. These relationships are usually established on the bases of: (1) line authority, (2) staff authority, and (3) functional authority. The organization manual or management guide defines each position.

Line Authority Relationships

Managers functioning in a **line authority** relationship to other persons or departments are involved with the direct supervision of subordinates in the chain of command. The **chain of command**, shown in Figure 6-3, indicates the formal authority relationships that run in a direct line from the top to the bottom of the organization.

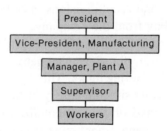

Figure 6-3   *A Chain of Command*

Line managers are in the chain of command because they are responsible for an activity that directly contributes to the earnings of the company. They usually are concerned with the accomplishment of quantitative objectives, cost control, and the on-going decisions that allow them to accomplish the tasks for which they are responsible.

Staff Authority Relationships

Line authority is derived from chain of command, or the organizational **hierarchy of authority**, based on superior-subordinate relationships. **Staff authority**, shown in Figure 6-4, is based on expertise in specialized activities and includes the authority to advise, plan, gather information, and provide guidance to line managers in the organization.

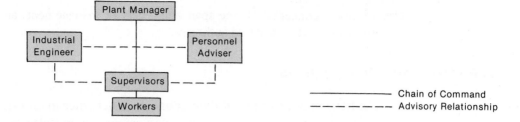

Figure 6-4   *A Staff Authority Relationship*

Functional Authority Relationships

Individuals who have **functional authority** have the right to issue policies and procedures for their functions or areas of expertise throughout the organization and to expect compliance. Staff persons prepare recommendations for the line manager. Persons with functional authority issue directives in their names instead of submitting them through the line manager. A production manager may, for example, have the authority to specify maintenance schedules for machines in any part of the company. Likewise, a personnel manager may have the right to establish policies and procedures used throughout a company in the hiring of employees.

A Caution

These distinctions between types of authority relationships are not as neat and clean as they appear at first glance. Most managerial positions are not solely line, staff, or functional in nature. A personnel manager, for instance, will be in a line relationship to the personnel department; in a staff relationship to the executive officers when serving on the advisory executive committee; and in a functional authority relationship to the total organization.

Therefore, every management job contains each of these three authority relationships to some degree. Understanding the changing authority of managers in their various relationships with others in the organization is a far more important issue than the attempt to impose the line, staff, or functional job category on a person.

DIVISION OF MANAGERIAL WORK

The section on departmentalization covered the horizontal differentiation of operating tasks. This section deals with the other necessary dimension of an organization's activities — the vertical differentiation of managerial activities. This specialization of managerial work is accomplished through two organizational concepts: (1) the span and levels of management, and (2) the decentralization of managerial authority.

Span and Levels of Management

The horizontal and vertical differentiation of activities in an organization are costly in terms of managerial and staff personnel and also in terms of communication and coordination. Nevertheless, they remain crucial factors in organizing because of the **span of management** or **span of executive control** — the number of subordinates a manager can effectively supervise.

As Figure 6-5 indicates, the span of management is clearly related to the number of levels in an organization. The narrower the span, the more levels that are needed and, of course, the more executives needed to manage the various levels.

The problem of the optimum number of persons that can be effectively supervised has been receiving increased attention in many firms. Sears and IBM are two firms that have broken away from the traditional narrow span of management and have moved toward a broader span. Generally the proper number of subordinates an executive can handle will depend on the complexity of the activity, the skill and experience of both the managers and workers concerned with that activity, and other related factors.

Decentralization of Managerial Authority

A broader span of management occurs when a manager decentralizes authority. **Decentralization** is the delegation of authority for making managerial

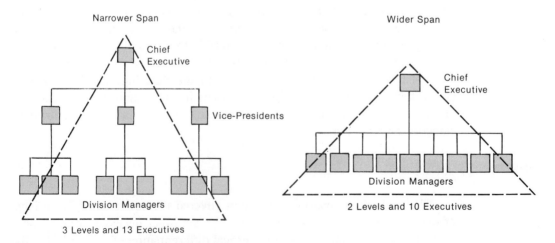

Figure 6-5 **Span and Levels of Management**

decisions to subordinates at lower levels in the organization. The degree of decentralization in an organization is not measured by the quantity of decisions that are passed down the managerial hierarchy, but rather by the importance and scope of the decisions and their impact on the entire organization.

DECENTRALIZATION AND PHYSICAL DISPERSION

The position is sometimes taken that a firm is decentralized when its management is physically dispersed. **Physical dispersion**, or **physical decentralization**, occurs when central managers are geographically separated from division or branch managers. This viewpoint is not entirely correct, as authority to make managerial decisions may be delegated by a manager to a subordinate sitting at an adjacent desk. Likewise, **centralized management** occurs when a central manager is heavily involved in the decisions that are made in distant divisions. Although decentralization of decision-making authority, or **decentralized management**, usually goes hand in hand with physical dispersion, one is not necessary to the other. Care should be taken, therefore, to distinguish between the two concepts.

FACTORS IN DECENTRALIZATION

There are no simple formulas to indicate the extent to which authority should be decentralized. The following factors are often considered when making this decision:

1. Are the persons at the lower levels capable of making sound decisions?
2. Which person down the line has the necessary facts to make a given type of decision?
3. Will changing conditions in the field require that speedy, flexible decisions be made at the local level?
4. How important is the decision in terms of dollars, its impact on other decisions in the organization, and the morale of the managers down the line?

THE PROCESS OF DELEGATION

None of the concepts discussed to this point — departmentalization, authority relationships, and decentralization — can be integrated and activated without the process of delegation, which is the heart of the organizing process. Each of these three concepts can be worked out on paper, but cannot be implemented without the willingness of a manager to delegate. Delegation is the process that ties together task responsibilities and the authority needed to carry out the tasks. As such it is a key management concept that must be incorporated into any organizational structure.

Basically, **delegation** is the managerial technique through which a manager assigns tasks or goals to subordinates, along with the authority to carry them out. The final step in this process is the subordinates' recognition of their responsibility or obligation either to perform the assigned work or explain to the manager why the job cannot be done. Thus, delegation is a two-way process in which carefully developed communication channels will encourage subordinates to discuss delegated tasks with the manager.

THE ORGANIZATION STRUCTURE

The formal organization, such as that shown in Figure 6-6 on page 111, does not simply evolve on a random or inevitable basis. This structure is the outcome of the many management decisions made throughout the organizing process to balance the organization's tasks, authority relationships, and human capabilities.

Only two basic forms of organization structure are commonly used today: line and line-and-staff, which are discussed in this section. Formal organization structures are being challenged by modern behavioral views of organization. The matrix organization is presented as a hybrid form straddling the formal and behavioral viewpoints, and it is used here to pinpoint some of the differences in premises underlying formal and behavioral organizational forms.

Line Organization

A **line organization** is a direct flow of authority from the top executive to the operations employee, usually through several executives at various managerial levels. It is sometimes called the **scalar** or **military type organization** because each person has an immediate supervisor. Although modern armies are too complex to rely exclusively on a line organization, they still use the direct chain of command.

ADVANTAGES

Figure 6-7, which is shown on page 112, is a line organization as applied to business. There are many advantages inherent in this form. It is simple and easy to understand. Responsibility is clearly defined, and every worker at every level reports to only one individual. Decisions can usually be rendered quickly, and executives must produce or they are replaced. As long as the orders of the immediate superior are carried out, each employee is relatively free from criticism.

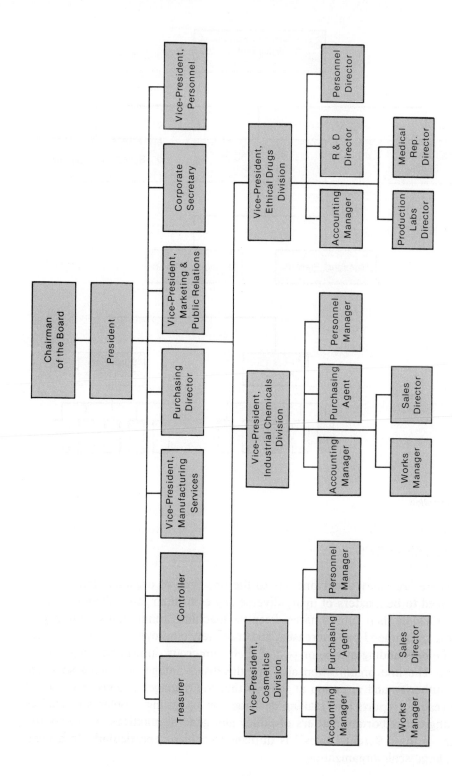

Figure 6-6   A Formal Organization Chart

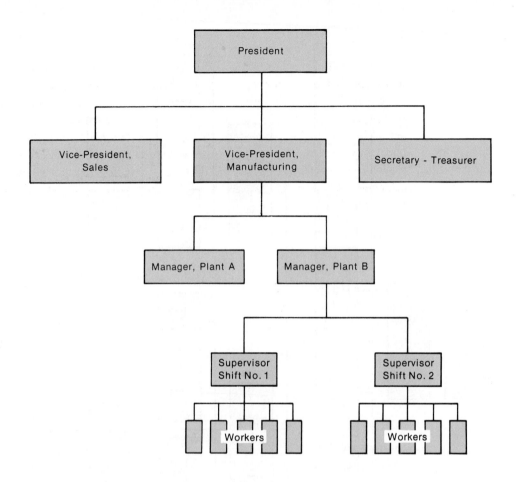

Figure 6-7 **A Line Organization**

DISADVANTAGES

There are many disadvantages to the line type of organization. Supervisors need to be masters of many diverse angles to their jobs. They should be able to handle their subordinates, keep the machines running, invent new processes, recommend pay increases, and train new employees. Frequently they may be outstanding at one or two of their numerous duties and very poor at others. The line organization also has the disadvantage of placing so much final authority and direction at the top that the manager spends most of the time reading reports and making decisions on operating problems instead of working out important matters of policy and general practices. Also, coordination of the different ''lines'' is difficult to achieve, particularly in a complex, large-scale organization.

Line-and-Staff Organization

The **line-and-staff organization**, shown in Figure 6-8, eliminates the problem of requiring managers to be highly competent in each phase of their jobs. Specialists in such areas as personnel, industrial engineering, market research, tax law, and the like are given staff or advisory authority instead of actual line authority. Their staff work is implemented through the line executives they support. Today's military services are essentially line-and-staff organizations in that extensive use is made of specialists in all lines who are attached to the various branches — for example, psychologists with branches of the military.

ADVANTAGES

The many advantages of the line-and-staff plan have made it the most popular form of business organization. It introduces a note of flexibility in the rigid line organization. The use of specialists can be incorporated without losing the advantages of the line plan. It incorporates the principles of division of labor and retains the important combination of authority and responsibility.

DISADVANTAGES

The so-called advice given by staff persons may be perceived as demands, which can lead to divided authority or serious friction. In some cases managers may try to shift responsibility to staff employees for unsuccessful actions taken on their advice. Also, managers may cease to consider issues that can be referred to staff members.

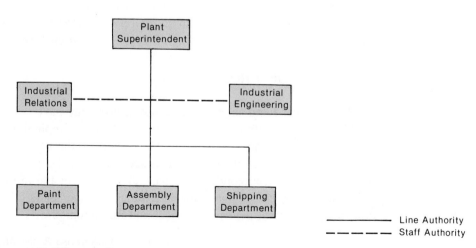

Figure 6-8 **Line-and-Staff Organization**

Formal Organization Premises

Formal traditional organization theorists accept the two basic premises of a rational person motivated by economic incentives and the formally-structured organization controlled by managerial authority. This **closed-system organization** viewpoint rejects environmental, behavioral, or human influences. Management is a necessary and sufficient integrative force, and the formal hierarchy is the mechanism for achieving coordination. The emphasis on clear, rigid structure and authority relationships reinforces such organizational principles as: (a) specialization and division of labor, (b) the scalar principle of authority and responsibility, and (c) a narrow span of management.

The Matrix Organization

Many modern organization theorists are critical of strict adherence to traditional theory and feel that it should be modified by behavioral and systems theories. The **matrix** or **project organization** is an interesting hybrid example of modern thinking, as it involves temporary, fluid work teams within the framework of the traditional pyramidal formal organization.

The concepts of matrix or project organization have emerged out of the needs of the Department of Defense and the National Aeronautics and Space Administration. New management and organization techniques were needed that could be applied across departmental lines to accomplish specific complex and finite undertakings, such as developing a missile system.

Many government agencies and nondefense industries have now adapted these concepts to their own needs. In 1970, for example, Chevrolet chose the project organization concept to develop and market the Vega. One section of the Chevrolet staff took total responsibility for the car from start to finish. This approach encouraged innovation and freedom from conventional organizational thinking and resulted in an entirely new manufacturing plant, a new aluminum engine, and the shipping of Vegas by new enclosed railroad cars.

A STREAM OF PROJECTS

Cleland and King suggest that today a firm may have a "stream of projects,"[1] each in a different stage of complexity and completion, and each with its own problems and peculiarities. Thus, there is the need for an individual designated as project manager and responsible for keeping abreast of and managing all the company's work on that project for the life of the project. With many projects on hand, the functional manager finds it extremely difficult to keep up with the many project and functional efforts.

[1]David I. Cleland and William R. King, *Systems Analysis and Project Management* (New York: McGraw-Hill Book Company, Inc., 1968), p. 15.

A MIXED-FORM ORGANIZATION

Figure 6-9 shows an abbreviated example of matrix organization with project management. As the figure suggests, project organization exists in a matrix or grid within the formal organizational framework that provides the functional expertise and centralized service activities required to support the projects and the company as a whole. In the matrix organization the various projects draw specialized expertise as needed from the functional departments on a temporary basis. The project effort reflects these work-oriented relationships; it is more concerned with the flow of work in horizontal and diagonal relationships than the vertical chain of command. A **diagonal relationship** would exist in Figure 6-8 if, for example, the manager of Project C should deal directly with the manager of the Instrumentation Department.

Some of the other departures of this hybrid form of organization from the traditional formal organization structures and relationships discussed earlier in this chapter are given here:

1. The authority of the project manager is a combination of technical expertise, charisma, political effectiveness, and formal authority, rather than merely the occupancy of a formal position in the chain of command. Therefore, this individual must rely heavily on persuasion and personal acceptance and must build alliances with peers, functional associates, and superiors.
2. The authority of the project manager goes outside the organization lines to relationships with suppliers, subcontractors, government agencies and the like, thus emphasizing an **open-system organization** that must be responsive to forces in its environment.
3. The project is finite in duration; if successful, however, it may be the start of a new formal organization division.

Project organization is an expensive, complex undertaking, and it should only be applied to infrequent and highly important jobs requiring the coordination of numerous specialties. There are various forms of matrix, project, and task-team organizations; this discussion has given some general insights into modern organization thinking.

Informal Organization

The projects discussed in the previous section are actually work groups or task teams that are formally established and appear on the organization chart. There are, however, many groups and interactions that form whenever people work together which do not appear on the organization chart. **Work groups** are formed by the workers themselves to accomplish a task. **Informal groups** are established on the job without official sanction. **Social groups** are established for purely social reasons and they may exist both in and out of the job situation.

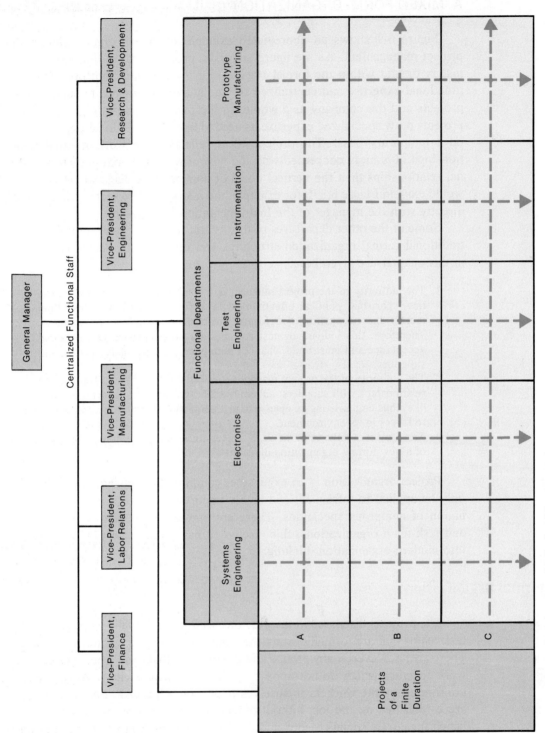

Figure 6-9 *Matrix Organization with Project Management*

In any type of group the members have something in common, and they believe that this "something" sets them apart from the general work force. Groups are not always beneficial to organizations, but often informal group membership helps decrease frustration and job monotony in the formal work situation.

An **informal organization** is formed, then, by activities and human interactions that are not formally established by the firm but nevertheless are naturally occurring, vital parts of the total organization. The wise manager carefully observes and interprets the dynamics of the informal organization.

ORGANIZATIONAL EFFECTIVENESS

Generally organizational behaviorists today see organizations as open social systems composed of a network of interdependent and dynamic groups. In this viewpoint the organization is a social interaction system that is structured by statuses and roles rather than by clearly structured formal hierarchy of tasks and authority relationships. **Status** is usually defined as the rank or position of an individual in a group or of a group in relation to other groups. **Role** refers to the behavior or activities of a person who occupies a certain status. A status is a set of privileges or duties; a role is the acting out of the set of duties and privileges.

Furthermore, the groups and the organization each have goals and these are not always compatible; thus, the possibility of organizational friction and conflict. However, as the firm's goals change, the organization is expected to remain fluid and change to accommodate these goals.

Criteria for Organizational Effectiveness

It is a narrow view to attempt to judge the effectiveness of a business organization by a single standard, such as profit maximization, high productivity, efficient service, or good employee morale. Modern theorists insist that a broad view must be taken. They define **organizational effectiveness** as the capacity of an organization to survive, adapt, maintain itself, and grow in the face of changing conditions. An effective business organization is one that meets the following criteria:

1. It has the managerial ability to solve problems and to react with flexibility to changes in the social, political, and economic environment. The current emphasis on environment places an increasing burden on management's ability and willingness to assume an active role in this vital area.
2. It has a sense of identity; it knows what its goals are and what must be done to achieve them; and this knowledge is widely shared by all members of the organization.

3. It is realistic in its planning in that it can judge correctly the impact of relevant changes in markets and technology on the company's future.
4. It provides for integration or fusing of personal, individual goals and enterprise objectives.

Organizational Development

The multidimensional viewpoint of organizational effectiveness is reflected in the currently popular area of **organizational development (OD)**. Many behavioral approaches, tools, and techniques are used in OD. Basically, however, OD enhances an organization's effectiveness by improving the internal growth and development of its human resources and also developing the organization's ability to cope with changes in its external environment.

As our society becomes more complex, dynamic, and interdependent, the organizing process will require greater managerial sophistication and awareness of both the formal and behavioral aspects of organization. The traditional organizational concepts explored in this chapter remain necessary and important. But they will probably be applied with considerable discrimination in the future, and modified to accommodate changing technological and human organizational requirements.

BUSINESS TERMS

QUESTIONS FOR DISCUSSION AND ANALYSIS

1. What basic guidelines should a manager have in mind when setting up departments in an organization?
2. Can the president of a company delegate responsibility to others down the line?

3. Would the average factory worker be concerned with whether he or she was working in a line or a line-and-staff organization? Explain.
4. A staff person may be able to help a line

supervisor by handling matters for the supervisor down the line in the organization. Do you see any possible problems in this practice? Explain.

5. If organizations are continually changing, then what is the use of having an organization chart?

6. Many small companies do not have organization charts. Do you think this is a desirable policy? Explain.

7. In a matrix organization with project management, how may the authority of the project manager differ from the authority of the manager in the traditional chain of command?

8. How does one differentiate between the formal organization and the informal organization?

9. If you wished to describe an informal group in an organization, what characteristics would you look for?

10. In what way does the concept of role govern, for example, the actions of an academic dean?

PROBLEMS AND SHORT CASES

1. The JetAir Corporation makes jet engines and employs 11,000 people. About ten years ago it adopted and implemented an active policy of decentralization because the top managers were unable to be sufficiently informed and knowledgeable about many complex problems and decisions at lower levels in the organization to make sound decisions. Now, however, JetAir has just obtained a large electronic computer that will be part of a major new information system for both engineering and business data. What impact do you think this will have on JetAir's decentralized decision making? Should this be recentralized?

2. Interview a business manager and determine (a) whether he or she occupies a position of line, staff, or functional authority, or perhaps a position involving all of these; (b) on what basis the division, unit, or department is departmentalized; and (c) if the company has a current organization chart. Note particularly the ways in which this manager's responses may differ from the discussion in the text.

3. Hillco was a simple organization long geared to handling one product line. Although successful, it felt the need to be alert to opportunities to diversify its product line. These broke rapidly, and in the short space of 18 months Hillco took on two new businesses. The president found himself with 20 executives reporting directly to him. Sales got a nice boost, rising from $300 million to $395 million in less than three years. But Hillco's profits went into a severe decline. What may have gone wrong? On the basis of your evaluation, what should the president do?

7 Management Activities

Two years ago the Klein Company was fat and happy. Orders were pouring in, new offices were being opened, and a large computerized data processing system was being installed to handle the expanded business. Then the roof fell in. Harry Klein's hand-picked successor quit and went with a competitor. The computer installation became snarled and costs were running wildly out of hand. Klein lost many good salespersons and fired other marginal producers, and orders fell way off. Klein blames the drastic situation on the "disloyal" manager who left and on "a lot of rotten luck."

Chapter 6 discussed the fact that our advanced society can only prosper by specializing — by pooling resources and exchanging the fruits of labor with others. The job of management in any organization is to make these cooperative specialized endeavors function properly — to combine and convert people, machines, money, and materials into a useful, goal-oriented enterprise. A manager cannot simply adapt after the fact to changing forces in the environment. A manager must be a dynamic innovating force — the activating element in the business enterprise.

LEVELS OF MANAGEMENT

Large businesses usually have three levels of management in the organizational hierarchy: (1) top or institutional management, (2) middle or administrative management, and (3) operating or technical management. These levels are shown in Figure 7-1; the arrows indicate the main function or orientation of each level.

Institutional Management

Institutional management, or **top management**, is composed of the board of directors, president, and group executives. The function or orientation of this

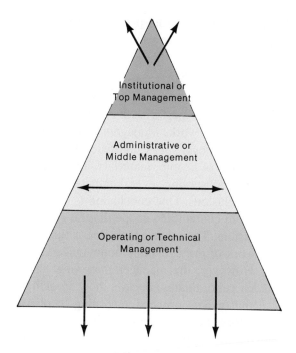

Figure 7-1   *Levels of Management*

level is to establish the relationship and role of the firm to other institutions in its environment. This includes the integration of the firm into the higher-order system of which it is a part, and the struggle for power and support among the many other organized interests of our society.

Administrative Management

Administrative management, or **middle management**, is composed of managers such as division general managers and service division managers. As the arrow in Figure 7-1 indicates, the orientation of this level is coordinative and integrative. It coordinates the work of the various departments in the operating level. It also provides a link between the production processes and the sale of the goods that are produced, thus mediating the technical organization and its customers.

Operating Management

Operating management, or **technical management**, is composed of department managers and persons of professional technical competence. This level is oriented downward to concrete operations — to producing the goods and moving them out the door. The technical expert, such as an engineer, often seeks recognition from peers and colleagues rather than from the managers at the administrative level.

THE MANAGER AS A SOCIAL MECHANIC

A manager performs a great variety of commonplace activities during a normal day's work. Managers make and receive telephone calls; go on trips; attend meetings; speak and listen to individuals and groups; and monitor the movement of people, materials, and machines.

After observing several managers at work, one may arrive at two conflicting conclusions. One conclusion is that the various managerial jobs differ so widely in content and scope that no generalization about managerial activities is possible. The other conclusion is that there is not much difference between the work of managers and nonmanagers.

However, the manager may view the work differently. When a person guides subordinates, decides how to achieve a particular goal, or checks to see that events proceed according to plans, that person acts as a manager. Therefore, various managers may have similar objectives in mind, but the constraints within which they must operate at any given time may require different approaches and the use of different techniques, concepts, and principles — i.e., the tools of the manager.

Thus, a manager can be seen as a social mechanic with the obligation to develop an awareness of the available tools and of the implications of the applicability of these tools in any particular situation. The tools of a manager — concepts, techniques, and principles — are potentially great in number. Is there any framework that will help the manager organize these tools for use? Certainly there is. Just as a toolbox with drawers and sections is used to separate pliers, socket sets, and the like, the manager may ''section off'' tools by the following major means: (1) the decision-making process, and (2) the functions of a manager.

Figure 7-2 shows the managerial functions and indicates that they are not discrete but interact with one another. Furthermore, decision making and communication are the coordinative processes that tie these various functions together.

The Process of Decision Making

Possibly the foremost responsibility of management at all levels, but especially top management, is decision making. It permeates all functions of management. In accord with the broad operational policies set forth by the board of directors, top managements are daily confronted with the necessity of deciding on courses of action that will best achieve the goals to which their

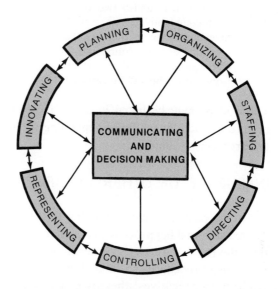

Figure 7-2   **Management Functions in a Coordinative Framework of Communication and Decision Making**

companies are dedicated. In many, if not most, instances the decisions involve choices between two or more alternative courses of action. And at the top echelon of management, from which the basic procedural orders for the companies' operations emanate, correct decisions may be vital to the continued success of the firms or even their survival. Farther down the managerial ladder, there is usually a decrease in the number and quality of alternatives available to the managers involved; but the importance of correct decisions at these levels is, nevertheless, essential to the well-being of the companies.

The ability to make correct decisions in business has long been recognized as a prime attribute of successful management, but until comparatively recently there has been little apparent need for inquiry into the process of decision making. However, with the growth of large corporations, with their vast resources in the areas of finance, productive capacity, and manpower, and the increased tempo of competition, the possible consequences of unwise decisions both on the companies involved and on the economy generally have focused the attention of business students on decision-making methods.

STEPS IN DECISION MAKING

The steps included in the decision-making process have been known for quite some time. They are:

1. Recognition of the problem.
2. Definition and analysis of the problem into its essential parts.

3. Attempt to establish two or more alternative solutions and to evaluate them comparatively.
4. Selection of the solution believed to be more favorable.
5. Adoption of this solution and the implementation of it through the issuing of the necessary orders and securing the needed acceptance of the plan from those who will be carrying it out.

These steps may be taken in a few moments by an executive or they may require a much longer time, depending on the complexity and importance of the problems at hand.

INFLUENCE OF OTHER DISCIPLINES

In the past few years a number of things have evolved that have brought the decision-making process into a sharper focus. From the purely mechanical side, the rapid and extensive development of high-speed computers and data processing procedures has added immeasurably to the quantity of information available to executives, thereby enabling them to base their decisions on far greater amounts of relevant data than previously. In addition to this, social and behavioral scientists have become aware that decision making by management is not only an economic activity dependent on accurate data, but it also reaches into the fields of sociology, psychology, anthropology, mathematics, philosophy, and political science. From each of these fields of knowledge have come theories and concepts which, it is hoped, will aid management in making its decisions and in bringing about results that will be beneficial not only to the firms involved but also to the society of which they are a part. Those who have been active in this area are hoping to develop a general theory of decision making that will synthesize the contributions from the various disciplines into a valid and useful whole.

Management Functions

The functions of managers that are truly characteristic of their work as managers may be broken down into categories in which managerial decisions are made. These are (1) planning, (2) organizing, (3) staffing, (4) directing, (5) controlling, (6) representing, and (7) innovating. It is in these functions that managers must be skilled if they are to accomplish their work through the efforts of other people.

PLANNING

Planning may be defined as the process of establishing and clarifying objectives and goals, determining the policies and procedures necessary to meet the objectives and goals, and preparing a plan of action.

Objectives. One way for a manager to identify areas in which a company should establish objectives is to consider the relationships and resources that are necessary to its survival and success. This will lead to objectives concerning the type and quality of goods produced and the desired relationship of the company to its customers, suppliers, employees, stockholders, and the surrounding community.

Policies. A broad guideline that says something about *how* objectives or goals will be attained is a **policy**. An **objective** is *what* one wants to accomplish; a policy is the practice or method used to achieve the objective. Figure 7-3 gives some examples of basic objectives and related policies.

BROAD OBJECTIVE	RELATED POLICY
An efficient, customer-oriented company.	Orders must be filled and shipped within three days of receipt.
A willingness to innovate.	A formal system for reviewing and rewarding employee suggestions.
Participation in civic improvement.	Time off without loss of pay to executives involved in desirable community programs.
Opportunity for qualified workers to advance.	All job openings posted; a yearly performance review conducted by each department head.

Figure 7-3 **Objectives and Related Policies**

Plan of Action. A predetermined course of action is a **plan**. Both objectives and policies are types of plans, as they prescribe broad future courses of action. But broad statements of what the company is trying to achieve are not enough. A **plan of action** must be prepared detailing the course of action and stating the specific resources required. This reflects the company's strategy. **Strategic decisions** are defined as major decisions regarding the utilization of resources that may have a long-run impact on the accomplishment of goals. Strategic considerations in the plan of action might include such factors as:

1. The firm's human, capital, and material resources.
2. The nature and importance of the work in process.
3. Future trends based partly on changing technical, commercial, and financial conditions.
4. The order in which each step of the plan is to be undertaken.
5. The timing of each step.
6. The communication and coordination needed so that each step is understood, accepted, and carried out.

An example of a strategic decision was Lockheed's decision in 1968 to compete against the McDonnell-Douglas DC-10 with its L-1011 "airbus."

This required an enormous marshalling of persons, materials, machines, and money. Over $40 million had to be committed to new buildings alone before a single L-1011 could be built.

Planning Information. At least three kinds of information are needed for planning, especially for top-level policy and strategic deliberations. **Environmental information** describes the social, political, and economic aspects of the climate in which a business operates or may operate in the future. **Competitive information** explains the past performance, programs, and plans of competitors. **Internal information** indicates the company's own strengths and weaknesses. Examples of environmental information are population trends, price level movements, transportation costs, labor force supply, and foreign trade forecasts. Competitive information includes organized data on the present and prospective profitability, return on investment, share of the market, and sales trends of competing companies. Internal information for planning should stress the elements of strength that give a company an edge over its competitors. Most frequently these are seen in cost variations relative to changes in sales volume, share of the market, delivery performance, community standing, reputation in the industry, and labor relations.

ORGANIZING

Once objectives and policies are established the manager must determine the activities necessary to achieve the objectives and provide for the coordination of authority relationships among the persons who will be performing these activities. If a firm is running smoothly, it may seem to an outsider that the whole process is relatively simple. Goods are shipped on time because they have been made and stored in advance of receiving an order and because the proper packaging and transportation facilities are available when needed. Actually this smooth flow could not have been accomplished without an efficient organization operating under competent managerial supervision. The specific elements of the organizing function of management were covered in the previous chapter.

STAFFING

Organizing establishes the positions within an organization and assigns duties to each. In **staffing** the manager attempts to recruit, hire, train, and develop the right person for each job. This is an ongoing managerial activity since people quit, are promoted, are transferred, are discharged, or retire. In the case of a growing company new positions are created that must be filled. Staffing is not solely the responsibility of the personnel department. Effective staffing requires that each manager observe his or her subordinates' performance, noting their strengths and seeking to remove weaknesses by careful counselling and training programs.

DIRECTING

The **directing** function of management involves the ability to guide and motivate subordinates so as to achieve the objectives of the enterprise, and at the same time to build an enduring, satisfying relationship between the subordinates and the enterprise. This important and basic function will be discussed more fully in a later section on managerial leadership.

CONTROLLING

Controlling may be defined as the managerial process that measures current performance against expected results and takes the necessary action to reach future goals. At all levels of management there must be control, all the way from knowing how much money the firm is making or losing to knowing the number of parts of a particular size and shape that are on hand. A proper organizational plan assigns control to individuals at various levels of management, depending upon the importance or type of factor involved. Top management should not be concerned with the problem of whether a minimum of 100 or 200 one-horsepower motors should be kept on hand, but it is concerned with the total dollars tied up in the parts inventory.

Steps in the Control Cycle. The control process consists of a cycle of four steps:

1. Deciding in advance what should be accomplished or what will constitute good performance.
2. Measuring current, actual performance in quantitative terms if possible.
3. Comparing current activity with the standards or norms of expected performance.
4. Taking corrective action, if needed, so as to achieve or exceed the desired results in the future.

There are many ways to check actual performance against standards. A few of the most common are: direct observation by the supervisor, consultation through informal contacts with subordinates, periodic audits or review of operations, special investigations, and formal management control reports. Because of the importance of this activity, Chapter 24 deals further with management control systems.

Since the first step in the control cycle is the result of planning activities, there must be feedback between control and planning. Feedback, in this instance, is the process of adjusting future actions based upon data gathered about past performance. Efforts at controlling will indicate whether past planning has been effective; these will indicate whether expected standards of performance are too easily achieved, reasonable, or unobtainable and will raise the question whether new plans should be formulated.

Special Control Problems. Two control problems frequently arise in large businesses that are not present in smaller organizations. One of these is that of **absentee management**, a condition that exists when executives of a large corporation have their offices in one city and their operating divisions are scattered throughout the country. Absentee management frequently requires the delegation of substantial authority to the personnel in the field, and considerable reliance must be placed on reports and occasional plant visits.

A related problem of a large firm is whether to operate on the basis of a centralized management or a decentralized management. This issue arises when a firm's operations are physically dispersed, such as the large chain-store organizations. Here the question refers to the measure of authority that is to be delegated to the field executives and how much is to be retained by the home office management. For example, in a firm embracing the philosophy of decentralized management, the branch offices might be permitted to handle their own personnel problems, to set quotas for their salespersons, to make local adjustments, and to conduct dealer relations. In a company that follows the practice of centralized management, these matters would be reserved for the home office.

REPRESENTING

At various times the manager must represent the company to the outside world. These outside groups include the general public, the local community banks, labor unions, trade associations, and numerous governmental agencies. Sometimes this function is merely to be accessible and pleasant to visitors; at other times it is a matter of subtle negotiations. **Representing** is the function that brings the manager into contact with the people outside the company.

Marcor and Federated Department Stores are among the many companies that regard participation in civic work as part of the self-development of an executive. Otherwise, top executives often are ill-prepared to take on the community, state, and national responsibilities as their part in a company's external relations at the institutional level.

INNOVATING

If the manager's job is to be creative, he or she must innovate. **Innovating** is finding new or better ways for people to achieve goals or discarding old procedures that are no longer needed. Managers can exercise this function in several ways: they may develop new ideas themselves; they may combine old ideas in a new way; they may adapt the ideas of others for their own use; or they may stimulate others to develop and carry out new ideas.

Many managers claim to encourage innovation but really do not, since they see innovation as a disruptive and unwelcomed process. Nevertheless, a congenial environment for creativity is increasingly essential to corporate growth and competitiveness. Some firms, such as duPont and Celanese, try to provide an environment for innovation by setting up small "venture" groups to research, develop, and test new products. These teams are managed outside of established product divisions and usually report to top management.

Alert managers realize that their companies cannot stand still. Remaining ahead of competition requires corporate leadership dedicated to the principle that innovation is the lifeblood of the company.

MANAGERIAL FUNCTIONS AND LEVELS

This outline of management functions has some hidden difficulties when one attempts to apply them to a specific managerial job. First, the list does not tell which functions are most important. It does not help managers allocate their time on the job. All functions are important parts of a manager's job, but the significance attached to each one may vary at different times in different organizations, and, as Figure 7-4 suggests, at different managerial levels in the same organization. Secondly, the terms used to name the function are vague and somewhat overlapping. It can be argued, for example, that planning is incomplete without innovating and controlling, and that organizing encompasses staffing.

The list of management functions does help, however, to distinguish managerial work from nonmanagerial efforts. It reveals to some degree the complexity of managerial tasks and helps the manager recognize the important role of decision making. It emphasizes that the manager's work is concerned with ideas and people, rather than with impersonal operations and things.

MANAGERIAL LEADERSHIP

When one thinks of management in general, one may think almost instinctively of the three basic activities that are formally regarded as elements of the directing function: (1) leadership, (2) motivation, and (3) communication. This is quite understandable since the directing function of management, as previously defined, involves the ability to guide and motivate subordinates in such a manner as to achieve the objectives of the enterprise and at the same time to build an enduring, satisfactory relationship between the subordinates and the enterprise. A relationship of this sort is based upon the recognition

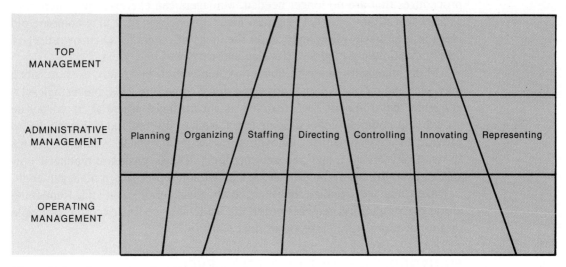

Planning	Organizing	Staffing	Directing	Controlling	Innovating	Representing

TOP MANAGEMENT

ADMINISTRATIVE MANAGEMENT

OPERATING MANAGEMENT

Figure 7-4 **Management Functions and Levels**

that the subordinates have differing goals that must be satisfied to some degree if they are to contribute effectively to the activity over time. These three elements which a manager must use to breathe life into the organization — to put into action the plans and organization that have already been discussed — will be considered.

Leadership

Managers may rely basically on the authority that has been officially or traditionally attached to the positions they occupy to mobilize the resources under their command. Beyond this formal authority, however, managers must also exert a degree of leadership to motivate subordinates to contribute willingly to the goals through good work. **Leadership** is defined as the ability to persuade or influence others in a dynamic, two-way process between the leader and followers. In this process the leader both influences the group members and is responsive to their desires.

The skillful leader realizes that various leadership styles may affect the performance of the organization or group with which he or she is dealing in different ways. The three basic **leadership styles** are autocratic, democratic, and laissez-faire. The **autocratic** (boss-centered) **leader** makes decisions without consulting others; the **democratic** (subordinate-centered) **leader** invites participation of subordinates in the decisions that affect them; and the **laissez-faire leader** leaves many of the decisions up to the subordinates to make by giving them a "free rein" over their activities. Figure 7-5 indicates seven representative gradations of leadership behavior in a continuum moving from boss-centered to subordinate-centered leadership.

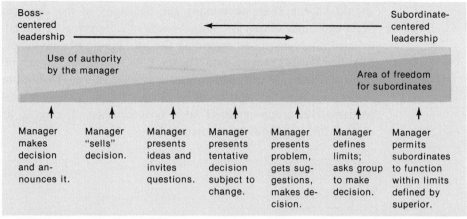

Figure 7-5   **Continuum of Leadership Behavior**

Tannenbaum and Schmidt suggest that no one of these styles is always the more effective but that the effectiveness of leaders will depend upon their ability to select correctly and employ a leadership style based upon an accurate assessment of three basic forces at any particular time: (1) forces in the manager, (2) forces in the subordinates, and (3) forces in the situation.

FORCES IN THE MANAGER

All managers view leadership problems in their own ways, depending on their particular background, knowledge, and experience. Four factors within the manager influence the pattern of leadership. These are:

1. The confidence placed in one's subordinates.
2. One's own leadership inclinations.
3. One's feeling of security in an uncertain situation.
4. One's value system.

In determining the degree of confidence placed in one's subordinates, the manager is likely to consider the knowledge, competence, and adaptability of each of them. There are managers who seem to act more comfortably and naturally when they can decide and direct their subordinates' activity; others operate more comfortably in a team role. If managers feel a great need for stability and predictability in their situations, they are reluctant to delegate work to others or to permit others to make decisions because releasing the control of decision making to others reduces the predictability of the results.

Perhaps one's value system is the major force within a manager that moves him or her toward either a boss-centered or a subordinate-centered leadership pattern. How strongly does a manager feel that subordinates should have a share in making the decisions of the department? Douglas McGregor, in his book *The Human Side of Enterprise*,[1] outlined two opposing managerial assumptions regarding the attitude and behavior of workers, and he called these **Theory X** and **Theory Y**. A manager who accepts the assumptions of Theory X will tend toward a work-centered, authoritarian pattern of leadership. Another whose values closely follow Theory Y will emphasize a participative, group-centered style of leadership. The basic assumptions of each of these theories are shown in Figure 7-6.

THEORY X	THEORY Y
1. Work is distasteful; it is an onerous chore to be performed in order to survive.	1. Work is as normal as play.
2. The average person has an inherent dislike of work and will avoid it if possible.	2. External control and the threat of punishment are not the only means for directing effort toward company objectives. People will exercise self-direction and self-control in working toward objectives to which they are committed.
3. Most people must be coerced, controlled, directed, or threatened with punishment to get them to put forth adequate effort toward the achievement of company objectives.	3. Commitment to objectives depends upon the rewards associated with their achievement.
4. The average person prefers to be directed, wishes to avoid responsibility, has relatively little ambition, and wants security above all.	4. The average person learns under proper conditions not only to accept but to seek responsibility.
	5. The capacity to exercise a relatively high degree of imagination, ingenuity, and creativity in the solution of organizational problems is widely, not narrowly, distributed in the population.
	6. Under the conditions of modern industrial life, the intellectual potentialities of the average human being are only partially utilized.

Figure 7-6 **Opposing Theories of Worker Attitude and Behavior**

FORCES IN THE SUBORDINATES

The second factor that influences the pattern of leadership exercised by a manager is the set of forces operating within the subordinates as a group. If a manager obtains affirmative answers to most or all of the following questions, he or she will probably be inclined to stress subordinate-centered approaches to decision making. The questions are:

1. Do the members of my department have a high desire for independence?
2. Are they ready to assume responsibility?
3. Can they tolerate uncertainty?
4. Are they deeply interested in the problem to be solved?
5. Do they understand and accept the company's objectives?
6. Do they have the knowledge and experience to deal with the problem?
7. Do they expect to share in the decision making?

[1]Douglas McGregor, *The Human Side of Enterprise* (New York: McGraw-Hill Book Company, Inc., 1960).

Negative answers to these questions move the manager toward a more boss-centered pattern of leadership.

FORCES IN THE SITUATION

A manager's pattern of leadership depends greatly upon the situation. The situation, in turn, depends on the type of organization, the effectiveness of the subordinates working together as a group, the nature of the problem to be solved or the decision to be made, and the pressure of time. Each company has its own concept of the "good manager," and this concept will push the manager in the direction of tradition. The subordinates as a group may lack unity and have little ability to work together. In this situation the manager is forced toward a dominating role. Problems differ in scope — some can best be handled by one person while others require the collaboration of a group for solution. If a problem calls for immediate solution, then it is difficult to involve other people. When the time pressure is less intense, the subordinate-centered pattern of leadership becomes more feasible.

Leadership cannot be conferred by promoting an individual to a management position. It is earned by the active understanding of (a) the factors that influence individuals and groups to act the way they do, (b) the dynamics of organizational life, and (c) the needs, goals, motivations, and prejudices of the individual as a manager.

Motivation

In the practice of management, the word "motivation" has a history that falls roughly into three phases. Up to the time around World War I, the typical manager gave little thought to motivation. The pattern of leadership was strongly boss-centered. Subordinates either did as they were told or were fired or transferred. In the years between World War I and II, motivation was based on various rewards. The typical view seems to have been, "Treat employees well and they will work harder out of loyalty and gratitude." Money was considered to be the chief means of spurring workers on toward superior performance. Changed social conditions and a deeper understanding of the attitudes of people at work have indicated that earlier ideas of work motivation were misleading. Behavioral scientists and effective managers now recognize that motivation depends more on internal or psychological incentives than on fear or rewards. **Motivation** is not coercing, coaxing, or persuading people to do what is wanted, but rather a process of creating organizational conditions that will cause employees to strive for superior performance.

Current management thinking about motivation has been strongly influenced by the findings of behavioral scientists. Neither the managers nor the scientists, however, believe that they have found the key to the complex problem of work motivation. At this time a considerable amount of practice and theory center around two concepts: (1) the relationship between morale and productivity, and (2) the hierarchy of needs.

MORALE AND PRODUCTIVITY

For a long time the connection between morale and productivity was thought to be direct and simple. It was believed that if morale were high, productivity would be high. Studies by the Survey Research Center of the University of Michigan indicate that employees may be happy and morale may be high, but productivity may be low. People may enjoy high morale and still fail to produce. This conclusion does not mean that morale can be ignored because it does not assure high levels of production. Employee morale does play a part in motivating people. It is the starting point, a springboard. Good morale, however, does not necessarily mean employees will jump to higher levels of performance.

HIERARCHY OF NEEDS

A. H. Maslow[2] proposed the theory that basic human needs may be arranged in an ascending order — in a hierarchy. Before his theory was developed, puzzling facts were noted. For example, it was generally assumed that people work to satisfy material needs. Money was thus assumed to be the great incentive. When, however, attitude surveys were taken and working people were asked what was most important to them in their jobs, good wages frequently took third or fourth place behind "challenging work," "chance for advancement," and even in some cases "a good boss."

Maslow's theory explains the seeming contradiction. He suggested that there is a **hierarchy of needs**. People give precedence to the first of these needs until it is relatively well satisfied. When the first need is almost satisfied, the second level of needs becomes dominant. Relative satisfaction of the second level leads to a third level, and so on through the series. Once a level is relatively satisfied, it ceases to operate as a primary motivator and is replaced by motivational forces created by needs of a higher order. Maslow's hierarchy of needs is shown in Figure 7-7.

The failure to understand the highest level of needs may cause a manager to complain, "I have given my people everything — good pay, pleasant working conditions, and the opportunity to have comfortable contact with one another — and yet they still are dissatisfied." Maslow's theory helps explain the situation. It is because the employees have the first four levels of needs at least partially satisfied that the fifth level — the need for self-fulfillment —

[2]Abraham H. Maslow, *Motivation and Personality* (New York: Harper & Brothers, 1954).

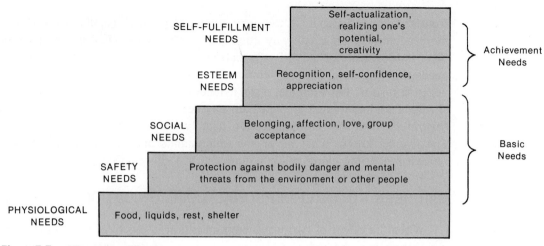

Figure 7-7   *Hierarchy of Needs*

arises. The emergence of this last level of needs will cause discontent unless the manager can find the ways and means of contributing to its satisfaction.

Communication

In recent years behavioral scientists have systematically studied the process of communication. They have found, for example, that the typical manager spends about 70 percent of the working day in writing, reading, speaking, and listening. Moreover, the greatest portion of this time is usually spent in face-to-face, oral communication. These studies also have pointed up the great complexity of **interpersonal communications**. By tracing step by step how an idea of one person is transmitted to another, they have identified many barriers that distort messages.

DIRECT AND FEEDBACK COMMUNICATION

Studies of interpersonal communications have shown that each oral exchange of ideas involves six different messages:

1. What the speaker means to say.
2. What the speaker actually says.
3. What the listener hears.
4. What the listener thinks he or she hears.
5. What the listener replies to the speaker.
6. What the speaker thinks the listener has replied.

The first four messages are direct messages and the last two are feedback messages. Without feedback messages there is only one-way communication from speaker to listener. A two-way communication is usually slower but is more accurate than a one-way communication. In two-way communication there is feedback not only of information but also of feelings. If the receiver heeds this feedback, two-way communication can produce both positive and negative results. For example, if the listener consistently feeds back that he or she does not understand, the speaker may begin to feel irritated, uncertain, or frustrated. Two-way communication usually permits more listener control. The listener knows what he or she understands and comprehends and can request repetition, clarification, examples, or a slower pace.

BARRIERS TO INTERPERSONAL COMMUNICATION

When the effect of two-way communication is positive, barriers to communication may be reduced. Barriers to interpersonal communications are factors that impede, distort, or cause a breakdown in the exchange of ideas and feelings. Barriers may be created in many ways. Some of the more common barriers are those generated by different meanings of words, by the lack of skill in listening, by the self-interest of the speaker, and by use of influence or authority to stop feedback.

Managers occupy positions of influence and authority over their subordinates. This position can be easily abused so as to "shut up" opposition or to block adverse questioning. Communication fails when managers obtain compliance with their directions by authority rather than by understanding.

MANAGERIAL PERFORMANCE

The findings of much of the research in managerial behavior point to the conclusion that the effective performance of management functions does not come about by chance or by some mysterious process. Sound decision making, competent leadership, the development of motivation, and good communications are not matters of birth or accident. Effective managerial performance depends directly on the skills of the managers, the level of their own motivation, and the environment of the organization in which they work. It is the combined effect of these three factors and not any one by itself that determines a manager's performance.

Skills of the Manager

Since managers direct the work of others and take responsibility for achieving results through these efforts, it can be seen that their effectiveness rests on three skills: technical, human relations, and administrative.

Technical skill implies a competence in a particular activity. It involves an understanding and proficiency in processes, procedures, techniques, and methods. Technical skill involves specialized knowledge and is readily recognized as important to the work of the tool and die maker, the computer programmer, the accountant, the tax lawyer, the engineer, and many others when they carry out their specialized work.

Human relations skill, or proficiency in human relations, is primarily concerned with working with people. It is this skill that enables a manager to work effectively as a group member and to build teamwork among the subordinates. It is based on an acute understanding of the differences and similarities among people. Human relations skill depends, on one hand, on an understanding of what subordinates mean by their words and actions and, on the other hand, on the manager's ability to communicate clearly with them. Human relations skill must be practiced continuously since it involves sensitivity not only when decisions are made and problems solved but also in day-to-day contacts with others.

Administrative skill, sometimes called conceptual skill, involves the ability to see the company as a whole and to understand the total situation relevant to it. This skill is exercised by recognizing how the various departments or divisions of a company are interrelated to one another and by perceiving how the company fits in the total fabric of society. A manager with administrative skill sees how various parts of the company work interdependently among themselves and are affected by outside changes in the social and economic environment. For example, when a major change is made in marketing policy, the change may have serious impact on the production, finance, research, and personnel of the organization. In turn, the change in marketing policy may result from, or even create, changes in governmental policy, labor relations, the location of plants, and consumer behavior. Administrative skill is concerned with integrating all the activities and interests of a company toward a common set of objectives.

As Figure 7-8 indicates, all of these skills have relatively different importance at different levels of management. Human relations skill is essential at every level. Technical skill has its greatest importance at the lower levels of management, while administrative skill becomes increasingly critical in top management positions.

Level of Manager's Motivation

Skills must be used, knowledge must be put into action, and this transformation depends on motivation. The motives of managers also follow Maslow's hierarchy of needs. Since managers generally have greater opportunity to satisfy the lower levels of needs, they can be expected to be more concerned with satisfying their esteem and self-fulfillment needs. It is for this reason that many managers are concerned with the impact and scope of their decision making.

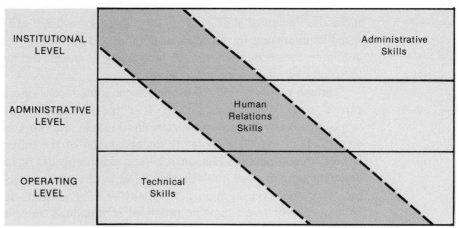

Figure 7-8   *Managerial Skills at Different Levels*

Work Environment of the Manager

A carefully developed organizational structure makes effective managerial performance more likely. The dynamics of the organizational process, however, create pressures upon managers. The effective manager learns to absorb or resolve these pressures.

Managerial pressures are those forces within a company that create change, conformity, uncertainty, or goal conflict. The pressures of change are those that cause a manager to be concerned over job transfers, reorganization, and geographic moves. While in every organization there are forces at work that will upset or change conditions, there are at the same time forces seeking stability and uniformity. Each manager faces the expectations of others in the organization that he or she should "fit the mold," or conform to the usual ways of operating and behaving. The third type of pressure tests the manager's tolerance of uncertainty. Many decisions must be made when information is unavoidably incomplete. Managers must risk their reputation and decide in the face of unknown future events. Finally, decisions to work toward one goal may have to be made at the expense of some other goal. A department head may wish to give raises to all departmental subordinates at a time when budget information indicates that costs should be reduced. A president may have to choose between maintaining good community relations by continuing production in an inefficient, high labor-cost plant or relocating the plant in a different city.

One might say that managerial activities are defined by a position description that states the manager's duties and authority and by a title that locates position in the organizational structure. In a formal sense this is true, but it is an oversimplification. This chapter has shown that the manager's activities are numerous and complexly interrelated. The way managers go about their work results from the interplay of the organization, their subordinates, and their own personalities. Their work abounds in both strains and possibilities. Finding a way to cope with the tensions and to grow in effectiveness is a genuine challenge to them.

BUSINESS TERMS

QUESTIONS FOR DISCUSSION AND ANALYSIS

1. Name several areas of decision making that might naturally be delegated to middle management. Can you justify your choices?
2. In what ways do you think that established policies can help in the decentralization of managerial decision making?
3. How do you think that informal channels of communication, sometimes called "grapevines," may affect decision making in an organization?
4. "Strategic decisions are so important that these should be made at the top level of the organization." Discuss this statement.
5. Discuss the question of whether or not the ultimate responsibility for staffing lies

with the personnel manager.
6. In staffing, would you say it is better to fit a person to a specific job description or to choose the person first and let her or him participate in working out the job description?
7. How may computer systems affect the elements of the control process?
8. Why does a successful manager have to be a leader of the persons in his or her department?
9. In what ways, if any, do you think that self-fulfillment plays a significant part in the average worker's attitude toward the job?
10. Why is verbal communication usually preferable to written communication?

PROBLEMS AND SHORT CASES

1. The Peerless Company is a successful, medium-sized producer of games, dolls, and novelty items. When asked how the company managed to succeed in such a competitive business, the president stated that the company wasn't greedy — it was willing to sit back and be "number two." It let others develop and test new

products, and then it watched the results to see if the product was worth copying. "Of course, we add our own little frills and goodies to the basic idea, and we sometimes lose out on the initial profits of a new item. But we also suffer far less flops than the front-row innovators, and it sure makes our planning and forecasting a heck of a lot easier." Discuss the advantages and disadvantages of this approach to managerial strategy and innovation.

2. Analyze the style and attributes of a manager you feel is also an outstanding leader. Include the following points in your observations: (a) What leadership style does this person usually use? (b) Is this person especially effective as a motivator? A communicator? Both? (c) At what level in the organization does this person work, and which managerial function appears to be the more important to the job? (d) Is he or she effective in all situations, or perhaps more effective in certain kinds of situations or relationships? (e) How does this individual recognize and reward good work? Discuss your findings in an oral class report.

3. There are some companies that follow the practice of requiring its management personnel at all levels to be active participants in civic affairs in the communities where they have plants or branch offices. In some instances the managers' jobs with these companies are in no small measure dependent upon their identification with local civic activities.

Opposed to this viewpoint are those firms that are more or less indifferent regarding their managers' participation in the affairs of their communities. In some instances such firms prefer that their managers devote all of their energies to company business and disapprove of their being identified with local civic movements in any way. Prepare a short paper setting forth the advantages and disadvantages, from the companies' standpoints, of both of these contrasting points of view and indicate which you feel is preferable, giving reasons for your decision.

Part 3

Marketing

Marketing is the dynamic area of business which matches the product offerings of a firm to the needs of its customers. Marketing is the way in which our society has elected to supply its material needs. Part 3 illustrates the importance of marketing.

Chapter 8 introduces marketing as a productive system which creates values or utilities for consumers. The decisions which confront a marketing manager are illustrated. The basic types of consumer and industrial goods are identified in Chapter 9, and several types of product policies are discussed. Emphasis is also given to the distribution channels which transfer the goods from producers to consumers. Chapter 10 is concerned with the promotional aspects of marketing. The steps in the sales process are outlined, and the media available to advertisers are evaluated. The major criticisms of advertising are mentioned and responses to these criticisms are provided.

Prices and pricing policies are the subject of Chapter 11. Different pricing goals are studied, and the factors which determine specific product prices are analyzed. Chapter 12 highlights the rise and meaning of the consumer movement. The reasons for the movement and its implications to business and society are critically examined.

8

Marketing Management

"All right, now pretend you're a typewriter," the researcher tells a young typist.

The woman flings herself on the floor, lies on her back, and stretches out her arms.

"Are you a man or a woman?" asks the researcher.

"A woman."

"What are you doing?" the man asks.

"I'm waiting for somebody to type on me," she replies.

To some people this may seem like simply a bizarre exercise in play acting, but to Ernest Dichter, a pioneer in motivational research, it is full of significance. It suggests that many office workers subconsciously consider typewriters not as mundane machines but rather as passive 'receiving' objects, he says. "Type me, fly me, it's the same idea," Mr. Dichter maintains.[1]

A customer-oriented economy is marketing oriented, and the United States is such an economy. One authority has stated that marketing is the delivery of a standard of living to society.[2] The American Marketing Association has defined **marketing** as "the performance of business activities that direct the flow of goods and services from producer to consumer or user."[3] Marketing personnel have the responsibility to research and ascertain the needs of consumers, to plan and develop products to meet these needs, and to perform the major economic activities that move the products from producer to consumer.

[1]Reprinted with permission of *The Wall Street Journal*, © Dow Jones & Company, Inc. (1972). All rights reserved.

[2]Paul Mazur, "Does Distribution Cost Enough?" *Fortune* (November, 1947), p. 138.

[3]Reprinted from Committee on Definitions, *Marketing Definitions: A Glossary of Marketing Terms*, published by the American Marketing Association, 1960, p. 15.

142

IMPORTANCE OF MARKETING

The basic importance of marketing in our economy is readily understood by examining: (1) employment in marketing, (2) number of marketing establishments, and (3) marketing costs.

Employment in Marketing

According to the *1972 Census of Business*, the number of workers in retailing was 11.4 million; wholesaling, 3.9 million; and selected services, 5.3 million — a total of 20.6 million employees. This number represents nearly 30 percent of all individuals employed in this country.

Number of Marketing Establishments

A measure of the scope of marketing is the number of establishments engaged in distributive activities. The number of organizations supporting marketing, such as transportation firms, finance companies, advertising agencies, and advertising media, should also be included. The *1972 Census of Business* lists 1,934,466 retail establishments; 348,168 wholesale establishments; and 1,590,248 selected service establishments — a total of 3,872,882 units.

Marketing Costs

Marketing costs, which represent the outlay of funds to accomplish the marketing process, emphasize the contribution of marketing to our economy. An historic study of distribution costs indicated that the consumer dollar is allocated as follows:[4]

Cost of production		41.1%
Cost of marketing		
Retail costs	19.2	
Wholesale costs	10.7	
Manufacturers' marketing costs	13.9	
Transportation costs	13.4	
Other marketing costs	1.7	58.9
Total costs		100.0%

Other studies indicate that the proportion of marketing costs in the selling price of a consumer product ranges from 42 to 59 percent. If costs are a

[4]Paul W. Stewart and J. Frederic Dewhurst, *Does Distribution Cost Too Much?* (New York: The 20th Century Fund, 1939), pp. 117–118.

measure of importance, then the marketing process should be considered as economically significant as the manufacturing process.

MARKETING AS A PRODUCTIVE SYSTEM

Both marketing and manufacturing are systems or processes. A difference between the marketing system and the manufacturing system is that the satisfactions provided by marketing are intangible while the satisfactions provided by manufacturing are tangible. The manufacturing system creates **form utility**, which is the satisfaction derived from a physical change in the product. On the other hand, the marketing system creates time, place, possession, and information utilities which are distinct capacities of a product to satisfy a consumer want.

To create these utilities, costly marketing activities must be performed during the marketing process. Product storage creates **time utility**, transportation creates **place utility**, and promotion creates both **possession** and **information utilities**. For example, a refrigerator manufactured in Columbus, Ohio, has no value to a consumer shopping in Denver, Colorado, until it has been transported (place utility) to a dealer's store in Denver. Consumers desire to make their selection from among the various models displayed and stored (time utility) in the dealer's showroom. The dealer uses extensive advertising (information utility) to inform the consumer about the refrigerator and personal selling (possession utility) to complete the transaction.

MARKETING CONCEPT

During the 1950s the American economy moved from a seller's to a buyer's market. There was intra-industry competition among automobile companies, and inter-industry competition among automobile firms and boat manufacturers for the same consumer dollar. Businesspersons began to understand that to obtain a share of consumer expenditures it was necessary to research, plan, and construct products that satisfied the needs of consumers. This is the essence of the **marketing concept**.

An expression of the marketing concept was first described in the 1952 annual report of General Electric:

> The concept introduces the marketing man at the beginning rather than at the end of the production cycle, and integrates marketing into each phase of the business. Thus, marketing through its studies and research will establish for the engineer, the design and manufacturing man, what the customer wants in a given product, what price he is willing to pay and where and when it will be wanted. Marketing will have authority in product planning, production

scheduling, and inventory control, as well as in sales distribution and servicing of the product.[5]

MARKETING ORGANIZATION STRUCTURE

The objectives of a firm determine the composition of its organization structure. Typical organizations are difficult to diagram since no two companies, even in the same industry, have identical corporate objectives. The General Electric organization differs from Westinghouse Electric, and the General Motors structure differs from Ford Motors. Figure 8-1 shows the marketing organization of a representative business which has adopted the marketing concept.

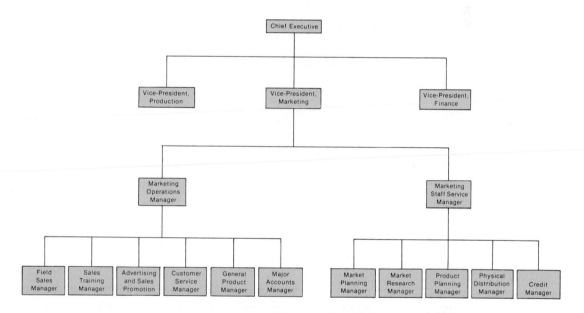

Figure 8-1 **Marketing Organization Under the Marketing Concept**

Since marketing, along with production and finance, is one of the three major functional areas of business, the vice-president of marketing or the **marketing manager** is frequently responsible to the chief executive of the firm. Figure 8-2 provides a profile of the typical chief marketing executive. To lessen the number of individuals reporting directly to the marketing vice-president, and to obtain a degree of specialization, marketing activities often are

[5] 1952 Annual Report of the General Electric Company.

THE POSITION: **Title:** Usually vice-president

Authority and responsibility: Both line sales and staff marketing services

Reports to: Usually the president or chairman and president

Most Important to the Success of the Marketing Function: Establishing objectives, with personnel selection and development second

THE EXECUTIVE: **Age:** Median is 50

Years in Present Position: Five or fewer

Most Important Attribute: Ability to contribute to top management decisions

Highest Educational Attainment: More than four out of five are college graduates, and almost one in five has a graduate degree, most often an MBA

Cash Compensation (including salary and bonus): $40,000-$59,999, with nearly 10 percent making $100,000 or more annually

Stock Option: Yes

Number of Directorships Held: None

Miles Traveled Annually: 25,000 or more, but usually no travel abroad

Time Spent Away from Office: Usually 25-49 percent

SOURCE: *Profile of a Chief Marketing Executive* (New York: Heidrick and Struggles, 1971), p. 3.

Figure 8-2   ***Typical Chief Marketing Executive***

grouped under a marketing operations manager and a marketing staff services manager. Sales and those activities most directly supporting sales are answerable to a marketing operations manager, while those activities less directly concerned with sales are accountable to a marketing staff service manager.

Marketing Operations

The **marketing operations manager** is responsible for: (a) field sales, (b) sales training, (c) advertising and sales promotion, (d) customer service, (e) product management, and (f) major accounts. The field sales manager, through an extensive sales organization, has charge of all the salespersons in the organization and has responsibility for all aspects of the firm's selling activities. Training programs on basic selling, product features, and company policies are developed and conducted for the salespersons by the sales training manager. Advertising and sales promotion programs which complement and intensify the selling activity are prepared by the advertising and sales promotion manager. The customer service manager attempts to correct consumer complaints concerning product defects. In a multiproduct company, product managers who are responsible for developing and marketing specific product lines report to the general product manager. In many large firms certain key or major accounts are handled by the major accounts manager at corporate headquarters rather than by salespersons in the field.

Marketing Staff Services

The **marketing staff services manager** is responsible for: (a) market planning, (b) marketing research, (c) product planning, (d) physical distribution, and (e) credit service. The market planning manager seeks to discover the best markets or customers for the company's products. Collecting, analyzing, and interpreting marketing data are the major activities of the marketing researcher. The product planning manager designs and creates new products to satisfy the ever-changing needs of consumers. The major responsibility of the physical distribution manager is to minimize the storage and transportation costs for a product and to maximize product availability to consumers. To enhance sales the credit manager must provide a variety of credit plans for prospective customers.

MARKETING FUNCTIONS

Marketing functions are those inescapable economic activities which are found throughout the marketing system. The marketing system includes eight basic marketing functions which are divided into three major categories:

1. Exchange
  - 1. Buying
  - 2. Selling

2. Physical Distribution
  - 3. Transportation
  - 4. Storage

3. Facilitating
  - 5. Financing
  - 6. Marketing research and information
  - 7. Risk taking
  - 8. Product standardization and grading

Functions of Exchange

The functions of buying and selling are concerned with the exchange of goods from seller to buyer. Buying involves the selection of the kinds of goods to be bought, the quality desired, the proper quantity, and the appropriate supplier. Selling, which is commonly considered the major function of marketing, includes searching for markets and influencing demand through personal selling and advertising.

Functions of Physical Distribution

The functions of transportation and storage are concerned with the movement of goods from the place of production to the point of consumption and with the storage of goods until they are needed by consumers. The transportation function involves the use of railroads, waterways, trucks, pipelines, and airplanes. The storage function is performed by manufacturers, wholesalers, retailers, and specialized firms such as public warehouses.

Facilitating Functions

The functions of finance, research and information, risk taking, and standardization and grading assist in the performance of the other functions. Financing provides the credit service which permits a buyer to pay for purchases over time. The research and information activity provides marketing data which marketing managers use in decision making. Risk taking, which is the exposure to a possible business loss, is present in all business activities. Standardization simplifies buying decisions by creating specific classifications of goods based upon criteria such as size, weight, color, and taste. Grading identifies the classification in which to place the goods.

Performance of Functions

The marketing functions must be performed at some point in the marketing process. Even though the responsibility for the performance of a function may be shifted from one point to another within the process, the function cannot be eliminated. For example, if a seller of refrigerators would not deliver the appliance to the buyer's home, the buyer would have to perform this transportation function.

As the marketing functions are shifted within the marketing system, companies develop different operating policies and varying cost structures. A firm manufacturing a retailer-branded lawn mower for a large retail chain, such as Sears, performs no mass advertising and incurs no other promotional costs. The promotional activities for the lawn mower and their costs are assumed by Sears. In contrast, a company that produces its own brand of lawn mower, such as Lawn Boy, needs an advertising budget and an advertising department in order to gain brand identity.

If none of the firms within a marketing system desire to perform a particular marketing function, a specialist may be utilized to accomplish the function. For example, if the transportation function is not performed by a firm within its system, the function may be shifted to a transportation specialist such as a trucking company.

MARKETING MIX

Marketing mix refers to the combination of decision elements in a company's marketing program. The combination is determined and controlled by marketing executives. The decision elements of marketing which are commonly identified as the four P's are:[6]

1. *Product*. Concerned with product planning, development, modification, branding, and packaging decisions.
2. *Place*. Concerned with decisions to determine which marketing establishments can be linked together most effectively in transferring product ownership from producer to consumer.
3. *Promotion*. Concerned with communicating to consumers and the related personal selling, advertising, and sales promotion decisions.
4. *Price*. Concerned with decisions regarding price determination, general and specific pricing policies, supply and demand relationships, and legal restrictions.

Marketing Strategy

Marketing mix and marketing functions are not synonymous terms. The marketing functions are inescapable activities in the marketing process; the marketing mix combines those marketing activities into purposeful marketing plans or strategies. In developing a **marketing strategy**, the combination of the marketing mix is determined by such factors as the market to be served, management objectives, competition, demand, social values, and legal restraints.

Different Marketing Strategies

The cosmetics industry illustrates how different marketing strategies can be developed by altering the marketing mix of a firm. Many cosmetic manufacturers, such as Coty and Maybelline, market through wholesalers who distribute to retailers. These manufacturers price competitively and promote extensively in consumer media, such as television, magazines, and newspapers, in an effort to stimulate a grass-roots consumer demand for their product.

[6]The four P's were popularized by E. Jerome McCarthy, *Basic Marketing* (5th ed.; Homewood, Ill.: Richard D. Irwin, Inc., 1975), p. 75.

In contrast, the marketing mix for Avon cosmetics is entirely different. Avon has carved a niche for itself in the cosmetics industry by catering to the person who desires to purchase a quality product directly from a salesperson. Although Avon advertises in the mass media, the bulk of its promotional expenditures are for commissions paid to a large sales force that taps on household doors and says, "Avon calling."

Market Segmentation and Product Differentiation

Market segmentation and product differentiation are complementary marketing strategies. Basically, market segmentation is a product development strategy, while product differentiation is essentially a promotional strategy.

When the market for a product is divided into two or more homogeneous groups of consumers, and variations of the product are developed to satisfy each group, **market segmentation** has occurred. Market segmentation allows a marketing manager to develop a strategy that will be responsive to the needs of a unique market sector.

Adequacy, measurability, and accessibility are the conditions that must be met for a strategy of market segmentation. Sales from the market segment should be large enough to justify the marketing effort directed to the segment. A firm that desires to sell a low-calorie salad dressing should be able to ascertain the adequacy of the market for the product. Life insurance industry statistics showing the number of overweight persons in this country would be a measure of this market. Assuming the market is adequate and measurable, management should decide if the prospective customers are accessible. Magazines directed to weight-watchers and morning television programs that feature exercise sessions are prime media for informing individuals on how to limit their calorie intake.

BASES OF SEGMENTATION

Markets are segmented on any of the following bases: geographic, demographic, or psychographic. For many years marketing managers have been aware of and have reacted to geographical differences in markets. For example, the management of one chain of shoe stores locates all of its retail stores in the broad-belted temperate zone of the midwestern United States, thereby eliminating the merchandising of shoes that appeal to clientele in either more southern or northern regions.

Demography is the science of vital and social statistics such as births, deaths, marriages, and population fluctuations. Socioeconomic variables — such as family income, age level, educational level, and family size — are types of demographic data often used to classify markets. Demographic data are very useful in segmenting markets since individuals can be grouped by factors that influence their purchases. Demographic information is also relatively easy to obtain and to classify.

Segmenting markets by identifying individuals who react similarly to a particular emotional appeal or who share common attitudinal or behavioral patterns is called **psychographic market segmentation**. Consumers who have been considered as belonging to different markets may be classified in the same market based upon similar behavioral patterns. A college professor and an unskilled laborer may be earning dissimilar incomes, may be of different ages, and may have contrasting educational backgrounds. One may be unmarried and the other a family person, yet both may hold common attitudes toward numerous products. On the other hand, two college professors may be earning identical salaries, may be of the same age, may have equal education, and may have similar size families; yet their behavioral patterns toward many products may be at opposite extremes.

PRODUCT DIFFERENTIATION

As an element of marketing strategy, **product differentiation** is an effort by marketing managers to secure a measure of control over the demand for a product by promoting distinctions between their products and the products of competing sellers. Product differentiation is characterized by utilizing promotional efforts, such as advertising and packaging, to shift consumer demand toward the firm's product. Producers of detergents, such as Cheer, Tide, All, and Dash, are quite skilled in the use of this strategy.

APPLICATION OF SEGMENTATION AND DIFFERENTIATION

The first step a firm takes when planning to introduce a new product is to research the needs of the prospective markets. The next step is to develop a product that satisfies the requirements of a particular market. If the company has executed its market segmentation strategy successfully, its product may be unique to this market sector. When the Ford Motor Company introduced the Mustang in 1964, it had no effective competition for nearly two years in the youthful, middle-income market segment to which the Mustang appealed. With 418,812 units sold, Mustang set a first-year sales record for any American car.

As the sales of a company's new product increases, other manufacturers begin introducing competitive products into the same market sector. These competitors effectively reduce the market share held by the original firm. In the case of the Ford Motor Company, Camaro, Barracuda, and Javelin were developed by other automobile manufacturers to compete with the Mustang.

In an effort to recapture its original share of the market segment, the initial producer develops additional products. The new products of the initial producer are differentiated from the original product through promotion, packaging, branding, and minimal physical changes. For example, in addition to the standard Mustang, for the 1969 model year Ford introduced the Mustang Mach I; and in 1970 the Mustang Boss was added.

When the sales of a product reach a steady decline, a firm must make a decision either to modify extensively or to drop the product. To justify the redesigning of a product, the company must determine if a sufficient need exists. After a critical evaluation of the market sectors which are served by compact cars, Ford introduced a redesigned Mustang II line for the 1974 model year. With the updated model, Ford was hopeful of repeating its success of a decade earlier.

UNCONTROLLABLE FACTORS IN THE MARKETING ENVIRONMENT

Marketing managers make their decisions within a social, economic, and political environment. Although they cannot control this environment, they seek as much information as possible about it so that they may make more accurate decisions. In the long run the decisions of marketing managers modify their environment. In the short run, however, they do not significantly change the environmental influences surrounding them. There are five **uncontrollable marketing factors** which are particularly significant to a marketing manager. They are (1) competition, (2) demand, (3) marketing legislation, (4) nonmarketing costs, and (5) structure of distribution.

Competition

''Macy's won't tell Gimbels, but Gimbels always knows'' is a familiar story in retailing. Any marketing manager is interested in knowing the plans of competitive firms. The marketing manager should be knowledgeable about the pricing, promotion, product, and place policies within the firm's industry. Ford executives should be aware of the advertising being done by Chevrolet and Plymouth. In addition, marketing executives should be aware of competition among industries. In the construction of high-rise buildings where poured concrete forms are replacing steel girders, executives in the steel industry should carefully assess the threat of competition from the concrete industry.

Some firms develop marketing intelligence systems in an effort to gather knowledge for better decision making. A major portion of the intelligence activity is devoted to accumulating information about competition. Important sources of intelligence for the marketing manager of a firm include:

1. The firm's salespersons.
2. The company's suppliers.
3. Government sources.
4. Trade associations.
5. Industry and competing company publications.
6. Marketing research.
7. Expert opinions.
8. Rumors.

Demand

Demand refers to the potential sales volume for a product or service in a given period of time. In order to forecast demand, a marketing manager should be conscious of: (1) population trends, (2) income patterns, and (3) buying behavior of consumers.

POPULATION

Population is the underlying market factor for consumer demand. From 1900 to 1973 the population in the United States grew from 76 million to 211 million, an increase of 178 percent. Rather than looking at total population, it is more significant to a marketing manager to segment the population by age groups. For example, the young population segment is the group which marries, forms families, purchases sports cars and other new products, and generally determines the fashions.

The migration pattern of population by state is important to marketers. The resulting shift in consumer markets during the decade of the 1960s is indicated in Figure 8-3. While Nevada, Florida, and Arizona experienced over a 15 percent increase in population, North Dakota, South Dakota, New Mexico, Mississippi, West Virginia, and Wyoming had more than a 10 percent decrease. Factors that frequently draw individuals to an area are: (a) employment prospects, (b) high wages, (c) appealing climate, and (d) attractive social environment.

INCOME PATTERNS

The aggregate amount for spending and saving in this country during a particular period of time, **disposable personal income,** is a prime factor in determining consumer demand. Personal income is the most important source of consumer purchasing power. Other sources include credit and wealth.

Figure 8-4, page 155, discloses that between 1962 and 1972 the southeast sector of the country sustained the greatest increase in personal income. A

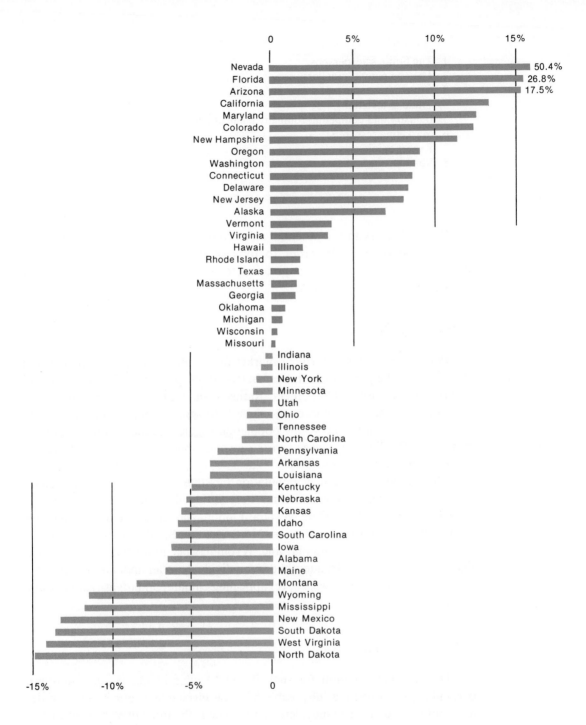

SOURCE: "Geographic Mobility in the Sixties," *Road Maps of Industry*, No. 1666, The Conference Board (May 15, 1971).

Figure 8-3   *Net Migration of Population by State, 1960–1970 .*

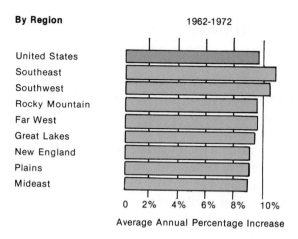

By Region   1962-1972

United States
Southeast
Southwest
Rocky Mountain
Far West
Great Lakes
New England
Plains
Mideast

0 2% 4% 6% 8% 10%

Average Annual Percentage Increase

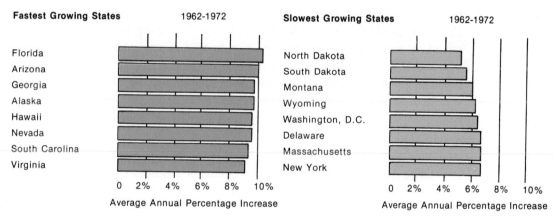

Fastest Growing States   1962-1972

Florida
Arizona
Georgia
Alaska
Hawaii
Nevada
South Carolina
Virginia

0 2% 4% 6% 8% 10%

Average Annual Percentage Increase

Slowest Growing States   1962-1972

North Dakota
South Dakota
Montana
Wyoming
Washington, D.C.
Delaware
Massachusetts
New York

0 2% 4% 6% 8% 10%

Average Annual Percentage Increase

SOURCE: *"Personal Income by Region and State," Road Maps of Industry*, No. 1723, The Conference Board (October 1, 1973).

Figure 8-4   ***Growth Rate of Personal Income by Region and State***

faster-than-average expansion of apparel, textile, nonautomotive transportation equipment, electrical machinery, and military payrolls in the Southeast contributed to this rise in income.

Most families spend the greatest proportion of their income on necessities such as food, shelter, clothing, and basic transportation. The income available after necessities have been purchased and a given level of living requirement has been met is called **discretionary income**. A family's discretionary income is contingent upon family size, composition of the family, total income, social environment, and life-cycle stage. As the income of a family increases, the discretionary portion usually has more than a proportionate rise. One study reveals that after average consumers spend for necessities, they have over 40 percent of their income remaining for discretionary spending or investment.

BUYING BEHAVIOR

Buying motives, generally in combination, are the initiating forces toward purchasing behavior. A **buying motive** is aroused when bodily energy is activated and selectively directed toward satisfying a need. If an individual's car is destroyed in an accident, the loss of the car activates a desire to purchase another car.

In most cases more than one motive guides human behavior. The purchase of a Pontiac Grand Prix may be spurred by the need for a high-performance automobile, a symbol of prestige, convenience for the family, and possible future savings resulting from a high resale value.

Information on the directions of consumer demand is acquired from economic forecasting and from surveys of buyer intentions. Family buying intentions are periodically measured by organizations such as the Survey Research Center of the University of Michigan. Industrial buying intentions are determined by the McGraw-Hill Survey of industrial expenditures and the Securities and Exchange Commission Survey of capital investments. Models of buyer behavior constructed by behavioral scientists assist the marketing manager to understand the buying activities of consumers.

Marketing Legislation

Since the marketing manager must make decisions within the fabric of the law, a knowledge of marketing legislation is a necessity. Management should also understand the laws so that the effect of their decisions upon public policy and social welfare can be evaluated. A body of marketing law has been developed to protect the public interest, which is designated as: (a) protecting the buyer from the seller, (b) protecting the seller from the buyer, and (c) protecting one competitor from another. The dominant American conviction is that uncontrolled competition among firms is an economic liability. Consequently, the bulk of marketing legislation is concerned with competition. In an effort to maintain some influence on marketing legislation at all levels of government, companies join trade associations and employ public relations personnel and lobbyists.

Nonmarketing Costs

In most cases the decisions made by a marketing manager have an impact on both marketing and nonmarketing costs. For example, a decision to employ an additional 50 salespersons in an effort to intensify coverage in all major markets will involve not only marketing costs but also manufacturing costs. The extra expense of manufacturing the additional products which are needed because of the intensified selling effort are **nonmarketing costs**. Although both costs are affected by the managerial decision, only the employment of additional salespersons is controllable by the marketing executive. Cost accountants and financial planning committees help marketing managers develop an awareness of how their decisions affect costs in other areas such as production and finance.

Structure of Distribution

The **structure of distribution** refers to the alternative channels of distribution that are available to move goods from producers to consumers. A channel of distribution is the path taken in the transfer of title to a good from producer or manufacturer to the final user. The structure of distribution is considered an uncontrollable marketing factor since the manufacturer must typically choose the firm's channel from among those in existence. For example, a new manufacturer of electric garbage disposal units may desire to grant an exclusive franchise to appliance wholesalers in large metropolitan areas. An investigation discloses, however, that the desired wholesalers are already handling competitive lines and that they do not care to add any additional lines. The manufacturer considers selling directly to appliance retailers, but a cost analysis reveals that this type of selling is not economically feasible. The attention of the manufacturer then turns to searching for other types of middlemen to handle the firm's line. The manufacturer finally decides to use hardware wholesalers to provide the needed distribution.

Studies of market potential, distribution cost analyses, and the application of mathematical models guide the marketing manager in selecting the most efficient route available for a product in its movement from the producer to the consumer.

Different Environments for Decision Making

Marketing managers in different industries make decisions within an entirely different framework of uncontrollable environmental conditions. For example, managers in the steel industry are confronted with environmental conditions largely different from those of the pleasure boat industry.

The few domestic competitors within the steel industry are all large organizations. General economic conditions affect the overall demand for steel, but the division of sales among individual firms in the steel industry is fairly stable from year to year. The major customer of the steel companies is the Detroit automobile industry, which uses about 20 percent of all steel shipments. Antitrust legislation and the threat of its use have prevented mergers and consolidations within the industry, and the actions of the administrative branch of government have been relatively effective in restraining unreasonable price increases. Rising demand for steel results in the greater utilization of inefficient, open-hearth manufacturing facilities rather than the more efficient oxygen furnaces, an action that causes higher nonmarketing costs. The distribution alternatives are few since the mills sell either directly or through warehouses to their customers.

In contrast, the pleasure boat industry is relatively fragmented with numerous small manufacturers in competition with each other. Consumer demand for boats is a direct result of increased leisure time and discretionary income. In general, this industry has been free of antitrust harassment. The facilities for constructing small boats are not too complex; and, in comparison to a steel mill, capacity can be increased easily and inexpensively. Although boat manufacturers would like to have their product distributed through franchised boat dealers, many alternative sales outlets are available. In addition to marinas and sporting goods dealers, some department stores, gasoline service stations, and even drugstores sell boats.

MARKETING RESEARCH

Marketing information is needed so that the marketing manager and others within the marketing organization can intelligently plan their strategies. The marketing research function provides this information.

The American Marketing Association defines **marketing research** as "the systematic gathering, recording, and analyzing of data about problems relating to the marketing of goods and services."[7] This definition adequately describes the processing of the data, but additional knowledge is needed concerning the type of facts to be assembled. Data are gathered and analyzed for the controllable marketing factors of product, place, promotion, and price, and the uncontrollable marketing factors of competition, demand, marketing laws, nonmarketing costs, and structure of distribution. The purpose of the data gathering is to improve decision making within the marketing system.

The following research activities are frequently conducted by a majority of firms that have a marketing research department:

1. Developing market and sales potentials.
2. Establishing a firm's share of total industry sales.
3. Determining market and customer characteristics.
4. Constructing sales analyses.
5. Developing competitive product studies.
6. Determining the acceptance of new products.
7. Developing short-range sales forecasts.

[7]*Op. cit.*, Committee on Definitions, *Marketing Definitions: A Glossary of Marketing Terms*, pp. 16–17.

Sources of Data

Both internal and external data gathered by or for a firm for its use are known as **primary data**. If these facts are published or otherwise released, they are known as **secondary data** in the hands of subsequent users. Since additional handling of the figures allows more chances for errors, and time is likely to have elapsed since the data were first collected, secondary data should be used with caution. Another difficulty with secondary data is that since they frequently are collected for a specific purpose, they may not completely fit the needs of subsequent users. They are, nonetheless, widely used in marketing research because of the enormous quantities of data available, frequently without cost, from government and private agencies. Important government sources include the U.S. Census reports, the yearly *Statistical Abstract of the United States*, the *Survey of Current Business*, the *Federal Reserve Bulletin*, and the *Monthly Labor Review*. Private sources of secondary information comprise publications issued by newspapers and magazines, trade journals, trade associations, private agencies, and colleges and universities.

Data-Gathering Methods

The marketing researcher has three basic ways to gather primary data: (1) observation, (2) survey, and (3) motivation research. The purpose of the research and the availability of money, time, and personnel influence the selection of the data-gathering method.

OBSERVATION

The **observation** technique relies on viewing and/or noting the activities of the respondents. Since consumers are unaware that their actions are being observed, it is assumed that they act in a normal manner. A difficulty with this technique is that it does not explain the reasons, attitudes, and behavior behind the action.

Observation may be accomplished through personal or mechanical means. A study on the frequency of shoplifting employed personal observation. A total of 226 customers were followed from the time they entered the store to the time they departed. The observers reported that 23 individuals (or 10 percent) stole merchandise. The appropriate site for a new gasoline service station can be partially determined by the mechanical technique of placing an electric recording cable across a street and recording the number of vehicles driving over it.

FACTORS TO EVALUATE	MAIL	TELEPHONE	PERSONAL INTERVIEW
Flexibility of the Interview	None	High	High
Length Limitation of Questionnaire	Moderate	Moderate	Long
Assurance of Accurate, Unbiased Response	High	Moderate	Moderate
Speed of Collecting Information	Slow	Fast	Moderate
Overall Cost per Response	Moderate	Low	High
Cost of Interviewer Administration	Low	Moderate	High

Figure 8-5   **Factors to Evaluate in Choosing Among Three Survey Techniques**

SURVEY

In the **survey** method the researcher gathers facts directly from a sample of respondents. Surveys are the most frequently used means to gather primary research information. The data may be collected by either (1) mail, (2) telephone, or (3) personal interview. As shown in Figure 8-5, a marketing researcher evaluates these three survey techniques on the following criteria:

1. Flexibility.
2. Length of questionnaire.
3. Accuracy.
4. Speed.
5. Cost per response.
6. Cost of administration.

Mail. A mail questionnaire is most suitable when a large, geographically dispersed group is being contacted. The replies to a mail survey may be more truthful than for the other two types since respondents frequently have the opportunity to keep their identities concealed. Although the questionnaire may be completed at the respondents' leisure, many of them are never returned and many others are not returned until one or two follow-up messages are sent. Even then, a 10 to 15 percent return is considered good.

Telephone. Telephone interviews are effective when responses to a series of short questions are needed immediately. A telephone interview is flexible and timely since the interviewer, in addition to the written questions, may also insert any comments that are appropriate. Accuracy may be compromised, however, since interviewer bias may occur and respondents may provide the answers they believe the interviewer desires. Another limiting factor is that in some communities 10 to 20 percent of the households either do not have phones or have unlisted numbers.

Personal Interview. When a long, complex questionnaire is used, a personal interview is most suitable. The personal interview provides an opportunity for the researcher to obtain complete answers and to judge the socioeconomic condition of the respondent. Interviewer bias may occur if the interviewer rewords the questions so that the respondent provides anticipated responses. Respondent bias may occur, too, when the respondent relates to the interviewer what the interviewer wants to hear. Personal interviewing is relatively expensive in terms of time and money. One study disclosed that this method was five times as expensive as a mail survey and over six times as costly as a telephone interview.

MOTIVATION RESEARCH

The application of the techniques of the behavioral sciences, such as sociology and psychology, to the solution of marketing problems is called **motivation research**. Motivation research is differentiated from the survey method by its reliance on sample sizes generally no larger than 50 respondents and on probing interviews that may last an hour or longer. Motivation research techniques attempt to discover the relationship between consumer attitudes and buying behavior. Emphasis is placed on discovering why consumers act as they do.

A basic limitation of motivation research results from the attempt to interpret accurately data from a small sample size. The following case illustrates this difficulty. Two research organizations were employed independently of each other by two different groups to study the problems encountered in merchandising prunes. One of the research agencies concluded that, since its respondents related prunes to unattractiveness and old age, prunes should be glamorized as a specialty food and renamed black diamonds. The other research firm found individuals recognizing and accepting the laxative effect of prunes, so this organization recommended that prunes should be promoted as a laxative.

These two studies, with their contradictory conclusions, point out how motivation research can be used best. It is most effective in seeking ideas and generalizations which may be further tested with larger samples by either the observation or survey techniques.

BUSINESS TERMS

QUESTIONS FOR DISCUSSION AND ANALYSIS

1. Should a firm be more interested in making a profit or meeting the needs of consumers with its products? Discuss.
2. How would you respond to an individual who declares that marketing personnel are leeches on society and create no tangible values for consumers?
3. In what respects would the marketing organization at U.S. Steel differ from the organization at Procter and Gamble?
4. Explain how a limited-service discount department store reduces its costs by shifting the performance of some marketing functions to consumers.
5. Discuss how market segmentation is practiced in the automobile industry. Is segmentation practiced in the magazine industry? Explain.
6. Is it ethical for a firm to engage in marketing intelligence? Under what conditions does marketing intelligence become unethical?
7. Indicate several reasons why states such as North Dakota, West Virginia, and Mississippi experienced more than a 10 percent decrease in population during the decade of the 1960s. How does a decrease in the population in a state affect marketing?
8. Is a color television set a necessity or a discretionary purchase? What criteria are used to distinguish between a necessity and a discretionary purchase?
9. Provide an example in the following cases where: (1) the buyer needs protection from the seller, (2) the seller needs protection from the buyer, and (3) a competitor needs protection from another competitor.
10. What basic data-gathering method would you use to determine the most popular television program? Would you use the same method to discover why the program is the most popular one? Explain.

PROBLEMS AND SHORT CASES

1. The Purfine Milling Company was one of the first producers of white enriched presifted flour. During the 1950s and the 1960s this medium-sized company diversified into cake, biscuit, pizza, and other flour-based mixes. In addition, the company developed a line of frosting mixes to complement its cake mixes. In the past the ability of the company to utilize its current plant and equipment determined the type of new product to be produced.

By 1976 management recognized the need to develop new products based upon studies of consumer needs. This acceptance of the marketing concept by the company meant a change in the marketing organization. In the present organization the director of sales, who is the chief marketing officer, reports to the president of the company. An advertising manager, a sales training manager, and a product planning manager report to the director of sales. There are no other positions in the marketing organization.

Draw a chart of a revised and broadened marketing organization showing each marketing position and the marketing activities which should be performed in each position.

2. In a large metropolitan community City Cola bottles and distributes its own brand of cola, root beer, and orange drink. The company was organized in the late 1940s and had a successful growth until the mid-1970s when competition from nationally-branded and advertised soft drinks began to reduce its market share. Drugstores, supermarkets, and other grocery outlets sold the City Cola drinks in two bottle sizes, 12-ounce and quart. The 12-ounce bottles were packaged six to a carton while the quart bottles were sold individually. To keep its investment in containers to a minimum, only nonreturnable bottles were marketed. By the mid-1970s the management of City Cola was concerned about a slight sales decrease and a loss of relative market share to other bottlers. Management believed that the company should look for specific markets to serve with either its current drinks or other soft drink products.

   Identify the various market segments which the company could serve and indicate the type of soft drink which each segment would purchase.

3. In Grand Rapids, Michigan, a group of interested citizens desire to establish a nonprofit television station which would be affiliated with the Public Broadcasting Corporation. This station would be supported by public donations. Programs would include children's shows, musical entertainment, dramas, documentaries, and talk shows. Design a questionnaire that you believe would be helpful in answering the following questions for the management of the proposed television station:
   a. Who will constitute the viewing audience?
   b. What type of programs will the viewer desire?

9 Products and Their Distribution

The safety pin was invented in 1849 by that king of ill-fated inventors, Walter Hunt of New York City. The idea came to Hunt in a flash, and it took him only three hours to work out the U.S. Patent No. 6,281 on his invention. The rest is history. Billions of safety pins have rescued millions of people from trillions of embarrassments. And Walter Hunt made his fortune, right? Wrong. Walter Hunt made exactly $100. Because on the same day he invented the safety pin, he sold his patent rights for that amount to a chap he met in the Patent Office.[1]

Providing products which satisfy consumer needs ensures an organization of a profitable and continuing existence. To remain competitive in the marketplace, manufacturers, wholesalers, and retailers are dependent upon consumer acceptance of their product offerings. The innovative products of some firms, such as the Polaroid camera and the Xerox copier, are instant successes; while the new products of other organizations, such as Ford's Edsel and RCA's computers, bring only disappointments.

PRODUCTS: TYPES AND LIFE CYCLES

A **product** is more than a physical combination of steel, aluminum, plastic, and other components; it is a bundle of satisfactions or utilities for the consumer. A consumer considers a refrigerator as an efficient operating mechanism for keeping food cold, but also views the refrigerator as an attractive addition to the kitchen decor. When a homemaker buys a refrigerator, she purchases all the intangible and psychic values as well as the tangible product.

[1]Reprinted with permission from the April 7, 1974, issue of *Family Week*, p. 30.

Basic Types of Goods

All goods can be placed into one of two broad categories: (1) industrial goods, or (2) consumer goods. **Industrial goods** are destined to be sold primarily for use in producing other goods or in rendering services.[2] **Consumer goods** are destined for use by ultimate consumers or households, and these are in such form that they can be used without further commercial processing.[3] Because of their use by both individual consumers and industrial consumers, goods such as tires and typewriters fall into both categories.

INDUSTRIAL GOODS

Industrial goods are generally classified according to their usage in a business. Industrial buyers frequently purchase goods for economic motives such as cost savings or expected future gain. When purchasing industrial goods, buyers often provide prospective suppliers with a description of the desired items and ask them to submit formal price quotations.

On the basis of use there are three major categories of industrial goods. One category is that of **unprocessed and processed materials** entering directly into the production process such as raw materials, semimanufactured goods, and parts. A second grouping, **MRO items**, is composed of maintenance, repair, and operating supplies which are used to support the production process. A final classification is capital goods, which consist of the major installations and equipment that are utilized to form the product.

CONSUMER GOODS

Consumer goods are usually characterized by the shopping effort required to obtain the goods. For some goods the consumer will readily accept a substitute if a particular good is not available. For other goods the consumer will accept no substitutes and will conduct an extensive search until the specific item is located. Consumers frequently purchase products for noneconomic motives such as prestige, pleasure, and conformity.

Consumer goods are classified into several categories. **Convenience goods** are goods that are bought by the consumer after little shopping effort, purchased frequently, bought by habit, and sold in numerous outlets. Generally convenience goods such as candy bars, cigarettes, and milk have low unit prices. Goods that are bought after comparing the features of several brands, purchased infrequently, and sold in a limited number of selected outlets are known as **shopping goods**. Usually shopping goods have a higher unit price

[2]Reprinted from Committee on Definitions, *Marketing Definitions: A Glossary of Marketing Terms*, published by the American Marketing Association, 1960, p. 14.
[3]*Ibid.*, p. 11.

than convenience goods. Examples of shopping goods are men's suits, automobiles, and furniture. **Specialty goods** are goods bought by the consumer after a special shopping effort, purchased very infrequently, and sold in a few exclusive outlets. Generally specialty goods carry a high unit price; but since no substitutes are considered, price is not a major consideration. Fine jewelry, prestige automobiles, and expensive perfume are examples of specialty goods.

Since not every consumer relates to a product the same way, the buying habits of the majority of consumers determine the classification for a particular good. As the buying habits of consumers change over time, goods shift from one classification to another. The usual movement is from the specialty, to the shopping, to the convenience goods category.

Product Life Cycle

In an earlier stage of our economy, products had a relatively long life cycle; but in the 1970s the changing life styles of consumers and technological advances have shortened the life cycle of numerous products. In the early 1960s the life expectancy of a frozen food or dry grocery product was 36 months, but a decade later its life span had slipped to 12 months.

As shown in Figure 9-1, a **product life cycle** encompasses five distinct phases:

1. Introduction stage.
2. Growth stage.
3. Maturity stage.
4. Saturation stage.
5. Decline stage.

The color television market illustrates the movement of a product through its life cycle. In the late1950s, when the color television market was in the introduction stage, RCA was practically alone in marketing color television sets. Since RCA was the major brand in the market, individuals who sought to buy a color receiver generally purchased an RCA. Recognizing its dominant market position, RCA promoted heavily to create consumer demand for color television.

During the early 1960s the color television market moved into the growth stage. Although RCA sales and profits increased, new competitors began entering the market. Prices remained high with console models selling for $500 or more. By 1965 nearly 10 percent of American homes had color television sets.

In the late 1960s the color television market reached maturity. Companies such as Zenith, Magnavox, Admiral, Sears, General Electric, and Motorola encroached on the commanding market share originally held by RCA. Mass

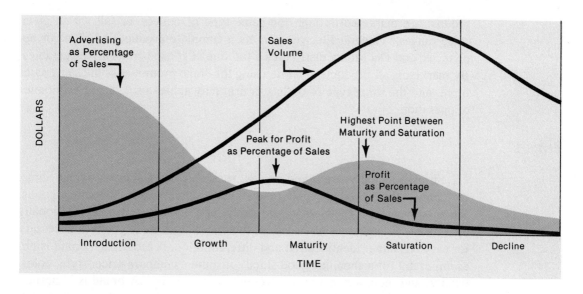

SOURCE: Adapted from *Management of New Products* (New York: Booz, Allen & Hamilton), p. 4.

Figure 9-1 *Product Life Cycle*

production and new technology lowered prices. Less expensive table models and consoles opened sales to new segments of the market. In 1970, 42 percent of all American families were enjoying color television.

By 1972, with 63 percent of the households having color television, the market approached the saturation stage. Amid strong foreign and domestic competition, the growth in sales slowed. Small portable models priced under $350 became popular. RCA began differentiating its product from competing products by promoting its Solid State Accu Color models. During the late 1970s the color television market remains in the saturation phase.

PRODUCT POLICIES

Product policies serve to guide management in the development of new products and in the modification or elimination of existing products. The product policies of a firm should be compatible with the policies of the remaining three P's (place, promotion, and price) in a firm's marketing mix.

Product Line

Multiproduct firms frequently market a complete line of products. A **product line** is a group of products that are closely related either because they satisfy a class of needs, are used together, are sold to the same customer groups, are marketed through the same type of outlets, or fall within given price ranges.[4] General Electric markets a complete product line of major appliances, and Del Monte distributes a full line of canned fruits and vegetables. By marketing all products in a line using the same promotions, the same sales force, and the same type of outlets, a firm may achieve significant economies of operation.

Brands

Firms frequently use brand names, such as Coca Cola or Virginia Slims, to identify their products and to distinguish them from competing goods. Since convenience goods, such as candy bars and cigarettes, are nationally advertised, but sold by self-selection, the branding of these goods is necessary for easy consumer identification and differentiation. A recognized brand is not as important for a shopping good since consumers compare price, style, color, quality, and other aspects of the product before buying. A brand is important for a specialty good since consumers recognize high-priced specialty products, such as Jaguar E-type cars or Lenox fine china, by their brand names.

Several alternative branding policies are available to a firm. A brand, such as Frigidaire, promoted and distributed by a manufacturer is known as a **national** or **manufacturer's brand**. When a middleman, such as a wholesaler or a retailer, sponsors a brand, it is called a **private** or **dealer's brand**. Most of the merchandise offered by Sears is one of the many Sears' private brands such as Craftsman, Kenmore, or Kings Road. Private brands permit a middleman to obtain closer control of the marketing effort and to avoid direct product competition with other merchants.

Trademarks

A brand may serve as a company trademark, but a **trademark** also may be a distinguishing symbol or some other company identification. Both the USS abbreviation of United States Steel and the distinctive bunny of the Playboy Club are trademarks. Brands and trademarks may be registered for 20 years with the U.S. Patent Office and may be renewed indefinitely for 20-year periods.

Labels

Labels on a product or package should provide information which will assist the consumer in making a buying decision. By using words, letters, or numbers, a **grade label** specifies the quality of a good. *Prime* is the highest

[4]*Ibid.*, p. 18.

quality designation for beef, *Grade A* identifies the best quality of canned corn, and *Number 1* indicates the top grade of wheat. An **informative label** furnishes data on the care, use, and preparation of the product. The Federal Trade Commission, recognizing the importance of informative labeling, requests manufacturers to place permanent care instructions on the labels of all textile apparel. A **descriptive label** lists the important attributes of a product. Nutritional labeling, which the Food and Drug Administration requires for some products, is a form of descriptive labeling.

Product Obsolescence

As fashions shift and technology advances, new products cause old ones to become obsolete. Critics have charged that businesspersons seeking the sales of new products purposely plan for the phasing out of old products, or **product obsolescence**. This criticism probably overstates the influence of product promotion and understates the influence of our cultural and value system on product acceptance.

There are three different forms of product obsolescence: (a) fashion obsolescence, (b) quality obsolescence, and (c) function obsolescence. The majority of the criticism of obsolescence is directed at fashion and quality obsolescence.

Fashion obsolescence is caused by a change in consumer wants. Marketing efforts, such as the annual model changes in automobiles, frequently hasten this obsolescence. If modifications in a product are merely superficial and are an inaccurate reflection of consumer values, these changes will generally not be accepted by consumers. **Quality obsolescence** is indefensible if the quality of a product is purposefully lowered so that the item will wear out faster. Lower quality, however, may be accompanied by lower prices and still provide a good value.

Function obsolescence, which is applauded by most consumers, is the result of technological change. For example, homemakers prefer the comfort of an automatic gas furnace to a manually-fired coal furnace, and they enjoy the convenience of an automatic washer compared to a wringer washer.

New Product Development

The success of a product is dependent upon the proper development and management of the product. It has been estimated that a single product failure in the food and drug lines may cost from $75,000 in test markets to $30 million after introduction into the national market. The importance of effective product development is illustrated by research showing that less than 2 out of 100 new product ideas ever attain commercial success.

ECONOMIC JUSTIFICATION FOR NEW PRODUCTS

A firm may have numerous motives for developing new products, but an economic or cost justification should be present to sustain these motives. The presence of any of the following conditions establish this justification:

1. Possession of specialized product knowledge.
2. Production of a complete product line.
3. Use of a common channel of distribution for all products.
4. Ability to share costs of new products with older products.

Several illustrations will depict conditions that lead to successful product development. As a result of building the B-47 and B-52 bombers and the KC-135 tanker, Boeing Aircraft acquired a large amount of specialized product knowledge which was easily transferred to the construction of commercial jets. With very little additional marketing costs Whirlpool added a trash compactor to its line of appliances. When low-sudsing laundry detergents were introduced to the market, Procter and Gamble experienced no difficulty in marketing its low-sudsing detergent, Dash, through its normal retail distribution channels. By using the same components in several different cars, an automobile manufacturer is frequently able to share the production costs of a new model with many of the present models.

PRODUCT MANAGER

Multiproduct companies often assign the following product line responsibilities to a **product** or **brand manager**: (a) sales planning, (b) product and market development, (c) promotion, and (d) pricing. Although product managers do not supervise any salespersons, they assist their sales departments by providing salespersons with specific information about a particular product. An oft-repeated criticism of the product managers' role is that their authority is not equal to their responsibility. The product manager is held accountable for the success of a product, but does not possess the direct supervisory authority over salespersons which will ensure this success. Large consumer product companies, such as Procter and Gamble, Scott Paper, and General Foods, used the product or brand manager concept many years before it was adopted by manufacturers of industrial goods.

DISTRIBUTION POLICIES

After consumer needs have been identified and a product has been developed to meet these needs, a distribution system is necessary to move the product from producer to consumer. In the early history of our country when markets were small and compact, producers sold directly to final consumers. As markets grew and the distance between major markets increased, a system of wholesale and retail middlemen evolved between producers and the final consumers.

Channels of Distribution

The routes that goods take in their progress from producers to consumers are known as **channels of distribution**. Each middleman in the channel needs to work closely with all other middlemen to move goods from producers to consumers in the least expensive and most expeditious manner.

CHANNELS FOR CONSUMER GOODS

The most direct channel of distribution for consumer goods is found where the producer sells directly to the consumer. This channel is used by many house-to-house selling firms, such as Fuller Brush and Avon Products, and by some producers who distribute by mail order such as the New Process Company.

Producer → Consumer

In another channel producers sell to retailers, who in turn sell to consumers. This channel represents the path taken by goods handled by department stores and chain stores.

Producer → Retailer → Consumer

A third channel is utilized where the wholesaler enters the picture between the producer and the retailer. This is the traditional method whereby goods have been distributed in this country. It is still the prevalent system for goods that reach the consumer through the small independent retailer such as a grocer, druggist, hardware dealer, or clothing specialty shop.

Producer → Wholesaler → Retailer → Consumer

Producers may adopt any one or more of these channels to have their goods reach the final consumers in as large quantities as possible. Many producers sell direct to the chains and larger independent stores and at the same time utilize wholesalers to reach the small independent retailers. The channel of distribution pattern then would be the following:

```
Producer ────┬──→Wholesaler ───────→Small Retailer ───────→Consumer
             │                     →Large Retailer ───────→Consumer
             └─────────────────────→Chain Store ──────────→Consumer
```

CHANNELS FOR INDUSTRIAL GOODS

The major difference between the channels of distribution for industrial goods and consumer goods is that typically a retailer is not present in the industrial channel. The two commonly used channels in industrial marketing are:

Producer ———————————————————→Industrial Consumer
Producer ————————→Wholesaler————————→Industrial Consumer

The first of these two channel patterns may include manufacturers' branch offices with or without stocks for delivery to customers. Frequently a manufacturer's salespersons work from a branch office without stock, but they fill their customers' orders directly from the factory.

Channel Decisions

The initial step in determining the channels of distribution for a product is to determine the market for the product. Because of the numerous markets to be reached and the complexity of our distribution system, numerous products are marketed through more than one channel of distribution. Many packaged food products, such as breakfast cereals, move through two or more channels of distribution. For cereals one typical channel is from producer to large grocery retail chain to consumer; another is from producer to grocery wholesaler to small grocery retailer to consumer.

Channels differ for different industries and even differ among companies in the same industry. The following factors are considered by management in selecting a channel of distribution: (1) market, (2) channel member, (3) product, and (4) environmental.

MARKET FACTORS

In addition to whether a good is directed to the consumer or industrial market, there are several other market factors that determine channel selection. If the product is sold in large quantities to customers in a densely concentrated market, such as New York or Chicago, a short channel of distribution may be utilized. There may be many consumers in a concentrated market; but if these consumers buy in small quantities, a longer channel is necessary. A longer channel is also appropriate when numerous customers are dispersed over a wide geographical area.

CHANNEL MEMBER FACTORS

An understanding of the capabilities and motivations of each channel member from manufacturer to consumer helps to explain the development of distribution channels. For example, financially strong manufacturers who desire to retain complete control of their marketing efforts may shorten the channel for their products by performing some or all of the middlemen's activities. The motivations of middlemen influence channel selection, too. Some retailers, such as large department stores, often desire to buy directly from producers; while others, such as small drugstores, desire to buy from nearby wholesalers on a hand-to-mouth basis. In most industries traditional channels of distribution develop; and if a new product is to be successfully marketed, it should follow these traditional channel patterns.

PRODUCT FACTORS

Because of their characteristics, some products move through shorter channels of distribution than others. Perishable items, such as fresh produce and dairy products, typically require a short channel of distribution. Goods which are custom designed for a specific use, such as large electrical transformers or computer installations, commonly utilize a short channel of distribution. The expense of physical handling requires a short channel for products such as coal and concrete blocks, which have a low cost relative to their bulkiness. Because a manufacturer's direct selling costs are a relatively low percentage of sales, one who markets either an expensive product or a complete product line is frequently able to sell directly to retailers and bypass wholesalers.

ENVIRONMENTAL FACTORS

Social, economic, and political forces frequently alter the planned channels of distribution. Management has discovered that certain middlemen do a better job than others in marketing to the urban poor. During an economic recession manufacturers seek the least expensive way to get their products into the hands of consumers. In some cases this may mean changing or eliminating certain middlemen. Dropping middlemen from a channel, however, may lessen competition and may pose the threat of an antitrust suit by the government.

WHOLESALING

Wholesaling includes all of the marketing functions and activities that involve the sale of goods where the purpose for making the purchase is a business or profit motive. This broad segment of marketing embraces all sales to retailers, other wholesalers, industrial users, government, service establishments, building contractors, and farmers for farm use. In other words, wholesaling includes all sales transactions except those made to the ultimate consumer which are known as retailing. The extent of wholesaling is revealed in

Table 9-1 which shows the number, sales volume, and operating expenses of selected types of wholesalers.

Table 9-1   **Number, Sales Volume, and Operating Expenses for Total Wholesale Trade and Selected Types of Wholesalers in the United States, 1972.**

	Establishments (Number)	Sales ($1,000)	Operating Expenses as Percentage of Sales
Wholesale trade, Total	369,791	695,223,644	10.2
Merchant wholesalers, Total	289,974	353,918,969	13.9
Groceries and related products	29,910	64,081,866	10.0
General line groceries	2,818	21,572,586	7.1
Voluntary group wholesalers	396	6,458,693	6.3
Retailer cooperative wholesalers	225	6,938,617	5.4
Other general-line wholesalers	2,197	8,175,276	9.2
Manufacturers' sales branches, Total	47,197	255,678,995	7.2
Manufacturers' sales branches — with stock	32,611	124,678,995	7.2
Manufacturers' sales branches — without stock	14,586	131,220,523	4.1
Merchandise agents, brokers, Total	32,620	85,625,680	4.2
Auction companies	1,769	8,060,207	2.5
Merchandise brokers	4,770	20,397,799	3.2
Commission merchants	6,940	18,970,904	3.8
Manufacturers' agents	16,529	23,344,579	7.1
Selling agents	1,722	6,493,714	3.2
Other agents and brokers	890	8,358,477	1.9

SOURCE: U.S. Department of Commerce, *1972 Census of Wholesale Trade, Area Statistics, United States*, pp. 8 and 10.

Reasons for the Wholesaler

Wholesaling performs a necessary marketing service in our competitive, profit-motivated economy, the cost of which is broadly equated to the economic values that it creates. A large number of producers located in many different areas must move their products to numerous, widely scattered industrial consumers and retailers. Figure 9-2 shows why wholesalers may be able to perform this allocation activity more economically than producers. It is less costly for a producer of packaged cereals to sell through 2,800 grocery wholesalers than directly to nearly 194,000 grocery retailers.

The services rendered to manufacturers by wholesalers are:

1. Establishing a strong contact with retailers.
2. Storing for the manufacturer.

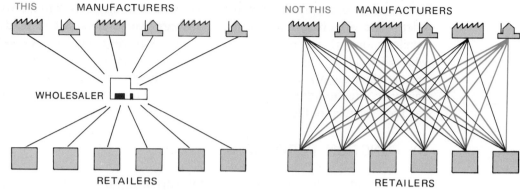

Figure 9-2 *Reasons for the Wholesaler*

3. Dividing large shipments into smaller quantities.
4. Assuming the credit risk.
5. Providing transportation economies.

The services performed for retailers by wholesalers include:

1. Serving as a purchasing agent for retailers.
2. Storing for the retailer.
3. Assembling goods from numerous suppliers.
4. Maintaining balanced stocks.
5. Providing prompt delivery services.
6. Financing the retailer.
7. Furnishing promotional and managerial assistance.

Merchant Wholesalers

Merchant wholesalers are wholesale establishments that buy and sell merchandise on their own account. They take title to the goods which they handle, and they experience all the risks of owning these goods. When the bulk of their business is to industrial users, they are known as industrial distributors. Merchant wholesalers are commonly classified by (1) the line of goods handled or (2) by the functions performed.

BY LINE OF GOODS HANDLED

Based upon the line of goods handled, there are three types of merchant wholesalers. The **general merchandise wholesaler** handles a variety of goods in diverse lines such as health and beauty aids, home furnishings, clothing, hardware, and automobile accessories. The customer for this type of wholesaler is frequently a rural general store, a variety store, or a small department store. The **general line wholesaler** markets a single line of goods, such as hardware or groceries, and typically sells to retailers who limit themselves to the wholesaler's line of goods. For example, hardware wholesalers sell to hardware retailers; and grocery wholesalers distribute to grocery retailers. A **specialty wholesaler** carries an assortment of goods in a portion of a general line. There are plumbing supply distributors selling only the plumbing supply part of the hardware line, and there are frozen food distributors marketing only the frozen food segment of the grocery line.

BY FUNCTION PERFORMED

Merchant wholesalers are frequently categorized as either (1) service or full-function wholesalers, or (2) limited function wholesalers. **Service wholesalers extend a broad range** of services to their customers. **Limited function wholesalers** restrict their services and functions, thus reducing their costs.

Service Wholesalers. Among the types of merchandise handled by service wholesalers are groceries, drugs, hardware, and dry goods. Their customers are principally retailers. Most general merchandise, general line, and specialty wholesalers operate as service wholesalers. A **rack jobber** or **rack merchandiser** who supplies supermarkets with nonfood items, such as health and beauty aids, housewares, records, magazines and greeting cards, is a unique type of service wholesaler. Rack jobbers typically warehouse their merchandise, install their own display racks, replenish store inventories, and price their goods.

Limited Function Wholesalers. Limited function wholesalers include drop shippers, wagon distributors, and cash-and-carry wholesalers. The more important factors contributing to the usage of these middlemen include the nature of the product and the desire to reduce the costs of distribution. The **drop shipper** or **desk jobber**, operating mainly in the lumber and coal industries where the product is bulky, takes orders, contacts suppliers, and has the product shipped directly to the customer. A **wagon** or **truck distributor**, who uses a truck as a warehouse, sells perishable items such as fruits, vegetables, tobacco, and candy to supermarkets and restaurants. A **cash-and-carry wholesaler** keeps operating expenses low by using self-service and central checkouts and by eliminating credit and delivery service.

Functional Middlemen

The term **functional middlemen** is used as a group designation for the wholesalers who do not take title (become the legal owners) to the goods which they sell. They are in business for themselves and negotiate purchases and sales in domestic and international trade on behalf of their principals who do take title to the goods. These middlemen are usually compensated in the form of commissions or fees. They may or may not take possession of the goods involved. An additional activity that some of them perform for their principals is the furnishing of marketing information. The important wholesalers in this classification are: manufacturers' agents, selling agents, merchandise brokers, commission merchants, and auction companies.

Integrated Wholesaling

Manufacturers' sales branches and chain store warehouses are forms of **integrated wholesaling**, which occurs when two or more typically separate business operations are combined under one ownership. In establishing sales branches manufacturers integrate forward in the channel of distribution, and in establishing chain store warehouses retailers integrate backward in the channel. Manufacturers with financial and managerial capability, such as Nabisco and General Electric, often establish wholesale branches as a means of gaining greater control over the marketing of their products. In chain organizations such as Kresge and Safeway the chain store warehouse is a collection point for goods before the merchandise is distributed to their retail stores.

RETAILING

Retailing is that segment of marketing where the products of the consumer goods industry are purchased by ultimate consumers for their or their families' personal use. It is the point in the channel of distribution where the offerings of manufacturers of consumer goods are accepted or rejected. It is where the validity of the total marketing concept is either proved or disproved. The marketing institutions which operate in this field are retailers. Figure 9-3, page 178, indicates the percentage of retail stores, retail sales, and population in each of the continental 48 states. The sales and profits as a percentage of sales for the ten largest retail firms in the United States are shown in Table 9-2, page 179.

Classification of Retailers

Retailers are classified on the basis of: (1) lines of goods handled, (2) ownership, (3) geographic location, and (4) type of operation.

LINES OF GOODS HANDLED

The extent of the lines of goods handled by a retailer frequently determines operating policies and practices. Based on the lines of goods handled,

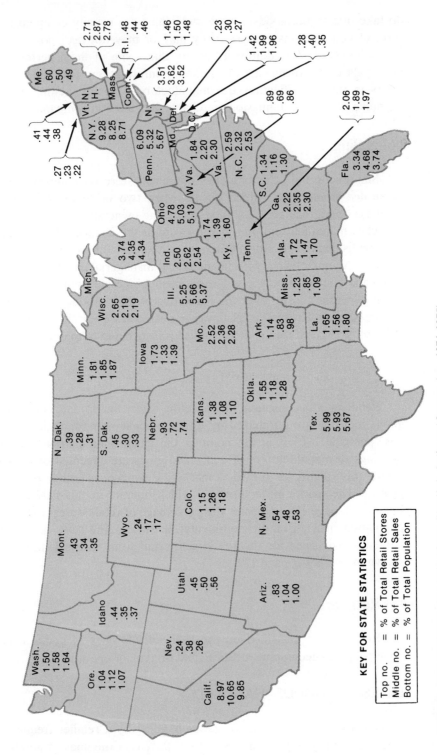

SOURCE: *1975 Retail Map of the United States* (New York: Audits and Surveys, Inc., 1974–1975).

Figure 9-3 **Retail Map of the United States**

KEY FOR STATE STATISTICS

Top no.	=	% of Total Retail Stores
Middle no.	=	% of Total Retail Sales
Bottom no.	=	% of Total Population

Table 9-2 **The Ten Largest Retailing Companies Ranked by Sales, 1974**

Rank	Company	Sales (In Thousands of Dollars)	Net Profit as Percentage of Sales
1	Sears, Roebuck (Chicago)	$13,101,210	3.9
2	Safeway Stores (Oakland)	8,185,190	1.0
3	J. C. Penney (New York)	6,935,710	1.8
4	Great Atlantic & Pacific Tea (Montvale, N.J.)	6,874,611	loss
5	S. S. Kresge (Troy, Mich.)	5,612,071	1.9
6	Kroger (Cincinnati)	4,782,449	0.9
7	Marcor (Chicago)	4,667,479	2.5
8	F. W. Woolworth (New York)	4,177,104	1.6
9	Federated Department Stores (Cincinnati)	3,273,282	3.6
10	Lucky Stores (Dublin, California)	2,701,771	1.5

SOURCE: "Fortune's Directory of the Fifty Largest Retailing Companies," *Fortune* (July, 1975), p. 122.

three classes of stores may be identified: (1) general merchandise, (2) single line, and (3) specialty.

General Merchandise Stores. The large variety of goods which they offer characterizes **general merchandise stores.** Several types of these stores will be examined. A **general store**, usually found in sparsely populated rural areas, is a small nondepartmentalized store that carries a wide range of staple goods, including groceries, clothing, dry goods, hardware, and sporting goods. The Hudson Bay Company of Canada and the Northern Commercial Company of Alaska continue to operate many general store-trading post combinations. A **department store**, which is a large departmentalized establishment handling a wide variety of shopping goods, is usually the dominant store in a community. Macy's in New York is the world's largest store, Filene's in Boston draws crowds to its automatic-markdown bargain basement, and Neiman-Marcus in Dallas supplies the wealthy with elegant merchandise and lavish promotions. In 1879 F.W. Woolworth established the first 5 and 10 cents store which, after many decades of price inflation, is more aptly called a **limited-price variety store.** Nearly 90 percent of these stores are operated by retail chains such as Woolworth, Kresge, and Newberry.

In the mid-1950s the **discount store**, which sold a mix of hard and soft goods, priced merchandise at a relatively low markup above cost, advertised extensively, minimized free customer service, maximized use of self-service, utilized relatively inexpensive facilities, and emphasized discount prices, appeared on the retailing scene. By the 1970s, having adopted many of the operating policies of department stores, numerous discounters such as K-Mart and Zayre desire to be known as low-priced department stores.

Single Line Stores. A **single line store** which may carry a variety of merchandise in several related lines is usually recognized by its most important line. Single line establishments include grocery, appliance, drug, hardware, and sporting goods stores. **Scrambled merchandising**, where a retailer carries lines of goods traditionally stocked by another retailer, has caused the identity of many single line stores to become blurred. A unique form of single line store is the grocery supermarket, which introduced self-service operations and central checkouts to retailing in the 1930s.

Specialty Stores. A **specialty store** offers a depth of assortment in one portion of a line of goods. Specialty stores such as meat markets and dairy stores are directly competitive with single line stores such as supermarkets. In some lines of trade, such as books, records, and automobiles, practically all the establishments are specialty stores. Most retail service establishments, such as beauty salons, bowling alleys, and theaters, are specialty operations.

OWNERSHIP

A retail establishment is either independently owned or is a unit in a chain organization. Chains account for over 35 percent of retail sales, but they operate less than 15 percent of all retail stores.

Independents. Most stores that are individually and usually locally owned — principally small stores such as grocery, drug, shoe, and hardware stores — are **independents**. The typical independent retail store is a small operation usually managed by the owner or owners. It is rarely incorporated; sole proprietorships and partnerships predominate. These stores are usually rather inadequately financed, and many of them are seldom very far from insolvency. As a general rule they buy through wholesalers and do little advertising or aggressive selling. In every community, however, there are capable independents whose methods are up-to-date and whose profits reflect their ability. The term "Mom and Pop stores" is occasionally used to designate those small, family-owned and operated grocery stores that are found in many communities.

Chain Stores. Two or more stores in the same general line of business which are centrally owned and managed by a corporate chain are known as **chain stores**. Fifty percent of the following types of establishments are operated by chains: department stores, discount stores, limited-price variety stores, grocery stores, and women's ready-to-wear stores. The advent of suburban shopping centers in the 1950s and their reliance on strongly financed tenants such as chains has increased the number and strength of chain organizations.

Chain organizations customarily centralize many of their activities, permitting specialization and efficiencies in operation. They commonly practice

central buying, whereby nearly all of the merchandise for the stores is purchased in large quantities by a central office rather than by each store. Many chains, particularly those in the grocery and drug fields, maintain chain store warehouses to which most of their merchandise is shipped and from which it is distributed to the stores. Other central office activities include installing uniform accounting systems for all stores, operating a real estate department, preparing store advertising, and training prospective store managers.

Voluntary Chains. There are two types of **voluntary chains**: those sponsored by independent wholesalers, and those promoted by groups of cooperating retailers who establish and own the wholesale establishment that serves them. The voluntary chain practices, which closely resemble those of the corporate chain, have permitted thousands of independent retailers to achieve operating economies. The strength of the voluntary chains lies in the cooperative spirit of the members and, by the same token, their principal weakness lies in the lack of positive control within the group. Voluntary chains are found mainly in the grocery, variety goods, and automobile accessory lines. IGA food stores, Ben Franklin variety stores, and Western Auto dealers are members of voluntary chain organizations.

Franchisers. Since the 1960s the franchising of complete businesses has provided many independent businesspersons with the operating expertise of a corporate chain. Under a **franchise contract** the retailer (franchisee) usually agrees to purchase the equipment and supplies from approved sources and to conform to standardized operating procedures imposed by the supplier (franchiser) of the business, whose compensation is typically a franchise fee for rendering managerial services. Franchised organizations have been particularly successful in retail services such as fast-food restaurants (e.g., McDonald's hamburgers), motels (e.g., Holiday Inn), auto rentals, (e.g., Hertz), and employment agencies (e.g., Kelly Girls).

GEOGRAPHIC LOCATION

Until 1950 nearly all the major retailers in a city were located in the downtown area. Since the 1950s many retailers have followed the consumer to the suburbs and located in planned shopping centers.

Shopping center developers plan and manage the center, leasing space to a variety of retailers. In the late 1970s it is estimated that half of all retail sales will be transacted in shopping centers. The downtown area that suffers the most from the development of a shopping center is in a city of about 100,000 population which is just large enough to support a center.

Shopping centers have been classified into three different types: (1) the neighborhood center, (2) the community center, and (3) the regional center.

Neighborhood Shopping Center. The shopping center which generally serves 7,500 to 20,000 people living within a 6- to 10-minute drive is the **neighborhood shopping center**. The major store — and the prime traffic generator — in the center is a supermarket. The other stores in the center, which may include a drugstore, hardware store, bakery, and beauty shop, offer convenience goods and services.

Community Shopping Center. A market of 20,000 to 100,000 people living within a 10- to 20-minute drive is handled by the **community shopping center**. The dominant store is generally a small department store or a large variety store. A majority of the stores stress shopping goods such as wearing apparel and appliances.

Regional Shopping Center. Over 100,000 consumers are served by the **regional shopping center**; some of these consumers may drive long distances to get to the center. One or more department stores are its major tenants, and frequently the center is an enclosed mall with a department store at each end. Some large regional centers, such as the Southdale Shopping center near Minneapolis and the Northridge Fashion Center near Los Angeles, have received nationwide acclaim.

TYPE OF OPERATION

Although the majority of retailers stock a variety and assortment of goods and operate from a store, there are some merchants who are nonstore retailers. Their **nonstore operations** include: (1) house-to-house selling, (2) mail-order houses, and (3) vending machines.

House-to-House Selling. Since 1960 the desire of many consumers for the convenience of shopping in their own homes has resulted in the success of aggressive new house-to-house selling organizations such as Amway and Avon. Older firms, such as Fuller Brush and Electrolux, remain in the field, too.

In many communities house-to-house salespersons are confronted with **Green River Ordinances**, so named because they originated in Green River, Wyoming. These ordinances which restrict house-to-house selling reflect both the fear of local merchants toward this type of competition and the suspicion of householders toward house-to-house salespersons. An additional restriction is the 1974 **"cooling off period" rule** of the Federal Trade Commission which permits a buyer to cancel a house-to-house sales contract of $25 or more within three days from the date of agreement.

Mail-Order Houses. Mail-order houses sell and deliver goods by mail, making use of catalogs, media advertising, direct mail, and the telephone to attract customers. Originally the mail-order house served the rural consumer who lacked adequate retailing facilities; but in recent years, by accepting telephone orders, the large mail-order houses with their numerous local offices have attracted the urban consumer who desires to save the time and the effort of a shopping trip. Only a few of the houses are very large, and these are often retailers who also operate stores, such as Sears, Penney's and Montgomery Ward.

Vending Machines. Although vending machines date back to the 1880s, their greatest growth has come in recent years. Vending machines permit the sales of small convenience items to be made at times and in places where another type of retailing is not possible. In a recent year nearly $7 billion of sales were generated from more than 5 million vending machines. Cigarettes, coffee, candy, and soft drinks account for two thirds of their volume.

BUSINESS TERMS

QUESTIONS FOR DISCUSSION AND ANALYSIS

1. When a woman buys a new sofa for her living room, is she buying only the fabric, wood, and steel construction? If not, what is she buying?
2. Is a portable, black and white television set selling for under $100 a convenience, shopping, or specialty good? Would your answer be the same if the set was a $300 console model? Discuss.
3. How should a manufacturer of microwave ovens expect the marketing strategy to be different in the saturation phase of the product life cycle as compared to the introduction stage?
4. To a critic of product obsolescence, explain how the obsolescence of products may actually benefit society.
5. Why would you expect the following products to have different channels of distribution: fresh vegetables, canned vegetables, and frozen vegetables? What channels do you believe each of the products would use?
6. Why is it less expensive for a producer of candy bars to sell through wholesalers than to sell directly to retailers, while it is more expensive for a large manfacturer of fine furniture to sell through wholesalers?
7. Describe several operating methods adopted by independent wholesalers and retailers to meet the competition of corporate chain store organizations.
8. Over the last decade, in response to changing life styles and environmental factors, department stores have added many new goods and services. Over the next decade what new goods or services do you think department stores will add?
9. Will the downtown retailers be able to survive the competition from suburban shopping centers? What actions have the downtown retailers taken to meet the competition from shopping centers?
10. Can vending machines be used most effectively to replace or complement present retailing establishments? Discuss.

PROBLEMS AND SHORT CASES

1. Astroline Appliances, a small manufacturer of portable appliances, has developed a new ultrasonic food mixer that uses sound waves rather than a mechanical beater to mix food. Some components of this revolutionary appliance are patented, but Astroline management believes that the technology is available for the large appliance manufacturers to produce a similar product within two years. The cost to manufacture the ultrasonic mixer is nearly 50 percent more than for a conventional mixer although future cost reductions are expected. Management has budgeted a substantial sum of money to promote the new product.

   Suggest to management the problems that the product will face during each stage of the product life cycle and advise management on a marketing strategy for the product as it moves through each stage of its life cycle.
2. In Chicago Tom Fought operates a small cereal factory that produces Crackling Cornups, a cereal which contains corn, wheat germ, sea salt, soy oil, ground fish powder, and sesame seeds. To some, the cereal tastes similar to a combination of Listerine and vinegar. To health food enthusiasts, however, it is truly the breakfast of champions. Because of its laxative effect, some consumers of the cereal recommend eating it only on weekends.

   Crackling Cornups was introduced in 1972 and sold through health-food stores in the Chicago area. Because of the rising interest in health foods, sales rose rapidly to over $1.5 million in 1976. Tom Fought has expanded his distribution to include several grocery stores within a few miles of his factory. Other grocers in the Chicago area have expressed an interest in selling the cereal. At this time Fought is considering more extensive distribution for his product throughout Chicago, the state of Illinois, and surrounding states. He feels Crackling Cornups should be sold wherever consumers buy cereal.

Prepare a distribution plan for the product that will indicate the distribution channels that should be used and the types of wholesalers and retailers who should handle it.

3. A developer of a large regional shopping center has assigned you the job of designing a new enclosed mall to be built in suburban St. Louis. There will be four major entrances and several secondary entrances to the mall. You realize that stores in the center handling convenience goods and services frequently maintain longer hours than the other stores and should be in easily accessible locations. You recognize, too, that numerous smaller shopping goods stores will usually locate between the major stores in order to take advantage of the traffic flow.

Draw a floor plan of the center showing the location of one or more of the following types of stores: department store, supermarket, variety store, drugstore, women's apparel store, men's apparel store, shoe store, jewelry store, appliance store, tire store, dry cleaner, bank, bakery, beauty shop, fabric shop, bookstore, and fast food restaurant. Include in your drawing the location of the entrance and parking areas.

10 Sales Management and Advertising

While the industry average is the sale of 18 to 20 cars and trucks a month, Joe Girard of East Detroit's Merollis Chevrolet sells over 100 units a month or over 1,200 units a year. Girard owes his success to what he calls "Joe Girard's Secret of Selling." His major selling secrets include: (a) follow up after the sale so the customer is not forgotten; (b) provide the same deal to everyone; (c) relax the customer by not exerting pressure; (d) understand the "little guy"; and (e) let your satisfied customers sell others.

To accomplish the last secret, Girard pays $25 to each individual who sends him a customer. In a recent year these payments amounted to $14,000. Of course, this sum was a small proportion of the $180,000 compensation he received during the same year.

In developing a promotional strategy, management commonly uses three basic forms of promotion: personal selling, advertising, and sales promotion. **Personal selling**, which accounts for the majority of promotional expenditures, is the oral presentation in a conversation with one or more prospective purchasers for the purpose of making sales.[1] **Advertising** refers to any paid form of nonpersonal presentation and promotion of ideas, goods, or services by an identified sponsor.[2] **Sales promotion**, which receives less emphasis than the other two forms of promotion, is identified as those marketing activities, other than personal selling, advertising, and publicity, that stimulate consumer purchasing and dealer effectiveness, such as display, shows and exhibitions, demonstration, and various other nonrecurring selling efforts.[3] In most firms

---

[1] Reprinted from Committee on Definitions, *Marketing Definitions: A Glossary of Marketing Terms*, published by the American Marketing Association, 1960, p. 18.
[2] *Ibid.*, p. 9.
[3] *Ibid.*

advertising and sales promotion are used primarily to reinforce the personal selling effort. In some instances, however, such as in mail-order selling, advertising becomes a major selling force. It is estimated that for manufacturers the cost of personal selling averages about 12 to 13 cents of each sales dollar, while the cost of advertising averages only 1 to 3 cents of every dollar.

PERSONAL SELLING

"Nothing happens until someone sells something" is a slogan of the Sales and Marketing Executives Club. This statement vividly illustrates the point that a product may be properly planned, priced, and distributed; but until the product is sold, there is no return to the company. In a survey of 400 company presidents there was common agreement that personal selling was the most important aspect of marketing.

Types of Salespersons

Just as there are many kinds of doctors, such as in medicine, philosophy, and jurisprudence, there are many kinds of salespersons. The salesperson in the hosiery department at Sears differs greatly from the IBM salesperson who sells a computer installation to a large bank. Depending upon the degree to which they solve problems for their customers, the duties of salespersons range from simple clerking to creative selling.

A truly **creative salesperson** obtains, analyzes, and evaluates information from a prospective customer, and then incorporates the information received in the sales presentation. Although found in all types of selling situations, creative selling frequently occurs in industrial selling, particularly in the sales of complicated installations and equipment such as machine tools and electric generators. Creative salespersons who employ engineering knowledge in their sales presentations are known as **sales engineers**.

A manufacturer's salesperson who promotes a product to those influencing its sale to the ultimate consumer is known as a **missionary salesperson**. Often a manufacturer who uses a wholesaler-to-retailer-to-consumer channel of distribution employs missionary salespersons to call directly upon retailers and to inform them about the specific advantages of a product. They do not secure orders for a manufacturer's product, leaving this assignment to the wholesaler's salespersons; but they do enhance a retail salesperson's ability to sell the product to the ultimate consumer. A missionary salesperson who is employed by a pharmaceutical manufacturer, such as Eli Lilly or Upjohn, to explain the benefits of the firm's products to prescribing physicians is known as a **detailer**.

Sales Organizations

A sound organization structure is a requirement for the effective management of the sales activity. A sales force is frequently organized on one or more of the following bases: (1) geographic, (2) product line, or (3) customer.

GEOGRAPHIC SALES ORGANIZATION

The most common method of organizing a sales force is by geographic areas. A **geographic sales organization** is particularly appropriate for firms which distribute a broad product line over a wide geographic area. A major advantage of this type of organization is that sales management is able to respond rapidly to serve its customers and to meet competition. The disadvantages relate to the costs and the complexity which arise from the geographic dispersion of the sales force.

The intensity of the geographic coverage determines the number of levels of management in this type of organization. As depicted in Figure 10-1, some large organizations with national distribution may have as many as four layers of sales management. For example, at the home office there may be a **field sales manager** who has responsibility for the entire field sales organization. Accountable to the field sales manager may be six to ten **regional sales managers**. Each regional sales manager may be responsible for the sales in several states. Reporting to each regional sales manager may be a number of **district sales managers** each of whom may supervise the sales efforts within a particular state. Answerable to each district sales manager may be several **territory sales managers**. Each territory manager may be responsible for sales within a group of counties. Reporting to each territory manager are the field salespersons. The line of advancement for an ambitious salesperson with managerial aspirations is a gradual climb up this vertical ladder of sales management.

PRODUCT LINE SALES ORGANIZATION

When a firm markets two or more full lines of products, the sales force is often specialized by product line. A **product line sales organization** benefits from specialization. Since the activities of a salesperson are limited to a particular product line, the individual becomes a specialist in that line. On the other hand, a disadvantage of this form of organization is the duplication of selling effort. As a result of employing more than one sales force, selling and administrative expenses increase. Another form of duplication occurs when more than one salesperson from a product-organized company calls upon the same customer.

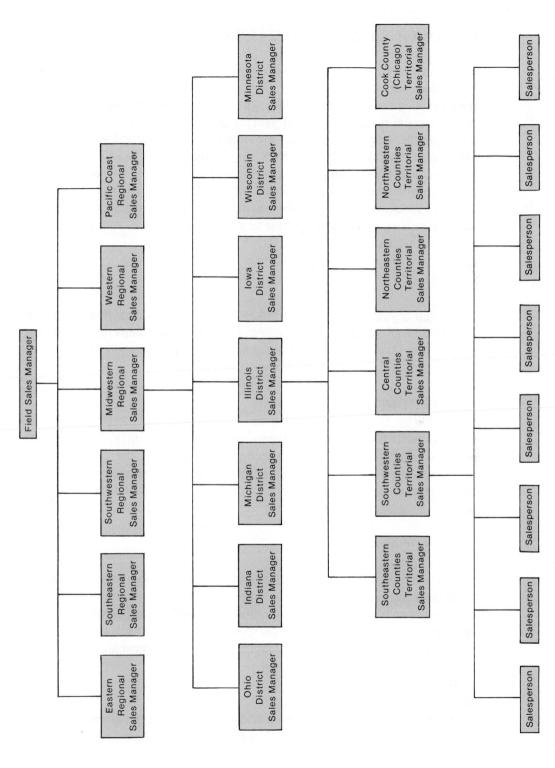

Figure 10-1   *Illustration of a Geographic Sales Organization*

CUSTOMER SALES ORGANIZATION

A third way in which the sales force is organized is by type of customer. A **customer sales organization** best illustrates the organizational application of the marketing concept since it places the focus of the sales effort on serving the customers' needs. The use of several sales forces to serve different customer groups, however, increases a company's marketing and administrative expenses. In the mid-1970s, the NCR Corporation shifted its sales force from a product-line base to four customer-oriented sales groups specializing in (a) retailing; (b) financial; (c) commercial, industrial; and (d) medical, education, and government customers. Within their broad market groupings, a salesperson who sells an accounting machine to a bank, for instance, may also sell it a computer installation.

Steps in the Sales Process

A well-organized sales effort follows a step-by-step plan that should be flexible enough to meet most selling situations. The steps in the selling process are: (1) prospecting, (2) preapproach, (3) approach, (4) presentation, (5) trial close, (6) answering objections, and (7) close.

PROSPECTING

In order to replace old customers and acquire new ones, a salesperson needs to conduct systematic prospecting. **Prospecting** is the activity which develops new sales leads. Sources of prospects include friends, business associates, present users, paid informers known as **bird dogs**, and **cold canvassing**, in which a salesperson contacts completely unknown individuals.

PREAPPROACH

After the prospects have been identified, a **preapproach** investigation determines if the prospects qualify as potential customers. Another purpose of the preapproach is to gather information which will permit a salesperson to tailor the sales presentation to the prospect. This use of the information builds a salesperson's self-confidence and increases sales effectiveness.

APPROACH

In the **approach** the salesperson attempts to capture the attention and interest of the prospect. The approach is especially important since it provides the prospect with the first impression of the salesperson. If the salesperson is successfully received, he or she can proceed with the sales presentation.

PRESENTATION

The sales presentation is the key element in the selling process. In the **presentation** a salesperson demonstrates to the prospect how the product features produce customer benefits. Some companies provide prepared, or canned, sales presentations for their salespersons. Generally the most effective presentations are the ones which are adaptable to a prospect's situation. Through questioning, a salesperson may be able to identify a problem confronting the prospect and then indicate how the product can provide a solution to the problem.

TRIAL CLOSE

A **trial close** is used during a presentation to see if the prospect has made a mental commitment to purchase. By gauging a prospect's reaction during the presentation, a salesperson receives some indication of the prospect's willingness to buy. In some instances a single trial close may lead to a sale; in other cases several trial closes may be necessary.

ANSWERING OBJECTIONS

Many different types of objections may arise during a sales presentation. The presence of **objections** is often viewed as a favorable factor since it indicates that the prospect is attempting to resolve various questions as he or she moves toward a purchase decision. Some objections, however, may just be excuses for not buying. Knowledgeable salespersons are aware of the usual objections they will encounter and they are ready to respond to them. Commonly expressed objections relate to:

1. Product features.
2. Product cost.
3. Need for the product.
4. Timing of the purchase.
5. Seller of the product.

CLOSE

Whenever a prospect expresses a definite interest in the product, the salesperson should **close**. Several effective closing techniques are utilized by successful salespersons. These include the *assumptive* close where the salesperson asks a final question such as "To which address do you want this shipped?" Another type of close is the *choice* close where the salesperson poses a question such as "Would you prefer to pay cash or use credit?" A third type of close occurs when a salesperson overcomes a final objection. A statement may be made to the prospect such as "Will you agree that if we can resolve this final objection, you will complete the purchase?" A fourth common type of closing involves presenting a summary of the product benefits and then asking for the order.

ADVERTISING

A definition of advertising which reflects some of the latest thinking is that advertising is constructive communication with consumers. This interpretation includes the concept that advertisers should try to make a purposeful contact with consumers. This circumstance is mutually beneficial in that consumers are informed of the availability of goods for which they have a need and the advertisers secure a profit through providing these goods. It also assumes that the advertising appears in the right media, with the right appeals, at the right times, and at the right prices for the consumers whose needs will be best satisfied by the goods involved.

Objectives of Advertising

An advertising manager for a company needs to set forth carefully the objectives of its advertising. Advertising which is directed to create a familiarity with the name and activities of a large diversified company, such as the Transamerica Corporation, is different from advertising which is designed to evoke immediate sales in a retail store. Common objectives of advertising include:

1. To provide information. By advertising their toll-free reservation number, Holiday Inn provides information to prospective travelers.
2. To create interest. In their advertising the Honda Motor Co. attracted the interest of women to their cars by attacking myths about women car buyers with statements such as "Women only drive automatic transmissions."
3. To persuade. By offering in their ads to pay $5.00 to all applicants who had an American Express credit card, the Diner's Club credit card organization sought to persuade the American Express cardholders to apply for a Diner's Club card.
4. To generate immediate sales. When Macy's department store advertises a pre-holiday sale of women's coats, they want to generate immediate sales.
5. To establish a favorable image. The Hallmark Greeting Card Company desires to establish a favorable company image by sponsoring the "Hall of Fame" television specials.

Types of Advertising

The two basic types of advertising are product and institutional. **Product advertising** is designed to sell one or more definite, identified products and usually it describes and extols their good qualities, satisfaction-giving features, or their prices. **Institutional advertising** is created for the purpose of getting some message across to the public which may or may not be related to the sale of any particular merchandise.

PRODUCT ADVERTISING

Within the general category of product advertising are several subtypes. **Primary advertising** is intended to stimulate an interest in and a desire for a certain class of goods, particularly some new type of product that has just come on the market, or in which the public has yet to indicate any appreciable interest. **Selective advertising** is supposed to impel consumers toward the purchase of a particular brand of goods, such as a Ford Pinto or a pair of Nettleton shoes. It is quite common to find primary and selective advertising in the same advertisement. **Mass advertising** is advertising that appeals to a cross section of the populace. **Class advertising**, on the other hand, is directed at special groups of people, such as newly married couples, golfers, or college students.

INSTITUTIONAL ADVERTISING

By means of institutional advertising a firm may announce a change in location, the adoption of a new policy, the acquirement of a new line of goods, or anything else that might be of general interest to its customers. Another form of institutional advertising exists when several advertisers issue a joint advertisement for their mutual benefit. The advertisements of the American Petroleum Institute, the American Gas Association, and the Florida Orange Growers are examples of group institutional advertising.

Publicity is information about a product that is supplied to the advertising media, usually newspapers or magazines, by the producer, which the publisher may or may not use. It usually appears in editorial or news form and frequently does not include the name of the maker. Since publicity is not paid for, it is not really a form of advertising.

Advertising Media

Of paramount importance to advertisers is the selection of the media that will carry their advertising. The term **media** refers to the different types of vehicles or devices by which advertising reaches its audience. These include:

(1) newspapers, (2) magazines, (3) radio, (4) television, (5) direct mail, and (6) other media.

In the discussion of media types that follows, four of the bases of comparison that will be utilized require some preliminary explanation. They are:

1. *Geographic selectivity*, which refers to the ability of a medium to deliver the advertiser's message to a particular geographic area such as a designated city or metropolitan community.
2. *Interest selectivity*, which means the capacity of a medium to deliver the advertiser's message more or less exclusively to groups of consumers who would presumably be interested in the product being advertised, such as homeowners for room air conditioners or farmers for tractors.
3. *Flexibility*, which refers to the ability of the advertiser to change the message, if need be, a relatively short time before the advertisement is to appear.
4. *Identity of the audience*, which means the extent to which the pertinent characteristics of the audience are known to the media.

Table 10-1 lists the 10 leading national advertisers in major media for 1974. Table 10-2 shows a comparison of the advertising volume by media for 1973 and 1974. In 1974 total advertising expenditures in all media were over $26.5 billion.

Table 10-1   **The Top Ten National Advertisers of 1974 in Major Media**

Rank	Company	Total Expenditures
1	Procter & Gamble Co.	$325,000,000
2	General Motors Corp.	247,000,000
3	Sears, Roebuck & Co.	220,000,000
4	General Foods Corp.	189,000,000
5	Warner-Lambert Co.	156,000,000
6	Bristol-Myers Co.	150,000,000
7	American Home Products Corp.	135,000,000
8	Ford Motor Co.	132,000,000
9	Colgate-Palmolive Co.	118,000,000
10	U.S. Government	110,800,000

SOURCE: Reprinted with permission from the August 18, 1975, issue of *Advertising Age*. Copyright 1975 by Crain Communications, Inc.

NEWSPAPERS

Newspapers are quite selective from a geographical standpoint because through them it is possible for advertisers to pinpoint their advertising to the metropolitan areas that they wish to reach. From the standpoint of interest selectivity or ability to reach special groups, newspapers reach all economic and social levels of the people and have a general rather than a special appeal.

Table 10-2   *Advertising Volume in the United States in 1973 and 1974*

Medium	1973		1974		Percentage of Change
	Millions of Dollars	Percentage of Total	Millions of Dollars	Percentage of Total	
Newspapers	7,595	30.3	7,910	29.8	+4
Magazines	1,448	5.8	1,525	5.7	+5
Farm publications	65	0.3	65	0.2	0
Television	4,460	17.8	4,850	18.3	+9
Radio	1,690	6.7	1,790	6.7	+6
Direct mail	3,698	14.7	3,920	14.8	+6
Business papers	865	3.4	915	3.5	+6
Outdoor	308	1.2	335	1.3	+9
Miscellaneous	4,951	19.8	5,240	19.7	+6
TOTAL	25,080	100.0	26,550	100.0	+5.9

SOURCE: Reprinted with permission from the December 16, 1974, issue of *Advertising Age*. Copyright 1974 by Crain Communications, Inc.

Most papers, however, contain specially edited sections, such as sports, the women's section, school news, and church notices, which may help the advertiser with a message for consumers interested in such topics.

A favorable characteristic of newspaper advertising is its flexibility or timeliness. In most cases changes in advertising copy can be made within a few hours of the time the paper goes to press. This permits advertisers to follow national or local events, the weather, or changes in their own internal situations with great speed. It is even possible in times of great urgency to alter advertising insertions between editions.

A substantial portion of the readers of daily newspapers are known through home delivery lists. Many daily papers maintain research departments that attempt to classify their known readers on the bases of income, education, religion, age, and many other characteristics that are useful for advertisers to know.

MAGAZINES

For the advertisers with nationwide distribution, the fact that most magazines have countrywide coverage makes these media singularly advantageous. For advertisers with a more limited geographic distribution of their goods, regional editions of many magazines provide access to these smaller markets without requiring them to pay for circulation in the areas where their products are not sold. Among the magazines of general editorial interest, *Time, Newsweek,* and *Reader's Digest* offer regional editions.

Since the general editorial magazines reach individuals with many different interests, they are effective media for products with a wide appeal.

Most others, however, are consciously directed toward readers who are included in rather specifically defined interest groups. In this class of magazines are those appealing to farmers, women, young people, homemakers, and the various trade journals. Magazines in the last group circulate only within the trades affected, such as groceries, drugs, and metals.

Magazine advertising is not flexible, in that the lapse of time between the deadlines for advertising copy and date of publication is sometimes great enough to make the themes of the insertions out of date by the time they reach the readers. *Reader's Digest* requires nine weeks and *Time* requests seven weeks for four-color advertisements to be submitted before the date that they will reach the readers.

As with newspapers, magazines have their subscription lists, which are classified according to the pertinent factors involved and which reveal important information for advertisers.

RADIO

Although the advent of television in the 1950s nearly caused the demise of network radio, local or spot radio continues as a profitable advertising media both for station owners and advertisers. Its effectiveness, however, appears to be greater during the daylight hours than at night when television commands the larger audience.

Radio is an excellent medium for territorial selectivity because advertisers can select just those stations that broadcast into the areas that they wish to reach. For any radio station the outer limits of its listening audience can be determined quite accurately. This may differ somewhat at night from the daytime, but research has convincingly defined the territorial coverage for most stations.

Interest selectivity, on the other hand, is somewhat less certain because the makeup of the listener group for any one program cannot be ascertained with any great degree of accuracy. Advertisers customarily assume that listeners of various types will be attracted to programs that offer entertainment that will appeal to them, for example, sports broadcasts for sports fans.

Radio advertising is exceedingly flexible because it is possible to change the copy if necessary even while a program is in progress. This permits advertisers to capitalize fully on sudden events to which they may wish to tie their messages.

Several research organizations identify the listening audience for radio stations. The Pulse, Inc. research organization selects a sample of homes and then sends an interviewer to each home to elicit from respondents an estimate of when they listened to the radio. The American Research Bureau checks the listening habits of the radio audience through the use of entries in diaries which are maintained by the listeners.

TELEVISION

The newest medium in advertising, television, has assumed a most important place. While still behind newspapers in percentage of total advertising it has passed direct mail, magazines, and radio. The combination of the spoken word and the visual presentation of products and their benefits which television offers has been most intriguing and alluring to many advertisers.

Because of the dominance of nationwide networks in television programming, actual geographic selectivity is limited to locally produced shows and commercials. During the early 1970s the Federal Communications Commission expressed its displeasure at the television networks' monopoly of prime evening time by making it mandatory for local stations to originate their own shows during a portion of this time period.

Interest selectivity is in conflict with the quest for large viewing audiences by television networks. High audience ratings attract advertisers to a network. Numerous amply-financed advertisers are needed to sponsor the many costly television shows. For example, a one-minute commercial on the football Super Bowl costs over $200,000. Certain programs provide some interest selectivity, such as the Saturday morning cartoons, the afternoon "soap operas," the evening news, and sports events.

Television commercials which may cost as much as $20,000 and take a month or longer to produce do not lend themselves to flexibility. Commercials and shows originating at the local level, however, may retain the dimension of timeliness and flexibility.

Although audience identification is not as exact as in the printed media, various sampling techniques are utilized to infer the characteristics of the television audience. One technique is the **coincidental method** whereby telephone calls are made to a sampling of homes during a telecast. Another form of measurement is conducted with the Audimeter. This automatic recording device was developed by the A. C. Nielsen Company, which is known for its Nielsen audience rating of television programs. The unit is attached to a television set and electronically records the viewing habits of a household.

DIRECT MAIL

A widely used advertising medium, direct mail, takes a number of different forms. Postcards, letters, catalogs, folders, and booklets are commonly used. The basis of all direct-mail advertising is the **mailing list**. Lists may be compiled from a variety of sources and may be classified almost endlessly. It is most important that the lists be assembled with the utmost care and that they be kept up-to-date. Through the manipulation of the list, direct-mail advertising can be made extremely selective, regarding both geographical location and consumer interests. Depending somewhat upon the elaborateness of the copy, this medium can be changed or discarded entirely until the copy is actually mailed. There are many companies who compile and classify lists of businesses and consumers which are available on a fee basis to sellers who wish to use direct mail solicitation.

OTHER ADVERTISING MEDIA

Other common advertising media include: **business papers**, which circulate only among members of a particular profession or industry; **outdoor advertising**, which consists of billboards and signs; **transportation advertising**, which is found in buses, taxis, and subways; **point-of-purchase aids**, such as display racks, demonstrations, and product samples; and **advertising specialties**, which include calendars, matchbooks, pencils, and other items containing an advertising message.

The Advertising Agency

The **advertising agency** is a specialized institution that assists businesspersons in all phases of their advertising effort. Advertising agencies were originally space sellers for the media, but they now help to create advertising for business firms that seek their services.

An advertising agency is equipped to undertake all phases of the preparation and execution of advertising for its clients. It handles the complete advertising campaign, which includes writing copy, creating art work, and selecting and making contracts with the media. Such secondary activities as product and market research, designing of packages and labels, and consultation on marketing matters generally are among the services of the larger agencies. Practically all national magazine and newspaper advertising is produced by agencies, whose specialized talents enable them to perform these functions better than the advertisers could.

Figure 10-2 shows the organization of a typical advertising agency on the basis of the functions performed. Table 10-3, page 200, identifies the top ten advertising agencies in the United States in terms of **billings**, which represent the total of all advertising space, time, and service charges billed to clients.

Oddly enough, the principal method by which the agencies are compensated dates back to the period when they operated as space brokers for the publishers. Under this system they are paid a 15 percent commission by the media on the basis of the space or time cost of the advertising placed by them in behalf of their clients, the advertisers. For example, assume that an agency acting for a client buys space in a magazine that costs $30,000. The magazine bills the agency for $30,000 less the 15 percent commission of $4,500, or a net of $25,500. The agency in turn bills the client for the full $30,000; and when

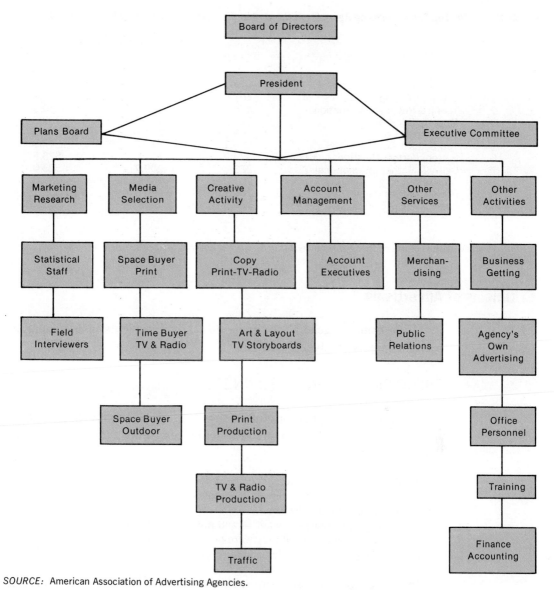

SOURCE: American Association of Advertising Agencies.

Figure 10-2 *A Typical Advertising Agency Organization Chart by Functions*

this is paid by the client, deducts the $4,500 and remits the $25,500 to the magazine. Over the past several years some agencies, viewing service charges as a fairer method of compensation than commissions, have switched to this form of compensation. The service charge to a client is composed of charges for materials, services, and a fair profit.

Table 10-3   **The Top Ten Advertising Agencies in the United States Ranked by World Billings, 1974**

Rank	Agency	Domestic Billings	International Billings (Millions of Dollars)	Total World Billings
1	J. Walter Thompson Co.	$401.5	$466.0	$867.5
2	Young & Rubicam International	468.9	281.6	750.5
3	McCann-Erickson	211.3	492.0	703.3
4	Leo Burnett Co.	366.1	211.6	577.7
5	Ted Bates & Co.	255.1	310.8	565.9
6	Batten, Barton, Durstine, & Osborn	373.9	151.6	525.5
7	Ogilvy & Mather International	223.3	299.7	523.0
8	Grey Advertising	290.0	101.0	391.0
9	Doyle Dane Bernbach	265.1	90.0	355.1
10	Foote, Cone & Belding	238.8	100.4	339.2

SOURCE: Reprinted with permission from the February 24, 1975, issue of *Advertising Age*. Copyright 1975 by Crain Communications, Inc.

Criticisms of Advertising

Advertising in general and individual advertisements in particular have been the targets of adverse criticism.

CRITICISMS AGAINST BUSINESS

Some of the expressions of disapproval have actually been criticisms against business itself and many of its practices. Among these have been the following claims:

1. Much advertising is merely competitive.
2. It stresses minor differences in products which serve the same purpose and are essentially the same.
3. It causes consumers to want — and presumably to purchase — goods that they would not desire if they were not exposed to the advertising.
4. It is designed to create demand for products.

In answer to these criticisms it should be noted that competition is a fundamental principle of capitalism, that product differentiation is a method by which producers of homogeneous products endeavor to make their goods appear slightly different from those of their competitors, and that in many instances consumers would not know of the existence and availability of many products if they were not advertised.

In answer to the criticism that advertising creates demand, it must be admitted that many, if not most, advertisers believe that demand creation is one of the main functions of advertising. A demand for a product cannot exist without a knowledge of the availability of the product on the part of potential users. But demand must be more than mere knowledge of the existence of a product; it must involve the desire for the product on the part of prospective purchasers.

OTHER CRITICISMS

Other criticisms of advertising are:

1. Advertising makes the advertised goods cost more than would be the case if they were not advertised.
2. Certain advertisements are in poor taste or offensive to the public.
3. Many advertisements are false or misleading.
4. Many advertisements are pointless and only casually related to the products involved.
5. Advertising creates monopolistic power.

Various answers can be given to these criticisms. In many instances advertising increases sales volume and generates additional earnings which more than offset the cost of advertising. Occasionally some advertisers who are under pressure of competition have exceeded the bounds of good taste for some segments of the public. Both advertising agency executives and media representatives, however, endeavor to prevent the appearance of any advertisement that might provoke displeasure.

Unfortunately false or misleading advertising by a few tends to undermine public confidence in all advertising. This damages the creditability of those advertisers who follow the policy of checking their copy carefully to make certain that it contains nothing but the truth. Some advertisements are pointless and unrelated to the product being advertised. It is doubtful if any harm results from these ads, but the extent to which they induce customers to purchase is certainly subject to question.

Research into the potential monopolistic power of advertising reveals that one cannot generalize that large-scale advertising creates monopolistic power. Rather, the situation for each product should be analyzed on the basis of factors such as capital requirements, lack of product and/or marketing ability, prospective earnings, and failure to have a line of related products.

Ensuring Truth in Advertising

There is no single method of ensuring that a certain amount of untruth will not appear in the advertising of the country as long as a system of free private enterprise continues. The following are a number of steps that have been taken to protect the public and ethical business leaders from some of the more flagrant and harmful types of false advertising: (1) industry self-regulation, (2) action by media, (3) Better Business Bureaus, (4) action by federal agencies,

(5) *Printers' Ink* statutes, and (6) action by consumer groups. These and other methods have helped to upgrade the advertising picture, which is unquestionably on a far higher plane than it was some years ago.

INDUSTRY SELF-REGULATION

Recognizing that false or misleading advertising reflects unfavorably on all members of the trade, some industries, such as the Cosmetic and Toilet Preparations Industry, have cooperated with the Federal Trade Commission in setting up Trade Practice Rules which may prohibit false advertising, misbranding, and deception on the part of its members. In 1971 the National Advertising Review Board was created by the major advertising trade associations to police advertising by reviewing complaints from the public and by operating its own monitoring program.

ACTION BY MEDIA

Nearly all media have certain minimum ethical standards to which all advertising must conform in order to be acceptable for publication. They recognize that false advertisements reflect not only on the advertisers but also on the media in which they appear.

BETTER BUSINESS BUREAUS

Originally established by businesspersons to defend themselves against unethical competition, **Better Business Bureaus** are well known for their activities to protect consumers. The weapons for the nearly 140 local bureaus have been twofold — publicity for the offending firms and recourse to the federal courts when false advertising is sent through the mails.

ACTION BY FEDERAL AGENCIES

The two principal agencies for fighting fraudulent advertising are the Federal Trade Commission and the Food and Drug Administration. The Federal Trade Commission Act of 1914 established the Commission and gave it authority to prevent the use of unfair methods of competition in interstate commerce. In 1938 the Wheeler-Lea Act (an amendment to the Federal Trade Commission Act) added to the duties of the FTC by giving it authority to prevent unfair or deceptive acts or practices in commerce, which includes false advertising of food, drugs, cosmetics, and therapeutic devices. The Federal Food, Drug, and Cosmetic Act of 1938 assigned to the Pure Food and

Drug Administration the power to prohibit false labeling and deceptive packaging of foods, drugs, and cosmetics.

PRINTERS' INK STATUTES

In 1911 *Printers' Ink*, a former advertising trade paper, set forth a model statute that was designed to aid in eliminating dishonest advertising. As a result, 44 states have adopted some form of this statute. **Printer's Ink statutes**, of course, are confined in their application solely to intrastate advertising, and their value has been lessened in some instances by poor enforcement.

ACTION BY CONSUMER GROUPS

Various consumer groups have been successful in getting deceptive or distasteful advertising changed. The ban on television cigarette advertising can be partially attributed to consumer advocates. Other consumer groups have successfully caused advertisers to modify their hard-sell commercials on children's television shows and to indicate when a product demonstration on television is a simulation rather than an actuality. Chapter 12 more fully describes all aspects of the consumer movement.

BUSINESS TERMS

personal selling	186	objections	191
advertising	186	close	191
sales promotion	186	product advertising	193
creative salesperson	187	institutional advertising	193
sales engineers	187	primary advertising	193
missionary salesperson	187	selective advertising	193
detailer	187	mass advertising	193
geographic sales organization	188	class advertising	193
field sales manager	188	publicity	193
regional sales managers	188	media	193
district sales managers	188	coincidental method	197
territory sales managers	188	mailing list	197
product line sales organization	188	business papers	198
customer sales organization	190	outdoor advertising	198
prospecting	190	transportation advertising	198
bird dogs	190	point-of-purchase aids	198
cold canvassing	190	advertising specialties	198
preapproach	190	advertising agency	198
approach	190	billings	198
presentation	191	Better Business Bureaus	202
trial close	191	Printer's Ink statutes	203

QUESTIONS FOR DISCUSSION AND ANALYSIS

1. Explain why a knowledge of the communication process is valuable in other areas within the company besides the promotion area.
2. Examine the implications for a retailer of the statement that "nothing happens until someone sells something."
3. Identify the most effective way to organize the sales force of a large computer manufacturer.
4. Which of the seven steps in the selling process is the most important one? What are the reasons for your choice?
5. List three of the common objections voiced by prospective new car buyers. As a car salesperson, what statements would you make to a prospect to overcome these objections?
6. Which is the most important factor in causing a customer to buy: the personality of the salesperson, the quality of the product, or the company's reputation? Defend your answer.
7. Is it ethical for an automobile manufacturer to stress noneconomic buying motives in advertising, such as prestige and "keeping up with the Joneses," rather than economic motives, such as low operating costs and resale value? Discuss.
8. As an advertising manager for a brewery, how would you justify to the company president the purchase of a one-minute commercial for $200,000 on the Super Bowl?
9. Do the polls which rank the popularity of television programs, such as the Nielsen ratings, result in better quality television productions? Explain.
10. Since cigarette advertising is banned from television, should it also be banned from all other advertising media? Explain.

PROBLEMS AND SHORT CASES

1. Famous Appliances manufactures and markets a full line of major appliances, room air conditioners, and television sets. Prior to World War II the company was a leading producer of wringer washing machines. After World War II the firm rapidly diversified into other lines of appliances. As a result of a merger in 1969 with a Japanese electronics manufacturer, a complete line of television sets was added to the firm's product offerings.

    In 1970 the company suffered a significant loss of sales volume. Although part of the decline was blamed on an economic downturn, the decrease was attributed mainly to an antiquated sales organization. The sales force was organized geographically and each salesperson sold the full line of Famous Appliances. This same form of organization had been used since the time that the company marketed only washing machines.

    Some of the older salespersons still considered the firm to be a washing machine company and they pushed washers to the exclusion of the other products in the line. In fact, nationwide sales of the company's washers accounted for a hefty 20 percent of total industry sales. On the other hand, sales of the company's television sets were a meager 2 percent of total industry volume. Appliance dealers in small and medium-size communities accounted for nearly two thirds of Famous Appliances sales.

    Structure a new sales organization for Famous Appliances and provide an explanation for your action.
2. Choose a well-known product with which you are familiar and prepare a step-by-step sales plan. To enhance your accuracy gather as much information as possible about the product. Include in your plan the following steps: (a) how to prospect, (b) type of information for the preapproach, (c) approach, (d) sales

presentation, (e) trial close, (f) anticipate and answer objections in the presentation, and (g) close.

3. A major producer of vitamins and cold remedies has developed a new, pleasant-tasting vitamin tonic which is designed to restore the vigor of youth to those past middle age. Since the tonic contains an alcoholic base, its rejuvenating effects are immediate, if not lasting. The producer believes that the past-fifty age group is the major market for the tonic. For the first year $2 million has been appropriated to introduce the tonic.

As advertising manager for the company: (a) formulate your advertising objectives, (b) develop an advertising plan which allocates the advertising appropriation to the different media, (c) justify your allocation to each media, and (d) indicate how you would measure the effectiveness of your advertisements in each media.

11 Prices and Pricing Policies

The Union Bank of Switzerland has studied prices in 37 cities around the world and found that men's clothing is cheapest in Bombay and Istanbul, but expensive in Copenhagen, San Francisco, and Beirut. Unfurnished three-room apartments are most expensive in Hong Kong and Tokyo, about 25 percent or more above the New York rate. TV sets are cheapest in the U.S.

When prices are matched against local incomes, the Swiss bank concludes that "the U.S. is still clearly in the lead as the most affluent nation." Bogota, Bombay, and Istanbul, it says, can "be found at the lower end of the scale."[1]

The concept of prices and the procedures of pricing practices are the end results of centuries of long evolutionary processes. Primitive human beings subsisted on the fruits of their own labor, a situation which can still be observed in some of the more remote areas of the world. A step above this situation came about when an individual ceased to raise or make all of the things needed but relied on neighbors for some of them. This condition brought about the concept of value in which a unit of one person's product was considered to be worth the same, more, or less than that of a neighbor. The equating of values gave rise to the practice of **barter**, in which a bargaining procedure was usually the basis for establishing the value of one product in terms of another. Aside from this, there was the necessity for a person with a product to offer to find someone who not only wanted it but had, in turn, something that the former required. Both of these situations were cumbersome and time-consuming. As time passed, money evolved and provided a common and acceptable medium of exchange for expressing the values of goods and services. These values were expressed in **prices**, which greatly facilitated purchases and sales. It is with prices and pricing practices that this chapter is concerned.

[1]Reprinted with permission of *The Wall Street Journal*, © Dow Jones & Company, Inc. (1974). All rights reserved.

PRICING OBJECTIVES

The pricing objectives of a firm should reflect both its specific marketing objectives and its broader company objectives. Table 11-1, page 208, which was derived from a study of pricing objectives in large companies, illustrates the pricing goals in ten major American corporations. This study and other research reveal that typical pricing goals include: (a) obtaining a target return on investment, (b) stabilizing prices, (c) maintaining or increasing market share, (d) meeting or reducing competition, (e) promoting the product line, (f) serving a desired market segment, and (g) optimizing profits.

Pricing goals vary from industry to industry and from company to company. When a firm prices its products so that the earnings from product sales yield a predetermined percentage return on investment, the firm is following a **target-return-on-investment objective.** Companies in industries where there is one firm that assumes price leadership frequently have price stability as a goal. These companies attempt to avoid ruinous price wars within their industry. In some firms, maintaining or increasing market share is a pricing goal. Industry sales may decline, such as in a business recession, but if a company maintains or increases its market share during the recessionary period, its marketing efforts may be judged successful.

Since competition is the essence of our enterprise system, a pricing goal of meeting competition or reducing its effectiveness is a normal expectation. A company with several different items in its product line may desire to promote its entire line through pricing. The pricing goal of some firms is to serve certain segments of the market. By developing products for various market segments and pricing to these segments, a company may be able to charge prices that yield a greater-than-average margin. As a pricing goal, the optimization of profits should be a long-run expectation. Short-run profit maximization may cause a company to focus narrowly on the profit which can be achieved on each transaction rather than on the optimum profit which can be achieved over a period of time.

PRICE DETERMINING FACTORS

The two basic approaches in determining selling prices are (1) the cost approach, and (2) the market or competitive approach. In the **cost approach** management sets a price after determining the product cost. In the **market** or **competitive approach** a price is established by referring to the current market price for similar items.

Cost Approach

Since all firms desire to set a price which will cover their costs and make a profit, some type of cost approach is used by the majority of businesses.

Table 11-1 **Pricing Goals of Ten Selected Industrial Corporations**

Company	Principal Pricing Goal	Collateral Pricing Goals
Alcoa	20% on investment (before taxes); higher on new products (about 10% effective rate after taxes)	a. Promotive policy on new products b. Price stabilization
American Can	Maintenance of market share	a. "Meeting" competition (using cost of substitute product to determine price) b. Price stabilization
A&P	Increasing market share	a. General promotive (low margin policy)
Du Pont	Target return on investment — no specific figure given	a. Charging what traffic will bear over long run b. Maximum return for new products — "life cycle" pricing
General Electric	20% on investment (after taxes); 7% on sales (after taxes)	a. Promotive policy on new products b. Price stabilization on nationally advertised products
General Foods	33⅓% gross margin ("⅓ to make, ⅓ to sell, and ⅓ for profit"); expectation of realizing target only on new products	a. Full line of food products and novelties b. Maintaining market share
Goodyear	"Meeting competitors"	a. Maintain "position" b. Price stabilization
Sears, Roebuck	Increasing market share (8–10% regarded as satisfactory share)	a. Realization of traditional return on investment of 10–15% (after taxes) b. General promotive (low margin policy)
Standard Oil (Indiana)	Maintenance of market share	a. Stabilize prices b. Target return on investment (none specified)
Union Carbide	Target return on investment	a. Promotive policy on new products; "life cycle" pricing on chemicals generally

SOURCE: Adapted from Robert F. Lanzillotti, "Pricing Objectives in Large Companies," *American Economic Review*, Vol. 48 (December, 1958), pp. 924–927.

The various cost approaches include: (1) markup on total costs, (2) rate-of-return pricing, (3) variable cost pricing, (4) break-even analysis pricing, and (5) average cost pricing.

MARKUP ON TOTAL COSTS

At all levels of business, but particularly at the wholesale and retail levels, it is customary for sellers to arrive at their prices through the use of

markup percentages. These markups are expressed as percentages either of cost or of selling prices. Most large stores and chains compute markup on selling prices, whereas smaller stores determine markup on cost.

There are two methods of using markup as a means of setting prices. One involves the use of a markup table as shown in Table 11-2. The other requires the use of one or more of the basic formulas shown in Table 11-3.

Table 11-2 **Retail Price Markup Table**

How to Use This Table: Find the desired markup percentage based on selling price in the column at the left. Multiply the cost of the article by the corresponding percentage in the column at the right. Add this amount to the cost in order to determine the selling price.

Desired Markup Percentage (Based on Sales Price)	Equivalent Percentage of Cost	Desired Markup Percentage (Based on Sales Price)	Equivalent Percentage of Cost
5.0	5.3	20.0	25.0
6.0	6.4	25.0	33.3
7.0	7.5	30.0	42.9
8.0	8.7	33.3	50.0
9.0	10.0	35.0	53.8
10.0	11.1	37.5	60.0
12.5	14.3	40.0	66.7
15.0	17.7	42.8	75.0
16.7	20.0	50.0	100.0

A markup is supposed to cover the cost of handling the article to be priced, a portion of the firm's expenses, and a certain amount of profit. Because of the difficulty of establishing these costs accurately for individual articles, like items are grouped into classes for which costs can be discovered, and the average or group markup to establish the retail price for a single item is used. Thus, in a store using the retail price markup method and having established an average markup of 50 percent for a given merchandise group,

Table 11-3 **Formulas for Markup Calculations**

$$\text{Cost} + \text{markup} = \text{Retail}$$
$$\text{Cost} = \text{Retail} - \text{markup}$$
$$\text{Markup} = \text{Retail} - \text{cost}$$
$$\frac{\text{Markup}}{\text{Retail}} = \text{Markup expressed as a percentage of retail}$$
$$\frac{\text{Markup}}{\text{Cost}} = \text{Markup expressed as a percentage of cost}$$

If a seller wishes to translate markup as a percentage of retail into a percentage of cost, or vice versa, the two formulas shown below are useful:

$$\frac{\text{Markup as a percentage of retail}}{100\% - \text{markup as a percentage of retail}} = \text{Markup as a percentage of cost}$$

$$\frac{\text{Markup as a percentage of cost}}{100\% + \text{markup as a percentage of cost}} = \text{Markup as a percentage of retail}$$

the person setting the price for an article in the group that costs $5 per unit would arrive at $10 as the selling price of a unit. This relationship can be determined through reference to the appropriate columns in Table 11-2.

Or, if one were using the formula method:

$$
\begin{aligned}
\text{Cost} + \text{markup} &= \text{Retail} \\
\$5 \quad + 50\% \quad &= 100\% \\
\$5 \quad &= 100\% - 50\% \\
\$5 \quad &= 50\% \\
\$5 \quad + 50\% \quad &= \$10 = \text{Retail}
\end{aligned}
$$

If this store were using the cost markup method, however, and wished to secure a retail price that would involve a markup of 50% on cost, the resulting price would be $7.50.

$$
\begin{aligned}
\text{Cost } (100\%) + \text{markup } (50\%) &= \text{Retail} \\
\$5 \quad + \quad \$2.50 &= \$7.50
\end{aligned}
$$

RATE-OF-RETURN PRICING

One way of obtaining the pricing objective of a target return on investment is by using the **rate-of-return pricing** method. This type of price determination relates selling price to sales volume. The desired rate of return may be attained through either a low selling price and a high volume or a high selling price and a low volume. The two approaches may yield similar results since the return from the sales of five items for a profit of one dollar each is equivalent to the sale of one item for a profit of five dollars. Discount department stores follow the former approach, while traditional department stores adhere to the latter approach. If the unit sales of a product can be estimated, then a selling price can be determined which will achieve the desired return on investment.

VARIABLE COST PRICING

Although management generally desires a selling price that covers variable costs, fixed costs, and a profit, circumstances may arise where only covering variable costs is used as a basis for pricing a product. **Variable costs** are the escapable or out-of-pocket costs such as labor and materials, which are only incurred when units are produced. **Fixed costs** are the inescapable costs, such as plant, equipment, and other overhead expenses, which are present regardless of the number of units produced.

In some instances a private brander secures goods from a national brand manufacturer who determines the selling price for the private brand on a variable cost basis. Since the national brand manufacturer already has the plant and equipment to produce its own brand, it only needs to add another shift of workers and to purchase additional materials in order to produce the private brand. If the manufacturer can sell the private brand item at a price greater than the variable cost, the additional markup received is a contribution to the fixed costs. The use of variable cost pricing provides a partial explanation of why private brand goods are often lower priced to the consumer than similar national brand goods.

BREAK-EVEN ANALYSIS PRICING

The break-even point for a product is the amount of volume needed to cover its total variable and fixed costs. When sales move beyond the break-even point, profits begin to generate rapidly. **Break-even analysis** is intended primarily to furnish management with information concerning the outcome of different combinations of prices, costs, and quantities. Its major importance is not in price determination, but in comparing alternative prices in reference to their effect on the break-even point.

AVERAGE COST PRICING

The **average cost** is determined by dividing total costs by the total units sold. Total cost is composed of both total variable and fixed costs. In determining a price based on average cost, management assumes that forecasted sales will be similar to past sales. If actual sales are less than the forecast, the fixed costs may not be completely covered and losses may occur. On the other hand, if sales are much larger than the forecast, profits will be greater than expected. The requirement by the government to seek sealed bids on many of its procurements frequently finds prospective suppliers submitting bids which were determined by the average cost pricing method.

Market or Competitive Approach

Although management desires to cover its costs, market factors may exert strong influences on pricing. The basic market approaches include: (1) prevailing market prices, (2) customary or convenient prices, (3) competitive factors, (4) what the traffic will bear, and (5) price leadership.

PREVAILING MARKET PRICES

If a particular price for a product becomes accepted, a manufacturer may be compelled to price the product at the **prevailing market price**. Working backward from the selling price, the manufacturer is forced to determine the costs. Many producers of standardized products conform to established market prices. Because of the nature of agricultural products, the prices received by farmers are usually those prevailing in a central market.

CUSTOMARY OR CONVENIENT PRICES

A variation of prevailing market prices is **customary** or **convenient prices**. Some convenience goods which have a low unit price and are purchased frequently adapt themselves to customary prices. Candy bars and soft drinks are usually sold for a customary amount which is a multiple of five, such as 15, 20, or 25 cents. In some cases a producer will adjust the size or the quality of the product rather than change from the customary price.

COMPETITIVE FACTORS

In instances where a new product effectively competes with an older product, the price of the older product will often determine the price of the new product. As explained on page 219, this is a form of cross-elasticity of demand. In the carpet industry the different synthetic fibers, such as olefin, kodel, dacron, and nylon, may be substituted for one another. Consequently, all of these fibers have similar pricing structures.

WHAT THE TRAFFIC WILL BEAR

Although this phrase has a rather unpleasant sound since it implies excessively high profits, it is nevertheless a rather widely used indicator of the upper limits to the prices that may be set by sellers. Sellers who know their market are aware of the price limits above which they cannot go and retain their customers. These limits cut across many of the other factors that enter into the price-determining procedures. **What the traffic will bear** reflects the attitude of the users of the product toward its value to them. Thus, a special instrument that will aid a surgeon in performing a difficult operation might be worth $100, even though it might cost only $15 to produce. The value may be in greater safety or comfort for the patient, more effective performance by the surgeon, or improved operating techniques.

PRICE LEADERSHIP

In any business field there may be certain acknowledged leaders who apparently set their prices without too much regard for the other members of the trade but whose price moves are rather quickly followed by their competitors. To a considerable extent the United States Steel Corporation in the steel business and the various Standard Oil companies in the field of gasoline and oil have been price leaders. The reasons for this **price leadership** are usually prestige, size, aggressiveness, and prominence.

PRICING POLICIES

Carefully designed pricing policies provide assurance that everyone involved in pricing within an organization will make similar pricing decisions. Product managers, sales managers, and others are involved in determining prices in a large organization with several product lines. Several of the more prominent pricing policies that will be discussed include: (1) high prices, competitive prices, and low prices; (2) skimming versus penetration pricing; (3) odd prices; (4) delivered prices; (5) price lining; (6) one price versus varying price; (7) leader pricing and bait pricing; and (8) discount policy.

High Prices, Competitive Prices, and Low Prices

A seller caters to different segments of the market by choosing either a high price, a competitive price, or a low price policy. Some firms produce a quality product and charge a high price, in the hope that it will become known as the "Cadillac of the industry." Many manufacturers and merchants such as Sears and J. C. Penney's price their products competitively to appeal to the majority of American consumers. Some sellers such as discount department stores use low prices as their principal sales appeal.

Skimming Versus Penetration Pricing

Skimming the cream pricing is a high price policy generally associated with a product in the initial stages of its life cycle. If a high price will not necessarily restrict demand or result in the emergence of potential competitors, a skimming policy may be quite appropriate. Du Pont has found price skimming to be very successful when introducing new specialty products.

Penetration pricing, a type of low pricing policy, is used by some firms to secure a dominant position in the market for a new product. When a new product is introduced into a highly competitive market, penetration pricing, which discourages potential competition, is the most appropriate pricing strategy. For product introductions the Alberto-Culver Company, an important producer in the competitive health and beauty aids industry, uses a market penetration policy.

Odd Prices

One school of merchandising thought believes that $2.95 is a more appealing price than $3, that 19 cents will sell more goods than 20 cents, and

$99.95 is more effective than $100. The underlying theory of this **odd-price policy** is that $1.98 makes the prospective buyer think of $1 plus some cents, rather than of a price slightly less than $2. That this concept is widely held is apparent from an inspection of the price lines of many stores of all types.

Delivered Prices

Some manufacturers adopt the policy of establishing their prices on what is called a "delivered basis." This means that the price quoted to buyers is **f.o.b.** (free on board) **destination**. It includes all transportation costs and is the price that buyers must pay to take delivery of the goods at their receiving docks or the freight terminal in their cities.

Opposed to this plan is the practice of quoting **f.o.b. shipping point** (or factory), that is, the seller will place the goods on a common carrier at the factory loading dock and all further transportation charges over and above the quoted price are to be paid by the buyer. The pricing of automobiles is an example of this latter policy. Some sellers located in the eastern part of the country take account of transportation costs by advertising "prices slightly higher west of the Mississippi River."

Price Lining

By limiting the prices for their goods to a few specific pricing points, retailers adopt a policy of **price lining**. Edward A. Filene, founder of Boston's Filene's department store, advocated only three major price points for each class of merchandise. For example, in the case of men's sport coats there would be only three price points: $49.95, $59.95, and $69.95. The advantages cited for a policy of price lining are that it: (a) simplifies consumer buying decisions, (b) makes the retail buyer's job easier, and (c) produces more rapid stock turnover.

One Price Versus Varying Price

Most retail pricing uses the **one-price policy**, that is, the established price applies to all comers and is not subject to haggling by individual customers. At other sales levels, however, this policy does not always hold true. Although some manufacturers and wholesalers follow it rather rigidly, many others may lower their prices from time to time in favor of particular purchasers. This flexibility of price may come about because of the superior bargaining skill of certain buyers or because of the size of their purchases.

A **varying price policy** has the effect of enabling large buyers to secure lower prices than their smaller competitors. To prevent this practice from placing small buyers at too great a disadvantage, the Robinson-Patman Act, which forbids certain types of uneconomic price discrimination, was passed by Congress.

Leader Pricing and Bait Pricing

Both leader pricing and bait pricing are examples of promotional pricing policies. In **leader pricing** a high-demand good, such as most convenience goods, is priced low and promoted highly to attract customers into a store. The leader item may be sold at cost or even below cost, making it a **loss leader**. Once a customer is in the store to purchase a leader item, there is a high probability that he or she will make numerous unplanned purchases.

Bait pricing involves advertising a low-priced model of shopping goods, such as furniture or appliances, to lure customers into a store. Once the customers are in the store, a salesperson attempts to persuade them to purchase higher-priced models. In many cases the compensation plan for the retail sales personnel strongly encourages them to trade a customer up from the bait model to a more expensive product. When the Federal Trade Commission becomes aware that the "bait and switch" practice is being used, the Commission orders retailers to discontinue its use.

Discount Policy

Sellers who elect to pursue a varying price policy have two principal methods by which they may put this plan into effect: (a) through simple price concessions, and (b) by means of a discount policy. An example of the first method is the lowering of a price of $1.50 per unit to $1.35. A **discount** may be defined as a reduction in price made by a seller to a buyer. Trade discounts, quantity discounts, and cash discounts are frequently offered by sellers to buyers in commercial transactions.

A **trade discount**, which is based on the list price of the product, recognizes the different functions performed by wholesalers and retailers. For example, if the list price, which is frequently the price charged the retail customer, is $45 and the trade discount is $33\frac{1}{3}$ percent, the wholesaler's price to the retailer is $30.

A **quantity discount**, which may be either cumulative or noncumulative, is often granted to buyers who order in large quantities. Presumably the large sales which occur as a result of this policy save the vendors storage, shipping, and billing costs. Cumulative quantity discounts permit buyers to utilize two or more separate purchases in the computation of the quantities to which discounts may apply, whereas the noncumulative type is applicable only to single purchases.

A **cash discount** is an inducement offered by the seller to encourage buyers to pay their bills within a short time after the goods have been delivered. The cash discount takes many forms, the most common of which is 2/10, net 30; that is, if the invoice is paid within 10 days after its date, the buyer may deduct 2 percent from the amount of the invoice; otherwise, the full amount is due in 30 days.

PRICE LEGISLATION

In a number of instances both federal and state legislation affect prices directly or indirectly. The federal price-control plans that were in effect during the periods of World War II, the Korean War, and the post-Vietnam War were intended to prevent prices from rising under the stress of an unbalanced supply-demand situation. After its involvement in the various wage-price control programs of the early 1970s, the federal government, aside from persuasion and threats, has restricted its activities in this area to legislation providing support prices for certain agricultural and dairy commodities and petroleum products.

The actions of the various states in regard to price legislation fall into two categories: fair trade laws, which legalize resale price maintenance; and unfair trade laws (with some variations on this title), which endeavor to establish minimum price levels below which goods cannot be sold. The major federal legislation on pricing is the Robinson-Patman Act, which attempts to prevent certain types of price discrimination.

Fair Trade Laws

Acting under the authority of the various state **fair trade laws**, passed in most states during the depression of the 1930s, manufacturers could execute contracts with retailers specifying the prices below which their branded products may not be sold. Two pieces of enabling legislation, the Miller-Tydings Act of 1937 and the McGuire Act of 1952, exempted the state fair trade laws from the federal antitrust statutes which prohibit price-fixing. During the 1960s a U.S. Justice Department economic survey found that consumers in fair trade states paid from 19 to 27 percent higher prices on fair traded goods than consumers in the other states. In the mid-1970s, as an anti-inflation move, Congress repealed the enabling legislation which permits fair trade pricing.

Unfair Trade Laws

Unfair trade laws, operative in nearly half the states under such diverse titles as unfair trade practices act, unfair sales act, unfair practices act, unfair sales practices act, and fair sales act, have a common theme. Under them, sellers — producers, wholesalers, and retailers — are forbidden to sell goods at less than their cost plus, in many states, certain specified percentage markups. These laws, like the fair trade laws, are designed to prevent price cutting and have sometimes been called "anti-loss-leader" laws, since the form of price cutting against which they were ostensibly enacted has been the loss leader. Unlike the fair trade laws, however, which affect only goods bearing a producer's brand and then only if the manufacturer wishes the price maintained, the unfair trade laws apply to all products branded or not. Several states have similar laws applicable to specific commodities, such as cigarettes, dairy products, gasoline, bakery products, and alcoholic beverages.

Robinson-Patman Act

At the time when the Robinson-Patman Act was passed in 1936, small businesses were pressing legislators for laws against price-cutting by chain stores. Between 1920 and 1930 chain operators had dramatically increased their share of total retail sales from 5 to 30 percent. Many individuals felt that there was a need to curtail all uneconomic practices conducted by large chain organizations. In fact, the Robinson-Patman Act was initially referred to as the anti-A&P act, since one of the most famous cases under the act involved the A&P chain. The major provision of the act makes it unlawful for a seller to discriminate in price between different buyers of goods of like grade and quality where the effect of such discrimination may be substantially to lessen competition or to create a monopoly.

PRICING THEORY

Economists have advanced several theories to explain how the price of any given commodity is set, the movement of prices, and why the price level is where it is at any one time. The equilibrium theory of prices, which is based upon the assumptions of pure competition (see Chapter 1, page 11), probably has the largest number of adherents among economists.

Equilibrium Theory

The **equilibrium theory of prices** assumes that two forces operate in the field of price — supply and demand. These forces bring about a price at which the quantity demanded by buyers equals the quantity that sellers are willing to supply. Some of the units of the commodity that are necessary to make up this quantity are produced by those whose costs of production are so high that there is little or no profit, but who decide, nevertheless, to stay in business.

The theory further assumes that if the current price for a commodity is found to be above the theoretical equilibrium point, two things will happen which will force the price downward: (a) the higher price will discourage would-be buyers, thereby reducing the quantity demanded; and (b) the opportunity for profits afforded by the higher price will attract new producers into the field, whose added products will increase the quantity supplied. The effect of this reduced demand and increased supply will be to reduce the price, probably below the equilibrium point. When this takes place, the results are the reverse of the condition just described: (a) the lowered price attracts buyers, increasing the quantity demanded; and (b) the diminished profits which then occur force some high-cost producers to leave the field, thereby reducing the quantity supplied. This brings about an upward movement of price toward the equilibrium point.

Figure 11-1 shows a graphic representation of the operation of the equilibrium theory. Curve *D-D'* represents the quantities of the product that could be sold at the various price levels. Curve *S-S'* represents the quantities that sellers would be willing to supply at the different price levels. Point *P*, where 500 units would be demanded at $5 each, portrays the point of equilibrium where demand and supply are equal.

Certain circumstances exist in business today which reduce the significance of the equilibrium theory. For example, for some individuals the factors of quality, service, and vendors' prestige have as much influence as price on their purchases. In some instances firms enjoy certain aspects of monopoly

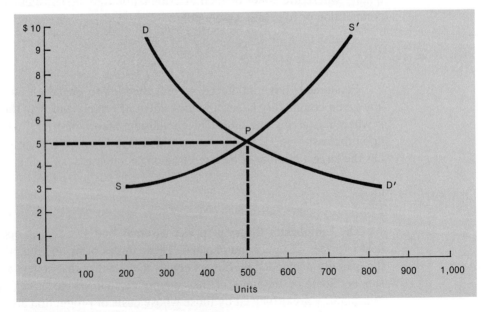

Figure 11-1   *Graphic Illustration of the Equilibrium Theory*

Part Three / MARKETING

because of location, control of natural resources, and patent protection. Brand influences cause many consumers to demand the products of certain manufacturers and to disregard the value of competing brands. The one-price system which prevails in most retail stores severely reduces the customer's ability to bargain for a good. Finally, numerous consumers show an indifference toward product prices by failing to heed informative advertising or by neglecting to make price comparisons at competing stores.

Demand Elasticity

Demand elasticity refers to the effect that a change in the price for an item has on the quantity demanded. If changing the price of an article produces a significant alteration in the quantity demanded, it has **demand elasticity** or an **elastic demand**. Likewise, if a price change does not bring about a significant difference in the quantity demanded, the article has **inelasticity of demand**. The assumption is, of course, that the quantity demanded will move in the opposite direction from price. Examples of goods with demand elasticity are the items advertised by grocery stores as weekend specials, such as breakfast foods. The classic example of demand inelasticity is salt; regardless of the price of salt, people use a fixed amount.

As used by many economists, the demand elasticity concept embraces the idea of an actual change in the total demand for a product. There is, however, another aspect of this subject that is reflected in the action of consumers who switch from brand *A* of a product to brand *B* when the price of the latter is lowered. In such a circumstance the total demand for the basic product remains unchanged, but the sales of brand *B* have increased at the expense of brand *A*. This is known as **cross elasticity of demand**. Although it is probable that most retailers have never heard of these terms, they are usually quite aware of the items whose sales can be increased through price cutting and act accordingly. The weekly specials of supermarkets embody this type of selective price cutting and are illustrative of price competition at the retail level.

Monopoly Price

The presence of a monopoly implies the complete control of the price by the monopolist and the absence of competition. In the business world at large there are very few pure monopolies. Those which do exist, such as the public utilities in most localities, are subject to governmental regulation to the extent that their freedom to set their prices is greatly if not completely curtailed. With this type of monopoly this discussion is concerned only to the extent of pointing out that prices are established or changed only with the consent of some governmental regulatory commission.

Oligopoly Price

In an industry where a few large firms are dominant, where all products are similar, and where total demand is relatively inelastic, an **oligopolistic pricing** situation occurs. Firms in the automobile, major appliance, and basic commodity industries, such as steel, aluminum, and petroleum, are confronted with this type of pricing. As shown in Figure 11-2, the demand curve for a company in an oligopolistic industry is a **kinked demand curve** rather than the gently curving one illustrated in Figure 11-1. The demand curve is kinked because if one firm reduces its price, all other firms in the oligopolistic industry follow. Since a price-cutting firm experiences no significant increase in demand or market share, other forms of competition, such as promotional or service competition, replace price competition in an oligopoly. Frequently a major firm in an oligopolistic industry assumes price leadership and maintains its price at the kink, which is the market price.

Monopolistic Competition

When two or more sellers of goods that satisfy the same needs or wants strive to persuade the same groups of buyers to purchase their wares, competition is said to exist. This applies to all levels of economic activity — manufacturers, wholesalers, and retailers. In the case of certain agricultural products, and possibly a few others, the fact that there is little if any difference

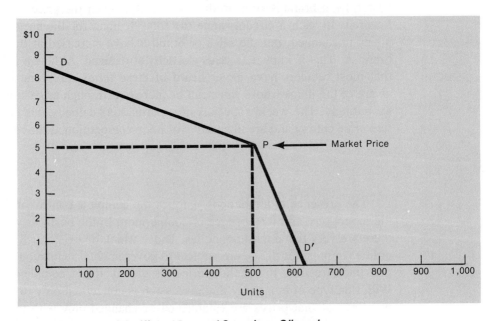

Figure 11-2   **Graphic Illustration of the Kinked Demand Curve in an Oligopoly**

between the products of different producers places competition very largely on a strictly price basis. This situation is probably as close to the economists' concept of pure competition as is to be found in our economic system. With most other products, however, producers can differentiate their products to a greater or lesser extent and, by engaging in monopolistic competition, escape the rigors of pure price competition.

PRICE INDEXES AND TRENDS

The federal government prepares two commonly accepted measures of the general price level: (1) the Consumer Price Index and (2) the Wholesale Price Index. These indexes are used widely as a reflection of inflationary or deflationary trends in the economy.

Consumer Price Index

Representing a market basket of about 400 goods and services purchased by city wage earners and clerical workers' families, the **Consumer Price Index** (CPI), which is prepared monthly by the Labor Department's Bureau of Labor Statistics, serves as a measure of the cost of living. In preparing the index, different prices are given different weights with food and housing prices given the heaviest weights. In recent years the CPI has been used widely as a measure of changes in the purchasing power of the dollar. Automatic wage adjustments known as escalator clauses and based on changes in the index are incorporated in numerous labor-management contracts. In addition, reference to the CPI is frequently used to adjust the following types of payments: (a) welfare, (b) pension, (c) rent on commercial buildings, (d) federal food lunch program, and (e) alimony.

Beginning in April, 1977, the Bureau of Labor Statistics will issue two consumer price indexes. The older index, which reflects the spending pattern of only the 45 percent of our population who are urban wage and clerical workers, is retained. The new index, which also includes salaried workers, professional workers, the self-employed, retired workers, and unemployed workers, covers about 80 percent of the population and provides a comprehensive measure of price trends for the entire economy. The expanded index is needed because an increasing number of groups are using the CPI for determining escalation payments and because it is the most widely used monthly indicator of inflationary pressures for the entire economy.

Wholesale Price Index

Representing the most broadly based measure of prices, the **Wholesale Price Index** (WPI) is an aggregate of price changes of nearly 2,500 specified

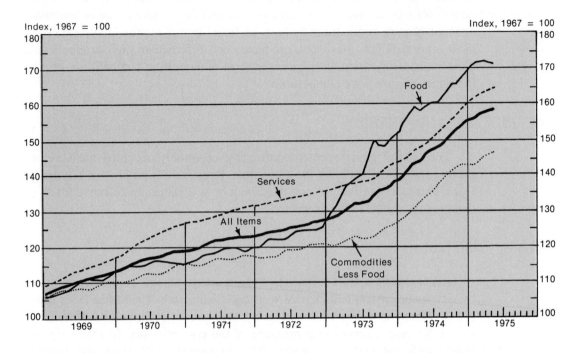

Index, 1967 = 100

Index, 1967 = 100

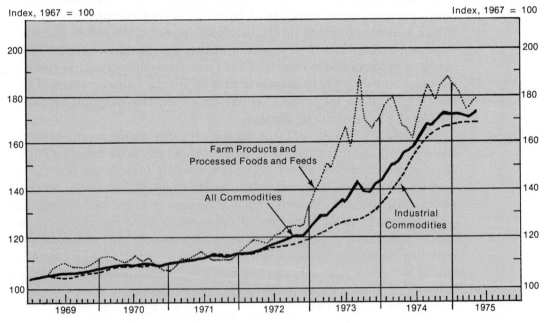

Index, 1967 = 100

Index, 1967 = 100

SOURCE: *Economic Indicators* (May, 1975), pp. 26–27. Prepared for the Joint Economic Committee by the Council of Economic Advisers.

Figure 11-3 **Price Development**

items. The WPI, which is usually the price paid to a producer or to a manufacturer, is designed to measure price changes at the first significant stage of commercial transaction. Included in this index are prices of items such as canned pork and beans, iron ore, milling machines, motor trucks, oil of lavender, and razor blades. Services (except for gas and electricity purchased for commercial use), transportation, and construction activities are excluded from the index. In this index intermediate products, such as parts and semi-manufactured goods, and finished products are given the heaviest weights, 45 percent and 44 percent respectively; materials are given a lesser weight of 11 percent. To provide the businessperson with specific measures of prices, the Bureau of Labor Statistics provides wholesale price change information for individual commodity groups and subgroups. Figure 11-3 illustrates the trend of consumer and wholesale prices since 1967.

BUSINESS TERMS

QUESTIONS FOR DISCUSSION AND ANALYSIS

1. Does nonprice competition at the retail level provide consumers with values as good as those provided by price competition? Explain.
2. Discuss why different companies have different pricing goals.
3. Is the cost approach in pricing a more justifiable approach than the market or competitive approach? Explain.
4. Should a hardware retailer take a uniform markup, such as 50 percent, on all goods sold? Discuss. How should the markup be established on the goods?
5. Explain how you would determine the price for a newly developed light bulb which is guaranteed never to burn out when used under normal operating conditions.

6. Do you believe that for a retailer an odd-price policy is an effective pricing policy?
7. Is leader pricing more ethical than bait pricing? Examine the reasons for your answers.
8. Should the government be allowed to control the prices of goods? What are the probable long-run effects of government-approved price controls?
9. Do retailers benefit more from fair trade laws than from unfair trade laws? Discuss.
10. Is the Consumer Price Index a better measure of the cost of living than the Wholesale Price Index? Explain. Would your answer be different if you were talking to a businessperson rather than a consumer?

PROBLEMS AND SHORT CASES

1. Using the retail price markup table or the formulas on page 209 that are applicable, calculate the answers to the following problems:
   a. Markup on cost is 25%, cost is $16. Find the retail selling price.
   b. Markup on cost is 66.7%, retail price is $8.95. Find the cost.
   c. Markup on retail price is 33.3%, cost is $20. Find the retail price.
   d. Markup on retail price is 35%, retail price is $50. Find the cost.
2. a. A cosmetic manufacturer receives from a retailer an order for 125 bottles of a particular cologne. The cologne is sold at a list price of $15.00 a bottle. The retailer receives from the manufacturer a 45 percent trade discount and an additional 2 percent quantity discount on the total order if it exceeds 100 bottles. How much should the retailer remit to the manufacturer?
   b. A retailer purchases $2,640 worth of merchandise; the terms are 4/10, net 30. The invoice is dated June 23 and is paid on June 30. How much is remitted to the seller?
   c. A manufacturer purchases a $5,000 conveyor for use in his plant. The supplier's terms are 2/10, net 60. The invoice is dated March 3 and paid May 1. How much is remitted to the supplier?

3. Within the past year, Dianne Diston opened a new dinner club in Grand Forks, North Dakota, called the Gourmet Inn. Although patronage was heavy on Saturday, holidays, and Sunday noon, business was very light on weekdays and Sunday evenings. Realizing she had a large overhead to cover, Ms. Diston developed and advertised the following promotional program to attract additional diners:

Gourmet Inn
Dinner Club Membership
The membership entitles you to receive 12 complimentary dinners of your choice as a member of the Gourmet Inn Dinner Club. You may dine twelve (12) times within the next year any day or evening, except Saturday nights, holidays, and Sunday before 3 P.M. in one of our elegant dining rooms. All you need to do is be accompanied by one guest. Then you pay for only one of the two dinners. The membership fee is just $20 for the entire year. To insure the finest service, the number of members in our Dinner Club membership must necessarily be limited. We suggest, therefore, that you place your order as soon as possible before the roster is filled.

As indicated by the promotional program, what are the pricing objectives of Ms. Diston? Identify and discuss the approach taken by Ms. Diston in determining her selling price for the Dinner Club membership.

12 Marketing and Consumer Issues

Bon Vivant Soups, Inc., is a family-operated business that was founded over 100 years ago. In July, 1971, a Bedford Village, N.Y., man died after consuming a can of its vichyssoise, a cold potato soup. The government charged that the soup was tainted with deadly botulin, a toxin that affects the nervous system. As a result, the government ordered the recall of nearly 1.5 million cans of soup from the firm's Newark plant, its wholesalers, and retailers across the country. The company suspended all operations and had to file bankruptcy. The president of the company, Maria Paretti, stated, "All we've ever been is quality. One human error and over 100 years of reputation goes down the drain. I'd say that's a bum rap."

The consumer movement of the late 1960s and the 1970s is not unique in the history of the United States. Consumer unrest occurred even during the early 1900s and the 1930s. During both of these earlier eras, rising food prices produced consumer boycotts, consumer protection groups, and crusading journalists who sought consumer protection legislation.

The latest era of consumer movement began in the middle 1960s when food prices began an upward surge. Since the price increases were on frequently purchased items, such as beef, pork, and eggs, they were particularly evident to homemakers. In October, 1966, homemakers in Denver expressed their dissatisfaction with rising prices by picketing supermarkets. During this same period politicians began initiating consumer protection legislation, and consumers began forming information and protection groups.

MEANING OF CONSUMERISM

Several definitions of consumerism have been advanced. Some individuals feel that the old expression of caveat emptor or "let the buyer beware" should be modified to "let the seller beware." After a thorough study of the reasons for the consumer movement, two marketing experts have aptly defined **consumerism** as "the organized efforts of consumers seeking redress, restitution, and remedy for dissatisfactions they have accumulated in the acquisition of their standard of living."[1] This definition conveys the sense of frustration which motivates consumers to protective action.

The present consumer movement is not a unified effort, but it is an alliance of many individual interests. The groups in this alliance include: (a) labor unions, (b) consumer cooperatives, (c) credit unions, (d) consumer educators, (e) product-testing groups, (f) consumer education organizations, (g) state and local consumer groups, and (h) other organizations with complementary interests, such as senior citizens' groups. The problem of maintaining harmonious accord in the consumer movement is extremely difficult because of the diverse groups within the movement. For example, any discussion which affects the vested interests of these dissimilar groups, such as the effect of the monopoly power of labor unions on consumer prices, is severely restricted.

There is not only a difference of opinion on the problems and priorities within the movement, but there is also a difference of views concerning the objectives of consumerism. The following three classifications identify these viewpoints:

1. The **Adaptationists**, who emphasize educating consumers to avoid fraud and deception and seek to prepare them to deal intelligently with the market as it is. This group sees little need for new consumer protection legislation and gets along comfortably with consumer service specialists in industry and with business and trade association representatives. Many consumer educators fall into this category.
2. The **Protectionists**, whose primary concern is with health and safety issues involving the possibility of physical harm to the individual. This group includes scientists, physicians, nutritionists, and other professionals.
3. The **Reformers**, who like the Adaptationists want to improve consumer education and who like the Protectionists want to insure the individual's health and safety, and who, moreover, seek to increase the consumer's voice in government and the amount of product information available to the public. This group consists chiefly of political liberals with a variety of professional affiliations.[2]

FACTORS GIVING RISE TO THE CONSUMER MOVEMENT

The major factors which contributed to the current consumer movement included: (1) rising consumer expectations, (2) increasing product complexity,

[1]Reprinted from Richard H. Buskirk and James T. Rothe, "Consumerism — An Interpretation," *Journal of Marketing*, Vol. 34 (October, 1970), p. 63, published by the American Marketing Association.

[2]Reprinted from Robert O. Herrmann, "Consumerism: Its Goals, Organization and Future," *Journal of Marketing*, Vol. 34 (October, 1970) p. 57, published by the American Marketing Association.

(3) expanding consumer demand, (4) continuing full employment, and (5) crusading consumerists.[3]

Rising Consumer Expectations

Consumers become frustrated when they seek products to enhance their individuality in a market which offers mainly mass-produced goods. Over the years businesspersons have promoted the increasing excellence of their products. Consumers have come to expect increasingly better products; and when they do not find better goods, they tend to suffer from unfulfilled expectations. For example, Consumers Union, a tester of consumer products, purchased 15 tape recorders costing several hundred dollars each and found nearly one third of them imperfect.

Increasing Product Complexity

Technological developments have permitted the production of more complex products. The malfunction of a complex product results in a service problem; and if the service is not properly performed, consumers become hostile toward the product and the servicing organization. For example, one survey of 90,000 owners of color television sets, of which most were less than three years old, revealed that 74 percent of the units had already received some type of repair.

Expanding Consumer Demand

During the 1960s business increased so rapidly that the resources of business could not be mobilized adequately to meet the expanding consumer demand. Firms were under pressure to move production into the marketplace regardless of cost and product quality. Elisha Gray II, chairman of Whirlpool Corporation, confesses that when a company makes or handles products numbering in the millions and involving budgets and sales of millions or billions of dollars, it's fairly easy to lose sight of the fact that it has to satisfy its customers one at a time.

Continuing Full Employment

Full employment has resulted in the employment of marginal workers who perform poorly, causing quality problems. This marginal performance is

[3]These factors were present during the late 1960s and the early 1970s.

particularly found in the product repair field. No one wants to be an appliance repairer or an auto mechanic when the pay and working conditions are better in factories. The director of General Motors' service division cited the problem in his statement that ten years ago management in a dealer's repair shop had reasonably good control over its personnel; but as labor shortages increased, there was a corresponding loss of control.

Crusading Consumerists

Individual crusaders have rallied political support for consumer protection. Ralph Nader, Vance Packard, Rachel Carson, David Caplovitz, and Maurine Newberger, each of whom has written one or more books and treatises on topics related to consumerism, gave impetus to the consumer movement. The success of the writings of these individuals can be attributed in part to an increasing social concern, which makes large corporations vulnerable to consumer attacks. Independent programs undertaken by two prominent crusading consumerists are discussed on pages 235–237.

CONSUMER COMPLAINTS

Certain types of consumer complaints are more widely voiced than others. Table 12-1 indicates that the key areas of consumer frustration are: (a) defective products, (b) defective service, (c) overcharging, (d) false and misleading ads, and (e) products or services that do not meet the requirements of consumers. As shown in Table 12-1, the importance of various consumer complaints changed between 1970 and 1974. A large decrease occurred in the

Table 12-1   **Types of Consumer Complaints**

	Percentage of Complaints[1]	
	1970	1974
Defective product or part	32	25
Defective service	16	25
Overcharging	23	16
False, misleading ad	17	14
Product or service did not measure up	3	12
Misrepresentation of financial arrangements	2	6
Deceptive or defective packaging	25	4
Shortweighting	5	2
Warranty or guarantee coverage	3	2
Deceptive pricing	5	1

SOURCE: Speech by Kenneth Schwartz, Opinion Research Corporation, Princeton, New Jersey, at American Marketing Association Regional Conference, Ball State University, October, 1974.

[1]Since consumers could identify more than one complaint, the columns total more than 100.

frequency of complaints concerning deceptive or defective packaging. Possibly this decrease is related to the passage and enforcement of the "Truth in Packaging" legislation.

Table 12-2 identifies the products or services which cause the largest number of consumer complaints. In 1974 automobiles and appliances accounted for nearly half of all consumer complaints.

Knowledge of the types of consumer complaints is particularly important for management, consumer groups, and legislators. As a result of recognizing the product and service problems within a company, the managers are able to take corrective actions. If consumer groups believe that the managers are unresponsive to consumer complaints, then these groups will publicize the unresponsiveness and seek remedial legislation.

GOVERNMENTAL RESPONSE TO CONSUMERISM

Legislators have reacted to the consumer movement by proposing various types of consumer legislation. The bills on consumer issues fall into three major categories. One category is designed to upgrade the effectiveness of existing consumer programs, such as those conducted by the Federal Trade Commission (FTC) and other regulatory agencies. Another group of laws involve the health and safety of consumers, such as safety standards for automobiles and safeguards for food, drug, and cosmetic products. A third category of consumer bills attempts to strengthen an individual's economic bargaining power in areas such as credit information and warranties. Some of the more significant legislation produced by the consumer movement is described in this section.

Truth in Packaging Act

In 1966 the Truth in Packaging Act, which was originally intended as a lever for use by the FTC and the Food and Drug Administration (FDA) in

Table 12-2   *Products or Services Causing Largest Number of Consumer Complaints*

	Percentage of Complaints	
	1970	1974
Automobiles	10	27
Appliances and electronic products	10	20
Food and groceries	37	18
Housing and home furnishings	4	12
Insurance	0	6
Other	39	17

SOURCE: Speech by Kenneth Schwartz, Opinion Research Corporation, Princeton, New Jersey, at American Marketing Association Regional Conference, Ball State University, October, 1974.

eliminating deceptive food, drug, and cosmetic packages and prices, was legislated by Congress. The law basically requires the weight or volume of consumer items to be clearly and prominently identified in simple terms, such as 23 ounces instead of 1 7/16 pounds. In addition, the Commerce Department is compelled to seek voluntary agreements from industry to reduce the number of package sizes. An example of the difficulties facing the regulators was illustrated in the toothpaste industry where a "medium" tube of Colgate, a "large" size of Crest, and a "giant" tube of Pepsodent all contained the same amount of toothpaste, 3.25 ounces.

Consumer Credit Acts

Since most consumers apply 18 to 20 percent of their disposable income to the repayment of credit obligations, legislation is needed to protect against credit abuses. The Truth in Lending Act of 1969 requires that consumers be informed of all direct and indirect costs of credit buying. Many of the problems women have experienced in getting credit are being corrected by the Equal Credit Opportunity Act of 1975. The Fair Credit Billing Act of 1975 eliminates certain unfair credit practices and assists consumers in resolving billing disputes.

Consumer Protection Act

During the early 1970s several consumer protection acts were placed before Congress. Each of the bills had similar provisions. Although the bills were initially defeated, the ultimate passage of a Consumer Protection Act was anticipated. Such a bill would provide legal underpinning to the White House's Office of Consumer Affairs, create an Agency for Consumer Advocacy to coordinate federal consumer programs and to represent the interests of consumers before federal agencies, and establish a Consumer Advisory Council to advise the Director of the Office of Consumer Affairs.

Broadened Powers of Regulatory Agencies

In addition to new legislation, the older regulatory agencies, such as the FTC, the Interstate Commerce Commission (ICC), and the FDA, under the prodding of consumer forces, have discovered that their powers are much broader than previously exercised.

The FTC has the authority to order **corrective ads** and to impose refunds to customers in cases where money was obtained by deception. One of the first corrective ads emerged from an FTC consent order imposed on the ITT Continental Baking Company and its advertising agency, Ted Bates & Company. The consent order provided that for one year at least 25 percent of the advertising expenditures should be devoted to FTC-approved ads which would indicate that Profile bread is ineffective for weight reduction.

In a related action the FTC announced that it supports the use of **counter-advertising** by consumer groups in broadcast media. This type of advertising would counteract product claims and advertising themes which raise controversial issues. In the early 1970s the FTC moved to require advertisers in selected industries to provide proof of certain advertising claims. Seven United States and foreign automobile manufacturers, eleven air conditioner producers, and four electric shaver companies were the first concerns requested to document their advertisements.

In 1974 the FTC adopted a regulation requiring house-to-house salespersons to give customers a three-day cooling off period in which they may cancel a sale. The purpose of the three-day period is to provide the consumer with an opportunity to discuss the purchase with others, to reflect upon the provisions of the contract, and to do some comparison shopping. In 1975 the Magnuson-Moss Warranty and Federal Trade Commission Improvement Act broadened the authority of the FTC over product warranties. Manufacturers of any consumer product costing over $5 are required to use simple and concise language in their warranty agreements. In addition, companies must clearly identify whether their warranty coverages are full or limited.

National Commission on Product Safety

In 1968 the National Commission on Product Safety was created to identify the risks in household products and to suggest ways to protect consumers. In addition, the Commission is to review the effectiveness of industry self-regulation programs and of current federal, state, and local consumer protection legislation. The agency is using both persuasion and compulsion to accomplish its goals. As an illustration, the Commission convinced appliance manufacturers to install door latches inside freezers to prevent the entrapment and suffocation of children. In another example, the Federal Housing Administration (FHA) in cooperation with the Commission mandated that nonshattering safety glass be installed in sliding glass doors and glass panels of FHA-approved homes.

Businesspersons are concerned about the costs involved in the Safety Commission's actions. A balance should be struck between a desired safety level and the costs for achieving this level, not only for the businessperson who markets products, but also for the consumer who pays for the products.

Class-Action Lawsuits

Class-action lawsuits allow all consumers with a similar complaint about a product or an illegal selling practice to pool their damage claims against the seller and file a class-action suit in a federal court on behalf of all the injured parties. In the mid-1970s class-action suits were not allowed in federal courts unless each individual claim was a minimum of $10,000. Another costly restriction is that those initiating the suit must notify at their expense all members of the class who can be identified with a reasonable effort. This notification provides all identifiable parties in the class with the opportunity either to join the case actively or to remove themselves from it if they prefer not to be bound by the suit's final decision.

Special Assistant to the President for Consumer Affairs

The closest communication the consumer has to the President of the United States is through the office of the Special Assistant to the President for Consumer Affairs. The major purpose of this office is to monitor and resolve consumer complaints. In 1964 President Lyndon B. Johnson named Esther Peterson as the first individual to serve in this post. Three years later Mrs. Peterson was succeeded by Betty Furness, a former television celebrity.

In 1969 Virginia H. Knauer, the former head of Pennsylvania's first State Consumer Protection Bureau, was appointed to the position. One of her goals was to survey all existing federal consumer programs with the intention of making them more responsive to the needs and desires of consumers. Her study uncovered 400 consumer programs administered by 33 government agencies.

Natick Project

In 1970 the federal government initiated a pilot project at the U.S. Army Laboratory in Natick, Massachusetts, to show how complex buying specifications can be simplified into language that the average consumer can understand. The government purchases thousands of consumer goods according to highly technical specifications and issues buying reports using the same technical language. For example, to the question of what makes a good sunburn cream the government's response is, "Assuming a film thickness of 0.001 inch (approximately 2.5 milligrams per square centimeter), a sunscreen formulation, for good protection, should transmit not more than one percent of the harmful ultraviolet rays at 2,967 Angstroms. . . ."

INDEPENDENT PROGRAMS FOR CONSUMER PROTECTION

In addition to the governmental agencies which protect and provide information to the consumer, several independent organizations serve consumer interests. An objective of the majority of their programs is to provide consumers with information which will permit more enlightened buying decisions.

Consumers Union

The Consumers Union (CU) is a nonprofit, product-testing organization which publishes *Consumer Reports*. Subscribers to this publication receive comparative test reports on a variety of well-known products. CU believes that an informed consumer makes more intelligent buying decisions. To maintain its creditability the magazine has steadfastly refused to permit its product ratings to be used in advertising. For example, in 1970 CU sued the Theodore Hamm Brewing Company for $500,000 in damages for indicating in an ad that CU gave a high rating to Hamm's Beer.

In recent years CU has moved into other areas of consumer protection. In 1974 CU became the first private consumer organization — rather than an industry group — to be selected by the Consumer Product Safety Commission to develop safety standards for a consumer product. CU was given the assignment to devise mandatory safety standards for lawnmowers. In another action CU brought a federal court suit against both BankAmericard and American Express, which both offer credit card services to retailers. The purpose of the suit is to outlaw the contract provision which prohibits retailers who use the credit card services from giving discounts to their customers who pay cash. CU contends that the barring of such cash discounts is illegal price fixing.

Consumers' Research, Inc.

Another consumer-financed organization operating similarly to CU is Consumers' Research Incorporated, which publishes its ratings in *Consumers' Research Magazine*. Consumers' Research was established in 1929, while CU was established in 1936 as an offshoot of Consumers' Research. The older *Consumers' Research Magazine*, however, has only one tenth the circulation of *Consumer Reports*.

Both Consumers Union and Consumers' Research have experienced some difficulties in rating products for consumers. One of the obstacles is the limitation of funds and facilities for testing purposes. Another problem is that the product tests are often conducted under artificial rather than actual conditions. A third difficulty is that since some buyers place more emphasis on fashion than on measurable technical standards, the product ratings are not valid for a certain segment of consumers. A final problem is caused by the reaction of a firm to a low product rating. The company may attempt to improve its rating by upgrading only the specific product features which are tested while no effort is taken to improve the overall quality of the product.

Institutional Guaranty Seals

There are several product testing groups which issue seals and allow their names to be used in advertising. The Good Housekeeping Institute, which issues a **Consumer's Guaranty Seal**, is one of these. The Institute is complementary to the *Good Housekeeping* magazine and it tests every product before the item is advertised in the magazine. *Parents' Magazine* provides advertisers in that publication with the use of the **Parents' Magazine Guaranteed Seal.** *McCall's* tests new appliances and furnishings advertised in it. The tested products are eligible for a **Use-Tested tag** which shows the product name, how the product is tested, a Use-Tested report, specific features, and an endorsement by *McCall's*.

Private Testing Organizations

Private laboratories and testing organizations supply many firms with invaluable objective information about their products. The Underwriters' Laboratories (UL), which was originally sponsored by the National Board of Fire Underwriters, will test any item, but only for fire and safety hazards. Although UL has no policing authority, its seal of approval is virtually mandatory for manufacturers who desire to have their electrical products accepted by consumers. UL provides manufacturers with both the information on the types of tests given a product and on the safety requirements or standards devised for a product.

Other private testing laboratories include the United States Testing Laboratories and the Nationwide Consumer Testing Institute. The results of product tests by these laboratories are not made public unless a company desires to release the findings. The major function of these independent laboratories includes analyzing product performance, noting structural flaws, and testing prototype products.

Better Business Bureaus

The Better Business Bureau (BBB) is, perhaps, unique as a nationally known business-sponsored agency which serves the interests of consumers. As stated in Chapter 10, it was originally established to defend business firms against unethical competition. The mission of the bureaus is to investigate consumer complaints and to focus attention on firms which generate numerous consumer complaints. Critics state that the bureaus concentrate their policing efforts on marginal businesses while often ignoring consumer complaints about the stronger firms, such as major auto dealers and other large retail firms, that are bureau sponsors. These bureaus, however, are not empowered or staffed to initiate lawsuits, make collections, rate products, evaluate pricing policies, or judge product quality.

In 1970 the Council of Better Business Bureaus was established to make the local bureaus more responsive to consumer needs. An unusual program instituted by the Council is a free arbitration service to consumers and businesspersons. If disputes cannot be resolved through the Council's mediation efforts, the disputants may empower an arbitration panel to determine a binding settlement.

Consumer Crusaders and Their Programs

During any type of social movement, certain individuals arise from the shadows of the movement to command respect and to assume leadership. The consumer movement has provided several prominent leaders, all with their own consumer programs. The activities of two of these leaders will be examined in some detail.

NADER ORGANIZATIONS

Ralph Nader is the best known of the consumer protection advocates. In 1969 Nader, who insists that he is not anti-business but simply "pro-people," was instrumental in General Motors' action to drop the Corvair. Sales of Corvairs plummeted 93 percent after Nader declared the car a safety hazard in his successful book, *Unsafe at Any Speed*. As an advocate, muckraker, and crusader, lawyer Nader has been influential in obtaining the enactment of the following major pieces of consumer legislation:

1. The National Traffic and Motor Vehicle Safety Act of 1966.
2. The Wholesome Meat Act of 1967.
3. The Natural Gas Pipeline Safety Act, the Radiation Control for Health and Safety Act, and the Wholesale Poultry Products Act, all of 1968.
4. The Federal Coal Mine Health and Safety Act of 1969.
5. The Comprehensive Occupational Safety and Health Act of 1970.

Nader's Raiders. In the late 1960s Nader's crusading efforts spawned several Nader-directed operations. To assist him in his investigations, he enlisted a corps of summertime student volunteers who became known as "Nader's Raiders." The Raiders have searched for mismanagement in such federal bureaucracies as the Department of Agriculture, the Food and Drug Administration, the National Water Pollution Control Administration, the Interstate Commerce Commission, and several others.

Center for Study of Responsive Law. Nader's Center for Study of Responsive Law was organized in 1968 to conduct research into violations of the public interest by business and governmental groups. Most of Nader's major reports have been released through the Center. The Center has conducted studies ranging from an investigation of the policies of a major New York bank to land development operations in California.

Center for Auto Safety. Nader's Center for Auto Safety is operated by a full-time director who is paid by a fellowship from Consumers Union. A complementary operation is an auto complaint center located in Cleveland, Ohio. As a result of the Center's investigations, the U.S. Transportation Department has issued many warnings about defective cars to auto owners and has issued demands for automobile manufacturers to repair auto defects.

Public Interest Research Group (PIRG). The 14-member Public Interest Research Group (PIRG) is a Nader organization which is an action-oriented public interest law firm. Research conducted by PIRG becomes the basis for legal action. A major project of this group is to find ways to make civil servants more accountable to the public for their decisions.

In the early 1970s PIRG began on a state level to mobilize student support on college campuses. To finance reform efforts on and off the campuses in a state, students vote at their school for a nominal amount to be added to their student fees each year. The reform group in each state is directed by a student board which includes lawyers, economists, ecologists, and other professional individuals.

Project on Corporate Responsibility. The Project on Corporate Responsibility is a Nader organization which encourages stockholder fights against companies which follow policies that appear to conflict with the public interest. The project attempts to convince universities, foundations, trusts, and others holding large blocks of stock in offending corporations to vote their stock for corporate policies and directors that represent the consumer interest. In the early 1970s the project mounted a stockholder campaign against General Motors known as "Campaign GM." The purpose of this was to make GM management accountable to the public on questions of pollution, safety, and hiring of minority groups.

Other Nader Groups. Other groups include the Corporate Accountability Research Group, the Tax Reform Research Group, the Health Research Group, and Public Citizen, Inc. By 1974 this latter organization, which serves as a fund raiser for the broad-based Nader complex, had received over one million dollars in donations.

Contribution of Nader Groups. The Nader groups believe their most important contributions have been in getting public officials to disclose more information about their operations and to enforce more strenuously regulations in such areas as pollution control and auto safety. Many consumer protection agencies and numerous government officials feel that Nader and his associates have provided a needed counterbalance to the interests of business. On the other hand, there is a sizable group of Nader critics who feel that, however well intentioned his motives are, the end result of his actions is the destruction of the corporate form of business.

JOHN BANZHAF'S CRUSADES

John Banzhaf, a George Washington University law professor who almost single-handedly initiated an antismoking campaign, is another important consumer advocate. Banzhaf is neither as austere nor as publicity-shy as Nader, but both men are lawyers who use knowledge of the law to right the wrongs committed against consumers. He states that his mission in life is to use the courts to remedy problems such as air pollution, unhealthy working conditions, and substandard housing. Banzhaf forced television stations to show antismoking commercials, and he established an organization which assisted in persuading the government to regulate cigarette advertising. Another crusade of his is to convince the Federal Communications Commission (FCC) to limit television commercial time to eight minutes out of each hour.

SOUP (Students Opposing Unfair Practices, Inc.) is a consumer action organization which was originally formed by five George Washington University law students for a practical law experience project in Professor Banzhaf's class. The first major action of SOUP was to oppose a provisional consent decree by the FTC against the Campbell Soup Company for false advertising. The complaint against Campbell was that clear glass marbles were dropped into the soup shown in some printed ads so that the vegetables and other solid ingredients would rise to the top.

BUSINESS'S REACTION TO CONSUMERISM

Businesspersons and consumer advocates tend to view the same marketplace from different vantage points. The two groups define several basic concepts in very different terms. As shown in Figure 12-1, each group perceives the consumer world differently. The concepts of competition, product, consumer needs, rationality, and information are defined one way by businesspersons and another way by consumer critics.

To close the gap between the viewpoints of businesspersons and consumers, companies have initiated various programs. Some of the programs

BASIC CONCEPTS	VIEWPOINTS	
	Businesspersons	Consumer Advocates
Competition	Product differentiation	Price competition
Product	Differentiation through secondary function	Primary function only
Consumer needs	Any customer desire on which the products can be differentiated	Must correspond point for point to primary functions of a product
Rationality	Any customer decision that serves the customer's own perceived self-interest	Efficient matching of product to customer needs
Information	Any data that will truthfully enhance the attractiveness of the product to the customer	Any data that facilitates the fit of a product's proper function with the customer's needs

SOURCE: Adapted from Raymond A. Bauer and Stephen A. Greyser, "The Dialogue That Never Happens," *Harvard Business Review* (November–December, 1967), p. 4.

Figure 12-1 **Two Different Viewpoints of the Consumer World**

serve to satisfy the complainants while others attempt to eliminate the source of the complaints.

Improved Consumer Communications

Some firms are installing toll-free telephone lines for consumers who desire to register their complaints directly to company headquarters. In 1967 the Whirlpool Corporation established the first toll-free telephone service in the country, which became the prototype for other firms. Whirlpool's telephone service, which is known as the **cool line**, resolves about 70 percent of the callers' questions and complaints over the telephone. The remainder of the 300 daily inquiries are handled by nearly 2,000 independent repairers across the country with whom Whirlpool works closely.

Automobile manufacturers have instituted telephone and letter-writing programs as means of handling consumer complaints. The Ford Motor Company indicated that it initiated at least one effective product change as a result of its "We Listen Better" letter-writing campaign which started in the fall of 1970. Numerous short, stocky drivers wrote that their Ford seat belts were too short when the seats were moved forward as far as possible. As a result,

Ford began to supply dealers with longer belts and with instructions to install them free of charge on customer request.

Consumer Ombudsman

Some firms have created the position of **consumer ombudsman**. This concept originated in the Scandinavian countries, where the ombudsman investigates complaints against administrative officials and procedures and reports the findings to the legislature. The function of a consumer ombudsman is to serve as an intermediary between a firm and the individual. The ombudsman investigates specific complaints, recommends an adjustment procedure, and follows up the recommendation to the satisfaction of the aggrieved individual.

In 1971 Chrysler Corporation created an ombudsman position with the title of vice-president, consumer affairs, so that its customers may take their complaints directly to top management. Chrysler officials believe that the ombudsman program centralizes the adjusting of complaints and helps the company gather specific information about product defects and the servicing capabilities of its dealers.

Marketing Policy Changes

An example of a company altering its marketing policies to become more compatible with consumer interests is Grolier, Incorporated. Grolier, which is a major publisher of reference books, significantly restructured its house-to-house sales operation. The firm now double checks each customer to be sure the individual fully understands the purchase contract. This checking is done by a representative of its credit department to guard against any misrepresentations by overzealous salespersons. Eight weeks after an order is shipped, calls are made from the Grolier home office in New York to a random 10 percent of its customers in order to determine the consumer reaction to both its books and salespersons. As an additional step, the revised purchase contracts allow dissatisfied customers to call collect to the New York office and discuss their complaints.

Organizational Changes

Several firms have adopted organizational modifications in an effort to better serve the consumer. For example, Ford Motors elevated its service division to the same organizational level as the sales division. Ford believed that this organizational change would provide district service managers with more authority to resolve repair and service problems at the local level.

Improved Product Quality

Many companies have improved the quality of their products and have established more accurate quality control procedures. General Motors states that in the 1937–1939 period the number of complaints received by the company and its dealers totaled 2.7 percent of car sales. Thirty years later in the 1967–1969 period, the firm received complaints equalling 2.5 percent of its sales, although many more cars were sold in the sixties than in the thirties.

Another approach companies have tried in an effort to improve product quality is a job enrichment program. Recognizing that assembly-line jobs are very monotonous, **job enrichment** restructures the job to make it more meaningful to the worker. Job enrichment allows a group of workers to assemble the complete product, relieving worker boredom and enhancing worker interest in the finished product.

Professor Stephen A. Greyser of Harvard Business School declares that the chance of a product failure is less in the 1970s than at any prior period. He points out that the consumer is utilizing many more items capable of breaking down than ever before, so that the cumulative probability of a product failure is greater. It is this cumulative effect which arouses consumer indignation.

Open Dating

Numerous food chains are providing open-dating information to their customers. **Open dating** is sharing with consumers the coded dates, such as numbers, letters, or combinations of both, placed on food items by either retailers or producers to indicate the shelf life of a product. For example, under open dating the shopper, as well as the store clerks, can determine if a package of bologna has one day or several days of shelf life remaining. In July, 1970, Jewel Food Stores of Chicago adopted an open-dating policy and claimed to be the first food chain with such a policy. The U.S. Department of Agriculture is requiring processors or retailers of meat and poultry to adopt open-dating programs.

Food industry officials have viewed the secret codes as management tools which have allowed them to maintain a high level of quality control at a relatively low cost. Some merchants maintain that open coding leads to higher prices because shoppers seek out the freshest food available, leaving the perfectly good older food on the shelves. Other merchants take the position that if an item is on their shelves at the time of the shelf-life expiration period, their inventory and stock turnover policies need to be corrected.

Unit Pricing

Unit pricing is another service numerous retailers have begun providing to their shoppers. Pricing in this manner enables consumers to compare costs by identifying the price of a product per established units, such as ounces, pounds, or quarts. Several states, such as Connecticut, Maryland, and Massachusetts, require unit pricing. A statute adopted by the Department of Consumer Affairs in New York City requires unit pricing on 18 grocery product lines, including canned and bottled vegetables and fruits, detergents, cereals, and soft drinks. The law was proposed after the Consumer Affairs Department sent a group of homemakers to supermarkets to determine the best buy on 14 products; these shoppers made the incorrect choice 40 percent of the time!

BENEFITS OF CONSUMERISM TO BUSINESS

In the 1970s leading businesspersons are aware of the basic rights of consumers, and they realize that to survive they must recognize these rights. The basic rights of the consumer include:

1. Protection from fraud, deceit, and misrepresentation.
2. Access to adequate information to make an intelligent choice among products and services.
3. Confidence that products will work as represented.
4. Assurance that health and safety will not be endangered by the goods bought.
5. Availability of a wide range of choice to meet individual tastes and personal preferences.[4]

Although the fifth consumer right is the strength of our enterprise system, it causes the most difficulty in implementing the other four. The availability of a wide range of choice means that products with varying levels of quality reach the marketplace. The government could prescribe standards for a host of perfect products, but is this really what all consumers desire? Excessively high standards could increase the price of a product to a point where the majority of consumers would be forced out of the market. Few consumers can afford the custom-built Rolls Royce, but many can afford the mass-produced Chevrolet. Since numerous consumers buy to satisfy psychological as well as physical needs, not everyone would desire the sameness of the perfect products. Even the Chevrolet comes equipped with many different options which permit it to be individualized to meet the desires of each purchaser.

Shared Goals

Consumerism is applied marketing with both the businessperson and the consumer activist seeking the same goal — continued consumer satisfaction. Business profits depend on continued sales, which occur only by marketing

[4]From a presentation to the National Marketing Advisory Committee, by Maurice H. Stans, U.S. Secretary of Commerce, December 4, 1969.

products that offer lasting consumer benefits. The compatibility of goals does not mean that consumerists can prescribe business policies. A company must set its own standard of performance, and over a period of time its performance builds its identity. In its planning each company must consider the impact of the consumer movement. Our competitive economy relies on consumers who make realistic choices between competing products.

Specific Benefits

There are several specific benefits that businesspersons can draw from the consumer movement. One benefit is that the consumerists can provide a firm with information about the strengths and weaknesses of its product line and service facilities. A second benefit is that through discussions with consumerists it is possible for businesspersons to determine how their products compare with competitive offerings. Another advantage results when management utilizes consumer groups to obtain reactions to company promotions and to evaluate the effectiveness of these promotions. A final benefit is that consumerism indicates to management the effect of a firm's goods and services on the quality of life. As a result, managers can develop products which reflect the goals of society.

BUSINESS TERMS

consumerism	226	*Parents' Magazine* Guaranteed	
Adaptationists	226	Seal	234
Protectionists	226	Use-Tested tag	234
Reformers	226	cool line	238
corrective ads	230	consumer ombudsman	239
counter-advertising	231	job enrichment	240
class-action lawsuits	231	open dating	240
Consumer's Guaranty Seal	234	unit pricing	240

QUESTIONS FOR DISCUSSION AND ANALYSIS

1. In order of importance identify what you consider to be the most significant goals of a consumer movement.
2. Why do buyers of industrial products not express as much dissatisfaction with their purchases as buyers of consumer products?
3. In what areas of business and services do you see the need for additional consumer protection legislation?
4. Should the present policy of submitting certain advertising claims to the Federal Trade Commission for substantiation after the ad is placed in the media be changed so that the substantiation is submitted before the ad is run? Discuss.
5. Do you believe the government's top consumer affairs position should be given cabinet rank? Discuss. What type of experience and education should such a cabinet officer have?
6. With both the Consumers Union and Consumers' Research testing and rating products, why are there still so many

products of mediocre quality on the market?

7. Examine the overall impact of a government-operated product testing and rating service in a free enterprise economy.

8. Do you believe that all marketers of perishable grocery products should be compelled to use an open-dating system? Explain.

9. There have been suggestions that automobile manufacturers reduce the list price of a new car so that the ineffective bargainer, as well as the effective bargainer, would pay the same price for a car. Do you agree?

10. What key topics should be covered in a course which is designed to create better-informed consumers?

PROBLEMS AND SHORT CASES

1. In the early 1970s the Federal Trade Commission announced that it supports the use of counter-advertising in broadcast media to counteract advertising claims which raise controversial issues. At that time a candy company in Tampa, Florida, was using a local television station to direct an extensive advertising campaign to the children's market. The firm's ads indicated that its product was a nutritional food supplement. A group of concerned mothers seriously doubted the product claims of the candy company. The mothers contacted the management of the television station and asked for free time to broadcast counter-ads. The mothers believed that the counter-ads would cause the young viewers to question the nutritional value of the candy.
   a. Should the television station provide free time to the mothers' group? What are the implications to the station and its advertisers if free time is granted?
   b. What criteria should the television station use for accepting a counter-ad?
   c. Indicate the type of information which the mothers' group should place in a counter-ad.

2. The Frank Harold automobile agency was located in Syracuse, New York. Over the years this agency, which sold mainly expensive, prestige-type autos, had established a loyal clientele among the business and professional persons in the area.

   In the summer of 1976, Kris Comart, a recent college graduate, purchased a sports model auto from the agency. Initially Kris was quite pleased with the performance of the auto. After a year, however, the driver's seat began ripping along the seams and the protective boot around the four-speed shift split open. After these problems had developed, Kris returned to the agency and showed the defects to the service manager. Kris stated that these defects were covered by the warranty. The service manager agreed that the seat could be fixed under the warranty, but the boot would not be covered. At this time the district representative of the automobile manufacturer was at the agency, so Kris asked him if the boot was covered by the warranty. To Kris's surprise, the representative stated that neither the boot nor the seat were covered by the warranty. Kris protested to the representative, to the service manager, and finally to the owner of the agency, Frank Harold. Her pleas were to no avail since Harold declared that the district representative is the one who decides if the manufacturer reimburses the agency for warranty repairs.

   Kris considered this entire incident as a big rip-off, and she decided to write directly to the president of the automobile company. An assistant to the president responded that since the auto was no longer under warranty, there was nothing the manufacturer could do. Kris returned several times to the agency to try to get a settlement, but she was told repeatedly that nothing could be done.

a. What alternatives are left for Kris?
b. Should Harold agree to repair the defects? What factors should Harold consider in making this decision?
c. What action could the automobile manufacturer take to make the company more responsive to consumer complaints?
3. Go into a store and select five products which come in different sizes, such as toothpaste, roll-on deodorant, detergent, applesauce, and dog food. Next, record the price and quantity for each size of the selected products. Finally, divide the price by the quantity to get the unit price for each size of package.
    a. Were you able to determine the unit price for each item visually without using paper and pencil or a calculator?
    b. Did the unit price change or remain the same for each package size?

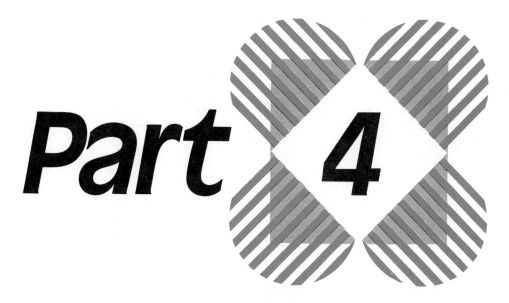

Part 4

Management of Human Resources

Business is a phenomenon of people rather than simply a collection of machine-like tasks. Capable, skilled human resources are the lifeblood of today's complex organizations. Part 4 recognizes that personnel managers face challenges from within and outside the organization in their efforts to build and maintain a productive, motivated work force.

Chapter 13 considers the structure and functions of the personnel department as it strives to staff the organization effectively. This is followed by a discussion of some issues and constraints in the environment of business that bear heavily on employee selection and training. These include the topics of minorities and women in the work force and affirmative action programs.

In Chapter 14 it is recognized that wage incentives are one important means of encouraging the effective performance of human resources. Economic theories of wages are discussed, as are the factors determining wage incentive plans and methods of wage payment. The impact of inflation on money wages and real wages is developed, and this chapter also notes the roles in programs of employee compensation of profit sharing, the guaranteed annual wage, and pensions.

Milestones in the growth and goals of organized labor that have helped to cast its present form are reviewed in Chapter 15. Tactics and tools in labor-management bargaining are examined, as are major labor laws. Consideration of current labor issues — including changes in traditional unionism, the generation gap, the emergence of women and minority unionists, and global unions — provides insight into the future of labor-management relations.

13 Employee Selection and Training

Bob Solomon was becoming increasingly concerned about his new job with the Ajax Corporation. During his recruitment into the company Bob was provided with biographical sketches of its stellar executives, glowing descriptions of the company's products, pages of prose about recreational opportunities in the area, and a leaflet on generous fringe benefits. All of these were laced with words like talent, teamwork, initiative, and creativity. However, in his first week of work Bob was given neither a general orientation nor specific job-related support. His enthusiasm for the new job was rapidly fading.

There was a time when a paycheck was the necessary and sufficient condition to tie a person to a job, regardless of its content. In the generally smaller companies of the past, this basic need for the paycheck led the worker to accept even a barely tolerable working relationship with the supervisor. Owner/managers often handled the basic personnel matters. They hired, paid, and sometimes fired their employees. Employees, in turn, did their jobs as long as they were physically able; for when their ability to work ceased, so did their jobs and paychecks.

More recently, however, two major factors have changed this relationship. First, the notable growth in the technological complexity of factory and office work has placed increased emphasis on finding, training, and keeping capable, skilled workers. Second, it has been recognized that business is basically a phenomenon of people, not simply a collection of machine-like tasks. As more workers have found their basic needs satisfied in our society, the recognition of the dignity of the individual and the importance of the opportunity for satisfaction and self-fulfillment on the job have underlined the expanded role of the personnel function in business and other organizations.

PERSONNEL MANAGEMENT

Personnel management involves recruitment, selection, hiring, training and development, and the general provision for the needs of the human resources in an organization. In this chapter the terms personnel and human resources are used interchangeably. The **human resources** approach recognizes that all persons in an organization, regardless of their level or job, are potential sources of innovation and talent. This approach differs markedly from the traditional viewpoint that the workers are basically lazy or unwilling to perform over the minimally-acceptable level and to contribute to the goals of the organization.

Unfortunately it is far easier to define personnel management than to pinpoint who in the organization performs this wide variety of personnel functions. Theoretically the existence of a personnel department does not relieve line managers of the responsibility for the staffing, morale, and effectiveness of their subordinates. In accepting this responsibility, however, managers may feel that they deal with people constantly and that they do not need to draw on the advice and support of the personnel department.

Likewise, personnel experts may be jealous of their prerogatives and look upon the management of human resources as the job of a specialist rather than as part of the manager's job. Ideally the many diverse and important areas of personnel management should be accepted as a combined effort of all line and staff managers in an organization.

CHALLENGES IN MANAGING HUMAN RESOURCES

The persons dealing with personnel management, regardless of their title, face challenges from within and outside the organization in their efforts to build and maintain a productive, motivated work force.

Internal Challenges

Within the organization a threefold problem is involved: (a) the right people must be found and the proper choice made from those available; (b) those who are hired must be trained to correct any skill deficiencies and retrained to maintain their skills at an acceptable level; and (c) the conditions on the job should benefit rather than frustrate the workers, thus contributing to the general morale or "espirit de corps" at all levels of the organization.

External Challenges

Challenges to personnel management from outside the organization are inescapable. These are found in social issues such as the hiring and training of women and minorities. Legal constraints in the environment exist in such forms as civil rights and safety legislation.

The balance of this chapter deals with these internal and external dimensions. First, the structure and functions of the personnel department as it strives to staff effectively the organization will be considered. This is followed by a discussion of some issues and constraints in the environment of business that bear heavily on employee selection and training.

THE PERSONNEL DEPARTMENT: STRUCTURE AND FUNCTIONS

Starting many years ago as an employment office, the personnel department has gradually expanded and added to its duties until it now covers a wide range of personnel matters. The director of personnel is one of the key persons in the firm, sometimes with vice-presidential rank. The other employees in the department are chosen for their interest in and ability to meet and resolve the personnel problems and challenges of present-day industry.

Structure of the Personnel Department

The many duties of the personnel department fall naturally into the following divisions: employment, training, personnel services, safety and health, personnel research, wages and salaries, and labor relations (see Figure 13-1). The functions performed in the first five divisions will be described in this chapter. Wages and salaries are discussed in Chapter 14, and labor relations in Chapter 15.

Functions in the Personnel Divisions

Figure 13-2 lists some representative functions performed by the five personnel divisions noted above. The scope and degree of these functions will

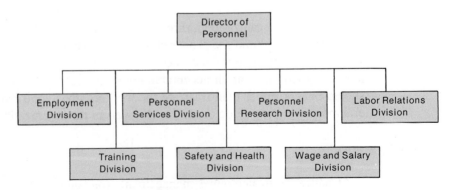

Figure 13-1   ***Organization Chart of the Personnel Department***

DIVISION	FUNCTIONS
Employment	Job analysis, description, and specification; developing sources of workers; administering the steps in the employment process; induction and orientation to the job; follow-ups and personal job evaluations; transfer, promotions, and involuntary terminations.
Training	Company or "vestibule" schools; sponsoring new workers; apprenticeship systems; job rotation; sensitivity training; retraining and upgrading skills.
Personnel Services	Eating facilities; recreational opportunities; insurance and hospitalization plans; employee counseling; legal advice; credit unions.
Safety & Health	Installation of safety devices in buildings and on machines; dissemination of safety information; conformance to requirements of workmen's compensation acts; periodic physical exams; programs to diminish industrial fatigue, including such measures as job enlargement and enrichment.
Personnel Research	Records and reports; statistical analysis of personnel records; publication of manuals for the guidance of other departments; develop systems and procedures, including computerized information retrieval systems for personnel; administer personnel audits and evaluations; research in employee motivation and productivity.

Figure 13-2   *Representative Personnel Functions*

vary from firm to firm. In a small company one person may perform only a few basic personnel functions. In a large company, however, the personnel staff may be quite large and may perform even more functions than noted here. The representative personnel functions in Figure 13-2 will be developed more fully under the headings of (1) selection and hiring, (2) training and development, (3) termination and dehiring, and (4) the internal environment of work.

SELECTION AND HIRING

Suppose a company spends a million dollars on a plant addition. Undoubtedly considerable thought will go into getting the most rapid and full return from that investment. Now suppose the same company spends a million dollars on its team of managerial and production workers. How often is the same kind of thought given to getting optimum value from this kind of investment? There is much more to it than showing that companies frequently succeed in recruiting good white- and blue-collar workers and then fail to give them the support they need to become effective quickly. What should be done in the pre-employment period and early weeks on the job to find and hire good people?

Job Analysis, Description, and Specification. The first step in securing the best people for a group of jobs is job analysis. **Job analysis** involves discovering the details of each position. Among the topics that should be covered in job analysis are the location of the job; its duties and responsibilities; the equipment, tools, and machines used; the working conditions; the pay; the opportunities for promotion; and whether job training is offered.

This information is written into a **job description**, a sample of which is shown in Figure 13-3. From the personnel data provided by the job analysis, a **job specification** is also prepared which lists the personal qualifications and special aptitudes required of the prospective employee. Armed with the job description and job specifications for a position, the employment division of the personnel department can then proceed intelligently with the task of finding the best available persons for the jobs.

JOB TITLE: PERSONNEL CLERK

Department: Personnel

Date: March 26, 197-

Employees in Department: 12

Employees on this Job: 3

General Description of the Job

Works under the supervision of the Personnel Manager; assists in clerical routine of induction which involves interviewing new workers; performs a variety of clerical and stenographic work.

Specific Duties of the Job

1. Interviews new workers after they have been given induction information such as hours, working conditions, services, etc., to verify personnel information and prepare records; checks information on application, statement of availability, draft, citizenship, and the like; obtains necessary information for income tax withholding, and determines classification; prepares forms for hospitalization, group insurance, and bond deductions; assigns clock number, makes up time card and badge card.

2. Calls previous employer to get reference information while applicant is being interviewed; may check references by mail after employee is hired, and occasionally records information from Dun & Bradstreet on personnel card.

3. Telephones employee's department or home after extended absence to determine when employee is expected to return, if at all; follows same procedure at end of leave of absence.

4. Handles stenographic work of Personnel Manager.

5. Does miscellaneous clerical work; assigns clock numbers and makes up time cards for employees transferred between departments; keeps record of equipment loaned to employees, such as micrometers, goggles, etc.; maintains current address file of employees in service; performs other clerical duties as assigned.

6. May substitute for Receptionist for short periods; give induction information to new employees in absence of Personnel Induction Clerk; escort new workers to departments; administer tests.

Figure 13-3 **Job Description**

Sources of Human Resources. The sources of supply for prospective employees depend on the nature of the business, the level of education and degree of skill needed for the jobs, and the nature of the population in the area in which the company is located. The sources of blue-collar resources include past and present employees, referrals of their friends and relatives, walk-in applicants, private employment agencies, trade and technical schools, classified advertising, and union headquarters and hiring halls.

Some firms have a policy of promoting from within their organization for all jobs above the lowest entry level. For example, the variety chains such as F. W. Woolworth Company and the S. S. Kresge Company have long done this, and they feel that it contributes to employee morale. More recently affirmative action programs have led an increasing number of companies to post job openings publicly for the employees to see. Affirmative action will be covered more fully later in this chapter.

In executive-level employment the two greatest sources of management candidates are a company's own personnel and referrals to people known personally by the company's own employees. These are followed in order by résumé advertisements in newspapers and technical journals; employment agencies; consultants or executive search agencies, known also as "headhunters;" placement services of professional societies and alumni groups; and career centers at conventions.

In some companies executives hire relatives or personal friends for attractive positions. This creates resentment among the other eligible employees, especially when more deserving in-house employees are ignored. The hiring or promoting of relatives solely on the basis of family connections is known as **nepotism**.

However, most companies set up their own set of recruiting ethics which may vary from company to company. Itek Corporation will not concentrate its advertising in the home city of a competitor. Gillette will not hire from a competitor. And many firms will not hire a person from a competitor without first talking with that competitor.

The Employment Process. Several steps are involved in the employment process. These are shown in Figure 13-4. Any combination of steps may be used in any given instance, depending upon the policies of the companies concerned. These include:

1. Submittal of a completed application form.
2. Preliminary interview.
3. Tests.
4. Investigation of applicant's background.
5. Physical examination.
6. The main interview.

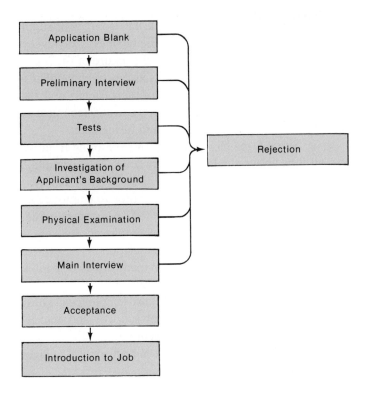

Figure 13-4 **The Employment Process**

The order of the steps in employment procedures is frequently based on placing those steps first that are less costly and that may result in a clear rejection of the applicant. The main interview is usually the occasion when the applicant is either definitely hired or rejected. In some companies the interviewer has a set form to follow with a fixed series of questions and remarks. Other companies allow their interviewers a free hand in conducting their discussions.

The responsibility of the personnel department for the new blue-collar or white-collar resource does not close when that person's name is added to the payroll. Haphazard procedures and gaps in needed information can invite worry and discouragement, so the personnel department launches the new employee into a program of induction and orientation.

Induction to the Job. The details of **induction**, which is the process of properly introducing a newly hired applicant to the details of the job and to fellow employees, vary with different firms. Many farsighted companies have found it worthwhile to make the induction process as careful and friendly as possible to encourage the best abilities and frame of mind of a person right from the start.

Job Orientation. New employees need to be oriented to certain policies, rules, and other matters concerning the company and their jobs to fit into the big picture quickly and effectively. **Job orientation** may include the daily work routine, safety rules, company pay practices, employees' organizations, recreational facilities, the availability and location of medical services, and the business of the company. All this information often is provided in a handbook that the new employee is given and asked to read. This step in itself provides only the most marginal orientation for most employees. Careful orientation programs may include group discussions, meetings, films, and tours to supplement the information in the handbook.

The orientation process sometimes includes periodic follow-ups on new workers throughout the first year to see how they are getting along with their jobs and co-workers. On a broader and more formal basis, some firms make an annual checkup of the records and achievements of all their employees, including supervisors; this is sometimes referred to as a **personnel audit**.

Proper selection and hiring should include an effective induction and orientation program that is carefully tailored to strengthen the security and sense of belonging of each new employee. The long-term relationship between the company and its human resources is too important to overlook these vital steps in the employment process.

TRAINING AND DEVELOPMENT

All employees require some degree of training to develop into effective, valued human resources. Training and development are related concepts, but are not synonymous. **Training** refers to the many various programs that may be offered to employees — both managers and workers — to help them develop their capabilities and to progress in their work. **Development** is the progress the person actually makes and may include conceptual or intellectual growth along with practical performance. Often the term "training" means vocational skill training in the short run, and managerial development is viewed as a long-run process.

Worker Training at the Operator Level. This training is of two types: training *for* the job and training *on* the job. Training for the job is given before the worker starts on the job. It is used where jobs may be complex and where inexperienced operators would interfere with the production flow. Training of a relatively brief duration often is given in **company schools**, which are called **vestibule schools** in some companies. Ford Motor Company and International Harvester, among others, have maintained schools of this type. They have been successful, for example, in the training and orientation of disadvantaged persons.

Certain types of work permit training on the job. These are usually fairly simple jobs where the presence of unskilled workers does not seriously affect the operations. Training may be given by supervisors, experienced operators, or by special instructors. In department stores, for example, the **sponsor system** is often used in which an experienced employee "sponsors" the new worker for the first few days and teaches her or him the details of the job. In building trades and crafts an **apprentice system** often is used in which inexperienced workers are apprenticed to master craftsmen for a period of time to learn their skills.

Managerial Training. The variety of managerial training techniques includes planned progression, job rotation among managerial training positions, "assistant-to" positions, committees and junior boards, conference programs, university management courses and programs, in-house workshops, and on-the-job training of an unspecified duration. In Chapter 6 three organizational levels were noted: the top or institutional level, the administrative or middle-management level, and the technical or operating level. Each of the training approaches mentioned here may be effective at one or another of these levels. A career plan that could lead to a position of top manager might resemble the model in Figure 13-5.

Operating-Level Management Training. Front-line supervisors and management trainees at the operating level are concerned with building the skills needed to carry out their programs and duties within the budget and getting the product out the door. On-the-job training by the managers is often the better type of training at this level, especially when accompanied by a clear effort to demonstrate and practice the techniques. Another procedure is **job rotation**, which is designed to familiarize junior executives with the details of the many positions that may be available and to reveal any special interests and abilities they may possess.

Middle-Level Management Training. Managers moving into the middle-management level need broader management theory and techniques than the specific techniques they have been using at the operating level. Possible means to develop the appreciation of broader managerial concepts are university "case courses," conference programs and workshops, and multiple-management miniboards such as those used by McCormick and Company. The **multiple-management miniboard** brings all levels of management into decision making by creating a chain of miniboards of directors throughout the company. Each of McCormick's major divisions has its own board of top management persons. Under these boards are a junior board of middle and lower managers and a factory board at the plant supervisory level. There are also

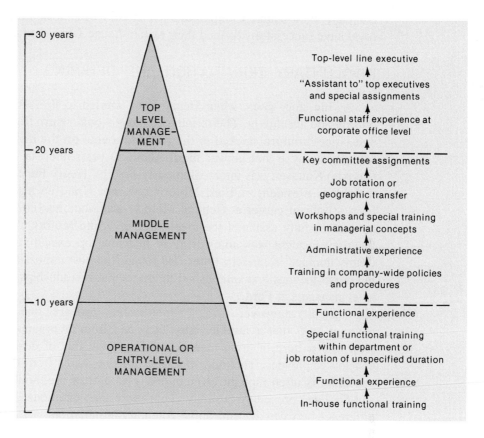

Figure 13-5   *Executive Career Model*

sales boards. The lower boards draw up their own bylaws, vote on membership, and pick their own projects. As one may imagine, these boards generate a host of proposals up through the company.

Top-Level Management Training. The demands at the top level are practically unknown to all but those who have made it to this level. Therefore, the best training techniques to share this knowledge with others is by creating "assistant-to" positions and special assignments carefully chosen and observed by the sponsoring executive.

Sensitivity Training. A recent training development involving interpersonal dynamics at all levels is **sensitivity training**, also known as T-groups. In this training program small groups of persons hold carefully and discreetly directed sessions, sometimes for several days, for the purpose of helping them to learn more about group processes, interpersonal relationships, and generally improving their effectiveness in dealing with their peers and associates in the company work teams. Companies such as Dow Chemical, Eli Lilly, and Uniroyal have successfully formed their own in-house T-group programs.

INVOLUNTARY TERMINATION AND DEHIRING

As the story goes, when Henry Ford wanted to fire someone he did it quickly and absolutely. The terminated party would return from a vacation to find office furniture stacked in the hall and a note on the door informing the former employee that he was fired! About 50 years later, in 1969, Semon E. (Bunkie) Knudsen was unceremoniously fired by Henry Ford II after only 19 months as president of Ford Motor Company. Knudsen had come to Ford from a brilliant career at General Motors, and since his termination at Ford has successfully assumed the presidency of White Motors Corporation. The Knudsen incident was noteworthy in that few top executives have been so clearly dumped in modern times. He found it almost impossible to overcome the harsh feelings and established interpersonal relationships of many higher level managers at Ford.

Generally, however, firing a subordinate is probably one of the most unpleasant tasks that a superior must face; and from an organizational point of view, the pattern of firing managers differs from that of dealing with lower-echelon employees. This undemocratic practice stems from the fact that the executive is often thought of emotionally as part of the family. At the rank-and-file level procedures usually count more than emotions. Thus, there is a difference between dehiring and involuntary termination.

Dehiring. Even though few executives are fired, many are dehired, outplaced, or selected-out. **Dehiring** is the process of getting an employee to quit voluntarily so that it is unnecessary to fire that person. **Outplacing** or **selecting-out** a person are simply genteel synonyms for involuntary, discreetly-executed job terminations.

Involuntary Terminations. The involuntary termination of an employee's services may take either of two forms: a discharge or a layoff. A **discharge** is a permanent separation from a company often accompanied by a stigma against the employee. While a **layoff** may be either a permanent or temporary separation, it casts no reflection upon the character or competence of the employee. Layoffs often result from the lack of work, and assure reemployment as soon as conditions improve. Layoffs and reemployment, particularly in plants operating under a union contract, are almost always based on **seniority**, which is the length of time the employee has worked for the firm.

Termination Responsibilities of the Personnel Department. It seems that managers fire subordinates, so where does the personnel department fit into all this? The personnel department has at least two duties involving job terminations. First, a personnel specialist should advise line managers on termination procedures that are fair to the parties concerned. Companies usually have a specified method for dismissals that includes: (a) a verbal warning informing the employee of what is being done incorrectly and of the possible consequences, (b) a written warning if the stated offense continues, and (c) a final warning that if the infraction has not ceased by a certain time, the employee may be dismissed. The personnel department may also keep a file on the employee throughout this process in case the decision is challenged.

Second, the personnel department should conduct a careful, constructive **terminal interview** with the terminated employee just prior to departure. This should be based as much as possible on facts rather than emotions. It may help the employee in self-evaluation and also may provide insights into questionable supervisory practices within the company.

THE INTERNAL ENVIRONMENT OF WORK

The idea that an employer should provide something more than acceptable wages and a safe place to work has gained considerable acceptance in the past few years. Part of this reasoning recognizes that not every employee will be able to have an enriched, challenging job. Therefore, anything an employer can do to enhance the physical environment of the job and the general interpersonal relations on the job may help the employees to identify with the company and with one another, and thus serve to maintain the productivity of the human resources at an above-the-minimum level. A few of the more basic personnel service activities that may contribute to this environment are discussed in the following paragraphs.

Employee Services. The services offered employees may include recreational and athletic programs, legal advice and assistance, insurance and retirement plans, child care, dining facilities, and full or partial tuition payments upon successful completion of course work at educational institutions. A comparatively recent development in the field of personnel services is employee counseling. Many companies now have counselors and professional psychologists with whom employees can discuss problems about their job, home, debts, education, retirement, and the like.

Safety and Health. The promotion of employee safety continues to make rapid strides, not only as a humanitarian concern for the quality of employee work life, but also because of the Occupational Safety and Health Act of 1970 (OSHA). Under this act, also known as the Williams-Steiger Act, Congress authorized the Secretary of Labor to establish mandatory health and safety standards for businesses engaged in interstate commerce. The act created a

National Institute for Occupational Safety and Health (NIOSH) within the Department of Health, Education and Welfare.

OSHA has had some impact on personnel departments. First, OSHA specifies that civil penalties can be assessed up to $10,000 per violation for willful and repeated violations. Since 1971, inspections have totaled about 159,000 resulting in about 106,000 citations alleging 549,000 infractions of the law. Almost $14 million in penalties has been collected. Therefore, safety training, including the dissemination of safety literature and the formulation and enforcement of safety programs, is a growing activity in personnel departments.

Second, despite the penalties to date, unions charge that the OSHA enforcement machinery has not been provided with enough money, inspectors, or impetus. As a back-up strategy, unions are increasingly raising health and safety issues in wage-bargaining sessions, asking that they be given more authority to set and police safety and health standards. Personnel departments must respond to the higher priority now being assigned to safety and health by union spokespersons. Also, OSHA may upgrade the working conditions in smaller businesses, which will place heavier burdens on those who handle the personnel functions in these businesses.

EXTERNAL ISSUES AND CONSTRAINTS

The discussion of OSHA legislation has already moved into the broad area of external issues and constraints faced by personnel departments. Occupational safety and health has not yet reached its zenith as a pressing social issue, and it is because of the affluence of our society that occupational safety and health and the broader issue of the quality of work life can become such important concerns.

But not every group in our society has a share of this affluence. White male America, which can be so enterprising in its individual and corporate pursuits, stands accused by women and minorities of neglecting the potential contributions of these integral parts of our society. This sense of frustration and inequity has become an inescapable problem for personnel departments in their policies and procedures for selecting and training employees. Hence, this section will consider these issues and key legislation imposing formal constraints on the actions of personnel departments and management in general. Finally, some implications of these issues and constraints on personnel selection and training will be suggested.

Women in the Work Force

The 1970 U.S. Census counted a female population of 104,299,724. This is about equal to the total population of Japan. Only three nations have larger female populations: China, India, and the Soviet Union. By early 1970 working women in the United States represented 42 percent of all women 16 years old or over in the population — close to double the proportion for 1920. As recently as 1962, there were 23,000,000 women in the work force. In 1970, as Table 13-1 indicates, this number exceeds 30,000,000.

Table 13-1 **The American Female Population**

Category	Number of Women	Percentage of Women in Category
White	91,027,988	51.2
Black	11,821,631	52.4
Spanish heritage	4,695,744	50.5
Other races	1,439,773	49.9
Under 18	34,161,180	49.0
Over 65	11,649,794	58.0
Voting age	70,138,544	52.5
In college	3,013,000	40.6
In other schools	25,931,000	49.0
In labor force	30,820,770	37.2
Family head	5,504,104	10.8
Living alone	7,234,000	67.7
Married	45,963,972	50.0
Widowed	9,624,679	82.1
Divorced	3,068,994	61.1
Below low-income level	14,841,000	58.1

SOURCE: U.S. Department of Commerce, Bureau of the Census, 1970.

OCCUPATIONAL SEGREGATION

Despite the dramatic changes in the participation of women in the work force in the past 70 years, there is little drama in most of the jobs women have. Although more than 250 distinct occupations are listed in the Bureau of Census tabulations, in 1969 half of all women workers were employed in only 21 of these occupations. About a fourth of all employed women were in five occupations: secretary-stenographer, household worker, bookkeeper, elementary school teacher, and waitress. As Figure 13-6 reveals, male workers are much more highly dispersed in occupations than women, with 50 percent in 65 occupations.

OCCUPATIONAL DISCRIMINATION

Women face an uphill battle in being identified, selected, and trained as managerial resources in the business organization, as the male executive is often opposed to women holding positions in what he has come to consider

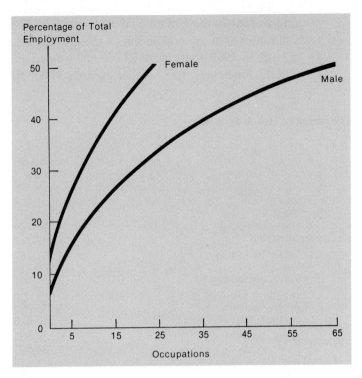

Percentage of Total
Employment

SOURCE: Hedges, *Monthly Labor Review* (June, 1970), p. 19.

Figure 13-6   **Occupational Dispersion**

the masculine domain. Based on Harriet Zellner's definitions of "discrimination," this attitude of male executives reflects two types of discrimination: "deliberate" and "erroneous."

✳ **Deliberate discrimination** is based on a subjective preference for males; that is, it is motivated by some sort of discomfort in dealing with women in certain occupational roles. **Erroneous discrimination** is based on an underestimation of female capacities in these roles; it is cognitive, or learned, rather than psychological in origin.[1] These attitudes have contributed to such myths as the following:

> "A woman's place is in the home."
> "Women aren't seriously in the labor force; they work for 'pin money,' not because they have to." (Income inequality will be covered in Chapter 14.)
> "Women should stick to 'women's jobs' and not compete for men's jobs."
> "Women are intellectually and emotionally unsuited for professional and executive work."
> "Women have a higher rate of absenteeism."
> "The employment of mothers leads to juvenile delinquency."

[1]Harriet Zellner, "Discrimination Against Women, Occupational Segregation, and the Relative Wage," *American Economic Review* (May, 1972), p. 158.

Clearly there is evidence that tends to overthrow or seriously modify many of these myths and misconceptions. Nevertheless, one of the most difficult areas in personnel selection and training is the need to change employers' attitudes and male attitudes in general with respect to women's roles and their desire to work.

Minorities in the Work Force

Of the 30 million Americans living below the poverty line, about 15 million disadvantaged Americans are white. Thirty percent are black or Spanish-speaking Americans. Thus, the problem of joblessness and poverty in the United States is not solely a race problem, but it certainly is closely related to the inner-city ghetto living of some blacks and other minorities such as American Indians and Spanish-speaking Americans.

BLACK PERSONS

The total population of 23 million blacks comprises 92 percent of the non-white population in the United States, and inner-city problems are often discussed in terms of black issues. By 1970 over 80 percent of the nation's blacks lived in metropolitan areas, with nearly half living in poverty areas as compared to 10 percent of the whites. As whites and industry have moved to the suburbs, blacks have faced shrinking employment opportunities. In 1970, for example, the unemployment rate for black teenagers was 32 percent, more than six times the national average.

SPANISH-SPEAKING AMERICANS

Americans with a Spanish-speaking heritage number close to 10 million in the mainland United States. Over 5 million are of Mexican origin or descent. A growing number of this group, especially the younger people in urban areas, prefer the name "Chicano" rather than Mexican-American or Hispano. "Chicano" denotes their desire to identify with and support an emerging movement based on a series of crusades to establish their social, economic, and political rights and power. It recognizes their Indian blood and is an expression of pride in their real self instead of a demeaning title imposed on them from an external source. More than 1.5 million of Spanish-speaking Americans are Puerto Ricans. Well over 600,000 are Cubans, and around 2 million come from or trace their descent to other Spanish origins such as Central or South America.

Nearly three fourths of the Spanish-speaking population live in the five states of California, Texas, New Mexico, New York, and Florida. Their urbanization is heavy; in 1970, 84 percent of this population lived in metropolitan areas, compared to 80 percent of the blacks and 69 percent of the total population. The relatively large proportion of Spanish-speaking workers in poorly paid jobs and their above-average level of unemployment contributed to the low average of income in 1971 of $7,250, as compared to $10,300 for whites and $6,400 for blacks.

AMERICAN INDIANS

The problems of our native Americans continue to be severe in the areas of employment, income, education, and health. The Bureau of Indian Affairs (BIA) estimates that unemployment on reservations averages about 40 percent, and in winter months goes to 90 percent of the labor force on some reservations. The average annual family income for reservation Indians is estimated at $1,500.

The 1970 census puts the national American Indian population at about 795,000, nearly half of whom live in urban areas and most of the remainder on federal or state reservations. Indians are widely distributed, but almost half live in western states, particularly in Oklahoma, Arizona, California, and New Mexico. Only seven large cities have Indian populations over 5,000: New York, Los Angeles, Tulsa, Oklahoma City, Chicago, Phoenix, and Minneapolis. The Indians concentrated in the cities are subject to the serious handicaps of poor health, deficient education, lack of marketable skills, high unemployment, and low income.

MINORITY JOBLESSNESS AND INSTITUTIONAL DISCRIMINATION

The concentration of disadvantaged blacks and other minorities in urban ghetto areas is one reason for their limited access to the job market. But it is a great mistake to equate joblessness to being a hopelessly disadvantaged person, or **hard-core**; for not every minority person out of work is educationally or motivationally unqualified to work at a decent job. Often that person is simply underemployed, as the most pervasive barriers he or she faces usually are not geographic but those resulting from discrimination.

Even when there is no overt intent to discriminate, institutionalized personnel arrangements such as the following may have a discriminatory effect:

1. A firm's existing employees form an important recruitment channel; when they refer friends or relatives to job openings, the effect is to perpetuate the racial and ethnic mix of the work force.
2. Unrealistic hiring standards are also a barrier. The high school diploma has frequently become a screening standard.
3. Widely different educational requirements are used for similar jobs from firm to firm throughout the country.
4. Written tests for hiring and promotion may exclude workers from jobs within their capabilities.

Since the Civil Rights Act of 1964, most overt forms of discrimination have gradually diminished. But substitute rules and informal customs in many firms have permitted racist employment patterns to exist.

Legal Constraints

The U.S. Government's efforts to end discrimination in hiring and training are carried out through the enforcement of: (1) the Civil Rights Act of 1964, as amended by the Equal Employment Opportunity Act of 1972; and (2) Revised Order No. 4, which sets out the content to be used in affirmative action programs.

THE CIVIL RIGHTS ACT AND THE EEOC

The key federal legislation on **equal employment opportunity** is Title VII of the Civil Rights Act of 1964. This act forbids discrimination based on an individual's race, color, religion, sex, or national origin. It also created the Equal Employment Opportunity Commission (EEOC), consisting of five members to administer Title VII. The EEOC reports to the President and generally covers business employers who have 15 or more employees, labor organizations, employment agencies, state or local governments, and educational institutions.

Prior to 1972 the EEOC was limited to informal conciliation efforts to eliminate alleged discriminatory employment practices. The Equal Employment Opportunity Act of 1972 amended Title VII of the Civil Rights Act of 1964 to permit the Commission to sue in a U.S. District Court on its behalf or for other claimants when it believes discrimination has taken place.

Of relevance to women workers is the EEOC's narrow interpretation of sex as a bona fide occupational qualification. The EEOC takes the position that protective laws, such as weight-lifting and night work, can no longer be used to discriminate against women. It places a burden of proof on the employer to establish that sex is a bona fide occupational qualification for a given position.

AFFIRMATIVE ACTION PROGRAMS

To ensure that the equal employment opportunity clause is observed by employers who have contracts with the federal government, Executive Order No. 11246 was issued in 1965 and amended by Executive Order No. 11375 in 1967. While these executive orders required "affirmative action" by employers with federal government contracts, they did not specify what it really meant. The new standards for affirmative action were set forth under Revised

Order No. 4, which requires that, within 120 days from the commencement of a contract, each prime government contractor and subcontractor with 50 or more employees and a contract of $50,000 or more must develop a written affirmative action compliance program for each of its establishments. The Office of Federal Contract Compliance (OFCC) considers an **affirmative action program** acceptable when it includes: (a) an analysis of areas within which the contractor is deficient in the utilization of minority groups and women, including managerial and professional areas; and (b) goals and timetables to which the contractor's efforts must be directed in achieving prompt and full utilization of minorities and women in areas where deficiencies exist.

IMPLICATIONS OF THE LEGAL CONSTRAINTS

Only through definite programs of affirmative action can most large-scale employers live up to today's standards regarding equal employment opportunities. Personnel administrators must be aware of the requirements concerning women and minorities in the following areas:

1. Recruiting. The advice and assistance of leaders from minority groups and women's groups should be sought in structuring a positive recruitment program.
2. Selection. All selection procedures (including written, performance, or oral tests; education and experience ratings; structured interviews; and application forms) must be designed to prevent discrimination against minority groups and women.
3. Appointment and Placement. Personnel managers must assure that the personnel representatives in the employment process have a commitment to equal opportunity principles and are competent to determine objectively the abilities of minority group applicants.
4. Job Structuring and Upward Mobility. Training classes for those below the current entrance level should be provided; minimum educational requirements should be based on the actual work to be performed; and career ladders should be available for lower-level employees along with counseling and training for the capable lower-level employee.
5. Top-Level Support. Affirmative action responsibility should be delegated to a high-level official. Supervisors at all levels should be trained in their affirmative action program responsibilities.

Implementation of an effective affirmative action program to remove discriminatory employment barriers rests on competent supervision, responsive personnel administration, and effective training. Since World War I, personnel administrators have provided an increasingly wide group of necessary services to their organizations in the efforts to hire and train productive human resources. Today their role remains equally important as they strive to do this while also responding to the social, political, and legal forces in their organization's environment.

BUSINESS TERMS

QUESTIONS FOR DISCUSSION AND ANALYSIS

1. Which employees of an organization should be regarded as human resources?
2. Suggest some circumstances under which nepotism might be considered a normal practice.
3. Discuss the statement that jobs in smaller firms, such as a bicycle shop, require far less job orientation than those in larger companies.
4. Should a person be trained *for* the job of a gas station attendant or trained *on* the job? Explain.
5. What problems do you see in a McCormick-type "miniboard" approach to training middle managers?
6. Discuss the viewpoint that whenever an executive's job is involuntarily terminated, it is best for both the executive and the company if the executive is asked to leave the job immediately.
7. Should the limited-price variety stores' policy of making promotions only from within the organization apply to women as well as men? Explain.
8. In what ways may a business firm benefit from hiring "hard-core" disadvantaged persons?
9. What effect may the Civil Rights Act have on the preparation of job specifications?
10. Evaluate the statement that affirmative action is simply another term for discrimination in reverse.

PROBLEMS AND SHORT CASES

1. Prepare a job description for a position with which you are familiar or for which you can secure the necessary information. Also prepare a job specification for this position.
2. Roger Weiss is now the purchasing director of a company for which he has worked 18 years. As the assistant purchasing director for the past 8 years, he was conscientious in his job and was a well-liked member of the company team because of his pleasant, cooperative manner. After the death of the purchasing director, Roger was promoted to that position. While Roger had been a good assistant, it now appears that his former boss had never really developed Roger's initiative, critical self-evaluation, and managerial skills. Roger is still 15 years from retirement. The company feels it has an obligation to Roger as a loyal employee whose professional and managerial training and

development have never really been stressed. Yet he cannot be allowed to hinder the ability of purchasing to respond to demands from the company and its broader environment. As his supervisor, what action might you take at this point?

3. Central City Electric, which specializes in commercial construction, has a problem. Because of a downturn in its business, it must lay off 50 workers of its 300-person work force. If it follows the seniority provisions of the contract with the union, the last hired will be the first fired. If it does this, however, it will probably get into trouble with the EEOC. About half of the last 50 workers hired are women and minorities; and if their jobs are terminated, the percentage of minority workers with Central City Electric will drop from 6 percent to about 3.5 percent. Prepare a report indicating what you think Central City Electric should do and why.

14 *Employee Compensation*

Jim Jackson had always paid the four full-time and two part-time employees in his gas station on the basis of a low hourly wage plus a generous commission on sales other than gasoline. The work force had worked well together when the economy was growing and sales were up. Now, however, with the new situation of recession combined with inflation, the employees were becoming more aggressive and competitive. Jackson noticed attempts to sell to each other's customers, and there was less willingness to help one another on the tougher jobs. He wondered if there were some other compensation plan that would help restore the previous cooperation without decreasing sales.

In ancient Rome different things circulated as money. When the emperors were firmly established, they issued coins of gold and silver and these were used throughout the Empire. In the early days of the Empire, however, Caesar paid his legionnaires in cakes of salt; and the Roman emperors did this again in the later days of the Empire when they began to run out of metal. This custom may be the origin of the saying that a person is — or is not — "worth his salt."

Our word **salary**, meaning a regularly paid compensation of a fixed amount, also finds its roots in this use of salt, as it comes from the Latin word "salarium" or "salt money." Over the long span of history money has assumed many other shapes and forms. Different societies at different times have been willing to exchange goods or services for seashells, whale's teeth, boar's tusks, stones, feathers, bricks, coconuts, cocoa beans, iron rings, beaver pelts, blankets, bronze axes, and stone wheels.

Any number of different materials, including paper IOUs, may serve as money. **Money** is anything that people will accept in exchange for goods or services in the belief that they may in turn exchange it at any time for other goods and services. For most people the satisfaction of human needs is the driving force that impels them to work for money by which they hope their needs and desires can be realized. In a capitalistic enterprise system these efforts are broadly known as production, and for employees the combined reward and stimulus is employee compensation, customarily referred to as wages.

The term "wages" is synonymous with "salaries" and is more commonly used than "employee compensation." "Wages" will be used in this chapter as an all-inclusive term to cover not only the pay received by the workers in stores, factories, offices, banks, mines, and farms, but also the salaries of executives and managers and the commissions paid to salespeople.

ECONOMIC THEORIES OF WAGES

Despite the fact that economists have theorized for many years on the manner in which wages and wage levels are determined, none of these theories is a complete and satisfactory explanation of the wage situation today. Many economists are still searching for new theories that will explain the current wage situation more adequately than has been done thus far. Because of this situation only three currently recognized economic wage theories are presented here: (1) marginal productivity theory, (2) bargaining theory, and (3) standard-of-living theory. They do not explain the entire wage picture, but they account for certain segments of it.

Marginal Productivity Theory

The rather complicated marginal productivity theory introduces two concepts: marginal productivity and marginal revenue. **Marginal productivity** is the value (selling price) of the goods produced by the last (or marginal) worker hired by a firm. **Marginal revenue** is the amount of increase in the total revenue (income) of a firm that results from the sale of one additional unit of output. The marginal productivity theory says that, under conditions of pure competition, an entrepreneur, whose objective is **maximization of profit**, will continue to hire additional workers until the point is reached where the value of the marginal product of the last worker hired just equals the wages paid to the last (or marginal) worker. Furthermore, the wages of all workers of the same ability in the firm will be determined by that paid to the marginal worker and the number of workers employed will be established at the point where their cost (wages) and marginal revenue are equal. Presented in another way, the point at which the wage of the marginal worker and the marginal revenue coincide will designate both the wage level of the workers and the number to be employed.

The major drawbacks to this theory are the almost total absence of pure competition in our economy and the great difficulty in accurately determining the productivity of the marginal worker in specialized complex business today. It appears reasonable to assume, however, that a manager will not continue to hire workers beyond the point where the return from the output of the marginal worker is less than the wages paid to this employee. A further difficulty is found in the suggestion that entrepreneurs do not always maximize their profits, but strive instead to increase their sales volumes or to maintain their competitive position in the industry.

Bargaining Theory

Many observers of the economic scene favor the bargaining theory of wages. The **bargaining theory** assumes that wages are set in a labor marketplace as the result of a bargaining process between labor, as sellers, and management, as buyers; and that the relative bargaining strengths of these two factors determine the wages to be paid. This theory has the virtue of describing an actual procedure that reasonably portrays the collective bargaining process.[1]

To assume, however, that an individual applicant seeking a job with an employer, particularly a large corporation, engages in a bargaining process, is to take a somewhat unrealistic view. The bargaining theory assumes, however, that there are lower limits below which the workers are unwilling to go and upper limits to the employers' offerings. Most jobs carry price tags, so to speak, or at least have a range of wage rates that are set by the employers on a take-it-or-leave-it basis. When there is a range, the employing officials are usually allowed to use their judgment, but they are rarely permitted to go above the upper limits.

The bargaining theory is a satisfactory explanation of one segment of the wage-determining process, but it is inadequate for the rest of the picture. It fails to explain high wages in unorganized industries or fields. It overlooks the relative productive value of skilled and unskilled workers, and does not explain the variations in wages between workers of equal skills in identical jobs. In plants where unions exist but where all workers are not required to join the union (the open shop[2]), the nonunion workers may receive the same benefits as the union members, frequently to keep them from joining the union. Also, in many plants senior workers receive automatic wage increases.

Standard-of-Living Theory

The **standard-of-living theory**, which is a comparatively recent development in wage theories, finds its roots in a pervasive belief that wages should be at least high enough to ensure workers a reasonable standard of living. The

[1]A further discussion of collective bargaining will be found on page 292.
[2]The open shop is further defined on page 290.

presumption of this theory is that all employers should pay wages high enough so that their employees may enjoy not only the necessities of life (food, clothing, and shelter), but also education for their children, adequate medical and dental care, and possibly savings.

This theory obviously is concerned with only the lower level of wages and seeks to establish a humanitarian, rather than an economic, basis for this level. It is therefore not to be considered as an overall wage-fixing theory. The apparent assumption with regard to firms that cannot afford to pay such minimum rates is that they must either find ways of so doing or go out of business as socially undesirable. The concept of standard-of-living wages is at the root of minimum-wage legislation.

FACTORS ACTUALLY DETERMINING WAGES

The shortcomings of all wage theories arise from the attempt that each makes to explain the whole wage-determining process, which tends to oversimplify an exceedingly complex situation. A larger number of different internal and external factors enter the wage-determining picture, and their relative weight in any situation varies with the peculiar conditions present in each instance. They include:

1. Demand for the various classes of labor.
2. Wage philosophy of the employers.
3. Stage of the business cycle — prosperity or recession.
4. Profit situation in the various businesses.
5. Degree of skill required.
6. Prevailing wage rates in the community.
7. Wage rates paid by other communities.
8. Degree of organization among the workers.
9. Bargaining skill of the workers' organizations.
10. Cost of living in the community.
11. Supply of the various classes of labor.
12. Relative mobility of labor.
13. Relative disagreeableness or attractiveness of the work.
14. Social desirability of the jobs.

These factors deal mainly with the nature of the industry, the company, and the job itself. Wages paid for different types of jobs within a particular industry or business are subject to wide variation. An automobile assembler receives about $5.50 an hour, including benefits; and the president of an automobile company like General Motors or Ford receives about $700,000 a year, including benefits. An unskilled laborer gets much less than a good salesperson; a filing clerk receives less than an expert typist, and so on.

Two basic reasons account heavily for these divergent wages: (1) the supply and demand of needed skills, and (2) competition.

Supply and Demand of Needed Skills

Many people whose capacities are limited or who are in situations which do not develop their latent capacities are able to do only unskilled labor. The ratio of these workers to the number of jobs available is high; hence, it is usually not necessary for management to pay high wages to secure as many workers of this type as it needs. As jobs become more complex and as the level of personal skills required to fill them rises, increasingly fewer individuals are qualified for these jobs; therefore, they are paid higher and higher wages. This is especially true in top executive positions, where the increasing need for competent managerial personnel has brought about not only very high salaries but also many additional rewards in the form of stock options, bonuses, retirement compensation, vacation allowances, and other incentives.

This explanation also applies to job variations between industries, as illustrated in Figure 14-1. A high degree of skill is required in contract construction (for example, carpenters, structural steel workers, plumbers, electrical workers, painters, and others in this area) along with strong union pressure and relatively small-scale contractors. The retail trade, by contrast, includes a large number of relatively unskilled people who, while unionized to some

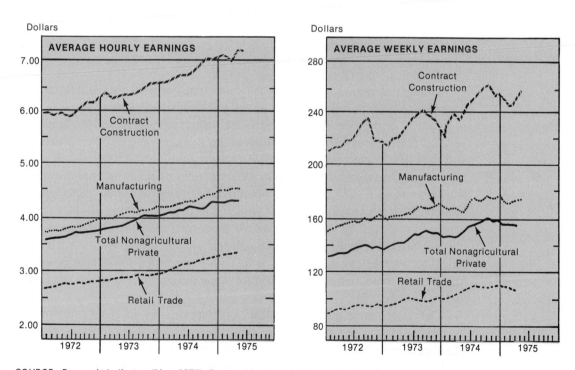

SOURCE: *Economic Indicators* (May, 1975). Prepared for the Joint Economic Committee by the Council of Economic Advisers.

Figure 14-1   ***Average Hourly and Weekly Earnings, Selected Industries***

extent, are unable to exert the upward pressure on their wage levels that is found in contract construction.

Competition

The second reason for the variation in wages is a corollary of the first and is based on the fact that the human and capital factors of production compete with each other on a cost basis for employment in the productive process. There is not only intergroup competition (labor competing with capital, worker versus machine), but also intragroup rivalry (laborers competing against laborers, executives against other executives).

Not only must a large number of laborers compete for the available jobs, but laborers as a group must compete against machines which can do the same things that they can do and frequently more cheaply. This situation tends to keep laborers' wages relatively low. On the other hand, not only are there comparatively few executives to compete for available jobs, but also there is practically no competition offered by land or capital. Hence, the remuneration of executives is relatively high. This same analysis can be made for all grades of jobs.

Other Factors

Among individuals performing the same types of work, wage differentials may be based on certain personal or geographic factors. One of these factors is seniority in the department, where the wage rates are based on length of service. Differences in the capabilities of the workers may also be reflected in varying rates of pay, the more skilled receiving the greater stipends. A situation of this sort serves a dual purpose — it acts as a reward for the better workers and as a stimulus to the poorer ones to improve their performance. Sometimes pay variations are due to the differing bargaining abilities of the employees when they were applying for their jobs; the better bargainers start out at higher levels than those who are less skilled at negotiating such matters. The warmer climate in the South, with a presumed lower cost of living, has often been advanced as a reason for wage differentials between the South and the North.

The unions have generally tended to disapprove of different rates of pay by the same firm for the same work, except where this reflects seniority. Their philosophy of "equal pay for equal work" assumes that the quality of work done by all workers will be the same, which is not always so. Such thinking tends to deaden the ambition of the better workers without providing any stimulus to the poorer ones.

WAGE INCENTIVES

Although productivity will be discussed in Chapter 17, it can be recognized here that a worker's performance is based both upon ability and motivation, or "will to do." Ultimately, however, productivity comes down to the manager's skill in promoting the effective and efficient use and combination of all the resources in the organization. Wage incentives provide one means of encouraging the effective performance of human resources.

The purpose of **wage incentives** is to induce workers to put forth greater productive efforts for which a cash reward is paid. The installation of a wage-incentive system in a company is a task that requires a high degree of skill, judgment, tact, and knowledge of the productive processes that are employed. Experience seems to indicate the desirability of "tailoring" each system to the plant in which it is to operate. The confidence of the workers must be gained, and they must understand thoroughly just how the system works. In unionized plants employees who are union representatives, known as **union stewards** or **shop stewards**, are brought into the operation and their approval secured.

Incentive plans can be used for office workers, salespersons, and even for executives. In each instance they must be fitted with care to the job to be done, and close attention should be paid to equalizing the extra reward to be paid with the additional effort required by the worker to secure it.

Desired Characteristics of Incentive Plans

The basic characteristics of a good incentive plan are: (a) it should provide a reward to the workers for the exercise of a reasonable measure of effort and attention, without creating a harmful physical or mental state on their part; (b) the production goals per worker should be reasonably attainable by the average employee affected; and (c) the added wage costs to the company should be at least balanced by the lowered production costs. A poor incentive plan would be lacking in one or more of these characteristics. A good incentive plan can do much to improve productivity and morale of an organization, whereas a poor one can have a devastating effect on personnel.

The Full Participation Plan

A common incentive plan for factory workers where extra effort on their part can result in additional production is known as the **full participation plan**. Where this plan is in operation, employees become eligible for incentive payment when their efficiency, as measured by the ratio of their output to an established standard, becomes 100%. For each 1% increase in output over 100%, an employee receives 1% increase in earnings. This is also known as the **1 for 1 plan**. To illustrate, in an operation where the standard time per unit is 2 hours and the base pay rate is $4.00 per hour, if an employee requires only 1.6 hours to complete 1 unit of work, efficiency is 2/1.6 = 125%. Since the employee has done 25% more work than is required, the rate of earnings would be $4.00 plus $1.00 (25%) or $5.00 per hour.

Group Incentive Plans

In an attempt to overcome some disadvantages of individual incentive plans, several companies have instituted **group incentive plans**, which include all or most of their employees. In some of these plans, representatives of the workers meet with management to discuss wage rates, machine speeds, and other details of shop practice. In several instances reports of these group efforts indicate quite favorable results from the standpoint of increased productivity, lower unit labor costs, improvement in product quality, reduction in scrap, and enhanced employee morale. Some observers believe that the extension of automation will bring about the replacement of individual wage incentives with group incentive plans.

METHODS OF WAGE PAYMENT

It is difficult to discuss incentives without also discussing pay methods, as these are closely related and, in fact, influence each other. There are many wage payment methods, just as there are many incentive systems, and established industry or management-union practices often determine which combination will be used. The most common of the different pay methods to workers are discussed in this section.

Straight Salary

A straight salary, which is the simplest form of wage payment, may be expressed in terms of a stated amount per day, week, month, or year. Straight-salary plans may or may not provide for deductions for absence or tardiness according to the policies of the companies using them. There is little in this system other than the possibility of a salary increase to serve as an incentive to an employee to exert extra effort on the job.

Time Wages

In this system payment is made on the basis of stated rates per hour or per day worked, without regard to quantity or quality of output. If a worker whose hourly rate is $3 works 8 hours, he or she receives a total wage of $24. Under the Fair Labor Standards Act employers must pay time and one half for overtime. Many contracts negotiated with management by labor unions also provide double time for work on Sundays and on holidays. It is customary for the regular working hours to be indicated either on a daily or a weekly basis. Except for the overtime feature and the possibility that markedly substandard work may involve discharge, there is nothing of the wage incentive in this system.

Shift Premium

A variant of time wages occurs when a higher rate is paid to workers on the afternoon shift and also on the night shift, which is called the **graveyard shift**. This system is known as the **shift premium plan**. Appearing during World War II when additional rewards were required to induce employees to work on these two shifts, the system has continued in most industries.

Bonus Payments

A mild form of incentive wages is found in the bonus payments that many firms make to their employees. These bonuses, which are frequently paid on a yearly basis, are customarily related to length of service rather than to output. They are used in banks, offices, stores, and other establishments where a record of each individual's production would be difficult, if not pointless, to maintain. They are incentives to employees to stay with the company but have little other value. Executive bonuses, which are sometimes related to the profitableness of the company, may take on the nature of incentives.

A notable example of a bonus plan that does have an incentive effect on the employees is that of the Lincoln Electric Company of Cleveland, Ohio. Since 1934, all of the company's personnel have participated in year-end bonuses which in many cases have equaled or exceeded the annual wages of the individual workers. In 1972, for example, a $19 million bonus was split, but not equally, by the 2,012 employees. The base for the bonuses is the company's success for each year, and the distribution to the employees is based on an evaluation procedure that measures each employee's worth to the company.

Piece-Rate Payment

The piece-rate payment plan involves payment at a stated rate per piece produced. Thus, if the piece rate for a given part is $.010 and a worker produces 2,500 pieces in a day, this individual will be paid $25.00. In many plants workers have a day (or hour) rate that becomes effective whenever they are not working on piece work. This allows for time consumed in setting up the machine, sharpening tools, machine breakdown, power failure, waiting for stock, and so on. Usually these plants guarantee their workers their day rate of pay as minimum wages. This is customarily well below what they can earn on piece work.

It is through piece-rate systems that wage incentives are usually established. A large number of such systems have been in force during the past several years, all of them varying slightly from the others but all designed to induce additional effort on the part of the workers and to reward them for it. Most of these systems establish a standard task that the workers must perform before they can begin to reap the additional remuneration that the system offers. One problem with this payment plan is deciding whether the worker should receive all of the earnings from the incentive or whether part should go to the worker and part to the supervisor.

Commission Payment

The **commission payment** type of wage payment is confined to salespersons and is, in effect, a piece-rate system. The salesperson's remuneration is a commission that is paid for each unit of product that he or she sells. The commission may be either a certain sum of money per unit, or it may be a percentage of the value of the item sold.

Since some companies pay only on a commission basis, a salesperson who fails to sell anything during any given period receives no pay for that time. Other companies pay a basic salary plus commissions. A number of firms give their salespersons drawing accounts, which are chargeable against commissions earned. For example, a salesperson who has a drawing account of $150 a week might, during a 4-week period, earn $800 in commissions. A common method of handling this situation is to pay this individual $150 weekly for the first three weeks, and then at the end of the fourth week to pay $150 plus $200 ($800 commissions minus $600 drawings) or a total of $350. If, however, commissions for the four weeks are less than $600, say $550, this salesperson would receive only $50 at the end of the fourth week.

A number of firms utilize a **guaranteed drawing account**. This operates in the same manner as the regular drawing account except that at the end of a stipulated period, such as four weeks, if a salesperson's commissions are less than the total of drawings, the debt is canceled and he or she starts with a clean slate. Thus, a guaranteed drawing account is quite similar to a salary.

In department and specialty stores the practice of paying commissions to salespersons, in addition to their regular salaries, is quite common. A variant on this system is the payment of **PMs (push money)** for the selling of certain designated items. Have you ever emptied a can of oil additive into your car's transmission and found a small metal tab or coin jingling around in the bottom of the empty can? This tab may have an amount ranging from perhaps 25¢ to $5.00 printed on it; the tab is redeemed by the manufacturer's salesperson to the service station or other retail outlet selling and servicing this product.

WAGE LEGISLATION

So far the discussion of various wage determinants has focused mainly on factors within the business system, but federal legislation often specifies wage provisions that establish the basic requirements or starting points for other wage and incentive systems. Three important acts in this area are the: (1) Fair Labor Standards Act of 1938, (2) Equal Pay Act of 1963, and (3) Employee Retirement Income Security Act of 1974.

Fair Labor Standards Act

The Fair Labor Standards Act, known as the Wage and Hour Act of 1938, was the first of a series of federal enactments designed to place a floor under the wages of labor and a ceiling on the number of hours of work per week for workers in private industry whose products enter interstate commerce. The philosophy behind the concept of minimum wages and maximum hours was that low wages constituted unfair competition and were detrimental to the health, efficiency, and general well-being of workers. Originally the minimum wage was 25 cents per hour and the maximum workweek, over which time and one-half rates had to be paid, was 44 hours, but this was soon reduced to 40 hours. Through several amendments, the minimum rate was advanced to $2.30 an hour beginning in January, 1976. Coverage has been extended to laundry and dry cleaning enterprises, construction enterprises, hospitals, nursing homes, and most schools. Hotels, motels, restaurants, retail and service enterprises, and gasoline service stations with sales above certain amounts are included. Federal government hospitals are excluded. Under certain specified circumstances, the minimum wage law is applicable to farm labor. In addition to the federal legislation, 40 states have minimum wage laws applicable mainly to women and children in selected industries.

The argument in favor of these laws is that employers should be compelled to pay employees the minimum wage rates required for a fair standard of living. The labor unions have been particularly active in bringing pressure on the Congress and the state legislatures to enact such legislation and to raise the minimum standard. Opposed to this argument have been claims that these laws do not benefit those whom they are ostensibly designed to help, namely, the unskilled; the effect has been to place their wage rates above those that they are capable of earning, with the result that they have been forced into the ranks of the unemployed.

Equal Pay Act

The Equal Pay Act of 1963, an amendment to the Fair Labor Standards Act of 1938, now requires equal pay for similar work, regardless of sex. The significance of this ruling can be seen in two cases involving Corning Glass Works and AT&T.

In the first case $1 million in back pay was awarded to women inspectors on the day shift who had been receiving a lower base pay than men inspectors on the night shift. The decision made it clear that higher rates of pay cannot be justified solely on the basis of the time of day the work is performed, although the law does permit **shift differentials**, or differences in pay for those working different shifts, based on other grounds.

In January, 1973, the EEOC filed charges of discrimination with the Federal Communications Commission against AT&T that resulted in the payment of $15 million in back pay to 15,000 employees, and salary increases of $23 million for approximately 36,000 women and minority workers who were paid less than white males. This decree was the first settlement under a 1972 amendment to the Equal Pay Act that extended its coverage to supervisors, professionals, and managerial employees.

In the past women have been socialized to expect only a certain niche in the occupational hierarchy. Now, with the help of legislation like the Equal Pay Act, they are beginning to fight "tradition" in matters of compensation and job promotion.

Employee Retirement Income Security Act

The product of almost a decade of legislative wrangling, this enormous 247-page Employee Retirement Income Security Act was signed into law by President Ford on Labor Day, 1974. The new law will have a great impact, as it affects in some way all of the 35 million persons presently covered by private pension plans. Private pension plans have grown greatly from $12 billion in assets in 1950 to almost $160 billion today. Unfortunately, some of the 350,000 plans have failed to deliver benefits to workers when the companies went out of business or were merged with other companies. This new law:

1. Guarantees that all employees 25 years old and over, with one year of experience, will be enrolled in the company's plan if the company has a plan.
2. Grants **vesting rights** to workers; that is, guarantees employees at least part of their pension benefits after a certain period of time even if they leave the employer.
3. Sets professional and financial standards for the management of pension plan assets.

4. Creates a federal Pension Benefit Guaranty Corporation to ensure, at the cost of $1 per worker per year, that pensions will be paid to workers even if the business fails.
5. Provides for self-employed persons to contribute to their own pension funds.

The act does not, however, provide for **portable pensions**, which allow for the transfer of benefits accrued on one job to the pension plan of another. Even without the portability feature, the amount of corporate profits that will have to go into pension funds to keep them healthy in the current inflationary climate will represent another cost for business at a time when most companies are trying desperately to hold down costs. And, conversely, inflation erodes the buying power of whatever rights — pension or otherwise — the worker may accrue.

WAGES AND INFLATION

Inflation is an economic condition existing when the purchasing power of money is diminishing. Inflation is brought about by an increase in money and credit relative to the available goods, resulting in a rise in the general level of prices and a reduction in what a dollar will buy. This commonly is referred to as "too much money chasing too few goods."

The recent reality and the future threat of **double-digit inflation** (an annual inflation rate of 10 percent or more) has an overriding effect on every topic that has been discussed so far in this chapter. Since 1966, our growing rate of inflation has hit every pocketbook in our society in some way or another; but wage earners and pensioners are especially hard-hit since inflation generally takes from the old, weak, and small, rather than from organized, wealthy interests who can shift their capital into whatever form of value escapes the inflationary erosion. The flight from paper money to things — real estate, art, gold — is an attempt to seek security against monetary depreciation.

In addition to falling hard on wage earners, middle-class persons with savings in their property or a few stocks, and pensioners, inflation reduces the real income of colleges, hospitals, libraries, other useful institutions, and the people working in them who usually are not protected by the bargaining power of trade unions.

Money Wages and Real Wages

Even when people get more income in an inflationary cycle, they think it belongs to them and they do not like to see it taken back by higher prices. Thus, many people today are becoming painfully aware of the important distinction that should be made between money wages and real wages. **Money wages** are, as the term implies, the actual dollars and cents that workers receive from their employers as payment for services rendered. **Real wages** are the goods and services that the money wages will buy at any given time. This means that real wages are dependent on the current price level as well as on the existing wage level. If money wages are high and the price level is relatively low, real wages are higher than if the price level were to be raised several points. In view of the fact that the value of money lies in the goods and services that it will buy, the test of the adequacy of any given wage level is in the real wage concept.

Real income or wages and prices are clearly related, as real income is the individual consumer's **purchasing power**. The United States Department of Labor publishes the Consumer Price Index (CPI) mentioned in Chapter 11, which portrays the real wage situation at any one time.

Inflation and Unemployment

Economists usually take the position that a credible disinflationary program cannot be accomplished without some rise in unemployment. Inflation must be controlled, but the cost of ending a high rate of inflation should not fall only on those who lose their jobs. Two avenues are possible. One is a program of public-service employment, paid for by the federal government. The other is a program of income maintenance including the strengthening of the unemployment compensation programs in terms of benefits, duration of payments, and coverage. These would be in addition to, or in conjunction with, existing company employee-benefit programs.

EMPLOYEE BENEFITS

During World War II and the years following, a group of so-called **fringe benefits** have come into being as additions to workers' direct wage payments. Among these are health, accident, and life insurance, and hospital and surgical care with the cost paid wholly or in part by the employers; paid vacations and holidays; paid time off for voting; rest periods; **severance pay**, which is sometimes given an employee upon employment termination over and above any unpaid wages; payments for work tools; and payment for work clothing.

In addition to these fringe benefits, which are now granted by most medium-to-large businesses, some companies have instituted plans which provide remuneration beyond their employees' basic pay schedules. The most common among these are the profit-sharing plan, the guaranteed annual wage system, and the pension plan.

Profit Sharing

An employee benefit that has had some vogue in this country is the distribution of some fraction of a firm's profits to its employees without requiring them to purchase stock. This is called **profit sharing**. It may be accomplished either through cash payments or through distribution of company stock. The purposes of profit sharing include inducements for greater production, lower labor turnover, economy in worker use of materials and supplies, loyalty to the company, and resistance to pressure for unionization.

Profits are distributed according to some predetermined pattern. They frequently recognize length of service, both in the matter of the amounts paid to individuals and in the requirement of a certain minimum period of employment as a prerequisite to participation in the distribution. It should be recognized that profit sharing is an expense of doing business and is really a bonus based on the size of the profits.

A profit-sharing scheme assumes the presence of profits available for distribution, which may not be realized in times of poor business or depression, or when it seems wise to plow a large part of the earnings back into the business. The effect on the workers of the failure of the company to continue to distribute the profit bonuses is said to be distinctly unfavorable and to more than offset any benefits that previous distributions may have afforded.

The Merrill Manufacturing Corporation of Merrill, Wisconsin, has had a cash profit-sharing plan since 1949 that is reported to be quite successful. Through the operation of an arithmetical formula, a certain percentage of the company's yearly profits are distributed quarterly to all employees, except officers, who have been continuously employed by the company for three months or more. The workers are kept informed of the profit-sharing plan through their supervisors and an annual meeting. A careful check is kept on quality control, and the employees responsible for spoiled material are informed about it. Suggestions for improvements in operations are invited by the management. A series of interviews with the employees by an outside agency indicated that the workers like the profit-sharing program, both because of the checks that they receive and because they understand how the plan operates.

Guaranteed Annual Wage

The concept of the **guaranteed annual wage**, an idea that has been gaining considerable attention for several years, is that the employer agrees to pay eligible workers (usually with one or two years' service) a certain guaranteed wage every week of the year or for 48 weeks, regardless of sales volume or the stage of the business cycle. The best-known plans are probably those of the Procter and Gamble Company, George A. Hormel & Company, and the Nunn-Bush Shoe Company. The plans of these concerns date to before World War II. Their products are consumer goods that have a considerable measure of stability in their sales volume. This means that there is a minimum of time when the plants are shut down or are working part time.

The big stumbling block to the widespread adoption of the guaranteed annual wage is the professed (and probably actual) inability of many employers to continue to pay wages when sales are low or nonexistent. Certain unions, however, have stated their intention to press for guaranteed annual wages from their employers. An early step in this direction occurred in 1955 when the United Auto Workers negotiated a guaranteed annual wage provision with the Ford Motor Company.

The Ford contract, which has been followed by contracts in the steel and rubber industries, has set the pattern for similar agreements in more than 100 companies. It actually provides for **supplementary unemployment benefits**, commonly known as **SUB**. While there is considerable difference in detail among these agreements, the basic pattern is that the employer will make payments to laid-off eligible employees, which, when combined with unemployment compensation from the state, will not exceed 65 percent of the employee's take-home pay for the first 4 weeks of unemployment, and will not exceed 60 percent of such pay for the next 22 weeks. Eligibility is based on length of service. The total time during which payments are made varies from 26 to 52 weeks.

The operation of these plans requires changes in state laws or rulings by state attorneys-general that will permit workers to receive both unemployment compensation and SUB in full amount at the same time. The funds from which the employers make the SUB payments are built up by contributions made by the companies on the basis of from 3 cents to 5 cents per employee for each hour worked. If the funds go below certain levels, the payments may be reduced or even suspended.

Under emergency legislation passed in 1974, unemployment compensation benefits were extended from 26 to 52 weeks in most states. Furthermore, an amendment to the 1974 federal tax cut bill added 13 more weeks for a temporary period. In March, 1974, 732,000 unemployed workers had been off the job more than six months, which introduced a real question on whether 65 weeks is enough for an "insurance" program. However, at some point such a program ceases to be insurance and becomes "welfare."

Pensions

The practice of employers' providing old-age pensions for their employees began in the 1800s; but since the passage of the federal Social Security Act in 1935, there has been a vast increase in the extent of such coverage. This has been particularly true in plants where the unions have contracts. Some pension plans are financed entirely by employers and others by joint contributions to the funds by both employers and employees. In either case a labor expense is involved for the companies concerned.

Recent pension legislation was discussed on pages 278–279. It seems probable that pensions will become a fixed part of the employee wage payment schemes in this country. The growth of pensions has been a potent instrument in the betterment of human resources in the companies that have adopted them, since pensions help satisfy the desire of workers for economic security.

As a means of providing jobs for younger persons, and also of enabling an employer to discontinue certain jobs, **early retirement** has become a provision of many retirement plans. This permits employees to retire at an earlier than normal age and still receive a relatively generous part of the usual pension. The pension is readjusted when the person becomes eligible for social security payments.

WAGE AND SALARY ADMINISTRATION

The overall control of all phases of employee compensation is usually performed by a management function known as **wage and salary administration**. The broad determination of wage and salary policies in any organization is a top management prerogative, but carrying out the details of wage and salary administration is entrusted to various departments of different companies, such as the industrial relations division, industrial engineering department, the treasurer or controller, and the personnel department.

The purpose of wage and salary administration is to provide adequate and equitable compensation to all employees. Wage and salary administrators face a distinct challenge in handling such important matters in the maintenance of a productive employee group. No employee — minority or majority, executive or operator, man or woman — is willing for long to tolerate poorly administered wage and salary plans. These must be carefully planned, clearly communicated, and consistently monitored and carried out.

BUSINESS TERMS

salary	267	standard-of-living theory	269
money	267	wage incentives	273
marginal productivity	268	union stewards or shop stewards	273
marginal revenue	268	full participation (or 1 for 1) plan	273
maximization of profit	268	group incentive plans	274
bargaining theory	269	graveyard shift	275

QUESTIONS FOR DISCUSSION AND ANALYSIS

1. Do you believe that the money value of the goods produced by the marginal worker in a firm can be accurately computed? Explain.
2. Which wage theory discussed in this chapter comes closest to explaining the actual wage determination process?
3. Why do workers of equal skills working in identical or similar jobs in different companies often receive different wages?
4. Labor leaders sometimes say that profits come out of wages, while managers maintain that wages come out of profits. Which of these, if either, is correct? Explain.
5. Presumably a worker does "a fair day's work for a fair day's pay." Why, then, are wage incentive plans often used?
6. A factory worker is on a "1 for 1" full participation plan. The standard time for each unit produced is one-half hour, and the base pay rate is $5.00 an hour. What would be the pay per hour if this worker produces a unit every 20 minutes?
7. How can a firm afford to have a guaranteed drawing account pay plan in which it "wipes the slate clean" if a salesperson's commissions are less than total drawings?
8. Why does the test of the adequacy of any given wage level lie in the real wage concept?
9. Should laid-off workers be permitted to receive supplementary unemployment benefits at the same time they are receiving state unemployment compensation payments? Explain.
10. Should pensions be provided as a reward for loyalty or as a matter of a worker's rights?

PROBLEMS AND SHORT CASES

1. Gus Olafsen is the owner of a large gas station employing 6 full-time and 3 part-time people over two shifts. He wants to establish a wage incentive plan to encourage the sales of tires, batteries, and accessories (TBAs). He is thinking of three possible plans: (1) an individual commission plan in which each person would be paid a commission on his or her TBA sales; (2) a group plan in which the commissions would be put in a pot and distributed on the basis of hours worked; and (3) a relatively high salary in comparison to other gas stations with the understanding that a certain sales quota was expected if the salary was to be justified and the job retained. Prepare a report indicating what you see to be the strengths and weaknesses of these various wage incentive plans.
2. The topic of minimum wage legislation, which has been prominent in Congressional circles, has created a considerable controversy between those who favor the minimum wage and those who oppose it. The issues involved cover

the question of whether the minimum wage increases the incomes of those whom it is ostensibly intended to benefit or merely prevents the unskilled from securing employment. There is also the question regarding employers who are unable to pay the minimum wage to their workers, and more recently the question of whether farm workers should be covered by this legislation.

Consult periodicals and newspaper articles in your school library and write a report covering this controversy, indicating your views on the subject and substantiating them.

3. Assume that you are an industrial (private) accountant at the middle-management level in a large corporation. Prepare a report suggesting what impact each of the three following conditions might have on your salary: (a) wage and price controls, (b) inflation, and (c) recession.

15 Labor-Management Relations

The first successful sit-down strike was directed by a Master of Arts from Harvard University. Clearly strike leader George Edwards had not expected to go from Harvard to the work force at Kelsey-Hayes Wheel Corp. in Detroit. The Depression that put him and others like him on production lines also motivated them to help relieve the hardships they shared with other workers. Beside them worked radicals of various stripes, eager to forge a labor movement capable of remaking society. Together, workers, ideologues, and displaced potential executives and professionals created the big industrial unions and, in some cases, rejuvenated the old-line craft unions.[1]

The term "labor" applies broadly to the human factor involved in the production and distribution of goods and services. Usually labor-management relations are concerned with the issues and matters arising through the collective action of employees, especially between company managers and the unions with which they deal. This is a relatively recent relationship, however, as the labor union movement has had a long and uneven history in the United States.

THE GROWTH AND GOALS OF LABOR

Even before the Declaration of Independence, skilled artisans in handicraft and domestic industries joined together in benevolent societies, primarily to provide members and their families with financial assistance in the event of serious illness, debt, or death of the wage earner. Although these early associations had few of the characteristics of present-day labor unions, they did

---

[1]"Why Labor Can't Find Young Leaders; A Labor Commentary," *Business Week* (October 31, 1970), p. 78.

bring workers together to consider problems of mutual concern and to devise ways and means for their solution.[2]

As recently as the late 1800s, however, workers labored 10 hours a day. The 6-day week was prevalent, and many workers in jobs requiring continuous operation had a 7-day schedule. Premium pay for overtime, paid vacations and holidays, and retirement benefits were almost unknown. The status of unions and the conditions of work have improved significantly since then.

The Growth of Modern Labor

Labor's dramatic past helped to cast its present form. This can be seen in four mileposts of modern union growth: (1) the Noble Order of the Knights of Labor, (2) the American Federation of Labor (AFL), (3) the Congress of Industrial Organizations (CIO), and (4) the combined AFL-CIO.

KNIGHTS OF LABOR

The Noble Order of the Knights of Labor was founded in 1869 by Uriah S. Stephens as a small local union of Philadelphia garment makers. At first it functioned as a secret society because of widespread bitterness against unions. By 1886 it claimed over 700,000 members throughout the country. The Order had a broad aim: the replacement of a competitive society by a cooperative one. More specifically, its program called for the 8-hour day, equal pay for equal work by women, abolition of convict labor and child labor, public ownership of utilities, and the establishment of cooperatives. Reliance was placed on educational and political methods rather than on collective bargaining.

This orientation led to an internal clash in the organization with stronger craft unions who wanted to bargain for the basic goals of higher wages and improved working conditions. When the Knights in 1886 refused to respect the jurisdiction of the large craft unions, several of the latter met in Columbus, Ohio, and founded the American Federation of Labor.

AMERICAN FEDERATION OF LABOR

Samuel Gompers was elected first president of the AFL, a position he held, except for one year, until his death in 1924. The AFL under Gompers' leadership was successful in developing along the lines of "pure and simple" unionism, and membership reached 4 million by 1920.

[2]Much of the material in this section on labor growth is from U.S. Bureau of Labor Statistics, *A Brief History of the American Labor Movement* (Washington: U.S. Government Printing Office, 1970).

The total union growth was hard-pressed by the economic depression of the early 1930s, but revived somewhat during the New Deal legislation that will be covered later in the chapter. Figure 15-1 shows the growth of the labor movement since 1930.

Around 1934 an internal struggle developed in the AFL over the question of whether unions should be organized to include all workers in an industry, or strictly on a craft or occupational basis. Efforts at compromise and concili-ation failed, and in 1938 nine unions expelled from the AFL formed the Con-gress of Industrial Organizations.

CONGRESS OF INDUSTRIAL ORGANIZATIONS

John L. Lewis, then president of the United Mine Workers, was elected to head the CIO. Its purpose was to promote the organization of workers in mass-production and organized industries such as the steel, automobile, and textile industries. Interestingly, the rivalry generated by the AFL and CIO stimulated the organizing efforts of both groups, and workers poured into the unions.

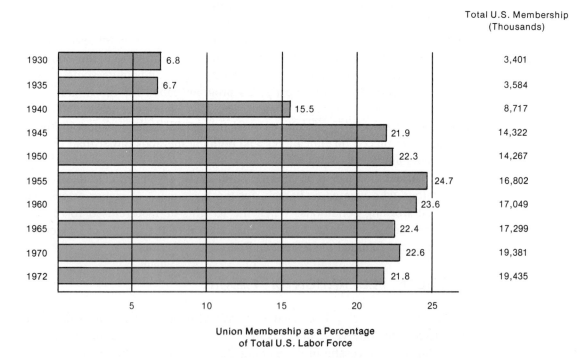

SOURCE: U.S. Department of Commerce, *Statistical Abstract of the United States* (Washington: U.S. Government Printing Office, 1973) and *Monthly Labor Review* (August, 1974).

Figure 15-1   **Union Membership in the United States, 1930–1972 (In Numbers and Proportions of Labor Force)**

THE AFL-CIO

A new era in American labor history opened in December, 1955, with the formation of the AFL-CIO. The merger of the two federations, rivals since 1935, brought into one organization unions representing approximately 16 million workers, or between 85 and 90 percent of the membership claimed by all unions in the United States. George Meany, former AFL president, was elected president; and Walter Reuther, former CIO president, became head of a newly created Industrial Union Department and a vice-president of the AFL-CIO.

But this marriage was short-lived. The United Auto Workers (UAW) became increasingly critical of the way the AFL-CIO handled such problems as unemployment and poverty, civil rights, and foreign policy issues. These differences, plus a personality conflict between Meany and Reuther, contributed to the latest split in the labor movement which resulted in the formation of the Alliance for Labor Action (ALA) in 1968. The Alliance's charter members — the two largest unions in the country — were the Teamsters and the United Auto Workers. In May, 1970, Walter Reuther died in an airplane accident; and the ALA later disbanded.

Goals of Organized Labor

The aims of organized labor are both political and economic. The political aspects of union activity, which appeared with the passage of the National Labor Relations Act of 1935 and have expanded to a marked degree in the past decade, include lobbying activities designed to secure the passage of favorable legislation and the rejection of unfavorable proposed laws in Congress and the state legislatures. Efforts have been made to "bring out the labor vote" for the purpose of electing so-called friendly candidates for public office and defeating unfriendly ones.

HIGHER WAGES AND SHORTER HOURS

Foremost among the aims of unions are the raising of wages and the shortening of the number of work hours. Any betterment in these factors is immediately recognized. In the long, slow movement toward higher wages and shorter hours since the early days of the Industrial Revolution, the unions have played a notable role.

SENIORITY PROVISIONS

Many agreements contain seniority provisions that specify the rights and privileges of the employees from the standpoint of length of service. These provisions are concerned mainly with layoffs, rehiring, transfers, and promotions. Obviously this objective disregards individual ability and ambition.

UNION SECURITY OR RECOGNITION

With **union security** employers admit the right of employees to choose their own representatives and agree to recognize the chosen union as the sole bargaining agent for the workers, or at least that portion of the workers who want the union. The items that follow indicate the ways in which unions have sought security.

Closed Shop. Under the **closed shop** the employer agrees to hire only persons who are union members, and all employees must remain members in good standing during their term of employment with the company. The Labor Management Relations Act of 1947, usually called the Taft-Hartley Act, outlawed the closed shop. It still exists in some industries, notably construction, printing, and maritime industries. The reason for this apparently illegal practice is that many workers in these industries get their jobs through **union hiring halls**. Employers who need qualified workers contact the local union business agent, who sends out individuals who are registered in the hiring halls as being available.

Criticism has frequently been directed against the construction unions for their rather rigid apprentice system, under which limited numbers of individuals are admitted to apprentice status to undergo extensive instruction and performance before being certified as journeymen in their various crafts. It has been charged that through this procedure and their reluctance to admit large numbers of apprentices, the construction unions virtually run an industry-wide closed shop. The unions that are involved have vigorously denied this accusation.

Union Shop. A **union shop** differs from a closed shop in that the employer may hire nonunion workers, but they must join the union after a prescribed period and remain in good standing as a requirement of continued employment. Right-to-work laws place a ban on the union shop in several states.

Open Shop. Most employers have been opposed to both the closed and the union shop, preferring instead the **open shop** in which, at least theoretically, both union and nonunion workers may be employed. Labor leaders, on the other hand, have been most violently opposed to the open shop.

Agency Shop. In the **agency shop** all employees for whom the union, the **bargaining unit**, negotiates are required to pay dues to the union, but they do not have to join it. The agency shop is legal except where the states forbid it, which they have the right to do. Thus, the agency shop is legal in Indiana but illegal in Florida. The agency shop was devised by the unions to circumvent state right-to-work laws.

Maintenance-of-Membership Arrangement. Under a **maintenance-of-membership arrangement** workers need not belong to a union in order to obtain a job, nor must they join it in order to retain their jobs. If they are members of the union at the time that the maintenance-of-membership shop becomes effective, however, or if they join after that date, they must maintain membership in good standing for the life of the existing contract as a requirement of continued employment.

Preferential Shop. In a **preferential shop** the employer agrees to give preference to union members in hiring and in layoffs. Thus, union workers, if available, are hired before nonunion workers and they are retained until the last when layoffs are necessary. The Taft-Hartley Act outlaws the preferential shop.

In some situations where not all employees are members of the union, the contract includes a provision by which the union is recognized as the sole or exclusive bargaining agent for all employees. Such a provision is characteristic of approximately one fifth of existing agreements. In some areas of public employment the union is recognized as representing only those employees who are members of the union. The employer deals with nonmembers on an individual basis.

CHECKOFF

The term **checkoff** is applied to the collection of union dues by the employer through payroll deductions. Provisions for this collection are contained in the agreement executed between the union and management.

RESTRICTION OF OUTPUT AND JOB RETENTION

One of the common economic aims of unions, which may or may not be admitted by labor leaders, is some form of restriction on the amount of work that will be turned out daily. The union thinking behind this action is the preservation of jobs, on the theory that there is only so much work to be done and that it should be parceled out so that all the present employees retain their jobs. The contract requirement stating that certain jobs be continued after management believes they are no longer needed is known as **featherbedding**, a practice that employers have been trying for years to eliminate.

FRINGE BENEFITS

In the past two decades or more the unions have also sought and secured such fringe benefits as pensions, employee insurance, hospitalization, and many other advantages for their members.

TYPES OF UNIONS

There are a number of independent unions that are not affiliated with the AFL-CIO. The AFL-CIO merger, nevertheless, reflects the fact that the two basic types of unions in this country are the craft union and the industrial union. **Craft unions** are organized according to crafts or trades, such as painters, plumbers, machinists, and teamsters. **Industrial unions** are organized according to industries, such as steel workers, clothing workers, and automobile workers.

Historically unionism in this country developed on the trade or craft basis, and only since 1935 has industrial unionism made much headway. The years since then, however, have witnessed a clear trend toward the industrial union; and even the craft unions are now admitting some unskilled and semi-skilled workers to membership.

COLLECTIVE AND COALITION BARGAINING

When a company becomes unionized, **collective bargaining** is substituted for individual bargaining. The union becomes the bargaining agent for its members and, in some cases, for some or all of the nonunion employees.

Advantages of Collective Bargaining

The collective bargaining agreement between a company and a union usually establishes procedures by which the union representatives in the shop can bring employee grievances to management's attention at any time. Likewise, management may consult with the union on subjects that concern both parties. Also, the necessity for the interpretation of clauses in the agreement calls for virtually continuous contact between union and management. Collective bargaining permits the unions to employ skilled negotiators in their bargaining activities, something that no individual could hope to do. It is through this process that labor is gaining a voice in the operation of industry.

Coalition Bargaining

In companies where several different unions have contracts, some unions have joined together in the bargaining process. This is known as **coalition** bargaining or **coordinated bargaining**. In one instance 26 unions bargained with and struck against the four largest companies in a single industry. The unions argue that because of the growth of industrial conglomerates, such tactics are necessary to balance union strength with that of their employers. The fear that this new maneuver may result in a superstrike, with its disruption of production and possible large-scale violence, has raised the question whether Congress should take action to outlaw joint bargaining by unions that represent different trades although they may be in the same industrial areas. The Industrial Union Department of the AFL-CIO has been promoting the idea of coalition or **conglomerate bargaining**, while the National Association of Manufacturers and the U.S. Chamber of Commerce have been strongly opposed to this concept.

BARGAINING TACTICS AND TOOLS

In many instances unions have been able to achieve their objectives through the process of negotiating with management. Unfortunately, however, there have been a large number of cases where labor and management have been unable to settle their differences on a peaceful basis and have had to resort to more strenuous practices.

Labor's Methods

The lifeblood of trade unionism in the United States has always been the representation of members in negotiations with employers, as noted above. And since World War II, the trend has been toward the peaceful resolution of disputes. Nevertheless, the strike continues to play a traditional, if not a somewhat moderated, role in collective bargaining. Other tactics include picketing, soldiering on the job, and boycotts.

STRIKES

A **strike** is a temporary refusal by employees to continue their work until their demands have been granted by management. The term **walkout** is used as a synonym for strike.

Usually the workers on strike remain away from the plant, but there have been two types of strikes in which they remain in the plant. These are the **sit-down strike**, in which the workers appear at their posts but refuse to perform their appointed tasks or to leave the premises until their demands are met; and the **slowdown strike** where the workers continue to work but at a markedly reduced tempo so that production is curtailed but not completely halted. The sitdown strike has been declared illegal by the courts in some states and has almost disappeared.

In a **jurisdictional strike** the union tries to force the employer to recognize it instead of another union for certain stated types of work. Under the Taft-Hartley Act most jurisdictional strikes are unfair labor practices and, as such, are prohibited. A **wildcat** or **outlaw strike** occurs when a group of workers go on strike without the official consent of the officers of the union or in violation of the terms of the contract. A **sympathy strike** involves a group of workers who go on strike because of sympathy with another group who are also on strike. The sympathy strikers usually have no grievance against their own employers but strike as a part of the union strategy to help the original striking group.

PICKETING

Picketing consists of posting one or more persons at the entrance to the struck plant for the purpose of dissuading or preventing persons from entering the plant and of informing the public that a strike is in progress. **Mass picketing** occurs when a large number of pickets assemble at the entrances to a struck plant and forcibly prevent persons who may wish to go to work from crossing the picket lines. This is mob rule and has generally been frowned on by the courts.

SOLDIERING ON THE JOB

Soldiering on the job occurs when one or more workers in a plant deliberately reduce the pace of their work to impede production. If this takes place on an organized basis, it is called a slowdown strike. The workers in this instance do not stop working, they merely slow down the tempo of their operations. **Sabotage** occurs when workers maliciously cripple or destroy the productive equipment of the plants where they work. This is illegal and is not often found.

BOYCOTTS

A **boycott** takes place when union members refuse to purchase products from companies whose employees are on strike or where some condition prevails to which the union is opposed. This type of boycott is called a **primary boycott**. A **secondary boycott** exists when workers apply these tactics against a secondary handler, who offers for sale the goods of a struck or a nonunion plant. The Taft-Hartley Act prohibits certain types of secondary boycotts.

There is often a very thin line between a secondary boycott and a product boycott. A **product boycott** involves picketing or other efforts of an informational nature not intended to affect a store's business, but to turn customers away from a boycotted product to others not opposed by labor. This strategy has gained recent prominence in labor's campaign to organize the Farah Manufacturing Company's plants in the Southwest. In this situation a nationwide boycott of the company's products — men's and boy's slacks — caused an $8 million loss for Farah in 1973 and forced Farah to recognize the union.

Management's Methods

Bargaining tactics employed by management have consisted mainly of lockouts, blacklists, injunctions, yellow-dog contracts, and strike insurance.

LOCKOUTS

A **lockout** consists of an employer's refusal to permit workers to enter the plant to work. This usually takes place because the employer resents some action on the part of the workers. At other times lockouts have occurred to deny union organizers access to the plants to prevent their holding organizing meetings.

BLACKLISTS

A **blacklist** is a secret list of names compiled by employers' associations and circulated among the members for the purpose of denying employment to the listed persons, who are known as union organizers and union members. Blacklisting is regarded as an unfair labor practice under a ruling of the National Labor Relations Board.

INJUNCTIONS

An **injunction** is a court order secured by the employer that aims to restrain the unions from interfering with the production of a plant in some manner, usually at the time of a strike. At one time injunctions were issued against almost all forms of strike activity, but in recent years they have been restricted to mass picketing, acts of violence, or damage to the employer's property.

YELLOW-DOG CONTRACTS

A **yellow-dog contract** is an agreement signed by workers, usually as a condition of securing jobs, whereby they promise not to join a union while working for their employers. The Norris-LaGuardia Act outlawed this type of contract.

STRIKE INSURANCE

Strike insurance funds have been established in the newspaper and air transport industries and in the railroads. Any member of these businesses can receive payments from the funds during a strike. Contributions are made by all members on a self-insurance basis. The purpose of this action is to strengthen the managements of struck firms and to enable them to hold out for long periods of time in the event of strikes. The unions, naturally, are bitterly opposed to strike insurance, although they have long had similar funds to aid strikers.

Methods of Settling Labor Disputes

Inasmuch as labor disputes are regarded as such only if management and labor are completely unable to agree on the points in question, the methods for settling them must of necessity involve the intervention of some outside agency or person, who may or may not represent some government agency. These methods for settling disputes are: (1) mediation, (2) arbitration, and (3) compulsory investigation.

MEDIATION

In **mediation** a third party attempts to bring both sides to a point of common agreement. This is done without coercion and purely on the basis of helpfulness and the disinterestedness of an impartial third party. The term conciliation is frequently used synonymously with mediation. In a strict sense **conciliation** means that the mediator reviews the proposals put forth by both parties, whereas mediation implies that the mediator also offers proposals.

The Federal Mediation and Conciliation Service, created in 1947, was established for the purpose of providing means whereby the good offices of a government agency could be made available to the parties of a labor dispute in an industry involved in interstate commerce, should these parties care to take advantage of them. Neither disputant is required to accept the agency's offer of assistance or to abide by its suggestions for solution of a dispute. The National Board of Mediation, established under the provisions of the Railway Labor Act of 1926 (amended in 1934), exists to mediate labor disputes in the railroad business.

ARBITRATION

Arbitration involves the submittal by labor and management of the disputed issue to an individual arbitrator or, more commonly, a board. Usually each side has one representative on an arbitration board, and a third party, someone acceptable to both disputants, is chosen as chairperson. This individual may be a public official or someone in the community who has a reputation for fairness and impartial judgment. Once both parties agree to submit the dispute, the decision becomes morally, if not legally, binding. This method of settling labor problems is known as **voluntary arbitration**. It is included as a possible procedure in some contracts between companies and labor unions. **Compulsory arbitration**, whereby both labor and management are required to submit to arbitration upon failure to settle their differences by other means, has made very little headway in this country, except in a few states and cities where employees of nonprofit hospitals, public utilities, and police and fire departments are prohibited by the law from striking and must submit their grievances to binding arbitration.

In a few cases, mainly in public utilities, impartial umpires have been appointed to whom all unsolved disputes are submitted for settlement. Their decisions are usually binding on both parties.

COMPULSORY INVESTIGATION

Either through legislation or by contract agreement, threatened strikes that may imperil public health and safety are postponed for varying periods while impartial third parties investigate the disputes and make reports on their findings, which may or may not include recommendations for settlement. This is known as **compulsory investigation and delay**.

LABOR LEGISLATION

Labor legislation has come to play an increasingly important role in the attempts made by both labor and management to secure and retain advantages in their dealings with each other. The history of the more important labor laws since the early 1930s reflects the relative success of these two parties in pursuing their objectives at both the national and state levels.

Over the years labor unions have emerged from being purely economic organizations into ones with strong political overtones. Many, if not most, national and international unions maintain lobbyists in Washington and in some of the state capitals whose function is to persuade legislators to vote favorably on measures that labor desires and against those that it opposes.

The AFL-CIO's Committee on Political Education (COPE) actively seeks prolabor legislation and supports favored political candidates. It is estimated that cash aid and services provided by COPE and other political union organizations amounted to over $7 million in 1974. By federal law unions can only use voluntarily contributed funds for political purposes, and not general funds from members' dues.

The following section will cover the key federal legislation having the most marked effect on labor-management relations. State laws are seen as secondary because of their variations and limited scope.

The National Labor Relations Act

In 1935 Congress passed the National Labor Relations Act, commonly known as the Wagner Act because of its sponsorship by Senator Wagner of New York. The purpose of this law was to help workers organize unions that were free from employer domination and to secure recognition for these unions from their employers. Employees were given the right to self-organization; to form, join, or assist labor organizations; to bargain collectively through representatives of their own choosing; and to engage in concerted activities for the purpose of collective bargaining or other mutual aid or protection. The specific provisions of the Wagner Act included a list of five so-called unfair labor practices in which employers were forbidden to engage. These are listed in Figure 15-2.

A National Labor Relations Board (NLRB) consisting of three members who were not to be affiliated with either labor or industry was established and empowered to prevent employers from engaging in any of the listed unfair labor practices. It conducts elections among the employees to determine the

UNFAIR FOR MANAGEMENT (WAGNER ACT)	UNFAIR FOR LABOR (TAFT-HARTLEY ACT)
1. To interfere with, restrain, or coerce employees in their collective bargaining or self-organizing activities.	1. A union may not coerce employees into joining a union (except in the case of a union shop) nor employers in the selection of their representatives for collective bargaining or handling employee grievances.
2. To dominate or interfere with the formation or administration of any labor organization or to contribute financially to its support.	2. A union may not try to force employers to discriminate against an employee except in the case of a union shop where the employee has not paid union dues and the initiation fee.
3. To discriminate in conditions of employment against employees·for the purpose of encouraging or discouraging membership in any labor organization.	3. If a union has been certified as the bargaining agent for the employees, it cannot refuse to bargain collectively with the employer.
4. To discharge or otherwise discriminate against an employee who has filed or given testimony under the act.	4. A union is not permitted to engage in secondary boycotts or jurisdictional strikes, or to force assignment of certain work to certain unions.
5. To refuse to bargain collectively with the chosen representatives of the employees.	5. A union may not charge excessive fees under union shop agreements.
	6. A union may not require an employer to pay for work that is not performed.

Figure 15-2   *Unfair Labor Practices*

representatives who will bargain collectively for them with the employers. The act also provided that representatives designated for collective bargaining by the majority of the employees in a plant should be the exclusive representatives of all the employees in the plant in matters of wages, hours of work, and other conditions of employment.

From 1935 until 1947, except for the period of World War II, the National Labor Relations Act remained in force without change. After the validation of this act by the Supreme Court in 1937, the unionization of large segments of American industry proceeded rapidly.

The Labor Management Relations Act

As time went on, many observers felt that the Wagner Act had gone too far in trying to remedy a situation that had been more favorable to management than to labor. Accordingly, the Labor Management Relations (Taft-Hartley) Act was enacted in 1947. Some of its more important provisions concern: (1) changes in the National Labor Relations Board, (2) unfair labor practices by unions, and (3) other provisions.

CHANGES IN THE NATIONAL LABOR RELATIONS BOARD

The Board was increased from three to five members. The position of the General Counsel of the Board with rather wide powers was created. In addition to having general supervisory authority over the board's attorneys, this individual has charge of the investigation and prosecution of all unfair labor practices. At the same time the Board no longer prosecutes cases of this sort, but merely hands down decisions regarding them.

UNFAIR LABOR PRACTICES BY UNIONS

The employer unfair labor practices listed in the National Labor Relations Act continue to be in force except that it is no longer considered an unfair practice for the employer to express an opinion on the issues of a labor dispute provided "such expression contains no threat of reprisal or force or promise of benefit." This same clause applies to unions.

A notable feature of the new act is that it contains a list of unfair labor practices in which the unions are forbidden to engage. These are also shown in Figure 15-2.

OTHER PROVISIONS

The Taft-Hartley Act also contains numerous other provisions relating to such matters as union shops and closed shops, Presidential strike injunctions in the interest of national health or safety, reports the union must file with the Secretary of Labor, and contributions to national political campaigns and candidates. Of particular interest is Section 14b of the act which permits states to pass legislation forbidding the union shop. Further reference to this topic appears in the section on state labor legislation.

The Labor-Management Reporting and Disclosure Act of 1959

Also known as the Landrum-Griffin Act, the Labor-Management Reporting and Disclosure Act of 1959 was enacted as a result of the findings of the McClellan Committee in regard to racketeering and financial irresponsibility in certain unions and as a result of public pressure. Under this act:

1. Every union must file a detailed annual financial report with the Secretary of Labor and make the information in it available to members.
2. Employers and labor-relations consultants must report annually to the Secretary of Labor on all payments made or received to influence employees on labor matters.
3. The financial and "conflict of interest" activities of union leaders must be disclosed.
4. Theft or embezzlement of union funds is a crime.
5. Union officers must be bonded by American companies.
6. New regulations were established for the election of union officers.
7. The NLRB is permitted to refuse jurisdiction over certain types of cases.
8. **Organizational picketing** (when a union places pickets outside a firm it is unsuccessfully trying to organize) is prohibited.
9. Certain aspects of secondary boycotts are eliminated.
10. The non-Communist affidavit clause of the Taft-Hartley Act is eliminated.

State Labor Legislation

In addition to federal labor legislation, laws affecting many phases of the labor situation have been enacted by several states. Among these are laws outlawing the closed shop; banning strikes by public employees and employees of public utilities; forbidding jurisdictional, sit-down, and sympathy strikes; and prohibiting compulsory unionism. Incidentally, the Taft-Hartley Act permits states to outlaw the closed shop, the union shop, maintenance of membership, and preferential hiring; and it does not authorize any of these practices in states where laws prohibiting them are in force. In the opinion of many students of the field of labor legislation, including many labor leaders, state laws are frequently harsher on labor in their provisions than are federal laws. This applies particularly to the so-called **right-to-work laws**, which stipulate that no one shall be required to join a union to secure or to retain a job.

The repeal of the right-to-work laws or the prevention of their being enacted by state legislatures continues as an objective of organized labor, as does also the repeal of section 14b of the Taft-Hartley Act.

CURRENT LABOR ISSUES

The American labor movement today is a product of the character and aspirations of workers as they have collectively sought to improve wages, hours, and working conditions, and generally to work toward a "better life for all."

Just as labor's past has been a prelude to its present, some insight into future labor-management relations can be gained by noting the major issues and trends that the labor movement faces today. Four such issues are: (1) changes in traditional unionism, (2) the generation gap in unions, (3) the emergence of women and minority unionists, and (4) global unions.

Changes in Traditional Unionism

The philosophy and structure of unions have changed through the years in response to changing economic and social conditions. Two aspects of traditional unionism that appear to be changing at present are discussed in the following sections.

CHANGING GOALS

Early unions concentrated narrowly on organizing workers and bargaining for economic gains. Now they have developed into complex labor organizations with ever-broadening horizons and commitments that extend far beyond the workplace — into areas of social reform, environmental improvement, group and race relations, humanization of assembly-line work, and taxation and other governmental policies. Economic goals will be no less important in the next decade, but at the same time the labor movement will work even harder for "social progress."

USE OF STRIKES

The essence of the labor movement is solidarity, as shown in the trade union anthem in Figure 15-3, page 302. And in no other way is solidarity better demonstrated than in the strike. To a union leader a strike can be fully as important a technique to build loyalty and improve relations with the rank and file as it is a tactic to force management to loosen the purse strings. Understandably most union leaders are sharply critical of an emerging view that the strike is a leftover from another age and is not suited to solve modern labor-management conflicts in an era of complex and diverse unions such as the AFL-CIO. This view, supported by some government officials, labor scholars, and even some union officials, holds that in many cases strikes should be replaced by voluntary arbitration or by national product boycotts.

> When the union's inspiration through the workers' blood shall run,
>
> There can be no power greater anywhere beneath the sun.
>
> Yet what force on earth is weaker than the feeble strength of one,
>
> But the union makes us strong.
>
> Solidarity forever, solidarity forever,
>
> Solidarity forever, for the union makes us strong.

Figure 15-3   *"Solidarity Forever" (To the Tune of "The Battle Hymn of the Republic")*

The Generation Gap in Unions

Many veteran unionists are retiring. The number of young members is growing year by year, and almost one half of all union members are under 35 years of age. Educated and the product of an age of affluence, they are sometimes described within labor as **silver platter unionists** because they have inherited good contracts and established unions. These younger unionists often have a political and psychological orientation much different from that of older members and labor leaders, and this suggests the type of future pressures within labor unions and between labor and management in the collective bargaining process.

CHALLENGES TO THE UNIONS

Within unions many young people are impatient with seniority systems; rebellious against the "establishment" as represented by older, entrenched labor leadership; and imbued with the idea that unions should use bargaining power for social progress along with economic gains.

CHALLENGES TO COLLECTIVE BARGAINING

With regard to collective bargaining issues, older workers are more interested in pensions and fringe benefits. Younger workers are primarily interested in more pay to support their growing families. This is simply one aspect of a general conflict between better educated workers and those who have accumulated job experience and seniority. Union negotiators must try to work out a delicate balance between industrial welfarism and wages — a compromise that may not be acceptable to either group. And, importantly, the rejection of negotiated settlements is a repudiation of leadership and a real barrier to the successful operation of the collective bargaining process.

Emergence of Women and Minority Unionists

The present shape and stance of the American trade union movement was challenged in 1974 by both women and blacks in their respective coalitions and conventions. The new Coalition of Labor Union Women (CLUW), established in 1974, and the Coalition of Black Trade Unionists (CBTU), established in 1972, both vow to win better representation within their unions and move toward such goals as equal pay and equal opportunity for better job slots.

COALITION OF LABOR UNION WOMEN

During the founding convention of the CLUW in 1974, its leaders charged that roughly one out of every five union members is a woman. There are approximately 4.5 million women in U.S. unions, but women are poorly represented on union boards. The AFL-CIO, for instance, has no women on its executive board. But the members of the CLUW do not reject existing trade unionism. Rather, they are aiming to push for such goals as equal pay, day care, and improved working conditions for women workers by remaining within the union movement and making it move their way.

COALITION OF BLACK TRADE UNIONISTS

Complaints raised during the CBTU 1974 meeting in Detroit paralleled those of the women. There are around 2.7 million blacks in unions, comprising roughly 15 percent of the unions' memberships. About one third of all blacks eligible for union cards have been organized, but few blacks have advanced to top union policy-making positions. The 1,300 blacks from 40 unions that attended the Detroit meeting voiced determination to acquire and exercise more power within the union movement.

Both the CBTU and the CLUW could become a threat to the AFL-CIO and labor generally if they bring together their closely related causes. Top union officials are worried that the labor movement could evolve into a **two-tiered union movement** of traditional unions and special interest blocs with contradicting objectives and positions. Business managers as well are considering the possible future impact of these evolving coalitions on collective bargaining. One point seems clear: women and blacks are increasingly unwilling to tolerate discriminatory paychecks and jobs.

Global Unions

International labor alliances, such as the International Metalworkers Federation (IMF) and the International Federation of Chemical and General

Workers, were formed to confront the enormous power and flexibility of multinational corporations with worldwide operations (to be discussed in Chapter 28). The viewpoint of international unions is that they must have a global orientation to apply pressure throughout a corporation's international operations when these employers are thought to be unfair in any dealings with labor, regardless of location. The IMF, for example, has successfully brought multinational pressure on such companies as Texas Instruments and Philips' of Holland.

The tools available to global unions include seeking legislative action in each country to regulate multinational corporations through tariffs, taxes, and nontariff barriers and collaborating through boycotts and strikes. These tactics suggest growing problems for multinational employers.

The present trend toward the extension of unionism is probably an inevitable consequence of prevailing conditions and has doubtless served to remedy some circumstances that could not have been altered by any other means. However, if there is ever to be any measure of industrial peace in this country, it will not come as the result of the mutual antagonisms of the representatives of both sides, but because labor and management recognize the basic identity of their aims and aspirations. Each must bring to the bargaining table a respect for the other's opinions, viewpoints, and responsibilities.

BUSINESS TERMS

QUESTIONS FOR DISCUSSION AND ANALYSIS

1. Discuss whether it is possible for workers to be loyal to both their employers and their unions.
2. Why might it be difficult to distinguish between a secondary boycott and a product boycott?
3. Do you think the management lockout is justified? Explain.
4. Suggest a reason why large employers in an industry group might need a strike insurance program.
5. Do you think strikes by public employees and employees in public-utility industries should be allowed where shutdowns may endanger the public welfare? Explain.
6. Discuss the viewpoint that U.S. labor unions should be allowed to contribute large amounts of money to help elect "friendly" political candidates.
7. Do you believe that additional labor legislation is needed? If so, in what areas? If not, why?
8. Do you think that the generation gap will tend to create disharmony between the rank and file of the unions and the union leaders? Explain.
9. On what basis may black trade unionists claim discrimination when there are almost 3 million blacks in unions?
10. On what bases might the potential power of international or global trade unionism be justified?

PROBLEMS AND SHORT CASES

1. Some earlier unions, such as the Knights of Labor, had social as well as economic goals, and emphasized political processes and education in achieving these goals. Later unions, such as the AFL-CIO, emphasize the purer union goals of better pay and working conditions, as espoused by Samuel Gompers, and base their efforts primarily on collective bargaining. Prepare a report suggesting: (a) which union goals will become important in the future, and (b) the impact these will have on management-labor negotiations.
2. Bill Riley is the owner-manager of a chain of electronics shops that carry a line of stereos manufactured by a company with an antilabor reputation. This manufacturer became the target of a union product boycott, and Riley's stores were picketed in a union "informational" campaign urging potential customers to buy other stereo products than the brand being boycotted. Riley noticed that some customers would not cross the picket lines and that the pickets were detrimental to the general walk-in business. He also received phone calls from unionists protesting his carrying the struck product. Although he enjoyed good relationships with the manufacturer, he decided to stop selling the boycotted product to get rid of the pickets and harassment. Later the union hailed its product boycott as successful. The manufacturer claimed that this was not a product boycott but an illegal secondary boycott. Prepare a brief report stating whether this was a secondary or product boycott, and support your decision.
3. Johnny Caldwell is a two-year UAW union man and a spray painter at an automobile plant against which the UAW is on strike. The union has set up strike schools at all its locals and has made attendance mandatory for anyone who wants to collect the weekly $40 union benefits. The union education official conducting Johnny's class is an old-timer with the union who is known for his ability to wax eloquently for prolonged periods on the American labor movement. In this session, after touching briefly on the status of the current bargaining, he reminisces and orates about the history of the union and the gains it has won in years gone by — gains such as paid holidays and supplemental

unemployment benefits. Films about the late Walter Reuther and films portraying the beginning of the UAW are also shown. The overriding theme is to teach the younger workers who have never experienced hard times that gains come only through struggle and unity. In mid-afternoon the education official is called to the phone and about one third of the class, including Johnny, head for the exit during the official's absence from the room. Upon his return the official is so flabbergasted and upset by the empty seats that he dismisses the balance of the class. Later he asks you, a younger union official, for your comments on the situation. Write a report suggesting some reasons why the strike school students walked out.

Part 5

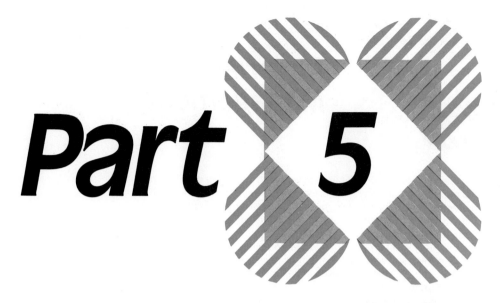

Production

In a broad sense production is a wider concept than manufacturing. Fundamentally production involves the changing and integration of a great variety of human and physical resources into goods and services. Part 5 deals with the many steps and processes in this expanded concept of production.

Chapter 16 discusses the activities relating to the acquisition, control, and movement of materials and supplies used in the production of a firm's finished products. These include the major topics of purchasing, materials handling and control, and materials movement.

The more common production processes and functions that are found in the manufacture of goods are described in Chapter 17. It recognizes, however, that an active manufacturing facility is not necessarily a productive one. The importance of productivity is developed along with the major factors affecting productivity growth: capital investment, technological innovation, and quality of labor.

16 Materials Management

Gary Nakamoto almost hated to leave the marketing department and move on to purchasing in his managerial training program. The marketing function seemed so much more dynamic and important to him, with the excitement generated by the introduction of new products and its real contribution to the company's profit and success. Gary was surprised to find that the purchasing function was rapidly gaining stature in this era of high prices and resource scarcity and, moreover, that a dollar saved in purchasing was a far greater contribution to the company's profit picture than the rather meager profit on each dollar of sales.

In the last 30 years the purchasing of materials and supplies has evolved from little more than a routine clerical job to a major function that is recognized as having a great impact on the success of a company. This is particularly true in an era of actual and potential resource scarcity, often on a world-wide basis.

The term **procurement** is a step up the ladder from basic purchasing. It is often used in business and government activities to describe the combined functions of purchasing, inventory control, and traffic control. Recently the term materials management has developed out of the expanded scope of purchasing and procurement to include the handling and control of the entire flow of materials in today's complex industrial organizations. **Materials management** includes all the activities relating to the acquisition, control, and movement of all materials and supplies used in the production of a firm's finished products. As shown in Figure 16-1, these generally include at least the following three basic activities: (1) purchasing, (2) materials handling and control, and (3) materials movement.

PURCHASING OF MATERIALS

Before products can be produced, the materials that make up the product must be purchased and brought to the plant. The typical corporate purchasing

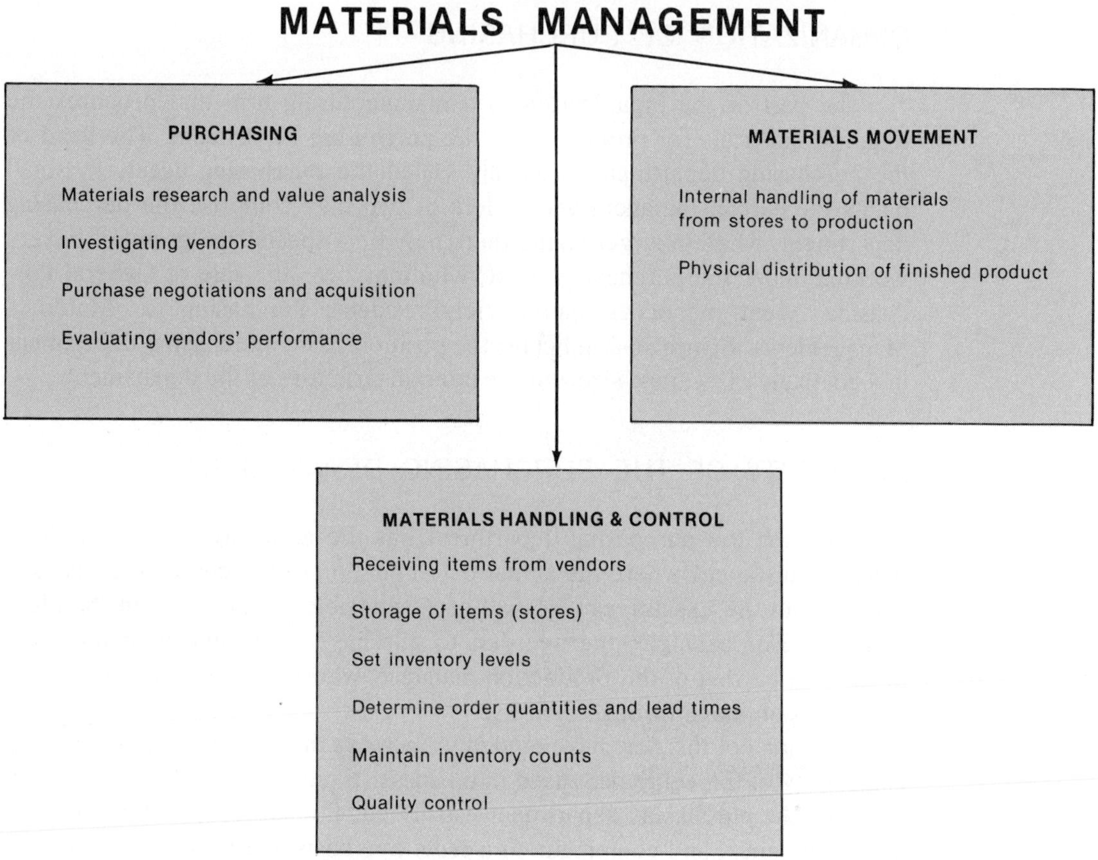

MATERIALS MANAGEMENT

PURCHASING	MATERIALS MOVEMENT
Materials research and value analysis	Internal handling of materials from stores to production
Investigating vendors	Physical distribution of finished product
Purchase negotiations and acquisition	
Evaluating vendors' performance	

MATERIALS HANDLING & CONTROL

Receiving items from vendors

Storage of items (stores)

Set inventory levels

Determine order quantities and lead times

Maintain inventory counts

Quality control

Figure 16-1 **The Three Elements of Materials Management**

department today is responsible for spending over half of every dollar that its company receives. Importantly, every dollar saved in purchasing is a new dollar of profit as compared, for example, to a dollar of sales that contributes only a small amount to profit. Consequently, in recent times an increasing emphasis has been placed on the effectiveness of the purchasing department.

The Purchasing Department

Every department in a business has certain prime objectives. In the case of a purchasing department, four such goals can be clearly stated. They are:

1. Buying the proper products for the purpose required.
2. Having the materials available at the time that they are needed.
3. Securing the proper amount as required.
4. Paying the right price.

ORGANIZATION OF PURCHASING

The part of the organization of a manufacturing firm that procures the required materials for production is the **purchasing department**. The head of the purchasing department is usually called the **purchasing agent**. In small plants the purchasing agent and a clerk or two may comprise the purchasing department, while in larger plants there may be a specialized group of buyers working under the purchasing agent, who may bear the title of General Purchasing Agent or, occasionally, Vice-President, Purchasing (or Materials Management). Figure 16-2 indicates the position of the purchasing department in a company of average size and the internal structure of the department.

AUTHORITY OF THE PURCHASING DEPARTMENT

Although the purchasing department has the authority to place orders, there are instances where the actual determination of the goods to be bought resides with the executives who will be responsible for their use in the plant or office. For example, the decision to purchase automated machine tools might well be that of the production manager, who would be accountable for the results obtained through their use.

Situations of this sort have tended to increase in number with the growing complexity of the equipment used in business. Except for circumstances such as these, the purchasing department usually has the authority to buy raw materials, supplies, and equipment on a repetitive basis and to make recommendations on sources of supply for other specific items.

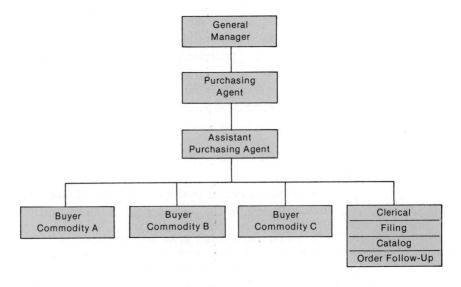

Figure 16-2   *Organization Chart of a Purchasing Department*

Some of the policies that govern the purchasing department may originate in that department and be decided by the purchasing agent, while others may arise in other parts of the plant and require that the executive heads of the company confer and establish the policies to be followed.

MANUFACTURING VERSUS BUYING

The decision to purchase a certain part required in fabricating a firm's product or to manufacture it, often referred to as **make-or-buy**, is obviously beyond the scope of the purchasing department and becomes a matter of company policy. For example, a manufacturer of washing machines must decide whether to purchase electric motors or to make them. The part that the purchasing department plays in formulating such a rule is to furnish the company executives with sufficient information concerning the supply market for electric motors so that the executives may make a wise decision. The purchasing department should be constantly alert to any changes in the supply market that might influence top management's decisions.

HAND-TO-MOUTH VERSUS FORWARD BUYING

The basic difference between hand-to-mouth and forward buying lies in the size and frequency of purchase. If a firm follows a policy of **hand-to-mouth buying**, it orders smaller amounts at more frequent intervals. On the other hand, **forward buying** involves orders for larger amounts issued less frequently. There is no sharp line of demarcation between the two; but purchasing departments tend to follow one or the other, depending on market prices. If prices tend to fluctuate rather unpredictably at frequent intervals, hand-to-mouth buying will probably prevail to minimize the risk of loss through inventory depreciation. On the other hand, if prices tend to be relatively stable over long periods of time, the company may be willing to make larger purchases at each ordering period, with longer intervals between orders.

Another factor to be considered in this policy is the amount of capital tied up in inventories of materials and parts. In recent years the concept of frequent turnover of inventories — with consequent savings in storage space required, minimized risk of spoilage and damage, and the release of capital for other uses — has gained support.

SPECULATIVE PURCHASING

In contrast to the buying that arises directly from the current need for certain items, there is **speculative** or **market purchasing**. This means that the purchasing department, believing that prices of certain items are going to rise appreciably in the near future, places orders for them in quantities in excess of their usual amounts. This is done to take advantage of the anticipated price rise. Or, fearing a strike by employees of a major supplier, the purchasing department may stockpile the raw material involved so that production can continue during the strike. In either case, if the amount ordered and the terms of buying bear little relationship to the current needs of the company, the speculative nature of the transaction is apparent. It is probable in many, if not most, companies that the purchasing agent would be required to secure authorization from top management before making a speculative purchase.

CONTRACT PURCHASING

Contract purchasing is the policy of a company that enters into contracts with its suppliers for certain materials to be delivered over a long period of time. There are two reasons for this practice — to protect the supply and to take advantage of low prices prevailing at the time the contracts are executed. Under some circumstances, where the vendor might have little control over costs of raw material or labor, the price might not be guaranteed for a long period of time. However, the buyer would be assured of a source of supply and regular shipments.

RECIPROCAL BUYING

Reciprocal buying, or **reciprocity**, means that a company buys from customers who, in turn, buy from that company. For example, a producer of motor trucks might buy coal only from a coal company that uses its trucks for delivery. This practice has been condemned as uneconomic and wasteful, and it is now illegal when restraint of trade can be shown. The arguments against it are that it narrows the field of suppliers with the result that the buyer pays higher prices and possibly fails to procure the exact goods required. The main argument in favor of reciprocal buying is that it helps to hold customers, a rather persuasive factor.

USE OF SEALED BIDS

Sometimes the selection of a source of supply is made on the basis of sealed bids. Under this method the purchasing agent provides to prospective suppliers complete information concerning specifications and quantities needed. The suppliers who are interested submit secret, written offers on or before a certain date, at which time the **sealed bids** are opened, the proposals are compared, and the order is given to the lowest bidder. The sealed bid procedure is quite common in the procurement practices of governmental agencies — federal, state, and local — and is gaining adherents in private business and among schools and hospitals.

PURCHASING ETHICS

Unfortunately the field of purchasing has not been entirely free from some rather sharp practices by the buyers. These practices have ranged from indiscriminate and pointless cancellations to the use of falsehoods in playing off one vendor against another. In some instances buyers favor salespersons who entertain them or give them valuable presents. Most firms recognize the value of ethical dealing with their suppliers as well as with their customers. The National Association of Purchasing Management has developed a set of rules known as the Principles and Standards of Purchasing Practice, to which its members adhere (see Figure 16-3).

PURCHASING FUNCTIONS

Purchasing departments, often in conjunction with engineering, marketing, and production, may perform a wide variety of functions from company

LOYALTY TO HIS COMPANY
JUSTICE TO THOSE WITH WHOM HE DEALS
FAITH IN HIS PROFESSION

From these principles are derived the N.A.P.M.
standards of purchasing practice.

1. To consider, first, the interests of his company in all transactions and to carry out and believe in its established policies.

2. To be receptive to competent counsel from his colleagues and to be guided by such counsel without impairing the dignity and responsibility of his office.

3. To buy without prejudice, seeking to obtain the maximum ultimate value for each dollar of expenditure.

4. To strive consistently for knowledge of the materials and processes of manufacture, and to establish practical methods for the conduct of his office.

5. To subscribe to and work for honesty and truth in buying and selling, and to denounce all forms and manifestations of commercial bribery.

6. To accord a prompt and courteous reception, so far as conditions will permit, to all who call on a legitimate business mission.

7. To respect his obligations and to require that obligations to him and to his concern be respected, consistent with good business practice.

8. To avoid sharp practice.

9. To counsel and assist fellow purchasing agents in the performance of their duties, whenever occasion permits.

10. To co-operate with all organizations and individuals engaged in activities designed to enhance the development and standing of purchasing.

WE SUBSCRIBE TO THESE STANDARDS

Figure 16-3 **Principles and Standards of Purchasing Practice Advocated by the National Association of Purchasing Management**

to company. The purchasing agent selects the company's suppliers, conducts negotiations, prepares specifications, places orders for goods and services, inspects incoming shipments, maintains balanced inventories, and also arranges for building repairs and externally-supplied maintenance services. Moreover, the purchasing agent is responsible for the continuing evaluation of vendor effectiveness. Many of these activities will be found in two of the more prominent purchasing functions: (1) ordering and receiving materials, and (2) value analysis.

ORDERING AND RECEIVING MATERIALS

The steps in the purchase and receipt of materials are: (1) establishing specifications, (2) activating the purchase negotiations, (3) investigating the supply market, (4) placing and following up the order, and (5) receiving the goods.

Establishing Specifications. Industrial purchasing relies on descriptive details or **material specifications** established by the purchaser. These specifications customarily originate with the engineering staff. Many industrial goods have industry-wide standards that are commonly recognized and accepted by all users. Nuts, bolts, screws, washers, steel bars, raw cotton, lumber, and many other finished or semifinished goods fall into this category. In specifying these items the engineering department merely indicates to the purchasing department the industry grades desired.

Activating the Purchase Negotiations. The actual purchasing process is initiated by a **purchase requisition** that is issued by a stock control clerk when the stock of an item falls to a predetermined minimum level. In the case of standardized or frequently purchased items, the order may be placed upon receipt of the requisition. In the absence of industry standards or when an item is not often purchased, the purchasing agent may send letters of inquiry to several prospective vendors inviting their attention to the company's needs.

Investigating the Supply Market. Over the course of time purchasing agents and buyers build up a knowledge of the markets for the materials they purchase. Buyers are expected to know about the suppliers with whom they deal — their products; their terms, prices, and discounts; the quality of their goods; their delivery reliability; and anything else that will help buyers perform their purchasing functions more effectively.

Placing and Following Up the Order. To place an order most companies complete a formal **purchase order** specifying a description of the goods wanted, the unit prices, the quantities desired, discount terms, shipping instructions, and the order number. To make certain that orders will be delivered on time, many firms use an order follow-up system designed to inform the purchasing agent of the current status of all outstanding orders.

Receiving the Goods. When the goods arrive, the receiving clerk checks them against a copy of the purchase order to verify that the order provisions have been met. If the shipment is correct in quantity, quality, and price, the goods are sent to stock and the vendor's invoice is certified for payment. If there are any discrepancies between the order and the shipment, the purchasing department must work this out with the vendor or shipper.

VALUE ANALYSIS

An activity that has attracted considerable attention in the past few years is known as **value analysis**. It involves a systematic appraisal and examination from time to time of products and parts to see if any cost-saving changes in design, materials, or processes can be effected, and to make sure the products or parts fulfill their functions at the lowest possible cost.

Value analysts usually apply the following tests to a product or service to determine whether maximum value is being obtained for each dollar spent on accomplishing its function:

1. Does its use contribute value?
2. Is its cost proportionate to its usefulness?
3. Does it need all its features?
4. Is there anything better for the intended use?
5. Can a usable part be made by a lower-cost method?
6. Can a standard part be found that will accomplish the function as well at a lower cost?
7. Is the product made on proper tooling, considering the quantities that are used?
8. Do material, labor, overhead, and reasonable profit equal its cost?
9. Will another dependable supplier provide it for less?
10. Is anybody buying it for less?[1]

The terms "value analysis" and "value engineering" are often used synonymously, although some authors prefer to define **value engineering** as the application of value analysis techniques in the engineering sphere of responsibility. Both terms are valid, for value analysis or value engineering is a team effort (often referred to as VA/VE) involving representatives of engineering,

[1]Fred Brewer, John Bartoletti, and Arthur Belter, "Value Analysis," Chapter 8 in *Purchasing Handbook,* edited by George W. Aljian (3d ed.; New York: McGraw-Hill Book Company, Inc., 1973), pp. 8-6 to 8-7.

production, and marketing as well as purchasing. In this team effort, purchasing must question engineering specifications, and engineering must question purchasing practices and policies such as awarding orders based solely on price.

MATERIALS HANDLING AND CONTROL

The second element of materials management is materials handling and control. From the moment that industrial materials arrive at the receiving platform or yards until they emerge as the completed product and are loaded for shipment to customers, they must be handled and moved from place to place in accordance with the nature of the production process and the actual materials.

Materials Control

Industrial materials are placed under a system of strict control as soon as they reach the receiving department; and they remain under it, in one form or another, until the finished product is delivered to the shipping department for transportation to a customer. **Materials control**, which takes the form of records and procedures, is designed to keep the management constantly informed of what materials and how many units of each are in the plant, and in what departments they are located. It provides a written record of the transfer of materials from one department to another and of the manufacturing processes through which the materials pass, and it serves as the authority for such movement. It is likewise important as a source of cost data for the cost accounting department.

Whenever materials move from one place to another within the plant, records are adjusted to reflect this transfer and to fix the responsibility for their custody. Identifying tags accompany all goods to allow accurate checking. The use of computers is rising rapidly in this area of materials control, as the location and quantity of each item can be quickly stored in and retrieved from their memory units.

Storage of Materials

The storage of materials, or **stores**, depends on their nature and how they are used in the manufacturing process. Coal and iron ore are usually stored on the ground; liquids, such as chemicals, paints, and oils, are kept in tanks; small metal parts are stored in bins in stock rooms; and so on.

Stock rooms may be centralized or decentralized. The basic idea behind the stock room operating policy should be to have the materials available for production when they are wanted, in quantities to ensure unbroken operation of production, and yet not to get in the way of the production operators.

Inventory Control

Most businesses cannot operate effectively without some stock of goods on hand. Generally companies must order goods ahead of customer demand. If a company does not maintain adequate inventories of merchandise or finished goods, customer relations are hurt, the reputation of the company as a dependable source of supply is damaged, and sales are lost. A manufacturer who does not avoid inventory shortages of raw materials and semifinished goods finds that the flow of production is interrupted, that machines and equipment are not fully utilized, and that costs are increased.

On the other hand, if inventories are excessive in comparison to customer demand, funds are tied up which could be used for other company purposes, storage costs are increased, and the inventories are likely to suffer deterioration, obsolescence, or theft. Because companies cannot accurately predict the amount of inventory needed to fulfill customer orders and the times at which these amounts will be sold, management faces the twin dangers of either too much or too little stock on hand. It is the goal of inventory management to find the optimum level of stock on hand under conditions of changing market demand, production requirements, and financial resources.

INVENTORY CYCLE

The level of goods on hand within a company rises and falls in a cyclical manner. The **inventory cycle** consists of two phases: the period in which goods are ordered and received and the period in which they are put into production or sold.

Some of the problems of inventory control can be seen in a very simple hypothetical situation. Suppose that Company X has annual sales of 20,800 units and that the sales are made uniformly throughout the year at the rate of 400 units a week. The units can be obtained from a dependable supplier in carload lots of 400 units. It takes one week to place and process an order and one week to deliver the order from the supplier to Company X. Lead time is therefore two weeks. If an order is placed for 400 units on the first day of the first week of the inventory cycle, the goods will be available for use on the first day of the third week. By the beginning of the fourth week, the inventory will be depleted. Therefore, if an **out-of-stock** is to be prevented, a second order must be placed at the beginning of the second week. This cycle of ordering and using goods must be regularly repeated throughout the year. Figure 16-4 illustrates the inventory cycle.

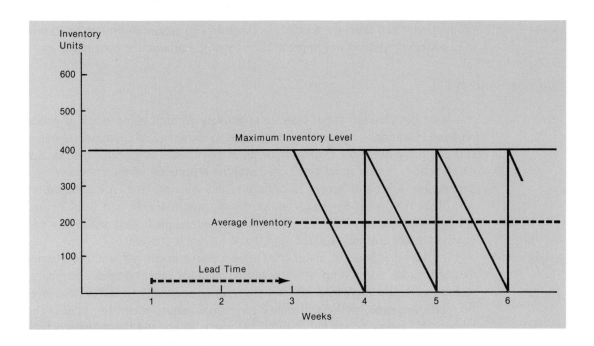

Figure 16-4   *Inventory Cycle*

The **average inventory** carried over the period of this regular cycle is equal to the minimum inventory plus one half of the order quantity. In this hypothetical situation there was no minimum inventory or **safety stock**. The average inventory was one half of the amount regularly ordered, or 200 units. If the minimum inventory were 200 units, the average inventory would be 400 units [200 + (400 ÷ 2)]. The size of the safety stock not only affects the average level of goods on hand but also has an important bearing on the cost of carrying the inventory.

Changes in lead time also affect the carrying cost of the inventory. If the lead time in this illustration could be reduced from two weeks to one week, the order quantity could be reduced and average inventory could be lowered.

MAXIMUM-MINIMUM SYSTEM

The average inventory is obviously between the minimum and maximum levels of inventory. In the previous example when the average inventory was 200 units, the minimum inventory was zero and the maximum inventory was 400 units. When the safety stock was set at 200 units, the maximum inventory was 600 units and the average inventory was 400 units. Thus, management may view the **minimum inventory** as the basic level necessary to provide uninterrupted production or good customer service and the **maximum inventory** as the level it can afford to carry in view of the costs involved. Maximum and minimum quantities of stock which are on hand are one set of guides for seeking the optimum level of inventories in view of the cost, timing, and policy considerations.

In the same example presented, the demand for goods was accurately predictable, and the supply was regular and dependable. In actual practice, however, numerous factors influence management's decision concerning minimum and maximum inventory levels. Different policies are called for with respect to finished goods, goods in process, and raw materials.

It is important to prevent the maximum-minimum system from being used in a rigid or automatic way. Checks against future requirements must be made to avoid reorders based only upon past experience and practice. The use of the computer and mathematical inventory control programs have allowed materials managers to gain a more sophisticated understanding of the relationships and constraints that exist between such factors as material requirements, carrying costs, order costs, lead times, and safety stocks.

PURCHASE AND CONTROL OF MERCHANDISE

Although this chapter deals with industrial materials management, it should be recognized that problems of purchasing and control are also encountered by nonmanufacturing enterprises, such as wholesalers and retailers, in connection with their merchandising activities. The problem of purchasing in wholesale and retail businesses differs from that in manufacturing businesses. Wholesalers and retailers buy only finished goods, and the major factor that determines which items shall be purchased is the probable demand for the goods.

Differences in terminology also exist. The term purchasing agent is replaced by **buyer**, and in retailing this individual is responsible for the sale of the goods as well as their acquisition. The term merchandise replaces raw materials and parts. As to storage, retailers generally have a substantial amount of the merchandise available for sale on display, and this inventory is called **forward stock**.

Despite these differences, many of the problems of materials management apply to all types of businesses including the discussion that follows on materials movement.

MATERIALS MOVEMENT

Materials management is not only concerned with the purchase and storage of materials and with the control of costs relating to these two operations; it also attempts to minimize the costs associated with the internal handling of materials and the shipment of goods to or from the company.

Internal Materials Handling

The in-house methods used in handling and moving materials are determined by the nature of the materials, by the layout of the factory, and by the type of product made. In the early days of manufacture most of the moving of materials was done by hand with trucks and skids, but recent years have seen a definite swing toward mechanical conveyors. Whenever possible, gravity has been harnessed for this purpose and in many industries it supplies almost the entire motive power for handling materials. Because of the many devices in common use and the specialized nature of the handling problems in each industry, the various conveying methods will be merely named here. No attempt will be made to describe them or to suggest the ways in which they might be employed. Chief among these devices are overhead cranes, conveyor belts, roller conveyors, pipe lines, trucks, overhead conveyors, forklift trucks, and driverless tractors.

External Traffic and Transportation

In addition to responsibility for the acquisition of materials, supplies, and services by the purchasing department, its duties may include the evaluation and selection of transportation to ship the finished goods. This area comes under the broader scope of materials management, although many companies do not have enough transportation volume to justify establishing a traffic department or hiring trained traffic personnel. However, no company that buys and sells goods is free from the costs of transportation, and most companies can achieve lower operating costs by giving careful attention to their traffic function and modes of transportation. In the absence of a traffic department this effort may rest on the purchasing manager.

THE TRAFFIC FUNCTION

The basic function of **traffic** is to secure delivery of materials and parts at the least possible transportation costs and to ship the finished goods by the most efficient means.

THE TRAFFIC DEPARTMENT

Transportation costs generally range from 6 to 20 percent of the total cost of goods sold, and for some companies they may reach 50 percent. This significant expenditure must be controlled. To provide transportation service for the company at costs consistent with services provided, traffic departments have been established in most companies. The traffic department is directed by a **traffic manager**.

The traffic department is principally concerned with the movement of incoming and outgoing freight. It commonly performs the following functions:

1. Packing, marking, and loading.
2. Freight rate negotiations.
3. Consolidation of shipments.
4. Preparation of bills of lading and other shipping papers.
5. Routing of shipments.
6. Handling of insurance coverage and claims against carriers.
7. Expediting and tracing shipments.
8. Warehousing.
9. Operating company-owned or leased transportation equipment.
10. Providing information on transportation aspects of new plant or warehouse locations.

The management of traffic affects many other departments of the company. The processing or manufacturing departments expect an adequate flow of materials scheduled at the right time. Careful scheduling of inbound and outbound shipments is required in controlling the size of inventories. The traffic department shows the purchasing department the most advantageous purchasing areas from the standpoint of transportation costs and services. Since the transportation rate for small quantities is relatively greater than that for large quantities, information from the traffic department can help the purchasing department determine the most economical size of purchase. The traffic department can show, for example, how small shipments can be consolidated and shipped in carload or truckload lots at lower cost and better service.

METHODS OF TRANSPORTATION

The external transportation factor in materials management involves decisions concerning costs, speed, and the selection of a particular carrier from among those that are available in a given locality. If the products concerned, such as lumber and cement, can be moved by water, the problem may take on quite a different aspect than if that form of transportation is not available. The expansion of the country's network of highways, which has greatly facilitated the development of truck transportation, has served to widen the markets for companies that are able to ship their products in this manner. Figure 16-5 is a summarization of the strengths and weaknesses of the various methods of transportation.

Railroads. The railroads handle the largest part of the transportation in this country, embracing a total trackage of some 390,000 miles and carrying between 2 and 3 billion tons of freight each year. Railroad rates are generally expressed in rates per 100 pounds or per ton from the point of origin to the destination. A distinction is made in the rates applicable to goods shipped in

METHOD	STRENGTHS	WEAKNESSES
Railroads	Low cost for moving a wide variety of goods over long distances Maintain fairly reliable schedules Rail system has wide coverage	Usually not speedy Deliveries often infrequent to any one point Wide variations in dependability Shortages of special shipping cars
Trucks	Great flexibility and adaptability as to points served and goods carried Short hauls are relatively inexpensive Usually a speedy method Can be combined with rail service	Often more expensive than rails on long hauls Lack of uniformity in truck regulations Trucks can be polluters
Waterways	Great flexibility in moving a wide variety of goods Low cost for high-bulk items	Slow, and deviates from established delivery schedules Water transportation may be seasonal
Pipelines	Moves high number of units per unit of time Dependable and safe	Pipeline construction is very costly Inflexible, and limited purposes Needs processing or other transportation facilities at end of line
Airplanes	Speedy between major cities Less damage to goods and fewer stolen goods	Relatively high costs and low flexibility as to goods that can be economically flown per transportation dollar Lack of terminals in smaller cities

Figure 16-5   ***Strengths and Weaknesses of Various Transportation Methods***

carload lots (CL) and those shipped in **less-than-carload lots (LCL)**. LCL rates are generally between 15 and 30 percent higher than the rates for carload shipments.

Motor Trucks. For relatively short hauls up to 300 miles, motor trucks compete with railroads. They are of particular importance for communities with infrequent or no railroad service. Their rates vary from levels lower than those applied by the railroads to those measurably higher. In many parts of the country a combination truck and rail service, known as **piggyback freight**, is available. In this instance goods are loaded on trucks which, in turn, are driven up onto special railroad flat cars. These cars are then made a part of a train moving in the direction of the trucks' destinations, frequently overnight. Later at a predetermined point the trucks are driven off the cars and proceed under their own power to the points where the goods are consigned.

Waterways. The waterways of the country — rivers, the Great Lakes, and the coastline routes — are of considerable importance in the movement of certain kinds of freight, such as goods of large bulk and low value, like coal, grain, oil, lumber, sugar, and cotton. Water transportation is the cheapest but also the slowest method of moving goods. It also affords a type of service called **fishyback freight**, similar to the piggyback freight of the railroads, in which trucks can be driven onto ships and transported to points nearer their destinations.

Pipeline. A network of around 160,000 miles of pipelines is used to transport crude petroleum, natural gas, and even coal in slurry form. If the cost of building a pipeline is to be justified, there must be continuous processing of the material transported at each end of the line. For this reason companies owning the pipelines consider them to be extensions of their productive facilities rather than as transportation devices. While pipelines have the disadvantages of governmental regulation and inflexible routes, they have a distinct cost advantage over transportation by railroad or motor carrier.

Airplanes. Air transportation is noteworthy for its speed, its advantage in long-distance hauling, its relatively high cost, and the fact that its cargoes usually consist of items of relatively small bulk and high value or quick perishability to justify the high expense. More recent developments seem to indicate that some larger commodities can be flown to their destinations. Many of the major airlines of the country offer air-freight service to and from the bigger cities, utilizing large jet aircraft.

MATERIALS MANAGEMENT IN THE FUTURE

The use of the computer and the development of a more comprehensive management viewpoint have caused many companies to consider the possibility of a totally integrated system of **physical distribution management** or **business logistics**. The goal of this managerial concept is better customer service at lower costs. It emphasizes the control of total costs of transportation, warehousing, inventory control, protective packaging, and materials handling. It seeks to achieve its objective by a detailed analysis of the total cost of each stage in the flow of materials from the raw state to finished goods in the hands of customers. Within each stage of the physical distribution of goods there are alternative choices. Through this detailed study, the business logistician seeks to point out the decision which will lower total costs and improve service.

Not every organization will adopt an integrated system of physical distribution, and an acceptance of the overall logistics management concept is constrained at present by limits in management sophistication and data processing systems. Nevertheless, one purchasing expert suggests four developments that seem likely to accelerate the acceptance of materials and logistics management in the coming decade. In a condensed form these are:

1. *Increased competition.* As economic pressures increase and profit margins shrink, greater attention will be directed to materials and their flows as a possible avenue to decreased operating costs.
2. *Increasing managerial competence.* The general competence level of managers in the individual materials functions is increasing. As they develop greater competence, they likely will become dissatisfied with present methods of handling and controlling material flows.
3. *Increased adoption of electronic data processing.* It will become more evident that this equipment has great capabilities in furnishing timely and adequate data necessary to manage materials efficiently.
4. *Greater complexity of organizations.* Business organizations are growing more complicated as technology advances and as greater attention is placed on providing higher levels of customer service. Integrated materials management enables the organization to maintain and increase efficiency even as the demands placed upon the materials functions increase.[2]

It seems clear the materials manager must be an innovative, dynamic, and broad-gauge professional who can draw on the skill, technical knowledge, and professional competence of many specialists and not be simply a materials specialist, regardless of his or her competence. It will take a most effective manager to meet the demands of the materials management organization in the future.

BUSINESS TERMS

[2]Harold E. Fearon, "Materials Management: A Synthesis and Overview," *Journal of Purchasing*, Vol. 9, No. 1 (February, 1973), p. 45.

QUESTIONS FOR DISCUSSION AND ANALYSIS

1. If the profit margin on sales before taxes is 8 percent, how much sales should be generated to net as much profit as a purchase saving of $1000?

2. Discuss whether the purchasing agent for a factory should be a member of top management.

3. What factors might influence a firm's decision to make or buy a component used in its final product?

4. Why may a purchasing manager find it hard to control material costs in a period of rapid economic growth?

5. Should a company have a policy prohibiting the purchasing agent from speculative purchasing? Explain.

6. Do you think the arguments for reciprocal buying should carry greater weight than those against it? Explain.

7. How are "value analysis" (VA) and "value engineering" (VE) similar? How do they differ?

8. What is the difference between materials control and inventory control?

9. What factors prevent inventory control from becoming a routine and stable activity?

10. Indicate the methods of transportation that you would select for each of the following products: (1) coal — in large amounts from Cleveland, Ohio, to Buffalo, N.Y.; (2) petroleum — on a regular basis for a distance of 90 miles; (3) expensive suits — from Chicago to New York; and (4) a computer — from Minneapolis to London.

PROBLEMS AND SHORT CASES

1. Vic Bartley, purchasing agent for Clean-Rite Products Company, was under continuing pressure from the company's president to cut costs. To do this, Bartley usually dealt with numerous suppliers on a low-bid basis. For example, he divided the orders for large amounts of boron, used in the preparation of washing powders and disinfectants, among four suppliers on a 55-15-15-15 percentage basis. He enjoyed a cordial relationship with the major supplier and businesslike relationships with the others. Each supplier knew that price was a prime consideration. Problems arose for Bartley, however, when the workers for the major boron supplier voted to strike, and the other suppliers informed him that they could not increase their allocations to Clean-Rite during that period. Also, the usual allocations would be supplied only at a higher price. Bartley located another vendor who would supply the boron, but at a stiff price premium. The president just about came unglued when Bartley told him of the situation, and accused Bartley of improper purchasing practices. Prepare a report discussing whether Bartley was at fault here and how he might handle future boron purchases.

2. The MidWest Petroleum Company is a medium-sized independent oil refiner. Recently it needed to purchase 20 pipeline gate-valves to use in enlarging the refinery capacity. Its purchasing agent issued specifications for the order and told bidders they could submit two sets of figures — a price for each valve and an overall price for the entire order.

    The Falworth Valve Company, a local firm, bid $500 for each valve and $10,000 for the entire order. Superb Valves, a competitor located about 300 miles away, also bid $500 per valve but $9,500 for the entire order. The valves were equal in quality, and the sales and service departments for each bidder were regarded as adequate. When the bids were made public, MidWest's purchasing agent was in a bind between his company's loyalty to local firms and the integrity of the company in the eyes of Superb Valves and other vendors with which it does business. Prepare a report suggesting the arguments in favor of (a) giving the order to the local firm, and (b) giving the order to Superb Valves.

3. The Denver district parts depot of the Black Motor Truck Company receives an urgent request to ship a certain truck gear to Muleshoe, Texas. The request comes from a moving company using Black tractors to pull its moving vans. On this particular job the incapacitated tractor is moving a colonel's household furniture on a military contract. If the moving company does not perform as agreed, it may lose further government contracts. Speed is of the essence. In an oral report discuss what method of transportation you would use to ship this truck part from Denver to Muleshoe, Texas. (Hint: check on a map the routes from Denver to Muleshoe.)

17 Production and Productivity

Replacing the assembly lines at the recently-built Saab-Scania auto engine plant in Sodertalje, Sweden, are teams of three persons each who complete the engine assembly, determining among themselves their individual responsibilities for each operation. Saab-Scania management feels that the quality of each engine will be more uniform and the increase in job satisfaction and worker involvement will result in higher productivity and a better engine.

The word "production" is often used in the sense of making things. This is, however, a narrow definition of the word. In a broader and more fundamental sense, production is the transformation of the inputs from human and physical resources into outputs desired by consumers. The outputs may be either goods or services. In this sense production is a wider concept than manufacturing, which is but a special form of production. Likewise, wholesalers, retailers, and service organizations are engaged in production. Thus, any business firm is an organization for converting skills and materials into goods or services which satisfy customers and which, hopefully, will result in a profit to the owners.

Also, "production" is often seen to include "productivity." Although these terms are closely related, it is a mistake to assume, for instance, that an active manufacturing facility is necessarily a productive one. The most commonly used definition of productivity at the plant level is real output per hour of work. Productivity in this sense is a rough measure of the effectiveness with which our most important productive resources are used.

Production, then, is the process by which goods and services are created. **Productivity** is a concept that expresses the relationship between output — the quantity of goods and services produced — and inputs — the quantity of labor, capital, land, energy, and other resources that produced the output. In this chapter both the production process in manufacturing and the basic components that contribute to an environment of high productivity will be considered.

PRODUCTION

Production involves the changing and blending of a great variety of inputs into goods and services to be sold. It is the job of **production management** to make the decisions necessary to transform inputs into salable outputs. The two major types of decisions required will be the main topics in this section. One set of decisions relates to the design of the manufacturing production system, and the other set pertains to the operation and control of the system in both the long and short run.

Manufacturing Production System

The long-run decisions affecting the design of the production system are:

1. *Location of the production facility*. Where will the factory be located in reference to nearness of markets, closeness to adequate supplies of labor and materials, environmental pollution controls, and other factors?
2. *Layout of the facility*. How shall the factory be arranged so that its operations are efficiently carried on?
3. *Selection of equipment and processes*. What equipment will be purchased so that goods or services may be produced at minimum cost?
4. *Production design of items processed*. In what form (pattern, style, quality) will goods and services be made?
5. *Job design*. How shall the human work of production be subdivided among people in view of skill, health, and costs involved?

These complex decisions are further complicated by the fact that the **manufacturing processes** may be classified in three different ways: (1) according to the nature of the process, (2) on the basis of the time of production, and (3) in reference to the character of the product manufactured.

NATURE OF THE PROCESS

The classification of production processes according to their nature identifies types or forms of substances used in manufacturing a product.

Extractive Process. In some industries the basic production process, known as the **extractive process**, is one of extracting substances from the earth or the sea. Examples of this process are the mining of coal, iron ore, lead, gold, and silver; drilling for petroleum; and the extraction of magnesium and other chemicals from the ocean. Farming and fishing may be called extractive industries, but they are on an ownership and operating basis different from the industries mentioned here.

Analytic Process. The **analytic process** is one in which a basic substance is broken down into a number of other materials, which may or may not bear any resemblance to the parent substance. In this category are petroleum refining, meat packing, and lumber milling.

Fabricating Process. The term **fabricating process**, although used principally in the structural steel business, refers to a process that is rather widespread in industry wherein a material has its form changed to some extent by being machined, woven, cut up, pressed, finished, or treated in some other manner. It is sometimes called the **converting process**, particularly in the textile field. Examples of the fabricating process are found in the manufacture of clothing, shoes, certain types of furniture, nuts, and bolts.

Synthetic Process. The **synthetic process** refers to the method of combining different materials to form a single product. In the manufacture of steel, glass, rayon, and dinnerware the final products are quite different from the original ingredients because of physical or chemical changes. In other industries, such as in the production of automobiles, electrical appliances, or radios and television sets, where the materials are merely assembled without undergoing physical or chemical change, this process is sometimes called the **assembly process**. This is particularly true in industries employing the assembly line as a part of their manufacturing process.

TIME OF PRODUCTION

Some production processes are characterized by the periods of time during which the productive facilities are kept in operation.

Continuous Process. The term **continuous process** is used to describe a manufacturing situation where long periods of time may elapse before any radical changes are made in the set-up of the machinery and equipment involved; that is, most or all of the machines will perform the same operations indefinitely. The production of automobiles where model changes occur only once a year is an example of the continuous process. The term ''continuous process'' may include industries where production may be halted every night — a one-shift operation — and resumed the next morning, and also those where the characteristics of the production pattern require the operation to run without stopping for long periods of time — months or even years — depending on the demand for the products.

Intermittent Process. The term **intermittent process** involves manufacturing conditions in which the duration of each run is sufficiently short so that the machines are shut down rather frequently and retooled to produce some different product. Most so-called job shops come under this category. A **job shop** has certain manufacturing facilities, such as machine tools or foundry equipment, that are available to make almost anything that its customers want. What is being produced in a plant of this type at any given time is what the current customers have ordered; and it may differ radically from what will be made six months hence.

CHARACTER OF THE PRODUCT

Other production processes are characterized by the presence or absence of customers' specifications for a particular product.

Standard Manufacture. The production of articles which are frequently originated, developed, and branded by the manufacturers is called **standard manufacture**. Some common examples of standard articles are television sets, refrigerators, and toothbrushes. Standard manufacture often involves producing for stock, as well as for immediate shipment to customers and dealers. This raises questions of securing enough capital to carry the inventories, providing adequate storage space and guards, and the risk of loss through market price declines, fire, or theft.

Custom Manufacture. To firms engaged in **custom manufacture**, the problems raised in standard manufacture are not usually present since the customers specify the quantities to be made and the firms limit their production to these amounts. Custom manufacture includes the production of such commodities as made-to-measure men's clothing, machine tools designed for special jobs, counters and fixtures for retail stores, and elevators and escalators.

Moreover, knowledge of existing processes, although necessary, is not enough. Production management must also be aware of new materials and processes. Recent developments in materials include the discovery of new alloys through the combination of various metals into compounds that possess greater strength than any of them alone and the finding of new uses for materials that have long been known to production engineers and metallurgists, such as the utilization of titanium alloys, cermets (metal-filled ceramic materials), beryllium, and chromium-based alloys. Some examples of new production processes are discussed later in the section on technological innovation.

The On-Going Production Function

Decisions relating to the daily operations and control of the production system pertain to the improvement of efficiency of operations, the control of the quantity and quality of output, and the reliability of the system. Topics that are of particular interest to production managers dealing with such questions are: (1) the organization of production, (2) work improvement, (3) production control, (4) maintenance of equipment, and (5) quality control and inspection. How well a production manager can solve the problems arising in each of these areas greatly determines the cost of each unit of output produced.

ORGANIZATION OF PRODUCTION

In a manufacturing company the responsibility for producing the goods that the firm makes is placed with the production division, which is composed of groups of specialists, each of whom is expert in planning, supervising, or performing one or more of the various steps in the production process. The extent of the production organization involved in these activities depends on both the size of the companies concerned and the relative complexity of the manufacturing processes required. Figure 17-1 shows the organization of a medium-sized firm that makes a fairly simple product. It should be noted that the production control and inspection divisions, while subordinate to the production manager, are completely independent of the actual manufacturing division, whose work they control and whose products they inspect.

WORK IMPROVEMENT

The goal of **work improvement** is the reduction of effort, time, and cost in productive operations. Attaining this goal depends on understanding what each operation in a production system involves, studying details of each work step, and then trying to find a better way of performing the tasks. Work improvement seeks the answers to four questions: (a) Can some part of the work be eliminated? (b) Can some parts of the task be combined? (c) Can the sequence of work steps be changed? and (d) Can the operation be simplified? The answers depend on knowing in precise detail why the work is done and how it is done.

Motion Study. This is the first step in analyzing a job and consists of a careful scrutiny of all the motions that comprise a task. Examination is made not only of the actual motions that the observed worker makes, but also of the physical conditions surrounding the job site, such as the distance from the machine to the boxes holding the incoming and outgoing work, the lighting, and anything else that may affect the job.

The principal purpose of **motion study** is to establish the most effective way of doing a job from the standpoint of the motions involved. A skilled observer can quickly detect waste movements that can be corrected in the interest of better performance. From this study comes a series of elemental

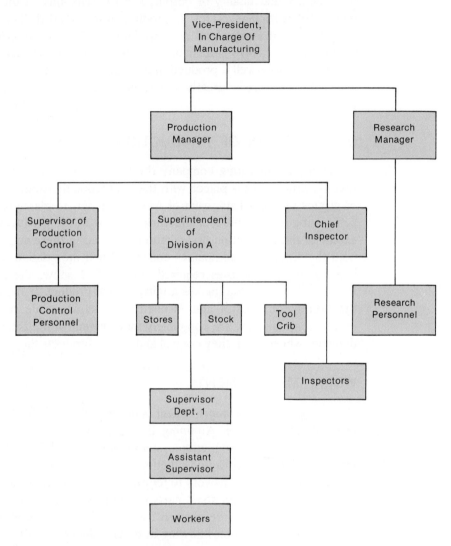

Figure 17-1   **Organization Chart of a Production Department**

motions that will produce the best method of doing the job. Each of these elemental motions can then be timed.

Time Study. The mechanics of **time study** is a rather technical process that requires considerable experience and training. Equipped with a special stop watch, an observation sheet for recording data, and a special board to hold the watch and sheet, the observer is stationed where he or she can see everything that the worker does during a **job cycle**. Each elemental motion is timed and the findings are recorded on the observation sheet. When the observations have been completed, a time-study clerk calculates the time allowance for a unit of work by adding the periods of time required for the elemental motions that make up that unit. The standard thus determined can be used as a measure of efficiency in production as well as a base for determining the worker's compensation.

Micromotion Study. A refinement of the time-study method is **micromotion study**, which involves the use of a motion-picture camera. Instead of an observer who watches the worker and records the times of the elemental motions, a camera captures the actions as well as the times, which are taken from a clock with a large dial that is placed in focus with the operator. The analysis of the film is made later by trained engineers. This method is valuable when the operation involves a great many motions that are too rapid or complicated for the human eye to follow. Micromotion study is used on a limited scale probably because of the cost involved, as compared with the gains achieved, and the relative shortage of competent observers and analysts.

PRODUCTION CONTROL

In its highest state of development, **production control** consists of a well-defined set of procedures that has as its objective the coordination of all of the elements of the productive process — workers, machines, tools, and materials — into a smoothly flowing whole, which results in the fabrication of products with a minimum of interruption, in the fastest possible time, and at the lowest obtainable cost. The details of the various systems of production control differ according to the characteristics of the industries in which they are used, but the basic principles are the same. The present discussion will be limited to (1) types of production control, (2) steps in production control, and (3) a management tool known as Program Evaluation and Review Technique.

Types of Production Control. There are two types of production control: order control and flow control. **Order control** is used by manufacturing concerns that operate their plants only when they receive orders from their customers. **Flow control** is used in factories that produce for stock and are prepared to make immediate deliveries from their finished goods inventories as soon as customer orders are received. The procedures in both types are approximately the same, and it is their function either to make certain that the flow of materials through the factory is such that the promised delivery dates are met or that the delivery to stock is so timed that a proper balance of stocks to sales may be maintained at all times.

Steps in Production Control. The basic steps in production control, in the order in which they occur, are described in the following sections.

Planning. When a customer's order or a company stock order is received by the production planning department, it is broken down into its component parts. This involves a **bill of materials**, which lists the finished parts, subassemblies, and assemblies that are called for by the order. This list, in turn, is broken down into those parts that are purchased in finished form from other manufacturers and the materials that are bought for fabricating and processing in the company's own factory. After reference is made to the inventories, purchase requisitions for the parts and materials needed are issued to the purchasing department, which issues purchase orders to the proper vendors.

Routing. The stage of production control which determines the route that the work will take through the shop and where and by whom the processing shall be done is called **routing**. It specifies the sequence of operations pertaining to a single part and also in regard to its relationship to other parts. Routing is sometimes regarded as part of the planning process.

Scheduling. The third step, **scheduling**, involves the setting up of the timetables that will govern the movement of the work as it is subjected to the various fabricating processes. A **master schedule** indicates the number of finished products that will come off the assembly each month or week until the order is completed. **Weekly departmental schedules** set forth the expected production of all parts in each department for each week of the production cycle. **Load ahead schedules** are made up for each department. These indicate the amount of work that lies ahead of the department until the present run is completed.

Performance Follow-Up and Control. Various follow-up routines are established, particularly for purchases, tools, and production. **Schedule performance reports** are issued by the production control department on the basis of parts and schedule follow-up reports received from the operating departments. These reports compare the performance of all departments to the schedules. **Scrap reports,** received from the inspection department, relate the number of pieces rejected and the reasons. These reports permit the production control department to notify the production department of an unusually large number of pieces scrapped so that arrangements can be made for additional production to take their places to prevent shortages from occuring at some later stage, with a possible consequent delay in delivery of the products to customers.

As the flow of production progresses and the processed parts move to the subassemblies and to the final assembly and finally emerge as finished units, the paper work routine indicates this to the production control department and the records are marked accordingly. When the entire order is completed, the schedules are terminated, the whole project is wound up, and the records are filed for future use.

Program Evaluation and Review Technique (PERT). In 1959 the U.S. Navy and Booz, Allen & Hamilton, a management consulting firm, developed a new management tool for production control of the Polaris guided missile project. This method of control is called **PERT** (Program Evaluation and Review Technique). It is a means of minimizing production delays and interruptions, of coordinating the various parts of the overall project or job, and of expediting the completion of the work. It seeks to achieve the completion of projects on time.

No longer is PERT confined to military projects. Manufacturers, builders, and advertising agencies find PERT a useful tool in making the best use of time, money, and manpower.

The Critical Path Method. One of the interesting and beneficial aspects of PERT has been the development of the **critical path method** (CPM). This is particularly helpful in estimating the length of time required to complete an order for a customer. In brief, the procedure in establishing the critical path is to note the different times required for each separate productive operation and to add the times for operations that cannot be performed concurrently to arrive at the greatest amount of time that will be required to finish the order. In this way it becomes possible for a producer to quote reliable delivery dates with a greater probability of being able to meet these dates than might otherwise be the case.

Network of Events and Activities. Figure 17-2 is a simple example which may be used to illustrate the fundamental characteristics of PERT and CPM. Suppose that in a five-step process the first two steps, A and B, may be performed simultaneously. Steps C and D depend on the completion of Step A. Step E depends on the completion of A, B, and C. This type of sequence of

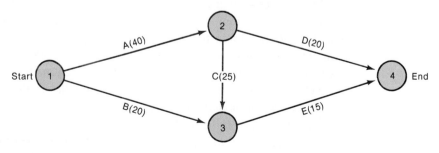

Figure 17-2   *Simple PERT Network*

steps or activities may arise in the making of parts in a machine shop, in arranging a meeting, in planning a trip, or in devising a promotion campaign. The pattern of events and activities may be represented graphically as a network.

The lines represent activities, or steps in the work; the circles indicate events, the point in time when an activity starts or is completed. At event 1, activity A begins and is scheduled to be completed in 40 hours; and at the time of completion of step A, event 2 occurs. Event 2 is the end of step A and also the beginning of both steps C and D, which are estimated to require 25 and 20 hours, respectively.

One of the first questions that should be asked of a network diagram is how long will the entire process take. What is the longest way through the network; in other words, what is the path with the least slack time? In the example shown in Figure 17-2, inspection indicates that the series of steps A, C, E, is the longest route, requiring 80 hours. The route of A-C-E is called the *critical path*. These three steps determine the completion time of the process. Activities B and D are slack steps: they allow leeway in the time of their completion and need not be strictly controlled. For example, step B could last as long as 65 hours without delaying the overall process. Activities B and D are noncritical in contrast to the path A-C-E which must be completed on time if the scheduled time of 80 hours is to be met. If the process is to be made more efficient in order to beat the scheduled completion time, activities A, C, and E are the steps which must be critically examined and streamlined.

In practice the PERT network consists of many hundreds of thousands of steps or activities, and the critical path cannot be found by inspection. The largest networks yet analyzed — those concerned with the production of new automobiles, rockets, or manned space vehicles — may be made up of from 20,000 to 30,000 different activities. The computer becomes a necessary instrument in finding the critical path in these situations.

MAINTENANCE OF EQUIPMENT

Modern factories are highly mechanized. Machine failure can have very serious effects and may result in the loss of thousands of man-hours of productive labor or even in the shutdown of the plant. Preventing breakdown of major equipment is a prime responsibility of any production manager. **Maintenance** includes all the activities involved in keeping machinery and equipment working at a desired level of reliability. **Reliability** is the probability that a production system or individual piece of equipment will function properly for a specified time after it is installed.

Three direct methods of attaining a satisfactory level of equipment reliability are: establishing a repair facility, using preventive maintenance, and providing redundancy. The company that uses its own people and equipment to provide repair service can usually shorten the **downtime** created by machine breakdowns. Also, a repair facility is necessary for preventive maintenance. **Preventive maintenance** depends upon periodic inspections and systematic care of machinery. If the cost of downtime is high and preventive maintenance is difficult and expensive, a company may turn to redundancy to avoid downtime and shutdowns. **Redundancy** is the use of a parallel or **backup system** so that breakdowns will not paralyze the factory operations.

QUALITY CONTROL AND INSPECTION

In all manufacturing operations the work must meet certain standards if the finished products are to meet the buyers' requirements. These standards are usually set forth in writing for the guidance of production and inspection personnel. The function of **inspection** is to measure the extent to which these standards have been observed and to detect and reject any part of the product that is not up to the standard. The establishment of these standards and the subsequent inspection is called **quality control**.

Inspection is performed by a special department that is set up for that purpose and that is frequently under the supervision of the works manager; but only rarely are the inspectors under the control of production department supervisors. The reason is that the duty of the inspectors is to "call them as they see them"; and as the rejection of material is somewhat of a reflection on the supervisor in charge, a more objective determination of quality can be obtained if the supervisor is not the inspector's immediate superior.

Most incoming parts and materials are inspected as they arrive from the vendors. After this point the minimum inspection requirement is one made of the finished article before it is shipped to the customer. The maximum number of inspections would include an inspection after each separate operation with a 100 percent final inspection. In most cases the prevailing practice is somewhere between these extremes, depending upon the nature of the manufacturing processes, the tolerances permitted, and the past history of defective material and workmanship. The term **tolerance** refers to the practice of permitting a certain leeway in the measurements of manufactured parts.

PRODUCTIVITY

In general, the concept of productivity refers to a comparison of the output of a production process to one or more of its inputs. The production process analyzed can be anything from a single factory assembly line to an entire economy. The ratio of output to the measured inputs of a production process is called **total productivity**, and the ratio of output to a single input is called **partial productivity**. In most discussions productivity simply means labor productivity or output per man-hour[1] where both output and man-hours refer to a private economy.[2]

Why Productivity Is Important

The meaning and measurement of productivity has important social implications because it takes into account not only the chief source from which social desires are met — that is, the total output of the economy — but also the major source of getting that output — namely, work.[3]

Knudsen suggests that in most cases both managers and workers have incentives to increase the output per man-hour obtained from the production process. Managers have an incentive to lower the man-hour requirements for producing a given output, since this frequently reduces costs of production and provides an opportunity for either increasing profits or lowering market prices to capture a wider market.

Workers also have an incentive to increase their output because increased productivity usually enables them to obtain higher wages. A relationship between real wages and output per man-hour is generally recognized.[4] Productivity movements are an important factor in determining price and cost stability, as the output per man-hour, reflected in unit labor costs, is a critical link between the cost of labor and the price of goods.

Factors Affecting Productivity Growth

Labor is quantitatively the most important factor in the economy. But output per man-hour indexes do not imply that labor is solely or primarily responsible for productivity growth. In a technologically advanced society, trends in output per man-hour also reflect technological innovation, changes in capital investment and capacity utilization, scale of production, materials flow, management skills, the state of labor relations, competitive pressures, and many other factors whose contributions often cannot be measured. Of these, the three more important determinants of output per man-hour are: (1) increased capital investment, (2) technological innovation and change, and (3) the quality of labor.[5]

[1]The term "man-hour" is used to denote the amount of production a man or a woman can turn out in one hour of work.

[2]John W. Knudsen, "Productivity Changes," *Monthly Review of the FRB of Kansas City* (April, 1971), p. 3.

[3]Herbert Stein, "The Meaning of Productivity," in *The Meaning and Measurement of Productivity*, prepared for the National Commission of Productivity by the U.S. Department of Labor, Bureau of Labor Statistics (September, 1971), p. 1.

[4]Knudsen, *op. cit.*, p. 5.

[5]Much of this discussion is based on U.S. Department of Labor, Bureau of Labor Statistics, *Productivity and the Economy* (Washington: U.S. Government Printing Office, 1973).

INCREASED CAPITAL INVESTMENT

Growth in capital per man-hour has been an important factor in productivity improvement since more and better equipment allows a worker to perform his or her job more effectively. Since growth in output per man-hour is closely related to the investment in plant, machinery, and equipment, the ratio of capital investment to output, or the **capital-labor ratio**, is a forerunner of potential growth in productivity. Likewise, as Figure 17-3 indicates, productivity is more likely to increase rapidly in countries where this ratio is high than in countries where it is low.

Estimates of capital investment include the constant dollar value of structures, plants, and equipment currently available for production. But a capital investment measure does not account for differences in how well the capital capacity is used over time. For productivity analysis, therefore, the flow of capital services is a preferred measure. A **flow-of-capital measure** reflects how effectively the capital investment is used to achieve various levels of output.

TECHNOLOGICAL INNOVATION AND CHANGE

Productivity growth is directly affected by the spread and acceptance of a new technology known as **technological diffusion**. Researchers generally agree that the rate of diffusion of any major new technology varies considerably within and between industries and nations, but disagree as to the specific factors causing this variation and their relative importance. Factors which are reported to affect the diffusion rate include cost and profitability of the innovation, size of the firm, and level and output of the firm.

Since World War II a number of noteworthy developments in production have emerged that may conceivably rank in importance with the introduction of the large-scale assembly line shortly after World War I. In addition to the new materials mentioned earlier, these include the general areas of (1) automation, and (2) key technological innovations.

Automation. The term automation is applied to circumstances where computers control the operation of machine tools, with the assistance of a feedback by which information regarding the progress of the operation is relayed to the computer to enable it to make any necessary adjustments or corrections. If the computer is capable of making the requisite adjustments in the machine without human assistance, this is known as **closed-loop control**. When the computer is not connected with the instruments that can make machine adjustments, it will signal for the operator to reset the machine. This is known as **open-loop control**. The fundamental purpose of automation, which has been called the "second industrial revolution" by some observers, is to raise production output, or productivity, in relation to the costs of production.

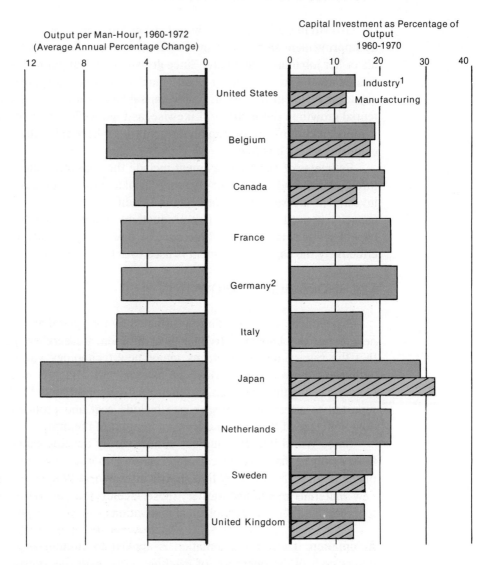

Output per Man-Hour, 1960-1972
(Average Annual Percentage Change)

Capital Investment as Percentage of
Output
1960-1970

United States
Belgium
Canada
France
Germany[2]
Italy
Japan
Netherlands
Sweden
United Kingdom

Industry[1]
Manufacturing

SOURCE: U.S. Department of Labor, Bureau of Labor Statistics.
[1]Includes manufacturing, mining, construction, and public utilities.
[2]Capital investment as a percentage of total output.

Figure 17-3 **Growth in Output Per Man-Hour in Manufacturing and Rate of Capital Investment in Ten Countries**

Key Technological Innovations. Figure 17-4 shows trends in the diffusion of four major technological innovations of the post-World War II period. These are: (a) the electronic computer, which has achieved significant productivity

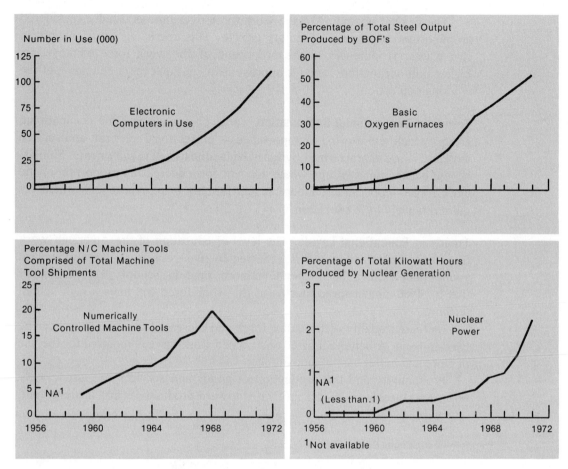

Number in Use (000)

Electronic Computers in Use

Percentage of Total Steel Output Produced by BOF's

Basic Oxygen Furnaces

Percentage N/C Machine Tools Comprised of Total Machine Tool Shipments

Numerically Controlled Machine Tools

NA¹

Percentage of Total Kilowatt Hours Produced by Nuclear Generation

Nuclear Power

NA¹

(Less than .1)

¹Not available

SOURCE: U.S. Department of Labor, Bureau of Labor Statistics.
¹Not available.

Figure 17-4 **Growth in the Use of Some Key Technological Innovations, 1956–1972**

gains in industry, business, and government; (b) the basic oxygen furnace (BOF), a steel-making process which reportedly lowers production and capital costs and increases output; (c) **numerical control** (N/C), a system for the automatic operation of machine tools which has increased productivity in the metalworking industries; and (d) the production of electricity by nuclear energy.

Productivity improvement that results from technological change is an important element in international competition. For example, the United States leads other major industrial countries in both computer installations and the production of numerically-controlled machines, but trails Japan and West Germany in the proportion of steel produced in basic oxygen furnaces.

QUALITY OF LABOR

The general upgrading of the work force over time is usually considered an important factor in productivity growth. This upgrading occurs mainly in two ways: (1) increases in the proportion of the work force employed in higher skill occupations, and (2) improvements in the level of education of the working population.

Trends in Occupational Composition. Table 17-1 shows that the occupational groups which are growing in importance — professional, clerical, and service workers — are characterized by fairly high educational requirements. Similarly, the occupational groups which account for a decreasing proportion of the work force — operatives, laborers, and farmers — represent jobs which require relatively little education.

Trends in Educational Levels. The level of education of the American work force has risen steadily and is expected to rise even more, largely because young people have been spending more time in school. It is estimated that by 1980 almost three fourths of the work force will have a high school diploma.

Increased quality of the labor force and increased capital per worker go hand-in-hand. A better educated and trained work force is required for the use of more and better capital innovations.

Productivity and the production of goods and services are also closely related, as most workers are motivated toward productivity and achievement.

Table 17-1   *Trends in Occupational Composition*

Occupational Groups	Occupational Distribution of Labor Force (In Percentages)		
	1960	1970	1980
Professional, technical, and kindred workers	11.4	14.2	16.3
Managers, officials, and proprietors	10.7	10.5	10.0
Clerical and kindred workers	14.8	17.4	18.2
Salesworkers	6.4	6.2	6.1
Craftsmen, foremen, and kindred workers	13.0	12.9	12.9
Operatives and kindred workers	18.2	17.7	16.2
Service workers	12.2	12.4	13.7
Laborers, except farm and mine	5.4	4.7	3.9
Farmers and farmworkers	7.9	4.0	2.7

SOURCE: U.S. Department of Labor, Bureau of Labor Statistics.

Increasing productivity can provide the means of improving the standard of life for families at the low end of the income scale. It can also provide the resources for improving the physical quality of our environment.

The United States may now be entering a new period in which sustaining the rate of growth of productivity will be more difficult than in the past. Innovation in technology and work methods may provide only a partial answer to this problem, because workers' attitudes are the real key to productivity improvement. In this sense, increasing productivity is a way of increasing the ability of people to do what they want to do. It appears that much thinking along this line will be required of production managers in the future.

BUSINESS TERMS

QUESTIONS FOR DISCUSSION AND ANALYSIS

1. Do you think the term "production" should be used for activities outside the factory? Explain.
2. Give an example, other than those in the text, of products produced by each of the four manufacturing processes: extractive, analytic, fabricating, and synthetic.
3. How does intermittent production differ from continuous production?
4. Give examples, other than those in the text, of custom manufacture.
5. Do you believe that workers, when subjected to motion and time study, will put forth their best efforts in the manufacturing operation being studied? Explain.
6. Name some types of manufacturing businesses where modern methods of production control would not be necessary.

7. Discuss whether PERT and CPM are essentially the same method.
8. Discuss some circumstances where workers might be permitted to inspect their own work.
9. Explain how automation and productivity are related.
10. Would you anticipate a completely automated plant ever coming into existence? Explain.

PROBLEMS AND SHORT CASES

1. The Burngood Company manufactures cookware of a current and sometimes faddish nature. The great variety of possible items that the sales manager wants puts heavy pressure on the production manager and factory operations. Each manager feels that the other should recognize the problems the other manager faces instead of making demands. Prepare a report discussing whether manufacturing or sales should decide what should be produced.
2. Arthur Gates, the president of a medium-sized manufacturing company, makes it a practice to tour the plant area at least once a week. Over the course of about a month, it seemed to him that the workers were generally goofing off and not performing their work at an acceptable level. He told the plant manager to get some motion and time study analysts out there and "get those clowns on the ball." Prepare a report discussing whether or not this approach will work.
3. Consult current issues of such periodicals as *Business Week, Forbes*, and *Fortune* in your school library and prepare a portfolio of reproductions of at least five advertisements or articles that are illustrative of recent advances in production procedures. These could include such items as machine tools, automation, machinery, new inventions, electrical controls, etc. Write a brief report on your findings, estimating the probable importance of each item to the field in which it will be used.

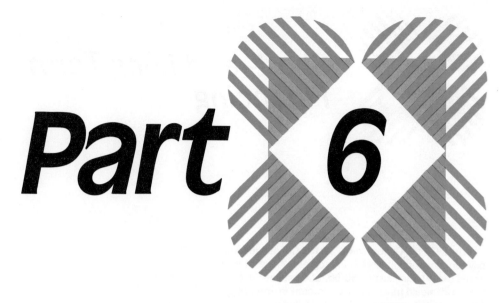

Part 6

Finance

Financial management is always important and is frequently crucial to the success of a business enterprise. Business decisions can rarely be made without reference to the money cost of alternate courses of action. For corporations with large numbers of stockholders, there is widespread interest in such items as net profit, dividends paid, share prices, and other dollar figures.

The methods available for obtaining both short-term and long-term funds are described in Chapter 18. The instruments used and the institutions involved are explained. This background provides information necessary for understanding the topics covered in Chapter 19. In this chapter emphasis is placed on the decisions that result from the recognition of financial problems and the establishment of policies concerning them.

Chapter 20 explains the markets that are available for trading in securities and commodities, which are vitally important to open corporations and to those firms that use certain raw materials in their production processes. Chapter 21 examines some of the risks that businesses face and indicates how these can be managed, which usually involves transfer to insurance companies.

18

Short- and Long-Term Financing

In 1974 the Central Iowa Electric Co. needed $50,000,000 to pay for construction already in progress. If a debt were created, it would disturb the existing 50/50 ratio between debt and equity and the bonds would have to pay 11 percent in order to be sold at par. The company's common stock was selling at less than one half of book value. It was questionable whether buyers could be found for a preferred stock issue unless an exorbitant dividend rate was stated. The management of Central Iowa wished it had not signed contracts in 1972 for its first nuclear plant even though there was already a demand for the additional capacity.

All businesses, from newsstands to giant oil refineries, have to be financed. Each enterprise must own some combination of cash, inventories, buildings, and equipment. These items, as well as other properties, are called **assets**. When a firm first begins business, it secures funds from its owners or creditors to purchase the necessary assets. Later, profits may be retained in the business or, if the firm is expanding, owners and creditors may make additional investments. These funds comprise the firm's **capital**, which is one common use of this term.

There are two major types of assets: current and fixed. **Current assets** include cash, accounts receivable, inventories, and marketable securities. In general, current assets other than cash will, in the normal course of business, be converted into cash within one year. Or, in some instances, these will be consumed within this period of time. There tends to be a continuous flow of current assets to cash as inventories are sold and receivables are collected. Because of this constant movement, current assets are also called **circulating capital**. **Fixed assets** consist of real estate, machinery and equipment, and other tangible items that have a useful life of one or more years. For many businesses funds that have been invested in these assets constitute the **fixed**

capital of the firm, although this category may also include investments and intangible assets.

The distinction between the two types of capital is important because short-term financing is better suited to satisfying circulating capital needs, except for a minimum permanent supply that must always be maintained, whereas long-term financing is more appropriate for supplying fixed capital needs. It is usually satisfactory for a business to borrow money from a bank on a 60-day note to purchase merchandise that will be sold in less than 60 days because the receipts from the sale of these goods will provide the cash with which to repay the loan. On the other hand, the purchase of land and buildings, for example, should be financed with funds secured from the owners of the business or from lenders who do not expect to be repaid for a number of years.

FORMS AND SOURCES OF SHORT-TERM FINANCING

Short-term financing involves obligations, or debts as they are ordinarily called, that have a maturity date of less than one year. Typical debts include amounts owed for goods purchased on credit terms, outstanding loans from banks that are due within a year, and accrued payables such as amounts owed for salaries or income taxes. These are called **current liabilities**. The difference between the total current assets and the total current liabilities is called **working capital**. This dollar amount represents the total of circulating capital that has been obtained from long-term financing sources.

Management of working capital is extremely important to the success of a firm. It is a task usually assigned to the treasurer or controller. It is inefficient to have too much cash on hand, but it is also hazardous not to have enough to pay wages, salaries, and outstanding bills when they are due. Too large an inventory is expensive, but not having enough may cause lost production time or sales. Money borrowed, except on trade credit terms, involves an interest cost. The job of financial management is to have the right amount and types of current assets on hand at all times and to provide these at the least possible cost, which generally involves the use of one or more of the different types of debt instruments available.

Types of Short-Term Obligations

Short-term obligations may take several forms, with open-book accounts and notes payable to a commercial bank being by far the most common. An examination of the following types of obligations will clarify the distinctions among them and indicate their appropriate uses: (1) open-book accounts, (2) notes payable, (3) commercial drafts, (4) bank acceptances, and (5) commercial paper.

OPEN-BOOK ACCOUNTS

When a manufacturer, wholesaler, or retailer buys materials, equipment, supplies, and merchandise from a supplier with the implied obligation to pay the invoice at a later date, an **open-book account** is entered on the books of both companies. Somewhere between 85 and 90 percent of all business transactions in the United States involving the sale and purchase of goods use an open-book account. Although not usually thought of as a loan, the net effect is that the seller is financing the buyer for the period of time between the receipt of the goods and the payment of the bill. Between retailers and consumers the term **charge accounts** replaces open-book accounts.

The smooth flow of business transactions in this country could not be maintained without the use of open-book accounts. The manufacturer buys raw materials on credit terms, converts them into finished goods, and sells them to wholesalers on open account. The wholesaler sells the merchandise to retailers without requiring immediate payment, and retailers may do likewise in their sales to consumers. When consumers pay for their purchases, the cash received permits the retailer to pay the wholesaler who, in turn, can pay the manufacturer.

Length of Credit Terms. Because of the added amount of time needed by those farther back in the flow of goods from maker to user, credit terms granted to manufacturers are usually longer than those extended to the wholesaler, and so on to the retailer and consumer. For example, raw materials may be sold to the manufacturers on credit terms of 90 days, the manufacturer may extend 60-day credit to the wholesaler, the wholesaler may allow the retailer 30 days, and the retailer expects customer charge accounts to be paid once a month, which means credit from 1 to 30 days. Actually credit terms vary by industries and by different suppliers. Granting more liberal credit terms may be one of the elements of competition.

Frequently the maximum length of the credit terms is not used because the seller allows the purchaser a cash discount. As described in Chapter 11, if an invoice carries the terms 2/10, net 30, the buyer can deduct 2 percent if the account is paid within 10 days after the date of the invoice. Although the payment of an open-book account within a cash-discount period shortens the duration of the use of this source of short-term financing, the saving is so substantial that many firms have a policy of taking advantage of every cash discount offered.

Credit Information. Most established businesses have a proven reputation for prompt payment of their accounts, and sellers are willing to ship goods to them on an open-book account basis. New firms do not have this advantage and, in some cases, older firms are not acquainted with the credit reputations of new customers. In these circumstances a business wishing to secure credit usually furnishes the name of its bank and invites correspondence to verify its financial responsibility.

There are also credit-rating agencies to whom a supplier can turn to check on the desirability of shipping goods on open account. Of these, Dun & Bradstreet, Inc., is outstanding. This is a nationwide mercantile credit-rating agency that lists thousands of large and small business organizations in its publications. Another organization that operates on a national and international basis is the Retail Credit Company. It specializes on individuals rather than business firms. In many cities there are mercantile credit interchange bureaus and retail credit bureaus. Most of these belong to the National Credit Interchange System or the Associated Credit Bureaus of America so that information between bureaus is available on a nationwide basis.

NOTES PAYABLE

Next to the use of open-book accounts as a source of short-term debt capital is the use of notes that are payable to commercial banks or to individuals or firms. A **promissory note**, which is a note payable by the issuing party, is a written instrument in which the maker promises to pay to the party named a definite sum of money at a determinable future date. The **maker** is the signer of the note and eventually becomes the one who pays the note. The bank or individual or company in whose favor the note is drawn is the **payee**. Most promissory notes bear interest at a rate that is stated on the face of the instrument. As used in short-term financing, most notes have a maturity date of from one to six months.

The words "pay to the order of," which appear on a promissory note, make it possible for the payee to pass the note to a third party by signing on the reverse side of the instrument. Such a signature is known as an **endorsement**, and the note qualifies as a **negotiable instrument**.

Business Loans from Commercial Banks. If a firm wishes to borrow $100,000 from a bank for 90 days or 3 months, it will sign a note payable to the bank for this amount and insert the rate of interest the bank agrees to charge. Assuming that this rate is 8 percent, the total cost of borrowing $100,000 for one fourth of a year would be $2,000. The bank may subtract this amount from the face of the note, in which case the borrower will receive $98,000 instead of $100,000. Interest deducted in advance by a bank is known as **bank discount**.

Some business firms, anticipating that they may need to borrow at some indefinite future time, submit detailed information to their banks covering such items as financial statements, names of officers and directors, and certain details about their operations. If an investigation of these facts seems to warrant making a loan, the firm will be notified that the bank has granted a

line of credit for a specified amount such as $25,000 or $500,000. The obvious advantage in having established a line of credit is the advance knowledge of how much can be borrowed quickly at any time the need arises.

Installment Purchases of Equipment. Notes are also used in connection with purchases of machinery and equipment on an installment basis. Although the bulk of installment buying is done by consumers, businesses may purchase such items as delivery trucks, drill presses, and other forms of heavy machinery on an installment basis. This involves a down payment and the signing of a note specifying monthly payments, which may extend over a period as long as three years.

To the extent that the repayment of such a note is not completed within one year, the unpaid amount is neither a current liability nor does it qualify as short-term financing. Loans that have a maturity of one to ten years fall into a time period to which the term **intermediate credit** is assigned. Because business needs for intermediate credit are relatively infrequent and a portion of the original loan is normally repayable within one year, such loans are usually handled as extensions of short-term financing.

The payee of an installment sales contract may hold the note or, as is more likely, sell it to a **sales finance company**, a financial institution that purchases installment sales contracts from dealers who have sold merchandise to consumers. In this respect sales finance companies differ from other types of loan companies that make loans directly to consumers repayable on an installment basis.

Loans from Federal Agencies. In the field of agriculture the Commodity Credit Corporation makes loans to farmers on their crops, and federal banks are available to make loans to rural cooperatives. Better known to businesspersons is the Small Business Administration (SBA), which was created to make short-term working capital loans to small businesses unable to secure funds elsewhere at reasonable rates of interest.

COMMERCIAL DRAFTS

A **commercial draft** is a credit instrument similar to a promissory note except that it is created by the person who is to receive the money. A **drawer**, usually the business firm that originates the draft, sends it to a **drawee**, the person who is obligated to the drawer, or to the drawee's bank. Upon acceptance of the draft, the drawee writes his or her name across the face of the instrument. Commercial drafts may be **time drafts**, in which case the drawer will indicate the length of time on the face of the draft; or they may be **sight drafts**, which means that the drawee pays upon presentation of the draft. A time draft that arises in connection with a shipment of merchandise is known as a **trade acceptance**.

Commercial drafts are sometimes used by manufacturers to sell a sizable quantity of goods to a customer who is either unknown or has a doubtful credit standing. The procedure is to make a shipment by freight on a cash-on-delivery basis, which involves the use of a sight draft. The shipper secures a receipt called an **order bill of lading** from the railroad company at the time the goods are shipped. When this document is used, the railroad agent at the destination cannot release the goods until the order bill of lading is presented. The shipper attaches a sight draft to the order bill of lading and mails both papers to the bank of the purchaser of the goods. To secure delivery of the shipment, the purchaser must accept the sight draft by paying it. The order bill of lading is given to the customer, who can then secure the goods from the railroad company.

BANK ACCEPTANCES

Bank acceptances provide a method of borrowing from a bank that has the advantage of securing only those funds actually needed and at the time of need. For example, the Foss Manufacturing Company wishes to purchase some raw materials and, before ordering, arranges with its bank to accept drafts drawn against the bank for the goods to be purchased. The bank issues statements to the effect that it will accept the drafts, which are known as **letters of credit**. The Foss Manufacturing Company then sends the letters of credit to the producers of the raw materials with instructions to send the bills of lading to the bank and to draw on the bank for the purchase price.

When the materials arrive, the bank accepts the drafts and, in return for the bills of lading, the purchasing company signs a note in favor of the bank and also a financing statement. A **financing statement**, as prescribed by the Uniform Commercial Code, describes the property that is pledged as security for a loan. By filing the financing statement with the secretary of state or at a county courthouse, or both, other creditors are placed on notice that although a firm has title to and possession of certain assets, there is a lien against them in favor of the lending company.

COMMERCIAL PAPER

In the financial world **commercial paper** refers to unsecured promissory notes that well-known corporations sell on the open market. These notes are issued in such denominations as $5,000, $10,000, and $25,000. They amount in total to a substantial sum, run from two to six months, and are sold to **commercial paper houses** who, in turn, sell them to such buyers as industrial corporations, pension funds, and financial institutions. Only large corporations with an unquestioned credit standing, such as the General Motors Acceptance Corporation or the C.I.T. Financial Corporation, can use this source of short-term financing. To those who qualify, the advantages are that money can be borrowed at a lower rate of interest than would be charged by a bank and that the borrower can secure more funds than most banks would be willing or legally able to lend.

Security for Short-Term Loans

In some instances firms engaged in short-term financing are either required to pledge assets as security for the loan or do so because they may then benefit from a lower interest cost. The common types of assets that are used in this manner are: (1) accounts receivable, (2) inventories, (3) movable property, and (4) other assets.

ACCOUNTS RECEIVABLE

Accounts receivable, or the open-book accounts owed to a firm by its customers, may be used as security for short-term loans in two ways: pledging and factoring.

Pledging. The usual procedure in **pledging** involves the allocation of a selected number of the accounts to the lending agency and receiving in return a loan of 75 to 80 percent of their total value. The borrower promises to forward all cash received from these customers until such time as the loan plus interest has been repaid. Customers of the borrowing firm are not aware that their accounts have been pledged as security for a loan. Furthermore, the lending company has recourse to the borrowing firm even if the debtors of the latter default.

Financial institutions that make short-term loans on pledged accounts receivable include commercial banks and commercial finance companies. A **commercial finance company** is a financial institution operating on a local or national basis that makes loans to businesses by discounting accounts receivable or by taking chattel mortgages on inventories or machinery.

Factoring. In **factoring**, accounts receivable are purchased outright by a financial institution known as a factoring company or **factor**, which takes title to the accounts and collects them. The factor makes a service charge and also charges interest on the money loaned to the borrowing firm. This procedure requires that the customers of the borrowing firm be informed of the sale of their accounts so that they will make their payments to the new owner of the receivables. Factors have no recourse to the borrowing firm in the event of default by the debtors.

INVENTORIES

Inventories may be used as security for a loan in several ways. When the lending firm has a lien on all the inventories of the borrower, it has a **blanket inventory lien**. This is a weak method, however, because the borrowing firm retains physical possession of the inventories and is free to sell them, although the use of a financing statement provides some protection to the lender.

A more common method of inventory financing involves the issuance of a **warehouse receipt** by the owner of goods that are stored in a warehouse owned by an independent warehousing company, or **bonded public warehouse**. The warehouse receipt specifies that the goods will be released to the person who rented the space, or to order or bearer, upon payment of the storage charges. This wording makes warehouse receipts negotiable and allows firms to pledge the goods owned as collateral for a loan, which is usually secured from a commercial bank. For example, the Crescent Candy Company purchases 100 tons of sugar on terms of 2/10, net 30. The shipment arrives and is stored in a bonded public warehouse. The warehouse receipt is endorsed in favor of the firm's bank, thus serving as collateral for a promissory note. The cash received from the bank allows the candy company to pay the invoice within the discount period. When the note is due, the borrower will have to pay it or sacrifice the right to have the warehouse receipt returned. In the latter event the bank will sell the sugar to other users to avoid loss on the defaulted note.

MOVABLE PROPERTY

The most widely used form of security for short-term loans is movable property such as automobiles and trucks, equipment, supplies, and even livestock if ownership of animals is involved in the business. The procedure used for obtaining a loan secured by movable property involves signing a note that specifies the terms of repayment and also a financing statement. The seller of the pledged goods can repossess the article or articles if payments are not made in accordance with the terms of the loan. For automobiles, trucks, and mobile homes, a financing statement isn't necessary as a certificate of title is issued for each of these durable goods. The lending institution, by keeping physical possession of the title certificate until the loan is repaid, effectively prevents the borrower from selling the pledged property.

OTHER ASSETS

Although receivables, inventories, and movable property are the common types of security used in connection with short-term financing, some other assets are also acceptable. For example, if the firm owns marketable securities, it may assign these to a bank as security for a loan. If the need for funds will only last a month or two, it may well be preferable to borrow against assets of this type rather than to sell the securities to raise the cash needed. Another asset sometimes available is the cash surrender value of life insurance policies carried on the lives of partners or executives of a company. The insurance company or companies involved will loan an amount equal to the cash surrender value of the policies, or a bank will accept an assignment of this asset as security for a loan of the same amount.

Cost of Short-Term Financing

Sound financial management dictates that short-term funds should be secured at the lowest possible cost. The least expensive method of borrowing is the open-book account. Whereas some retailers add an interest charge of 1½ percent a month on unpaid monthly balances on customer charge accounts, interest on open-book accounts, even when overdue, is a rarity. The rate on interest-bearing obligations is affected by money rates generally and by the amount of risk assumed by the lender. The lowest charge, called the **prime rate**, is the interest rate quoted by large city banks on loans made to their most credit-worthy customers.

In computing costs, business firms as well as consumers need to be aware of the difference between nominal and effective rates of interest. The **nominal rate of interest** is the one stated on the instrument used in connection with the loan, while the **effective rate of interest** is the true interest cost. Bank discount and the not uncommon requirement that a business obtaining a loan from a commercial bank must maintain a checking account balance equivalent to, for example, 20 percent of the loan, are examples of the higher cost of the effective rate since the interest is based on a larger total than usable funds. More commonly, the effective rate on loans repayable on an installment basis, e.g., most automobile financing, is almost double the nominal rate due to calculating interest on the full amount of the loan for the entire borrowing period despite the gradual reduction in the size of the loan.

To illustrate, assume that a business buys a new delivery truck for $7,000. It turns in an old truck as a down payment of $1,000 and agrees to pay $280 a month for two years for a total of $6,720. The monthly payment was calculated by adding the nominal interest rate of 6 percent a year on the $6,000 unpaid balance:

$$[2(\$6,000 \times .06)] = \$720; \$6,720 \div 24 = \$280.$$

To determine the effective rate of interest, the following formula can be used:

$$E = \frac{2 \times p \times f}{a(n+1)}.$$

where E = effective rate of interest, p = the number of payments in a year, f = the cost of the loan in dollars, a = the amount of the loan, and n = the number of installments.

Substituting the facts given in the example for the letters in the formula, the effective rate of interest is 11.52%:

$$E = \frac{2 \times 12 \times \$720}{\$6,000 \times (24+1)} = \frac{\$17,280}{\$150,000} = .1152 = 11.52\%.$$

Importance of Commercial Banks

Of the several types of financial institutions that serve the short-term capital needs of business, commercial banks are by far the most important. A **commercial bank** is a financial institution that loans money, maintains checking accounts, and renders several other services. There are approximately 14,000 commercial banks in this country; these have commercial loans outstanding in excess of $160 billion.

In addition to extending credit, commercial banks provide businesses, as well as most individuals, with a service known as a **checking account**. This results from accepting money for deposit and paying out these funds on order of the depositor by means of checks. A **check** is a negotiable instrument signed by the bank customer directing that the amount of money specified be paid by the bank to the payee or order. With the exception of cash sales at the retail level, checks are used for the settlement of practically all business transactions.

Other services of a commercial bank that are relevant to short-term financing include:

1. Handling the conversion of foreign currencies.
2. Collecting notes, drafts, and bond coupons.
3. Renting safe-deposit boxes.
4. Preparing and mailing dividend checks.

FORMS AND SOURCES OF LONG-TERM FINANCING

As stated earlier in this chapter, the fixed capital needs of a firm should be financed with funds secured from the owners or from creditors who do not expect to be repaid for several years. If a firm borrows on a long-term basis, the debt or debts it owes are classified as **fixed liabilities**, and the total debt comprises the **debt capital** of the business. Funds originally contributed by the owners plus subsequent additions either by way of additional investments or by allowing net income to remain in the business are classified as the **net worth** of the firm and comprise its **equity capital**. These two sources comprise the area of **long-term financing**.

Small businesses, including most sole proprietorships and partnerships and many corporations as well, are limited in their ability to raise funds. Consequently, long-term financing for these firms is restricted to mortgaging fixed assets and securing funds from the owner-managers of the business. Because small businesses frequently face an uncertain future, debt capital should be relatively small in relation to equity capital. Starting a business on a shoestring means a high ratio of debt capital to equity capital, and is very risky.

Larger corporations are able to sell securities to the public, which is basically the explanation for most of our giant enterprises that exist today. Two types of instruments are used: bonds and stocks. Although some corporations do not issue bonds, most do; in the case of railroads and public utilities, over one half of their total capital comes from this source. All corporations must issue stock as it alone represents ownership.

Bonds

A **bond** is a type of security that is a debt of the issuing corporation that matures at a stated future date and on which interest is paid annually or semiannually. All bonds issued by private companies contain some common features. In addition, there are many special provisions, one or more of which may apply to a particular issue.

GENERAL FEATURES OF BONDS

Considerations applying to all bond issues sold by industrial firms, railroads, public utilities, and financial enterprises are: (1) provision for trustee, (2) denomination of bonds, (3) maturity dates, and (4) registered versus coupon bonds.

Provision for Trustee. Bonds, which represent a debt of the issuing corporation, are usually held by a large number of investors. These investors may be widely scattered over the country and may not be acquainted with each other. They need someone to act in their behalf and to safeguard their interests. Such a person is known as a **trustee** and is chosen by the corporation at the time the bond issue is sold. Today a trust company or large bank usually serves in the capacity of trustee.

The duties of the trustee are included in the agreement under which the bonds are issued. This legal document is called the **indenture**. Under it the trustee certifies that the bonds are genuine, holds any collateral that may be used as security for the issue, and collects money from the corporation to pay the interest and also the principal. In addition to these specific duties, the trustee undertakes, in behalf of the bondholders, to make sure that all provisions of the indenture are carefully followed during the lifetime of the issue.

Denomination of Bonds. Most industrial, railroad, financial, and public utility bonds are issued in units of $1,000. Sometimes the denominations of part of the issue will run higher, such as $5,000, $10,000, and $50,000 units, or may be printed in lower amounts, usually $500 or even down to the $100 level. If bonds have a face value of less than $500, they are frequently referred to as **baby bonds**. Despite these varying denominations, the price of a bond is quoted in terms of a ratio to 100, such as 101½. This quotation means that a $1,000 bond would cost $1,015.

The savings bonds issued by the federal government, particularly the Series E for individuals, are an exception to the usual denomination of bonds. Bonds with a maturity value as low as $25 are sold at a 25 percent discount, and interest is not paid until the bond matures. Securities that pay interest in this fashion are known as **accumulation bonds**.

Maturity Dates. Because bonds are a debt, they must be repaid at some future date. The length of time between the issue and repayment varies considerably, but practically all bonds will run for at least 10 years and may not mature for as long as 100 years. As an instrument of long-term financing, a period shorter than 10 years would hardly be satisfactory. Common lives of bond issues are 20, 30, and 40 years.

Registered Versus Coupon Bonds. A **registered bond** shows the name of the owner on the face of the security; a record of the owner is kept by the issuing corporation; and interest checks are mailed to the holder. A **coupon bond** shows no evidence of the owner; the corporation does not know who holds it; and interest is paid to the party who presents the dated coupons which are clipped from the bond.

SPECIAL FEATURES OF BONDS

Practically every bond issue is different in some respect from one issued by another company or from another series that is sold by the same organization. The names by which bond issues are advertised and sold frequently contain a descriptive phrase indicating the inclusion of one or more of the following special features: (1) security, (2) method of repayment, (3) callable or redeemable bonds, and (4) convertible bonds.

Security. Since bonds are a debt of the corporation, investors usually expect some type of security as protection in case the issuing party finds it impossible to live up to the terms of payment of interest or principal. Bonds usually run for a long period of time, and a corporation that is prosperous today may fall on hard times before the maturity date of the issue. Some of the common types of security offered to bondholders are real estate mortgages, chattel mortgages, stocks and bonds of other companies, or merely the excellent credit standing of the debtor corporation.

Bonds backed by mortgages on real property are described as **real estate mortgage bonds**, and when movable property is pledged they are called **chattel mortgage bonds**. An exception occurs when the chattel mortgage is on rolling stock of railroads such as engines, freight cars, and passenger coaches. These bonds are known in financial circles as **equipment trust certificates**. When stocks or bonds of other companies are pledged as security, the bonds are called **collateral trust bonds**. If the only security backing a bond issue is the good name of the debtor, the bonds are known as **debenture bonds**. All bonds issued directly by the federal government, as well as the issues of many corporations, are debenture bonds.

Method of Repayment. At the time a bond issue is sold, purchasers are informed as to how the debt is to be liquidated. There are two common methods of repayment. One is to issue bonds that mature in different years so that the impact of the full amount will not be felt at a given date. Such bonds are known as **serial bonds**. For example, a 20-year $1 million issue might run for 10 years without any bonds maturing. At the end of the eleventh year and annually thereafter during the life of the bonds, $100,000 worth mature as specified when the bonds were first sold.

Another method of repayment is the establishment of a sinking fund. Under this plan, the issuing corporation deposits annually with the trustee an amount of money that, at the expiration of the bond issue, will equal the amount due. Using the same size of issue as that in the preceding illustration, the corporation might deposit $50,000 a year with a trustee. At the end of 20 years, the deposits would amount to the face value of the total issue. Actually, the size of the annual deposits could be smaller because of interest earnings on the funds in the hands of the trustee. Such bonds are called **sinking-fund bonds**.

Some corporations, particularly railroads and public utilities, do not expect to liquidate their debt other than by retiring one issue with the proceeds received from another. Bonds sold for this purpose are called **refunding bonds**.

Callable or Redeemable Bonds. Although bonds must be retired when they mature, it may be desirable for the debtor corporation to liquidate the debt at an earlier date. To make this possible, a clause is frequently inserted in the indenture providing that the bonds can be called at the option of the issuer in accordance with announced terms that usually state a price higher than the face value. For example, a 40-year bond issue might not be callable for 10 years; between 10 and 20 years it could be called at a premium of $75; between 20 and 30 years, at a premium of $50; and thereafter at its face value. The exact amount at which the bonds can be redeemed is known as the **call price**. Bonds that have this feature are known as **callable** or **redeemable bonds**.

Convertible Bonds. Bonds, as an investment, appeal to insurance companies, savings banks, and individuals who desire a stated rate of return coupled with a high degree of safety. To attract buyers who desire some speculative possibilities as well, some bond indentures provide for the exchange of bonds into common stock at the option of the holder during the life of the bond issue. These are known as **convertible bonds**.

A typical convertible feature would allow the holder of a $1,000 bond to exchange this security for 25 shares of common stock. If at the time the bond issue is sold the shares are selling for $30 each, the conversion privilege is of no value. If the stock advances to $50 per share, the bond will rise in value to approximately $1,250; but the dividend which is paid on 25 shares may well exceed the fixed yield on the bond. If a considerable portion of the bond issue is converted, the firm has solved a large part of its redemption problem.

BOND PREMIUM OR DISCOUNT

If the corporation selling a bond issue is highly regarded by investors, or if the bond market is favorable, or if the interest rate offered is higher than prevailing rates on comparable bonds, an issue may be sold initially for more than its face value. The amount by which the price exceeds the stated value is called a **bond premium**. If a bond with a face value of $1,000 is sold for $1,062.50, the $62.50 is the amount of the premium. If conditions are the reverse of those indicated above, a $1,000 bond may be sold for $987.50 and, in this case, the $12.50 reduction from the face value is known as the **bond discount**.

Stocks

Equity capital in a corporation includes all funds contributed by the owners. The evidence of this ownership consists of stock certificates that, among other details, show the name of the owner, number of shares, and type of stock. There are two basic types of stock, preferred and common. Some firms have never sold any preferred stock; others have issued several separate series. All corporations, however, must have common stock outstanding as it represents ownership at the residual level. Unlike bonds, stocks do not have a maturity date.

PREFERRED STOCKS

Certificates representing **preferred stocks** show a stated rate of return that, when paid, is known as a dividend. Because of the stated dividend rate and other possible features, such as convertibility, some investors feel that preferred stocks occupy a middle ground between bonds and common stocks. Legally there is no justification for this viewpoint as preferred stocks are a form of ownership rather than debt. Furthermore, although a preferred stock shows a rate of return, such as 6 percent, even this dividend is not owed until so declared by the board of directors. Also, unlike bonds, the authority to issue preferred stock must be obtained from the state in which it is incorporated. The number of shares to be authorized and a brief description of the type or types of preferred stock that may be issued are contained in the original application for a charter or might, at a later date, be the subject of a charter amendment.

As described in the following paragraphs, preferred stock may have a number of different features. Owners would need to refer to their certificates to determine which features apply to their shares.

Preference as to Dividends and Assets. The very name "preferred stock" indicates that such shares of stock must have a preference or preferences over another type. Without exception, preferred stockholders receive dividends before common stockholders. Although the board of directors of a corporation has the right to **pass the dividend**, which means that the dividend is not declared, it could not take this action and still declare a common stock dividend. Also, if a corporation were liquidated, the preferred stockholders would be reimbursed before any distribution to the common stockholders.

Cumulative or Noncumulative. Dividends on preferred stock are usually declared on a quarterly basis although some companies pay on a semiannual or annual basis. If a dividend is passed by the board of directors, the question arises as to whether the amount is forever lost to the preferred stockholders. If the stock is **cumulative preferred stock**, the dividends omitted in previous periods must be declared before any action can be taken which leads to a distribution of profits to the common stockholders. If the stock is **noncumulative preferred stock**, such omissions need not be taken into consideration at a later date.

Participating or Nonparticipating. Preferred stocks have an established dividend rate. For example, an issue may state that the return shall be $6 a year per share. When the firm is particularly successful, however, the preferred stockholders will be limited to an annual return of the amount stated unless the stock is participating. In other words, **participating preferred stock** allows the owners to share in excess earnings, whereas **nonparticipating preferred stock** limits the annual dividends to the amount stated at the time of issue.

Callable or Redeemable. A feature of many preferred stocks, which is similar to a common provision in bond issues, is the inclusion of a call price at which preferred stocks may be redeemed at the option of the issuing corporation. If no such feature is included in the original agreement, there is no legal means by which a corporation can call in any outstanding preferred stock. The only possibility in this case is to buy the shares on the open market; but if some owners refuse to sell, these shares will remain outstanding as long as the corporation is in existence.

Convertible. Preferred stocks, particularly if they are nonparticipating, may not be overly attractive to investors. The lack of assurance that the dividend will be declared more than offsets the slightly higher yield frequently available in comparison with bonds issued by the same corporation. To induce investors to purchase a preferred stock issue, the contract may include a clause providing for conversion into common stock at the option of the owner. If a preferred stock selling for $100 a share is convertible into four shares of common stock, and the common stock is quoted at $22 a share, there is no value to the conversion privilege. Should the selling price of the common stock rise beyond $25, the preferred stock will increase in value. At some point the holder might decide to convert if he or she did not object to owning common stock and if the yield on four shares of common was higher than the income from one share of preferred.

Par or No-Par. All shares of stock, preferred or common, which are issued with a stated value printed on the face of the certificate known as its par, are classified as **par stock**. If a par is not indicated, it is classified as **no-par stock**. The difference between the two types is simply whether the stock certificate does or does not have a stated monetary value. As far as owners are concerned, there is practically no difference between par and no-par stocks.

When the preferred stock has a par value, for example $100 a share, the dividend rate is given as a precentage such as 5 percent. Also, the stock may be sold at a premium or discount, above or below par, as in the case of bonds. If the stock has no face or par value, the dividend rate must be stated in terms of dollars, such as a $5 preferred stock.

Voting or Nonvoting. Common law holds that since stock is ownership, all stock is entitled to vote. In the case of preferred stocks this privilege is frequently removed or restricted by the contract under which it is issued. It is a right that is sacrificed in return for securing other favored treatment.

If preferred stock does not have regular voting power, that is, one vote for each share, it may be given voting privileges on special matters, such as when a bond issue is proposed that might jeopardize the favored position of the preferred stockholders. An even more common provision is the extension of voting rights when a stated number of quarterly preferred dividends have been passed by the board of directors.

Series Issues. Some corporations have more than one issue of preferred stock outstanding. Because each issue was originally sold on different dates involving varying market conditions, the stated rate of return is different for each series. Otherwise, the various issues are almost always on an equal footing. Series issues of preferred stocks are more widely used by public utility and railroad companies than by industrial corporations.

COMMON STOCKS

Common stocks represent ownership and are the least complicated of all securities used for long-term financing. No dividend rate is ever stated. They cannot be convertible, participating, cumulative, or callable. Voting rights are rarely restricted. Common stockholders take the greatest risks but stand to make the maximum gain if the corporation is successful.

Common stocks can be of the par or no-par variety. Many corporations have issued common stock with low par values such as $1, because under some circumstances these shares reduce incorporation fees, annual franchise payments, and the tax on the transfer of shares. Occasionally a corporation will issue Class A and Class B common stock with voting rights denied to one of the classes.

The characteristics of common stocks, and of preferred stocks and bonds as well, are important factors that enter into the decision-making process about the type or types of securities a corporation should use. Figure 18-1 highlights the differences between the two major types of long-term financing instruments — bonds and stocks.

Long-Term Capital Institutions

The only financial institutions that are exclusively concerned with the long-term capital needs of business are investment banking companies.

INVESTMENT BANKING COMPANIES

The primary function of **investment banking companies** is to market securities for corporations that have long-term capital needs. Such banking companies are sometimes called security houses and this title describes, in part,

BONDS	STOCKS
1. Represent debt of issuing corporation.	1. Represent ownership in corporation.
2. Must be repaid at some future date.	2. No obligation to repay although sometimes stock is retired.
3. Definite rate of interest due at stated intervals.	3. Unless and until dividends are declared, no return is due stockholders even though preferred stock may state a specific rate of return.
4. Interest on bonds is an expense of doing business.	4. Dividends are a distribution of profits.

Figure 18-1   *Major Differences Between Stocks and Bonds*

their operations. The "merchandise" they purchase for subsequent sale to investors consists of bonds, preferred stocks, and common stocks of old and new companies.

Suppose the Stoddard Manufacturing Co. decides to construct a new factory building and equip it with the necessary machinery through additional capital funds of $50 million. If a decision is reached to obtain the funds needed from an issue of mortgage bonds, the problem of selling these securities to the public would loom as almost insurmountable to a company unfamiliar with this field of finance. An investment banking company can be contacted and, if it agrees to market the bonds, the entire problem is solved as far as the manufacturing company is concerned.

The investment banking company would make an investigation of the Stoddard Manufacturing Co. prior to making a commitment regarding the proposed bond issue. If reports received from engineers, accountants, and other experts were favorable, the investment banking company would then enter into negotiations to underwrite the bond issue. This means that an offer would be made to the Stoddard Manufacturing Co. to buy the bonds. An acceptance would result in immediate access to the cash needed. The price that the investment banking company would be willing to pay would depend on the amount that it anticipates can be realized from the sale of the bonds. If its experts conclude that the bonds can be sold at par, the company might pay $49,600,000 for the issue. The discount of $400,000, which would represent the gross profit to the investment banking company, is called the **spread**.

If the issue is not too large in relation to the size of the investment banking company, the institution may handle the entire transaction through its central office and branches. If the issue is too large for one firm, or if the risk is too great, several other investment banking companies may be invited to participate in the financing as an underwriting syndicate. Some investment banking companies specialize in organizing syndicates and in wholesaling blocks of securities to smaller dealers located in various cities. Other investment banking companies, such as the well-known firm of Merrill Lynch,

Pierce, Fenner & Smith, Inc., operate many retail outlets and employ large numbers of salespersons.

OTHER LONG-TERM FINANCIAL INSTITUTIONS

The financial institutions described in the following sections normally render only indirect assistance although they are essential components of the long-term capital picture.

Brokerage Firms. Brokers are persons who buy and sell for others, charging a commission for their services. They are found in many areas of business activity, especially in finance where a number of brokers frequently join together to form a **brokerage firm**. A member of the firm is officially known as a **registered representative** since he or she has been required to pass examinations and to register with the National Association of Security Dealers.

The chief activity of a brokerage firm is to serve its clients by buying and selling securities that have previously been issued and are currently outstanding. Because such facilities are available, long-term securities are more attractive than they would otherwise be. Investors are more willing to buy a new issue when they know there will be a subsequent market for it. Also, brokerage firms will loan limited amounts to those who buy securities from them, thereby increasing the amount of money entering the long-term financing area.

Trust Companies. Financial institutions that specialize in assuming the capacity of trustee for business firms and individuals are called **trust companies**. In today's financial world most trust companies also operate as commercial or savings banks, and the majority of large commercial banks maintain a trust department. Consequently, the functions of a trust company are frequently carried out by a department of a larger financial institution.

As explained on page 356, trust companies serve as trustee for bond issues. In connection with issues of stock, they frequently function as a **transfer agent**, which involves recording changes in ownership following each sale of shares. For large corporations with thousands of outstanding shares of stock which are traded daily on exchanges, the service of a transfer agent is usually a necessity.

Investment Companies. Companies that sell shares to individual investors and use the capital raised to purchase securities of other firms are known as **investment companies**. The holdings of some investment companies, called the **portfolio**, are diversified among bonds, preferred stocks, and common stocks; while others purchase and sell common stocks only. These companies provide a method by which an investor can own, indirectly, an interest in different corporations.

Investment companies can be organized as business trusts or as corporations. There are two main types — the **open-end investment company** and the **closed-end investment company**. Most of the largest companies are the open-end type and are the ones commonly called **mutual funds**. Shares can be purchased at any time and in any quantity by contacting a salesperson. Subsequently, at the request of the shareholder, the mutual fund will redeem the shares by paying the liquidation price of each share computed on a daily basis. Closed-end investment companies issue shares only when first organized. Afterward, unlike mutual funds, these shares can be bought and sold on a security exchange or on the over-the-counter market.

Insurance Companies. Organizations that insure individuals and businesses against many types of risks are known as **insurance companies**. The cash they receive from premiums paid by policyholders normally exceeds the payments on claims, policy loans, and other business expenditures which leaves them a balance on hand. This excess is invested in mortgages on business and residential properties, in bonds issued by corporations and governments, and to a lesser degree, in stocks. The amounts involved are so large that insurance companies are important sources of long-term capital for many corporations. In some instances an entire bond issue can be sold at a private sale, thus avoiding underwriting costs.

Savings and Loan Associations. Although savings and loan associations specialize in making mortgage loans on residences, they also extend long-term credit to businesses for such structures as office buildings, warehouses, and retail stores. Savings and loan associations can join the Federal Savings and Loan Insurance Corporation which insures accounts in eligible associations up to $40,000, and may also join the Federal Home Loan Bank Board, which extends credit to its member mortgage-lending institutions.

Savings Banks. Except in states that permit mutual savings banks, the common situation is to find a savings department in a commercial bank. **Savings banks** accept deposits from savers on which an announced rate of interest is paid. These funds are then invested in mortgages, bonds, and other securities permitted by law. Membership in the Federal Deposit Insurance Corporation is available to savings banks as well as commercial banks. At the present time deposits are insured up to $40,000.

BUSINESS TERMS

QUESTIONS FOR DISCUSSION AND ANALYSIS

1. Why is it not possible for a firm to increase its working capital by use of short-term financing?

2. Is the fact that a high percentage of business transactions involve open-book accounts an indication that most businesspersons are honest?

3. Why do the payees of installment sales contracts usually sell these notes to sales finance companies? Don't they sacrifice the interest they could earn?

4. Certificates of title are issued for such durable goods as automobiles and mobile homes but not for home furniture and

appliances. Is there any logic to this inconsistency?

5. Does the fact that most bonds have a face value of at least $1,000 indicate that the firms issuing such securities are not interested in small investors?

6. If a corporation issues bonds and plans to repay them by selling refunding bonds, why would it not be more satisfactory to issue bonds without a maturity date?

7. Why would any investor buy preferred stock of a well-established company rather than bonds or common stock of the same corporation?

8. Interest on bonds is an expense of doing business while dividends on stock are a distribution of profits. Is this an illogical distinction?

9. There are food brokers, real estate brokers, insurance brokers, and other types of brokers. Why, then, does the public generally associate the term broker with a person who will buy or sell stocks or bonds for individuals?

10. A business maintains a pension fund. What are the arguments for and against its investing all receipts in mutual funds?

PROBLEMS AND SHORT CASES

1. The Solax Manufacturing Co. purchased raw materials at an invoice price of $180,000. Terms were 3/10, net 90. The firm does not have cash available to take advantage of the discount although it expects to be able to pay in full at the end of 90 days. The commercial bank with which the Solax Manufacturing Co. does business is willing to loan up to $200,000 for 80 days at 10 percent, but it requires that the borrower maintain a balance of 20 percent of the loan in its checking account.

Show calculations to indicate the net saving if the minimum necessary amount is borrowed for 80 days to take advantage of the cash discount.

2. The capital structure of the Welco Corporation consists of the following:

Preferred stock 500,000 shares, par value $100 per share, 7%, cumulative, nonparticipating
Common stock 3,000,000 shares, no par

Through 1975 dividends were paid on both classes of stock, but net profits after taxes were only $700,000 in 1976 and the board of directors passed the dividends. In 1977 profits increased to $2,800,000 and the board declared a dividend of $5 a share on the preferred stock. In 1978 profits increased sharply to $7,600,000 and the board of directors wished to resume dividend payments on the common stock.

Show calculations to determine the maximum per share dollar distribution available to the common stockholders in 1978, assuming that all profits earned in 1976, 1977, and 1978 are paid out.

3. A group of ten businessmen have decided to form a corporation to be called Funland Enterprises, Inc. Living in a community that has had very limited recreational facilities, these men came to the conclusion that the population of the area was more than adequate to support an amusement park. They have taken an option on 160 acres of land located a half mile from the city limits and only a quarter of a mile from an exit on an interstate highway.

Their plans for the area include a large swimming pool, a dance hall, a roller coaster and other rides, concession stands, and a midget car racetrack. The total cost of the entire project, including land, access roads, and a parking lot, has been carefully estimated at $24,750,000. The promoters feel that they should raise $25,000,000 to proceed with construction.

Publicity about the project, which has been widespread due to an article in a financial newspaper, has aroused considerable interest among various financial institutions and investors. It would appear that there would be no difficulty in marketing mortgage bonds, preferred stock, and common stock. Also, local banks have indicated that they would be willing to loan up to $1,000,000 for one year at 9 percent with an understanding that the note could be renewed for another year if the principal were reduced by $100,000. Each of the ten incorporators is in a position to invest $500,000 of his own money in the corporation.

On the basis of the information given, present a financial plan for Funland Enterprises, Inc., and indicate the financial institution or institutions you would use. Justify the details as to debt and/or equity as well as the financial institutions named.

19

Financial Policies and Problems

A pension fund managed by Wilbur Wallace owned 10,000 shares of the Essex Tool Co. that had cost $60,000. Unknown to anyone, the Norwich Drilling Co. had quietly been buying Essex shares for several years and now owned 32 percent of the 3,000,000 shares outstanding. The stock, traded on the New York Stock Exchange, was currently selling for approximately $8.00 a share. The Norwich company suddenly made a dated tender offer for 1,500,000 shares at $10.00 each, which was quickly followed by a strongly-worded letter from Essex management advising against acceptance. Mr. Wallace faced a difficult decision that could not be postponed.

Money is the lifeblood of a business. It flows in mostly from sales of goods or services and flows out for numerous types of expenditures. This circulation of money must be managed efficiently. It is imperative that numerous financial policies be established and that frequent financial problems be solved. These responsibilities are usually assumed by the owner or owners in small firms. In larger corporations the officer in charge normally carries the title of Vice-President of Finance or Controller.

This chapter will examine the major types of financial policies and problems that are peculiar to profit-seeking business enterprises. These include selecting external sources of funds, policies concerning the distribution of profits to the owners, factors that influence the allocation of funds, and refinancing plans. In addition, the financial implications of various forms of combinations and, conversely, the sale of portions of a business will be examined. Finally, attention will be devoted to procedures available to salvage or liquidate firms that find themselves in critical financial trouble.

SELECTING EXTERNAL SOURCES OF FUNDS

When a firm decides to raise funds from external sources, several complications arise. One major problem is the selection of the proper types of securities. Once this decision has been reached, the question arises as to how these can be sold. Although these two problems are closely related, they will be discussed separately.

Security Selection Factors

Several factors must be considered in arriving at a choice of securities when a large corporation decides to raise additional funds from external sources. These are (1) debt or equity capital, (2) taxes, (3) voting control, (4) market conditions, (5) stability of earnings, and (6) rate of earnings.

DEBT OR EQUITY CAPITAL

As explained in Chapter 18, if bonds are issued, the amount involved becomes a debt of the corporation, which requires repayment at some future date. If stock is issued, there is no problem of repayment. For bonds, interest must be paid, and in the case of mortgage bonds there is the danger of foreclosure if interest and principal payments are not maintained on schedule. On the other hand, more stock means sharing the expected profits with more owners.

TAXES

From the viewpoint of reducing taxes, raising funds by selling bonds is to be preferred over the sale of stock. Interest on bonds is tax deductible as a business expense. Dividends are not a business expense. They are a distribution of profits and therefore are taxable as part of earnings. Also, a tax on the total stock outstanding is assessed by the state in which the corporation is organized.

VOTING CONTROL

In deciding whether to issue stocks or bonds, a corporation must consider the problem of voting power. Bondholders are not owners and rarely assume any voting rights. Although the voting rights of preferred stockholders are sometimes restricted, the general rule is that all stockholders are entitled to vote. Unless the existing stockholders buy new issues in proportion to their former holdings, voting control may pass to new investors in the firm.

MARKET CONDITIONS

Market conditions may be an important factor when the sale of securities is to be made to existing stockholders or to the general public. As a general rule when business conditions are prosperous, most investors prefer common stocks because these offer a potentially high return; and because the price of the stock may go up, they provide a hedge against inflation. When business conditions are depressed, the surer and probably higher return on preferred stocks and bonds is of greater interest.

In some instances special inducements are offered to market any type of corporate security. The most common of these is to make either bonds or preferred stock convertible into common stock as was explained on pages 359 and 361. Another incentive involves issuing warrants with the security being sold. A **warrant** provides the holder with the option of buying a share of common stock at a specified price within a stated period. For example, warrants attached to a $1,000 bond might allow the bond purchaser to buy five shares of common stock of the issuing company at $20 a share, provided the warrants were exercised within a three-year period. At the time the bond is sold, the stock is probably selling for slightly less than $20 a share; but should the price advance over the three-year period to $25 or $35 per share, the warrants would prove valuable to the bond buyer.

STABILITY OF EARNINGS

The total amount of funds that can safely be secured from bonds varies directly with the stability of the earnings. A corporation that has stable earnings year in and year out can best afford to sell bonds. Such a concern can finance yearly interest payments and yearly deposits into a sinking fund for the retirement of the issue. A firm with highly fluctuating profits, on the other hand, can pay interest one year with ease and yet be seriously handicapped by this fixed charge in the next year.

This factor, together with a large investment in fixed assets available for mortgaging, explains why public utilities, such as gas and electric companies, frequently secure one half to two thirds of their total capital from bond issues. Their earnings are unlikely to fluctuate since consumers use about as much gas and electricity in one year as another. On the other hand, a firm that manufactures a luxury item is likely to have high profits one year and low profits another. Unless the amount of the bond issue outstanding is small in proportion to total capital, the financial burden imposed by fixed interest charges and sinking-fund payments might cause the firm to fail.

RATE OF EARNINGS

Rates of interest on bonds are fixed and have no relationship to the profits that may be earned on the capital contributed by bondholders. If a firm expects that it can earn 15 percent on any amount of capital employed in the business and it can borrow money from bondholders at a rate somewhere between 5 and 9 percent, the difference between what it pays for money and what it earns on these funds is available for the stockholders. The principle of borrowing money at a lower rate than the rate of expected earnings on these funds, with a resulting excess available to the stockholders, is called **trading on the equity**.

For example, if a corporation has $100,000 in assets acquired from the sale of common stock and earns, after taxes, 15 percent on these assets, it has $15,000 in profits available for distribution to the owners. The corporation now decides to double its size and secures an additional $100,000 by selling bonds with an 8 percent interest rate. If net profits remain at 15 percent of assets, there will be $30,000 in earnings before bond interest is paid and $22,000 available to the owners after the interest payment. Without any additional investment on their part, the owners can share in an additional $7,000 profits.

Selling the Securities

One method of selling the securities that have been selected for issue involves the use of an investment banking company. The underwriting activities of this type of financial institution were described in Chapter 18 on pages 362 to 364. Two other methods are (1) selling directly to the public, and (2) making a rights offering.

SELLING DIRECTLY TO THE PUBLIC

If a new and relatively small corporation is being formed and the decision has been made to sell stocks, its promoters may have enough friends, relatives, and wealthy acquaintances to market the stock among these individuals. If the amount to be raised is sizable or involves bonds, the chances are excellent that the corporation will find it necessary to contact an investment banking company as mentioned in the previous paragraph.

MAKING A RIGHTS OFFERING

The charter of many corporations requires that existing stockholders have the first opportunity, or **preemptive right**, to buy a new issue before it is offered to nonstockholders. (A preemptive right does not apply to bond issues because its purpose is to protect stockholders against a dilution of their percentage of ownership.) This legal safeguard would be especially important to an individual owning voting control of a corporation. Thus, if a corporation already in existence decides to expand by selling additional shares of stock and the preemptive right is not waived by its stockholders, it would make what is known as a **rights offering**. Under this method the corporation mails each stockholder a certificate called a **subscription warrant** that indicates the number of rights to which the investor is entitled. One **right** is allotted to each share of stock outstanding, and it customarily takes more than one right to purchase a share of the new stock.

Suppose a corporation with 500,000 shares of common stock outstanding, which is currently selling at $90 a share, has decided to sell an additional 100,000 shares at a subscription price of $70 a share. In this example it would take 5 rights (500,000 ÷ 100,000) to have the privilege of purchasing one share of the new stock. Thus, the holder of 100 shares of the existing stock can acquire 20 shares (100 ÷ 5) of the new stock by surrendering the subscription warrant showing 100 rights and paying $1,400 (20 × $70).

As shown in the illustration just given, under a rights offering it is customary to set the subscription price of the new stock somewhat below the market price of the old stock. This differential encourages existing stockholders either to exercise their rights or to sell them to nonstockholders during the rights offering period. In this illustration each right would sell for approximately $3.33.[1] If a stockholder has only 4 rights, he or she will have to buy another right or sell the 4 rights because fractional shares of stock are not issued. If the stock involved is listed, rights are traded on national exchanges. In any event the corporation or its agent will usually buy and sell rights for its stockholders.

DISTRIBUTION OF EARNINGS POLICIES

Another financial problem faced by all business enterprises requires a decision regarding the distribution of earnings. In the case of sole proprietorships and partnerships, the owners usually pay themselves a modest salary if they are actively engaged in the operation of the business. This amount probably covers their normal living costs. Any withdrawal beyond a salary allowance may or may not be prudent, depending upon the size of the profits and the extent to which borrowed capital is used. By retaining a portion of the profits in the business, it will either automatically grow in size or some of its debt will be paid off.

The dividend policies of corporations are of more importance because thousands of stockholders may be affected. Dividends represent a distribution of earnings by a corporation to its stockholders. If a company has not earned a profit and has no retained earnings from former years to distribute, or if the

[1]The formula for calculating the value of one right during the rights offering period is:

$$R = \frac{\text{market value of the existing stock} - \text{subscription price of the new stock}}{\text{number of rights required to purchase one share} + 1}$$

board of directors feels that it is unwise to declare a dividend, the owners will receive no income from their investment. Most successful corporations, particularly those whose securities are listed on an exchange, do pay dividends regularly. These may be paid in (1) cash, (2) stock, or (3) securities or scrip.

Cash Dividends

The vast majority of all dividend-paying corporations or their agents mail dividend checks to their stockholders every quarter. Very few corporations pay dividends on a monthly, semiannual, or annual basis. Recently many large corporations have offered their stockholders a plan, called the Automatic Dividend Reinvestment Plan, under which their dividend checks are sent to a bank or retained by the company for investment in additional shares of stock. Stockholders who wish to buy more shares have an opportunity to do so at low commission rates and are able to own a fraction of a full share.

The amount of a quarterly dividend check depends on the number of shares owned and the rate per share. In the case of nonparticipating preferred stock, the amount paid per share is one fourth of the stated annual rate of return for these securities. For example, the owner of one share of a $100 par, 6%, nonparticipating preferred stock would receive a quarterly check for $1.50. As for common stock, the rate per share depends on the dividend policy of the corporation.

REGULAR DIVIDEND POLICY

Some corporations have a reputation for paying quarterly dividends of a fixed amount every year, regardless of their current profits. If preferred stocks are outstanding, they are probably nonparticipating and the stated rate is paid. In a somewhat comparable manner a steady dividend rate is paid on common stocks. A variation of this type of dividend policy is used by the board of directors of many corporations in years of high profits. It consists of the declaration of the regular dividend plus a so-called extra, frequently added to the last quarterly payment of the year. Actually this means a higher yield to the stockholders, but from the psychological viewpoint the investors realize that they should not expect a like sum the following year unless operations are again unusually profitable. If the extra dividend is sizable, the declaration may be termed **cutting a melon**.

VARIABLE DIVIDEND POLICY

A variable dividend policy is the exact opposite of a steady yield in that in some years no dividends may be declared, and in others the amount paid out may be a handsome return on the investment. If operations are not profitable, no distribution is made even though the corporation could do so legally with no damage to its financial structure. On the other hand, if profits are large, dividend payments are generous. In some instances every dollar earned in a given year is distributed to the stockholders that year.

CONSERVATIVE DIVIDEND POLICY

A modification of the variable dividend policy is the plan of declaring a certain percentage of earnings in the form of dividends and retaining the rest as a reinvestment of earnings. The board of directors might decide that approximately 35 percent of the earnings should be distributed each year and that 65 percent should be retained by the business. Under this policy, dividends vary from year to year and are rarely generous. Figure 19-1 shows how General Electric's regular dividend policy from 1965 through 1970 turned conservative from 1971 through 1974.

Stock Dividends

Although about 90 percent of all dividend payments are made in cash, some companies either substitute stock dividends for cash distributions or

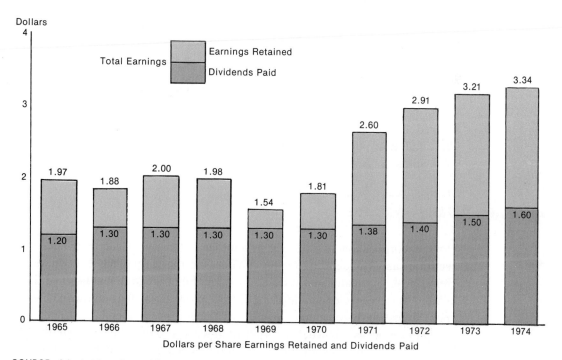

SOURCE: Adapted from General Electric Company 1974 Annual Report.

Figure 19-1   **General Electric's Dividend Policy, 1965–1974.**

supplement the cash dividend with shares of stock. The rate may be low, such as a 3 or 5 percent stock dividend, or as high as 50 or 100 percent. For example, if a firm declares a 10 percent stock dividend, each stockholder will receive one new share for each ten already owned. Unlike cash dividends, stock dividends do not constitute taxable income to the stockholders unless these individuals sell the shares received. The main reason for stock dividends is that the corporation has urgent needs to retain the cash that would otherwise go to its owners but feels an obligation to distribute some tangible return to keep faith with those who have invested in it.

Although frequently confused with a stock dividend, a stock split is legally entirely different even though in both instances the investor receives additional shares of stock. A **stock dividend** is a distribution of profits earned in the current or prior years in the form of stock rather than cash. A **stock split**, or **stock split-up**, consists of dividing the common stock outstanding into additional units such as a two-for-one or three-for-one split, which could be done even if a corporation had never operated at a profit. It merely increases the number of shares of stock represented in raising capital. For example, common stock may originally have been sold at $100 a share. Assuming no change in its market value, a two-for-one split would give each stockholder twice as many shares but the value of each would be $50.

The rationale behind a stock split-up is to bring the market price of a share of stock into a **trading range**, which is a price that is attractive to most investors and speculators. The trading range is usually thought of as falling between $20 and $80 a share. If the stock of a corporation is quoted on the New York Stock Exchange at $240 a share, it is considered out of the trading range. But if a stock split of 4 for 1 is approved by the stockholders, the price will drop to around $60 a share. Actually, because the dividend rate is usually not reduced in proportion to the split ratio, the market price would more likely fall to around $65 rather than $60. Consequently, stockholders favor stock splits because of increased demand for shares and a higher yield.

Securities or Scrip Dividends

If a corporation owns stock in another company, it can distribute these securities as a dividend to its stockholders. In the early 1960s E.I. duPont de Nemours & Company was ordered by a federal court to divest itself of the 63 million shares of General Motors Corporation stock that it owned, and it chose to distribute these to its owners as a securities dividend.

On rare occasions when a corporation wishes to distribute a cash dividend but does not have an adequate balance in its checking account, it may issue a scrip dividend. A **scrip dividend** is a short-term paper similar to a note payable, which may or may not bear interest, and is usually due in a few months.

Since a scrip dividend is clear evidence of a weak cash and credit position, its use is generally confined to close corporations.

ALLOCATION OF FUNDS

Once decisions on sources of external funds and on an appropriate dividend policy are made, they usually continue for several years. The day-to-day activities of those who manage the financial affairs of a firm are more likely to be concerned with the allocation of funds among current assets and fixed assets. The management of cash, receivables, and inventory requires constant supervision; and appropriate actions must be taken in light of established policies. For example, a firm must decide on the length of the credit terms it will grant and, even more important, whether it should offer a cash discount. Terms of 3/10, net 60 will certainly increase cash and reduce receivables over what they would have been without a cash discount. Other policies that affect cash and receivables would include such items as extension of credit, overdue accounts, lines of bank credit, and frequency of meeting payrolls, to name a few.

Managing and Valuing Inventories

The finance division of a firm is interested in inventories because of the huge sums most firms have invested in this current asset. Although inventory management may be considered a production or sales function, sound financial management requires that the amount of capital used for this purpose should be carefully controlled. Every dollar that is needlessly tied up in inventory could be producing income for the firm if invested elsewhere.

Also, the method of valuing inventories can have a substantial effect on profits, income taxes, and cash available for corporate use. In the mid-1970s many firms shifted from an inventory valuation policy of FIFO to LIFO. **FIFO** stands for "first in, first out" and assumes that raw materials, parts, and finished goods first acquired or manufactured are priced out ahead of more recent acquisitions. **LIFO**, or "last in, first out," assumes that the most recent prices paid will be used in price computations. This change was made to eliminate profits arising solely from inflation. The end result was to increase costs, reduce profits and taxes on them, and provide funds for internal use.

Fixed Assets

Decisions concerning the acquisition of fixed assets range from the purchase of a single machine to the building of a new plant. Management must be alert to the availability of new equipment that can cut costs, but at the same time must consider the loss incurred when old machines are scrapped before their useful life has expired. Plant expansion plans that involve the expenditure of millions of dollars must strike a balance between estimated future production needs and the cost of the necessary funds.

REFINANCING PROGRAMS

On occasion a corporation may decide to make substantial changes in its capital structure. The original plan may have proved to be faulty or market conditions may now be ripe for issuing some types of securities that were not previously in public favor. Also, in some instances the firm may see an opportunity for purchasing some of its own securities at bargain prices. Common refinancing plans are: (1) bonds for bonds, (2) stock for bonds, (3) stock for stock, (4) long-term for short-term financing, and (5) tender offers for bonds or stocks.

Bonds for Bonds

The indenture of many bond issues includes a provision that the bonds may be called or redeemed prior to maturity at the option of the corporation. Usually a premium must be paid, which varies with the length of time the bonds have been outstanding. For example, a 40-year bond issue may not be callable for 10 years; then it may be redeemable at 110 percent of face for the next 10 years, and then at 105 for the remaining life of the issue.

Since issuing bonds for bonds does not change the financial structure of a firm, it might seem that there would be no point in refinancing on this basis. Actually there are two occasions when replacing old bonds with a new bond issue would be justified. The more common situation is the opportunity to replace a high-interest bond issue with one carrying a lower interest rate. The saving in the annual interest cost may well equal the bond premium in two or three years and, aside from the expense of exchanging or selling the new bonds, the reduced expense will prove to be a profitable move over the life of the issue. Another occasion when bonds might replace bonds arises when an old issue matures and no provision has been made for its retirement. The proceeds from a refunding issue are used to pay off the old bonds and the corporation's financial structure remains intact. The debt of the federal government is largely managed in this manner; and some corporations, notably railroads, follow this practice.

Stock for Bonds

A number of bond issues outstanding are convertible into common stock and, if the conversion feature is both worthwhile and has an expiration date, there is a possibility that this shift will take place almost automatically. Usually, however, when a shift from debt capital to equity capital is contemplated, the bonds outstanding are redeemed with the proceeds from a stock issue. The procedure is quite simple. The corporation sells preferred stock or common stock for cash by methods previously described. The money received is used to redeem the bonds either at maturity or earlier if the bonds are callable and the company exercises its call privilege.

Stock for Stock

As mentioned in Chapter 18, a preferred stock issue may be callable or redeemable. The provision under which this stock was issued may state a single premium at which the stock can be called at any time. For example, a $100 par preferred stock may have a permanent redemption price of $110.

The purposes of redeeming a preferred stock issue are to refinance with a new issue carrying a lower dividend rate or to eliminate this class of stock. If a corporation has outstanding a sizable issue of 7 percent preferred stock, the company may decide to replace this stock with an issue of 5 percent preferred. The change will increase common stock dividend possibilities, assuming that the preferred stock is nonparticipating. Or, the corporation may decide that the market is strong for common stocks and that now would be a good time to eliminate the preferred class. The advantage in this shift would be to remove a security senior to the common stock so that, if more capital is needed at a later date when the market is strong for preferred stocks, the way would be open for such an issue.

Long-Term for Short-Term Financing

Some refinancing plans are undertaken to convert, on a relatively permanent basis, a portion of the short-term debt into long-term securities. For example, a corporation may find that its cash balance does not improve to a point where the short-term bank indebtedness can be liquidated out of current receipts at any time during the year. As a result, the problem of paying these notes presents a constant source of financial difficulty. Although this problem is usually met by more short-term borrowing, a more satisfactory solution is to sell bonds or stock, thereby reducing the short-term debt to a manageable size.

Tender Offers

When interest rates are high and the stock market is in the doldrums, securities issued by many corporations are quoted at low prices. If the company has cash on hand, it may make its security holders an offer, called a

tender, to purchase its own outstanding bonds or stocks. (Offers from outsiders, as illustrated on page 383, are also called tenders.) Bonds must be repaid eventually anyway, and if the issuing corporation can buy them before maturity at a discount, it may find such a course of action very advantageous. For example, in 1974 UAL, Inc., made an offer to buy $32,500,000 of its 4½ percent debentures due July 1, 1992, at $52 for each $100 principal amount.

The reasons for making a tender offer for shares of stock vary from company to company. Sometimes a corporation wishes to hold some of its own shares, called **treasury stock**, to be used later for acquisitions. More commonly, if the stock is selling below its **book value**,[2] the purchase of shares increases the book value of the ones that remain outstanding. Also, earnings per share, with fewer shares participating, are likely to show an improvement.

COMBINATIONS AND SPIN-OFFS

The last 20 years have witnessed a marked trend in the growth of many corporations. In most instances this growth has been achieved by one company buying or joining forces with one or more previously independent firms. Also, there have been a number of instances where, following a combination, a reverse action has taken place either voluntarily or at the direction of the federal government. For example, the Procter & Gamble Company acquired the Folger Coffee Company, the Duncan Hines Companies, the Charmin Paper Products Company, and the Clorox Company. The federal government then stepped in and required Procter & Gamble to divest itself of the Clorox Company on the grounds that this acquisition was detrimental to competition in the bleach industry.

Types of Combinations

A **horizontal combination** takes place when separate companies doing exactly the same business activity are combined. A chain of drugstores, restaurants, motels, hotels, supermarkets, lumberyards, or department stores, if under one ownership and management, provides an illustration of this common form of combination. By contrast, a **vertical combination** joins types of companies doing different but related activities in the production and distribution of a product. For example, the United States Steel Co. owns coal and iron ore companies, shipping lines, railroads, blast furnaces, rolling mills, and fabricating plants.

Sometimes two businesses are combined because their activities are so closely interwoven that it seems preferable to be under one management.

[2] Book value = $\dfrac{\text{net worth of a firm} - \text{preferred stock value}}{\text{number of shares of common stock outstanding}}$

Such a combination is called a **complementary combination**. Meat packers have joined forces with fertilizer factories; business machine companies have bought electronic data equipment manufacturers; and in some cases the need to dispose of by-products, such as gas from coke production, makes it advantageous for two formerly separate companies to join forces. In other instances the companies combined are in allied lines, which is a **circular combination**. For example, when Standard Brands, Inc., was formed, it combined diverse food products into one organization.

Since the early 1960s there has been a rash of companies joining forces that have little or no logic in their association together. These are called **conglomerate mergers**. Textron, Inc., for example, has bought up companies manufacturing helicopters, eyeglasses, wristwatch bands, golf carts, chain saws, ball bearings, home and industrial staplers, and a host of other consumer, industrial, and military products.

Methods of Financing Combinations

As might be expected, financing these various types of combinations can be extremely complex, particularly if the companies concerned are sizable in their own right. Occasionally when one large firm buys a relatively small company, it may do so for cash. In this case the financing may be no more of a problem to the buyer than would the purchase of a new piece of heavy equipment. More commonly, securities are involved as noted in the following examination of three major methods used to form combinations: (1) mergers, (2) consolidations, and (3) holding companies.

MERGERS

When a **merger** takes place between two or more companies, the dominant one absorbs the smaller units and they disappear as separate entities. If Company A makes an offer to Company B to purchase its assets and liabilities and the offer is accepted, Company B ceases to exist as a separate organization, and Company A is then a larger concern. If the payment to Company B is entirely in cash, the only financial problem may be to arrive at a mutually agreed-upon price. If, however, the payment is to be made in bonds, preferred stock, or common stock of Company A, or some combination that may even involve part cash, long hours may be spent by the financial managers of both firms in arriving at an equitable settlement.

Although there is no single dominant pattern, the most widely used technique is to make payment in common stock, partially because this method is tax free to the stockholders of Company B. If, for example, on the date of the sale, Company A's stock is selling for $40 a share and Company B's shares are quoted at $60, Company A will issue 1½ shares of its stock for each share of Company B stock outstanding. Company B will then be dissolved and, quite possibly, be operated as a division of Company A.

A **consolidation**, also known as an **amalgamation**, results in the formation of a new company by combining two or more existing firms. If Company A and Company B decide to combine but neither one cares to merge with the other, a Company C can be organized to buy up the assets and liabilities of A and B. In this event, both of the old companies disappear and a new company is born. For example, the American Motors Corporation is a consolidation that combined the Hudson Motor Car Company and the Nash-Kelvinator Corporation.

Since a new company is formed in a consolidation, its financial structure can consist of any desirable combination of debt and equity capital. The size of the new firm obviously will be dictated by the amount paid for the companies forming the consolidation. The kinds of securities issued will, however, be influenced by what the stockholders of the old companies are willing to accept. If they wish a tax-free exchange, the new company will issue its common stock for the common stock of the original companies at some agreed-upon exchange ratio.

HOLDING COMPANIES

A popular device for combining a number of concerns is the **holding company**. In its pure form a holding company, known as the **parent company**, is organized for the sole purpose of acquiring enough of the voting stock in other companies, called **subsidiaries**, to insure control. Theoretically this should be more than 50 percent, but in actual practice some holding companies own all of the stock of their subsidiaries and in other cases much less than one half. When a corporation has a large number of stockholders, none of whom is a large stockholder, the current system of management-secured proxies is such that a 20 or 30 percent ownership is adequate for effective control. Also, in actual practice many holding companies conduct operations in their own names and also function as holding companies.

Although practically every large corporation is a holding company to some extent, the best known is the American Telephone & Telegraph Company (AT&T). In addition to operating the long-distance lines within the United States and from the United States to other countries, AT&T owns between 16.8 percent and 100 percent of 22 large telephone companies operating in 48 states. Western Electric Company, AT&T's manufacturing division, is wholly owned; it and AT&T jointly own the Bell Laboratories.

Suppose a holding company is organized to buy stock of Company A, which it wishes to control. It can raise the necessary funds by selling bonds, preferred stock, or common stock, or some combination of the three. The cash received is then used to buy voting shares in Company A. If the management of Company A has resisted offers to merge or consolidate, the holding company may extend to each stockholder of Company A an offer to buy shares at a price that is usually in excess of the current market quotation. This price can be in cash or a stated number of shares of the holding company's stock. If enough stockholders accept the tender offer, the directors, and probably the officers of Company A, will suddenly discover that their services are no longer wanted.

Spin-Offs

In recent years many corporations, particularly those classed as conglomerates, have found it either necessary or advisable to dispose of one or more of their operating units. The divestiture by a firm of a segment of its business is known as a **spin-off**. Although the most common reason for a spin-off is a decision that the business activity is incompatible with the other operating units, sometimes the federal government or a foreign government is responsible. In 1973, for example, the W. R. Grace & Co. divested itself of tin and tungsten mining operations in Bolivia, and Libya took over 51 percent of the company's petroleum holdings in that country.

The most common method of accomplishing a spin-off is to sell the business to some other corporation that is willing to buy it. Another possibility is to transfer the unwanted assets to a newly created corporation in exchange for its shares of stock, which are then distributed to the stockholders of the original corporation. When expropriation by a foreign government is involved, the hope is that adequate compensation will be paid, preferably in cash.

FAILURES AND REORGANIZATIONS

Every year some businesses, including new and well-established ones, meet with financial reverses. The fault may lie with the present management or may be caused by outside factors over which no control can be exercised. For example, a neighborhood grocery store that had been prosperous for many years found its profits changed to losses when a large supermarket opened in the vicinity. Regardless of the reasons, continued losses will usually weaken the financial structure of a firm to a point where some action must be taken by the owners or managers.

Under the National Bankruptcy Act, **insolvency** exists whenever the aggregate of a person's property is not, at a fair valuation, sufficient to pay his or her debts. Anyone who reads the financial pages of a local newspaper has probably noted that a corporation has been adjudged bankrupt, for example, with assets of $62,400 and liabilities of $3,295,000. An individual or a firm may also become insolvent under state laws merely because of inability to pay current debts. A manufacturing firm may have assets valued at more than its liabilities, but because most of its capital is tied up in special machinery the assets cannot be liquidated to pay accounts and notes payable that are due.

After a business becomes insolvent, there are two major avenues open for either salvaging or liquidating it: (1) voluntary creditor agreements, which assume that the firm can again be profitable, and (2) legal action, which can result in liquidation or reorganization.

Voluntary Creditor Agreements

When the owner or owners of a business realize that the firm is in dire financial straits, the first step is to call a meeting of the creditors. At this time a decision can be reached as to whether to seek a solution with or without court assistance. The creditors know that if the company is adjudged bankrupt by a court, the legal costs will be high and it is most unlikely that they will receive full payment for their claims. Furthermore, a former customer who might otherwise be saved for future business is probably lost.

If the creditors believe that the business can operate at a profit in the future, despite past reverses, they may agree to postpone the due date of their claims. An **extension agreement** must be signed by all creditors to give the plan a fair chance to work out successfully. A variation of the extension agreement is a **composition settlement**, by which the creditors accept a reduction in the amounts due them. These amounts may be paid in cash immediately, or settlement may be postponed for a few months.

In these voluntary agreements the creditors usually elect a representative who assumes active management of the firm for a long enough period of time to guarantee that the plan will be followed. As soon as the organization is operating smoothly and successfully, the creditors' representative withdraws and allows the original managers to operate without supervision. If the creditors cannot agree on a voluntary solution or if there seems to be no hope of successful operation of the business, the only alternative is to turn to a court for help. Such a step can be taken by the insolvent firm, or the creditors may force the issue.

Legal Action

When the Constitution of the United States was written, it provided for a national and uniform bankruptcy law. Consequently, even though states have insolvency laws, legal actions involving bankruptcy are usually taken under the federal law and are brought in federal district courts.

DECLARING BANKRUPTCY

An individual or a corporation, with certain exceptions such as banks and insurance companies, may go into bankruptcy by declaring under oath that liabilities owed exceed the value of assets owned. Or, if an act of bankruptcy is committed, such as assigning assets to a favored creditor, three other creditors (if there are more than 12) with claims of $500 or more can file a petition asking that the firm be declared bankrupt. Unless the business can refute the charges, the court will approve the petition.

If creditors fear that assets might disappear, the judge may appoint a **receiver** who serves as a temporary custodian of the firm's assets until they can be turned over to a trustee. At this stage the court appoints a **referee in bankruptcy** who serves as the court's representative in subsequent proceedings. The referee calls a meeting of the creditors and they elect a representative known as a **trustee in bankruptcy**. In most instances this trustee with approval by the referee liquidates the assets, pays preferred claims, and distributes the balance, if any, to the general creditors. The debtor is legally discharged from obligations, and the creditors are given impartial treatment in accord with their legal status. The priority of claims by different classes of creditors is discussed in Chapter 25 on page 506.

REORGANIZATION

Under the National Bankruptcy Act, as amended, liquidation of a bankrupt firm is not mandatory. If a corporation is basically sound but has become insolvent because of a capital structure that it cannot support, provisions of the act provide for a possible financial reorganization. **Reorganization plans** usually involve the scaling down of amounts owed or the interest or dividend rates, with more sacrifices being taken by the common stockholders and other unsecured interests. For example, first-mortgage bondholders owning 6 percent securities might agree to accept 4 percent bonds in exchange. Second-mortgage bondholders might agree to a reduction in the interest rate and also in principal amount. Preferred stockholders might be given new preferred stock with a lower dividend rate or even common stock. Common stockholders are sometimes eliminated entirely or are given a small amount of new stock in exchange for their previous holdings. The net effect is to reduce the annual fixed charges for interest and debt retirement to the point where normal operations of the business will allow for these charges and still leave a profit margin.

BUSINESS TERMS

warrant	371	preemptive right	372
trading on the equity	372	rights offering	373

QUESTIONS FOR DISCUSSION AND ANALYSIS

1. If a corporation has to issue warrants to buy common stock when selling senior securities, is it likely that the warrants will prove worthless? Discuss.

2. Explain why public utilities must trade on the equity in order to attract buyers of its common stock.

3. Why shouldn't corporations be required to pay out all, or at least a high percentage, of net earnings to their stockholders?

4. As a stockholder would you prefer to receive a 100 percent stock dividend over a two-for-one stock split?

5. In a period of rising prices, is the use of LIFO as a device for measuring the value of raw materials, semi-finished goods, and finished goods on hand likely to understate the true worth of these inventories?

6. What type of a combination is the Federal Trade Commission most likely to oppose as having the greatest potential for reducing competition?

7. Conglomerate mergers, which were very popular in the late 1960s and early 1970s, seem to have lost their glamour. What reasons can be given for this change?

8. If a holding company owns 100 percent of the stock of a subsidiary, why shouldn't it dissolve the corporation and operate the subsidiary as a division of the parent company?

9. As one of several creditors of an insolvent business, would you prefer that it work out a voluntary creditor agreement or declare bankruptcy? Present arguments to support your position.

10. If an insolvent corporation does not have either bonds or preferred stock outstanding, would an owner of common stock prefer liquidation of the company over a refinancing plan?

PROBLEMS AND SHORT CASES

1. Every year the Osgood Mattress Company has been able to average a 15 percent operating profit, before interest, on its $25,000,000 in total assets. Debt and equity capital consists of $2,000,000 in open-book accounts, $5,000,000 borrowed from commercial banks at 8 percent interest, and $18,000,000 in common stock and retained earnings represented by 1,500,000 shares outstanding. The corporation decides to expand by selling $6,000,000 in 9 percent bonds and $4,000,000 in 7 percent nonparticipating preferred stock. The bank loans are to be paid off and, in view of the increase in size, it is contemplated that the open-book accounts will grow to $2,500,000.

Assuming a continuation of the 15 percent return on operations and that all earnings are paid out either as interest or dividends, what dollar dividends per share were available to the common stockholders before and after the expansion? Show calculations.

2. The major sources of capital for the Early Bird Canning Company are as follows:

Commercial paper, 7%, maturing in one year	$10,000,000
First mortgage bonds, 8½%, callable at 105, due in 1985	40,000,000
Preferred stock, 6%, $100 par, nonparticipating, convertible, redeemable at 110	10,000,000
Common stock, no-par, 10,000,000 shares authorized, 8,000,000 shares outstanding	50,000,000

The firm has been prosperous and has established a regular dividend policy of $2 a share on its common stock, which is listed on a national exchange. Recent trading in this stock has hovered around $52 a share, although the price range has fluctuated between $40 and $60 a share within the past year. The bonds and preferred stock are also listed and usually sell at or slightly above par.

The management of the Early Bird Canning Company wishes to raise enough new capital to retire the commercial paper and to buy a large manufacturer of dried fruits as a step toward diversification. The stockholders of the dried fruits company are willing to accept $20,000,000 in cash for their business or to exchange 400,000 shares of the common stock of the Early Bird Canning Company. The reputation of this company is such that it appears certain that the market will absorb any type of securities that it offers for sale, and more than one investment banking company has indicated an interest in forming a syndicate to sell appropriate issues.

Present a financial plan for the Early Bird Canning Company that will accomplish the two stated objectives. Explain why your plan is preferable to alternate methods that could be used.

3. The Offshore Oil Drilling Corporation's long-term capital came from $15,000,000 in 7 percent bonds and $20,000,000 in common stock represented by 1,250,000 no-par shares. For several years the corporation has been unable to show a net profit although it has averaged $900,000 in profits from operations (before bond interest). All retained earnings from former years have now been exhausted and the firm is in default on its bond interest for last year and this year. Currently relief is being sought under the National Bankruptcy Act.

A reorganization plan has been proposed and approved under which the bondholders accept $7,500,000 in 5 percent bonds, $7,500,000 in a $100 par 6 percent preferred stock, and 1,000,000 shares of common stock with the understanding that the $2,100,000 in interest owed will be cancelled. The common stockholders are required to turn in four shares for each one retained.

Assuming the continuation of operating earnings of $900,000 annually, can the corporation meet its obligations on the bonds and preferred stock and still pay a dividend to the old stockholders? If so, how many dollars or cents per share will be available?

20 Security and Commodity Markets

Gary Bell, an investor, recently purchased 100 shares of the Ajax Manufacturing Co. for $3,600, which used up his surplus cash. In today's morning paper he noted that Ajax lost $2.50 a share in yesterday's trading. Immediately after arriving at his office he called his broker for an explanation. The broker assured him that Ajax was an outstanding company but that its shares of stock were, of course, subject to the ups and downs of the stock market. Despite this reassurance, Bell was in a foul mood all day even though he had bought Ajax intending to hold it for the long pull.

In this country millions of shares of stock and millions of bushels of grains are bought and sold on each working day. Most of these purchases and sales take place on organized security and commodity exchanges. Details on both volumes and prices are not only reported daily in metropolitan newspapers but also summarized on radio and television news broadcasts.

The security markets are very important to publicly held corporations. For example, if a corporation's common stock is selling for $28 a share, an offering of additional common shares will have to be priced near this figure. The commodity markets are also of intense interest to all businesses that use such items as soybeans, sugar, cotton, corn, copper, and other similar raw materials. A manufacturer of flour, for example, is vitally concerned with the current price being paid to farmers for the wheat they have grown.

Businesspersons are not the only individuals who follow the market. In the United States approximately 30 million men and women are curious about the value of shares of stock they own, and 3 million farmers are concerned with grain and feed prices. Many persons turn to the financial pages of a newspaper before reading any other section to observe the daily price movements in the security and commodity markets (see Figure 20-1). These markets, with emphasis on the exchanges and governmental regulations concerning them, will be discussed in this chapter.

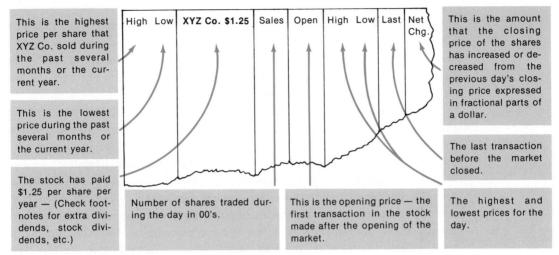

This is the highest price per share that XYZ Co. sold during the past several months or the current year.	High	Low	**XYZ Co. $1.25**	Sales	Open	High	Low	Last	Net Chg.	This is the amount that the closing price of the shares has increased or decreased from the previous day's closing price expressed in fractional parts of a dollar.

This is the highest price per share that XYZ Co. sold during the past several months or the current year.

This is the lowest price during the past several months or the current year.

The stock has paid $1.25 per share per year — (Check footnotes for extra dividends, stock dividends, etc.)

Number of shares traded during the day in 00's.

This is the opening price — the first transaction in the stock made after the opening of the market.

This is the amount that the closing price of the shares has increased or decreased from the previous day's closing price expressed in fractional parts of a dollar.

The last transaction before the market closed.

The highest and lowest prices for the day.

¹Stock prices are generally quoted in dollars and ⅛ fractions of a dollar per share. For example, 51⅜ is equivalent to $51.375.

Figure 20-1 *How to Read the Financial Page (Assuming Your Newspaper Is Quoting the "Final" Prices for the Day)*

SECURITY EXCHANGES

A **security exchange**, commonly called a stock exchange, is an organization that provides facilities for its members to buy and sell stocks and bonds. Stocks and bonds that have been approved for trading on a security exchange are known as **listed securities.**

National and Regional Security Exchanges

The most famous and largest of the national security exchanges, the New York Stock Exchange (NYSE), lists approximately 2,000 stocks and a like number of bond issues of over 1,400 corporations. Despite this small number in relation to the total number of existing corporations, almost every sizable industrial company is represented on the NYSE. On a normal trading day around 20 million shares of stock in more than 1,300 corporations change hands.

To qualify for listing on the NYSE, in addition to securing approval from the Securities and Exchange Commission (SEC), a corporation must meet the following standards:

1. It must have a minimum of 1,000,000 shares publicly owned.
2. It must have a minimum of 2,000 stockholders, each owning at least 100 shares.
3. Its annual earnings should exceed $2½ million currently and $2 million for each of the previous two years.
4. Its common stock publicly held must have a minimum value of $16 million.

The NYSE has a limited membership of 1,366. Its members are individuals, many of whom are partners in a brokerage firm. A membership is called a **seat**, and it can be sold if the prospective member has been approved by the board of directors of the exchange. The price of these seats has been as low as $17,000 and as high as $625,000 during this century.

There are approximately a dozen other exchanges in the United States. Of these the American Stock Exchange (also called **Amex** or **Curb Exchange)** located in New York City and the Midwest Stock Exchange located in Chicago are important enough to have their daily transactions reported in *The Wall Street Journal*. With the exception of the Pacific Coast Stock Exchange and the Philadelphia-Baltimore-Washington Exchange, the other exchanges are not too important. The stocks handled by these regional exchanges are usually some combination of a few local companies and a selection of the same stocks available on the **Big Board**, which is a nickname for the New York Stock Exchange.

Operation of Security Exchanges

The chief function of a security exchange is to provide a convenient means by which individuals and organizations can buy or sell outstanding securities of well-known corporations. A security exchange is not a source of capital to the corporation that has its stocks and bonds listed. These securities have already been sold, usually through investment banking companies; and subsequent sales that take place on a stock exchange are between such diverse security holders as individuals, corporations, banks, insurance companies, pension funds, investment trusts, churches, hospitals, trust funds, and endowment funds.

For every buyer there must be a seller. The statement that "everybody is buying stocks" merely means that the demand is greater than the supply, with a resultant increase in prices. When an investor thinks a stock is going up in price, he or she would not be able to buy if a security holder did not believe it was a good time to sell. Conversely, even in a severely depressed market there is always a buyer if the seller is willing to accept the offering price.

TRADING PROCEDURES

An order to a stockbroker to buy stocks on an exchange, regardless of the residence of the potential investor, is routed to the trading floor of the exchange. Here it is given to a member of the exchange, who is known as a **commission broker**.

On the floor of the exchange are a number of **trading posts** at which a specified list of stocks are bought and sold. If the order placed by a customer is for 100 shares of common stock of United States Steel Corporation, the member locates the post and makes an offer to buy under terms specified by the customer. Assuming the customer is willing to pay the current, or even a somewhat higher, price per share, a **market order** would be placed, which is usually filled immediately since someone is always willing to sell if the offering price is accepted. If, however, the customer placed a **limited order**, such as $60 a share and the stock is selling at $62 a share, the member leaves the order with another broker who is known as a **specialist**. A specialist spends most of the time at one post and concentrates on a limited number of securities. The specialist will make a memorandum of the customer's order and if at a later time in the day or at a later date an offer is made to sell U.S. Steel shares at $60, the order will be executed.

Trading is conducted in **round-lots** that normally are 100-share units. If the order is for 25 shares, it is placed by the member with an **odd-lot broker** who makes a specialty of handling such orders, for which he or she receives a special commission. By grouping several odd-lot orders, odd-lot brokers may be able to buy one or more round lots, which are distributed to the several purchasers, or they may decide to purchase the additional shares for their own account.

A Sample Transaction. Betty Hall, who lives in a suburban area near St. Louis, has decided to buy 25 shares of International Harvester Company (IHC) common stock. One of her neighbors is Ted Samuels, a stockbroker employed by a large brokerage firm with offices in many cities including downtown St. Louis. After reaching Samuels by telephone, Ms. Hall places an order to buy at $33, and this purchase request is immediately teletyped to the New York office of the brokerage firm. From there it is telephoned to the floor of the New York Stock Exchange (on which IHC is listed) and delivered to a partner on the trading floor.

This member goes to the post at which IHC is sold and, because the order is for only 25 shares and the trading unit is 100 shares, the broker turns the buy order over to an odd-lot specialist operating at that post. At this particular moment IHC has dipped to $32½, so the odd-lot specialist buys 100 shares and allocates 25 to the exchange member with whom we are concerned. This individual reports to the New York office that the stock has been bought, the teletype carries the news to St. Louis, and Samuels notifies Ms. Hall that her order has been executed. A seller rather than a buyer of IHC stock would go through a similar process.

The machinery for buying or selling stocks is well established, and transactions are completed in a relatively short time. A buyer or a seller in a broker's office in a large city can expect to complete a transaction within one or two minutes if he or she is willing to do business at market quotations.

Stock Quotations. How did Betty Hall decide on a buying price of $33 a share? She may have been following the daily reports in her newspaper, or her stockbroker may have recommended the stock as a good buy at this price. If Ms. Hall had been in the St. Louis office of the brokerage firm that executed the order, she could have watched the electronic **ticker tape.** By means of electric letters and numbers, about the size of electric basketball scoreboards, that move from right to left, actual transactions on the NYSE can be seen in brokerage offices within a few seconds.

Figure 20-2 shows a small segment of ticker tape. Each stock has an abbreviation which may or may not be easily recognizable. Below the symbol is the sales price for 100 shares or, in the case of sales up to 1,000 shares, the number of hundreds is indicated. For large sales the exact quantity is shown.

GIS	XON	GT	IBM
$59\frac{5}{8}$	$3s87\frac{1}{2}$	$3,000s21\frac{1}{4}$	$215\frac{3}{4}$

Figure 20-2   Ticker Tape Segment

The letter "s" separates the size of the sale from the sales price when more than a single round-lot is involved. The reading of the tape shown is:

> 100 shares of General Mills, Inc., common at 59⅝
> 300 shares of Exxon Corp. common at 87½
> 3,000 shares of Goodyear Tire & Rubber Co. common at 21¼
> 100 shares of International Business Machines Corp. common at 215¾

More recently, many large security brokers have also installed electronic devices placed on the desks of account executives that provide almost instantaneous information about stocks and their price quotations.

PRICE VARIATIONS AND AVERAGES

As noted in the ticker tape segment, stock prices are quoted in eighths, quarters, and halves. Bond prices are quoted in relationship to 100 regardless of the denomination of the bond, which is usually $1,000. A bond quoted at 112 ¾ would cost $1,127.50 to purchase. Government bonds are an exception to the variations in price. For these securities the quotations are in thirty-seconds, such as 98²⁴/₃₂. For convenience in printing, this figure is usually shown as 98.24 but the bond will cost $987.50 (98¾).

To judge whether the stock market is up or down, averages are published in the financial pages of newspapers and aired on radio and television. The best known is the Dow Jones average of individual stocks, which is based on only 30 corporations. Standard & Poor's index uses 425 industrials, 25 rails, and 50 utilities. Since 1966 the NYSE has issued an average based on all of its stocks. Also, each trading day the NYSE makes a report every half hour on the number of cents an average share has gained or lost.

Averages for the over-the-counter market, which is discussed on pages 398–400, are also released daily. Bond averages are likewise reported; again, the best known is the Dow Jones, which is based on 40 issues.

COST OF TRADING

Whether they are buying or selling, customers of a brokerage firm pay a commission for the services rendered to them. Commissions charged by members of the NYSE vary by the amount of money involved and by the number of shares in the transaction — odd-lot, single round-lot, or multiple round-lots. For many years brokers charged uniform commission rates, but since May 1, 1975 these have been competitive. In general, the commission a customer pays for a single round-lot will amount to more than one percent but less than two percent of the purchase or sale price. For example, one firm charges $77.50 for executing an order for 100 shares of stock selling for $50 a share.

In addition to commissions, the state of New York levies a tax on the transfer of shares. This tax is paid by the seller. As shown below, the rates are less for out-of-state residents not employed in New York.

Shares Selling at	Sales by Residents (Tax per Share)	Sales by Nonresidents (Tax per Share)
Less than $5	1.25¢	0.625¢
$5 but less than $10	2.5¢	1.25¢
$10 but less than $20	3.25¢	1.875¢
$20 or more	5.0¢	2.5¢

Florida is the only other state that levies a tax on stock transfers.

A final item of the cost of trading is a transaction fee levied by the SEC. It is a modest charge of 1¢ for each $500 or fraction thereof of the money involved.

SPECULATIVE TRANSACTIONS

In every market one finds investors and speculators. An **investor** is one who buys securities in order to hold them on a more or less permanent basis.

The **speculator** hopes to make a profit buying and selling them within a few weeks, days, or within the trading hours of a single day. Speculators who buy stocks in anticipation of a rise in price are known as **bulls**; and those who sell, expecting the market to go down in the days or weeks ahead, are known as **bears**.

Short Selling. As illogical as it may seem, a bear often sells shares he or she does not own. This market operation is known as **short selling**. The bear sells today expecting to buy, or "cover the short sale" as the process is called, within a relatively short time after the market goes down to a price at which a profit can be made. For example, Bob Smith, a speculator, might sell 1,000 shares of AT&T at $55 a share on Monday morning. On Friday afternoon, noting that shares are now available at $53½, Smith covers the short sale by buying 1,000 shares at this price. These transactions result in a profit of $1,500 minus the costs of trading. Of course, if the market does not go down, Smith will eventually incur a loss. Because Smith must deliver shares of stock to the Monday morning purchaser, he borrows these from the broker who handled the sale. In return for the use of the cash proceeds from the sale, the broker usually loans these shares without charge. They may be shares owned by the brokerage firm or, more likely, shares that the firm is holding for one of its customers.

Margin Trading. Another possibility for a speculator to increase profits is to buy stocks on a margin. If a buyer can **margin** his or her account with a broker up to 50 percent, it means that only one half of the purchase price is required. A speculator who has $1,000 can buy either 100 shares of a stock selling at $10 or 200 shares at the same price by borrowing the extra $1,000 from a broker. In case the stock rises to $15, the shares could be sold for a profit of $500 in one case and $1,000 in the other, minus commissions and taxes (and, in the latter instance, minus interest on the money borrowed). On the other hand, if the stock declines in value, the broker will call for an additional deposit to protect the broker's firm against loss. If the margin trader cannot put up additional funds, the broker will sell the stock no later than when the price drops to $5 to protect the loan, and the speculator's original $1,000 deposit will be lost.

From the foregoing discussion it might appear that speculators are using stock exchanges as a type of gambling casino. Although there is some truth in this accusation, speculators render a real service to investors and to the exchanges. They not only keep the market active but also hold price variations between sales of a particular stock to fractions of a point. Speculators are one important reason why an investor can always find a buyer or a seller for a stock or bond listed on an exchange.

Value of Security Exchanges

Security exchanges render an extremely valuable service in the field of finance. The maintenance of a free market, with prices established at all times by the forces of supply and demand, make listed securities more useful than unlisted stocks and bonds. They can be used as collateral at a bank for a loan or as the security for collateral trust bonds. Estates are easier to appraise to the extent that they contain listed securities.

For a corporation large enough to qualify, it is a matter of some prestige to have its stocks and bonds listed on an exchange. The chances are good that the number of stockholders will increase after listing, thus helping its sales and certainly making it easier for the "in group" to retain control. Of even greater importance is the added bargaining power a corporation has with an investment banking company when negotiating for the sale of additional securities. The market for new issues of bonds and stocks of well-known companies is much stronger than for unknown corporations.

Security exchanges have provided a marketplace where an individual can invest savings at a relatively low commission charge. The United States seems to be in a period of ever-increasing prices resulting in a steady shrinking in the purchasing power of the dollar. Although there is no perfect hedge against inflation, over the long run common stocks do tend to increase in value when prices go up because corporations increase their prices to offset higher costs of labor and materials to such an extent that their profits also increase proportionally. Furthermore, individuals can feel confident about the reliability of their brokers. The Security Investors Protection Act passed in 1970 insures customers of a brokerage firm against losses caused by the insolvency of the broker up to $50,000 in securities and $20,000 in cash.

Regulation of Security Sales and Exchanges

In the early part of the twentieth century less than a half million people owned corporate stocks and bonds, and no effective regulations covered security sales. The doctrine of caveat emptor — let the buyer beware — held full sway. Unscrupulous promoters sold shares of stock in ventures having scant, if any, hope of success, and the public was the victim of many security swindles. When an aroused public finally demanded legislation to curb these swindles, both the states and the federal government enacted appropriate laws.

STATE REGULATION

Although in 1909 the United States Post Office secured the passage of a law that made it a criminal offense to use the mails to defraud, this legislation did not prevent crooked security salespersons from operating in various cities and communities. In 1911 Kansas passed a law regulating security sales in that state. At the time it was under consideration, a member of the legislature remarked that some promoters would sell stock in the "blue sky" itself. Today, the laws regulating security sales that have been passed in most states are known as **blue-sky laws**. These blue-sky laws frequently cover the following items:

1. New security issues must be registered with an appropriate state official.
2. Dealers, brokers, and salespersons must obtain annual licenses.
3. Individuals charged with fraud in connection with the sale of stocks and bonds are prosecuted.

Unfortunately, state regulation provides little or no control over interstate sales, a situation that the federal government had recognized as early as 1920 when it gave the Interstate Commerce Commission (ICC) jurisdiction over the sale of railroad securities. Need for further controls was apparent, and since 1933 the federal government has played a dominant role in regulating security sales.

FEDERAL SECURITIES ACT OF 1933

The Securities Act of 1933 was based on the belief that potential investors had the right to know all pertinent facts about a company issuing new securities and that the officers, accountants, engineers, and lawyers providing such information should be held legally liable for supplying such facts. It has been called the "information law" because full disclosure of relevant financial facts is the major requirement of the act. This is accomplished by (a) requiring the filing of a **registration statement**, which contains extensive details about the company and the proposed issue of securities, and (b) the preparation of a condensed version of this statement, called a **prospectus**, that must be furnished to each prospective purchaser of the stocks or bonds offered for sale.

Since 1934 the enforcement of this law has been under the jurisdiction of the Securities and Exchange Commission (SEC). The SEC is given 20 days after the registration statement is on file to issue a **stop order** if it believes the proposed offering should not be made to the general public. Even though a stop order is not issued, the SEC does not guarantee the correctness of the information supplied and can request the Department of Justice to institute criminal proceedings if, at a later date, the law seems to have been violated.

Some security issues are exempt from registration. These include all forms of government securities, railroad issues subject to the ICC, and stocks and bonds of cooperatives and nonprofit institutions. Also, sales not involving the use of mails or interstate commerce are exempt, as well as those in which there has been no public offering. In recent years many issues have been sold at private sale for the express purpose of avoiding registration under this law.

FEDERAL SECURITIES EXCHANGE ACT OF 1934

The Securities Exchange Act of 1934 is notable because it established the powerful SEC. In addition it provided for several major reforms which are discussed in the following paragraphs.

Company Registration. Every corporation whose stock is listed on one of the national exchanges is required to file a registration statement with the SEC. Furthermore, it is specified that this statement must be kept up-to-date by the filing of annual reports. Whether or not a company is in the process of selling new securities, an investor is able to find out the same type of information that formerly was available only when new securities were to be sold.

National Stock Exchanges. Practically all of the security exchanges, including the large ones previously mentioned, were classified as national and placed under the jurisdiction of the SEC. The SEC employs a competent staff to watch sales on these national exchanges and to investigate those who might violate its trading regulations.

Margin Requirements. A third purpose of the Securities Exchange Act of 1934 was to restrict the amount of credit that would be available for financing the purchase of stocks. Control over this feature was placed in the hands of the Federal Reserve Board, which governs the federal reserve banks. This Board determines the extent to which a purchaser can margin his or her account and also limits the amount of loans that can be made by a member bank or by a broker for the purpose of financing stock purchases. During the past 25 years the margin requirement has been placed as high as 100 percent, which results in the equivalent of outright cash purchases, and as low as 50 percent.

Other Provisions. Further provisions of the law require the registration of all securities brokers and dealers with the SEC, and members of security exchanges have to indicate whether they are operating for their own account or as brokers and also whether they are **floor traders** (members who buy and sell for their own accounts), odd-lot dealers, or specialists. Proxy statements are subject to scrutiny to make sure they are truthful and not misleading. Corporate officers who own 10 percent or more of the stock of a company that is listed on a national exchange must list their holdings with the SEC, must not sell the company's securities on a ''short'' basis, and any profits made by them through the purchase and sale of securities of the corporation that are completed in a period of less than six months must be paid to the company.

OVER-THE-COUNTER MARKETS

Over-the-counter markets encompass all transactions involving the purchase and sale of outstanding public and corporate securities that do not take place on an organized security exchange. The bonds and stocks that are traded over the counter are known as **unlisted securities**. In contrast to the approximately 4,700 different issues of stocks and bonds traded on all security exchanges, it has been estimated that there are about 50,000 different bonds and stocks traded over the counter.

Unlike the technique used on security exchanges where brokers representing buyers and sellers meet face to face, the over-the-counter market is based on bid and asked prices. The **bid prices** are those that would-be buyers of over-the-counter securities are willing to pay, and the **asked prices** are those at which would-be sellers are willing to part with the bonds or stocks they own (see Figure 20-3). One or more of the approximately 4,000 security dealers who function in this market customarily establish the bid and asked prices. These dealers, who can also be classified as either investment banking companies or brokers or both, usually carry an inventory in several different unlisted bonds and stocks. They publicly announce that they "make a market" in these securities and will buy them at a bid price or sell them at an asked price. The difference represents their gross profit.

In the past one of the problems that faced security dealers operating in the over-the-counter market was the difficulty of obtaining bid and asked prices at the moment when a customer wished to buy or sell. Telephone calls made to market-making brokers were a partial solution, as were the daily reports of the National Quotations Bureau, a commercial service for subscribers. In 1971 the National Association of Security Dealers, a trade association to which most brokerage firms belong, began operation of its Automated Quotations known as NASDAQ. This is a computerized communications system

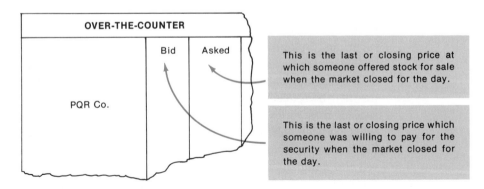

Figure 20-3 **Over-the-Counter Bid and Asked Prices**

that provides constant information on approximately 3,500 companies. A broker equipped with a desk-top quotation unit can obtain up-to-the-second information on any of the stocks on line in the central computer.

Securities Traded Over the Counter

Securities traded on the over-the-counter market include United States government and other public bonds and notes, most corporate bonds, mutual funds, foreign securities, bank stocks, insurance stocks, and a large number of industrial and public utility stocks that, for the most part, do not qualify for listing on an exchange. Whereas there are no specific requirements for a security to be traded over the counter, the National Association of Security Dealers has established the following standards for a company to be listed on NASDAQ:

1. It must have at least $1 million in assets.
2. It must have 500 or more stockholders.
3. It must have a minimum of 100,000 shares outstanding.
4. There must be at least two broker-dealers who make a market in its stock.

It has been estimated that the dollar volume of securities traded over the counter is substantially higher than the comparable figure for stocks and bonds traded on all security exchanges combined. It is difficult to obtain accurate figures because the transactions take place in thousands of locations in all 50 states and are not reported to a central agency. Also, in addition to the thousands of corporations on which either NASDAQ or a telephone contact with an appropriate broker will provide bid and asked prices, a broker is always willing to attempt to locate bonds or stocks of any publicly held corporation for a customer. Since transactions in these securities do not occur regularly, the bid and asked prices will be established by the potential buyers and sellers.

The Third and Fourth Markets

Sometimes transactions in listed securities take place off the organized exchange on which the bond or stock is listed and thus become a part of the over-the-counter market. When large blocks of listed securities are traded off the floor of the exchange with a brokerage firm acting as an intermediary between two institutional investors, the transaction is said to take place in the **third market**. The same transfer of securities without the use of an intermediary broker is referred to as the **fourth market**. Such transactions pose a threat to commission earnings of members of security exchanges although they may diminish now that commissions can be negotiated.

Regulation of Over-the-Counter Markets

In 1938 Congress passed legislation known as the Maloney Amendment to the Securities Exchange Act. It authorized investment banking companies to form associations for the purpose of self-regulation. The only association ever formed under this authority was the National Association of Security Dealers, Inc. This is a nonprofit corporation composed of broker and dealer members each of whom has been required to pass a qualifying examination as a Registered Representative or Principal and to subscribe to extensive and detailed Rules of Fair Practice.

The Federal Securities Acts of 1933 and 1934 were both amended in 1964. One amendment gave the SEC and NASD disciplinary authority over brokers and security dealers, which means that the Rules of Fair Practice can now be enforced. Of even greater importance was the provision that publicly held companies whose shares are traded in the over-the-counter market must, unless specifically exempted, provide the same type of information formerly required only of corporations with shares listed on organized exchanges. All industrial corporations engaged in interstate commerce with total assets of $1,000,000 and 500 or more stockholders were included and came under the same requirements as to registration, proxy solicitation, and other trading provisions as those applicable to listed securities.

OPTION EXCHANGES

A **stock option** gives the holder the privilege of buying or selling a named stock at a specified price within a stated time period. Stock options are frequently granted to corporation executives as a means of attracting and keeping persons of outstanding ability. Warrants are also a form of an option, and these were explained on page 371 in Chapter 19. A distinguishing feature of these two types of options is that both are issued by the corporation whose stock is involved.

An **option exchange** is an organized market for options that are sold by individuals or security dealers to investors or speculators who believe that the price per share of the specified stock will increase in as short a time as 30 days or as long a time period as 6 months and 10 days. With a relatively small outlay of cash, an individual can obtain the right to buy many more shares than personal resources would otherwise permit. If the stock goes up, profits will be large; if the stock goes down, the option will be allowed to expire and its cost will be a loss.

For example, a speculator who has $5,000 on hand believes that Xerox, which is selling for $50 a share, will make a substantial advance in the next six months. This individual can make an outright purchase of 100 shares. Or, assuming that a 50 percent margin requirement is in effect, he or she can acquire 200 shares. If, however, the speculator purchases an option to buy Xerox at $50 a share for the next six months and the cost is $10 per share, the right to purchase 500 shares can be acquired for $5,000. If the stock advances to $75 a share, profits (ignoring commissions and interest) would be $2,500, $5,000, or $12,500 depending on which of the three alternate actions was taken. If the stock falls to $40 in this same time period, losses would be $1,000, $2,000, and $5,000, respectively.

The Chicago Board Options Exchange (CBOE) was the first organized market for options and has since been followed by option trading on the American Stock Exchange. The CBOE deals in only 40 stocks, all listed on the New York Stock Exchange. At present only options to buy, known as **calls**, are available although it is contemplated that options to sell, called **puts**, will be added. The CBOE moved into new facilities in 1974 and is equipped to handle 200,000 option contracts daily, which would be a total of 20,000,000 shares since a sales unit is 100 shares.

COMMODITY EXCHANGES

A **commodity exchange** is an organized market for a selected list of commodities. In general, these products are produced in large quantities by thousands of suppliers and can be stored. There are many users of the commodities for which specific standards have been established. These users do not care about or know who grew, mined, or manufactured the actual goods purchased and delivered to them. Such products as wheat, corn, soybeans, sugar, wool, cotton, oats, rye, silver, lead, gold, zinc, tin, rubber, coffee, and cocoa are examples of commodities traded on exchanges. In addition, some livestock and vegetables are listed on certain commodity exchanges.

The oldest and best known commodity exchange is the Chicago Board of Trade on which grains, soybean meal and oil, silver, plywood, iced broilers, and steers are traded. Other exchanges handling grains are located in Minneapolis, Kansas City, and Winnipeg, Canada. The leading exchanges that handle cotton, wool, cocoa, rubber, hides, and potatoes are located in New York City. There are also overseas markets, notably the London metals markets.

Functions of Commodity Exchanges

Buying or selling on commodity exchanges is conducted by members of the exchange, who are usually brokers or partners in brokerage firms. These individuals execute orders for customers in a manner similar to the operation of stock exchanges. On the floor of a commodity exchange, instead of trading posts, the grain exchanges have central locations for each grain called **pits**. On cotton exchanges the central location for trading is called a **ring**.

An individual or firm who wishes to make a purchase or sale on a commodity exchange proceeds in much the same manner as in buying or selling shares of stock. A broker, who might be the same person used to buy securities, is contacted. The broker's firm probably holds a membership on the commodity exchange, so an order can be executed in a few minutes in a manner very comparable to the procedure for buying or selling stocks and bonds. The commission charged varies with the commodity and quantity, and is generally reasonable.

On a commodity exchange there are two markets — spot and futures. The **spot market** is the cash market. A buyer in the spot market usually expects delivery of the commodity and the seller usually owns the product sold. In the **futures market** contracts for purchase or sale call for delivery some months in the future. Actually, delivery is rarely made as the buyer of a contract will normally close the account by selling a contract; and the original seller of a contract follows a reverse procedure.

A SAMPLE FUTURES TRANSACTION

In December, Don Burns, a speculator, believes that corn is underpriced. He instructs his broker to buy 10,000 bushels for May delivery. By this transaction Burns takes a **long position**; if he had sold May corn, he would have taken a **short position**. If the December price of corn is $3.00 a bushel, Burns must margin his account with his broker as he has made a $30,000 purchase. Unlike security exchanges where the margin requirements have been established by the Federal Reserve Board at 50 to 100 percent, in this case a margin of approximately 10 percent is more common. In this specific transaction the broker would probably require Don Burns to make a deposit of no less than $3,000.

After this December purchase, Burns follows the market and is pleased when, in March, May corn is selling for $3.75 a bushel. At this time he instructs his broker to sell a contract for 10,000 bushels and to use this contract to cancel his purchase contract. He has made a profit of $7,500 less commissions on an investment of $3,000. If the price had gone down to $2.70 a bushel, he would have been forced to cover his May sale unless he supplied additional cash to increase his margin account. In any event he would have had to buy a contract no later than May.

HEDGING

The main useful purpose of the futures market is to protect the legitimate manufacturing profit of a processor who uses one of the commodities traded on an exchange. This is called **hedging**. It becomes necessary because the selling price of the processed product tends to follow the cash price of the raw material despite the time gap between its purchase and the subsequent sale of the finished product. The classic example of a hedging transaction involves wheat because flour sells in close relationship to the day-by-day price of wheat rather than on the basis of the cost of the grain that may have been purchased two or three months earlier for conversion into flour.

A typical hedging transaction, illustrated below, might work in the following manner. On February 1 the Minneapolis Milling Company buys 100,000 bushels of wheat in the spot market at $5.00 a bushel. At a processing cost of $200,000 and an estimated profit of $50,000 it expects to convert the wheat into flour worth $750,000 in today's market. As a hedge, on February 1 it sells 100,000 bushels of wheat at $5.00 for May delivery, which provides adequate time in which to have the flour ready for sale. During February and March the wheat is manufactured into flour but, because the price of wheat has declined to $4.00 a bushel, the Minneapolis Milling Company finds that it cannot sell the flour in April for more than $650,000, which represents an overall loss of $50,000. However, it now buys a contract for 100,000 bushels of wheat for $400,000, which offsets the contract sold on February 1 and results in a profit of $100,000. This profit, less the $50,000 loss on the sale of the flour, allows the Minneapolis Milling Company to earn the $50,000 that it originally hoped to make on its manufacturing operations.

CASH TRANSACTIONS		FUTURES TRANSACTIONS	
February 1		February 1	
Purchased 100,000 bushels of wheat @ $5.00 per bushel	$500,000	Sold May contract 100,000 bushels @ $5.00	$500,000
February and March			
Paid manufacturing costs	200,000	In April	
Total cost of flour	$700,000	Purchased May contract 100,000 bushels @ $4.00 to	
In April		offset Feb. 1 sale	400,000
Sale of flour	650,000		
Loss on sale of flour	$ 50,000	Profit on futures transactions	$100,000

Profit on futures transactions	$100,000
Less loss on sale of flour	50,000
Net profit	$ 50,000

Regulation of Commodity Exchanges

Although a Commodity Exchange Authority was created under the Secretary of Agriculture in 1936, the supervision and control over commodity exchanges fell far short of the authority of the SEC over security markets. Only futures in grains, livestock, and potatoes were covered, which left about one third of all transactions completely unregulated by any governmental agency. The exchanges had enforced rules necessary to the smooth functioning of their markets. Units of trading were established such as 50 tons for sugar, 100 bales for cotton, and 5,000 bushels for grains. Maximum price variations for one day's trading were established by the Commodity Exchange Authority, such as 20 cents a bushel for wheat and soybeans and 2 cents a pound for cocoa. The Authority also limited the holdings of speculators to 2,000,000 bushels of one grain or 30,000 bales of cotton.

In 1974 the Congress passed the Commodity Futures Trading Commission Act, which abolished the Agriculture Department's Commodity Exchange Authority and created a five-member commission to regulate all trading in commodity futures. The Commodity Futures Trading Commission (CFTC) has authority to seek court injunctions against violators of the law and the right to assess fines up to $100,000. Trading regulations for the various exchanges must be submitted to the CFTC for approval. Additional delivery points for commodities can be established to prevent or reduce price manipulations. Many other technical provisions were also included in this act. In general, the CFTC will oversee the markets for commodity futures in much the same manner as the SEC watches the stock exchanges.

BUSINESS TERMS

security exchange	389	prospectus	396
listed securities	389	stop order	396
seat	390	floor traders	397
Amex or Curb Exchange	390	over-the-counter markets	398
Big Board	390	unlisted securities	398
commission broker	390	bid prices	398
trading posts	390	asked prices	398
market order	391	third market	399
limited order	391	fourth market	399
specialist	391	stock option	400
round-lots	391	option exchange	400
odd-lot broker	391	calls	401
ticker tape	392	puts	401
investor	393	commodity exchange	401
speculator	394	pits	402
bulls	394	ring	402
bears	394	spot market	402
short selling	394	futures market	402
margin	394	long position	402
blue-sky laws	396	short position	402
registration statement	396	hedging	403

QUESTIONS FOR DISCUSSION AND ANALYSIS

1. What reasons can be advanced for owning shares of a listed stock rather than shares of an unlisted stock?

2. Might a large corporation that could fulfill

the requirements of the New York Stock Exchange prefer not to be listed on this exchange?

3. Why would a person who wishes to buy a particular stock give a broker a limited order rather than a market order?

4. Does a commission rate on stock purchases and sales of between one and two percent of the dollar amount of the transaction seem low, reasonable, or high?

5. Is a margin requirement even as low as 50 percent for the purchase of stocks contrary to the generous extension of credit available for buying automobiles, homes, and numerous other goods?

6. Would it be satisfactory to abolish all security exchanges and rely on NASDAQ, or some modification of this communication device, for trading in stocks and bonds?

7. Is any purpose other than speculation served by an option exchange?

8. Could the commodity exchanges function without the activities of speculators?

9. Why should margin requirements for purchases made on a commodity exchange be lower than those required for the purchase of stocks?

10. Does hedging necessarily protect a manufacturing profit?

PROBLEMS AND SHORT CASES

1. Refer to a current issue of *The Wall Street Journal* or a metropolitan newspaper and itemize the following information:

   a. Closing average, Dow Jones Industrials
   b. Closing price per share of American Telephone & Telegraph Co. preferred stock
   c. High for the year of International Business Machines common stock
   d. Closing quotation of Exxon bonds, 6s due in 1997
   e. Bid price for American Express Co. stock
   f. Asked price for Safeco Corp. stock
   g. Cash price for corn
   h. Closing price for December futures, Chicago wheat

2. The widow of Kermit Drake received $75,000 from the proceeds of her late husband's life insurance policies. Since she already had substantial amounts in savings accounts, she decided to acquire some common stocks. Assuming that she purchased the following securities at the prices indicated, and that commissions averaged 1.75 percent of the cost of the stocks, how much of her $75,000 inheritance did Mrs. Drake invest in stocks including commissions?

Shares Purchased	Corporation	Price per Share
200	American Telephone & Telegraph Co.	52⅜
100	E. I. duPont de Nemours & Co.	125½
150	Exxon Corp.	83⅞
300	General Motors Corp.	48¾
200	Xerox Corp.	80⅝

3. Charles Clemson, a farmer, has just sold his farm to a gravel company for $475,000. After paying taxes, Clemson expects to clear $400,000. Since he is 62 years old and his two children are grown and married, he decides to retire. Not knowing very much about financial matters Clemson consults you about investing his $400,000.

   In discussing this problem with Clemson and his wife, you discover that they live modestly, have no other resources as they only recently completed paying for the farm, and that they would expect to live on the income from investments hoping to turn over the principal to their children when they die. In your conference you also discover that Clemson is fearful that he may become bored in retirement and would like to spend some time each day checking over his investments. Although he is not sure how to go about it, an investment in commodities would be welcome as this is one area, insofar as grains are concerned, that he feels he knows something about.

Draw up an investment plan for $400,000. Be as specific as possible; if you include bonds, preferred stocks, and common stocks in your recommended investments, you do not have to name the exact company selected.

21 Risk Management and Insurance

George Walton had received a call at home at four o'clock in the morning informing him that a fire had broken out in his firm's factory building. Now, two hours later, he was gazing at a rubble of brick, glass, pipes, and machinery. His thoughts were on company insurance policies, safely stored in the undamaged office building, and on orders promised for prompt delivery. Would the fire insurance policies cover reconstruction costs? What about the profits he had expected to make on orders in process? How would his employees get along without work? And, above all, how soon could the factory get back into production?

Businesses that operate in a capitalistic system are constantly faced with **risks**, which may be defined as exposure to losses. Since it is not possible to avoid every exposure, risk management becomes essential to assure the continued success of all going concerns. When a potential loss is identified, managers will, first of all, take steps to determine if the risk can be avoided. Usually this is not possible, and management will attempt to reduce the possible impact or, preferably, transfer the burden to someone else despite the cost of this solution.

Assume, for example, that one of our industrial giants has plants and offices in all 50 states. Management consists of five key executives. If this corporation has a rule that none of the five may fly, it has avoided the risk of a fatal airplane accident. Since such a regulation would not be practicable, a policy that not more than one of the five may fly in any one airplane is more realistic. Furthermore, if the company carries a $1,000,000 life insurance policy on each of the five executives with the proceeds payable to the corporation, should one be killed in an accident the payment might well equalize the loss of profits for which this individual would have been responsible.

Unfortunately not all business risks are subject to as satisfactory a solution as was suggested in the preceding hypothetical case. Because some risks must be absorbed, and because reducing the impact of others only lessens the loss, sound business management dictates the transference of all that are capable of being shifted. This is usually accomplished by carrying **insurance**, which can be defined as a social device by which many share the losses of a few. To carry out the mechanics involved, financial institutions known as insurance companies have been organized. By a process called **underwriting**, an insurance company will enter into an agreement with a business to reimburse it for certain stated losses that may be incurred. In return for a payment, known as a **premium**, which usually covers the cost for a limited period of time such as one year, the insured receives a printed document, called an **insurance policy**, that specifies the terms of the insurance contract.

BUSINESS RISKS

Businesspersons must be aware of all of the different types of risks attached to the operation of their firms and must decide the best course of action for each type. Some risks are uninsurable, some can be avoided or reduced without buying insurance, and others have to be appraised in light of required characteristics before an insurance company will issue a policy.

Uninsurable Risks

The major uninsurable risk facing any business is the ever-present possibility that it cannot be operated at a profit. If the income from sales or services is inadequate to meet necessary expenses, losses result. If these continue for any length of time, sooner or later the business will have to discontinue operations. From 1970 to 1976 industrial and commercial failures averaged approximately 10,000 each year including many small retail stores and such giants as the Penn Central Railroad.

In addition to management's inability to insure against operating losses, there are numerous other internal risks that are not insurable. For example, a manufacturing business may have been built on ownership of a patent that is about to expire. Employees may cause losses by striking and closing down operations. Perfectly good merchandise, such as high-priced fur coats, may have to be sold at a loss because of the public's concern about endangered species. This list may seem endless to management, but fortunately businesses are usually able to keep losses of these types within acceptable limits.

The most serious types of risks that are uninsurable are external rather than internal. A business unit frequently has little or no control over a course of events that may bring disaster to it. On the other hand, disaster may strike because a company refused to anticipate the future or adjust to change. Some of the different categories of risks that must be assumed are: (1) development of new products, (2) changes in distribution methods and customer preferences, (3) fluctuations in prices and price levels, and (4) changes in laws.

DEVELOPMENT OF NEW PRODUCTS

The development of automobiles, television, and the jet airplane has changed the American way of life. Companies that fail to anticipate the future or adjust to change tend to continue to make products that have become obsolete, and sooner or later they are compelled to go out of business. In recent years the demand for steam locomotives has all but disappeared, and airplane propellers seem doomed. If the automobile of the future is powered by electricity or steam, the continued existence of thousands of service stations selling gasoline could be in jeopardy.

CHANGES IN DISTRIBUTION METHODS AND CUSTOMER PREFERENCES

The growth of chain stores, supermarkets, and shopping centers has forced many "mom and pop" retail stores to close. The advent of food franchisers, for example, McDonald's and Kentucky Fried Chicken, has dealt a death blow to many restaurants. Motels, particularly chains such as Holiday Inns, have taken their toll on hotels in many cities.

FLUCTUATIONS IN PRICES AND PRICE LEVELS

If raw materials are an important element in the overall cost of a finished product, a sharp price increase may cause losses to a firm unable to make offsetting increases in their selling prices. In 1974 newly hatched chickens were slaughtered and some feeder cattle were given away because of the high cost of feed grains.

CHANGES IN LAWS

When changes are made in tariffs that permit increased imports of competitive goods, the local firm may be unable to price its products above its costs. Likewise, when a city, a town, a county, or a state votes to prohibit liquor sales, taverns, night clubs, and restaurants in that area may be forced out of business.

Noninsurance Risk Protection

For a limited number of firms, there are two devices that provide protection against certain types of risks without making use of an insurance company. One of these is hedging, which was explained in Chapter 20. However, this technique is not available to many firms as most manufacturing does not involve the use of commodities in which futures are available. The other device is self-insurance.

When a risk that could be transferred to an insurance company is deliberately retained and a method of paying losses is provided, the firm involved is engaged in **self-insurance**. For example, a large corporation might own hundreds of factories, warehouses, and office buildings valued at millions of dollars and scattered among the 50 states. An insurance policy covering these properties against loss by fire would demand a substantial premium payment year by year. By eliminating the costs and profit of an insurance company, the chances are excellent that a smaller amount set aside each year will prove adequate for the payment of such losses if they do occur. Governmental bodies, such as states, frequently do not carry insurance on buildings or vehicles owned.

Characteristics of Insurable Risks

An understanding of business risks would not be complete without the realization that, before an insurance company is willing to underwrite possible losses, each risk must have the following characteristics:

1. The annual loss must be predictable. The number of people who will die each year or the number of houses that will burn each year can be predicted with amazing accuracy. An exception to this statement could occur if a nuclear war killed millions of people and laid waste miles and miles of buildings of all types. Insurance is written with the expectation that a catastrophe of this magnitude will not take place.
2. The risk must be spread over a wide geographical area. A fire insurance company could not afford to insure all the houses in one city only. A disastrous fire such as occurred in Chicago in 1871 would bankrupt the company.
3. Risks must be selected. No company can afford to insure only people who are seriously ill, have heart trouble, or make their living testing new airplanes.
4. The risks must be numerous enough to make the law of averages work. Insuring one life for a small annual premium could not be done on a scientific basis, but insuring the lives of 100,000 people can.
5. The premium cost must be low in relation to the insured's recovery possibilities. If the annual cost of a policy insuring a $5,000 truck against loss by theft was $1,000 instead of approximately $10, a business would try some method other than insurance to secure protection against this risk.

On the basis of these requirements the question may well be asked as to how some policies, such as insuring the hands of a concert pianist for $100,000, fit into the classification of insurable risks. The answer is that such policies are not written except by Lloyd's of London, an organization that is not an insurance company but rather an association through which members offer to underwrite hazards of all types. Marine insurance, which falls within the classification of insurable risks, forms the bulk, though not the spectacular portion, of the underwriting business of Lloyd's.

THE INSURANCE BUSINESS

An understanding of the different types of insurance policies available to businesses and individuals will be aided by an examination of the insurance business. Although frequently taken for granted, the separation between public and private insurance underwriters is extremely important. Also, within the private sector the specialization of insurance companies helps to explain why most firms and individuals purchase numerous insurance policies.

Governments as Underwriters

The extent to which government underwrites various risks, sometimes in competition with private industry, is startling for a capitalistic system. All states participate in a nationwide plan of unemployment insurance, which is required by federal law. Workmen's compensation insurance, now required by all states, is frequently a monopoly of state government. Although not universal, many states operate retirement plans for state employees including public school teachers.

The federal government has been in the insurance business for many years. It insures mail and deposits in banks, in savings and loan associations, and in credit unions. Through the Federal Housing Administration it insures private lending agencies against loss on FHA-approved loans made to buy, build, or remodel homes. The U.S. Department of Agriculture owns and manages the Federal Crop Insurance Corporation that insures farmers against hail and other causes of crop failure. The Department of Labor operates a Pension Benefit Guarantee Corporation. Low-cost life insurance has often been available to members of the Armed Services, and career military personnel can draw retirement pay after 20 or more years in uniform. Railway employees have separate retirement and unemployment insurance programs operated by the federal government as do federal civil service employees.

By far the most extensive entry of the federal government into the insurance business began in 1935 when the first Social Security Act was passed, and this activity was expanded in 1966 with the introduction of the related Medicare program. The Old-Age, Survivors, and Disability Insurance System, commonly called **Social Security**, provides a program of monthly payments to retired or disabled workers or their surviving dependents. **Medicare** covers hospital and medical insurance for those 65 years of age or older who are drawing retirement benefits. These programs require contributions on the part of the insured both before and after retirement, although the cost of the programs is shared by employers and the United States Treasury.

It is probable that the Congress of the United States will enact some form of national health insurance. The direction this legislation will take and just how it will be financed are not now apparent.

Types of Private Insurance Companies

Private insurance companies can be classified as to ownership. The two major types are mutual companies and stock companies, both of which were explained in Chapter 5. In the life insurance field, in 1973 over 90 percent of some 1,821 companies were owned by stockholders. However, the 151 mutual companies owned two thirds of all of the assets of United States insurance companies and accounted for slightly over one half of the life insurance in force. By contrast, stock companies are predominant in all areas of property and liability insurance. In the area of hospital costs and surgical fees, non-profit Blue Cross and Blue Shield associations play an important role.

Another classification of insurance companies can be made on the basis of the types of policies they write. Until a few years ago, partly because of state legal restrictions, companies tended to specialize in a limited area such as life, fire, or surety bonds. In recent years all states have liberalized their regulatory laws to permit a single insurance company to write many different coverages. This change has reduced specialization to two distinct types of insurance companies: property and liability, and life. One coverage, health insurance, is written by both categories of insurance companies, but otherwise the areas are quite distinct.

The division of insurance companies into property and liability, and life is in line with the sales outlets of insurance companies. Individuals or firms engaged in the business of selling insurance are customarily either general insurance agents or life insurance agents. A general insurance agency represents a number of different companies, including competing firms. The agency may represent a life insurance company, too, but it does not stress this area of its business. The life insurance agent normally sells policies on a commission basis for only one company.

Further evidence of these two classifications is found in the professional designations that are granted to individuals who qualify for and pass certain examinations. The **CLU** (Chartered Life Underwriter) certificate is granted by the American College of Life Underwriters. In a similar manner the American Institute for Property and Liability Underwriters grants the designation **CPCU** (Chartered Property and Casualty Underwriter).

HEALTH INSURANCE

Health insurance, sometimes identified as **accident and sickness insurance**, covers one or any combination of the following: (a) hospital, surgical, and other medical expenses; (b) loss of income during the period of disability; and (c) major medical expense. It is sold by life insurance companies, nonprofit associations such as Blue Cross and Blue Shield, and by property and liability underwriters.

Assume that Jerome Green, married, with three children, is involved in a serious automobile accident while driving home after work. He is hospitalized for three weeks and another four weeks elapse before he can return to his job. While in the hospital, if he was properly insured, all or substantially all of his expenses including surgeon's fees would be covered. He would also receive a stated weekly income for the entire seven weeks, such as two thirds of his regular salary. If he owned a major medical policy and if his personal medical expenses exceeded an agreed upon deductible amount such as $300, he would receive reimbursement for the excess. Health insurance policies also may provide that, if the insured loses an eye or a hand or a foot, he will receive either a flat sum or weekly amounts for several weeks.

A substantial percentage of all types of health insurance is written on a group basis with employers providing the entire cost as a fringe benefit; in some instances, employees bear all or a share of the cost under a payroll deduction plan. The extent of the use of health insurance is far greater than most people realize. Approximately 85 percent of the entire population of the United States is covered by some type of health insurance.

In 1973 life insurance companies paid $10.3 billion in health insurance benefits; Blue Cross plans, with 80,000,000 members, paid out $7.4 billion. Property and liability companies contributed another $1.3 billion to bring the total to $19 billion. This amount does not include the substantial Medicare payments for hospital and medical care for people 65 years of age or older.

Recently dental care has been added to some health insurance policies, usually on a group basis paid for by the employer. Also, Health Maintenance Organizations, known as HMOs, are growing in number. Members of these groups receive complete medical care in return for an annual payment.

PROPERTY AND LIABILITY INSURANCE

Approximately 3,000 insurance companies sell property and liability insurance and related lines. They own about $50 billion in assets and are responsible for employing nearly 600,000 people. The major classifications of property and liability insurance are: (1) fire, (2) automobile, (3) burglary and theft, (4) workmen's compensation, (5) marine, (6) fidelity and surety bonds, (7) liability, and (8) other coverages.

Fire Insurance

Homes, apartment houses, store buildings, factories, and almost every type of building can be insured against loss resulting from fire. The same thing is true of the contents, whether it be furniture, merchandise, machinery, or supplies of any type and description. Policies are sold on a one-, three-, or five-year basis with a strong preference for the three-year maturity. The advantages of a three-year policy over a one-year policy are that the buyer is guaranteed against a rate increase in the second and third years and that a discounted rate may be granted.

Premium rates are relatively low but vary considerably in different geographical areas and among types of construction (see Figure 21-1). For example, cities are graded on such items as water supply, fire alarms, building laws, and the efficiency of the fire department. Within the city the location of a building is important as it may stand between two old buildings or at some distance from other structures. If the construction is considered fireproof, the rate will be lower than on frame buildings. The lowest rates are in the neighborhood of 10 cents for each $100 of coverage, and more hazardous risks may cost $2 for each $100.

COINSURANCE CLAUSES

Fire damage to industrial property resulting in complete destruction of the property insured is rare. If it were permissible to buy an insurance policy for one third or one half of the total value of the property owned, the annual saving in insurance premiums would probably offset a fire loss in excess of this coverage. Insurance companies protect themselves against this reduced premium income by inserting **a coinsurance clause** in the policy. This clause requires that the insured buy coverage up to a stipulated percentage of the

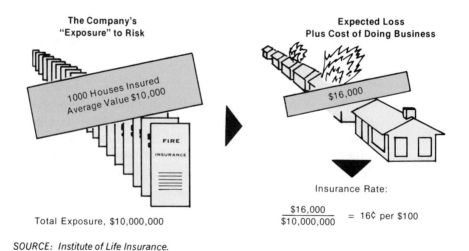

The Company's "Exposure" to Risk

1000 Houses Insured Average Value $10,000

FIRE INSURANCE

Total Exposure, $10,000,000

Expected Loss Plus Cost of Doing Business

$16,000

Insurance Rate:

$$\frac{\$16,000}{\$10,000,000} = 16¢ \text{ per } \$100$$

SOURCE: *Institute of Life Insurance.*

Figure 21-1 **How Fire Insurance Rates Are Set**

value of the property, usually 80 percent, or assume a proportion of each fire loss. In most states residential property is not subject to coinsurance clause restrictions.

If a factory is properly valued at $100,000 but is insured against fire for only $50,000, the risk is only partially covered because the minimum insurance for full protection against partial losses is 80 percent or $80,000. If a fire occurs with a total damage of $20,000, the insurance company will pay $50,000/$80,000 or ⅝ of the loss. This means a payment of $12,500 even though the loss was $20,000.

By the addition to a Standard Fire Policy of a variety of special agreements, known as **riders** or endorsements, the insuring company will cover a multitude of other perils related to the ownership of property. For example, additional coverages can include protection against damage caused by lightning, explosion, riots, aircraft, vehicles, smoke, vandalism, glass breakage, theft, falling objects, weight of ice or snow, freezing of plumbing, collapse of buildings, and liability of the property owner for injuries suffered on the insured's premises. When all or most of these riders are added, a deductible of $50 or $100 is usually included in the contract to reduce the cost of the policy.

Of particular interest to businesses are a variety of additional endorsements that are available. A common coverage is **business interruption** that protects the insured against loss of earnings following a total or partial shutdown resulting from property damage. **Depreciation insurance** is another coverage important in periods of inflation. This pays for the cost of replacing a property over and above the actual cash value of the insured building. Numerous other types of losses that are consequential to a fire or allied loss can also be covered if the insured wishes to pay the additional cost.

Automobile Insurance

The usual types of automobile coverage include fire and theft, bodily injury liability, property damage, and collision insurance. If the policy covers fire and theft, the amount paid the insured in case of total loss is the value of the car at the date of the fire or theft.

COMPREHENSIVE COVERAGE

Automobile insurance companies also offer **comprehensive coverage**, which is a contract that covers practically all damage to the insured's automobile, including fire and theft, except that resulting from collision and upset. For example, claims have been paid for accidental damage to upholstery and for windshields broken by flying stones.

BODILY INJURY LIABILITY

Bodily injury liability insurance will pay the policyholder's legal liability for injury to one person or to a group. If a driver hits a pedestrian or causes injury to persons in another car, the insurance company will pay damages up to the amount of coverage carried. A common policy fixes a maximum of $5,000 for liability resulting from the death or disability of one person, and $10,000 for similar reasons to more than one person. This type of policy is frequently identified by the fraction 5/10. Higher maximum coverages than 5/10 can be obtained in amounts such as 10/20 or 100/300 by paying a higher premium.

A **medical payments endorsement** can be purchased that will pay hospital and doctor bills up to a specified maximum for each occupant of the insured's car who is injured in an accident, including the policyholder. In many states legislation that relieves drivers from liability for injury to their passengers arising from an accident has been enacted. Such "guest laws," as they are termed, were passed to prevent friendly suits against car owners with the knowledge that the insurance companies would finance the settlements.

PROPERTY DAMAGE LIABILITY

Property damage liability insurance is stated at a single amount, such as $10,000. If the insured car damages another car, or runs into a house, or damages any property not belonging to the insured, the insurance company will settle the claim up to the amount of the policy. It will not pay anything for damages to the policyholder's car unless **collision** or **upset insurance** is carried. This type of coverage protects car owners against any damage to their automobiles resulting from accidents, but it is relatively expensive unless they purchase collision insurance with a deductible allowance, such as $50 or $100. In this event the insurance company pays for damages that are in excess of the stipulated deductible amount. Many drivers do not carry collision insurance because of the relatively high cost, although cars purchased on the installment plan are so covered to protect the finance company.

PROTECTION AGAINST UNINSURED MOTORISTS

Another coverage common to family automobile policies is protection against an uninsured motorist who causes bodily injuries to the occupants of the insured's car. In an effort to get such drivers off the roads, some states have passed **financial responsibility laws.** Such legislation usually provides that the driver of an automobile at fault in an accident must show evidence that he or she has taken care of the resulting costs to the innocent car driver. Owning an insurance policy covering bodily injury and property damage liability is the preferred method of demonstrating the required financial responsibility.

NO-FAULT RULE

Currently a substantial change is taking place in automobile insurance as one state after another enacts some form of a **no-fault rule**. Under this plan an injured party collects from his or her insurance company rather than from the company that wrote the policy carried by the driver who caused the accident. Advocates of the no-fault rule maintain that most litigation is avoided; that the individual receives a prompt reimbursement for medical expenses, loss of income, and possibly the cost of repairs; and that the cost of a policy would be less. Opponents of no-fault insurance dispute these claims.

Burglary, Robbery, and Theft Insurance

Burglary involves the unlawful taking of property within premises closed for business, and evidence of forcible entry must be visible. **Robbery** is the forcible taking of property from another person. **Theft**, or its legal synonym **larceny**, covers any act of stealing without regard for forceful entry or violence and hence includes both burglary and robbery.

Although residence burglary insurance is the most common type written, the businessperson is more interested in other forms. These include mercantile open stock, business safe, office burglary and robbery, and paymaster protection. Small retailers can obtain a comprehensive storekeepers' burglary and robbery policy that will cover safe and mercantile open stock burglary; damage to money, securities, merchandise, or equipment caused by burglary or robbery; theft of money or securities from a residence or night depository; kidnapping an employee to gain entrance; and robbery inside or outside the business premises. Insurance covering shoplifting losses is not usually carried because such losses are frequently difficult to prove and the cost is high.

Workmen's Compensation Insurance

The purpose of **workmen's compensation insurance** is to guarantee medical expenses and salary payments to workers who are injured on the job unless it can be shown that the employee's injury or death was willful or caused by intoxication. The usual practice is to specify weekly benefits. These are set at a fraction of the regular wage, such as one half or two thirds, to discourage those who might prefer to draw benefits rather than work. A waiting period of from a few days to two weeks is also a common provision of many laws. This means that no benefits can be drawn until the expiration of the waiting period, which eliminates claims for minor accidents. In case of death, weekly payments are made to the dependents of the deceased for a specified period, frequently eight years.

Workmen's compensation insurance is compulsory in all 50 states although the laws are not uniform. Certain classes of workers, notably farm and domestic employees, are frequently exempt as are employers of less than a stated number of employees. In some states workmen's compensation insurance is a monopoly of the state; in others, private insurance companies compete with state plans; and in still others, private insurance companies write the policies unless the employing company is large enough to warrant approval for self-insurance. Rates vary with the hazard of the industry.

Marine Insurance

Two general types of marine insurance are ocean marine and inland marine. Both are transportation insurance and, despite the connotation of the word "marine," inland marine insurance need not involve shipment by water.

OCEAN MARINE INSURANCE

The oldest form of insurance is that on ships of all types as well as their cargoes. An **ocean marine insurance** contract covers practically all perils of shipments on the high seas, including all degrees of loss from injury to the vessel and contents up to a complete loss of both as a result of sinking. Fire insurance is included as a part of the policy.

INLAND MARINE INSURANCE

A typical **inland marine insurance** policy provides protection against loss on movable goods while being transported by rail, truck, airplane, inland and coastwise steamers, and barges. Such a policy covers a variety of risks, such as hazards of water and land transport, fire, and theft. Of interest to many businesses is a form of inland marine insurance designed to cover shipments of merchandise by parcel post. One method is to buy a coupon book that provides insurance tickets to be inserted in each parcel shipped; another is a blanket policy that covers all parcel post shipments. Both methods are less expensive and less bothersome than insuring each package at the post office.

A type of inland marine insurance that has become quite popular in recent years is the **personal property floater**. This policy provides protection of personal property from all hazards wherever located — in the home, in transit, or abroad. It is a comprehensive type of coverage that includes fire and theft protection as well as other risks. Under such a policy the personal effects of students attending college away from home can be covered while in transit or at their college residences.

Fidelity and Surety Bonds

Fidelity bonds are usually written to cover employees occupying positions of trust in which they have jurisdiction over funds. The employer is guaranteed against loss caused by the dishonesty of such employees, and the insurance company will reimburse the policyholder for losses up to the amount specified in the policy. Coverages may be individual, or group, or may name positions. For example, a business firm may secure a fidelity bond on certain employees for the amount of funds to which each has access. Or, the company may secure a policy covering a group of employees in a particular department. Still another possibility is to purchase a policy in which positions and the amounts of coverage are specified, such as treasurer — $50,000. Whoever is hired for a specified task is bonded for the stated amount.

Surety bonds are written to protect the insured against loss from the nonperformance of a contract or the nonperformance of any agreed-upon act or business transaction. A building contractor, for example, who agrees to erect a factory according to specifications and within a certain time, might be required to furnish a surety bond guaranteeing performance of the contract.

Liability Insurance

Bodily injury liability and property damage liability resulting from the operation of a motor vehicle have been discussed as a part of automobile insurance. It was also noted that a rider could be added to a Standard Fire Policy covering a home to cover the liability of a property owner for injuries suffered on the insured's premises. In recent years damage suits of astronomical amounts have frequently been filed against both car owners and homeowners. For example, assuming that a child lost an arm and a leg in an accident, the parents may sue for $1,000,000. In making an award, even if for a lesser sum, a jury may exceed the liability insurance incorporated in an automobile or homeowner's policy. To guard against this hazard, a personal excess liability policy can be purchased that supplements other liability insurance.

Manufacturers, contractors, retailers, and other businesspersons find it advantageous to protect themselves from claims arising from injuries, real or fancied, to the person or property of others. For example, the owners of buildings are subject to elevator accident risks, people stumble and fall in darkened movie theaters, and visitors to an industrial plant may be hit by a moving crane. All of these hazards can be covered by a liability policy.

Businesses that produce consumer products are constantly faced with the risk that they may be sued for damages. For example, the use of a faulty food or drug product may be alleged to cause illness or even death even though it passed inspection. Insurance against this risk is known as **products liability insurance**.

Physicians and surgeons, dentists, lawyers, accountants, architects, pharmacists, and hospitals are constantly being sued for malpractice. These claims frequently involve six or seven figures, so it is understandable that all of these professional persons and institutions purchase extensive liability insurance policies.

Other Coverages

The different kinds of insurable risks inherent in operating a business are so extensive that it becomes difficult for management to determine proper coverage. One of the common types carried as a result of today's architecture is glass breakage. Another common type is boiler and machinery insurance, which features preventative engineering service provided by the company writing the insurance.

Other coverages include false arrest, product warranties, rain insurance, forgery, power interruption, title insurance, and so on. A number of these risks can now be incorporated in a special multiperil policy that covers most of the property and liability insurance needed by a business.

LIFE INSURANCE

Life insurance policies are written by more than 1,800 different companies that own assets of approximately $252 billion and employ 1,575,000 people. In the United States there are 145,000,000 policyholders whose lives are insured for $1,778 billion and who, in a recent year, paid $33 billion in premiums. Benefit payments to policyholders and to the beneficiaries of policyholders who died were in excess of $20 billion. The life insurance industry is truly gigantic in all dimensions.

As in the case of other forms of insurance, life insurance is based on the law of averages. No one can predict whether a particular individual will die during any given year, but the number of persons living at the beginning of a year who will die within 12 months can be computed within narrow margins. The annual premium on a life insurance policy is related to statistics covering deaths as compiled by actuaries. An **actuary** is an individual employed by an insurance company who is an expert at computing risks and the size of insurance premiums necessary to the profitable operation of the company. Although insurance companies rely on more than one table, many states require the use of a mortality schedule compiled by the National Association of Insurance Commissioners, an organization of state insurance commissioners. In 1958 this body adopted the Commissioners Standard Ordinary Mortality Table, which is shown in Table 21-1.

Note that the CSO 1958 Mortality Table covers the life history of ten million people beginning at birth and continuing to the age of 99. For each year there is shown the number living at the beginning of the year, the number who will die during the year, and the death rate per 1,000 for that year. For example, at the age of 18 a total of 9,698,230 young men and women will be living out of the original group of 10 million. During the year 16,390 will die, which is a death rate of 1.69 per 1,000.

Life insurance policies can be classified in several different ways. Categories used by the Institute of Life Insurance are: (1) ordinary, (2) group, (3) industrial, and (4) credit.

Ordinary Life Insurance

Ordinary life insurance consists of individual policies of $1,000 or more that usually require passing a physical examination. Typically bought from a life insurance agent, ordinary policies account for over one half of all life insurance in force. With only a few exceptions these policies can be further classified as either whole life, endowment, or term.

WHOLE LIFE POLICIES

A **whole life policy** pays its face value to a beneficiary when the insured dies provided that premium payments, due annually, semiannually, or quarterly, are current and that a loan on the policy is not outstanding. If premiums are payable every year as long as the insured lives, the insurance is known as **straight life**. If premiums are payable for only a stated number of years, such as 20, the policy is called **limited payment life**.

Straight life is the most widely used form of life insurance; it accounts for three fifths of all ordinary policies in force. It provides more protection than limited payment life for the same premium. A disadvantage is that, unless the insured dies before retirement, premiums continue to be due every year despite a probable reduction in income.

Both straight life and limited payment life policies have level premiums that depend on the age at which the policy is purchased. Under a level premium plan the cost when an insured is young is higher than is needed. The excess payments are held in reserve by the insurance company to make sure that there will be funds available to supplement the level premium when the insured is old. Since the policyholder has a rightful share in the reserve, if the

Table 21-1   Commissioners 1958 Standard Ordinary Mortality Table

Age	Number Living	Deaths Each Year	Death Rate per 1,000	Age	Number Living	Deaths Each Year	Death Rate per 1,000
0	10,000,000	70,800	7.08	50	8,762,306	72,902	8.32
1	9,929,200	17,475	1.76	51	8,869,404	79,160	9.11
2	9,911,725	15,066	1.52	52	8,610,244	85,758	9.96
3	9,896,659	14,449	1.46	53	8,524,486	92,832	10.89
4	9,882,210	13,835	1.40	54	8,431,654	100,337	11.90
5	9,868,375	13,322	1.35	55	8,331,317	108,307	13.00
6	9,855,053	12,812	1.30	56	8,223,010	116,849	14.21
7	9,842,241	12,401	1.26	57	8,106,161	125,970	15.54
8	9,829,840	12,091	1.23	58	7,980,191	135,663	17.00
9	9,817,749	11,879	1.21	59	7,844,528	145,830	18.59
10	9,805,870	11,865	1.21	60	7,698,698	156,592	20.34
11	9,794,005	12,047	1.23	61	7,542,106	167,736	22.24
12	9,781,958	12,325	1.26	62	7,374,370	179,271	24.31
13	9,769,633	12,896	1.32	63	7,195,099	191,174	26.57
14	9,756,737	13,562	1.39	64	7,003,925	203,394	29.04
15	9,743,175	14,225	1.46	65	6,800,531	215,917	31.75
16	9,728,950	14,983	1.54	66	6,584,614	228,749	34.74
17	9,713,967	15,737	1.62	67	6,355,865	241,777	38.04
18	9,698,230	16,390	1.69	68	6,114,088	254,835	41.68
19	9,681,840	16,846	1.74	69	5,859,253	267,241	45.61
20	9,664,994	17,300	1.79	70	5,592,012	278,426	49.79
21	9,647,694	17,655	1.83	71	5,313,586	287,731	54.15
22	9,630,039	17,912	1.86	72	5,025,855	294,766	58.65
23	9,612,127	18,167	1.89	73	4,731,089	299,289	63.26
24	9,593,960	18,324	1.91	74	4,431,800	301,894	68.12
25	9,575,636	18,481	1.93	75	4,129,906	303,011	73.37
26	9,557,155	18,732	1.96	76	3,826,895	303,014	79.18
27	9,538,423	18,981	1.99	77	3,523,881	301,997	85.70
28	9,519,442	19,324	2.03	78	3,221,884	299,829	93.06
29	9,500,118	19,760	2.08	79	2,922,055	295,683	101.19
30	9,480,358	20,193	2.13	80	2,626,372	288,848	109.98
31	9,460,165	20,718	2.19	81	2,337,524	278,983	119.35
32	9,439,447	21,239	2.25	82	2,058,541	265,902	129.17
33	9,418,208	21,850	2.32	83	1,792,639	249,858	139.38
34	9,396,358	22,551	2.40	84	1,542,781	231,433	150.01
35	9,373,807	23,528	2.51	85	1,311,348	211,311	161.14
36	9,350,279	24,685	2.64	86	1,100,037	190,108	172.82
37	9,325,594	26,112	2.80	87	909,929	168,455	185.13
38	9,299,482	27,991	3.01	88	741,474	146,997	198.25
39	9,271,491	30,132	3.25	89	594,477	126,303	212.46
40	9,241,359	32,622	3.53	90	468,174	106,809	228.14
41	9,208,737	35,362	3.84	91	361,365	88,813	245.77
42	9,173,375	38,253	4.17	92	272,552	72,480	265.93
43	9,135,122	41,382	4.53	93	200,072	57,881	289.30
44	9,093,740	44,741	4.92	94	142,191	45,026	316.66
45	9,048,999	48,412	5.35	95	97,165	34,128	351.24
46	9,000,587	52,473	5.83	96	63,037	25,250	400.56
47	8,948,114	56,910	6.36	97	37,787	18,456	488.42
48	8,891,204	61,794	6.95	98	19,331	12,916	668.15
49	8,829,410	67,104	7.60	99	6,415	6,415	1,000.00

insurance is cancelled the individual receives what is known as its **cash surrender value**. This is also the amount that can be borrowed at a stated interest rate from the insurance company by the insured. If the cash value is not used, it can be compared with some differences to a savings account.

ENDOWMENT LIFE INSURANCE

Endowment life insurance is similar to limited payment life insurance with the exception that it emphasizes the savings element in a contract over the protective features. The annual premium is larger than for straight or limited payment life, and consequently the cash surrender value of the policy increases at a faster rate. At the expiration of a stated number of years, which may be an even figure such as 30 or the number of years before the insured reaches 65, the cash value of the policy equals its face. If at the age of 30, Ruth Roberts takes out a $50,000 endowment policy running for 30 years, she has automatically created an estate of $50,000 by the time she is 60. If she dies within this period, the insurance company will pay the face of the policy to her beneficiaries. If she lives to the age of 60, however, the company will pay her the face of the policy at that time, or she may elect to receive annual payments. Endowment is the only type of life insurance that allows the insured rather than a beneficiary to collect the face value of the policy.

TERM LIFE INSURANCE

Term life insurance bears a similarity to fire insurance in that the insurance company is obligated to pay only if a loss (death in this case) occurs within the time limit covered by the policy. If the insured is living at the end of the specified term, all premiums paid are the property of the insurance company and the policy automatically expires. If term life insurance policies were written on an annual basis, the CSO 1958 Table can be used to compute a basic cost. Referring to the figures in the CSO table, if all of the 9,698,230 eighteen-year-old individuals were insured for $1,000 for one year, the insurance company would pay out during the year $16,390,000 to the beneficiaries of the 16,390 individuals who would die during the year. If a premium payment of $1.69 were made for each $1,000 policy ($16,390,000 ÷ 9,698,230), the insurance company would have just enough money to meet the necessary outlay. The actual premium would obviously need to be higher for several reasons, including meeting the expenses of doing business. Note that the costs of term insurance computed on this basis would increase year by year amounting to $3.53 per $1,000 at age 40 and increasing to $20.34 at age 60. Rather than changing the rate every year, term insurance is usually purchased on a 5-year, 10-year, or 20-year level premium plan. These policies are customarily renewable up to the age of 65 without the necessity of providing evidence of insurability.

The chief advantage of term life insurance is its low cost. More protection can be purchased by an individual for a given premium payment than is available under any other type of life insurance policy. Since most term life insurance policies are convertible into more permanent forms of life insurance, they are frequently sold to young persons with family and home mortgage responsibilities.

Table 21-2 shows the comparative annual premiums per $1,000 charged by one company for four different types of life insurance policies involving total coverages of $10,000 to $25,000.

Group Life Insurance

The most extensive business use of life insurance in recent years has centered on **group life insurance**, which is simply a policy covering each employee of a single firm for a sum such as $5,000, or the amount may vary with different categories of employees. Such insurance is usually written on a one-year renewable term plan. It is distinctive in that no medical examination is required. This is possible because of the number, as well as the composition, of the group covered. Most employers do not hire workers who are not physically fit, and most workers are in a relatively healthy age bracket.

The employer usually pays at least a portion of the premium, which really constitutes a bonus to the employee. Rates are lower than for any form of an individual policy because the premiums are paid by the company in one check, which greatly reduces collection costs; there are no medical examination fees; and commission rates are lower than on other types. The $708 billion in group term insurance outstanding at the end of 1973 provides some idea of the extensive use business makes of this form of life insurance.

Industrial Life Insurance

Industrial life insurance has substantially the same subdivisions as ordinary insurance but differs in that policies are usually for less than $1,000 and

Table 21-2   *Comparative Annual Premium Costs per $1,000 Insurance*

Age	5-Year Renewable Term	Straight Life	20-Pay Life	20-Year Endowment
20	$ 4.88	$15.21	$26.71	$47.96
30	5.41	20.00	32.29	48.58
40	7.90	27.85	40.12	50.86
50	15.20	41.09	51.74	57.05

the agent collects the premium weekly or monthly from the policyholder, frequently at his or her home. A physical examination is not customarily required. Rates are quoted at such figures as 10 cents or 25 cents a week rather than in dollars per year per thousand.

Despite the small size of policies, which average slightly over $500 each, industrial life insurance in the United States amounted to over $40 billion in 1973.

Credit Life Insurance

The extensive purchase of goods on the installment plan and the use of short-term borrowing by consumers has made credit life insurance the fastest-growing form of life insurance. **Credit life insurance** guarantees repayment of amounts due on installment contracts or personal loans in case the debtor dies. It has assumed one of the risks of consumer financing, both for the lender and the borrower.

Banks, finance companies, credit unions, retailers, and some mortgage lenders are the chief purchasers of credit life insurance. It is written on a one-year basis, and the amount applicable to a borrower decreases as the debt is repaid. Practically all credit life insurance is written on a group basis, although individual policies are available. The extensive use of credit life insurance has resulted in outstanding policies in excess of $101 billion.

Credit life insurance should not be confused with **credit insurance**, which is a type of policy which insures a firm against unusually high losses resulting from the extension of credit on open-book accounts. An interesting feature of credit insurance policies is the requirement that the insured must bear part of each loss, which keeps the firm from being too generous in extending credit.

Business Uses of Life Insurance

Life insurance can be and is used by sole proprietorships, partnerships, and corporations. The most common type is group life insurance, which many firms believe necessary to remain competitive in the labor market. For businesses extending credit to individuals, credit life insurance is another form that is widely used. Both of these types of insurance policies have been explained. Two additional adaptions of life insurance to the needs of business are: (1) insurance on owners or executives, and (2) retirement and pension plans.

INSURANCE ON OWNERS OR EXECUTIVES

If a sole proprietor dies, the firm may have to be sold to pay funeral and administration expenses and taxes. An adequate term life insurance policy payable to the estate can avoid the necessity for a sale, and the business can be continued by the spouse, son, daughter, or other heirs. A straight, limited-payment, or endowment policy might be preferable, since any one of these types could be used during the lifetime of the owner as a support for credit, as collateral for a bank loan, and as a basis for a retirement plan.

When a partner dies, the partnership must be dissolved; but the question remains as to who will buy the deceased's interest in the firm. A term life insurance contract payable to the surviving partner or partners can provide a fund with which to buy this interest and avoid the necessity of taking in a new partner. Likewise, if it is assumed that the partner will retire at a given age, an endowment policy maturing at the agreed retirement age guarantees that necessary funds will be available.

Some corporations have found that their profitability is closely connected to the abilities and contacts of one or two key executives. Carrying an insurance policy on their lives payable to the corporation can provide a cushion to absorb the reduction in earning power that might result from the death of one of these individuals.

RETIREMENT AND PENSION PLANS

Firms interested in providing a continuing income to retired employees beyond the benefits from the federal social security system can finance such a program through insurance companies. Currently some 9 million employees are covered by insured pension plans and the number is growing rapidly each year.

There are three commonly used methods of insuring pensions. The most widely favored by business is a so-called deposit administration plan in which a single fund is established with an insurance company that covers all employees. As each employee retires, money is withdrawn from the fund to purchase an annuity for these individuals. Another method involves the purchase each year of a fully paid annuity benefit for each employee. Smaller firms frequently make use of a pension trust plan, which requires the purchase of a life insurance policy for each covered employee.

In 1974 Congress passed a pension reform act known as the Employee Retirement Income Security Act. The provisions of this law, which were detailed on pages 278 and 279, included mention of vesting rights. These necessitate that pensions be funded. Although alternative methods can fulfill local requirements, the use of one of the plans available from life insurance companies provides a safe haven for pension-fund assets.

BUSINESS TERMS

risks	407	underwriting	408
insurance	408	premium	408

QUESTIONS FOR DISCUSSION AND ANALYSIS

1. What are some of the risks, in addition to those mentioned in the text, that businesses must absorb? Give a specific example of both an internal and external risk.

2. On what grounds can government justify its extensive activities in the insurance business?

3. Why does Congress seem to feel that some type of national health insurance is necessary, especially in view of the high percentage of the population already covered?

4. What reasons might be given for not requiring a coinsurance clause in a homeowner's fire insurance policy?

5. A recent college graduate has just purchased a new automobile. What types of coverages should be included in a related insurance policy?

6. Is no-fault insurance in conflict with the generally accepted premise that a person at fault should pay resulting damages?

7. A thief hides in a store during open hours and after closing steals valuable merchandise. What type of policy would the owner need to protect the business against this risk?

8. Liability suits against physicians and surgeons have grown yearly in number as have the size of jury awards. What explanations can be given for this continuing upsurge?

9. Why should individuals not buy life insurance on a term basis only, which they are required to do when purchasing fire insurance?

10. Assuming a business is fully insured, what are the various types of risks that management has transferred to insurance companies?

PROBLEMS AND SHORT CASES

1. The Stockton Manufacturing Co. owns a building that has been appraised at $12,000,000. Assuming that the corporation takes out a fire insurance policy with an 80% coinsurance clause, how much insurance can be collected in each of the following situations?

	Fire Loss	Insurance Coverage
a.	$ 2,000,000	$4,800,000
b.	4,000,000	6,000,000
c.	6,000,000	7,200,000
d.	8,000,000	9,600,000
e.	10,000,000	9,600,000

2. A company wishes to purchase a $10,000 one-year term life insurance policy for each of its 5,000 employees. It is determined that the average age of the group is 38. If the insurance company needs a 30 percent margin on total premiums to cover its costs with a reasonable margin of safety, what would be a single premium cost for a group insurance policy? Refer to the Commissioners 1958 Standard Ordinary Mortality Table on page 422 to compute your answer.

3. Last year the Colfax Manufacturing Co. earned an after-tax profit of $2,300,000. It distributed $1,200,000 of this amount to its 8,000 stockholders who hold the 500,000 shares outstanding.

Recently management became aware that efforts were being made to organize the 4,200 employees. Because the firm has always paid good wages and because of its location in a small nonunion town, the workers have been content with a company-sponsored committee organization that has settled the few labor disputes that have arisen from time to time.

A friendly worker who attended a meeting called by the union organizers reported to management that it was agreed that current wage rates were satisfactory as well as the policies on vacations. The union people did, however, stress that some fringe benefits, particularly insurance coverages, were sadly lacking and would be obtained if the employees would vote to join the union.

Management would prefer the status quo on labor relations. They believe that a voluntary offer of an insurance program will defeat the union, which imposes a $50 initiation fee and membership dues of $10 a month. It has been determined that the annual cost per employee of various types of coverages would be:

Pension Program (Deposit Administration Plan)	$200
Blue Cross (Hospital Charges)	
Family Plan	250
Single Coverage	115
Blue Shield (Surgeon's Fees)	
Family Plan	50
Single Coverage	23
Major Medical (All costs in excess of $300)	28
Health and Accident Insurance	
Supplement to Workmen's Compensation	46
Group Life ($10,000 per employee)	32

On the basis of the above facts, what action should the Colfax Manufacturing Co. take? If a company-financed insurance program is offered its employees, what should it cover?

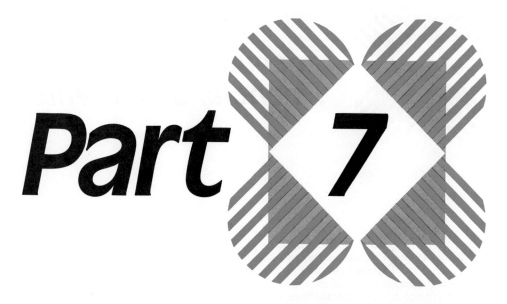

Part 7

Business Controls

Business controls represent an important aspect of business operations. Planning creates a pathway for managerial action, and controls provide a check on the progress along the pathway. Control techniques assist managers in determining if their operations are within acceptable standards of performance.

By recording, classifying, summarizing, and interpreting large amounts of financial data, the accounting system of a firm generates a picture of the financial strength of an enterprise. Chapter 22 provides an overview of the accounting function. Stress is placed on the managerial uses of financial information for purposes of control and planning rather than on accounting techniques.

Chapter 23 relates the importance of the computer to numerous and varied business activities. A section on computer security indicates the risks which confront business-persons who store and retrieve data from computers. The social implications which result from an expanding network of computer systems are examined in the final paragraphs of this chapter.

Several types of management control systems are recognized in Chapter 24. Although there are both qualitative and quantitative controls, this chapter focuses on quantitative controls. The chapter concludes with illustrations of the business applications of several operations research techniques.

Chapter 25 establishes the need for a body of business law which facilitates the operation of our complex business system. The two major types of legal systems are described, and the areas of business law which have the most significant impact on business are examined.

22

Accounting and Financial Statements

C. Rodger Whitman had recently been promoted from
Vice-President of Sales to President and Chief Executive Officer of
the Benton Cement Corporation. He had always had a healthy respect
for the accuracy of figures furnished him by company accountants,
but his faith had just been shaken. A report submitted by his chief
accountant recommended that the firm change from a FIFO to a LIFO
method of inventory valuation. Reasons given were that this change
would reduce profits by $18,400,000 for the year and save almost
$9,000,000 in taxes. It was difficult to believe that such substantial
differences could be achieved by changing accounting procedures.

Practically all business transactions, such as making sales or meeting
payrolls, are measurable in dollars and cents. **Accounting** may be defined as
the recording, classifying, and summarizing of these business transactions,
and interpreting this compiled information. A satisfactory accounting system
is an absolute necessity for a successful business. Management cannot make
intelligent decisions without knowing, for example, its cash balance, how
much is owed both to and by the firm, and whether operations are profitable.
Outsiders are also interested in the financial summaries prepared from adequate accounting records. Various governmental bodies assess taxes on the
income reported, investors decide whether to become stockholders, and
banks and suppliers make credit decisions based on financial statements.

Because accounting is so important to outsiders as well as insiders, efforts
are being made to standardize procedures and to require greater disclosure by
open corporations. A Financial Accounting Standards Board has been established and it can be assumed that pronouncements by this body will be followed by accountants. A Cost Accounting Standards Board is tackling the
problem of proper accounting in this area with particular reference to government contracts, and an international group is concerned with the diverse standards existing in foreign countries. The Securities and Exchange Commission

also specifies acceptable practices for the firms listed on exchanges. Even the Federal Trade Commission is now requiring that companies operating in more than one type of business, such as an airline owning a chain of hotels, must show the accounting details of each operating unit. All of these efforts should lead to a meaningful uniformity and greater acceptance by the public of figures released by all types of accountants.

TYPES OF ACCOUNTANTS

The owner of a small firm may keep the accounting records, employ a part-time accountant, or use an outside bookkeeping service. In large enterprises the accounting department is organized into numerous functions and each of these is headed by a specialist. As a result **industrial accountants** may become known by such terms as cost accountant, tax accountant, systems accountant, internal auditor, or budget accountant. Figure 22-1 shows the organization of the accounting department of a large manufacturing concern.

In addition to the broad classification of industrial accountants, other categories are public accountants and governmental accountants. **Public accountants** are independent firms who offer their services to the public. If they have complied with the state rules governing certification, which includes passing a rigorous examination, they are called **certified public accountants.** CPAs, as they are generally known, audit the books and perform various services for the clients who employ them. Their work is professional in nature and requires a high order of ability and integrity. **Governmental accountants** are those employed by local, state, and national governmental units including such federal agencies as the Federal Bureau of Investigation, the Bureau of Internal Revenue, and the General Accounting Office.

ACCOUNTING PROCEDURES

The first step in accounting procedures is the recording of business transactions. Some small firms rely on pen-and-ink records, but the use of adding

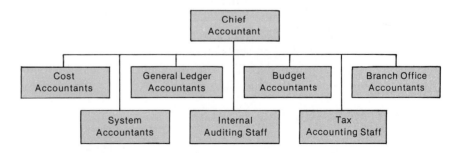

Figure 22-1 **Organization Chart for an Accounting Department**

machines, cash registers, and other types of business machines is widespread. More recently electronic data processing has made rapid strides in recording business transactions as well as classifying and summarizing these more rapidly than was formerly possible. In this first step, summarized or individual transactions are entered into some form of a **journal**, a book of original entry in which transactions are recorded in chronological order.

The next step is a procedure by which the transactions are classified. By a process known as **posting**, the entries in the journal are transferred to a **ledger**, which is a book of accounts. Each account brings together all transactions affecting one item, such as cash or sales. At stated periods — monthly, quarterly, semiannually, or annually — the ledger accounts are totaled or balanced; these provide the basic information for financial statements.

The third step in accounting procedures, summarizing, is provided by constructing the financial statements. The income statement and the balance sheet are the principal ones prepared at regular intervals. Since they are the result of and the reason for much of the work done by an accounting department, they will be examined in some detail. Other supplementary financial statements that may or may not be required (cost of goods manufactured schedule, capital statement, retained earnings statement, and statement of changes in financial position) will be illustrated and discussed briefly before the final step in accounting procedures — interpretation — is explained.

The Income Statement

The statement that summarizes the incomes and expenses of a business for a stated period of time is the **income statement**. It shows such information as the total merchandise purchased and sold, expenses incurred, and miscellaneous sources of income. Other names given to this statement are the **profit and loss statement**, **operating statement**, **income summary**, and **income account**.

The income statement is dynamic, whereas the balance sheet is static. This means that the income statement reflects summaries of operations over a period of time such as a year, six months, a quarter, or a month, while the balance sheet is a picture of the business at a given instant of time, usually the close of business on the date of the balance sheet. Both statements are prepared at the same time, and the net income or loss shown on the income statement is reflected in the capital section of the balance sheet.

Figure 22-2 presents an income statement for Simon's Hardware Store, a sole proprietorship. Each of the main sections of this income statement is explained in the following sections.

REVENUE FROM SALES

The major source of income for most firms is the sale of merchandise, and this is the first section on the income statement. The **sales** figure includes the

SIMON'S HARDWARE STORE
Income Statement
For Year Ended December 31, 1976

Revenue from sales:			
Sales		$440,650	
Less sales returns and allowances		8,100	
Net sales			$432,550
Cost of merchandise sold:			
Merchandise inventory, January 1, 1976		$ 86,310	
Purchases	$284,300		
Less: Purchases returns and allowances	$7,860		
Purchases discount	3,100	10,960	
Net purchases		273,340	
Merchandise available for sale		$359,650	
Less merchandise inventory, December 31, 1976		78,400	
Cost of merchandise sold			281,250
Gross profit on sales			$151,300
Operating expenses:			
Selling expenses:			
Sales salaries	$ 42,100		
Advertising expense	14,400		
Store supplies expense	2,170		
Depreciation expense — store equipment	3,240		
Miscellaneous selling espense	5,150		
Total selling expenses		$ 67,060	
General expenses:			
Office salaries	$ 18,150		
Office supplies expense	1,320		
Taxes expense	6,200		
Depreciation expense — building	6,000		
Depreciation expense — office equipment	2,310		
Insurance expense	2,450		
Uncollectible accounts expense	2,000		
Miscellaneous general expense	1,700		
Total general expenses		40,130	
Total operating expenses			107,190
Income from operations			$ 44,110
Other income:			
Dividends on stock		$ 300	
Other expense:			
Interest expense		6,980	6,680
Net income			$ 37,430

Figure 22-2   *Income Statement*

amounts paid by customers and the amounts they have agreed to pay if sales have been made on account. It is a total for the year or for a shorter period of time if statements are prepared more often. From this total must be subtracted the value of the merchandise returned or reductions in price granted following complaints by the customer as to quality or quantity received. The resulting figure is called **net sales**.

COST OF MERCHANDISE SOLD

The **cost of merchandise sold** represents the purchase price of the merchandise that was sold by the firm during the year. The formula used for arriving at the cost figure is usually the one shown on the income statement. Merchandise on hand at the beginning of the year plus purchases, adjusted for returns and allowances and discounts, gives the total cost of all the merchandise that might have been sold. Subtracting the inventory figure at the end of the year from this total results in the cost of the merchandise sold.

The beginning and ending inventories are determined by a physical count of each item in stock and a valuation of these quantities (see page 377). The purchases of merchandise made during the year can be secured from the ledger account in which have been posted all of the invoices covering the various shipments received. Returns and allowances follow the same pattern as indicated previously for sales.

Carl Simon, a retail hardware merchant, usually purchases all the merchandise that he has available for sale. By contrast, manufacturing firms produce their goods from raw materials and semifinished goods which they have purchased. In this situation the line titled ''Net purchases'' in the income statement would be replaced with ''Schedule No. 1 — Cost of goods manufactured'' and finished goods inventories would be shown instead of merchandise inventories. Figure 22-3 shows a **schedule of cost of goods manufactured**.

GROSS PROFIT ON SALES

The difference found by subtracting the cost of merchandise sold from the net sales is termed the **gross profit on sales**. If there were no expenses in connection with the sales, gross profit would be the amount of net income earned. For business firms that have substantial operating expenses, the gross profit on sales should be one third to two thirds of the total sales figure. In retail circles the gross profit on sales is known as the **gross margin** and reflects the average overall markup percentage on goods sold.

OPERATING EXPENSES

Payrolls for salesclerks and office employees, supplies used, depreciation on plant or fixed assets, advertising costs, taxes, and expired insurance are

BLACKSTONE MANUFACTURING COMPANY
Schedule No. 1 — Cost of Goods Manufactured
For Year Ended December 31, 1976

Work in process inventory, January 1, 1976			$ 29,000
Raw materials:			
Inventory, January 1, 1976		$ 61,000	
Purchases	$184,900		
Less purchases returns & allowances	2,500		
Net purchases		182,400	
Total cost of materials available for use		$243,400	
Less inventory, December 31, 1976		70,000	
Cost of materials placed in production		$173,400	
Direct labor		152,000	
Factory overhead:			
Indirect labor	$ 14,800		
Repairs	12,000		
Heat, light, and power	19,600		
Depreciation — machinery & equipment	25,350		
Factory supplies expense	10,400		
Patents expense	7,250		
Insurance expense	3,600		
Total factory overhead		$ 93,000	
Total manufacturing costs			418,400
Total work in process during year			$447,400
Less work in process inventory, December 31, 1976			34,800
Cost of goods manufactured			$412,600

Figure 22-3 **Schedule of Cost of Goods Manufactured**

examples of **operating expenses**. All of the costs that a business firm incurs in its normal operations are grouped under this classification. Individual items are shown so that the owner or owners can note the amount spent for each purpose. If certain expenses appear too large, as brought out by comparison with previous income statements, corrective steps can be taken.

Operating expenses are usually subdivided into selling expenses and general or administrative expenses. **Selling expenses** are those that are incurred as a direct result of the sales activities of the firm. Such items as salaries of salesclerks, advertising, store supplies used, depreciation on store equipment, and delivery costs are examples of selling expenses. The advantage of segregating these from general expenses is that the total for one year compared with the total for another year may be significant. If selling expenses have increased in total, it is then possible to analyze the individual items to locate the cause or causes.

Office salaries, rent, taxes, insurance, office supplies used, depreciation on buildings and office equipment, and the cost of bad debts resulting from uncollectible account sales are examples of **general expenses**. They are costs connected with the general operation of the business. If an expense is difficult to allocate between the selling and general classification, such as fire insurance on merchandise inventory, it is usually assigned to the general expense classification.

INCOME FROM OPERATIONS

The difference found by subtracting the total of the operating expenses from the gross profit on sales is known as the **income from operations**. If there are no other items of income and expense, this figure is also the net income, but most businesses do have nonoperating incomes and costs. In some instances the total operating expenses may exceed the gross profit on sales. Should this occur, the difference between the two amounts would be known as the **loss from operations**.

OTHER INCOME AND OTHER EXPENSE

Most firms secure some income and incur some expenses of a financial, rather than an operating, character. These are classified as **other income** and **other expense** and are added to or subtracted from the net income from operations. Other titles used for these sections are nonoperating income and expense and financial income and expense. The most common items are interest received and paid on notes, mortgages, and bonds.

NET INCOME

The final figure on an income statement and the one that represents the result of all operations of a business, both operating and nonoperating, is called the **net income** or **net loss**. It is naturally the most interesting single figure on an income statement. Although the amounts used in arriving at the final result are of interest to those connected with the management of the firm, other persons are more concerned with the amount of net income or net loss.

Income statements for unincorporated and incorporated businesses are identical with the single exception of the determination of the net income figure for corporations. As legal entities they must pay income taxes, assuming that operations have been profitable. Consequently, an income statement for a corporation ends as follows:

Net income before income taxes	$225,000
Income taxes	88,900
Net income	$136,100

The Balance Sheet

A **balance sheet** lists the assets, the liabilities, and the capital of a firm as of the close of business on a specific date, which is frequently the end of a month, a quarter, or a year. As explained in Chapter 18, assets consist of the property owned and used in the operation of the firm, such as land, buildings, merchandise, office equipment, and cash. Some of these assets may have been acquired by buying on open account or by the use of borrowed funds secured from a bank or from the proceeds of a bond issue. Until these debts are paid, creditors have a claim against the property owned by the business. The claims of these creditors against the assets of the business are known as **liabilities**, which may be either current or fixed. The remaining and secondary claim against the assets, which is the right of the owner or owners in the property, is an amount identified in Chapter 18 as equity capital. The word capital when used in this sense is also called net worth, **proprietorship**, or **owner's equity**. Corporations often use the term **stockholders' equity**.

Because all the assets of a business are subject to claims by creditors and owners, it follows that total assets equal the total claims of creditors and owners. The statement that assets equal liabilities plus capital is known as the **balance sheet equation** and is expressed as follows:

$$\text{Assets} = \text{Liabilities} + \text{Capital}$$

By transposing the liabilities the equation can be made to read:

$$\text{Assets} - \text{Liabilities} = \text{Capital}$$

The balance sheet equation stresses the fact that a business has an entity of its own in showing the amount of its obligation to its owner or owners.

Figure 22-4 shows the balance sheet for Simon's Hardware Store, whose income statement is shown on page 433. Note that the balance sheet items not only have been grouped according to the three major classifications — assets, liabilities, and capital — but also have been divided into subclassifications. Assets have four classifications: (1) current assets, (2) plant assets, (3) investments, and (4) intangible assets. Liabilities are classified into: (1) current liabilities, and (2) long-term liabilities.

CURRENT ASSETS

Cash and other assets that will be converted into cash or consumed within a short time are current assets. The maximum length of time for conversion is

SIMON'S HARDWARE STORE
Balance Sheet
December 31, 1976

Assets

Current assets:			
Cash			$ 14,080
Accounts receivable		$ 28,340	
Less allowance for doubtful accounts		3,200	25,140
Merchandise inventory			78,400
Store supplies			1,560
Office supplies			1,270
Prepaid insurance			930
Total current assets			$121,380
Plant assets:			
Store equipment		$ 32,400	
Less accumulated depreciation		8,300	$ 24,100
Office equipment		$ 23,100	
Less accumulated depreciation		7,040	16,060
Building		$150,000	
Less accumulated depreciation		30,000	120,000
Land			9,000
Total plant assets			169,160
Investments:			
Stock in Steelcraft, Inc.			5,000
Intangible assets:			
Goodwill			7,500
Total assets			$303,040

Liabilities

Current liabilities:			
Notes payable			$ 14,000
Accounts payable			33,900
Taxes payable			2,680
Total current liabilities			$ 50,580
Long-term liabilities:			
Mortgage payable			90,000
Total liabilities			$140,580

Capital

C. R. Simon, capital			162,460
Total liabilities and capital			$303,040

Figure 22-4   Balance Sheet

usually one year, and it is expected that this process will take place in the normal operations of the business. If merchandise is sold on open-book account or for notes, it is reasonable to assume that the accounts receivable or notes receivable will be collected in less than one year from the date of the sale. Such items as office supplies on hand will be used within a year, and insurance currently prepaid will expire in the months ahead.

PLANT ASSETS

Assets that possess a degree of permanence extending beyond one year and which are intended for use rather than for sale are known as **plant assets** or fixed assets. Some assets, such as automobiles or trucks, may not last more than three to five years, while land for a building site may last forever. Although such assets are sold when they are no longer useful to the firm, they are not purchased for this purpose.

With the exception of land, plant assets deteriorate in value with use and the passage of time. Because it is desirable to show the original cost of the asset as well as its reduced value year by year, two separate figures are required. The accumulated depreciation is increased each year until it equals the value of the asset from which it is subtracted. At that time, if the estimate of the useful life of the asset was accurate, the balance sheet value will be zero and the asset will be discarded. Scrap values are taken into account when warranted.

INVESTMENTS

Stocks or bonds of other organizations that are purchased with the intent to hold them for income or for other reasons are known as **investments**. It is unusual for a sole proprietorship, such as Simon's Hardware Store, to list investments because stocks or bonds would normally be purchased personally rather than by the business. It may be that an investment in a tool manufacturer is necessary for Simon to become a dealer for its products. The presence of investments on balance sheets of corporate holding companies is common.

INTANGIBLE ASSETS

Assets in the nature of a legal right or some other value without physical substance that have been purchased are classified as **intangible assets**. The most common of these is **goodwill**, which is the price paid for a firm above the net fair value of its assets over its liabilities because of the good name, trade connections, or earning capacity of the operating business. Patents purchased by a firm are valuable for the 17 years for which they are granted by the United States Patent Office. Copyrights are another example of an intangible asset with a somewhat longer life as they are granted for 28 years and can be renewed for a like period of time.

CURRENT LIABILITIES

Debts that are owed and payable within a short time are classified as current liabilities. Amounts owed to trade creditors, banks, employees, and other debts of a similar nature are common current liabilities. For example, purchases of merchandise on open-book account are due in 30, 60, or 90 days, depending upon the terms of the transaction. As in the case of current assets, the usual rule is that liabilities that will come due and be payable within one year after the date of the balance sheet should be included under this heading.

LONG-TERM LIABILITIES

Debts that will not be due for several years are called **long-term liabilities**. Money borrowed by selling bonds, long-term notes, or by assuming a mortgage payable results in such liabilities. Adding the long-term liabilities to the current liabilities gives a total that represents the amount of capital employed by a business that is secured from outsiders.

CAPITAL

If a business is being operated as a sole proprietorship, a single line shows the amount of capital at the date of the balance sheet. Supporting this figure is a **capital statement** that shows changes which have taken place since the date of the last balance sheet. Figure 22-5 presents this information for Simon's Hardware Store.

SIMON'S HARDWARE STORE Capital Statement For Year Ended December 31, 1976		
Capital, January 1, 1976		$143,030
Net income for the year	$37,430	
Less withdrawals	18,000	
Net increase in capital		19,430
Capital, December 31, 1976		$162,460

Figure 22-5 **Capital Statement**

If a business firm is operating under a partnership agreement, the interests of the partners are shown in the capital section of the balance sheet. For example, if Carter, Nelson, and Prince own and operate a business under the name of the Carter Drug Company, the capital section of the balance sheet for this firm might appear as follows:

C. D. Carter, capital	$ 68,400
H. H. Nelson, capital	35,250
S. R. Prince, capital	19,800
Total capital	$123,450

The supporting capital statement for a partnership would be similar to the one shown for Simon's Hardware Store, with the exception that it would show changes that had taken place during the year in each partner's capital account.

On corporate balance sheets the individual interest of each stockholder is not shown even though the company may have only one, two, or three owners. Instead, dollar values for the different types of stock outstanding, as well as for paid-in surplus and the amount of retained earnings, are shown. The stockholders' equity section of a balance sheet for a corporation with both preferred and common stock outstanding might appear as follows:

Preferred stock	500,000
Common stock	1,200,000
Paid-in surplus	2,435,000
Retained earnings	14,177,236
Total stockholders' equity	$18,312,236

In much the same manner that a capital statement supplements a balance sheet for a sole proprietorship or partnership, a **retained earnings statement** for a corporation presents details of changes that have taken place in this account during the year. Figure 22-6 shows such a statement for the Blackstone Manufacturing Company.

Statement of Changes in Financial Position

A recent development in the statements prepared from accounting data and published in the annual reports of corporations mailed to stockholders is the **statement of changes in financial position**. This statement shows the sources that provided working capital, what this working capital was used for, and the components of the resulting increase or decrease in working capital.

As shown in Figure 22-7, the customary major source of working capital is the net income of the business. Next in order is the total of depreciation charges, as these reduce net income but do not require an outlay of cash

BLACKSTONE MANUFACTURING COMPANY
Retained Earnings Statement
For Year Ended December 31, 1976

Balance, January 1, 1976		$3,486,750
Net income for the year		649,000
Total		$4,135,750
Less cash dividends:		
Preferred stock	$300,000	
Common stock	200,000	500,000
Balance, December 31, 1976		$3,635,750

Figure 22-6 *Retained Earnings Statement*

BLACKSTONE MANUFACTURING COMPANY
Statement of Changes in Financial Position
For Year Ended December 31, 1976

Sources of working capital:		
Net income	$649,000	
Depreciation	38,400	
Sale of subsidiary	750,000	$1,437,400
Application of working capital:		
Cash dividends paid	$500,000	
Purchases of property, plant, and equipment	277,400	
Reduction in long-term debt	620,000	1,397,400
Increase in working capital		$ 40,000
Changes in Working Capital Components:		
Increase (decrease) in working capital		
Current Assets:		
Cash	$ (1,800)	
Receivables	14,300	
Inventories	36,700	
Prepaid expenses	2,100	$ 51,300
Current Liabilities:		
Accounts payable	9,400	
Taxes payable	1,900	11,300
Increase in working capital		$ 40,000

Figure 22-7 *Statement of Changes in Financial Position*

during the current year. Other sources include the sale of securities and unneeded assets. This working capital is commonly used to pay dividends, retire long-term debt, and acquire additions to property, plant, and equipment.

The difference between the sources of working capital and its uses will either increase or decrease the amount on hand the previous year. To show in detail the effect on each current asset and current liability, the increase or decrease from figures reported a year ago are shown in the lower portion of the statement. This section provides a reconciliation for the amount shown as the year's change in working capital.

Interpretation of Financial Statements

After the income statement, balance sheet, and any other desired statements are prepared, the fourth and last step in the work of an accountant, that of interpretation, can be performed. The fact that a business may or may not have been operated at a profit is of vital concern, but this one figure fails to tell the whole story. For example, a bank may be willing to extend a loan to a firm that has a strong financial structure despite recent operating losses. Judicious use of such borrowed funds might correct conditions so that future business operations would be profitable. On the other hand, a firm may be headed for financial trouble even though it is currently operating profitably.

By means of percentages, ratios, and other techniques, it is possible to analyze the financial status of a business. The directions such an analysis may take are varied and extensive. The current statements offer definite possibilities for interpretation, and comparisons with previous statements and those of competing firms can be made. For example, an analysis of the income statement of Simon's Hardware Store on page 433, with 100 percent being assigned to the net sales, would show that the business made less than nine cents on each dollar of sales ($37,430 ÷ $432,550 = $0.087). An examination of the balance sheet on page 438 shows that 53.6 percent of the funds used in the business were contributed by the owner ($162,460 ÷ $303,040 = .536). There are also a number of important relationships between the two statements, and the other statements and schedules offer analytical possibilities taken alone or in conjunction with the income statement and the balance sheet.

Some of the most useful techniques for analyzing financial statements are: (1) current ratio, (2) acid-test ratio, (3) number of day's sales in receivables, (4) turnover of merchandise inventory, (5) ratio of ownership to debt, (6) rate of net income on capital, (7) rate of net income on total assets, and (8) earnings per share of common stock. With the obvious exception of the last item, these ratios and percentages will be calculated for Simon's Hardware Store, whose statements have been illustrated. No attempt has been made to show trends, to contrast the efficiency of Simon's firm with other hardware stores by using available industry figures, or to rely on data not contained in a single income statement and balance sheet.

CURRENT RATIO

The ratio of current assets to current liabilities is the **current ratio**. It is found by dividing the total current assets by the total current liabilities. This ratio is very important to the owners and to short-term creditors because the current assets constitute a source of funds to pay current liabilities. An acceptable minimum ratio is usually 2 to 1, which takes into consideration the fact that current assets sometimes shrink in value whereas current liabilities do not.

By referring to the balance sheet on page 438, the current ratio for Simon's Hardware Store is calculated as follows:

$$\frac{\text{Current assets}}{\text{Current liabilities}} = \frac{\$121,380}{\$50,580} = 2.4 \text{ to } 1$$

ACID-TEST RATIO

The **acid-test** or **quick ratio** is a refinement of the current ratio in that it determines the ability of a firm to meet its current debt on very short notice. It recognizes the fact that the conversion of merchandise inventory into cash takes more time than is true for other current assets. To find the acid-test ratio, divide the total cash and net receivables by the current liabilities. If the firm owns marketable securities purchased on a temporary basis, these may be added to the cash and net receivables. An acceptable minimum acid-test ratio is 1 to 1.

Using information from the illustrated balance sheet, the acid-test ratio for Simon's Hardware Store is:

$$\frac{\text{Cash} + \text{Accounts receivable (net)}}{\text{Current liabilities}} = \frac{\$14,080 + \$25,140}{\$50,580} = .8 \text{ to } 1$$

Whereas the current ratio was comfortably in excess of the minimum, the acid-test ratio falls short of the 1 to 1 requirement. This indicates an area in which Carl Simon should take corrective action.

NUMBER OF DAYS' SALES IN RECEIVABLES

A measure of efficiency of collecting amounts owed the business and of the firm's policies on extending credit can be computed by determining the number of days' sales in receivables resulting from charge sales. This is done in two steps. First, the net charge sales for the year are divided by 365 (366 in leap years) to provide a daily charge sales figure. Second, the daily charge sales are divided into the gross accounts receivable (or net accounts receivable if the gross amount is not given) to find the number of days' sales tied up in receivables.

Assuming that 80 percent of all sales are charged, the calculations for Simon's Hardware Store are:

$$\text{Step 1.} \quad \frac{\text{Net charge sales}}{366} = \frac{\$432,550 \times .80}{366} = \$945.46 \text{ daily charge sales}$$

$$\text{Step 2.} \quad \frac{\text{Accounts receivable (gross)}}{\text{Daily charge sales}} = \frac{\$28,340.00}{\$945.46} = 30.0 \text{ days}$$

Assuming that credit terms provide for payment by the tenth of the month following the charge and that the middle of the month is the average date for credit sales made during the month, it could be expected that the gross receivables would total approximately 25 days of charge sales (15 + 10). On the basis of this line of reasoning, Carl Simon seems to be slightly lax in extending credit and collecting receivables.

TURNOVER OF MERCHANDISE INVENTORY

A retail establishment must always be alert to "turn over" its stock of salable goods as rapidly as possible; in other words, to sell present stock before it loses its maximum value. The frequency with which this move is accomplished is called the **inventory turnover** and is a measure of efficiency.

The preferred method of determining the turnover of merchandise inventory is to divide the cost of merchandise sold by an average monthly inventory. In the case of Simon's Hardware Store, only the beginning and ending inventories are available for averaging. Its inventory turnover would be calculated in two steps:

$$\text{Step 1.} \quad \$86,310 + \$78,400 = \$164,710$$

$$\$164,710 \div 2 \quad = \$82,355, \text{ average inventory}$$

$$\text{Step 2.} \quad \frac{\text{Cost of merchandise sold}}{\text{Average inventory}} = \frac{\$281,250}{\$82,355} = 3.4 \text{ turns}$$

For a retail grocery store 3.4 would be a poor turnover, but for a hardware store it is excellent. A comparison with previous years' turnovers and also with other hardware stores of the same size would be helpful.

RATIO OF OWNERSHIP TO DEBT

Practically every business is financed by a combination of funds secured from the owners and by borrowed capital. The ratio of ownership to debt shows the relative proportion of capital secured from the two sources. A mark of conservative financing is substantial ownership on the part of the proprietors or stockholders. This means that the ownership equity is large enough to absorb extensive and continued losses, and there is less danger of insolvency.

The ratio of ownership to debt for Simon's Hardware Store is calculated as follows:

$$\frac{\text{Ownership equity}}{\text{Creditors' equity}} = \frac{\$162,460}{\$140,580} = 1.2 \text{ to } 1$$

This is an unsatisfactory ratio as sole proprietors ought to contribute at least twice and preferably three times as much capital as is secured from creditors. Assuming the continued profitability of the firm, a conservative policy on withdrawing these profits, and a gradual reduction in the mortgage payable, this ratio should improve.

RATE OF NET INCOME ON CAPITAL

The reason that individuals invest their own funds in a business is to secure a return on their investments. Because of the risks involved, this rate should be higher than if a similar amount were invested in conservative securities. Furthermore, in the case of a sole proprietorship, the net income may also include a personal service factor. Despite the fact that an owner may devote full time to the business, a personal salary is not included as an operating expense.

As shown in the capital statement on page 440, Simon's investment in his business was $143,030 at the beginning of the year and $162,460 at the end of the year. An average of these two amounts is $152,745. The rate of net income on capital is calculated by dividing the net income by the average investment. For Simon's Hardware Store the computation shows the following:

$$\frac{\text{Net income}}{\text{Average investment}} = \frac{\$37,430}{\$152,745} = .245 \text{ or } 24.5\%$$

Although Simon's rate of net income on capital shows a very satisfactory yield, it must be remembered that personal service is included.

RATE OF NET INCOME ON TOTAL ASSETS

Another measure of the efficiency of a firm is the return on total assets. This percentage is found by dividing the net income by the total assets as shown for Simon's Hardware Store in the following computation:

$$\frac{\text{Net income}}{\text{Total assets}} = \frac{\$37,430}{\$303,040} = .124 \text{ or } 12.4\%$$

Since the cost of the borrowed capital is between 6 and 7 percent, Simon's Hardware Store enjoys a very satisfactory rate of net income on total assets.

EARNINGS PER SHARE OF COMMON STOCK

A dollar-and-cents figure that is frequently shown in the printed annual reports of corporations and widely used by security analysts is the **earnings per share** of common stock, or **EPS**. EPS is computed by dividing the amount available to common stockholders by the number of shares of common stock outstanding.

No EPS can be computed for Simon's Hardware Store, a sole proprietorship; and the same situation exists for all partnerships. However, an example of an EPS calculation can be made for the Blackstone Manufacturing Co., whose retained earnings statement is illustrated on page 442. The only additional information necessary is that the Blackstone Manufacturing Co. has 800,000 shares of common stock outstanding. The EPS is computed:

Net income	$649,000
Less: Preferred stock dividends	300,000
Income available to common stockholders	$349,000

$$\frac{\text{Income available to common stockholders}}{\text{Number of common stock shares outstanding}} = \frac{\$349,000}{800,000} = \$0.44, \text{EPS}$$

BUSINESS TERMS

QUESTIONS FOR DISCUSSION AND ANALYSIS

1. What are some specific types of problems that management would attempt to solve by the use of accounting data?
2. Why is it desirable that the accounting treatment of business transactions be uniform in this country and also in the rest of the world?
3. The only truly professional designation in the entire field of business is that of a Certified Public Accountant. What reasons can be given for this restriction?
4. Are exact figures shown on an income statement or are they estimates?
5. Under what circumstances could a firm show a loss from operations on its income statement and yet show a net income?
6. Are exact figures shown on a balance sheet or are they estimates?

7. Why would one business show goodwill on its balance sheet while a much more highly regarded competitor's balance sheet might not show this asset?
8. If a business shows a net loss for the year, would it have any source of working capital for that year?
9. As a stockholder you would like to judge the efficiency of the management of your company. What ratios, percentages, or turnovers would you apply to the financial statements?
10. Financial analysis produces precise measurements such as 1.8 to 1, 58.6%, and $1.34. Can management rely on these specific figures as a basis for making decisions?

PROBLEMS AND SHORT CASES

1. **a.** The following account balances were taken from the books and records of the Clark Furniture Co. on December 31, 1977. Prepare an income statement using Figure 22-2 on page 433 as a guide for form and arrangement.

Sales	$385,400	Depreciation expense, store equipment	$ 1,850
Sales returns & allowances	1,680	Office salaries	18,300
Merchandise inventory, January 1, 1977	46,110	Uncollectible accounts expense	2,730
Purchases	283,300	Depreciation expense, office equipment	1,500
Purchases returns & allowances	2,870	Depreciation expense, building	2,880
Purchases discount	4,190	Taxes expense	5,100
Merchandise inventory, December 31, 1977	51,900	Insurance expense	3,800
Sales salaries	35,770	Miscellaneous office expense	1,650
Advertising expense	12,120	Interest expense	1,740
Store supplies expense	2,060		

b. The following additional account balances were taken from the books and records of the Clark Furniture Co. on December 31, 1977. Prepare a balance sheet using Figure 22-4 on page 438 as a guide for form and arrangement.

Cash	$ 6,450	Store equipment	$ 18,500
Accounts receivable	13,700	Accumulated depreciation, store equipment	3,700
Allowance for doubtful accounts	4,170		
Merchandise inventory	51,900	Office equipment	15,000
Store and office supplies	3,160	Accumulated depreciation, office equipment	3,000
Prepaid insurance	2,490		

Building	$ 72,000	Notes payable	$ 22,200
Accumulated		Accounts payable	9,100
depreciation, building	8,640	Taxes payable	1,660
Land	9,300	Mortgage payable	30,000
Goodwill	10,000	James Clark, capital	120,030

c. The following additional account balances were taken from the books and records of the Clark Furniture Co. on December 31, 1977. Prepare a capital statement using Figure 22-5 on page 440 as a guide for form and arrangement.

James Clark, capital,		James Clark, drawing	
January 1, 1977	$112,260		$ 16,000

2. The following figures were taken from the statements of the Ten Percent Store, Inc., for the year ended December 31, 1977. Compute the (a) current ratio, (b) acid-test ratio, (c) number of days' sales in receivables, (d) turnover of merchandise inventory, (e) ratio of ownership to debt, (f) rate of net income on capital, (g) rate of net income on total assets, and (h) earnings per share of common stock.

Current assets	$ 240,000	Current liabilities	$ 100,000
Cash	37,200	Total liabilities	170,000
Receivables	71,400	Capital, January 1,	
Merchandise inventory		1977	417,000
January 1, 1977	101,800	Capital, December 31,	
Merchandise inventory,		1977	460,000
December 31, 1977	125,700	Net sales	1,290,000
Total assets	630,000	Cost of merchandise	
		sold	775,000
		Net income	83,000

Number of shares of common stock outstanding = 40,000

3. Jim and Ethel Walsh have been operating the Walsh Paint Store in rented quarters in a suburban shopping center. The business has produced a good living for the Walsh family, but every cent not needed for living expenses has been invested in the store. For some time the Walshes have wanted to add a line of unpainted furniture for which they have adequate unused display space. Recently they were approached by Bill Stone, the owner of a downtown variety store, who offered to sell them his entire stock of unpainted furniture at 50% of his cost, as he wanted the space for a more profitable department. An examination of Stone's purchase invoices indicated that the amount involved would be $28,000. The Walshes were delighted to accept the offer with terms of cash at the end of 30 days. They were confident that, over a period of time, the inventory could be sold for between $75,000 to $100,000.

Prior to the purchase of the unpainted furniture, the balance sheet of the Walsh Paint Store showed the following current assets and current liabilities (the value of a few fixed assets was minimal):

Current assets:	
Cash	$ 6,400
Accounts receivable	18,700
Merchandise inventory	26,300
Total current assets	$51,400

Current liabilities:

Accounts payable	$14,600
Notes payable	10,000
Total current liabilities	$24,600

The purchase of the furniture increased the merchandise inventory to $54,300 and the accounts payable to $42,600. When the Walshes approached their bank for an additional loan of $28,000, they were shocked to be turned down because their current ratio was now less than 2 to 1 and their acid-test ratio was less than 1 to 1. The loan officer agreed that the purchase was a bargain but explained that his hands were tied by bank policy. He indicated that if the ratios were met he would gladly approve a $28,000 loan.

Assuming that no other source of credit is available, what should the Walshes do in the next 30 days?

23 Data Processing

"How in the world can I ever have complete knowledge about all the drug products which I sell," declared Doris Frederick, a detail salesperson for a large pharmaceutical manufacturer. Doris, who recently graduated from college, was completing a sales training program which was conducted by her sales manager, Ted Stills. Ted replied to Doris, "You do not need complete knowledge because for about $3,000 the company is supplying you with auxiliary brainpower!" "What do you mean?" responded Doris. Ted explained, "For each salesperson the company is investing in portable computer terminals which are about the size of a typewriter. You can easily connect the terminal to a telephone — even a pay phone — and gain instant access to information which is stored in the company's computer hundreds of miles away."

As society grows more complex, the need for information increases. Managers require a wide range of information for effective decision making. Data which are stored and available to managers are collected from numerous sources both inside and outside an organization. The orderly method of gathering, storing, and processing these data is called a **data processing system**.

NATURE OF DATA PROCESSING

Data processing begins with the origination or collection of data and ends with the communication of information to the people who will use it. Between the gathering and reporting steps, the processing of data may involve classifying, sorting, calculating, summarizing, recording, storing, retrieving, and reproducing them. All data processing, whether done manually, mechanically, or electronically, is an application of one or more of these operations. If both mechanical and electronic equipment are employed, the term **automated data processing (ADP)** is applicable; if all processing is done electronically, the term **electronic data processing (EDP)** is more descriptive.

Data are the raw facts that must be converted into information. There are many classes of data, but the common ones used in business are those which identify individuals, locations, objects, quantities, and monetary values. The word "data" may be defined as all the facts that have been gathered, and the term "information" then denotes the particular facts management wants to know. **Information** is the result of data processing and may be made available to company personnel as operating documents, reports, and analyses of problems. The procedure used to convert data into information is **information processing**. The goal of an efficient system of data processing is to produce the maximum amount of useful information for people within an organization in minimum time at reasonable cost.

HISTORY AND IMPORTANCE OF DATA PROCESSING

The first data processing tools were simple — a person's fingers, pebbles, notched sticks, and knotted ropes. Primitive nomads could classify their wealth into cattle, sheep, and chickens. By using different colored cords for each class of livestock and by tying knots in the cords, they could count and record the number of animals they owned.

The evolution of these simple counting and recording devices into high-speed electronic data processing systems took several thousand years. During this time many inventions helped to pave the way to the present level of development; notable among these were the following:

The abacus	1860 — Babbage's differential analyzer
1642 — Pascal's calculator	1889 — Hollerith's punched card equipment

The first truly electronic computer was made at the University of Pennsylvania in 1946; it was called ENIAC (Electronic Numerical Integrator and Calculator) and was conceived to produce mathematical tables required for the accurate firing of projectiles. ENIAC weighed nearly 30 tons, contained almost 19,000 vacuum tubes, and required an operating area of 1,500 square feet.

Within the past 25 years the growth of computer utilization has been phenomenal, increasing from a few hundred in the 1950s to 5,400 in 1960; 90,000 in 1970; and 200,000 in 1975. Computers process a wide range of data from that used in routine business operations to the calculations upon which the astronauts depend.

TYPES OF COMPUTERS

There are two general classes of computers, analog and digital. There are also hybrid computers that combine the features of both.

Analog Computers

An **analog computer** carries out its calculations by making measurements. It deals with continuous quantities; it translates such physical conditions as temperature, pressure, angular position, or voltage into related mechanical or electrical quantities.

The operating principle of an analog computer may be compared to the operating principle of an ordinary weather thermometer. As the weather becomes cooler or warmer, the mercury in the glass tube rises or falls. The graduated marks on the tube permit the interpretation of the climatic changes. The expansion and contraction of the mercury has a relationship to the conditions of the weather. The thermometer provides a continuous measurement that is analogous to the climatic temperature. Other examples of devices that make analogous measurements include the slide rule and the automobile speedometer.

Analog computers are used in industry to make scientific computations, to solve equations, and to control manufacturing processes. An analog computer is used by the National Aeronautics and Space Administration to measure the speed, direction, and trajectory of manned space vehicles.

Digital Computers

Digital computers deal solely with numbers. Whereas analog computers measure physical relationships, digital computers count numbers. A digital computer differs from the ordinary rotary calculator in four ways:

1. It is faster; it can perform arithmetic operations according to directions at speeds measured in billionths of a second.
2. It has the capability to make logical decisions, such as comparing one number with another and determining which is larger.
3. It has the capacity to store data and have them available for almost instantaneous recall.
4. It can follow a set of written instructions.

The remainder of this chapter will be devoted to digital computers because they are the type most commonly used in business.

COMPONENTS OF A COMPUTER SYSTEM

A computer system consists of a central processing unit, one or more input devices, and one or more output devices. The heart of the computer system is the **central processing unit (CPU)** which is the computer. The three sections or units of a CPU are: (1) memory, (2) arithmetic, and (3) control. The CPU processes the data which are received from an input device and then transmits the processed data to an output device. A schematic diagram of the basic components of a computer system is shown in Figure 23-1.

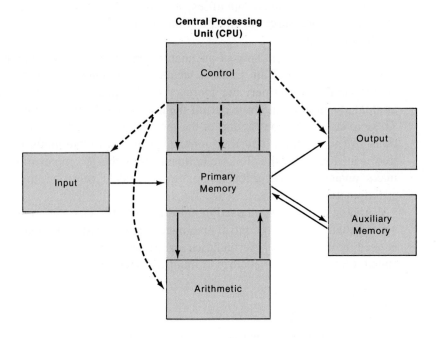

NOTE: Solid lines indicate information flow; broken lines indicate control.

Figure 23-1 **Schematic Diagram of Basic Digital Computer Components**

Input Unit

The purpose of the **input unit** is to permit the computer operator to "communicate" with the computer. It carries out its function by translating codes from the external form in which the data are represented, such as holes in a punched card, to the internal form in which data are stored in the memory unit. The data thus translated and stored may be numbers used in calculations, instructions that tell the computer what to do, or numbers or letters to be used as names and addresses.

Input consists of data to be processed and the instructions required to process the data. The input unit of a computer involves devices that "read in" data and instructions from various media. The **input media** include punched cards, punched paper tape, magnetic tape, magnetic disks or drums, optical characters, and magnetic ink characters. Various types of input media are illustrated in Figure 23-2.

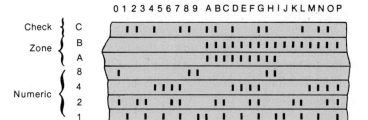

0 1 2 3 4 5 6 7 8 9   A B C D E F G H I J K L M N O P

Check { C

Zone { B

A

8

Numeric { 4

2

1

Magnetic tape is tape upon which data are recorded by the presence and absence of mag-
netized areas arranged according to code. Actual tape is one-half inch wide.

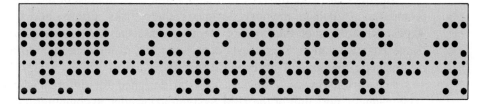

0 1 2 3 4 5 6 7 8 9   A B C D E F G H I J K L M N O P Q R S T U V W X Y Z   ' . / & $

Punched paper tape is a special tape upon which data may be stored in the form of punched
holes. Holes are located in columns across the width of the tape. Each column usually
contains 5 to 8 positions, which are known as channels.

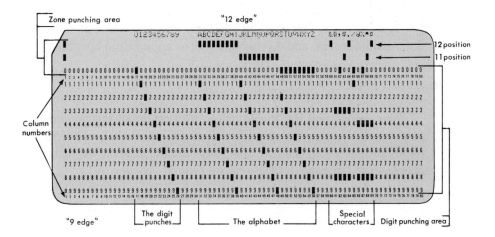

A **punched card** is made of heavy, stiff paper of constant size and shape. Data are stored in
the form of punched holes arranged in 80 vertical columns. All holes in a single column are
sensed simultaneously when a card is read by automated equipment. In each column there
are 12 punching positions; (0-9) are identified as numeric punches and 11 and 12 are
identified as zone punches.

Figure 23-2   ***Input Media Containing Data***

Chapter 23 / DATA PROCESSING   **455**

Memory or Storage Unit

The **memory** or **storage unit** is the distinguishing component of a CPU. It is the center of operations. All data being processed by the computer pass through the memory unit. By means of this unit immense quantities of data are immediately available to the commands of the computer. The memory holds:

1. The input data.
2. The intermediate results of calculations.
3. The final results to be "read out."
4. The program of instructions telling the computer what to do.

Magnetic cores are the type of memory unit used in most of the high-speed computers. Auxiliary memory devices include disks, drums, and magnetic tapes. Regardless of the type of memory unit, the computer performs the same basic operation. It converts data according to instructions into a series of magnetic charges and stores these charges.

The various memory devices may be designed for different capacities. The magnetic core unit of the IBM System/360 Model 30 computer has 32,768 storage locations. A magnetic disk assembly which contains 25 disks has a storage capacity of over 100 million characters of information.

Arithmetic Unit

The **arithmetic unit** of a CPU performs the operations of addition, subtraction, multiplication, and division, as well as comparison operations.

Control Unit

The **control unit** has the function of interpreting the program or instructions stored in the memory. It directs the various processing operations, issues proper commands to computer circuits to execute instructions, and checks to see that the instructions are properly carried out.

Output Unit

The **output unit** has the function of reading out or translating into convenient form the results of processing or the contents of the memory. The **output** is the end product of the computer system. The output media used to read out may be punched cards, magnetic or paper tapes, or printed pages. Printed pages are the most important medium for obtaining information from a computer if the output is going to be used solely by human beings. High-speed printers are capable of printing 1,200 lines a minute. Some of the types of information that can be produced by a printer are accounts, journals, financial statements, bills and invoices, and checks.

COMPUTER HARDWARE

The term **hardware** describes the central processing unit and its peripheral equipment. The CPU contains the circuits that control and perform the execution of instructions. **Peripheral equipment** is the collective term for input and output units and auxiliary memory units that are linked to the CPU. For example, a system may consist of seven pieces of hardware: the computer, console, card reader, card punch, high-speed printer, magnetic tape units, and disk storage units. The last five of these are classified as peripheral equipment. One or more pieces of peripheral equipment may be located a few feet or many miles away from the central processing unit.

Terminals

A **terminal** which is a special-purpose input/output device is a form of peripheral equipment. It satisfies the need for users in remote locations to communicate with the computer. A terminal permits the input of data to the computer and/or the output of information to the user. Types of terminals include paper tape devices, visual display units, voice response units, touch-tone devices, and console typewriters.

In stores with computerized checkouts, a terminal has replaced the cash register. On each package in these stores there is a special rectangular label which is composed of thick and thin bars and spaces known as a **Universal Product Code (UPC)**. When the checker slides each item's UPC over a laser-beam scanner, the terminal is instructed by a computer to print the code number of the item, the department, the price, and the tax on the transaction slip.

Computer Generations

It is convenient to speak of the developments in computer hardware in terms of three generations. In the first generation of computers beginning in 1955, the circuitry was based on vacuum tubes, such as were used in radio sets. The speed of operations was in the neighborhood of 500 additions a minute. By 1960 the vacuum tubes were replaced by transistors which identified the second generation computers. Speed increased sevenfold. In the third generation of computers, the circuits are based on silicon chips much smaller than the eraser of a pencil and speed has reached the level of millions of instructions per second. Other recent improvements in computer hardware have been the development of larger memories; **optical scanning devices**, which can read printed matter or handwritten material and convert it into data for the computer; data transmission equipment, which links distant computers over standard communications facilities; and information-retrieval instruments, which automatically store and recall filed data.

Electronic Calculators

An important hardware category, although perhaps less exciting and powerful than the large computer, includes the modern desk-top and pocket calculators. These are a far cry from the noisy, clanking machines used to grind out relatively simple arithmetic calculations. Although today's **electronic calculators** can be used to perform simple adding-machine calculations, many of them are capable of silently and swiftly performing complex operations encountered in business, scientific, and engineering problems. Although the calculators fail to match the speed of computers, they have the advantage of simplicity over the computer. Using the keyboard to give instructions to the calculator is easy compared to the complex programs that most computers require.

COMPUTER SOFTWARE

Various programming aids that help make effective use of a computer are known collectively as computer **software**. A **program**, which is a software item, may be defined as a series of operating instructions to be performed in processing the data supplied to the computer, the results of which will give the required answer. The actual writing of a program is done by a person called a **programmer**. A program is prepared by listing in complete detail the logical steps which the computer must take to obtain the desired results. There are four basic considerations in the preparation of a program:

1. Defining the problem to be solved.
2. Outlining each logical step required to reach the solution.
3. Writing the program in a symbolic language.
4. Translating the program into machine language.

Machine language is a basic combination of characters which a particular computer "understands." **Symbolic languages** enable the programmer to write instructions in English and algebraic symbols. Three of the most popular of the symbolic languages are COBOL, FORTRAN, and RPG. **COBOL (Common Business Oriented Language)** employs business terminology and is written in English-like words. **FORTRAN (Formula Translation)** is a widely accepted language for scientific and mathematical use. It is written in a combination of arithmetic expressions and statements in English. For example, to indicate addition in FORTRAN a plus sign would be used, and in COBOL the word "ADD" would be used. **RPG (Report Program Generator)** language provides an easy method for programming a small computer to write a business report. The program is placed on a special specification form which is translated by RPG into machine code instructions.

FLOW CHARTS

The importance of outlining the logical steps required to arrive at the solution of a problem has been mentioned. One way to do this outlining is by means of flow charts. Not only in computer programming, but also in general logical thinking, flow charts are most useful.

A **flow chart** is a graphic representation of the logical steps to be used in solving a problem. It helps the programmer to do the following:

1. To break down a problem into workable segments.
2. To ensure that each step is accomplished in correct sequence.
3. To discover areas of the problem that need further clarification.
4. To prevent or to detect errors in a proposed solution.
5. To discover laborsaving and timesaving shortcuts to the solution.

Basically a flow chart is a drawing of boxes, lines, arrows, and comments which indicate what is to be done. A well-designed flow chart will reveal all of the specific steps that are necessary for a completely logical solution to a problem.

For example, there may be as many as eleven distinct steps in solving the problem of crossing an intersection where there is a traffic light but no oncoming automobile traffic. The problem may be stated: How does one go from corner *A* to corner *B* without diagonal crossing? The diagram of the problem and its flow chart are shown in Figure 23-3.

THE SYSTEMS CONCEPT

Commonly the installation of electronic data processing equipment has been for the piecemeal application of routine subsystems. These subsystems are those which are best understood by the firm's employees. They are usually characterized by a high volume of transactions and a large amount of routine processing (sorting, calculating, etc.) that must be performed with each transaction. The potential cost savings from the application of electronic data processing is high. For these reasons it is typical to include accounts receivable, inventory control, the payroll, and similar subsystems in developing programs for a computer as first steps toward integrated data processing.

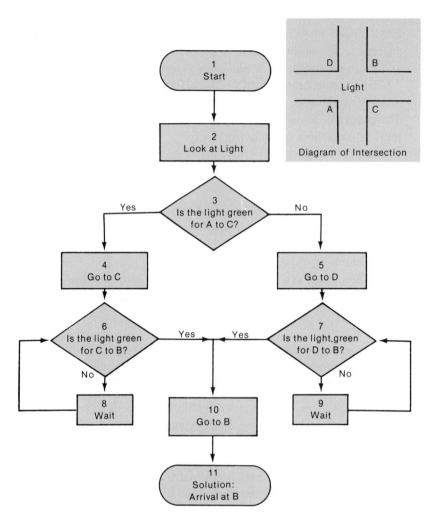

Figure 23-3   **Flow Chart for Crossing Intersection from A to B with No Automobile Traffic**

As the flow chart and its related program are developed for each data processing operation, computer specialists, called **systems analysts**, seek ways of combining, expanding, and coordinating them into larger units of operation. The systemization of data processing operations for the purpose of eliminating the duplication of data and of limiting the rehandling and resorting of data from one stage to the next is called **integrated data processing (IDP)**. The term is broadly used and may be applied to a particular group of operations of a company or to its entire operations. When the integrated data processing system is very comprehensive, it is called a **total systems concept**.

A growing number of companies are developing and experimenting with plans for a total systems concept. These comprehensive plans would give unity and coherence to the financial, production, marketing, and personnel functions of an enterprise. The total systems concept can properly subordinate departmental goals to the overall objectives of the company and give top management a broad, critical perspective of all the operations of the company. This section illustrates how subsystems may be coordinated into larger integrated data processing plans.

Retail Order Subsystem

At the J. C. Penney Company a central office computer records individual store sales, prepares store reports, and makes out the purchase orders for each store. In writing a purchase order the computer selects the correct vendor for the store on the basis of merchandise availability and cheapest transportation. The computer then assigns the cost, selling price, and unit weight for the item and checks the order quantity so that it meets the vendor's requirements. If a store's inventory of an item is larger than it should be, the computer does not write the order. Finally, the computer decides if this order is to be consolidated with other orders to the same vendor for the same store, and also selects the method of shipment from the vendor to the store.

Factory Subsystems

The possibility of operating a completely automated factory system has been enhanced by the development of the **minicomputer** which is a cabinet-sized, limited-storage computer. This type of computer is cheap enough to be used for single tasks, such as operating molding machines and controlling heat-treating processes, and it is run without the direction of a large centrally controlled computer. In addition to controlling individual operations, the minicomputers can communicate information to a higher-level supervisory computer which can assemble and analyze all the production data such as production costs, number of defective parts, and inventory needs.

The Phillip Morris cigarette plant in Richmond, Virginia, has minicomputers in place to operate a completely automated factory, but the firm desires to gain more experience before linking the units together. The eventual goal for the company is to make this plant 50 percent more productive than the firm's other three factories. By increasing machine utilization only one percent, Phillip Morris would save $250,000 annually. If computer control of the blending operation could improve tobacco usage by one percent, the company could save an additional two million dollars annually.

Real-Time Systems

One term frequently occurring in discussions of the total systems concept is real time. **Real time** is a type of data processing performed concurrently with a physical process or business transaction. The purpose of this type of information for management is to produce results that are immediately useful in controlling a physical process or business transaction as it occurs. A real-time computer system has three major characteristics. First, data are maintained **on-line**; that is, all data and instructions to be used in the processing are directly available to the computer by either being stored in the memory of the computer or being read in as required. Second, data are updated as events occur. Third, the computer can be "questioned" from remote terminals; that is, information stored in the computer can be obtained on request from a number of locations at a distance from the computer.

One of the first commercial applications of real-time data processing is SABRE, a system built by IBM for American Airlines. Updated with new equipment in 1972 and 1975, this information system receives data pertaining to airplane passenger reservations from the company's agents throughout the country. It can immediately process the information and send a virtually instantaneous output message to the agent. SABRE is designed to handle tens of thousands of telephone inquiries every day together with requests for prices, passenger reservations, inquiries regarding seat availability to and from other airlines, sales of tickets, and specific flight seating location assignment. On certain days American Airlines has nearly 1,000,000 passenger records in its electronic files. The processing of a reservation through SABRE takes approximately 1 to 2 seconds from agent input until the response is received.

COMPUTER-BASED SERVICES

The computer software industry is evolving into a computer services industry, and over the past few years many firms have been created to sell computer services to other firms. These firms own the computer hardware and employ skilled personnel in data processing, programming, and systems design. Some banks have entered this new industry by providing payroll, accounts receivable, billing, and other accounting and clerical services to their clients.

The financial burden to a company which is considering a computer application has frequently dictated the decision to use a computer service firm. As shown in Table 23-1, the cost of purchasing computer hardware adequate to serve the needs of a medium-sized business will run approximately $250,000 to $1,000,000. If most of the units are leased, rentals will be from $5,000 to $20,000 a month. The cost of hiring competently trained programmers and operators can be expected to equal rental costs. Unless the firm is large enough to require the full capacity of its computer, it should be able to save money by using the computer service market. Some managers are hesitant to

Table 23-1   **Rental and Purchase Price Ranges of Computers**

Computer Size	Average Monthly Rental Price Range, Including Maintenance	Purchase Price Range
Minicomputers	$ 300– 1,200	$ 5,000– 50,000
Small	1,200– 5,000	50,000– 250,000
Medium-sized	5,000– 20,000	250,000– 1,000,000
Large	20,000–250,000	1,000,000–12,500,000

SOURCE: From *Principles of Business Data Processing*, 2d edition by V. Thomas Dock and Edward Essick. © 1974, Science Research Associates, Inc. Reprinted by permission of the publisher.

use the computer services facilities, however, as these methods involve turning over important business information and functional responsibilities to persons outside their company.

Three differing and significant aspects of the computer service market are: (1) time-sharing, (2) facilities management, and (3) service bureaus.

Time Sharing

Time sharing is a means of allowing many customers to share the capabilities of a large, central computer through the use of remote terminals hooked up to the computer. Although the computer actually services each user in sequence, the high speed of the computer makes it appear that the users are being serviced at the same time. This service benefits small businesses as well as large ones. For the smaller business the most powerful computers in the world are as accessible as the nearest telephone, which can be adapted for access to the distant computer. This multiple-access system allows large service corporations to provide these very sophisticated EDP resources to a small business which may neither be able to afford nor to utilize such resources fully on its own.

Facilities Management

An executive may wish to start a computerized system of some type but may not feel financially nor technically capable of selecting the hardware, of training programmers to write the software for particular needs, and generally of installing and overseeing the system. If executives do not wish to use time-sharing, then they may turn to a computer service company specializing in **facilities management**. This company would set up and operate the complete function for them.

Service Bureaus

Another way for a small business to process data is through a service bureau. The **service bureau** has trained programmers and computer operators on its staff and it either has its own computer or leases time from other computer owners. In the usual arrangement the data to be processed, such as sales slips, checks, and receipts, are delivered or mailed by the business to the service bureau. The service bureau staff places the data on cards or tapes to be used as input. The computer then processes the input and prints the reports according to programs which were prepared earlier in the service bureau.

COMPUTER SECURITY

There are several reasons why computer security has become a topic of increasing concern to management. One reason is that usage of computer services facilities means trusting important business data to individuals outside the firm. Another factor is that the storage of substantial amounts of valuable data in a single location increases the risk of a large loss. Since the computer system can be programmed both to illegally retrieve valuable data and then to cover the theft, computer larceny is hard to detect.

Examples of Inadequate Computer Security

Several examples will indicate the threat to computer security. Officials at the Encyclopaedia Britannica accused three night-shift workers of copying nearly three million names from the firm's most-valued customer list and selling them. Britannica claimed three million dollars in damages. At the Dow Chemical Company several years ago, antiwar demonstrators broke into the Dow Chemical center and used magnets to destroy $100,000 worth of tapes. In another instance, a young man stole about one million dollars worth of supplies over a two-year period from the Pacific Telephone and Telegraph Company. In the company's trash cans he found a set of instructions which gave him the entry code to the company's computerized ordering system. By using the code and punching the correct beep tones on his touch-tone phone, he successfully outwitted the system until an unhappy confederate informed the police. After serving time in jail, he formed a business to advise clients on computer security.

Measures to Promote Computer Security

It has been estimated that nearly 90 percent of the computer installations have inadequate security. The managements of many companies, however, are now turning to computer security experts for assistance in safeguarding the computer. System commands and passwords are being utilized to protect computers against illegal entry. One computer manufacturer, Honeywell, Incorporated, has devised a way to restrict the total amount of information available to any one user of the computer. Other schemes seek to control access to the computer location through a system of electrically-locked doors, electronic sensors, and closed-circuit television.

SOCIAL IMPLICATIONS OF THE COMPUTER

The impact of the computer has created change both inside and outside the organization. Inside the organization the computer has altered work assignments and provided management with new tools for decision making. Outside the organization the computer is significantly changing our way of life and will continue to exert a force for change. Some of the social concerns that are related to the computer are: (1) generation of masses of information, (2) organizational changes, (3) automation, (4) invasion of privacy, and (5) depersonalization.

Generation of Masses of Information

The computer has the power to gather rapidly, record, analyze, and distribute masses of information. This information can be transmitted to and from a computer at speeds of over 150,000 characters per second. The ability of the computer to process a large amount of data forces management to select only the data which are necessary. Some managers are overwhelmed with computer printouts which are unnecessary and go unheeded. Someone has referred to this misuse of information as GIGO — garbage in, garbage out. Management needs information of real value to assist in decision making. The procedure for collecting and organizing facts rapidly into separate areas of information and acting upon these data is known as a **management information system**.

Organizational Changes

The computer makes it possible to centralize decision making in a decentralized organization. Through the use of terminals, managers in remote locations have instant access to a central computer. When a firm replaces its decentralized filing and record system with a centralized processing center, a greater centralization of power occurs in the organization.

Since the computer operates most efficiently with routine programs and procedures, it becomes a force in the standardization of some work assignments. After a computer program is prepared, it is used repetitively whenever possible. It is too costly and time-consuming to write a separate program for each decision-making situation.

The computer has also restructured various work assignments. Many of the routine tasks of lower and middle management have been transferred to the computer. This action has freed middle managers to supervise creatively rather than to become involved with the numerous routine details of a job. For example, the computer relieves credit managers from determining if their customers are approaching their credit limits. Only in exceptional cases are credit managers needed to resolve problems concerning credit limits.

Finally, the computer alters both managerial and departmental responsibilities. The electronic data processing function is giving rise to a new group of specialists, such as systems analysts, programmers, and computer operators. As the computer reaches into all levels and activities of an organization, the data processing manager becomes a more important part of the management team. The utilization of the total systems concept within an organization may result in the elimination of some departments and the creation of new departments. In some cases the computer will serve as a focal point around which the activities of a firm will be organized.

Automation

For workers, one of the most fearful aspects of the computer is its capability of controlling machinery to perform tasks that were formerly accomplished by human labor. The unemployment that results when machine labor is substituted for human labor is called **technological unemployment.** Employees who are eliminated by automation are generally unskilled and semiskilled workers who find difficulty in seeking new employment. Because of the growing use of computerized checkouts in supermarkets, the Retail Clerks union fears a loss of 25 to 30 percent of supermarket jobs.

Numerous firms have established retraining programs for workers who are replaced by automated equipment. In some instances union contracts provide that workers who suffer from technological unemployment are entitled to a lifetime job with the company. This type of agreement causes management to weigh carefully the economic and social consequences of adopting new technology.

Invasion of Privacy

By bringing many separate pieces of information together in one central location, the computer is able to create massive **data banks.** These banks create the potential for an invasion of a person's privacy. It has been proposed that the federal government create a centralized data bank on all individuals. Thus, any agency of the government would have access to all the information compiled on a person. However, it is doubtful that this bank will ever materialize since Congress and others have expressed opposition.

Various types of data banks are already in existence. The federal government has 11 centralized data banks, the largest of which is in the Social Security Administration and contains information on 50 million persons. Credit bureaus also gather and computerize a variety of information on individuals. The need for maintaining accurate data is stressed in a provision of the Consumer Credit Protection Act which provides individuals with the right to check and validate the information collected on them. As data banks are assembled by other organizations, safeguards need to be developed to protect a person's privacy.

Depersonalization

When the computer replaces the human element in decision making, an impersonal computer program is substituted for human judgment. **Depersonalization** occurs when individuals feel they are viewed as numbers rather than separate personalities. Individuals become frustrated when they are informed that a particular action cannot be taken because there is no computer program for it. They express even more displeasure if the computer makes a mistake, such as underpayment on a check or terminating electrical service for alleged nonpayment.

Some organizations are taking actions to reverse this tendency toward depersonalization. The Aerojet-General Corporation is eventually going to eliminate all computers from management control operations. Executives of the company point out that the specialists operating the computers are not decision makers, but these specialists and the computers have usurped many of the functions of the manager. The firm wants more personal involvement from its managers. Computers, however, will continue to perform many other operations in the firm.

BUSINESS TERMS

QUESTIONS FOR DISCUSSION AND ANALYSIS

1. Does the continuing growth of the computer market mean that computer manufacturers are in a low-risk and a high-profit industry?
2. Identify several types of industries in which you foresee increased usage of the computer. Explain the reasons for your choice.
3. Identify a practical application for computer terminals in each of the following kinds of businesses: (a) manufacturing, (b) wholesaling, and (c) retailing.
4. Indicate the subsystems which are necessary for the efficient scheduling of production in a factory.
5. What are the characteristics of a company that would have the most success in adopting a total systems concept?
6. Explain how a real-time system could be used by a railroad to determine in which railroad yards its freight cars are located.
7. Are computer-assisted crimes as serious as other types of criminal actions? Explain.
8. Are the adverse social implications of the computer more imagined than real? What is the basis for your belief?
9. How may data banks provide benefits to society?
10. What actions can companies that use computers extensively take to avoid the depersonalization of their customers and employees?

PROBLEMS AND SHORT CASES

1. Joan Allen's alarm awakened her at 7:00 A.M. She dressed rapidly, ate a hurried breakfast, and rushed out of the house to catch the Bay Area Rapid Transit (BART) car which would take her into San Francisco where she attended college. After disembarking from BART, she stopped by a branch bank to withdraw some money. Although the bank was closed, she inserted a card into a machine which provided her with the necessary cash. On arrival at school, she picked up her schedule for the next semester. As usual, she discovered that the schedule had several errors. After correcting her schedule at the registrar's office, she went to the business office to pay her fees. She wrote a check for the full amount. Then she proceeded to her exciting business simulation class. In this course the students were divided into teams and companies. Each team made managerial decisions which simulated the operation of a real company. After class Joan did some shopping and purchased some new shoes. She noticed at the checkout that the checker passed a coded tag on the shoes over a concealed beam of light instead of punching keys on a cash register. Joan decided to save her cash and pay for her purchase with a bank

credit card. Since it was time to go home, Joan headed for a BART station. On the way, she saw a man in a phone booth typing on what appeared to be a portable typewriter. She knew office space was scarce in the metropolitan area, but this was too much!

    a. From the preceding paragraph identify how the computer touched Joan Allen's life.

    b. Trace a day in your life, hour by hour, and indicate how your activities were affected by the computer.

2. In five years Excello Plastics has grown from a small plastics operation with only three employees to a firm which employs 150 individuals. The firm manufactures a variety of extruded plastic products. As the firm has grown, its number of customers has expanded, its accounting problems have become more complex, and its personnel records have multiplied.

    For some time Excello management has recognized the need to process more efficiently and expediently the increasing amount of data which the firm generates. In the past management considered the purchase of a computer but rejected it because of cost factors. At this time a member of the management team suggested that the company consider the use of one of the following types of computer services: time sharing, facilities management, and service bureaus.

    As a consultant, you have been asked to: (a) evaluate the pros and cons of each of these three types of computer services, and (b) provide sufficient reasons for a specific recommendation.

3. Last year, Autoequip, Incorporated, a medium-sized producer of automobile parts, began to study the feasibility of installing a company-operated computer system. The committee that has been conducting the study has gathered data to indicate that the company should gradually progress toward a total systems concept. James C. Hall, the financial vice-president of the firm, believes that the committee's recommendation is completely unrealistic. He contends that it calls for more hardware and software than the company can efficiently utilize. He favors the immediate installation of a simple computer system for handling accounts receivable, accounts payable, payroll, and inventory since he believes that the computer is primarily a device to perform accounting operations.

    Questions have arisen concerning who should head the new Electronic Data Processing (EDP) department. Hall favors a person from his own area who is presently chairperson of the task force. He states that the head of the EDP department should report directly to the chief accountant, who is a subordinate of the financial vice-president. The vice-president of engineering, Chris Bell, is opposed to this view. She believes that the arrangement will provide little or no time to use the computer for engineering studies. She is also concerned that the committee chairperson is not sufficiently acquainted with the engineering uses of the computer. The marketing vice-president, Gary Wood, is worried that he and his staff will not receive detailed sales and marketing reports promptly or that such reports might not be effectively presented. The task force chairperson is privately recommending that the head of the proposed EDP area should be independent of all functional area executives and should be a vice-president in charge of information services and report directly to the president.

    As chairperson of the board of directors, you are asked to resolve this conflict. What factors will you consider in arriving at a recommendation?

24 Management Control Systems

A typical reaction from a manager who has attempted to use operations research and failed is:

"All that I read and heard about operations research led me to expect miracles from it. I assumed that if we were not using it, we were not managing. Needless to say, we were quite disillusioned, and we scrapped the whole program.

"Frankly, I'm frightened away by all the esoteric terminology, the talk about computers, and the mathematical controversies those people engage in. I figure this operations research stuff is for the big companies, not us."[1]

Control is the basic management function which measures performance against a planned objective and, if necessary, seeks corrective action to ensure that the objective is achieved. In a small, uncomplicated organization visual controls are frequently adequate; but in a large, complex operation elaborate controls are necessary. Controls provide an assurance to management that work is progressing according to a predetermined plan. This assurance permits management to focus its energies on new challenges rather than on routine activities.

Control devices are either qualitative or quantitative in nature. Qualitative controls generally embody managerial reviews and subjective estimates. Quantitative controls — the focus of this chapter — involve mathematical computations or statistical techniques which are often desired since they are objective and precise. Regardless of the type of controls, the presence of controls and their continual monitoring is necessary for effective management.

To enlarge upon the discussion of the control activity which was considered briefly in Chapter 7, this chapter will examine: (1) various steps in the

[1]Adapted from J. D. Batten, *Developing a Tough-Minded Climate* (New York: American Management Association, Inc., 1965), p. 33.

control system, (2) different control techniques available, and (3) the decision-making technique called operations research, which supplies a framework for the planning and controlling efforts of a firm.

STEPS IN THE CONTROL SYSTEM

As indicated on page 127, there are four steps in the control cycle. Each of these steps will be examined in detail to provide a greater insight into the control system.

Deciding in Advance What Should Be Accomplished

Good performance is determined by establishing a standard. A **standard** is a unit of measurement or some other value which serves as a basis for comparison. Standards are frequently stated in specific units, such as dollars or man-hours; they may also be stated in qualitative terms, such as stable labor-management relations or a strong company image. The standard to be used should reflect the objective to be achieved. Standards are developed in the following ways: (1) rule of thumb, (2) industry experience, (3) past experience, and (4) management plan.

RULE OF THUMB

A **rule of thumb** standard is one which has achieved general acceptance, but is not necessarily correct for specific cases. For example, in financial analysis a current ratio (current assets divided by current liabilities) of 2 to 1 is usually considered satisfactory. Although a 2 to 1 ratio is suitable for some firms, it may be inappropriate for others. For electric utility companies the desired ratio is considerably less, and for department stores the ratio is ordinarily greater than 2 to 1.

INDUSTRY EXPERIENCE

The accumulated experience of many firms in an industry provides guidelines for setting standards. Trade associations, trade journals, and government agencies often gather performance figures for an industry. For example, the National Retail Merchants Association provides department store officials with information, such as average dollar sales per square foot of selling space, number of transactions per square foot of selling space, and salespersons' salaries as a percentage of net sales. Since each company has unique objectives and plans, an industry standard has limited application.

PAST EXPERIENCE

Management may accumulate information on a company's performance which is helpful in developing current standards for the firm. If present conditions differ from past conditions, then it would be unwise to use past experience in developing current standards. Past performance, however, can provide a point of departure for establishing new standards. Companies in cyclical industries, such as steel and automobiles, experience more difficulty in using past data to reflect the future than companies in industries with more stability, such as food and tobacco.

MANAGEMENT PLAN

The more useful type of standard is developed from a carefully conceived and properly prepared **management plan**. The planning process forces the planners to consider the many internal and external forces which affect the operations of a company. Employee participation in the planning and the standard setting emphasizes self-controls and often results in higher standards than would have been set solely by management.

A type of managment plan in the financial area is a budget which can be constructed from the forecasts of anticipated company sales. The budget becomes a financial standard from which other standards, such as ratios and operating expense percentages, can be developed.

Measuring Current, Actual Performance

In measuring current performance, some unit of measurement is necessary. In most instances the type of standard determines the kind of measurement. For example, if the standard for a salesperson is the completion of eight calls in a day, the unit of measurement is the number of sales calls. If the standard is a current ratio of 2.2 to 1 ($2.20 of current assets to $1.00 of current liabilities), then the measurement is in terms of dollars.

Although there are numerous qualitative measures of performance, management commonly prefers to utilize quantitative measurements. In Chapter 17 PERT and CPM were mentioned as two quantitative techniques for production control. In Chapter 22 ratio analysis was explained as a form of quantitative financial control.

Comparing Current Activity with the Standards

The frequent comparison of performance to a standard permits early discovery of any drift from the standard. The comparison should be completed as near to the area of performance as possible. This assures the rapid detection and correction of any variation in performance.

Managerial control should function as a **cybernetic system**. A thermostat which automatically shuts off a furnace when the temperature rises to the desired point illustrates a cybernetic system. This system uses some of its energy to feed back information which compares the system's performance with a standard.

Taking Corrective Action

The action step in the control system is the correcting of deviations from standards. If corrective actions are not taken immediately, then the control system becomes ineffective. Variations from performance are usually identified in a report which calls for corrective action within a specified period of time.

Authority for correcting any variations from the plan should be granted to the person who is responsible for monitoring the control system. Even without a formal plan, capable managers recognize when performance in their areas departs from a standard. Control devices tend to confirm managerial expectations.

In some instances even the strongest of remedial actions do not adequately correct deviations in performance. Careful study and review may indicate that the standard is imperfect and should be altered. Since businesses operate in a dynamic environment, it is necessary for managers continually to reexamine the suitability of their objectives and plans.

CONTROL TECHNIQUES

Several different control techniques are widely used in business. The following will be examined in this section: (1) forecasts, (2) budgets, (3) statistical data, (4) control charts, (5) break-even charts, and (6) management by objectives. Many of these devices aid both managerial planning and controlling. They provide a plan which contains a control system for detecting any variations from the plan.

Forecasts

Forecasting is an attempt to predict the future by evaluating the circumstances of today and anticipating the events of tomorrow. Although a forecast is not really a control device, it furnishes information which is useful in developing standards of performance. Actually making a forecast is frequently the initial step in developing a control system.

Forecasts may be classified as short-term or long-range. Because of the possibility of unforeseen events occurring over a long interval, short-term forecasts usually are more accurate than long-range ones. From a businessperson's viewpoint the three major types of forecasts are: (1) economic, (2) market or industry, and (3) company.

ECONOMIC FORECASTS

Businesspeople turn to economic forecasting more often than to any other type. All business executives know that it is important to gain some idea of what general business conditions will be in a number of months or years ahead. **Economic forecasts** attempt to make such estimates, and in so doing, place major reliance on the use of external data. Economic forecasting can be and frequently is a complicated process. It generally serves as a framework for the preparation of a budget for a company.

Of the many different methods of making economic forecasts, three of the more commonly used are: (1) projections, (2) leads and lags, and (3) the use of gross national product (GNP) data.

Projections. The extensions of known trends of the past into the future are called **projections**. Projecting is done by plotting data for past years on a chart and, from the latest date, extending a line that follows the pattern of prior years.

Leads and Lags. It is the aim of forecasters to locate among the various economic data available some that lead and others that lag behind general economic conditions. For **lead data** forecasters favor common stock prices, housing starts, and hours worked per week; for **lag data** common indicators include consumer debt, value of manfacturers' inventories, and expenditures for new plants and equipment.

Use of GNP Data. The total market value of all final goods and services produced during a stated period, such as a year or a quarter, is known as **gross national product (GNP)**. The four major components of GNP and the bases which are used by the Continental Can Company for forecasting each one are illustrated in Figure 24-1. A forecaster can project each component to any desired period of time and arrive at an estimate of the dollar value of the gross national product for that date.

INDUSTRY OR MARKET FORECASTS

The forecast of overall economic activity yields information which is valuable in the preparation of specific **industry** or **market forecasts**. Projections,

FORECASTING THE FOUR MAJOR COMPONENTS OF GNP	BASIS FOR FORECAST
1. Government expenditures (purchase of goods and services)	Data from the federal budget; recent rate and trend of government expenditures; planned programs of public works construction; and informed opinion of government personnel.
2. Private investment expenditures	Sum of estimates (a) through (d) below.
(a) Investment in producers' durable equipment	Survey information on industrial investment intentions: S.E.C., Department of Commerce, McGraw-Hill, *Fortune* surveys. These data are often adjusted by judgment for differences in coverage and for any changes that may have occurred since the data were gathered.
(b) Residential, nonfarm new construction	Contract award data; analysis of consumers' income and of credit regulations and conditions; and general considerations of the supply of housing required, and that available. Housing starts are also forecasted.
(c) Nonresidential new construction	Contract award data; analyses by experts in the construction industry; and capacity utilization.
(d) Changes in business inventories	Data on the rate of inventory change available from government statistics on current inventories; comparison of trends in production of goods, and the apparent consumption thereof; past cyclical behavior; and government surveys of intentions.
3. Personal consumption expenditures	Sum of estimates (a) through (c) below.
(a) Durable goods	Current rate and trend of sales of durable goods; analysis of credit conditions; and surveys of consumer buying intentions, which are also of some help. New automobile registrations are forecasted separately.
(b) Nondurable goods	Current rate and trend of sales of nondurable goods; and analysis of consumers' incomes.
(c) Services	Current rate and trend of expenditures for services; and analysis of consumers' incomes.
4. Net balance of international transactions	Imports are influenced by GNP cyclical phase; and exports by overseas economic developments.
Gross national product	Sum of 1 through 4.

SOURCE: *Forecasting Sales*, Studies in Business Policy, No. 106 (New York: National Industrial Conference Board, Inc., 1964), p. 77.

Figure 24-1   *Bases for Forecast of Gross National Product by Continental Can Company*

leads and lags, and the use of GNP data can be used for making industry forecasts as well as for general economic forecasts. To obtain the greatest degree of accuracy, however, different approaches generally are used in making an industry forecast. These include: (1) market surveys, (2) market tests, (3) market factor analysis, and (4) sales force opinion and expert opinion.

Market Surveys. Consumers are asked direct questions in the **market survey** method. For example, they may be asked if they plan to purchase a new car during the next year. Although expensive and time consuming, this type of forecast may be the only practical way to estimate the market.

Market Tests. Somewhat similar to the market survey is the direct **market test**. However, under this method the product is available to consumers and actual sales results are tabulated. As an illustration, after the introduction of a new automobile model the manufacturer carefully checks on initial sales of the model to project total sales for the year.

Market Factor Analysis. Attempts to relate overall industry demand to a particular market factor constitute **market factor analysis**. For example, the demand for replacement automobile tires is directly related to the number of automobiles in use. Although the logic of this method is simple to understand, it is frequently difficult to find the appropriate factor which can be used as a base.

Sales Force Opinion and Expert Opinion. Some similarities exist between the sales force opinion and the expert opinion methods. The former is sometimes referred to as the bottom-up method, while the latter is called the top-down technique. The **sales force opinion** method makes use of salespersons who have continuous contact with the market to estimate future sales. These estimates become the basis for the construction of a market forecast. In the **expert opinion** method, company executives and others who are keenly aware of developments in the industry are consulted for forecasts which, in turn, are filtered down to the operating units.

COMPANY FORECASTS

Any of the preceding forecasting methods which are used for industry forecasting may be appropriate for predicting the sales of an individual firm. A frequent starting point for the forecasting of future company sales is its past sales. The past sales can be adjusted to reflect changes in:

1. Economic conditions.
2. Industry trends.
3. Internal company programs and policies.
4. Efforts of competition.
5. Past nonrecurring events, such as strikes and weather.

Reasonably accurate **company forecasts** generally can be attained by the proper analysis and use of this information.

Budgets

All large companies and many smaller progressive concerns use budgets as an aid in management planning and control. A **budget** is a written plan of action, covering a specific period of time, against which actual performance may be compared. The customary coverage for an operating budget is a year, which is then broken down into quarters or months. This subdivision is particularly important for firms that have seasonal variations although the major purpose is to make it possible to check the budget against actual operations at frequent intervals.

BUDGET PREPARATION

Within a company budgets typically are prepared for: (a) sales, (b) sales expense and advertising, (c) production, (d) all major departments, (e) cash, and (f) estimates of the financial statements. Preparation of any budget should be completed prior to the first day of the budget period. As operations move into the budgeted period, controls should be established so that corrective measures or revisions can be made promptly.

The budget procedure is illustrated by examining the construction of the sales budget and the production budget.

Sales Budget. Since all the activities of a business depend primarily on the volume of sales, the first step in the preparation of a company budget is customarily to establish the **sales budget**. This involves the submission of the estimated sales volume by the sales manager, revision of this estimate by a budget committee in light of information furnished by the firm's statisticians, and the establishment of the revised figures as the goal for the sales budget. All of the other departmental budgets are then set up on the basis of their relation to the sales budget and involve only the single step of compiling and submitting the figures.

Production Budget. The drawing up of the **production budget** consists of determining the amounts of all products that will be made during the coming period and setting up the production schedules so that these goals can be attained. In most companies the production budget is dependent upon the development of the sales budget. In some firms the manufacturing division decides what and how much is to be made, and the sales budget is based on this estimate. This practice, however, is becoming less frequent.

Occasionally the manufacturing division takes issue with the sales department's budget figures, with the result that changes are made in the latter estimate. This situation may arise due to the production department's feeling that the sales department is asking it to do the impossible in agreeing to manufacture goods in the quantities asked. Perhaps a major alteration in the plant that will take a sizable part of the productive facilities out of action for a time is scheduled for the coming period. Or possibly a planned addition to the factory is behind schedule because of material or machine shortages. These or any number of other causes may force a revision of the sales budget to bring it in line with the productive capacity of the manufacturing division.

BUDGETARY CONTROL

When the budget committee has coordinated and reviewed the estimates received from divisions and departments, its final figures, assuming the approval of the firm's president or executive committee, become the goal toward which all activities are directed. The sales department subdivides its total into quotas for districts and individual salespersons, the production department sets up manufacturing schedules, and similar procedures are followed by other operating units. By the time all this has taken place, the chances are excellent that the beginning of the budgetary period is only a few days away.

Use of Performance Report Forms. Control is achieved by the use of forms, such as the one illustrated in Figure 24-2, that show the budget figures for a period of time, such as a month, with a space for inserting actual performance reports as soon as they are compiled. A comparison between the planned and actual results indicates how well each department and the entire organization is doing in measuring up to its budgeted figures. These performance reports are available to the budget committee and the chief executive officer of the company who may review them with the department managers concerned. Any variations will be noted and remedial steps, if required, can be instituted. For example, if sales in a certain territory are running below the budget, the sales manager can get in touch with the salespersons in that area to discover where the trouble lies.

Use of Flexible Budgets. There is another facet to budgetary control, and this occurs when estimated figures are out of line with actual performance. The variance can be either over or under although plans are more likely to be optimistic than pessimistic. Assuming that five months of a budgeted year have gone by and sales are consistently running 10 percent below estimates, a revision of the budget for the remaining seven months may be in order. This will have far-reaching effects on almost every department and division of the firm, but there is no point in adhering rigidly to goals that seemingly cannot be attained. Actually many firms prepare **flexible budgets** which are based on

LOOMIS DEPARTMENT STORES
Income Statement with Variations from Budget
For Month Ended January 31, 1976

	January Budget		January Actual		January Variation
Sales		$264,000		$271,000	$+7,000
Cost of merchandise sold:					
Merchandise inventory, Jan. 1	$ 66,700		$ 65,100		$−1,600
Purchases	190,000		194,000		+4,000
Merchandise available for sale	$256,700		$259,100		$+2,400
Merchandise inventory, Jan. 31	75,000		70,000		−5,000
Cost of merchandise sold		181,700		189,100	+7,400
Gross profit on sales		$ 82,300		$ 81,900	$− 400
Operating expenses:					
Selling expenses:					
Sales salaries	$ 26,000		$ 27,500		$+1,500
Advertising	9,000		10,200		+1,200
Delivery expense	3,200		3,400		+ 200
Misc. selling expenses	2,000		2,350		+ 350
Total selling expenses	$ 40,200		$ 43,450		$+3,250
General expenses:					
Office salaries	$ 9,000		$ 9,175		$+ 175
Rent	3,600		3,600		0
Taxes	2,000		2,000		0
Insurance	1,300		1,300		0
Misc. general expenses	900		830		− 70
Total general expenses	$ 16,800		$ 16,905		$+ 105
Total operating expenses		$ 57,000		$ 60,355	$+3,355
Net income from operations		$ 25,300		$ 21,545	$−3,755
Other expense:					
Interest expense		300		250	− 50
Net income		$ 25,000		$ 21,295	$−3,705

Figure 24-2   **Budgetary Control Statement Indicating Variations from Budget**

different sales estimates before the start of the budgetary period. In any event, the budget should be closely geared to actual conditions as they develop and necessary adjustments should be a part of the control process.

One of the most commonly used methods for handling quantitative data is statistics. A study of manufacturers in Ohio disclosed that 23 percent used elementary statistical techniques, and an additional 22 percent utilized some advanced statistical methods in their operations. **Business statistics** may be defined as: (1) the collection, (2) analysis, summarization, and measurement, (3) presentation, and (4) interpretation of numerical data that are related to the problems of business. A most important function of business statistics is forcing the manager to explain situations or to state problems in explicit and specific form.

COLLECTION OF DATA

Numerical data must be collected before they can be summarized and used. If the figures are concerned with operations of the company, without regard for outside influences, the source for these data lies within the records of the particular business. Financial statements, purchase invoices, sales reports, and payroll records can supply vital information that is subject to statistical analysis. As an illustration, a company may show an operating profit in the current year of $325,000 as contrasted with a corresponding figure of $300,000 for the preceding year. If these figures represent the output of a factory and no expansion took place during the current year, the conclusion might be reached that more efficient use was made of the production facilities or that the plant operated more hours. However, an analysis may show that 50,000 units were sold in the current year as contrasted with 60,000 in the preceding year and that the increased operating profit was due entirely to an increase in selling price. In this case, the sales manager rather than the plant superintendent may have deserved commendation.

Although internal data provide many useful figures, particularly for control at the executive level, external data are more helpful in arriving at sound solutions to many problems. If by chance the desired information is available from outside agencies, its use will save time and money. More often, the statistical department of a business must secure the facts it needs by its own efforts. As mentioned in Chapter 8, three methods commonly used to obtain original information are: (a) mail surveys, (b) personal interviews, and (c) telephone interviews.

ANALYSIS, SUMMARIZATION, AND MEASUREMENT

Once the data are available, the figures must be processed. Sometimes they need to be broken down into segments, and at other times they are summarized into usable totals. Various types of statistical measurement can then be applied to yield results ready for presentation and interpretation. When thousands of individual items have been collected, the task of summarizing the data can be simplified by the use of various business machines and computers.

Two types of statistical measurement — ratios and percentages — were illustrated in Chapter 22 in connection with the interpretation of financial statements. Both ratios and percentages are useful for data other than those secured from accounting information. For example, a firm had total sales of $1,000,000 of which $800,000 was derived in states east of the Mississippi River and $200,000 in states west of that dividing line. This fact could be expressed as a 4 to 1 ratio, or 80 percent.

Other common types of statistical measurements include: averages, index numbers, correlations, and time series. An **average**, which is a measure of central tendency, is the typical value in a group of data, such as weekly wages or daily stock prices. An **index number** is a device for measuring the change that has taken place in a group of related items over a period of time. Both the consumer and the wholesale price indexes, which were discussed in Chapter 11 and which are illustrated in Table 24-1, are index numbers.

If there is a definite affinity between two or more separate sets of figures, the measurement of the degree of relationship is known as a **correlation**. A correlation exists between gasoline sales and the number of cars on the highway. Measuring the changes that occur in a series of data over a period of

Table 24-1 **Consumer and Wholesale Price Indexes, Annual Averages and Changes 1967–1974**
(1967 = 100)

	Consumer Prices						Wholesale Prices					
Year	All Items		Commodities		Services		All Commodities		Farm Products, Processed Foods and Feeds		Industrial Commodities	
	Index	Per-centage Change	Index	Per-centage Change	Index	Per-centage Change	Index	Per-centage Change	Index	Per-centage Change	Index	Per-centage Change
1967	100.0	2.9	100.0	1.8	100.0	4.4	100.0	.2	100.0	−3.4	100.0	1.5
1968	104.2	4.2	103.7	3.7	105.2	5.2	102.5	2.5	102.4	2.4	102.5	2.5
1969	109.8	5.4	108.4	4.5	112.5	6.9	106.5	3.9	108.0	5.5	106.0	3.4
1970	116.3	5.9	113.5	4.7	121.6	8.1	110.4	3.7	111.7	3.4	110.0	3.8
1971	121.3	4.3	117.4	3.4	128.4	5.6	113.9	3.2	113.8	2.0	114.0	3.6
1972	125.3	3.3	120.9	3.0	133.3	3.8	119.1	4.6	122.4	7.6	117.9	3.4
1973	133.1	6.2	129.9	7.4	139.1	4.4	134.7	13.1	159.1	30.0	125.9	6.8
1974	147.7	11.0	145.5	12.0	152.0	9.3	160.1	18.9	177.4	11.5	153.8	22.2

SOURCE: U.S. Department of Labor, Bureau of Labor Statistics, Monthly Labor Review (July, 1975), p. 93.

time is known as a **time series**. A record of the number of cars which were produced in each year from 1970 to 1976 is a time series.

PRESENTATION OF STATISTICAL MATERIAL

To present statistical material in a manner that will be useful for purposes of analysis, two devices are commonly used. These are summary tables and graphic presentations.

Summary Tables. A considerable amount of statistical material is presented in Table 24-1. Years, geographical areas, types of products, age groups, income groups, nationalities, and the like may be the bases for comparisons in **summary tables**.

Graphic Presentations. The pictorial presentation of statistical data has the great advantage of interest to the reader by presenting a visual analysis of the facts. One of the most common graphic statistical presentations is the **line** or **curve chart**, which, as illustrated in Figure 24-3, uses a line or curve to indicate changes or a trend over a period of time. Other common forms of graphic presentations are: (a) the **bar chart**, which is used for the comparison of figures; (b) the **pie diagram** or **circular chart**, which divides a circle representing 100 percent or a dollar into many smaller portions; and (c) **statistical maps**, which are commonly used to present geographical information (see page 81).

INTERPRETATION OF BUSINESS STATISTICS

The final stage in the role that statistics may play in aiding management to make decisions and to control operations is that of interpretation. At this point two questions need to be resolved — What conclusions can properly be drawn from the data and who should be responsible for this interpretation?

As to the first question, considerable judgment needs to be used. People in this country have a great faith in figures, which in most cases is probably justified. If a controller reports to the board of directors of a company that its profits last year were $2.18 a share, this statistic is accepted as a fact. Caution, however, should be used in relying on statistical measurements to influence decisions, particularly those affecting the future operations of a firm. Despite the best of intentions, several types of errors can creep into a computation. Arithmetic errors are likely to occur, particularly when the quantity of data to be processed is extensive. In surveys the sample selected may not be representative of the whole. If a computer is used, the programmed instructions may be faulty. There have been instances where individuals have used only selected information which supported their views. In other cases they have manipulated accurate figures to arrive at faulty conclusions.

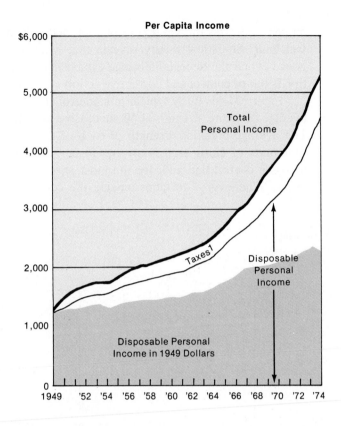

Per Capita Income

Total
Personal Income

Taxes[1]

Disposable
Personal
Income

Disposable Personal
Income in 1949 Dollars

SOURCE: "The Two-Way Squeeze, 1975," *Road Maps of Industry*, No. 1759, The Conference Board (April 1975).

[1]Mainly income taxes, personal property taxes, and inheritance taxes.

Figure 24-3 **A Line Chart**

The location of responsibility for interpreting statistical measurements to top management or for using such measurements in routine operations varies with the size and complexity of a firm's organizational structure. Most large businesses maintain a statistical department. Smaller firms usually subdivide this responsiblity among the various divisions of the company. For example, the sales manager interprets statistics based on market data while the controller analyzes financial facts and figures.

Control Charts

A **control chart** is a line chart which attempts to answer the question: Is the situation under control? In its simplest dimensions, a control chart consists of three horizontal lines: one shows average or normal performance, another indicates the **lower control limit**, and a third represents the **upper control limit**. Statistical theory reveals that when the measure of performance goes beyond the acceptable range established by the control limits the situation is out of control and corrective action is required.

Figure 24-4 is fairly typical of a control chart. Here, by means of dots, the average breaking strength of 50 successive samples of cotton cloth is shown. The average breaking strength of each of the samples was found by testing four units of cloth each hour. It will be seen that these averages fluctuate across a central line and, for the most part, that they are within the control limits. Whenever a dot goes outside the control limit (samples 30 to 35 and

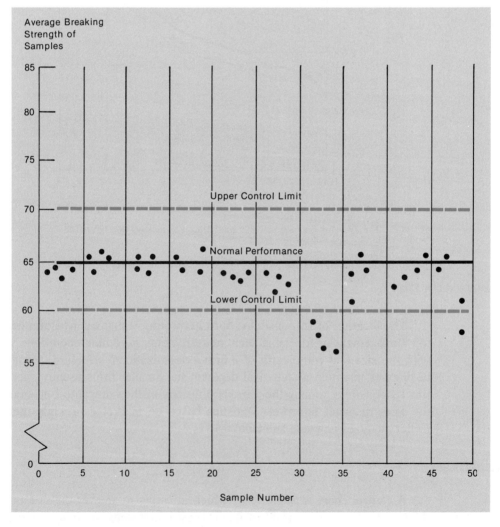

Figure 24-4   **A Control Chart**

48), trouble is indicated; and the first-line supervisor is immediately alerted to look for the source of trouble. If found, the trouble will then be corrected.

Statistical computations determine the location of the upper and lower control limits in such a way that the supervisor will look for serious trouble but will not be distracted by random variations in the production process. The control limits should strike a balance between two types of errors: (a) looking for trouble that does not exist, and (b) failing to look for trouble that does exist.

Control charts can be used not only for controlling the quality of production but may also be used in many other situations. For example, a marketing manager may construct a similar chart showing the ratio of the number of completed sales to the number of customers called upon. The credit manager may use a similar chart representing the average time required to receive payment on accounts receivable.

Break-Even Charts

The **break-even chart** graphically represents the relationship among costs, sales volume, and profits at a given time. In its simplest form it uses straight lines to represent sales income, variable costs, and total costs. It assumes that variable costs, which vary proportionally with sales, are clearly distinguishable and that fixed costs will not vary regardless of sales volume.

Figure 24-5 shows the construction of a break-even chart. The sales price of the product is $100. Variable expenses are 60 percent of the sales price, or $60 a unit. The monthly fixed costs are $50,000. The plant, under normal operating conditions, has a maximum productive capacity of 2,000 units a month.

Figure 24-5 shows that total costs equal total sales income when 1,250 units are produced and sold. If less than this amount is produced and sold, the company suffers a loss. By producing and selling more than 1,250 units a month, the company makes a profit. For this reason, an output of 1,250 units a month is called the **break-even point** — neither profits nor losses are incurred.

Management by Objectives

A **management by objectives (MBO)** program provides both a plan and a control over the activities of individuals. In an MBO program specific objectives are established for individuals prior to an operating period. After the period commences, continual evaluations are made to see if the objectives are being achieved. Since the objectives for individuals are determined jointly by themselves and their superiors, MBO is a form of participative management.

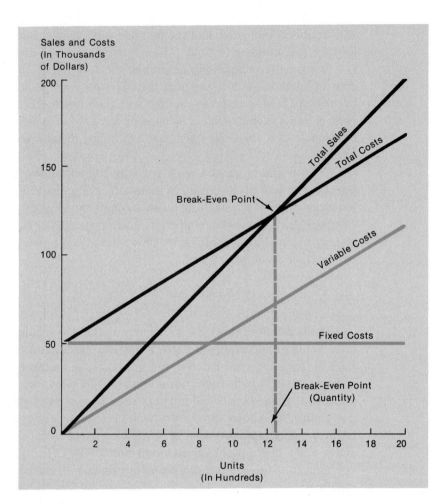

Sales and Costs
(In Thousands
of Dollars)

200

150

Total Sales

Total Costs

Break-Even Point

100

Variable Costs

50

Fixed Costs

Break-Even Point
(Quantity)

0

2   4   6   8   10   12   14   16   18   20

Units
(In Hundreds)

Figure 24-5 **A Break-Even Chart**

    The MBO goals should be specific, measurable, and reasonable. It is not enough for a sales manager to declare: "Sales will be increased." This manager should say: "Sales will be increased by 15 percent in the next year. Ten new customers, each contributing a minimum of $30,000 in sales, will be added. One new salesperson will be employed to develop these new accounts." This statement provides exact measurable goals. If a goal of adding ten new customers, each contributing a minimum of $30,000 in sales, is thought to be unrealistic, then it should not be stated. Unreasonable goals weaken the self-confidence of the individuals who utilize MBO.

    A major advantage of MBO is that it forces individuals to list their objectives and to prepare a plan of action to reach these objectives. Companies using MBO find that it causes individuals to establish goals which are in line with the overall goals of the company. A final advantage is the ability of MBO to provide a useful method of evaluating an individual. Comparing actual performance to stated goals increases objectivity and decreases subjective appraisals.

OPERATIONS RESEARCH

Operations Research (OR), which is the application of mathematical techniques to a wide variety of management problems, was originally used to enhance military efficiency during World War II. Frequently OR is conducted by a team of accountants, engineers, statisticians, economists, scientists, and mathematicians. The use of computers is almost a necessity; in fact, the ability to apply complicated mathematical formulas to business problems is interwoven with the programming of a computer to handle the data. In the OR process a problem is defined and analyzed, alternative solutions are tested, and a recommendation is made. Once the OR recommendation is placed into effect, it becomes a planning and controlling device.

In this section the following applications of OR will be discussed: (1) game theory, (2) simulation, (3) linear programming, and (4) queuing theory.

Game Theory

The purpose of **game theory** is to decide the strategy that is most likely to achieve maximum profits in a competitive situation. A business firm does not know what its competitors may do, but it must plan its moves to offset those of its opponents. For example, if the firm's goal is to increase sales, it may be able to do so by lowering prices, by launching an advertising campaign, or by employing more salespersons. The firm does not know what its competitors will do to offset any one or a combination of its moves, but it can make any number of assumptions and by mathematical computations arrive at a plan that indicates maximum profit potential. This decision may well determine the sales budget and most of the other budgets as well.

Simulation

Simulation provides a technique for observing the interaction of a number of important elements in a business problem. Various combinations of factors are studied in an attempt to see what will happen if some factors remain constant and others change. If these decisions were actually made one at a time, the possibility of expensive mistakes and the time required to note results would discourage making such experiments. By creating a model and by using a computer, the interaction of any number of variables can be observed promptly and without any danger of losing money. For instance, a Kent State

University economist developed a forecasting model employing 12,000 equations and 8,500 economic indicators.

In recent years several large corporations have sought to combine economic forecasting and budgeting with simulation into a unified **corporate financial model**. In one case a leading forest products producer assigned a group of economists, mathematicians, and financial analysts to a two-year project in building a corporate financial model.

Linear Programming

Linear programming is a mathematical device for determining the best way to allocate a limited amount of resources. In a linear programming problem all the relationships are expressed as linear or straight-line functions; that is, if it takes four sales calls to make one sale, then it takes eight sales calls to make two sales. Since in most problems several linear functions are present, a computer is generally used to perform the complex calculations.

Linear programming can be used to resolve problems such as the assignment of salespersons, location of facilities, and the nutrient mix of livestock feed. For example, a problem of the H. J. Heinz Company was that its eastern plants could not meet the market demand for ketchup while its western facilities produced more than the market required. With the help of linear programming, the firm developed a shipping schedule which provided the most economical way of matching the output of its six plants to the needs of its nearly 70 warehouses.

Queuing Theory

Queuing theory is a mathematical technique for solving problems caused by waiting lines wherever they may occur. It was originally developed in an attempt to determine the amount of central switching which was needed for the efficient operation of a telephone system. Queuing theory attempts to minimize expenditures by determining the proper balance between the cost of service and the cost of the waiting line.

To illustrate, one company's problem was that at lunch time employees from several floors took the elevators to the company cafeteria. As a result, two waiting lines developed, one at the elevator and another in the cafeteria. A management consultant used queuing theory to solve this problem by designing a staggered lunch hour program for this company.

BUSINESS TERMS

QUESTIONS FOR DISCUSSION AND ANALYSIS

1. If a management plan is a more useful type of standard, why do many firms rely on a rule of thumb, industry experience, or past experience type of standard?
2. Should trade associations have as one of their major responsibilities the gathering of information which can be used by companies to determine standards of performance? Discuss.
3. What criteria should management use to determine if a standard of performance should be changed?
4. Why is an accurate sales forecast essential for a firm? How can this accuracy be enhanced?
5. Critics of budgets indicate that they are too rigid and create unnecessary pressures on operating personnel. Present a response to these critics which justifies the use of budgets.
6. Cite several examples showing how statistics are used in each of the following

three functional areas of business: marketing, production, and finance.
7. Identify several situations in business, government, or some other field where statistics can be distorted to support a particular point of view.
8. What type of presentations would you use to display the following types of statistical material: (a) sales of a company over a five-year period; (b) proportion of total sales which is accounted for by the major product lines of a company; and (c) for two different years, the number of individuals employed as service workers, schoolteachers, salespersons, farmers, clerical workers, and laborers.
9. Explain how a break-even chart could be used by the administrators of a college or university.
10. What problems could management encounter in using and relying upon a simulation to solve a business problem?

PROBLEMS AND SHORT CASES

1. The Nationwide Chair Company produces institutional furniture for schools, churches, and hospitals. The sales of its school furniture has a definite seasonal sales pattern. The state of the economy has a marked influence on the marketing of its church furniture. Over the past decade, as interest in nursing

homes and geriatric centers has increased, the sales of its hospital furniture has shown a steady upward trend.

In the past 15 years the company has grown from $2 million to over $30 million in sales. When the company was smaller, it operated with a very loose budget. In recent years expanding volume has dictated tighter controls over expenditures. At this time Nationwide management is attempting to develop a procedure for sales forecasting which will provide concrete information for the preparation of a company budget.

Recommend the forecasting techniques which the company can use to project the yearly sales for each of its three major lines of furniture.

2. The Redd Products Company has recently purchased a completely equipped factory in Minnesota from a firm which ceased operations. Since the company is a manufacturer of small boats, it is considering the production of a small aluminum fishing boat in the factory.

A careful estimate of expenses indicates that fixed costs will amount to $152,000 in the first year and that variable costs will run 80 percent of sales. The proposed selling price at the manufacturer's level for each boat is $380. The marketing manager estimates that 1,600 units can be sold in the first year.

You are requested to make a report to management on the proposed course of action. What is your recommendation? Support this with a break-even chart.

3. For the next school term prepare for yourself a management by objectives program. Identify the objectives that you desire to accomplish during the next term. If possible, include objectives related to your college courses, work experiences, and extracurricular activities. For each objective that you list, identify an appropriate measure of performance.

25 *Business Law*

Irv Cohen was a partner in the B & C Plumbing Company. On March 31 he signed a contract for $2,800.00 to install by June 30 a specific make and model of a furnace in a new house under construction. B & C immediately ordered the furnace only to receive word from the manufacturer that delivery could not be made before August 1. When this information was conveyed to the contractor, his response was an emphatic "Either install the furnace as agreed or I'll sue you for damages." Cohen then contacted a lawyer who indicated that the contract was valid. Now he dreaded telling his partner about his mistake.

Law consists of constitutions, statutes, court decisions, rulings, and regulations that are administered by officials and enforced by various types of courts. **Business law** is concerned with the segment of the entire legal system that provides for a smooth and orderly flow of business transactions and the settlement of disputes concerning them that occasionally arise. It provides fixed rules of conduct that society, through the legal process, has decided are right and just in the conduct of business affairs.

Because ignorance of the law is no excuse, the managers of all firms need to have a general knowledge of business law. A partner should know that in signing a contract for the partnership he or she is legally binding all partners. A firm making shipments f.o.b. destination must realize that it will have to guard against losses incurred prior to delivery of the goods to the buyer.

In addition to a rudimentary and basic knowledge of business law, an owner or manager should also be aware that professional advice should be sought on many occasions. For example, a lawyer should be consulted when real estate is purchased, when articles of partnership are drawn up, or when a court appearance is required. Large corporations have so much legal work that they customarily maintain a legal staff; medium-sized firms frequently have a continuing relationship with a law firm on a retaining-fee basis; and small businesses normally employ a lawyer only when a need for legal assistance arises.

Following a brief description of law in the United States, this chapter will examine the various areas that comprise the scope of business law. It should be noted that legislation regulating business is not included. Some of these state and federal laws have already been discussed in previous chapters and others will be explained in Chapter 26.

LAW IN THE UNITED STATES

As a background to a consideration of the specific areas of business law, it is important to understand how law operates in this country. Therefore, our legal systems, types of courts, and legal procedures will be described and the differences between torts and crimes clarified.

Legal Systems

There are essentially two legal systems in operation throughout the world: civil law and common law. **Civil law** is based on codes which consist of compilations of laws, rules, and regulations. The Ten Commandments can be classed as civil law, and ancient Roman law was codified. The Code Napoleon was compiled in France in 1804. Today the legal systems of many European countries are based on civil law; and in this country Louisiana, long under the domination of France, still uses some civil law.

Common law began in England centuries ago. Considering the relationship of the thirteen colonies with that country, the United States logically inherited this system when it became an independent nation. A basic premise of **common law** is that each decision rendered by a court becomes a precedent for successive cases of a similar nature, which is known as the doctrine of **stare decisis**, a Latin phrase meaning "to stand by decided matters." Originally court decisions were based on custom, tradition, or on the few laws that had been enacted. Over the years these decisions, modified by changing times, found their way into constitutions and statutes drawn up or enacted by the people or their duly elected representatives. Further interpretation then followed, creating more precedents for guidance in subsequent decisions or as a foundation for further legislation.

Common law is frequently called unwritten law or case law. The term case law is in contrast to statutory law, which is written law as embodied in acts passed by federal, state, or local legislative bodies. Today the distinction between case law and statutory law, or even between common law and civil law, is inconsequential since practically every conceivable situation has been the subject of legislation.

Court Systems

Two court systems exist in the United States: the federal court system and the state court system (see Figure 25-1). If a case involves an alleged violation of a federal law or interstate commerce, it is heard in a federal court. Most legal disputes, however, are of such a nature that they are tried in state courts.

In both systems when a court has the authority to hear a case for the first time, it is known as a **court of original jurisdiction**. In the federal system the U.S. district courts and special courts, as well as the United States Supreme Court in a few instances, are courts of original jurisdiction. In the state systems the lower courts, and occasionally the state supreme court, are courts of original jurisdiction.

After a case has been decided by a lower court, the loser may appeal the decision to a higher court if it can be alleged that a principle of law has been violated. A court that has authority to review decisions reached in a lower court is known as an **appellate court**. If an appellate court believes that the case was improperly tried in the first place, it may dismiss the previous decision or refer it to the original court for a retrial. The United States Supreme Court is the highest appellate court for federal matters, and the supreme court of a state is the highest court for disputes with no federal implications.

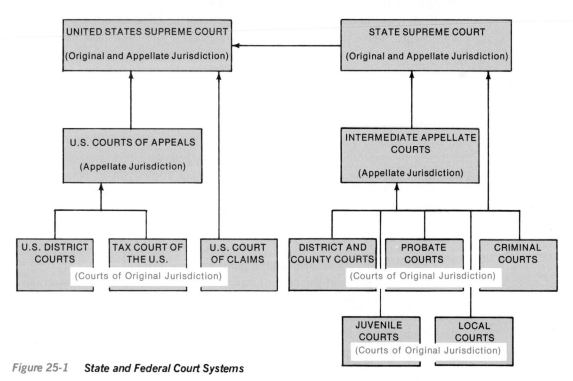

Figure 25-1 **State and Federal Court Systems**

One of the problems in resolving disputes brought before state courts has been the lack of uniformity among the laws of the 50 states. To improve this situation, a National Conference of Commissioners on Uniform State Laws was formed several years ago with representatives from each state. This Conference promotes uniformity in state laws and over a period of years has been successful in securing the passage by many state legislatures of a number of uniform laws.

In 1957 the National Conference of Commissioners on Uniform State Laws in conjunction with the American Law Institute drafted a Uniform Commercial Code. One of the stated purposes of this Code was to simplify, clarify, and modernize the law governing commercial transactions. It has been adopted in every state except Louisiana. In the ensuing discussion the provisions of this Code, where applicable, have been followed.

Legal Procedures

A businessperson who has been wronged, either because another party has broken a law or has taken an unfair advantage, may initiate legal action. The wronged individual is called the **plaintiff**, and the party accused of the wrong is known as the **defendant**. The plaintiff's attorney files a complaint with the proper court and a **summons** is issued, which requires the defendant to appear in this court to answer the charges.

If the case involves a point of fact, it will be tried before a jury unless both parties waive this privilege. Assuming that a jury does hear the facts as presented by witnesses for both parties, it renders a decision in favor of the plaintiff or defendant. If a jury does not hear the case, the decision is rendered by the presiding judge.

The above procedures apply to all types of legal cases other than those involving a crime. If a law is broken, the individual responsible can be arrested by a police officer and required to furnish bond or go to jail. For example, a dealer in radio and TV sets might be charged with receiving and selling stolen merchandise. If when brought to trial a conviction is obtained, the chances are that the judge will levy a fine and impose a jail sentence.

Torts and Crimes

Laws that apply primarily to the general public are not usually recognized as separate segments of the area of business law. At the same time, such laws frequently affect the conduct of businesspersons or provide them with protection and may be extremely important to their success or failure. Two such classifications are the law of torts and criminal law. It is essential that the business applications of these laws as well as the laws covering specific types of business transactions be understood.

BUSINESS TORTS

A **tort** is a private wrong resulting from a breach of duty created by law. Torts are primarily concerned with moral wrongs that one person may do to cause damage or loss to another. In business transactions torts arise from slander, libel, fraud, and the infringement of patents, copyrights, and trademarks. A person engaged in business may not indulge in deceit, make libelous statements, induce someone to break a contract, make threats, try to intimidate suppliers, or, in general, engage in unfair trade practices. For example, a restaurant owner in a small town repeatedly and untruthfully claimed that a rival establishment served horsemeat. It was proved that the intent was to destroy a competitor's business, and the restaurant owner was forced to pay damages.

A particularly vulnerable area for many businesses is the possibility of the infringement of patents, copyrights, and trademarks. If the federal government grants a patent, it gives the holder the exclusive right to its use for 17 years. Copyrights are good for 28 years and may be renewed for a like period. A registered trademark does not have an expiration date. Such well-known names as Kodak, Nabisco, and Frigidaire are the property of the corporations that registered these names, and others may not copy them or use any similar name that might mislead the public. Whether or not an infringement is deliberate or unintentional, the holder of a patent, a copyright, or a trademark can sue for damages, as it is the responsibility of each business to be sure that it does not commit torts of this nature.

BUSINESS CRIMES

A **crime** is a public wrong in that it violates a law that has been passed prohibiting certain conduct considered to be detrimental to the welfare of the state. As related to business, it includes forging checks or receipts, operating lotteries, selling goods on a short weight or measure basis, making fraudulent use of the post office, extortion, embezzlement, and bribery. For example, Congress has enacted legislation prohibiting the use of the mails to defraud. A promoter mailed literature to a "sucker" list describing a nonexistent company with an invitation to subscribe to shares of stock. Following a complaint from an individual who lost a sizable sum of money, the promoter was investigated by postal authorities, arrested, convicted, and imprisoned.

A crime can also be a tort and, obviously, some torts can also be crimes. Slander, for example, is a criminal offense in some states although generally it is thought of as a private rather than a public wrong. A distinction between the two types of offenses is that the state will bring an action to enforce a law when a crime has been committed, whereas torts require the injured party to bring an action against the offender. In some instances one action may follow the other if the wrong or injury is both a crime and a tort.

The major topics that are generally accepted as comprising the area of business law are contracts, agency, negotiable instruments,[1] bailments, sales, suretyship and guaranty, property, bankruptcy, partnerships, and corporations. Partnerships and corporations have been adequately covered in previous chapters. An examination of each of the other topics will indicate the types of legal information that the average individual engaged in business should understand. It will also furnish some indication of the importance to business of a comprehensive legal system.

Contracts

A **contract** is a voluntary agreement between two or more competent persons by which, for a consideration, one party acquires the right to have the other party do or not do some lawful act. In a general sense, the entire field of business law is one of contracts because agreements between parties are essential to practically all business transactions. This subject therefore is not discussed as something apart from other applications of business law but rather as a fundamental background. The following features of contracts will explain the terms used in the above definition as well as discuss other aspects of this important area of business law: (1) voluntary agreement, (2) competent persons, (3) consideration, (4) lawful acts, (5) forms of contracts, and (6) performance, discharge, and remedies.

VOLUNTARY AGREEMENT

The essence of an agreement is an offer and an acceptance. The offer must be communicated in definite terms and with the intent to create a contract, and the acceptance must be indicated within a reasonable time or before the offer is withdrawn. Any means of communication may be used and, if the mail or telegraph is involved, the contract is in force just as soon as the acceptance is deposited with the post office or telegraph company. A reply that fails to conform to the exact terms of the offer, known as a **counteroffer**, does not constitute an acceptance because there is no mutual agreement or common understanding of the subject matter of the contract.

Contracts must also involve agreements in which both parties act in good faith and of their own free will. The term "voluntary" is used in the sense that there has been no fraud, duress, or undue influence brought to bear on one or the other party. Tricking someone into signing a written contract or

---

[1]State laws applicable to negotiable instruments are contained in Article 3 of the Uniform Commercial Code which is titled "Commercial Paper." In the financial world, however, the term "commercial paper" has a more restrictive use as explained in Chapter 18.

threatening a person at the point of a gun to agree to a contract will provide grounds for relief. Even some mutual mistakes, such as agreeing to sell a building that, unknown to either party, burned down the night before will void the contract.

COMPETENT PERSONS

Most people are legally competent to enter into a contract, but some groups, such as insane persons, are without the capacity to make a contract. For many years most states classified persons under 21 years of age as **minors**, who could not make enforceable contracts with the possible exception of buying necessities. Because the right to vote in national elections has been granted to 18 year olds, many states have reduced the classification of minors to those under 18.

An exception to the inability of minors to make enforceable contracts is contained in the Uniform Minor Student Capacity to Borrow Act that has been enacted by several states. This law should be of particular interest to many college freshmen. It provides that a loan made to a minor for the purpose of furthering his or her education at an institution of higher learning is enforceable with the same effect as if the student were an adult at the time of the execution of the loan agreement, provided, however, that the lender has on file at the time of making the loan a certificate stating that the borrower is enrolled or has been accepted for enrollment at a specific institution.

CONSIDERATION

Consideration, which is something of value received by one party or parted with by the other party, is essential to every contract. If John pays Sam $50 for an option to purchase property at a certain price within 30 days, the payment of the $50 is the consideration for this option contract. Sam gives up his right to sell the property for 30 days and John parts with $50. Also, any possible gain to one party or loss to another will serve as satisfactory consideration. For example, a wealthy uncle agrees to pay $1,000 to his niece if she does not smoke until she is 21 years of age. The fact that the young woman gives up a legal right provides adequate consideration. An offer to sell merchandise at a stated price, followed by an acceptance, includes adequate consideration.

LAWFUL ACTS

The subject matter of a contract must involve lawful acts. A contract made with a person in which a promise is made to burn down a building illegally is not enforceable, nor is one with the intent to restrain trade unduly. Other contracts that are against public policy or that would violate specific laws are not enforceable. For example, most states have laws against gambling; and promises to pay gambling debts, whether written or oral, are not enforceable. Likewise, if a lender attempts to collect interest in excess of the legal rate permitted in the state, as a general rule this individual forfeits the right to collect any interest, although the debt is still owed.

FORMS OF CONTRACTS

Most contracts do not need to be written, and oral agreements are fully enforceable although there may be difficulty in proving the facts. Under what is known as the **Statute of Frauds**, certain types of contracts must be in writing, including sales of real estate, of personal property in excess of a certain value (usually $500), and agreements that cannot be performed within one year. The reason for the unusual name for this rule of law dates back to England when persons wishing to prove the validity of an oral contract would induce friends and relatives to give false testimony in court.

Both oral and written contracts may be either express or implied. An **express contract** is one in which the terms have been agreed upon such as a business signing an order to buy 100 units at $2.00 each to be delivered within ten days and payment to be made at the end of the month. An **implied contract** is one based on the conduct of the parties. For example, when an individual calls a broker requesting that the broker buy 100 shares of a named stock at the market price, there is an implied contract that is just as enforceable as an express contract.

PERFORMANCE, DISCHARGE, AND REMEDIES

Most contracts are discharged by full performance on the part of both parties. Some contracts are not completed, however, and this condition may or may not give rise to a court action. In some instances the defendant may be excused under the operation of a law, such as bankruptcy; or if special conditions, such as illness, have arisen in a personal service contract, the courts may excuse performance.

When a contract has been broken, the remedy is to obtain from a court an order that requires the payment of damages or, in a few instances, compliance with the terms of the contract. If damages are in order, the court issues a **judgment** in favor of the plaintiff, which can be executed against the defendant. If necessary, a sheriff will sell enough property of the debtor to satisfy the judgment.

Of interest to many businesspersons is the situation in which a person against whom a judgment has been rendered has no real or personal property that can be sold to satisfy the claim. If this person is a wage earner, it is possible in most states to force the employer to pay the amount owed by withholding a portion of the wage usually paid to the employee each payday. This is known as **garnishment**. Because a federal law limits the use of this collection device, it is not an entirely satisfactory way to collect a debt, particularly if the amount is sizable. The legislation passed by the Congress exempts weekly take home pay up to $63, and only 25 percent of weekly take-home pay in excess of $84 can be garnisheed.

Agency

An **agent** is one who is authorized by another person, known as the **principal**, to deal with third persons on behalf of the principal. By contrast, an employee, sometimes identified as a **servant**, does not have authority to act for an employer in contract situations. It should also be understood that the word agency is sometimes used to denote a type of franchise relationship, such as an automobile agency. Agency, in its legal sense, is a vital necessity to the business world, particularly for large firms, as otherwise it would be virtually impossible to delegate authority.

Principals are liable for all acts of their agents within the actual or apparent scope of the authority vested in the agents. For example, a bank officer made a $50,000 loan to a business. This amount exceeded the officer's authority, but since the business was unaware of any restrictions, the bank could not reject the commitment.

Agents are bound to follow instructions, to serve loyally, to render proper accounts, and to use intelligence and due care in the acts they perform. If they exceed their authority, they may become personally liable to their principals.

Negotiable Instruments

A negotiable instrument is a form of business paper that can be transferred from one party to another as a substitute for money. Under Article 3 of the Uniform Commercial Code, negotiable instruments can be classified as drafts, checks, certificates of deposit, and notes.

UCC REQUIREMENTS FOR NEGOTIABLE INSTRUMENTS

The Uniform Commercial Code provides that to be negotiable an instrument must conform to all of the following requirements:

1. It must be in writing and signed by the maker or drawer.
2. It must contain an unconditional promise or order to pay a sum certain in money.

3. It must be payable on demand, or at a definite future date.
4. It must be payable "to order" or "to bearer."
5. Where the instrument is addressed to a drawee or payee, this individual must be named or otherwise indicated with reasonable certainty.

Some of the acceptable forms of negotiable instruments, such as checks, promissory notes, drafts, and trade acceptances, have been described in Chapter 18.

Some instruments are not negotiable because they lack one or more of the above stated requirements. An I.O.U., for example, cannot be transferred to a third party because it does not contain the words "to order" or "to bearer." A note payable "when convenient" would not be negotiable because there is no definite future date. It should be noted, however, that a nonnegotiable instrument may be enforceable as an ordinary contract.

A person who receives a negotiable instrument is a **holder in due course** if the instrument is complete and regular on its face, if it is acquired before it is overdue, if it was taken in good faith and for value, and if there was available at the time of negotiation no knowledge of any infirmity in the instrument or defects in the title of the person from whom it was received. For example, when a merchant accepts a check from a student written by a parent, the chances are close to one hundred percent that the retailer is a holder in due course.

TYPES OF ENDORSEMENTS

By signing his or her name on the back of a negotiable instrument, whatever rights were originally granted to the payee can be transferred to a third party. This act is known as an endorsement[2] and can consist of the payee's name only, or certain words can be added above the signature. A **blank endorsement**, which consists merely of the appropriate signature, is the most widely used method of transferring a negotiable instrument. Care should be taken to make sure that the signature on the back conforms to the name of the payee stated on the face of the check, note, or draft. Care should also be taken not to lose the negotiable instrument after it has been endorsed in blank.

When words are added above the signature, the usual effect is to place some restriction on complete negotiability. A **special endorsement** specifies a named person to receive the negotiable instrument. An example would be "Pay to the order of Florence Jones" followed by the signature of the payee. A **restrictive endorsement** limits the purpose for which the endorsement was made, which most commonly requires that the instrument be deposited in the individual's or the firm's bank account. A **qualified endorsement** relieves the

[2]The spelling *indorsement* is used in the Uniform Commercial Code.

endorser from the usual contingent liability in case the maker defaults. For example, a check might be drawn in favor of a lawyer with instructions to endorse it to a third party when certain papers are delivered. Under such circumstances the lawyer should not be liable if subsequently the check is returned to the third party marked **N.S.F.** (not sufficient funds). Figure 25-2 illustrates each of these four types of endorsements.

Bailments

A **bailment** is a relationship in which one party, known as the **bailor**, leaves personal property with another, known as the **bailee**, for a certain purpose with the understanding that the goods will be returned to the bailor or delivered to someone else after the purpose is fulfilled. There is no passage of title, which means that a bailment is not a sale. Leaving a watch at a jeweler's shop for repairs or with a pawnbroker as security for a loan are examples of bailments.

As a general rule bailees are required to exercise reasonable care of the personal properties entrusted to their care. In return, in the case of business transactions, the bailor usually makes a payment for services rendered. Use of a parking lot or a public warehouse involves a fee paid by the bailor to the bailee.

The question of responsibility for damages varies with circumstances. In the dry cleaning business the firm is liable for damages resulting from negligence, but not from defects in a garment. Hotels attempt to avoid liability for losses by notifying guests to deposit valuables in their safes. Railroads and

Blank Endorsement

Restrictive Endorsement

Special Endorsement

Qualified Endorsement

Figure 25-2 *Various Types of Endorsements*

other forms of public transportation must pay for loss or damage to goods in transit unless excused for such reasons as a flood (act of God) or seizure (act of public authority or enemy).

Sales

A **sale** is an exchange of goods or personal property between two parties for money or other consideration paid immediately or to be paid in the future. It involves a contract and most of the comments already made about contracts are applicable to sales. In fact, sales are sometimes considered to be a specialized branch of the law of contracts. A **bill of sale**, which is a document signed by the seller giving evidence of the transfer of title to the buyer, may or may not be required. Sometimes it is a necessity for certain types of property; for example, a bill of sale may be required to obtain a certificate of title for a motor vehicle.

A substantial number of the legal problems that the average businessperson faces are concerned with sales. Manufacturers buy raw materials and then sell finished goods while retailers buy and sell the same merchandise. If retailers sell on the installment plan, they have the problem of repossession when payments are not made on schedule, a situation discussed in Chapter 18. Two other major problems that are created by sales are concerned with the (1) risk of loss and (2) warranties.

RISK OF LOSS

If merchandise is lost somewhere along the way from producer to consumer, there remains the question as to who bears this loss. For example, if a customer buys a pane of glass at a retail hardware store which, following payment for it, is dropped and broken, who assumes this loss? Since title generally passes immediately in a cash transaction, the purchaser in this illustration must absorb the loss. When goods are shipped f.o.b. factory, the risk of loss passes from the producer at the time they are delivered to a common carrier. As mentioned earlier in this chapter, if the terms are f.o.b. destination, the purchaser does not bear any risk until the goods are delivered to the purchaser's place of business. Sometimes a buyer specifies a **c.i.f.** contract, which means that the invoice covers the cost of the goods, insurance on them, and the freight charges, thus shifting the risk of loss to an insurance company for the time the goods are in transit.

On occasion manufacturers and wholesalers wish to sell their products through dealers whose credit standing does not warrant the use of an openbook account. In this case, goods can be sent on **consignment**, which means that title remains in the hands of the shipper, known as the **consignor**, until such time as they are sold by the retailer, called the **consignee**. The fact that title does not pass until the merchandise is sold is important to the retailer who neither needs to insure the goods against fire and other hazards nor pay personal property taxes on such merchandise. For like reasons, the ownership is important to the wholesaler or manufacturer. Other advantages to a manufacturer or wholesaler of selling on consignment are the right to repossess unsold goods should the retailer become bankrupt and the right to control the price at which the merchandise can be sold.

WARRANTIES

An **express warranty** is a statement on the part of the seller that the goods have certain characteristics, such as quality, which is made to induce the buyer to make the purchase. If an antique dealer states that a chest of drawers is over 100 years old and if it is subsequently discovered that 10 years is a more accurate estimate, the dealer can be sued for damages.

An **implied warranty** covers title and quality. The buyer has a right to assume that the seller delivered clear title to the goods and that the merchandise agrees with a sample or description and is usable for the purposes for which it was sold. A purchaser of stolen goods must return them to the original owner or pay for them, but has a right of action against the seller because there was an implied warranty of clear title.

Warranties have assumed increasing importance in recent years as a facet of the consumer protection movement. To attract buyers, many manufacturers advertise warranties such as free parts for an automobile for one year or 12,000 miles. Rulings by governmental bodies backed by legislation require that warranties be written in plain English so that they can be understood by the purchasers of these goods. The old theory of caveat emptor, or let the buyer beware, is being replaced by laws and court decisions favoring consumers who seek damages because products do not conform to express and implied warranties.

Suretyship and Guaranty

Suretyship is a contract by which a third party, known as a **surety**, agrees to be answerable for the payment of a debt or performance of some act or duty in case another person fails to meet the obligation. **Guaranty** refers to a contract under which a third person, known as a **guarantor**, undertakes to perform a contract or to fulfill an obligation of another provided the individual who was responsible for discharging the contract is unable to do so. The main distinction between the two is that suretyship involves primary responsibility coextensive with that of the debtor, whereas guaranty is a secondary liability.

The surety agrees to pay the debt or discharge the obligation if the principal does not, while the guarantor must discharge the obligation only if the principal cannot do so.

An example of the difference in responsibilities of a surety and a guarantor is afforded by the contrast between the comaker of a note and an accommodation endorser. An individual who signs a note on its face, even though he or she has no personal interest in it, is equally liable with the debtor who originated the instrument. On the other hand, if a person merely endorses a note, the holder at the due date must first look to the maker for payment, and only after the maker has failed to pay can the holder collect from the endorser. A surety need not be notified if the debtor defaults because the obligation to pay at maturity is just as direct on the third party as on the maker, whereas to be held for payment a guarantor must be notified of a default.

Sureties, and guarantors too, may be individuals or corporations. For example, a father wishing to assist his son in starting a retail business might agree to be responsible for the payment of invoices covering merchandise shipped to the new store. As noted in Chapter 21, there are surety companies in the insurance business who, in return for a premium, will contract to assume, if necessary, the obligations of the party purchasing the policy. The most common use of surety insurance is made by building contractors who are required to furnish a bond guaranteeing that they will complete a construction project according to plans and within the time allowed.

Property

Ownership of, or an interest in, anything subject to ownership is known as **property**. Businesspersons are vitally concerned with the laws on this subject because their daily transactions and the places in which they are carried on directly or indirectly involve rights and interests in property. When they buy merchandise, any subsequent loss that may occur falls on them even though payments have not yet been made for the goods. If they improve buildings on which they have a lease, such improvements become the property of the owner when the lease expires.

The term property, when it refers to possessions or things owned, may be given several classifications, but the most important distinction from a business viewpoint is that of real property and personal property. **Real property** normally refers to land and buildings or to things immovable in general. **Personal property** refers to things owned that are movable. Personal property may be further subdivided into **tangibles** and **intangibles**, the former referring to merchandise in stock, fixtures, machinery and equipment, and the latter to stocks and bonds, notes and checks, bank accounts, and accounts receivable. Businesspersons are interested in these classifications because, if for no other reason, they may be required to pay taxes at different rates on each grouping.

OWNERSHIP

Persons who have every possible right that can be attached to ownership have absolute ownership. In the case of real property, this is known as an **estate in fee simple**. Aside from the various types of restrictions that may be imposed by government, owners may use their properties as they wish. Properties can be sold, given away, left to heirs by drawing up a will to this effect, leased or rented, or used as security to borrow money. A customer who owns a fair amount of property usually has a satisfactory credit standing, but a businessperson will do well to remember the rights of this individual concerning the property that has been used as a basis for granting credit. If it is given away or used as security for a loan, it is no longer available to satisfy claims of general creditors.

Ownership rights in real property that fall short of the extent of absolute ownership are usually for a fixed period of time. A common example is the relation of landlord to tenant. When a proprietor leases a store building for 10 years, the tenant has a right in the property for that period of time if the stipulated rent is paid. Repairs and improvements that the tenant may make will usually revert to the owner at the conclusion of the 10 years.

SECURITY FOR LOANS

Property is frequently used as security for the extension of credit. If personal property is involved, a financing statement such as that described in Chapter 18 may be used or a chattel mortgage might be issued. Under the latter option, the buyer acquires title to as well as physical possession of the goods and, if the schedule of payments is completed, the mortgage is canceled. If the prescribed payments are not made, the seller can take legal steps to regain possession of the goods. Such an action is known as a suit in **replevin**. When intangible personal property, such as stocks and bonds, have been used as security for a loan, no mortgage is necessary because the lender can take physical possession of the securities.

If real property is used as security, the obligation created is a real estate mortgage. This mortgage, as well as a chattel mortgage, should be recorded in a county courthouse. If the loan is not paid in accordance with the terms, the mortgage is usually foreclosed and title is transferred to the creditor.

Bankruptcy

As noted in Chapter 19, an insolvent firm may go into bankruptcy on its own initiative, which is called **voluntary bankruptcy**, or it may be declared a bankrupt by a federal court, which is known as **involuntary bankruptcy**. In either case, the court-appointed referee calls the creditors together and they elect a trustee. As a general rule, the trustee then liquidates the assets and distributes the proceeds.

It would be very rare for the trustee to be able to pay all creditors in full, for a bankrupt owes more than is owned. The federal bankruptcy law has established a system of priority of claims that recognizes five classes of **preferred creditors** as follows:

1. The actual and necessary costs of preserving the estate subsequent to the filing of the petition.
2. Wages due to laborers, clerks, traveling or city salespersons, or servants, that have been earned within three months prior to bankruptcy, not to exceed $600 to each claimant.
3. Reasonable expenses of creditors in opposing an arrangement or a plan for the discharge of a bankrupt.
4. Taxes due the United States or any state or subdivision.
5. Debts owed to any person who by law is entitled to priority.

Court costs are included in (1) as are fees for the referee, trustee, and lawyers. Number (5) most frequently involves the holders of a first mortgage on the bankrupt's property. If this property is sold for more than the mortgage, the preferred creditors will be paid in full. If the property brings less than the amount of the mortgage, the lenders will receive the entire proceeds and join the general creditors for the balances due them.

Assuming that there is money available for distribution after preferred claims are settled, the **general creditors** will receive a percentage of their established claims. A final accounting is then filed with the court, and the debtor is legally discharged from further payments on the amounts owed. Although there are a few liabilities that cannot be discharged in a bankruptcy proceeding, such as alimony or child support payments, in general the bankrupt can start a new business or take employment with a clean financial slate.

A few types of businesses, such as banks, cannot become voluntary bankrupts nor can they be forced into bankruptcy. Other classifications, such as farmers and wage earners, can become voluntary bankrupts but cannot be forced into bankruptcy by creditors. Despite these exceptions, over 200,000 actions each year indicate that bankruptcy laws have wide applications.

BUSINESS TERMS

QUESTIONS FOR DISCUSSION AND ANALYSIS

1. Why should managers of businesses be expected to have a general knowledge of business law? Can't all legal problems be referred to a lawyer?
2. If a judge uses extremely poor judgment in making a decision, does this ruling create a precedent under common law that may influence subsequent cases?
3. Does the existence of appellate courts have a good or detrimental effect on courts of original jurisdiction?
4. Would it be illegal for a firm leasing a copier from IBM to advertise that it will make Xerox copies for seven cents each?
5. Why was 21 originally chosen as the age at which a minor became legally competent to make all contracts? Why is this age now being reduced to 18?
6. Are salespersons in retail stores agents of the establishments that employ them or are they servants? Does the type of merchandise sold make a difference?
7. Blank endorsements are widely used. Is this because they require minimum effort or because they are entirely satisfactory?
8. Do most consumers place considerable reliance on warranties when they purchase such items as automobiles and home appliances?
9. From the lender's point of view, what kind of property would be most satisfactory as security for a loan?
10. Why should a business or a person who owes debts be able to discharge these by bankruptcy proceedings? Does a moral obligation to repay still exist?

PROBLEMS AND SHORT CASES

1. a. For several years Vince Hart had rented the building in which he operated a retail shoe store. Fearing an increase in rent, he decided to make an offer to buy the property from the landlady, Clara Ronson. Mrs. Ronson agreed to sell the property for $100,000, an amount in excess of Hart's cash resources but one that he felt he could raise given a little time. Consequently he signed an agreement to buy within 90 days for $100,000 and sent it to Mrs. Ronson with a check for $50, which she cashed. Shortly before the 90 days had expired, Hart was able to complete financial arrangements and asked Mrs. Ronson to

name a time and place for signing the necessary papers. She replied that she had sold the property for $150,000 a week earlier and that his $50 was in the mail. Hart then instituted a suit to compel Mrs. Ronson to sell him the property for $100,000. What decision should the judge render?

  b. A student delivered a dark dress to a dry cleaning outlet near her residence hall and explained that she had spilled some fingernail polish on the front of the dress. After the dress was cleaned the polish was gone, but in its place was a white area so noticeable that the garment could not be worn. The student felt that she was entitled to payment for the dress, but the dry cleaning firm insisted that the material was faulty as it had used only solvents regularly employed to remove fingernail polish. Is the student entitled to a fair price for the dress?

2. Five years ago R. W. Fox quit his job as a cook and incorporated a restaurant called Red Fox, Inc. Fox's capital was adequate to finance start-up costs, and for three years the restaurant was profitable. For the past two years, however, competition and increased costs caused losses to the point where the firm cannot now pay its bills, its help, and the monthly mortgage payments. Consequently, the firm filed a petition in bankruptcy.

   The trustee elected by the creditors found that the corporate books showed the following:

Assets		Liabilities	
Cash	$ 110	Wages payable	$ 600
Inventories	1,850	Taxes payable	2,100
Fixtures and equipment	10,140	Accounts payable	14,500
Land and buildings (net)	60,000	Mortgage payable	78,000
	$72,100		$95,200

The trustee sold the inventories for $890, the fixtures and equipment for $7,300, and the building for $50,000. The cost of the sales, lawyer's fees, and court costs amounted to $3,150.

Compute the amount available to the general creditors. How much did they receive on a cents-on-the-dollar basis?

3. The building in which Leon Cline worked provided three floors as parking spaces for automobiles. Cline paid the owners of the building, the Standard Realty Corporation, $28 a month as rent for a parking space. He signed a standard contract that stated, "Ignition keys must be left in the car at all times in order that management may move your car if necessary to attain maximum use of the parking spaces."

   On several occasions Cline shopped during the noon hour and placed his purchases in his car. The parking attendant allowed him to lock the car and keep the key. Over a period of time, this practice became a regular procedure and was extended to the morning as well as the afternoon hours.

   One day Cline's automobile was missing when he was ready to drive home and it became obvious that it had been stolen. When the Standard Realty Corp. refused to pay the value of the stolen vehicle, Cline filed a suit on behalf of his insurance company asking for a judgment in the amount of the value of the automobile, court costs, and lawyer's fees.

   What claims could Cline make and what defenses could the Standard Realty Corp. offer? What decision should the judge render?

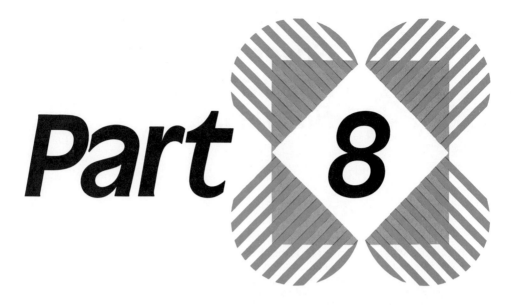

Part 8

Regulations, Multinationalism, and the Future

Although the chapters in Part 8 identify separate bodies of knowledge, they represent a prologue to the future of business. In the years ahead there will be increases in the regulation of business, taxation, and multinational trade. Each of these three factors will have a greater effect on managerial decisions.

Chapter 26 explores the impact of governmental regulations on business. A distinction is made between regulated competitive businesses and regulated industries. The body of law which affects competitive businesses is examined, and the characteristics of regulated industries are noted.

In Chapter 27 the principles of taxation are enunciated. The types of federal, state, and local taxes are discussed as they relate to business. A final section illustrates the influence of taxes on business decisions.

The importance of multinational trade and its implications to society are described in Chapter 28. The significance of the multinational corporation in worldwide business is clarified. This chapter also examines the reasons for erecting barriers to diminish trade and for establishing treaties to enhance trade.

Chapter 29 provides a point of departure into the future world of business. The role of the futurists in business and the techniques and information which a futurist uses to project future events are explained. A study of future expectations reveals that the environmental trends of the present serve as a prelude to the future.

26 Governmental Regulation of Business

The United States Department of Justice has asserted in court that it is necessary to break up the Internation Business Machines Corporation in order to achieve competitive conditions in the data processing industry. Frank T. Cary, Chairman of the Board of the corporation, stated in the 1974 Annual Report: "IBM continues to believe that there is no correlation between bigness and badness, or between success and monopoly. In its brief filed on January 15, 1975, IBM characterized the lawsuit as an attempt to change the whole thrust and purpose of the Sherman Act so that it fetters rather than encourages competition."

Among the powers the Constitution of the United States gave the federal government were the rights to tax and to regulate commerce among the several states. These two broad areas provide much, although not all, of the bases on which federal business regulation depends. Each of our 50 states has a constitution; and the right to regulate intrastate activities of business is at least as extensive, if not more so, as allowed by the federal Constitution. If laws regulating business passed by the Congress and by state legislatures are constitutional, which appropriate courts will determine, and if they are correctly enforced by administrative agencies, businesses must abide by their restrictions.

Although there never was any doubt about the right of government to regulate business, the federal government showed little interest in this subject for approximately 100 years. This same attitude was also true of the states although a few had exercised a measure of control over banks, insurance companies, canals, and railroads. It was essentially a century of laissez-faire capitalism that functioned smoothly because business in the United States was conducted by a large number of relatively small units. In this kind of social and economic environment, and with only the restricted use of such present-day necessities as electricity, gas, and the telephone, competition was an effective regulator of business and business practices.

Toward the close of the nineteenth century, conditions began to change. Railroads became important in the development of the country, and the need for regulating rates charged for rail transportation became apparent in the 1880s. Another development was the creation of monopolies. Competing firms turned their shares of stock over to trustees who then controlled and operated the formerly independent firms to minimize competition and maximize profits. These organizations became known as **trusts**, which were extremely successful in the oil, sugar, tobacco, and whiskey industries.

REGULATED COMPETITIVE BUSINESSES VERSUS REGULATED INDUSTRIES

When government finally decided that regulation of business was required, it became aware that it would be necessary to recognize two categories. The larger of the two categories encompassed enterprises that were expected to compete against one another with prices being determined by the forces of supply and demand operating in a competitive climate. The other included businesses such as gas, electricity, telephone, rail transportation, and similar areas in which it was in the public interest to permit monopolies to exist. For example, two telephone companies serving one community with subscribers of one unable to make a direct call to those of the other would not be satisfactory to the customers of either company.

Different methods of supervision and control were applied to each of the two types. In the case of competitive businesses, efforts were and still are directed toward enacting and enforcing laws designed to create an economic climate in which business units can and must compete in a fair and equitable manner. For businesses that function best as monopolies, specially created governmental agencies — usually called commissions — substitute for the marketplace in determining allowable prices and levels of service.

This chapter will first describe the regulation of competitive businesses at the federal level and then by state and local governments. Following this discussion, the methods and procedures used by both federal and state commissions to supervise regulated industries will be explained.

REGULATION OF COMPETITIVE BUSINESSES

The earliest laws regulating businesses, which were passed by the federal government between 1890 and 1914, were directed toward efforts to enforce competition. Laws that were directed to such functional areas of business as marketing, labor, and finance were enacted much later. The impact of most of the legislation of this type has been adequately described in previous chapters. For example, the federally prescribed minimum hourly pay rate was discussed in Chapter 14. Within recent years the federal government has passed a number of regulatory laws applying to consumer goods, as well as laws for protecting the environment as it is affected by business activities.

Federal Laws to Promote Competition

A law against trusts was the first of a series of acts and amendments passed by the Congress of the United States designed to protect the public by assuring a healthy competitive business climate. Then the emphasis in legislation shifted from monopolies to illegal or unfair trade practices, although both the Department of Justice and the Federal Trade Commission still watch for any signs of monopolistic practices. The laws in effect today that promote competition one way or another are the Sherman Antitrust Act, the Clayton Act, and the Federal Trade Commission Act.

SHERMAN ANTITRUST ACT

In 1890 the federal government moved against the trusts that had been formed by enacting the Sherman Antitrust Act. The extent of opinion favorable to such a measure can be judged by the fact that this law was passed by both houses of Congress with only one dissenting vote. It provided that "every contract, combination . . . or conspiracy in restraint of trade or commerce among the several states . . . is hereby declared to be illegal," and that "every person who shall monopolize or . . . combine or conspire to monopolize . . . shall be deemed guilty of a misdemeanor." Persons convicted of violating the act were subject to a fine not to exceed $50,000 and/or imprisonment for one year. Triple damages were to be awarded to those injured by the actions of trusts.

Adoption of the Rule of Reason. The Sherman Act was predicated on the fear, not without foundation in 1890, that large organizations were automatically detrimental to the best interests of the public. Bigness and badness were considered synonyms. The act gave the Attorney General of the United States the authority to take action against the trusts and, after extensive legal delays, most of them were broken up. The act was, however, weakened when the federal Supreme Court adopted the **rule of reason**. Under this rule a combination, contract, or conspiracy was judged as to whether or not it constituted an undue or unreasonable restraint on interstate commerce. Furthermore, as time went on, the fear of large corporations subsided as more than one giant company appeared in several industries such as steel, rubber, and oil. Today the Sherman Act is more likely to be applied to several firms who are in the same type of business and who conspire with one another.

Illegal Practices Under the Sherman Antitrust Act. One illegal device a group sometimes uses is **collusive bidding** in which supposedly competing firms either agree to submit identical prices or agree that one of them is to be the low bidder on a contract. In the latter case, geographical areas might be assigned for the exclusive benefit of each firm, resulting in a **territorial pool.** Another possibility for a conspiracy, **patent licensing**, which is an arrangement under which the owner of a patent allows others to use it upon payment of a royalty, can be illegal when used to restrain trade. Likewise, if several competing firms agree that it would be desirable to raise prices in a group consensus known as a **gentlemen's agreement**, a resulting increase in prices could be illegal if the government can prove a conspiracy in restraint of competition.

CLAYTON ACT

By 1914 it was apparent that the legislation of 1890 was not a complete answer to the trust problem. The Clayton Act was the second attempt by Congress to deal with monopolies. It was more specific than the Sherman Act and recognized that the trust problem was no longer one of size but rather one of business practices.

The act stated that it was unlawful for persons engaged in interstate commerce to "discriminate in price between different purchasers of commodities . . . where the effect of such discrimination may be substantially to lessen competition or tend to create a monopoly in any line of commerce." Exceptions could be made where such discrimination took into account differences in grade, quality, quantity, or cost, or where such discrimination was made in good faith to meet bona fide competition. The law also prohibited exclusive agreements "for the sale of goods, wares, merchandise, machinery, supplies, or other commodities . . . for use, consumption, or resale within the United States," if the result of such an agreement "may be substantially to lessen competition or tend to create a monopoly in any line of commerce." Furthermore, the act specifically prohibited **tying contracts** under which a buyer had to agree to buy other goods from the same vendor to obtain the merchandise desired.

Unlawful Practices Under the Clayton Act. The **interlocking directorate**, which exists when the majority of the members of two or more boards of directors are the same individuals, was declared unlawful if either corporation had assets in excess of $1 million and if the corporations were in competition with each other. The purchase by one corporation of another corporation's stock was prohibited if the effect was substantially to lessen competition or to tend to create a monopoly. Approximately a half century later this provision of the law was invoked against the du Pont company, which was required in 1962 to divest itself of the 63,000,000 shares of General Motors common stock that it owned. Somewhat similar to an interlocking directorate is a **community of interests**, in which a few stockholders dictate the composition of the boards of directors of two or more competing corporations.

Amendments to the Clayton Act. Two important amendments have been made to the Clayton Act. As described in detail in Chapter 11, the Robinson-Patman Act of 1936 was aimed at eliminating the favorable price treatment frequently accorded to quantity purchasers such as chain grocery companies. In 1950 the Celler-Kefauver Act prohibited mergers when the result might lessen competition or tend to create a monopoly. This law is one of the reasons for the rash of conglomerates in recent years. A company wishing to expand finds that it cannot legally acquire other firms engaged in the same line of business.

FEDERAL TRADE COMMISSION ACT

The Federal Trade Commission Act passed in September, 1914, a month earlier than the Clayton Act, provided that unfair methods of competition in commerce were illegal. To enforce this law, as well as many of the provisions of the Clayton Act, it also created the Federal Trade Commission.

The Federal Trade Commission (FTC). The FTC is a federal agency that consists of five commissioners aided by a large staff of accountants, economists, and lawyers. It investigates alleged unfair methods of competition, issues complaints against offending firms, conducts hearings, and, when necessary, issues cease and desist orders against those found guilty of engaging in forbidden practices.

Over the years the powers of the FTC have been expanded and its current activities include making surveys into various business practices, which sometimes result in "trade practice conferences" designed to secure voluntary agreement among firms in a particular industry as to what constitutes unfair competitive methods. Out of these may come a set of Trade Practice Rules that are mutually agreeable to the Commission and to the members of the trades affected. The mere fact that the FTC is in existence is a deterrent to the actions of firms that might be tempted to violate either laws or ethical principles, which is one of the reasons that the Commission is sometimes called "the policeman of the business world."

Amendment to the Federal Trade Commission Act. In 1938 the Wheeler-Lea Act was passed as an amendment to the Federal Trade Commission Act. It provided that unfair or deceptive practices that might prove harmful to the public, as well as unfair methods of competition, were illegal. It was no longer necessary to prove that competitors were injured if the unfair method was damaging to the general public.

Federal Consumer Protection Laws

In addition to the regulation of business through legislation designed to promote competition, in recent years the federal government has passed numerous laws for the specific purpose of protecting consumers. Two major categories of this type of legislation are concerned with (1) foods, drugs, and cosmetics, and (2) labeling and safety. The following applicable laws illustrate how the Congress has attempted to protect the best interests of consumers.

FOOD, DRUG, AND COSMETIC ACT

Although the Food and Drug Administration (FDA), now a part of the Department of Health, Education, and Welfare, was established in 1906, its authority was increased with the enactment of the Food, Drug, and Cosmetic Act in 1938. Powers of the FDA include insistence on sanitary methods of manufacture, purity of content, and proper labeling. The package must show the accurate weight, ingredients in proportion, and whether coloratives or preservatives have been used. Drugs must be labeled as to use and, if the drug is habit-forming, a statement to this effect must be included. New drugs cannot be distributed until they have been proved safe to use. Heavy penalties are provided with a limit of a fine of $1,000 and/or imprisonment for one year for a mere infraction of the law, and maximums of $10,000 and imprisonment for three years for deliberate intent to defraud or mislead.

Other legislation has given the Food and Drug Administration the power to control adulteration of insecticides, labeling of caustic poisons for household use, and maintenance of manufacturing standards. The FDA has authority to make semiannual inspections of drug factories, to make checks on the quality of products, and to withhold approval of new drugs until it has been demonstrated that these are safe and effective. Also, drugs already on the market can be removed from an approved list as was done in the elimination of cyclamates from many diet soft drinks.

LABELING AND SAFETY ACTS

To protect consumers against unfair or deceptive trade practices as applied to clothing, the Congress has enacted several laws requiring that labels attached to garments must show the types of materials used. The Wool Products Labeling Act of 1939 requires that each product be labeled to show the total fiber weight of the wool; whether it is new, processed, or reused; the percentage of nonwool filling; and the name of the manufacturer. The Fur Products Labeling Act of 1951 requires that the correct name of the animal that produced the fur, as well as manufacturing details, appear on the label of each such item offered for sale. Protection from burning fabrics was provided by the Federal Flammable Fabrics Act of 1953, and the Textile Fiber Products Identification Act of 1958 requires the use of labels that show the percentage of natural and synthetic fibers used in the manufacture of cloth and other materials. The protection of the public through proper labeling is further extended by the Hazardous Substances Labeling Act (1960), the Fair Packaging and Labeling Act (1966), and the requirement that cigarette packages carry a health warning.

Recent legislation designed to protect consumers has been extensive. Outstanding examples are the Child Protection and Toy Safety Act and several laws on safety devices for automobiles. Numerous federal agencies are involved and their activities cover diverse and wide-ranging fronts.

Environmental Control Laws

A relatively new direction in the federal regulation of business has been antipollution legislation covering air, water, noise, strip mining, and off-shore drilling for oil. Although states and groups of states as well as municipalities have attempted to reduce pollution for many years, it is generally agreed that federal standards will have to be established and enforced. Many businesses are substantial contributors to water and air pollution in particular; consequently, they are the target of much of the antipollution legislation discussed in Chapter 3.

To enforce the antipollution laws, an Environmental Protection Agency (EPA) was established by executive order of the President. The authority for this action was contained in a bill passed by the Congress known as the National Environmental Policy Act. This 1969 legislation created a Council on Environmental Quality (CEQ) that was to act as a policy-making group. It studies the impact of any proposal that may affect the environment such as the Alaska pipeline. Of late its findings are sometimes at cross-purposes with the needs of this country for local energy sources.

State Laws and Regulations

Cities, villages, townships, counties, parishes, and other governing units within a state are created and exist under the constitution of that state. Consequently, state regulation of business encompasses all legislation passed by the state legislature and any of its political subdivisions that have legislative authority. As long as these laws do not conflict with the state constitution, the federal constitution, or federal legislation, they are legal and enforceable.

Under what is known as the **police power**, it is not only the right but also the duty of a state to protect the health, safety, and morals of its citizens and to promote the general welfare. This power is not dependent upon state constitutions or enabling legislation but is inherent in the power to govern. For example, a state can establish a weighing station and stop overloaded trucks, even those moving in interstate commerce. There may or may not be a law covering this activity, although in general most business regulation is covered by specific legislation.

Considering that there are 50 states and thousands of political subdivisions, it is obvious that the regulation of competitive business varies considerably among these governmental units. There are, however, some areas that are quite commonly considered by governing bodies as proper restraints on business activities. These are: (1) labor legislation, (2) health and sanitation laws, (3) prices, (4) usury laws, (5) zoning ordinances and building codes, and (6) licenses.

LABOR LEGISLATION

State laws dealing with labor have long been recognized as a valid field for legislation. At the outset, the chief concern was with necessary minimum standards for working conditions. Most states provide that factory buildings shall be fireproof or have adequate protection against fire hazards to workers. Each employee is entitled to a certain amount of space. Adequate washrooms and other sanitary facilities must be available. Safety devices must be installed where the occupational hazard is excessive; for example, mines must be equipped with ventilating devices, emergency exits, and proper shafts.

With the advent of federal labor legislation and the broad interpretation of interstate commerce, most state laws are subservient to national provisions. Minimum wages, maximum hours, union recognition, and unemployment insurance are dictated by the federal government. One interesting exception is Section 14(b) of the Taft-Hartley Act that permits the states to pass right-to-work laws, which several have. The unions would like to have this section repealed.

HEALTH AND SANITATION LAWS

In addition to the application of health and sanitation rules to factories, laws to protect customers of retail establishments have been passed. For example, a restaurant is usually subject to a periodic inspection and, if certain minimum standards of cleanliness are not maintained, the owner's license to operate can be withdrawn. Employees who handle food may also be subject to annual health examinations.

PRICES

The price at which a retailer is permitted to sell a certain product may be affected by state legislation. As described in Chapter 11, fair-trade laws were passed by a considerable number of the states since the enactment of federal legislation which made state fair-trade laws possible. However, the number of states with fair-trade laws on the books had dwindled from 45 in 1951 to 25 in 1975. Furthermore, Congress repealed the enabling federal laws late in 1975 so that fair-trade laws are no longer legal. At the present time only state unfair trade laws, also described in Chapter 11, affect allowable retail prices.

Sellers of commodities in intrastate commerce are very likely to find that the state has copied many of the federal laws against monopolies, trade practices, and pricing policies. Goods of like grade and quality must be sold at the same price to all purchasers unless the difference can be justified on the grounds of manufacturing, selling, or delivery costs. Any other price practices that might tend to create a monopoly or in any other manner restrain trade would also be illegal.

USURY LAWS

Laws passed by states stipulating the maximum rates of interest that can be charged on different types of loans are known as **usury laws**. Many people find it necessary to borrow money, and those with little or no credit standing cannot expect lending agencies to compete for their business. If they do locate a source of funds, however, the interest and other charges that the financial institution can charge will be limited by the state usury law. These charges vary with the type of loan and terms of repayment.

ZONING ORDINANCES AND BUILDING CODES

Most people who build a home do not want their residential area invaded by hot dog stands, pool halls, and other similar types of business enterprises. Laws establishing areas that are available for business sites and others that are restricted to homes are known as **zoning ordinances**. Such laws are passed by village, town, or city councils, and recently townships and counties have established zoning boards to control the use of suburban and rural land areas. Zoning ordinances interfere with the right of property owners to use their land in any manner that they may desire, but this interference is considered a necessary protection for their neighbors and others who own land in the same geographical area.

Assuming that the requirements of a zoning ordinance have been met, there may still remain the restriction of a building code. **Building codes**, both state and local, are regulations that provide minimum specifications for construction details. For example, a code may provide that only fireproof buildings can be constructed in a certain area, or that electric wires must be laid within a pipe or cable. After work is completed, a building inspector checks it and, if the specifications provided by law have not been followed, necessary corrections must be made.

LICENSES

A **license** is a formal document issued by a governmental body to a business or a person authorizing the holder to engage in an activity. It is illegal to engage in such activities without the necessary license. Licenses are issued by states, counties, cities, and towns. Most licenses are on an annual basis although some are for an event only, such as a parade or carnival permit. Several states list over 100 different types of businesses that must secure a license, such as restaurants, barbershops, dry cleaning establishments, hotels, ice plants, laundries, motion-picture houses, soda fountains, and dealers in tobacco, fireworks, office machines, and automobiles. In some areas local licenses are more numerous than state licenses. Local licenses affect most commonly pool halls, bowling alleys, and other places of amusement.

The use of licenses as regulatory devices plays an important part for businesses that sell liquor, for the professions, and for some types of occupations. Stores that sell liquor in bottles, other than those that may be operated by a state, are required to secure a special license. Also, hotels, inns, taverns, and other places where liquor is sold for consumption on the premises are licensed. By refusing to issue a license or to renew one, the state can control the number and types of outlets. The practice of medicine, law, accounting, dentistry, and other professions is usually regulated in that the individuals concerned must secure a license from the state before they can offer their services to the public. Brokers, real estate salespersons, barbers, insurance agents, and many other workers in occupations not classed as professions must also secure a license from the state. The ability of the individuals concerned to continue in business is based on keeping their licenses in force.

REGULATED INDUSTRIES

The types of businesses currently considered to be desirable monopolies and hence qualifying as regulated industries can, in one sense, all be classified as public utilities. A **public utility** may be defined as a privately owned industrial firm that renders a service so essential to its customers that it is allowed to operate legally as a monopoly under governmental regulation of rates and standards of service. Under this broad definition electric, gas, water, telephone, and telegraph companies qualify as do railroads, metropolitan buses, subways, oil and gas pipelines, and air, water, and motor transport companies. Sometimes steam heating, cold storage, irrigation, and sewage disposal companies are also included.

In modern usage the term "public utility" refers to all of the preceding categories with a few exceptions that include the railroads and some other forms of transportation. The remainder of this chapter will be devoted in part to describing the characteristics and the regulation of public utilities, sometimes called public service companies, including an explanation of the general principles that apply to all types of regulated industries. Following an examination of the criteria used by commissions to make decisions affecting the various types of companies under their jurisdiction, the regulation of several specific industries will be discussed.

Characteristics of Public Utilities

The major classifications of public utility companies have certain characteristics that are lacking in other forms of private business.

PUBLIC NECESSITY

One characteristic is the public necessity of the service rendered. Under present-day living conditions most people expect to have access to water, electricity, gas, and a telephone. Furthermore, there is no acceptable substitute for these services, the need for them cannot be postponed, and consumers have no choice but to pay whatever bills they are rendered. Because of this public necessity, some municipalities operate the water system, street buses, and, less frequently, an electric generating station.

ECONOMIC EFFICIENCY

Public utilities also differ from other industries in that they function in business areas where competing units would be inefficient. For example, there is certainly no point in two gas companies serving one community. It would also be undesirable for two firms to build dams or generating plants or to lay wires or pipes to provide competition. Public utilities require large investments of capital and need all the business available in one territory to absorb depreciation charges and out-of-pocket costs.

RIGHT OF EMINENT DOMAIN

Another characteristic of many public utilities is the right to secure special privileges from governmental units. These include the **right of eminent**

domain, which is the power of a government to take private property for a public purpose by the payment of a fair price that, if necessary, will be determined by a court. This privilege may be and is commonly granted to telephone, telegraph, gas, electric-services companies, and other public utilities. For example, many long-distance electric transmission lines run overland on a straight line between two terminals, making use of private property for the erection of support towers regardless of whether or not such use of the land is agreeable to the owner.

Public Utility Regulatory Agencies

As previously pointed out, part of the burden that a public utility must carry for its special privileges, such as monopoly status and the right of eminent domain, is to be subject to much more extensive regulation than is imposed on any and all types of competitive businesses. Such additional regulation is largely centered on rates and service. The determination and enforcement of what constitutes fair rates and satisfactory service falls under one or more of three levels of government depending on the territory served by the utility.

CITY COUNCILS

If the public utility is a bus line, a local water or electric company, or any other privately owned organization selling its services exclusively within the confines of a municipality, it will be regulated by the city council or a comparable counterpart. At the time a **franchise**, which is an exclusive right to serve the community for a specified number of years, is granted, regulatory conditions are imposed. Customarily a committee of the council is charged with the responsibility for overseeing that the rates charged and the services rendered are in accord with the terms of the franchise.

STATE PUBLIC UTILITY COMMISSIONS

More commonly, a utility serves more than one community within a state. In this event its regulation will fall under the jurisdiction of a state public utility commission, which is a branch of the state government. Although the utility must still obtain a franchise to operate in each city, this commission can overrule the terms of a franchise if these would obstruct the overall regulation of the utility company. For example, if a city insisted on a very low rate structure before granting a franchise to a natural gas company, it might mean that the company would have to charge high rates in other areas it serves to earn a fair profit. Under these conditions the state commission could overrule the municipality, although it is more likely that it would have entered into the negotiations before the local franchise in question was granted. Although the competence of the commissions varies widely among the 50 states, the appointment of intelligent commissioners, who employ a staff of experts, has frequently resulted in efficient and capable state regulation.

From 1907, when the first state utility commissions were established in New York and Wisconsin, until 1935, when the first of several laws affecting utilities was enacted, the federal government did not regulate public utilities. During this time it became increasingly clear that the interstate operations of some utilities, notably electric and natural gas companies, were so extensive that state commissions could not regulate these companies effectively. The federal government, as will be discussed later, has now established several agencies that either regulate a phase of public utility company operations or the interstate rates and services of a particular industry.

State Regulation of Public Utility Rates

Of prime importance to the public utility and to its customers are the rates charged for its services. Although many business firms have found that a low profit on a high volume of sales produces maximum profits for the owners, there is a justifiable fear that a monopoly would not follow this price policy. Consequently, all of the states regulate the rates that public utilities may charge for their services.

As a general working principle, commissions have tried to establish rate structures that permit each public utility company to earn a fair return on a fair value of its property. This principle follows a line of argument adopted by the Supreme Court of the United States in a decision that read, in part, as follows: "A public utility is entitled to such rates as will permit it to earn a return on the value of the property which it employs for the convenience of the public equal to that generally being made at the same time and in the same general part of the country on investments in other business undertakings which are attended by corresponding risks and uncertainties."

FAIR RATE OF RETURN

A rate of return that is fair to the utility and to the public is extremely difficult to establish. In most instances the rates allowed have varied from 5 to 8 percent on the fair value of its property, with 6 and 7 percent favored over the extremes. Of course, once a rate of return is established, there is no guarantee that the return will equal the rate. If operations produce a loss or a very low rate of return, the company can apply for an adjustment in rates. If the commission should refuse to grant such a request, the courts on an appeal would probably decide that the allowed rates were too low.

Beginning in 1974 the operating costs of public utilities increased sharply and almost every company applied for rate increases. In many instances the state commissions allowed the utilities to pass on to consumers the higher prices they were paying for coal and oil but required that additional rate increases would have to be processed in the usual manner. Also, in view of the high cost of obtaining capital, the utilities took the position that they should be allowed to earn 10 to 12 percent instead of 6 or 7 percent. They felt that unless the higher rate of return was allowed they would not be able to obtain necessary funds for expansion.

FAIR VALUE OF PROPERTY

Assuming that a fair rate of return has been determined, it must also be decided what is a fair value of the property owned by the public utility that is used for the purpose of rendering services to the public. This involves placing a price tag on every item of such property, which is extremely difficult to do. Even if there is mutual agreement on the properties to be included, there is likely to be a lack of agreement as to a method to be used in arriving at a true value.

Two widely used measures are: (a) **original cost** less depreciation, and (b) **reproduction cost new** less depreciation. The first of these is known as **historical cost** and corresponds to values shown on the balance sheet. The reproduction cost method prices properties at current costs rather than at prices actually paid. Both methods have been approved by the United States Supreme Court.

RATE DIFFERENTIALS

One of the special problems that arise in determining fair rates is that all customers of a particular public utility cannot be charged the same rates. In a given locality, like users of the metropolitan buses, water service, electric service, and telephone service do pay the same amount. Rates may vary between two communities located some distance apart, however, even though they are served by the same company. This condition may result from negotiating franchises in different years or under other diverse circumstances. Of even more importance is the difference between rates charged to classes of consumers, such as the homeowner and a manufacturer. The kilowatt-hour rate charged for electricity in the case of the individual is much higher than that charged to the company.

State Regulation of Public Utility Services

Several features of the problem of service might not be apparent to a casual observer. The public takes most of these for granted without recognizing that its best interests are being protected by the commission.

One of the areas important to consumers is that a utility cannot choose its customers or render different classes of service to like users. A person who builds a house on a street that carries gas, telephone, water, sewer, and electrical connections has a right to demand these services. Except for possible overloads or nonpayment of outstanding bills, the desired connections will be made. In addition, the services must meet certain minimum standards. For example, the water must be pure and have adequate pressure, the electricity must be maintained at a standard voltage, and gas must have certain heating qualities.

Because utilities are monopolies, a company cannot enter a new territory without first securing permission from the appropriate commission. This usually involves securing a **certificate of convenience and necessity**. Also, a public utility cannot reduce or abandon the service it renders without first securing commission approval. The fact that one segment of its operations regularly operates at a loss is not sufficient reason for abandonment.

Federal Regulation of Public Utilities

Although the operations of public utilities are primarily intrastate, electricity and natural gas move across state lines and are thus in interstate commerce. Furthermore, between 1920 and 1935 there was a tremendous increase in public utility holding companies that created interstate transactions among its operating companies which formerly had been independent and domiciled in one state. Public recognition that state commissions lacked constitutional authority to cope with interstate utility problems led to a demand for remedial action by the federal government. In 1935 Congress responded by passing the first of several laws that brought the interstate activities of public utilities under federal supervision.

PUBLIC UTILITY HOLDING COMPANY ACT OF 1935

As the title of this law indicates, one of its purposes was to exert a measure of control over public utility holding companies. Too many of those organized in the previous 15 years were so far removed from operating companies that they were uneconomic and strictly speculative in nature. The act required all holding companies to register with the Securities and Exchange Commission and specified that a holding company could control two or more holding companies that, in turn, owned operating companies, but it could not be owned by another holding company. Holding companies that violated these limitations were required to dissolve and go out of business, which explains why this provision was commonly called the **death sentence clause** of the act.

As a means of forcing the holding companies to register, the law provided that unregistered companies were forbidden to use the mails and other instrumentalities of interstate commerce. Registered companies were not allowed to borrow from subsidiaries, to pay excessive dividends, or to make political contributions. Sales, service, and construction contracts between the holding company and subsidiaries were subject to review by the Commission.

The act also gave the Federal Power Commission (FPC), an existing federal agency, the right to regulate interstate electric rates. This eliminated one of the problems that had vexed state utility commissions. The law further provided control over charges for electric service through the creation of joint boards of federal and state commissions. The act also gave the FPC direction to coordinate and interconnect transmission lines in the United States and to control sales and purchases of companies transmitting electricity in interstate commerce.

NATURAL GAS ACT OF 1938

As in the case of electric service, the Natural Gas Act of 1938 gave the FPC jurisdiction over the rates charged by companies engaged in the interstate transmission of natural gas. The reason that manufactured gas was not included was that almost all gas so produced is consumed in the city in which it is manufactured or in nearby areas and does not, normally, enter into interstate commerce. This act added to the jurisdiction of the FPC another important interstate public utility operation.

An interesting application of this act came about when the FPC attempted to set the prices that natural gas producers could charge pipeline companies. In a decision rendered in 1954 by the Supreme Court of the United States, the position of the FPC was upheld. This indicates that courts sometimes are as important as commissions in the regulation of public utilities. At the present time there is some agitation to remove price controls on natural gas on the theory that they discourage exploration for new supply sources.

Regulation of Specific Industries

As indicated earlier in this chapter, modern usage of the term public utilities does not cover the areas of transportation and communication. These industries, however, are subject to varying degrees of regulation in a manner similar to that accorded other companies vested with a public interest.

RAILROADS

As early as 1870 the farmers in the midwestern grain-growing states became so incensed about the high rates charged by the railroads that they insisted in their state legislatures that commissions be created to control these monopoly prices. State commissions, however, could regulate only intrastate transportation, and practically all railroads operated in interstate commerce. Since the federal government is the only legislative body authorized to control interstate commerce, pressure was exerted on the Congress to take appropriate action. As a result, the Interstate Commerce Act was passed in 1887. This legislation, which was designed to regulate the transportation of goods across state lines, represents a milestone in the history of the federal regulation of business.

The 1887 law created the Interstate Commerce Commission (ICC) and gave it the right to end rate discriminations. The law stated that rates were to be just and reasonable, and required schedules of rates and fares to be published. It also included a **long-and-short-haul clause**, which made it illegal for a railroad to charge a higher rate for a short haul than for a long haul under substantially similar conditions. Some railroads had been charging a low competitive rate between two points served by another line, but between cities not served by another carrier they charged a high monopoly rate. Although the ICC was not given the necessary authority to enforce the provisions of the 1887 Act and several adverse court decisions further weakened the law, subsequent acts and amendments have corrected these deficiencies.

The early recognition of the public utility characteristics of the railroads and of the need for extensive regulation of common carriers in interstate commerce has resulted in more and more legislation over the years, expanding the scope and extent of ICC control. Currently the ICC has extensive jurisdiction over practically all facets of railroad operations. Rates, service, valuation, security issues, consolidations, safety appliances, accounting, and many other phases of this industry are controlled by the seven commissioners, aided by a large staff of experts. Problems involving both intrastate and interstate commerce are handled cooperatively with the state commissions.

MOTOR CARRIERS

Motor carriers engaged in interstate hauling are under the jurisdiction of the ICC, although those engaged strictly in intrastate traffic are subject only to regulation by state commissions. All of the states exercise a certain amount of control over trucks using the roads within their boundaries; that is, they regulate the length, width, height, and the gross weight of the vehicle and its contents. Safety regulations covering the operation of motor vehicles have been prescribed by the ICC, and the states generally follow such regulations.

Motor trucks and buses engaging in interstate traffic were first regulated by the federal government under the authority of the Motor Carrier Act of 1935. Under this act the ICC was given power over interstate motor transport carriers very similar to the extensive supervision that existed for railroads. The extent of control varies for common, contract, and private carriers. **Common carriers** operate on regular schedules and offer service to the general public. **Contract carriers** hire their services for special hauls, such as moving household goods. Trucks and buses used by the firm owning them are known as **private carriers**. Common carriers are subject to rate and service regulations and cannot do business without obtaining from the commission a certificate of convenience and necessity. Carriers holding such certificates have a franchised monopoly similar to that discussed earlier in this chapter. Permits and minimum rates are prescribed for contract carriers, while private carriers are subject merely to safety regulations.

Passenger buses operating within one city, if not publicly owned, are regulated by the governing body of the metropolis. In recent years efforts to bring mass transportation to commuters has resulted in subsidies and other concessions in an effort to reduce fares.

OTHER TRANSPORTATION SYSTEMS

In addition to interstate traffic by rail and truck, raw materials and other types of merchandise move by air, water, and pipelines. In each of these areas an appropriate agency of the federal government regulates rates, services, and other details in a manner more or less comparable to that described for railroads. In each instance a different regulatory body is involved insofar as the controls are on an interstate level.

Air Transportation. Air transport is subject to control by local, state, and federal agencies. The first two deal with the construction and operation of airports and regulations concerning their use. The federal regulation of air transport is primarily under the jurisdiction of the Civil Aeronautics Board (CAB). This five-member agency has the authority to prescribe rates for passengers and air mail, to approve domestic and overseas routes for airline companies, and to establish standards of service. The certification of aircraft and personnel as well as the development of airports are supervised by the Federal Aviation Administration, which is a division of the Department of Transportation.

Water Transportation. In 1940 water transportation between the states was placed under the control of the ICC, although from its beginnings this Commission had the authority to fix rates involving joint water-rail interstate transportation. Regulation of water transportation is similar to that for motor trucks, but several types of contract and common carriers are exempt from supervision over rates. Where rates are controlled, they are usually established at a 10 to 20 percent reduction from the charges allowed the railroads for similar classes of goods.

Pipelines. The interstate shipment of oil by pipelines has been under the jurisdiction of the ICC since 1906. Although many oil pipelines are owned by the users, on occasion they do become common carriers by transporting the oil of independent producers. As noted earlier, the interstate shipment of natural gas by pipelines is controlled by the FPC.

COMMUNICATIONS

In the areas of telegraph, interstate telephone, radio, and television, the federal government has established a regulatory agency with varying degrees of authority over companies engaged in these businesses. This is the Federal Communications Commission (FCC), which received most of its authority under the Communications Act of 1934. The FCC has the authority to regulate rates and services for interstate communications by wire, which includes telegraph messages and long-distance telephone calls. It also supervises charges for cable and radio overseas messages, satellite communications, and cable TV.

In the fields of commercial television and radio, since stations do not charge the public for their programs, there is no rate regulation. Rather, the FCC has concentrated on allocating television channels and radio frequencies. Each station is licensed for three years, and must follow prescribed rules or endanger its chances of having the permit renewed. One of the problems faced by the FCC was that only 12 channels were available in the VHF (very high frequency) band, which led to station interference in some areas of the country. To solve this problem, 70 new channels were allocated space in the UHF (ultrahigh frequency) band. To make effective use of these new channels, since many TV sets could not receive UHF programs, Congress amended the Federal Communication Act specifying that after April, 1964, all television sets manufactured had to be able to receive programs broadcast by stations using channels 2 to 83. This requirement is an interesting example of the effect regulation may have on the freedom an industry usually has regarding the products it manufactures.

BUSINESS TERMS

QUESTIONS FOR DISCUSSION AND ANALYSIS

1. Does the size of business units have a substantial impact on competitive conditions in various industrial and commercial areas?
2. If there were no governmental restrictions on business activities, would businesses form trusts today?
3. Are consumers in need of even greater regulatory efforts in their behalf? Is there a reasonable doubt about the value of some laws already enacted?
4. Do consumers always bear the costs incurred by industries to meet environmental control standards?
5. Would businesses be happier if the federal government would leave all regulation to the states?
6. Would consumers benefit if each community had, for example, one regulated gas station, one regulated supermarket, and one regulated drug store?
7. Are there any reasons that justify extending the right of eminent domain to public utilities in light of the importance of the private ownership of property in a capitalistic society?
8. What incentives does a public utility have to operate efficiently considering that it is guaranteed a fair return on its fair value?
9. Why should utilities and railroads not be allowed to abandon losing segments of their businesses? Is this restriction unfair to its other customers?
10. There has been considerable recent agitation to eliminate many federal regulatory agencies on the premise that they have done more harm than good as evidenced by the plight of many railroads. Is this country ready for a return to laissez-faire capitalism?

PROBLEMS AND SHORT CASES

1. Mrs. Mary Romano took out a franchise from the Leaning Tower of Pizza Corporation, which was located in another state. Her contract specified that she would construct a building from plans furnished and that she would purchase all raw materials, equipment, and supplies from the franchiser.

   All went well for several months but deliveries were frequently slow on a number of meat items. To serve her customers, Mrs. Romano made local purchases of missing ingredients and, to her surprise, discovered that she could purchase more advantageously from a local meat wholesaler than from the franchiser. Consequently, she continued this practice to the enhancement of her profits.

When the Leaning Tower of Pizza Corporation became aware of what Mrs. Romano was doing, it ordered her to stop on the grounds that she was violating the terms of her franchise. She, however, refused to do so, and was sued for breach of contract. A lower court held for Mrs. Romano on the grounds that the provisions of the franchise violated both the Sherman and Clayton Acts.

The Leaning Tower of Pizza Corporation is now considering what action it should take. It can appeal the case and hope for a reversal from a higher court, it can make changes in the contractual relationships with its franchise holders, or it can allow the decision to stand and hope that other franchise holders will not follow the lead of Mrs. Romano. What should it do?

2. **a.** A personal loan office located in a state with a usury law that specified a maximum rate of 3 percent a month made a loan to a customer on the following terms:

Size of note signed	$600.00
Less: Interest at a discounted annual rate of 20%	120.00
Cash proceeds	$480.00
Length of loan	1 year
Monthly payments required	$50.00

Was this loan made at usurious rates? Show calculations to justify your answer.

b. An electric public utility company has had the following rates approved for residential customers:

First 100 kilowatt hours	5.0¢/kilowatt hour
Next 300 kilowatt hours	4.0¢/kilowatt hour
Next 600 kilowatt hours	3.5¢/kilowatt hour
Additional kilowatt hours	2.5¢/kilowatt hour
Minimum monthly rate	$2.00

Compute the monthly bill if the consumer uses the following number of kilowatt hours: (1) 35, (2) 90, (3) 200, (4) 600, (5) 3,000.

3. The Northwestern Electric Co. has filed a rate increase application with the Ohio Utility Commission. The company has been valued for rate-making purposes at $400,000,000 based on original cost less depreciation, and its earnings for the past year were $22,000,000. The company contends that it should have been allowed to earn at least $34,000,000, and it also disputes the method used to value its facilities. It has produced detailed figures to show that its present value based on reproduction cost new less depreciation is $600,000,000.

An examination of the company's financial statements shows that it secured (a) $200,000,000 from a 4% bond issue sold several years ago that does not mature for another 20 years, (b) $100,000,000 from a 5 percent nonparticipating preferred stock, and (c) $100,000,000 from the sale of common stock.

Lawyers for the company contend that the decision of the United States Supreme Court is not being followed; that the company is in competition because of the optional use of gas, oil, and company-owned generating plants; and that risks are somewhat comparable to those faced by manufacturing firms. Evidence presented indicated that other firms operating in the same territory average earnings of over 10 percent.

How should members of the Ohio Utility Commission form an opinion on this request for a rate increase and what should their decision be?

27 *Business and Taxes*

Intending to get married early in 1976, Donald Dalton, a $22,000 a year man, filed a new withholding allowance certificate with his employer claiming two exemptions. Although the marriage was called off, Dalton did not correct his reported status as the smaller amounts withheld for state and federal taxes resulted in a larger paycheck, which he enjoyed spending. In 1977 Dalton had his 1976 tax forms filled out by a tax-preparation firm and was shocked to learn that he owed his state $195 and the federal government $910. A bank account of $376.40 that yesterday seemed more than sufficient suddenly appeared woefully inadequate.

The environment in which businesses operate in the United States includes substantial taxes levied on incomes, sales, properties, employees, securities, business activities, and other bases that will produce revenue for one governmental unit or another. Most corporations, for example, are required to pay more than one half of their earnings to various taxing authorities. To their credit, businesses do not attempt to evade legitimate levies despite this heavy tax burden. They do, however, avoid paying more taxes than are legally necessary. Consequently, many business decisions are made only after consideration has been given to the tax consequences of the alternate courses of action available.

As an aid to understanding the exact nature of the tax burden carried by businesses, this chapter will examine some principles of taxation and explain the types of taxes levied by local, state, and federal governments. Specific examples will illustrate various ways in which the impact of tax burdens does enter into, and on occasion dictate, the most advantageous solutions to certain business problems.

Although specific rates have been used in the discussion that follows, it should be understood that these are constantly being changed as legislative bodies meet and pass new laws. Furthermore, it should also be kept in mind that new sources of revenue may be found. For example, a **value added tax**, which is a sales tax levied on each sale of a good to the extent of its increased value as it moves through successive manufacturing and distributive channels, may well be adopted by the federal government. Such a tax is already used in several European countries.

PRINCIPLES OF TAXATION

The problem of enacting a suitable program of taxation for any governmental unit is most difficult. The total revenue secured should be adequate to meet necessary current expenditures. The burden should be distributed on an equitable basis. The tax law must be reasonably simple and the funds easy to collect. In some instances it may be desirable to use the tax as a means of regulation as well as revenue.

At the federal level, taxation is also used in an attempt to exercise some control over the economy. In 1975, for example, Congress reduced income taxes on individuals by $20 billion to provide consumers with additional buying power. At the same time, as a stimulus to capital spending, businesses were allowed a 10 percent credit on the cost of new equipment against income taxes otherwise owed.

Bases for Taxation

Some tax rates remain constant regardless of the size of the tax base. Any tax fulfilling this specification is known as a **proportional tax**. For example, in a taxing district the same tax rate on the appraised value of property is used regardless of the amount of property owned by one person. Rates of a **regressive tax** become lower as the tax base increases in size. The cost of securing a corporation charter, when based on the number of shares authorized, involves lower rates on the shares in excess of a stated minimum. The opposite of a regressive tax is a **progressive tax**, which applies higher and higher rates as the tax base grows in size. Income taxes are usually designed so that higher rates apply to the upper brackets of income. Likewise, inheritance and estate tax rates are higher for large bequests or estates.

The reasons for selecting certain bases for purposes of taxation are not always apparent. Obviously, broad bases, such as sales, income, or property, offer an opportunity to raise sizable sums without using excessively high rates. Taxes on gasoline have the advantage of raising funds from those who use the highways that are maintained and improved with these revenues. Taxes on liquor and tobacco are types of **sumptuary taxes**, which are taxes designed to discourage consumption of the items taxed by increasing their retail prices.

Impact and Incidence of Taxes

From the businessperson's point of view the impact and incidence of taxes are important. **Impact** refers to the person who is liable for the tax and who keeps the necessary records and mails out a check in payment of the amount due. In many instances it is possible, through a process known as shifting, to pass the tax on to others, usually the final consumer. The place at which the ultimate burden falls is known as the **incidence** of the tax. A gasoline tax may be paid by the owner of a service station but, if this tax is added to the purchase price paid by the customer, the proprietor is merely serving as a collection agency for a governmental unit. If the tax cannot be shifted, the businessperson must absorb the amount. If the incidence can be made to fall elsewhere, the tax, aside from the burden of record keeping, does not affect operations except to the extent that prices are necessarily higher.

TYPES OF STATE AND LOCAL TAXES

The taxes that are most frequently levied by the several states and their various political units include: (1) sales and gross receipts taxes, (2) income taxes, (3) property taxes, (4) corporation taxes, (5) death and gift taxes, (6) severance taxes, (7) payroll taxes, and (8) miscellaneous licenses. Some of these are duplicated by the federal government while others are not.

Sales and Gross Receipts Taxes

Sales taxes are levied on the retail price of goods or services at the time they are sold. If the rate applies to all or nearly all items, it is known as a **general sales tax**. If the rate is restricted to one or a few items, it is known as a **selective sales** or **excise tax**. For companies selling goods and services, a **gross receipts tax** may be identical to a general sales tax; but for others, such as financial institutions, the interest they receive, which does not arise from the sale of goods or services, would not be subject to a sales tax.

GENERAL SALES OR GROSS RECEIPTS TAXES

General sales or gross receipts taxes provide the largest single source of revenue for most states, and several cities and counties also make use of this tax. Forty-five states have enacted some form of a general sales or gross receipts tax. Rates vary from 2 to 6½ percent, with three fourths of the states using either 3 or 4 percent. City and county rates vary between 1 and 3 percent. Some states allow exemptions, such as food purchases not consumed on the premises or sales under a minimum amount.

To supplement the general sales tax, most states have enacted a **use tax**, which is a sales tax on goods entering the state from another state. Out-of-state firms that are licensed to do business in a state must collect the use tax on sales to customers living in a state that has a general sales tax despite the fact that a particular transaction is interstate in character. Other out-of-state merchants do not collect use taxes but, when a title is necessary, such as for an automobile, the purchaser who went out of state to buy the car is required to pay the tax.

SELECTIVE SALES OR EXCISE TAXES

Common examples of selective sales or excise taxes are those levied by all states on tobacco and alcoholic beverages. Rates can be specific, for example, 18.5 cents for a package of cigarettes; or rates can be ad valorem, such as 10 percent of the selling price.

The taxation of gasoline and other motor fuels sold for consumption on the public highways is another widely used source of income as all states secure revenue from this type of tax. Rates vary from a low of 5 cents a gallon to a high of 10 cents, with more than one third of the states using a 7-cent levy. Substantial revenues are derived from this tax and, in general, these funds are used for building and improving highways, roads, and streets. Payments are made to the state, but a common practice is to return a proportion of the amount collected to the county, township, city, or village on the basis of the collections originating in the various political subdivisions.

SELECTIVE GROSS RECEIPTS TAXES

States levy selective gross receipts taxes on insurance companies, public utilities and railroads, pari-mutuel betting, and amusements. For example, a customary method of taxing insurance companies is to make an assessment of 2 percent of all premiums collected within the state. Since an insurance company must be granted permission to operate within each state, an agreement to pay the tax is required before a license is issued. Public utilities and railroads are frequently taxed on gross receipts attributable to operations within the state, which may or may not involve a problem of allocation. Railroads frequently operate interstate whereas public utilities generally do not.

In certain states a good revenue producer is the tax levied on pari-mutuel betting. Over one half of the states collect a share, which is usually 5 percent, of the money that is wagered on each race. Taxes on the price of a ticket to entertainments of all sorts, such as movies and athletic events, range from 3 to 10 percent of the admission charge.

Income Taxes

An **income tax** is one that is levied against wages, salaries, commissions, dividends, interest, rents, and other similar sources of income to individuals, and against net profits of businesses including corporations. Forty-four states have enacted some type of personal income tax, and 45 states tax the incomes of corporations. In several of these states, income taxes are the major source of revenue (see Figure 27-1).

STATE INCOME TAXES

For individuals most states allow certain deductions and exemptions from gross income, such as $750 for each member of a family; after this deduction, rates are graduated upward with a range from .75 percent on the first $1,000 of taxable income to 19.8 percent on income over $100,000. A few states levy a percentage of the family or person's federal income tax liability. Typically a taxpayer with an income of $50,000 living in a state that taxes the first $2,000 at 1 percent, the next $2,000 at 2 percent, and so on until a maximum rate of 6 percent is reached, would owe $2,700.

For corporations the tax rate is most commonly a flat percentage of all net income, ranging from 3 to 12 percent, although some states apply graduated rates. Foreign corporations are taxed in the same manner as domestic corporations to the extent that the taxable income of the foreign corporation can be allocated to its activities within the boundaries of the state levying the tax.

CITY INCOME TAXES

Within recent years more than 3,700 cities located in nine states have also enacted income tax laws. Rates are usually 1 percent on payrolls and profits of resident individuals and firms; nonresident individuals and firms pay the same rate on wages or incomes from employment or sales within the city limits. One of the justifications for a city income tax is that persons living in suburban municipalities but employed downtown are required to share the costs of the facilities they use during working hours.

Property Taxes

Property taxes are levied against the value of real estate, tangible personal property, and intangibles owned by a taxpayer. These three types of property are sometimes treated equally for purposes of taxation, but separate rates more commonly apply to each. Counties, cities, villages, school districts,

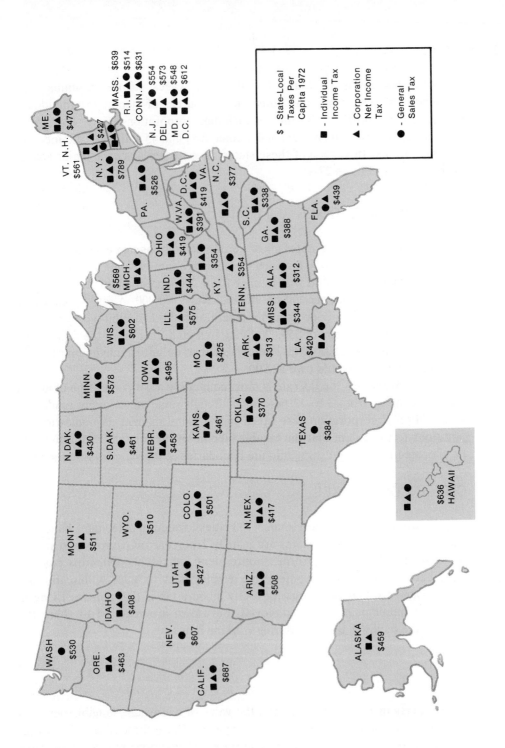

SOURCE: Tax Foundation, Inc., *Monthly Tax Features*, Vol. 18, No. 5 (May, 1974).

Figure 27-1 **Where the Money Comes From – Major Tax Sources**

drainage districts, etc., rely on one or more forms of property taxes as their major source of revenue whereas these are a minor source of income for states.

REAL ESTATE TAXES

To tax real estate, local assessors value both land and buildings, frequently from one third to one half of true market value. A rate is then applied on an annual basis. For example, in a particular school district the rate might be $42.16 on each $1,000 of assessed value. This would mean that a factory building and land valued at $2,000,000 for tax purposes would have an annual real estate tax of $84,320.

TANGIBLE PERSONAL PROPERTY TAXES

For businesses the classification of tangible personal property usually includes the value of machinery; stocks of raw materials, goods in process and finished goods; and office, store, and factory equipment. The usual valuation procedure is to use cost minus depreciation against which either a special rate or the real estate rate is assessed.

INTANGIBLE PERSONAL PROPERTY TAXES

Intangibles subject to taxation include stocks, bonds, mortgages, and notes. The value of these intangibles can usually be determined from market quotations or from the amounts stated on the instruments. Taxes on intangibles are the weakest form of property tax since it is easy to conceal assets of this type. However, an interesting development in recent years has been the trading of tax information between state governments and the federal government. Businesses and individuals who report dividends and interest on their federal income tax returns soon discover that their local and state tax returns are being checked against this information.

Corporation Taxes

As explained in Chapter 5, to secure a charter a business is charged an organization tax called an incorporation fee. An **entrance tax** is similar except that it refers to a foreign corporation that wishes to conduct business in states other than the one from which it received its charter. Incorporation fees are usually based on the amount of stock authorized, and some states assess their entrance taxes on the same base. More commonly, entrance taxes are a fixed amount such as, for example, $100.

In addition to incorporation fees and entrance taxes, states levy an annual tax on both domestic and foreign corporations. The amount of the tax for domestic corporations is normally based on the amount of stock either outstanding or authorized. For foreign corporations the base may be the amount of stock owned by residents of the state, the value of the assets located within the state, or a flat fee. The annual fee levied on domestic corporations is known as a franchise tax, whereas for foreign corporations the term **privilege tax** is commonly used.

Death and Gift Taxes

Death duties include both estate and inheritance taxes levied on the transfer of wealth of a deceased person. **Estate taxes** are assessed against the entire net value of the holdings formerly belonging to the deceased, while **inheritance taxes** are based upon the separate bequests made to individual heirs. Inheritance tax rates usually vary depending upon the directness of descent; for example, widows and children pay a lower rate than do nephews and grandchildren.

All states except one levy inheritance and/or estate taxes. Because the rates vary in the several states, businesspersons have sometimes found it advantageous to transfer their holdings and legal residences to a more favorable state prior to the time at which they expect to die. Another possibility of avoiding estate taxes is to make substantial gifts while still living. To close this loophole, however, many states have enacted a **gift tax** on such transfers of property.

Severance Taxes

A **severance tax** is a fee levied upon the owner of timberland or mineral deposits whenever the timber is cut or the minerals are removed from the ground. The advantage of a severance tax is that it encourages conservation. For example, if a real estate tax is assessed against timberlands on which trees are being allowed to mature, the owner might find it necessary to conduct logging operations to raise enough money to pay the taxes. If a severance tax is substituted, the owner pays it only during the years when revenue is being received from the property.

Payroll Taxes

Two types of payroll taxes may be paid by employers into the state treasury. The federal Social Security Act of 1935 provided for a nationwide plan of **unemployment insurance**, which is a program designed to pay partial wages to workers while they are involuntarily unemployed. Unemployment insurance is a federal-state program and each state has its own rates, schedules of benefits, and rules and regulations. A 1970 amendment to the Federal Unemployment Tax Act provided for a levy of 3.2 percent on the first $4,200 of wages earned by each person covered by the act. A credit of 2.7 percent of this amount is allowed for payments made to state funds that are used to finance payments to unemployed individuals.

Unemployment insurance taxes do not provide general revenue funds to a state as collections are held for one specific purpose. In 1975 several states exhausted their funds and had to be bailed out by the federal government to continue weekly payments to unemployed workers.

Another payroll tax for workmen's compensation, which is a form of accident insurance for employees who are injured on the job, is compulsory in most states. Although some states permit employers to purchase a policy from a private insurance company, several states operate the fund from which such benefits are paid. The cost is assessed against employers as a percentage of their payrolls, with rates that vary according to the hazard of the industry. A contractor who builds bridges and skyscrapers pays a higher rate than does a retail merchant. The subject of workmen's compensation insurance was discussed in greater detail on pages 417–418.

Miscellaneous Licenses

Although strictly speaking a license fee is not a tax, licenses produce substantial revenues for states and local subdivisions. Ranking first in importance in all states is the sale of license plates and renewal stickers for motor vehicles. Fees are usually lowest for motorcycles and highest for large trucks. Charges for passenger cars average around $10, but there is no uniformity among the states. For businesses that maintain their own fleets of passenger cars or trucks or both, the annual cost for license plates is a substantial expense. Less costly to individuals and businesses is the closely related fee for drivers' licenses.

Other licenses issued at the state level include liquor sales permits and licenses for certain types of business activities such as the manufacture and wholesale distribution of beer and other similar malt beverages, bottling operations, and the manufacture and wholesale distribution of tobacco products. Chain-store taxes, when based on the number of stores in the chain, are another example of singling out a specific industry as a source of revenue.

Of interest to certain businesses are such state licenses as those issued for hunting and fishing. At the local level, licenses are commonly required for such businesses as bowling alleys, pool halls, taverns, and so on.

TYPES OF FEDERAL TAXES

While tax collections by state and local governments are substantial, they can only be termed modest when compared to the dollars that flow into the federal treasury each year. For example, federal taxes collected in 1974 were estimated at $260 billion as contrasted with a $74 billion total estimate for all states. An examination of the following types of taxes levied by the federal government will indicate the sources from which billions of dollars are collected each year as well as the relative importance of the various bases used: (1) income taxes, (2) excise taxes, (3) employment taxes, (4) estate and gift taxes, (5) customs duties, and (6) miscellaneous taxes.

Income Taxes

Income taxes are levied on the gross receipts of individuals not engaged in business and on the net profits of businesses organized as proprietorships, partnerships, or corporations. They comprise the largest source of revenue for the federal government, in recent years producing receipts in excess of $150 billion annually. Of this huge sum, individuals pay almost three fourths and corporations the remaining one fourth. The rates and methods of computation vary considerably between taxes for individuals and for corporations.

PERSONAL INCOME TAX

Every citizen or resident of the United States, whether an adult or a minor, who has annual income in excess of a prescribed amount must file a federal tax return and may be liable for taxes on personal income. The income level at which an individual must file a return is currently as follows:

Single individual who can be claimed as a dependent on another taxpayer's return and who has investment income	$ 750
Single individual, under 65	2,350
Single individual, 65 or over	2,800
Married couple, under 65, living together and filing jointly	3,400
Married couple, with one spouse 65 or over, living together and filing jointly	3,550
Married couple, both 65 or over, living together and filing jointly	4,300
Married individual, filing a separate return or not living with spouse	750
Self-employed individual	400

Of particular interest to students is the need to file a return, regardless of the amount of income reported, to secure a refund. Many college students work during the summer but do not earn $2,350. Since their employers must withhold income taxes from their paychecks, unless a Form W-4E is used, filing a return is the only way they can secure a refund of the withheld tax.

Sole proprietors or partners have their net incomes taxed on the basis of such profits forming all or a part of the income of the individuals concerned. Owners of close corporations having 10 or fewer stockholders may elect to be taxed in the same manner as if they were organized as partnerships.

The individual income tax is far more involved than this discussion might indicate. The computation of net profits from businesses, the taxation of capital gains and losses, a tax credit against dividends received, and allowable deductions for persons not using the standard deduction are just a few of the complications that face many taxpayers. Penalties for failure to report the correct amount of income and to pay the tax thereon may result in severe monetary penalties as well as imprisonment.

Example of Personal Income Tax Calculation. An illustration of the actual tax calculation of a married businessman will show the application of 1976 rates on 1975 income. Roger Wilson operates a book and record shop and also owns a one-fourth interest in a restaurant. The income statement for this store shows a net income of $37,460 and the partnership return allocated $8,390 to Wilson as his share of the profits of the restaurant. In addition, Mrs. Wilson received interest from savings accounts in the amount of $4,200 plus $2,000 from United States bonds. These items comprise their entire income. The Wilsons have one daughter attending college and a son in high school. The calculation of their taxable income, exemptions and deductions, and tax is as follows:

Income from book and record store	$37,460	
Share of profits from partnership	8,390	
Interest income	6,200	
Total income		$52,050
Exemptions, 4 at $750 each	$3,000	
Deductions for contributions, etc.	2,600	
Total exemptions and deductions		5,600
Taxable income		$46,450
Computation of tax: (Married Taxpayer's Table)		
Tax on $44,000	$14,060	
Excess over $44,000 ($2,450 at 50%)	1,225	
Tax on $46,450 based on table		$15,285
Less: Tax reduction on 1975 income, 4 at $30 each		120
Net federal income tax		$15,165

Declaration of Estimated Taxes. Personal income taxes are on a pay-as-you-go plan that requires employers to withhold a portion of each salary or wage payment. If an employee has no other source of income, the amounts withheld over a year will approximate his or her total tax liability. Individuals, such as the Wilsons mentioned previously, who receive taxable income from sources other than salaries and wages are required to estimate their total tax a year in advance and make quarterly payments that, in combination with withholdings, will approximate their tax liability. These payments are due on April 15, June 15, and September 15 of the taxable year, and January 15 of the following year. If income prospects change during the year, an amended declaration can be filed on any of the dates just mentioned.

CORPORATION INCOME TAXES

Corporations engaged in industry or trade pay a tax rate of 20 percent on the first $25,000 of earnings, 22 percent on the next $25,000, and 48 percent on earnings over $50,000. Larger corporations do not benefit to any great extent from the lower rates on profits of $50,000 or less as the tax on $1,000,000 of net income amounts to $466,500.

Prepayment of Taxes. Corporations also prepay their income taxes. One fourth of the estimated total is payable on the 15th of April, June, September, and December. Such prepayments are required if it is estimated that taxes will exceed $40.

Tax-Exempt Corporations. Some types of corporations do not pay income taxes. Examples of exempt organizations include those operated exclusively for religious, charitable, scientific, literary, or educational purposes or for the prevention of cruelty to children or to animals. Labor unions, fraternal societies, some mutual companies and cooperatives, and civic organizations and clubs are also exempt. In all cases no part of the net earnings of these organizations can benefit any private stockholder or individual, nor can the organization engage in political activities. Furthermore, if any of these corporations has income from the operation of a business enterprise which is not related to the purpose on which its exempt status is based, such income is taxable. Tax-exempt corporations are required to file an annual information return which is examined to make sure that they are entitled to retain their favored status.

Excise Taxes

The federal government levies excise taxes at both the manufacturing and retail levels, although the latter classification is currently of little consequence. Because only specific items are taxed, federal excise taxes correspond to state selective sales taxes.

MANUFACTURERS' EXCISE TAXES

A federal tax that applies to the prices charged by manufacturers on selected items is known as a **manufacturers' excise tax**. Examples are the 8-cent tax on a standard package of cigarettes and the 10 percent rate applied to fishing equipment.

Manufacturers' excise taxes raise over twenty billion dollars for the federal treasury, with the largest amounts coming from taxes on tobacco and distilled spirits. Items subject to tax also include gasoline and oil, tires and inner tubes, truck and trailer chassis, firearms, fishing equipment, and bows and arrows.

RETAILERS' EXCISE TAXES

A federal tax that applies to the retail price of goods or services is known as a **retailers' excise tax**. A well-known example is the 6 percent tax on local and toll telephone service, which is scheduled to be reduced 1 percent each year until it reaches 1 percent in 1981.

Retailers' excise taxes have been eliminated from many products but still apply to special fuels such as diesel oil, telephone and teletypewriter service, and the transportation of persons or property by air. In addition to the charge of 8 percent for airplane tickets, there is a $3 per head charge for international travel.

Employment Taxes

Every employer and each employee subject to the provisions of the Federal Insurance Contributions Act (FICA) must pay a tax on wages paid or received to finance old-age, survivors', and disability insurance benefits and for hospital insurance (Part A of Medicare). For 1976 the law provided a schedule of rates to be applied to the first $15,300 of earnings amounting to 4.95 percent for Social Security and .90 percent for hospital insurance levied on both the employer and employee. As opposed to this combined rate of 11.70 percent, self-employed persons pay a rate of 7.90 percent. Because questions have been raised about the solvency of our Social Security system, it is likely that Congress will raise rates or the top figure, or both.

In addition, as explained earlier in this chapter, under state unemployment insurance taxes the federal government levies an unemployment insurance tax of 3.2 percent on the first $4,200 paid to a covered employee. Against this tax the government allows a credit of 2.7 percent for payments made to the states.

Estate and Gift Taxes

The federal government taxes estates and gifts that exceed stated amounts. These laws complement each other in that it is no longer possible to avoid estate taxes by making gifts prior to death. Despite the fact that there is an exemption of $30,000 for gift tax purposes, plus $3,000 each year to any number of donees and an exemption of $60,000 for estates, these two taxes produce almost $5 billion annually.

Gift tax rates start at 2¼ percent and increase by brackets to a high of 57¾ percent on taxable amounts in excess of $10 million. The estate tax rate is 3 percent for the first bracket and reaches a high of 77 percent at the $10 million level. The effect of these taxes is to make it almost impossible for large concentrations of wealth to remain in one family for many generations.

Customs Duties

Customs duties, commonly called tariffs, are taxes levied on the importation of foreign goods. Unlike all other federal taxes, they do not constitute a part of the internal revenue system of the United States and are not supervised by the Internal Revenue Service. Congress enacts separate legislation on customs duties, and the collection of these taxes is under the jurisdiction of the Bureau of Customs of the Treasury Department.

During the early history of the United States, the receipts from customs duties were considered a major source of income to the federal government. More recently, newer forms of tax legislation have overshadowed the receipts from this source, even though the amount collected has grown in total. At present the receipts from customs duties approximate $4 billion annually.

Miscellaneous Taxes

In searching for suitable sources of revenue, the federal government has singled out a number of miscellaneous sources on which taxes are levied. Motor vehicles are charged $3 for each 1,000 pounds of weight in excess of 26,000 pounds. Wagers placed with bookmakers and lottery operators are subject to a 2 percent tax, and persons accepting wagers must pay a fee of $500 each year. Occupational taxes are assessed against brewers and rectifiers of distilled spirits as well as retail and wholesale dealers in liquor and beer; and fairs, outings, etc., selling beer or wine must pay a fee of $2.20 a month.

In some instances a tax seems to have been levied primarily for purposes of regulation rather than income, in which case it is known as a **regulatory tax**. An example is the annual tax of $250 for all slot machines. Other regulatory taxes are 2 cents per hundred for white phosphorus matches and 10 percent on state bank notes. In these two instances the result has been the elimination of each item from circulation.

TAXATION AND BUSINESS DECISIONS

The tax burdens carried by businesses enter into many business decisions. According to fiscal experts, taxes ideally should not affect courses of action; but the fact is that they do. When a business has to absorb all or a part of a tax levy, its profits are reduced, thus restricting its ability to expand without resorting to outside financing or decreasing its dividend payments. If the tax can be shifted to consumers, the resulting higher prices usually reduce sales; so, if a business can control its prices, it has to decide whether to absorb all or part of the tax in order not to lose sales volume.

Decisions Influenced by State and Local Taxes

State and local taxes are usually not high enough to dictate the answer to any specific business problem. As illustrated in the following paragraphs, however, decisions on such matters as business locations and on a choice between buying or leasing equipment may be influenced by state and local income, property, and sales taxes.

BUSINESS LOCATIONS

A firm that plans to build a new factory would be interested in a state that preferably does not have an income tax and in a county or township where property taxes are relatively low. A related development in recent years has been the creation of industrial parks by municipalities and the building of factories to the specifications of businesses attracted to the location by favorable lease terms. This result is attained because the city can issue tax-free revenue bonds which allow it to secure funds to buy land and build buildings at a low interest cost.

The location of certain types of retail stores, particularly in cities close to a state line, will be affected if tax rates vary between the two states. For example, if the gasoline tax in one state is 6 cents a gallon as opposed to 9 cents a gallon in a neighboring state, it might not be wise to open a service station in the high tax state. Taxes on liquor and cigarettes have similar effects on retail store locations.

States that have a sales tax usually supplement this levy with a use tax. If an enterprise needs to be licensed to do business in these states because of the location of a branch or sales office, it must collect the use tax on sales to consumers resident in such states even though the goods are shipped in interstate commerce. Firms that are not registered generally do not pay use taxes, and states cannot prohibit shipments that cross state lines. A business may well find it costly to open a sales or branch office in a state that has and enforces a use tax.

LEASE OR PURCHASE OF EQUIPMENT

Property taxes on tangible personal property are affected by not only rates but also by the method used to arrive at the taxable value. If the burden is heavy, a firm may find it advantageous to lease rather than own certain items of equipment.

Decisions Influenced by Federal Taxes

Federal taxes are frequently such a heavy burden that they either dictate or strongly influence many types of business decisions. The examples cited here illustrate the importance of federal taxes in several different areas.

LONG-TERM FINANCING

When a business needs new capital, it may well have the option of borrowing the required funds or securing the same amount from the owner or owners. In the case of corporations, this choice usually involves issuing either bonds or stocks. Interest on bonds, or any type of debt capital, is a legitimate business expense; whereas dividends on stocks are considered a distribution of profits after taxes. If the corporation is in the 48 percent bracket, that is, it has income in excess of $50,000, the advantage of securing this interest deduction is obvious.

FORM OF BUSINESS OWNERSHIP

In some instances the double taxation of corporate income distributed to stockholders works a hardship on the owners. Where this situation exists, if the corporation is not eligible to be taxed as a partnership, it might well consider the tax-saving advantage of changing to this form of ownership. Likewise, partnerships owned by wealthy individuals might find it advantageous to incorporate.

ACCOUNTING PROCEDURES

Most businesses have some flexibility in allocating income to one year or another. Depreciation charges, the write-off of worthless accounts, selling machinery or investments, and even sales can be routed to the year that seems better taxwise. Contributions to charitable and educational organizations, bonuses to employees, and payments to pension plans must be examined in light of their reduced cost when taxes are considered.

EXECUTIVE COMPENSATION

The compensation of executives in many corporations is closely related to tax consequences as usually one half of the amount of a raise will become a tax liability of the officer. Consequently, stock options, generous pension plans, long-term employment contracts, and other devices are substituted for cash salaries and bonuses. There is no question that tax consequences influence and usually dictate decisions on executive remuneration at the $50,000-and-up levels.

PRODUCTION OF GOODS

Customs duties have a tremendous impact on firms whose products are in competition with goods imported into this country. A change in rates could lead to a decision to start or to abandon production of a part or a product. Customs duties also have a marked effect on some industries because of the different rates that customarily apply to certain goods imported in either a finished or semifinished state. The decision as to whether to build a factory in this country may hinge on whether it is cheaper to import parts than finished goods.

BUSINESS TERMS

value added tax	532	entrance tax	537
proportional tax	532	privilege tax	538
regressive tax	532	death duties	538
progressive tax	532	estate taxes	538
sumptuary taxes	532	inheritance taxes	538
impact	533	gift tax	538
incidence	533	severance tax	538
general sales tax	533	unemployment insurance	539
selective sales or excise tax	533	manufacturers' excise tax	543
gross receipts tax	533	retailers' excise tax	543
use tax	534	customs duties	544
income tax	535	regulatory tax	544
property taxes	535		

QUESTIONS FOR DISCUSSION AND ANALYSIS

1. Businesses seem to carry a heavy tax burden. Is this situation equitable?

2. Are progressive taxes discriminatory? What are some justifications for their use?

3. Are businesses able to pass on all of their tax costs so that eventually the consumer pays? Discuss.
4. Is a general sales tax progressive, proportional, or regressive? Justify your conclusion.
5. States that do not have a personal income tax are Florida, Nevada, South Dakota, Texas, Washington, and Wyoming. Those that do not have a general sales tax are Alaska, Delaware, Montana, New Hampshire, and Oregon. What reasons can be given why these states are exceptions to the general rule of levying both types of taxes?
6. Why are real estate taxes the major source of revenue for local governmental units?
7. What are some reasons that can be given to explain why corporations are taxed almost one half of their net earnings by the federal government?
8. Why should such items as TV sets, diamonds, sports cars, and yachts not be taxed by the federal government along with tobacco products and distilled spirits?
9. Young men and women starting business careers at age 22 will pay Social Security taxes for 43 years more or less. Is the resulting pension a bargain considering that the employer matches the employee's payments?
10. Would it be preferable not to have tax consequences enter into business decisions? Could this result be achieved?

PROBLEMS AND SHORT CASES

1. A group of 15 men and women plan to form a corporation in Pennsylvania to manufacture a revolutionary type of lawn sprinkling system. A site is to be purchased and a factory building constructed. A labor force of 300 will be needed for production, and 50 salespersons will cover the territory east of the Mississippi River. The plan is to sell the system house-to-house although service centers will be established in ten locations. Automobiles will be furnished to the salespersons.

   Assuming the success of this undertaking, itemize the types of taxes this corporation will pay to: (a) states and local subdivisions, and (b) the federal government.

2. In 1975 Eugene Garcia earned a net profit of $21,400 from his drugstore. In addition, he received $1,200 for serving on the board of directors of a local bank and $600 for his services on the city council. During the year he received $2,600 in interest from United States government bonds, and his wife received $8,340 in interest from deposits in savings banks and savings and loan associations.

   The Garcias have five children. The oldest child, a daughter, is 21 and is married. A son, 19, is in college, and the younger three are in grade and high schools. In preparing a joint federal income tax return Mr. Garcia elects to take a standard deduction of $2,600 for such items as charitable contributions, taxes, interest, and medical expenses. During the year the Garcias made four payments to the federal government on a quarterly basis of $1,750 each.

   Using the appropriate rate from those listed here and additional information shown in the example on page 541, how much tax did the Garcias owe on April 15, 1976?

Over	but not over		of excess over
$20,000	$24,000	$4,380 + 32%	$20,000
$24,000	$28,000	$5,660 + 36%	$24,000
$28,000	$32,000	$7,100 + 39%	$28,000
$32,000	$36,000	$8,660 + 42%	$32,000

3. At a session that lasted most of one night, the legislature of a state, in a rebellious mood against the governor, took action to repeal all taxes that produced revenue for the state. The next day responsible legislators realized that this situation was intolerable, but they also recognized an opportunity to enact a tax law that would be an improvement over the former patchwork series of laws. It was decided by leaders of the legislature that, while adequate income for the state was a necessity, the new law should take into account the federal tax system and also the taxes currently levied by local governmental units to support their functions.

You are called in as a tax consultant to a legislative committee appointed for the purpose of recommending a new law to the state legislature. What would be your recommendations, and what reasons would you advance for each type of tax selected?

28 *Multinational Trade*

Annie Bradshaw's Labor Relations class had been discussing the movement of the United States toward becoming a "service" economy. It had been noted that manufacturing employment had not increased significantly in the postwar period, while employment in wholesale and retail trade, services, and government had grown. Annie wanted to be a production planner and she wondered what this trend would mean to her and the country. Would manufacturing in a post-industrial era be able to provide jobs for additional workers? And what about those huge petroleum-related deficits — how can the U.S. balance its international accounts if it loses its competitiveness in manufactured exports?

One does not have to be a business wizard to realize that the United States and many other nations are heavily involved in global trade relationships. That American-label sportshirt or blouse you are wearing may have been made in Thailand; your new pocket calculator, assembled in Mexico from American parts; your bike rack, in Austria; your deluxe camera, in Japan; and your stereo, in Taiwan. And in a few years countries like Paraguay and Tanzania will probably be more heavily involved in this trade activity.

WHY TRADE IS NECESSARY

In the United States our complex and dynamic system of corporate capitalism is based on specialization and gain, and both workers and the owners of productive capital must benefit or gain from their relationship in this capitalistic framework. Thus, an equivalent exchange exists in which an individual sells personal skills on the market and in return is able to acquire goods and services with the money earned. In this way people are able to live much better than if they had to provide all of their own needs such as clothing, food, and shelter.

Specialization

Countries work the same way. Just as workers combine their talents and training with the available natural and capital resources to specialize, so countries specialize on the basis of their labor, energy supplies, climate, and management. They use the earnings from this effort to buy the goods provided more efficiently by other countries. In this way each country benefits from the fruits of its specialization.

Principle of Comparative Advantage

Each nation can, however, produce a wide variety of items with different levels of efficiency. How does each decide what items to produce? The argument for world trade rests on the principle of comparative advantage which, in turn, is based on the concept of specialization. The **principle of comparative advantage**, or **comparative costs**, argues that the goods a country should produce, as opposed to those it should buy, are determined by the relative efficiency with which these items can be produced elsewhere.

For example, assume that two countries, *A* and *B*, each produce wheat and steel. *A* produces both products at less cost than *B*. For *A* the relative saving in production costs for steel is greater than for wheat. In this situation *A* enjoys an **absolute advantage** over *B* in the case of both products; and in the case of steel, when the relative saving in production costs is greater, *A* enjoys a **comparative advantage** over *B*.

Despite the fact that *A* can produce both steel and wheat cheaper than *B*, it might concentrate its resources on steel for which it enjoys the larger relative saving, and import wheat from *B*. Otherwise, *B* might not have the dollars to buy steel from *A*. In other words, products must be exchanged between countries if each is to benefit from the other's specialization and comparative advantage.

GROWTH OF MULTINATIONAL TRADE

During the past 25 years the world has changed from one of **international trade**, based on countries exporting goods to and importing from others, to a world of **multinational trade**, based on countries investing directly in plants in other countries. Between 1946 and 1973 the long-term investments of United States companies in foreign affiliates rose from $12 billion to $100 billion, an eightfold increase. Now the worldwide sales of foreign manufacturing affiliates of U.S. firms exceed $100 billion, almost three times the value of U.S. exports of manufactured products.

While U.S. direct investments abroad have been watched closely in recent years, little attention has been paid to the steadily growing amount of foreign investment in the United States. As Figure 28-1 shows, U.S. investments abroad are still many times greater in value than foreign investments in the United States, but the latter are growing vigorously.

THE MULTINATIONAL CORPORATION

In the United States multinational corporations (MNCs) began in the 1850s. They grew rapidly, and by 1900 about one half of the then-existing 50 largest corporations had significant overseas operations. This growth continued through the 1920s, but slackened in the 1930s as a result of worldwide depression.[1] Today the MNC is well-known despite the fact that there is no widespread agreement on a precise definition of the term "multinational."

Multinational Defined

Some purists distinguish between the **international** or **transnational company** that has operations in several countries but operates out of a parent country, and the MNC that is truly global in ownership and management. Few, if any, corporations have yet reached this stage, for such a company would remain nonpolitical and would resist being the instrument of any national policy.

Deviating from the purist's approach, the MNC can be defined as one that operates under a worldwide strategy. More specifically a **multinational corporation** is defined as one in which the managers think globally — coordinating and interchanging technology, production, sales, and distribution among the subsidiaries and with the parent company.

Scope of MNCs

It is difficult to generalize about the scope and activities of multinational corporations because they cover a diverse and heterogeneous group of companies. These activities may range from making thimbles in Mexico to exploring for oil off the coast of Africa, from wholly-owned U.S. subsidiaries to plants in which the U.S. ownership is only 10 percent, and from factories to sales outlets. Multinational corporations are different not only because of their diverse operations but also because of their degree of ownership, size, geographic distribution, management philosophies, and numerous other variables.

[1]Much material in this section is from the U.S. Department of Commerce, *The Multinational Corporation: Studies on U.S. Foreign Investment*, Vol. 1 (Washington: U.S. Government Printing Office, 1972), p. 7.

U.S. Cumulative Direct Investment Abroad

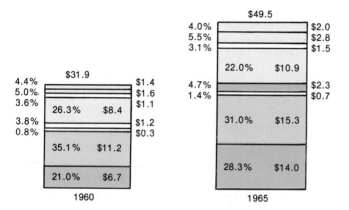
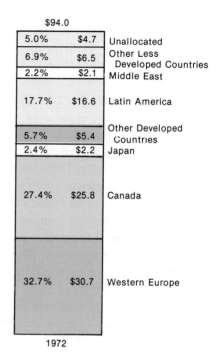

1960 — $31.9

%	$
4.4%	$1.4
5.0%	$1.6
3.6%	$1.1
26.3%	$8.4
3.8%	$1.2
0.8%	$0.3
35.1%	$11.2
21.0%	$6.7

1965 — $49.5

%	$
4.0%	$2.0
5.5%	$2.8
3.1%	$1.5
22.0%	$10.9
4.7%	$2.3
1.4%	$0.7
31.0%	$15.3
28.3%	$14.0

1972 — $94.0

%	$	
5.0%	$4.7	Unallocated
6.9%	$6.5	Other Less Developed Countries
2.2%	$2.1	Middle East
17.7%	$16.6	Latin America
5.7%	$5.4	Other Developed Countries
2.4%	$2.2	Japan
27.4%	$25.8	Canada
32.7%	$30.7	Western Europe

Foreign Cumulative Direct Investment in the U.S.

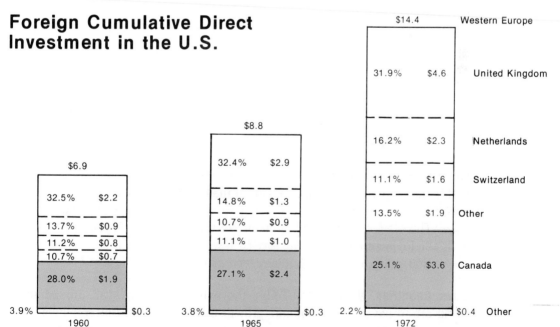

1960 — $6.9

%	$
32.5%	$2.2
13.7%	$0.9
11.2%	$0.8
10.7%	$0.7
28.0%	$1.9
3.9%	$0.3

1965 — $8.8

%	$
32.4%	$2.9
14.8%	$1.3
10.7%	$0.9
11.1%	$1.0
27.1%	$2.4
3.8%	$0.3

1972 — $14.4

%	$	
		Western Europe
31.9%	$4.6	United Kingdom
16.2%	$2.3	Netherlands
11.1%	$1.6	Switzerland
13.5%	$1.9	Other
25.1%	$3.6	Canada
2.2%	$0.4	Other

SOURCE: *International Economic Report of the President,* 1974.

Figure 28-1   **U.S. and Foreign Direct Investment (In Billions of U.S. Dollars)**

Role of the MNC

Until the 1930s most countries paid little attention to the capacity of multinational corporations for moving across international boundaries. In recent years as nations have more clearly defined their goals and priorities, they have been confronted by multinational entities that flowed through boundaries, established policies, and sometimes frustrated the national efforts. Thus, the question of national and commercial sovereignty arises. Who has final control over the actions of the multinational subsidiary, the parent or the host country? Who decides whether capital and profits flow freely from one subsidiary to another? Who decides whether a plant closes or stays open?

This friction between the MNC, with its supranational point of view, and the host country, with its national economic concerns, has invited political and economic scrutiny and questioning as to the desired role of multinational corporations. The major issue is the degree of freedom that MNCs should have or the extent of regulation that should be imposed on their present operations and future growth.

Three policy issues are especially visible in the relationships of the MNC to its parent and host countries: (1) employment, (2) transfer of technology, and (3) balance of international trade and payments. The perceptions of these issues will vary as seen from the eyes of labor, other trading countries, and U.S. business as a whole.

EMPLOYMENT

The expanding volume of foreign investment by U.S. business and the emergence of the multinational corporation as a force in international commerce have heightened interest in the effects of foreign trade and investment on domestic employment.

Labor's Viewpoint. In the eyes of American labor unions, the activities of U.S. multinational corporations result in the export of U.S. jobs. In the past, low-wage foreign labor produced generally low-quality imports in small volumes. The MNC has changed the nature of these imports and their impact on U.S. employment by combining foreign low-wage labor with modern American capital, management, technology, and marketing skills.

Other Countries' Viewpoints. Today the national pressures all around the world are to have rapid economic growth and to maintain full employment. Unlike the mercantilism of times past, the object of the **new mercantilism**[2] is

²See John Cobbs, "The New Mercantilism: Hoarding Jobs," *Business Week* (March 31, 1973), p. 38.

to hoard jobs rather than gold and other precious metals. Each trading partner of the U.S. feels that its trade surplus is essential, as trade surpluses provide job insurance.

U.S. Business Viewpoint. U.S. direct foreign investment is not contrary to the interests of U.S. workers but may, in fact, be a positive factor in stimulating U.S. employment and economic activity. U.S. multinationals produce one fourth of the total U.S. exports with their shipments to overseas affiliates. Nearly one job in eight in the U.S. production industries depends on exports. Furthermore, U.S. capital often moves abroad not because of cheap labor, but rather because of the market growth potential in developed countries or the threat of being denied access to foreign markets through exports.

TRANSFER OF TECHNOLOGY

The multinational firm has become one of the principal means for the exporting of capital, technical knowledge, and management know-how from the United States. Although the percentage of U.S. investment in Europe compared to all European investment is relatively slight, the effect of the MNC has at times been disproportionate to its size.

Labor's Viewpoint. Higher-technology production capacity and jobs are being exported by the MNC either through the construction of subsidiary plants abroad or by the licensing of production and patent rights. These technology transfers by multinational firms are closing the technological gap and eroding America's competitive advantage.

Other Countries' Viewpoints. On the one hand, it is often felt that by bringing technical knowledge and management know-how to Europe, for instance, the U.S.-based MNC has not only acquainted its potential customers with the benefits of high-technology products, but it has also presented a competitive challenge to European firms to strive for new technological products of their own. In these ways the multinational firm has assisted in narrowing the technology gap between U.S. and European countries that existed in the form of capital shortages and management skills.

On the other hand, critics in Europe, Canada, and some less-developed countries (LDCs) claim that the MNC undermines home-grown industry and leads to control of key sectors of their industrial base by U.S. capital.

U.S. Business Viewpoint. Advocates of the MNC see the transferring of U.S. technology abroad as a means for raising living standards abroad — in part through the **diffusion of technology** and in part through improving the world-wide allocation of resources. Furthermore, although the MNC has been an important means for diffusing technology, the primary cause for reducing the technology gap rests in the independent actions of foreign countries such as increasing their R & D (research and development) expenditures.

BALANCE OF INTERNATIONAL TRADE AND PAYMENTS

The **balance of trade** shows the difference between the money value of a nation's imports and exports of manufactured goods. A country's **balance of payments** refers to the difference between the total payments to foreign nations and the total receipts from foreign nations during a given time. Because it would easily take a book to cover the incredibly complex world of international trade and money flows, this section will only touch on the relationship of MNCs to U.S. trade performance and international payment balances.

MNCs and U.S. Trade Performance. Between 1950 and 1972 the persistent deficit in the U.S. balance of payments amounted to a cumulative total of over $88 billion. In 1972 the United States sustained a $7 billion trade deficit — the largest in its history — in manufactures. It is little wonder then that the effect of direct foreign investment on the U.S. balance of trade and payments has been questioned. Ironically it is impossible to measure the differences that would result if there were no multinational business. It is a fact, however, that U.S.-based multinationals have been a positive factor in our trade account and have not been responsible for the deterioration in our balance of trade.

To illustrate, manufactured exports related to multinational corporations increased from $13.7 billion in 1966 to $21.7 billion in 1970, accounting for about 65 percent of total U.S. exports. Imports of manufactures from U.S. multinationals rose from $6 billion to $11 billion, accounting for about 35 percent of total U.S. imports of manufactured goods. U.S. multinationals have continued to be positive factors in U.S. trade balances. The 1972 deficits mentioned here have been attributed to other factors such as:

1. The rapid growth in the U.S. economy, giving rise to a large increase in the demands for imports.
2. The effects of the dollar devaluation in 1971 which increased the value, but not always the volume, of U.S. imports.
3. The growing value of raw material imports, particularly petroleum.
4. The failure of our trading partners to provide meaningful access to their markets for U.S. products.

Figure 28-2 shows the variations in U.S. trade with some major trading partners, and Figure 28-3 reveals that U.S. trade made a recovery from the 1972 trough. In 1974, however, we were in the red again.

MNCs and U.S. Balance of Payments. The causes of the persistent U.S. balance of payments deficit are not rooted in U.S. foreign investment. Indeed,

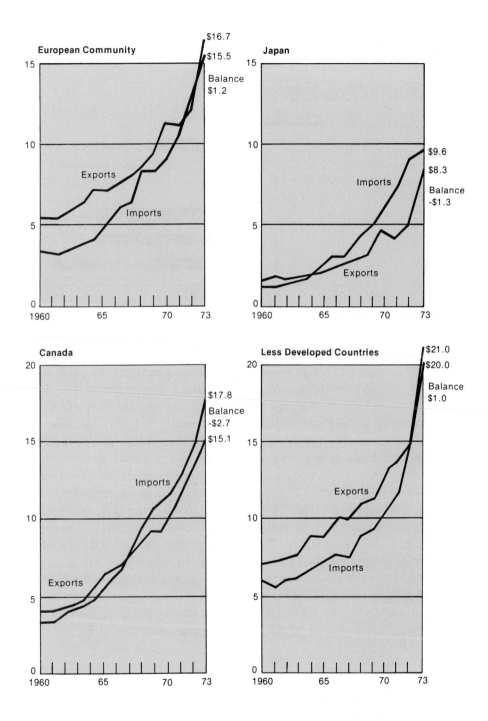

SOURCE: *International Economic Report of the President*, 1974.

Figure 28-2   **U.S. Trade with Major Partners (In Billions of U.S. Dollars)**

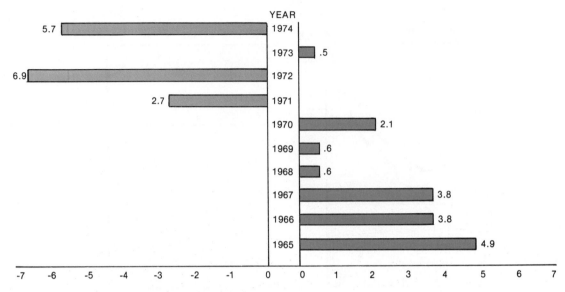

SOURCE: *Economic Report of the President,* 1975.

Figure 28-3 **U.S. Balance of Trade in Merchandise, 1965–1974 (In Billions of Dollars)**

the income on foreign investment is growing at a healthy pace; together with royalty and fee income, it exceeded direct investment capital flows by $6.7 billion in 1973. Rather, the cause is in the assumption by the U.S. government of massive political, military, and economic aid responsibilities around the globe. While the United States assumed the military and political role to protect the freedom of others, the countries we protected concentrated on developing highly technological advances and competitive economic structures which they protected from outside competition in various ways.

Whatever the cause, the chronic deficits in the U.S. balance of payments have created a glut, or **overhang**, of U.S. dollars in Europe and Japan amounting to about $100 billion. These huge holdings in the hands of foreign affiliates of U.S. corporations, foreign banks, and foreign branches of U.S. banks are known as the **Eurodollar** or **Eurocurrency market**. These funds are capable of flowing across national boundaries and of triggering monetary crises. A majority of MNCs are not necessarily speculative, but they have been a primary force in the growth of international money markets in both the supply and demand for funds.

Motives of Multinational Business

Criticisms of the motives of multinational corporations by some industry and labor groups abound. These criticisms have tended to oversimplify the motives for investing abroad or have sometimes implied suspect or hostile motives in certain investments. This chapter suggests, however, that success in multinational business does not come easily and that the U.S.-based MNC faces numerous, escalating pressures and barriers in its efforts to establish trade relationships throughout the world. Why does the MNC continue to pursue this?

If one were to inquire into the motives for international investment by multinational companies, the following might be typical:

1. A need to get behind tariff walls to safeguard the company's export markets.
2. Greater efficiency and responsiveness by producing in the local market as compared with exporting to it.
3. The possibility of lower production costs which make it cheaper to produce components abroad.
4. The fear that competitors going abroad may capture a lucrative foreign market or may, by acquiring cheaper sources of supply, threaten the domestic position of the company.
5. A need to diversify product lines to avoid fluctuations in earnings.
6. A desire to assist licensees abroad who may need capital to expand their operations.
7. A desire to avoid home country regulations such as antitrust laws in the United States.

In a general sense the fundamental forces impelling corporations to invest abroad are the quest for profit and the fear that their present or prospective market position will be lost to foreign or domestic competitors. Thus, U.S. foreign direct investment is not necessarily contrary to the interest of U.S. workers but may, in fact, be a positive factor in stimulating U.S. employment and economic activity.

INTERNATIONAL INSTRUMENTS FOR WORLD TRADE

In these days of wrangling between oil-producing and oil-consuming nations, often governments do the most talking about new forms of international organization and cooperation. The fact is that the internationalization of the world community has been at least as much the work of the multinational corporations as of governments. It has been the work of corporations with access to many credit markets, with a marketing know-how in many countries and cultures, and, above all, with managements capable of making decisions and pursuing new directions.

True, the multinational corporations have not done it all alone. They could not operate on a worldwide basis without relatively free flows of money and credit, without multilateral tax agreements, or with high tariffs that interfere with international trade. Two basic instruments of postwar economic policy have helped to facilitate the role of the multinational corporation for the past 30 years. These are the International Monetary Fund (IMF) and the General Agreement on Tariffs and Trade (GATT).

International Monetary Fund

In July, 1944, experts from 44 governments met for the United Nations Monetary and Financial Conference, or Bretton Woods Conference, to make financial arrangements for the post-World War II period. Two of the major actions of the Bretton Woods Conference were to establish: (a) the International Bank for Reconstruction and Development (IBRD), also known as the World Bank, to make long-term capital available to those urgently needing it; and (b) the International Monetary Fund (IMF) to cover short-term imbalances in payments between member nations.

ROLE OF THE IMF

The IMF was established to secure international cooperation, stabilize exchange rates, and expand international liquidity. It has currency reserves of the 125 member nations which were paid in by each nation on a quota basis determined by a country's volume of international trade, national income, and international reserve holdings. Under the Bretton Woods agreement, each government pledged to keep its currency within a certain range of an agreed dollar value. All currencies were officially denominated in terms of gold, although they were actually pegged to the dollar. The dollar was fixed to gold and was convertible to gold by official monetary institutions. The IMF provided the moral suasion and money credit that kept the system alive. As of January, 1975, the rule no longer holds that 25 percent of the quota for each member must be in gold.

Until recently a member nation with a temporary balance-of-payments problem could borrow a foreign currency from the fund by depositing a certain amount of its own national currency as collateral. The borrowing nation had an obligation to repay its loan within five years.

IMF CHALLENGED

Since 1968 numerous challenges to the IMF system have arisen. In 1968 central banks of surplus trade countries converted dollars into gold almost to the point of panic. In August, 1971, President Nixon declared that official dollar holdings were no longer convertible into gold and argued for a better break for the U.S. in the revaluation of currencies and in the tariff restrictions of stronger countries.

After a period of turmoil the new currency rates were set at the much-publicized Smithsonian Agreement in December, 1971. The year 1972 witnessed no improvement in the dollar flows, and by 1973 the U.S. faced another massive run on the dollar. At this point many nations felt the U.S. was not serious about voluntarily reducing its payments deficits. The Smithsonian Agreement lasted for a year, and the Bretton Woods system now is "inoperative."

Since 1973 the world's currencies basically have been **floating currencies**, which implies that their values are determined by supply and demand instead of by administrative decisions. More accurately we have a case of **managed floating** in which governments reserve the right to actively influence the money market. Today growing movements of **petrodollars,** or huge dollar supplies generated by some oil-surplus nations, make it especially important that nations devise a revamped monetary system in a cooperative way.

THE IMF AND SDRs

Special drawing rights (SDRs), or "paper gold," provide an important step toward a new international monetary system. In a move away from anchoring the currencies of IMF members to the U.S. dollar, special drawing rights were created to anchor IMF member-governments' currencies to the market value of a collection of 16 major world currencies. This permits the pegging of a currency to a more stable measure, or "peg," than to one currency, such as the dollar, that may vary widely on international money exchanges.

When SDRs were created in 1969, the dollar had a par value of $35 to an ounce of gold; so an SDR was defined as equal to one dollar or to an ounce of gold. But subsequent devaluations and the end of gold convertibility eroded the value of the dollar in terms of other currencies. Therefore, in 1974 the IMF began to define the SDR in terms of the composite of 16 currencies. One SDR now amounts to about $1.25.

An example of the importance of this change is found in world oil prices, which are valued in dollars. If the dollar falls in value in comparison to the SDR, oil-producing countries paid in dollars are able to buy fewer goods for their dollars. However, if the price of oil were measured in terms of SDRs, this would boost the price of oil for those who pay in dollars, and the oil producers would be able to buy more goods per barrel of oil sold.

General Agreement on Tariffs and Trade (GATT)

Tariffs refer to taxes on goods passing the borders of a country and will be discussed later. This taxation of trade as a source of revenue has its roots in ancient trade practices. According to Root, however, the Mercantilists of the eighteenth century were probably the first to make tariffs the instrument of national control of international trade.[3]

[3]Franklin R. Root, *International Trade and Investment: Theory, Policy, Enterprise* (3d ed.; Cincinnati: South-Western Publishing Co., 1973), p. 271.

During the depression of the 1930s industrial nations raised trade barriers to help domestic producers. The United States imposed the Smoot-Hawley Act and the others responded with retaliatory measures, thus effectively blocking world trade. To prevent a breakdown in world trade similar to the one that crippled trade during the 1930s and contributed to the buildup of World War II, the General Agreement on Tariffs and Trade (GATT) was established in 1948 by 23 countries. Today more than 80 countries responsible for more than 80 percent of the world's trade are members of GATT. Numerous nonmembers also apply GATT rules which are designed to encourage mutual tariff concessions and promote increases in the exports and imports of participating nations.

GATT does not rigidly bind its member nations. Article 19 of GATT provides protective tariff measures that countries can impose when their domestic industries are threatened by imports of specific products. Article 24 paved the way for customs unions or "economic communities," to be discussed later, by providing an exception to the principle of nondiscrimination in tariff arrangements.

TRADE EXPANSION ACT

Success of economic communities, such as the European Economic Community, in reducing internal trade barriers was partly at the expense of outsiders who were in an unfavorable position compared to the member countries. This was a big reason for the Trade Expansion Act of 1962, pursued by President John F. Kennedy, in which Congress authorized the President to negotiate multilateral tariff reductions up to 50 percent on an across-the-board basis rather than item by item.

THE KENNEDY ROUND

The Trade Expansion Act paved the way for the Kennedy Round of tariff negotiations held within GATT from 1964–1967. Fifty-four countries participated in this important step which covered 400,000 tariff headings. An average tariff reduction of 35 percent was realized on nonagricultural items.

INTERNATIONAL TRADE BARRIERS

While organizations such as the IMF and GATT were established to create a viable monetary mechanism and to lessen tax and tariff inequities in world trade, individual nation-states view the proposals and actions taken within these organizations in terms of what they regard as their national interest. Two examples of national-interest views have resulted in: (1) economic integration, and (2) nontariff barriers.

Economic Integration

Economic integration means the adoption of a common economic policy by a group of nation-states. When one thinks of attempts at economic integration today, the European Economic Community (EEC), or Common Market, naturally comes to mind. The major force pushing the Common Market together today is the need its members see for a united stand in economic negotiations with the United States. Also, through **industrial integration** involving national joint ventures, such as French and British development of the Concorde supersonic transport, the Common Market hopes to create European enterprises big enough to compete with U.S.-based multinational giants.

FORMS OF ECONOMIC INTEGRATION

The EEC is only one of many possible forms that efforts toward economic integration may take. Economic integration covers a wide scope of arrangements — from preferential tariffs to full economic integration, which has rarely been achieved.

Tariffs. A **tariff**, or customs duty, is a schedule of taxes levied upon goods transported from one country or political division to another. When the tariff on identical commodities differs according to the source of those commodities, it is a **preferential tariff**. An example is the eligibility of British Commonwealth members for special tariff treatment in trading with Great Britain.

Free Trade Areas or Zones. In a true **free trade area** or **zone**, no export or import duties or other regulations designed to reduce trade are established among the members. Today, however, most free trade associations reduce duties among members rather than removing them completely.

Customs Unions. A **customs union** goes a step farther than free trade areas. The member countries agree not only to abolish trade restrictions among themselves but also to adopt common policies regarding trade outside of the union.

Economic Unions. An **economic union** refers to an arrangement where member countries agree to coordinate their economic policies in matters of customs duties, fiscal and monetary regulations, and related subjects, as well as to permit the movement of capital and labor across their borders.

MAJOR TRADING COMMUNITIES

The three main world trade communities are the European Economic Community (EEC), the European Free Trade Association (EFTA), and the Latin American Free Trade Association (LAFTA).

European Economic Community. The first step in European economic integration was taken in 1950 and resulted in the formation of the European Coal and Steel Community as a common market for coal and steel. The members of this association were Belgium, France, West Germany, Italy, Luxembourg, and The Netherlands. In 1957 these six members signed the Treaty of Rome in which they agreed to establish the European Economic Community, or Common Market, and to expand the common import duties and economic policies believed to be of benefit to the members. In 1973 the Common Market was enlarged to include Great Britain, Denmark, and Ireland, which moved over to the EEC from the EFTA. The EEC remains a vigorous effort in economic integration.

European Free Trade Association. With the formation of the EEC in 1957, Great Britain was in a bind. Britain wanted the benefits of a common market on the European continent, but did not want to yield its sovereignty to the extent anticipated by the EEC as it moved toward the status of an economic union. So Britain promoted the European Free Trade Association, also known as the "Outer Seven," with Austria, Denmark, Norway, Sweden, Finland, and Switzerland. As a result, the EFTA was established by the Stockholm Treaty in January, 1960. In essence, it aimed for freer trade among the members without the common economic and political commitments made by EEC members. However, in 1973 Great Britain joined the Common Market over the continued protests of France, and Denmark followed. Today the EFTA is composed of Finland, Iceland, Norway, and Portugal.

Central and South American Free Trade Associations. The progress of European efforts at economic integration led republics in Central and South America, as well as Mexico, to think along the same lines. The earliest attempt was the Central American Common Market (CACM) formed by Costa Rica, El Salvador, Guatemala, Honduras, and Nicaragua. Patterned after the EEC, it likewise aims for the eventual industrial and economic integration of the trade area.

The Latin American Free Trade Association (LAFTA) followed on the heels of the CACM. It was formed in 1960 by Argentina, Brazil, Chile, Mexico, Paraguay, Peru, and Uruguay. Colombia, Venezuela, and Ecuador followed by 1970. The LAFTA emphasizes the principles of reciprocity and

most-favored-nation treatment[4] with special treatment provided to the least-developed member countries.

Since 1965 LAFTA has been followed by the Andes Development Corporation, a regional subgroup of LAFTA, and the Caribbean Free Trade Association comprised of the former British colonies of Antigua, Barbados, Guyana, Jamaica, and Tobago.

Nontariff Barriers

Recurring monetary crises have given new urgency to the problems of international economic relations. One problem assuming major proportions is that of nontariff barriers. A **nontariff barrier (NTB)** is defined broadly as any measure other than tariff, public or private, that significantly distorts international trade flows.[5]

TYPES OF NONTARIFF BARRIERS

Existing NTB regulations are frequently modified to meet new economic and political considerations, and new NTBs are arising in increasingly rapid succession. Examples of the major types of nontariff barriers are shown in Figure 28-4.

TYPE OF NTB	EXAMPLE
1. Government Participation in Trade	CANADA — government export subsidies on Michelin x-radial steel-belted tires
2. Specific Limitations on Trade	PHILIPPINES — arbitrary and excessive valuations, long delays
3. Standards	AUSTRALIA — margarine must be pink colored
4. Specific Limitations on Trade	EGYPT — dubbing of foreign motion pictures must be done in Egypt
5. Charges on Imports	LEBANON — all imports subject to: landing charges, wharf dues, handling dues, and storage fees

SOURCE: U.S. Department of Commerce, 1974.

Figure 28-4 **Examples of Nontariff Barriers**

[4]Under a most-favored-nation policy, any tariff reduction extended by one nation to another is extended to other nations included in the trade community.
[5]John W. Knudsen, "International Trade Policies — The Problem of Nontariff Barriers," *Monthly Review*, Federal Reserve of Kansas City (May, 1972), p. 11.

Antidumping regulation is a well-known subarea of customs administration that may create distortions in trade depending on how it is handled. **Dumping** refers to discriminatory pricing where exporters sell their products in a foreign market at a lower price than in the home market.

EFFECTS OF NONTARIFF BARRIERS

NTBs generally have the effect of interfering with and preventing the normal working of competitive forces. They also have the effect of directing more of a country's income to the protected domestic firms and workers than if these barriers did not exist. From the standpoint of the multinational corporation, it is often the uncertainty created by these barriers, as well as their effect of restricting access to foreign markets, that is important.

In all, our trading partners have been very effective in protecting their important domestic industries from what they consider to be disruptive imports. The recent demands that the United States retaliate against the foreign NTBs have contributed to a rising tide of protectionism in Congress.

THIRD WORLD TRADE

As multinational business spreads across the world, it is running headlong into economic nationalism in emerging nations as well as in developed ones. On the one hand, most of the less-developed countries (LDCs), often of the nonaligned Third World, are extending liberal inducements to invite foreign investment. On the other hand, the inducements are planned and controlled by governments that are suspicious and fearful of the giant multinational corporation.

This uneasiness is reinforced in the present period of resource scarcity where foreign investment, regardless of its intended benefits, is seen as exploiting the resources of the host country. Figures 28-5 reveals the reliance of the U.S. on mineral imports. The classical doctrine of comparative advantage is suspected by some of holding the LDCs in their impoverished states as providers of natural resources to developed nations. The poor countries subsidize the rich and are left behind in the world's race for prosperity. This feeling is especially strong in the Third World.

The Third World

What is meant by the "nonaligned Third World"? The term goes back to the Berlin Treaty at the end of World War II. Two major blocks emerged: the Western block and the Red block. The remainder were considered the

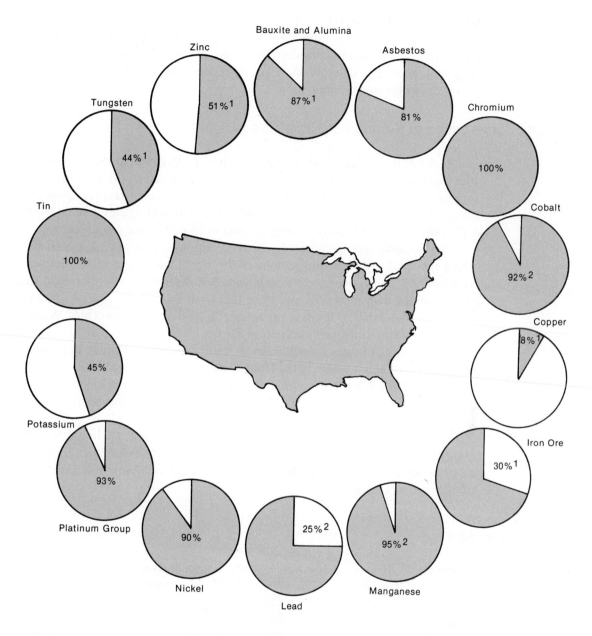

SOURCE: *International Economic Report of the President*, 1974

[1]Sufficient U.S. reserves to provide U.S. self-sufficiency at right price.

[2]Sufficient seabed reserve to provide U.S. self-sufficiency at right price.

Figure 28-5   **U.S. Mineral Imports as a Share of Consumption, 1972.**

nonaligned or **Third World** countries, partly in an economically disadvantaged sense. These terms have now been redefined to represent an international philosophy rather than relating only to specific nations. The **nonaligned philosophy** is defined as a determination not to become the satellite of any super-power or multinational corporation.[6]

Summit Conferences of Nonaligned Countries

At the first meeting of nonaligned countries in Belgrade in 1961, 25 countries were represented. The fourth such meeting in Algiers in 1973 brought together delegates from 76 of the world's nonaligned countries, representing about 2 billion people or two thirds of the world. These countries contain over half of the world's oil and two thirds of most of its other vital resources.

The foremost aim of the conferences to date has been to seek means by which the smaller and poorer nations of the world could protect themselves from political and economic encroachment. **Self-determination** — the right to develop one's own resources and to benefit from this effort — clearly is the thrust that the MNC will come up against in dealing with the Third World LDCs that comprise a significant part of the world.

The many challenges in multinational trade cannot be ignored, as a satisfactory level of employment in the United States depends basically on a vigorous domestic economy and the ability of U.S. industry to be competitive and profitable in the world economy. To achieve a healthy domestic economy, however, labor and business must be assured that they will be given the chance to compete fairly in foreign markets. Each country's interests and obligations must be carefully balanced, and the United States must continue to strive for a framework in which it can deal effectively with new problems of multinational trade.

BUSINESS TERMS

principle of comparative advantage		diffusion of technology	555
or comparative costs	551	balance of trade	556
absolute advantage	551	balance of payments	556
comparative advantage	551	overhang	558
international trade	551	Eurodollar or Eurocurrency	
multinational trade	551	market	558
international or transnational		floating currencies	561
company	552	managed floating	561
multinational corporation	552	petrodollars	561
new mercantilism	554	special drawing rights (SDRs)	561

[6]Richard D. Steade, *Business and Society in Transition: Issues and Concepts* (San Francisco: Canfield Press, 1975), p. 202.

QUESTIONS FOR DISCUSSION AND ANALYSIS

1. Assume that wristwatches and leather jackets both can be produced in Mexico and Japan. Which country would you guess would enjoy a comparative advantage in which product?
2. Explain whether General Motors and American Motors are both multinational corporations.
3. Discuss the following comment: "U.S.-based multinationals are simply flowing to the areas of the world in which there is cheap labor."
4. Explain how the U.S. can have a positive trade balance and a negative balance of payments at the same time?

5. In the term "Eurodollar," why is a dollar not a dollar?
6. Why did the Kennedy Round of tariff negotiations contribute to a rise in nontariff barriers?
7. What is the main difference between a customs union and an economic union?
8. Discuss whether everyone in a nation using nontariff barriers benefits from these barriers.
9. How would it be possible for a U.S. citizen to be a member of the Third World?
10. Why should the United States worry about or concern itself with Third World thrusts?

PROBLEMS AND SHORT CASES

1. Are the ten largest U.S. industrial corporations (on the basis of sales) also multinational corporations? Consult the May issue of *Fortune* magazine to determine the top ten companies, and then look up these companies in *Moody's Industrials* to see if they have direct foreign investments. Write a brief report noting the major products produced overseas and the geographical areas of investment of each company.
2. Suppose you are a citizen of a less-developed country and that you make only a subsistence-level income. Prepare a report indicating some positive and negative points that you would see in a multinational corporation investing in your country.
3. Protectionism is not a phenomenon of only past years. In the early 1970s labor mounted a major campaign to support the Burke-Hartke bill, an assortment of protectionist measures. The bill failed to pass, but its seeds are now sown in the minds of protectionist-leaning legislators. Prepare a brief report on the provisions of the bill and suggest the general impact of these provisions on foreign subsidiaries of U.S.-based MNCs.

29
Futurism and Business

In a time of increasing resource shortage the world has one substance of surpassing abundance for the future in the form of cellulose, an organic compound which is the chief constituent of all plant cell walls.

Alec Jordan, president of the Chemurgic Council, a nonprofit organization of scientists devoted to exploring ways for the better utilization of renewable resources, has made the following observation about cellulose: " If we can transform this vast resource with large-scale production into sugar, alcohol, and single-cell protein foodstuffs, the way would be clear for a decrease in world tensions arising from the imbalance between have and have-nots — the chief reason why countries go to war."[1]

The survival and growth for many businesses is dependent upon their ability to forecast the future. The heightened complexities and the faster pace of life have lessened the values of the past as an indicator of the future. Businesses are recognizing the need to project trends over the next decade or longer. By adapting their product line to the changing demands of the marketplace, managers can extend the life cycles of their products. If forecasters had correctly anticipated future trends, many discontinued products such as chlorophyll toothpaste, the Servel gas refrigerator, and even the ill-fated Edsel might still be around.

The focus of this chapter is on futurism and business. **Futurism** is the study of the possibilities of tomorrow and the effort to convert certain possibilities into preferred probabilities. Initially the methods which are used by business to forecast the future are examined. Next, some of the broad environmental trends which will affect business are discussed. Finally, several

[1]"The Ultimate Renewable Resource," *News Front* (Winter, 1975), p. 61.

of the resulting changes which will occur in management and the major functional areas of business are identified.

FORECASTING THE FUTURE

Corporate officials who determine how future trends will affect the operation of their firms are known as **futurists**. Futurists analyze the social, economic, political, technological, and other factors which will affect the stability and growth of the firm. They are frequently economists, sociologists, or marketing researchers who are given the broadened responsibility of counseling top management on the impact of future environmental developments. It has been estimated that 20 percent of the largest 500 companies in the country employ futurists.

In addition to gathering, digesting, and analyzing enormous amounts of information, the futurists use two formal techniques to project the future. One is a social forecasting technique called the scenario which attempts to discover future public-policy problems. Another is the Delphi method which supplies a technological forecast.

Scenarios

Scenarios are hypothetical sequences of events constructed for the purpose of focusing attention on causal processes and decision points. They attempt to answer two questions: How precisely could some hypothetical situation be created step by step? What alternatives exist for preventing, diverting, or facilitating this turn of events? For example, scenarios have been written to explain step by step how the cities of Boston, New York, Philadelphia, and Washington could merge into one megapolis and how Japan could rise to be the third strongest industrial nation in the world.

Delphi Technique

In an effort to reduce the range of disagreement over the feasibility of new processes and products and to predict more precisely the time of readiness for commerical development, some firms are now using the **Delphi technique**. The RAND Corporation, an independent research organization, devised Delphi forecasting which in its simplest form is a systematic procedure of arriving at a consensus of expert opinion concerning the potential and time of a technological advance. It depends upon an investigator acting as an intermediary and arbitrator among experts to prevent misunderstanding and to minimize the danger of submerging individual judgment in a vague majority view. The method has worked quite successfully in many situations, and its application to other types of forecasting seems promising at this time.

ENVIRONMENTAL TRENDS

Environmental factors will play a significant role in determining the future course of business. A study of the past indicates that the development of various business establishments (such as supermarkets), the adoption of major organizational changes (such as decentralization), and the use of new methods of supervision (such as democratic management) were the responses of businesspersons to environmental factors. Business fosters environmental changes as well as reacts to them. For example, the mass production and distribution of automobiles by Henry Ford significantly altered the tempo of American society. The construction of central electric power stations and the transmission of electricity caused profound changes in the home and in industry. Some of the important environmental trends which will affect the future of business are discussed in this section.

Zero Population Growth

A growth psychology has dominated the United States. This nation is deluged with growth figures for new home construction, automobile sales, population, gross national product, and many others. Managerial decisions are often predicated upon the sustained growth of a company; yet the future beckons **zero population growth (ZPG)**. This will occur when each adult woman bears an average of only 2.4 children. At ZPG the population will neither increase nor decrease but remain stable. Population experts have estimated that ZPG could happen in the United States by 1990. The movement toward ZPG will require company officials to reevaluate and adjust their actions to a stable or declining market rather than a continually increasing one. Gerber, a processor of baby foods, has already noted the decline in the birthrate and has begun developing products for other markets.

The concept of ZPG has been more readily accepted in the industrialized and affluent countries such as the United States, England, and The Netherlands. Somewhat surprisingly, it has not been widely received in underdeveloped and socialistic countries where poverty is a major concern. Evidently Maslow's hierarchy of needs, which was mentioned in Chapter 7, pertains to entire societies as well as to individuals. Before a society or a nation can think about indulging in a higher level of living through ZPG, its citizens should have satisfied their basic needs for food, shelter, and clothing.

Energy Conservation

The United States is moving from a period when energy was easy to find and easy to exploit to a period when new sources of energy are difficult to locate and costly to process. In the future, individuals and industries will be forced to adapt to an age of energy scarcity. It is doubtful if the annual growth rate in energy consumption of nearly five percent can be maintained. Some environmentalists advocate zero energy growth, but this action would virtually destroy our industrialized economy.

As illustrated in Figure 29-1, the United States is gradually reducing its dependence on fossil fuel to meet its total energy demands. Prior to the exhaustion of the fossil energy sources, it is hoped that technology will provide all countries with new forms of energy such as the breeder reactor, nuclear fusion, solar power, geothermal power, ocean gradient power, and cellulose conversion.

Over the next few years there will be a shift from the use of scarce fuels to the use of more plentiful ones. Whenever possible coal will replace petroleum, such as in the generation of electric power. If more efficient automobile storage batteries are developed, it is predicted that electrically powered automobiles will replace gasoline powered ones for much of our urban driving.

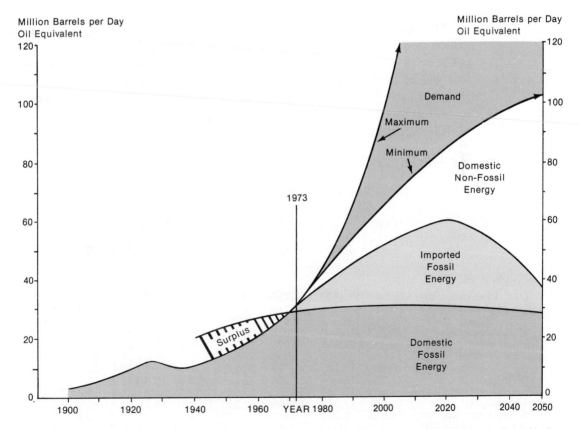

SOURCE: Understanding the "National Energy Dilemma" (Washington: The Center for Strategic and International Studies, 1973), Fold Out "P".

Figure 29-1   **Supply and Demand for Energy, 1900–2050 (In Barrels per Day Oil Equivalent)**

Ecology Preservation

Since eight out of ten Americans are in favor of rigorous antipollution controls, particularly of air and water, legislators will feel a compulsion to enact and sustain these forms of controls. In the future an increasing share of America's resources will be used to solve ecological problems. In the short run between 1972 and 1982, it is estimated that the cumulative expenditures for environmental protection will be about $290 billion. Over the long run this figure will be many times higher.

Although consumers want businesses to observe ecological safeguards, they often hesitate to sacrifice their own standard of living for ecological considerations. As environmental programs educate and regulations dictate a reallocation of essential priorities, consumers will be forced to modify their life styles.

Changes in the Labor Force

The labor force is expected to expand from 85.9 million in 1970 to 101.8 million by 1980, 107.7 million by 1985, and 112.6 million by 1990. In 1970 one out of every five employees was in the 25 to 34 age group; by 1980 one out of four will be in this age bracket. This same ratio will continue into 1990. As shown in Table 29-1, the average age of the labor force will fall from 38 years in 1970 to 35 years by 1980. These younger, better-educated employees will provide the future leadership for our enterprise system.

Table 29-1   *Distribution of Total Labor Force by Age, Actual 1970 and Projected 1980, 1985, and 1990*

Age Group	Number (In Thousands)				Percentage Distribution				
	Actual	Projected			Actual		Projected		
	1970	1980	1985	1990	1960	1970	1980	1985	1990
BOTH SEXES									
Total, 16 years and over	85,903	101,809	107,716	112,576	100.0	100.0	100.0	100.0	100.0
16 to 24 years	19,916	23,781	22,184	20,319	17.6	23.2	23.4	20.6	18.0
16 to 19 years	7,645	8,337	7,165	7,089	7.2	8.9	8.2	6.7	6.3
20 to 24 years	12,271	15,444	15,019	13,230	10.4	14.3	15.2	13.9	11.8
25 to 54 years	51,487	61,944	69,202	76,421	64.6	59.9	60.8	64.2	67.9
25 to 34 years	17,678	26,779	29,739	30,531	20.9	20.6	26.3	27.6	27.1
35 to 44 years	16,789	18,720	23,177	27,617	23.3	19.5	18.4	21.5	24.5
45 to 54 years	17,020	16,445	16,286	18,273	20.4	19.8	16.2	15.1	16.2
55 years and over	14,500	16,084	16,330	15,836	17.7	16.9	15.8	15.2	14.1
55 to 64 years	11,280	12,787	12,929	12,310	13.0	13.1	12.6	12.0	10.9
65 years and over	3,220	3,297	3,401	3,526	4.7	3.7	3.2	3.2	3.1
Median age	38.2	35.2	35.8	37.0					

SOURCE: Denis F. Johnston, "The U.S. Labor Force: Projection to 1990," *Special Labor Force Report 156*, U.S. Department of Labor, Bureau of Labor Statistics (1973), p. 5.

Women will continue to make great strides in business. By 1980 a larger percentage of women will be in the professions such as law, accounting, and medicine. Over 20 million, or 40 percent, of married women will be at work in 1980. Since in many families both the husband and the wife will be contributing to the family income, more than one half of all families will have incomes over $14,000 by 1980.

Rising Education Levels

As shown in Figure 29-2, from 1940 to 1973 the proportion of workers without a high school education declined greatly. On the other hand, the percentage of those in the labor force with college degrees is growing rapidly. In 1940 only 6 percent of all workers had finished four or more years of college. This proportion rose to nearly 15 percent in 1973, and it is expected to approach 23 percent by 1990. When the number of college graduates in the labor market exceeds the supply of available jobs, the purpose of a college education will need to be reevaluated. It will be necessary to demonstrate that college is an effective cultural and intellectual experience rather than merely a stepping-stone for a career.

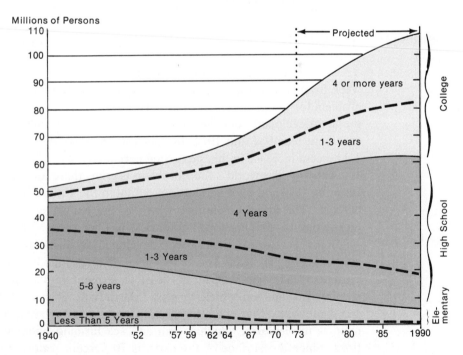

SOURCE: "Educational Attainment of the Work Force," *Road Maps of Industry*, No. 1758, The Conference Board (March, 1975).

Figure 29-2　**The Rising Educational Level of Workers in the Civilian Labor Force, 18–64 Years of Age**

The highly educated segment of the population will adopt more sophisticated and cosmopolitan tastes and values. Regardless of their type of work — banker, carpenter, or computer programmer — individuals will pursue lifestyles that are tailored to their individual choices. A relatively high standard of living and an affluent society will encourage the enjoyment of immediate wants rather than the yearning for future pleasures.

Persistent Urban Problems

Although urban renewal projects and mass transportation are attempting to halt the decay and congestion of the cities, it is doubtful if these actions will significantly improve the condition of the cities by 1980 or 1990. Some individuals in the higher- and middle-income brackets will be lured back to the cosmopolitan attractions of the city, but most middle-income families will choose to live in the less complicated environment of suburbia. Lower property values will reduce the tax base of cities at the very time that they will need increased revenues to pay for expanding maintenance and service costs. One expert estimates that it would take a minimum of $20 to $25 billion a year for at least a decade to revitalize our cities.

Challenges in Agriculture

Since it is estimated that throughout the world 10,000 people die each week from lack of food, the production of adequate food supplies is a critical problem for the present and future. The food shortage is particularly acute in the less-developed countries where food production increased only 0.3 percent between 1962 and 1972. In contrast, the developed nations exhibited a 1.7 percent increase in this same time period.

Although the world's food problem is grim, there are some hopeful signs. Between 1940 and 1971 agricultural output in the United States rose nearly 83 percent. The **green revolution**, which is the exporting of U.S. agricultural technology to less-developed countries, has been reasonably successful. The *single cell protein (SCP)* has been developed as an inexpensive and plentiful alternative to soybeans for animal feed. The production of SCP, which is created by allowing a strain of yeast to ferment in a petroleum derivative, requires no land on which to grow. Already English, Italian, and Russian companies are either operating or constructing SCP plants. Another development is **mariculture**, which is fish and sea farming under controlled conditions. Since the surface of the earth is 70 percent water, mariculture represents an enormous potential as a food source.

In the future, American agriculture will be dominated by larger and more capital-intensive farms. In 1960 only 23,000 farms had sales over $100,000; but by 1980 over 90,000 farms will have this volume, and several thousand farms will have revenues exceeding $1 million. As more equipment and less labor is used on farms, farm productivity will continue to rise. In 1960 labor accounted for nearly 30 percent of total productive resources used in agriculture, but by 1980 labor's share of this resource input will decline to 10 percent.

Public-Private Partnership

The responsibilities of the public and the private sectors of our enterprise system will become blurred in the future. As a result of consumer desires, government will enlarge its role in business. In 1975 a government-sponsored study of consumer attitudes toward our enterprise system indicated that 56 percent of the citizens want more government regulation while only 35 percent want less. Nearly 27 percent of those interviewed in the study identified that inflation was a principal source of their complaints. Another 18 percent shared the beliefs that big business caused shortages, received political tax advantages, and tended to be monopolistic. A disappointing aspect of the study was that 24 percent of the interviewees were unable to define what is meant by private enterprise.

As the public sector attempts to remedy the social and economic ills in our society, private enterprise will benefit, too. Since the government is not equipped to solve all our problems, private enterprise will be contracted to provide the necessary resources and expertise.

By 1990 new forms of business organizations will emerge to meet the needs of our complex society. Government organizations similar to the Amtrak railroad system will provide services in areas where the public need is present, but the risk and the capital requirements are high. Corporations which are incorporated and owned jointly by the government and private investors will be organized when the venture requires government control and large amounts of capital. Comsat, the communications satellite company, is an example of a corporation which, although owned by private investors, was incorporated by the government and has three directors appointed by the President.

Enlarged Social Responsibility

By the very act of forming a partnership with government, businesses become more responsive to society. In the future, corporate management will respond faster to changes in social values and priorities than in previous times. Through a corporate specialist in public affairs, a firm will monitor public opinion for shifts in the social consciousness.

Enlightened companies will adopt an annual **social audit** which will indicate the extent to which they have accomplished their social objectives. This audit will review a firm's achievements and its ability to adhere to previously established standards of social performance. Companies will develop a procedure for measuring the return on their social investment, just as they now measure the return on their plant, equipment, and other tangible assets.

Central Planning and Direction

By the 1980s, in an effort to reduce the frustration of inflation and the despair of recession, the federal government will be providing more planning and direction for private industry. Although a government planning office will not establish a stringent five-year plan, such as those used in communistic countries, it will attempt to coordinate and develop long-range production goals for private industry. Government planning will supplement rather than replace the market system. The planning agency will indicate the number of refrigerators or packages of detergent which it believes should be produced and then attempt to persuade corporate managers to accept the figures.

Internationalization of Business

In the future large multinational corporations will dominate business activity. Through the use of computers and telecommunications, the information systems of multinational corporations will have the capability to transfer immediately data to and from locations around the world. The chief economist for the United States Chamber of Commerce forecasts that within the next 25 years manufacturing will be concentrated within the factories of 55 worldwide corporations. To prosper, these large multinational companies will need to adapt to local cultures, to communicate their corporate goals to the local citizenry, and to discharge their social responsibilities in each host nation.

Another aspect of the internationalization of business is the prospect that less-developed countries will join together to form **cartels**. These cartels will regulate the prices and production of various raw materials which are needed by the industrialized nations. In 1973 the Organization of the Petroleum Exporting Countries (OPEC) demonstrated the effectiveness of their cartel by raising prices and restricting the output of petroleum. The success of OPEC will not go unheeded by other resource-rich countries.

Post-Industrial Society

The trend toward a service economy will intensify over the next several decades. In fact, some futurists identify a **post-industrial society** which is dominated by service industries. A continued increase in the services sector of the economy, however, does not mean that bowling alleys and beauty salons will replace General Motors and du Pont as the mainstays of our economy. Much of the increase in service employment is occurring because the number of workers who are employed by the government is increasing faster than in other areas of our economy. By providing employment and wages to millions, manufacturers will continue to sustain the affluent society which is necessary for the enjoyment of services.

In the future some services will grow more rapidly than others. There will be a strong demand for services which emphasize individualism and self-improvement. A persisting development will be the shifting of services from the home and homeowners to specialists who can perform them more efficiently. Examples of this movement are the popularity of home maintenance services, lawn care services, and condominium living. Other service industries which will expand are financial services, such as insurance and real estate, and professional services such as medical and health care.

Information Revolution

Although it is difficult to comprehend the masses of information which are being generated today, the future will bring even a greater flood of knowledge. Management information systems (MIS) will be needed to select, record, store, process, and retrieve the information which is necessary for decision making. As indicated in Chapter 23, the computer provides the capability for MIS. It is anticipated that in the near future for many companies MIS will move from the theory to the application stage.

During the 1980s there will be several new media which will disperse information to the public. The perfection of audiovisual television recordings will have a substantial impact upon the advertising, education, and entertainment industries. Cable television and satellite communications will bring consumers more diverse and specialized forms of information. Instant newspapers and other printed material will be available in the home through a subscription to an electronic facsimile service. Home facsimile units will provide for the immediate reproduction of printed matter which is generated thousands of miles away.

Reappraisal of Technology

Periodically this country looks to technology to save itself from an untimely adversity, such as the energy crunch, and at other times it considers technology as a bearer of social and economic misfortune such as technological unemployment. The 1980s will be a time to sit back and evaluate the consequences of implementing technical achievements.

Some futurists feel that the landing on the moon in 1969 marked the end of the old technology where the United States prodded ahead with new developments simply because the expertise was available. In the future the benefits to be realized from technology will be carefully weighed against the costs to society. The barring of support by the United States Congress for the development of a supersonic transport (SST) is a prelude of this new mood toward technology.

MANAGEMENT

The hard-nosed, bullheaded managers of the past are being replaced with humanistic, democratic administrators who attempt to match the goals of their organizations with the goals of their workers. The manager of the future will face many new and complex relationships and adjustments. Some factors which will confront a manager are discussed in the following paragraphs.

Increased Worker Participation

Although a basic management premise has been to place full authority and responsibility in the hands of one individual, in the future there will be more shared decision making. The better-educated, self-assured workers of the future will desire to share in the managerial decisions which affect their work. They will want less authoritative and more participative management. Authority will flow from the objectives which are agreed upon by the workers and their supervisors.

It is conceivable that management in this country will follow the pattern of management in several other nations and permit workers a voice in major policy decisions. In England the Chrysler Corporation offered to place labor representatives on the board of directors of their English operation in return for labor peace. In numerous European corporations, such as Volkswagenwerk AG, the ultimate authority on many key policy matters is determined by a **supervisory board** which represents management, workers, government, and other outside interests.

Growth of Systems

In the future more companies are going to adopt the systems approach. As pointed out in Chapter 23, in the systems concept every activity, such as marketing, production, and finance, is related to every other activity; and a change in one activity has an impact upon all other activities. An advantage of this approach is that it provides a method for coordinating separate operations into a unified company plan.

A system should retain flexibility so it is capable of responding to change. A rigid system could lead management to incorrect goals. An official of the General Electric Company illustrated this problem when he cited the person who chose the right course in school to gain admission to the right college where he could study the right subjects and move on to the right graduate school to work in the right career — only to discover that it really was not the right career for that person.[2]

Increased Professionalism

Some companies have a proud tradition of promoting from within; that is, only their own employees are considered for vacant positions in the corporate chain of command. In the future most companies will not be able to afford the luxury of ignoring qualified candidates from outside the company to fill managerial vacancies. Young, highly educated, professional administrators will be sought for their managerial expertise. These goal-oriented individuals, many of whom will be graduates of outstanding business schools, will be equally comfortable as managers in industry, government, or education. Paradoxically the increased professionalism of the manager presents a disadvantage to a company. The most important concerns of the professional manager will be the challenges of the profession, rather than those of a specific company.

The professional manager will get things done through people. According to one management expert, the manager of the future will need to be a leader-administrator, a visionary planner, a change-generating entrepreneur, a statesperson, and a designer of systems and structures. Because of these diverse requirements for a top administrator, some management authorities predict that the chief executive responsibilities in major firms will be shared. Presidential teams rather than single individuals will be employed to manage our giant corporations.

Rise of the Public Manager

The professional managers will be **public managers**, too. In addition to earning a profit for the shareholders of a company, a public manager will need to be responsive to society and to act as a spokesperson for the enterprise system. These managers will recognize and be sensitive to the impact of corporate decisions upon our life-style. The public manager will need to balance delicately a company's responsibilities to its employees, shareholders, government, customers, suppliers, and the community.

Increased Use of Temporary Organizations

The managers of the future will use extensively the matrix or project organization described in Chapter 6. This type of structure will permit managers to

[2]Reprinted from Robert J. Lavidge, "Marketing in 1980 — Management Must Look Ahead to Anticipate Changes," *Marketing News* (October 15, 1973), p. 1, published by the American Marketing Association.

shift their resources to meet the changing requirements of a firm. Meeting the challenges of a complex, fast-paced environment requires the establishment of temporary organizations which can be quickly disbanded after accomplishing their missions.

MARKETING

The marketing system will be called upon to translate the ecological and social concerns of consumers into goods and services. The marketing of services, such as health care, recreation, and entertainment, will rival the importance of the marketing of tangible products such as automobiles and appliances. In most organizations sophisticated marketing systems will replace the piecemeal application of marketing techniques.

Marketing in the Service and Nonprofit Sectors

Marketing in the service sector of the economy will increase in importance. Since the United States moved into a service-oriented economy in the early 1950s, the marketing of all types of services has gained momentum. Table 29-2 shows examples of services and new, improved methods of providing existing services. It has been forecast that in the near future Sears will be generating over half of its earnings from the sales of retail services.

In the nonprofit sector of the economy administrators will be challenged to market energy conservation, ecological preservation, and other similar

Table 29-2 **Examples of Service Product Innovations**

Nature of Service	New Service Product	Service Product Improvement
Communications	Communication satellite	Free-standing public telephone
Consulting and business facilitating	Equipment leasing	Overnight TV rating service
Educational	Three-year degrees	New curricula
Financial	Bank credit cards	"Bank by mail"
Health	Treatment with lasers	Intensive care
Household operations	Laundromat	Fuel budget accounts
Housing	Housing for the elderly	Motel swimming pool
Insurance	National health insurance	No-fault insurance
Legal	"Divorce Yourself" kit[1]	Legal services for the poor
Personal	Physical fitness facilities	—
Recreational	Dual cinema	New play
Transportation	Unit train	Flight reservation system

SOURCE: John M. Rathmell, *Marketing in the Service Sector* (Cambridge, Mass.: Winthrop Publishers, Inc., 1974), p. 62.

[1]Under court injunction in New York but being appealed.

programs to consumers. The Audubon Society and the Sierra Club have an intangible product to market, while General Motors and Ford have tangible products to market.

As the social welfare activities of government continue to increase, administrators will need to market these activities to the public. The need for marketing government services was illustrated in the mid-1960s by the initial failure of the elderly to participate in Medicare. Although Medicare provided at a very low cost abundant medical care benefits for the aged, an advertising campaign was finally necessary to achieve the desired enrollments.

Retailing in a Cashless Society

By 1990 many Americans will be participating in the cashless society. In the **cashless society** goods will be ordered, bills will be paid, and bank balances will be reduced without the physical handling of any cash or the writing of any bank checks. By using a touchtone phone and a special credit card, consumers will be able to place their orders with a merchant. With the assistance of a computer, the merchant will fill the order. Then the merchant's computer will bill the customer and the payment will be credited to the merchant's account by a computer in the customer's bank.

A modified form of the cashless society concept has been tested by the City National Bank in Columbus, Ohio, and the Hempstead Bank in Long Island, New York. In these tests the consumer presented a credit card to the merchant who, by using the computer swiftly and automatically, completed the transaction and transferred the funds to the proper accounts. This system is known as **electronic funds transfer**. Although City National realized a 7 to 10 cents saving on each test transaction as compared to conventional transactions, the bank concluded that this type of system will need wide usage to show overall cost savings.

Rise of Rentalism

In a society with a geographically, occupationally, and socially mobile population, the temporary possession and use of a good becomes more important than ownership for many consumers. In the future the rental of goods will become more important than at present. By renting, a consumer is freed from the worries of maintenance and obsolescence. Renting is more flexible and convenient than owning. In a study of the reasons for renting cars, convenience was identified as a major factor. Renting, which implies sharing the usage of a good among different consumers, will become an economically and ecologically efficient practice. Already numerous companies are preparing for an upsurge in rental demand. For example, RCA purchased Hertz, and the Greyhound Corporation acquired Boothe Leasing.

PRODUCTION

Within the past 25 years the use of quantitative techniques and automated equipment has changed considerably our manufacturing processes. In recent years a large proportion of expenditures by manufacturers has been directed to equipment which will reduce pollution and preserve our environment. Although the present trends in production will continue to be important, changing environmental forces will give rise to new developments.

Completely Automated Factories

The continued automation and computerization of factories will result in more capital investment per employee, but fewer employees. As stated in Chapter 23, the era of the completely automated factory is near. When these new factories go into operation, they will reduce significantly the demand for unskilled labor but expand the demand for semiskilled and skilled technicians. In petroleum refineries this change in the composition of the work force has already occurred.

Flexible Work Scheduling

Flexible work scheduling will be adopted by numerous companies. **Flexible work scheduling** allows workers to choose within a prescribed range their own working hours. A major requirement is that employees complete a certain number of hours of work within a given time period. Many young factory workers view their jobs as temporary necessities until they can locate more desirable assignments. For these individuals flexible work scheduling has the ingredients to make factory jobs look more attractive.

Between 1900 and 1940 the average workweek decreased from 60 to 40 hours. From 1940 to 1970, however, there was only a three-hour reduction in the workweek. Yet the demands of workers persist for increased leisure time. Flexible work scheduling permits a worker to free a block of time by working in more concentrated periods of time. By the mid-1970s Hewlett-Packard, a California electronics firm, and Control Data Corporation, a Minneapolis-based computer manufacturer, had initiated flexible work scheduling for several thousands of their employees.

By expanding the concept of flexible work scheduling beyond the workday or the workweek, some experts foresee work combinations, such as six weeks on and three weeks off or six months on and six months off. Although this kind of scheduling may not be appropriate for all jobs, this pattern of work may make the boring and routine jobs more acceptable to workers.

Job Enrichment

Manufacturers will need to enrich and enlarge the scope of work for a better-educated work force. The repetitious motions of the assembly line are hardly compatible with a worker's desire for recognition and self-expression. A job enrichment program, which was mentioned in Chapter 12, is a way to redesign the work to make it more interesting to employees. It permits employees to participate in goal setting, problem solving, and decision making. Job enrichment shifts the focus of the production system from industrial efficiency to social efficiency.

If labor organizations are receptive to job enrichment programs, they should be prevalent throughout industry by 1980. The Corning Glass Works in Medfield, Massachusetts, and Volvo, the Swedish automobile manufacturer, have adapted their production processes for job enrichment. If job enrichment is utilized in the Volvo assembly plant which is expected to be built in the United States, it probably would hasten acceptance of the concept by American manufacturers.

FINANCE

To many individuals finance often is believed to be an extremely conservative and unexciting field. To those who are employed in the field, it is a highly dynamic and stimulating area. In the future there will be changes in both the sources and the forms of financing.

Capital Shortage

By 1980 American firms will experience a shortage of capital. In the mid-1970s corporate capital expenditures for new plant, equipment, and other long-term expenditures were amounting to about $100 billion a year; but by 1985 capital needs are projected to be over $230 billion a year. All companies, but particularly the smaller emerging firms, will be hurt by the **capital crunch**.

One of the reasons for this capital shortage is that financial institutions, such as banks, life insurance companies, and investment companies, tend to ignore the smaller, less prominent firms and concentrate their investments in a few of the larger, more dominant corporations. For example, the ten largest banks in the United States have holdings of nearly $27 billion in only ten major American corporations. Another reason is that the private sector of the economy has received growing competition from the public sector which requires large amounts of capital to finance massive government deficits.

Foreign Investment in the United States

Since the end of World War II, companies in the United States have made numerous scattered and diverse investments throughout the world. In the future as foreign countries and foreign companies increase their surplus of dollars, they will be investing in United States corporations. Although many Americans will be displeased by this apparent untimely turn of events, during the 1980s foreign investment will provide much needed financing for capital-short American firms. Already there is evidence of this occurrence. In 1974 the Magnavox Company, an American television and electronics manufacturer, was purchased by a subsidiary of Philips Gloeilampenfabrk, a large, Dutch-based electronics firm. In another instance, an Arab investor purchased a controlling interest in a major Detroit bank.

Competition Among Consumer Financial Institutions

The various consumer financial institutions will be competing to provide many of the same types of financial services to consumers. Some of these institutions will be in nationwide competition with each other. Bank holding companies will either acquire or establish nationwide consumer finance companies and mortgage banking companies. Through the use of computer terminals and a telecommunications network, the holding companies will be able to offer to consumers throughout the country a wide array of financial services.

All consumer financial establishments, such as commercial banks, mutual savings banks, and savings and loan associations, will be seeking through innovation and enabling legislation to offer their customers checking accounts, consumer loans, and credit cards. For example, in the early 1970s some mutual savings banks creatively developed a financial instrument which permits them to offer the equivalent of an interest-bearing checking account. In another development savings and loan associations gained legislative authority to finance certain types of household goods in addition to homes and business properties.

BUSINESS TERMS

QUESTIONS FOR DISCUSSION AND ANALYSIS

1. What type of information and trends would a futurist who is employed by an automobile manufacturer be seeking?
2. Is the advent of zero population growth really going to prove beneficial to the United States? Explain.
3. In the future should the opportunity to enter college be made available to every person who is a high school graduate? Discuss.
4. What type of solutions would you propose to resolve the economic and social problems which threaten our major cities?
5. If a major company in a vital industry is on the brink of bankruptcy, should the government provide financial assistance? What are the implications of this type of government action?
6. Is it wrong for less-developed nations to form cartels that regulate the prices and production of raw materials which are needed by industrialized nations? Explain.
7. Assess the advantages and disadvantages of having key policy matters in a corporation determined by a supervisory board which represents management, workers, government, and other outside interests.
8. In the future will consumers desire to patronize retailers who do not adapt to the concept of the cashless society? Discuss.
9. When an employer adopts flexible work scheduling, what type of adjustments and problems does the employer face?
10. Should the United States enact legislation which would limit foreign investment in American companies? Discuss the implications.

PROBLEMS AND SHORT CASES

1. Scenarios are hypothetical sequences of events constructed for the purpose of focusing attention on causal processes and decision points. Write a step-by-step scenario to explain how major food chains, such as Safeway, A&P, and Kroger, will participate in the cashless society.
2. In recent years the publication of books about the future, such as *Future Shock* by Alvin Toffler, *The Year 2000* by Herman Kahn and Anthony J. Wiener, and the *Post-Industrial Society* by Daniel Bell, have evoked strong interest in expectations of the future. In 1966 the World Future Society was organized for the study of alternative futures. This society publishes the *Futurist* magazine every other month. Since the mid-1960s, articles about the future have appeared in numerous periodicals. Many of these articles can be located by consulting the *Readers' Guide to Periodical Literature* and the *Business Periodicals Index* in your school library.

   Prepare a short paper which examines in depth three trends of the future. Explain the reasons for the development and growth of these trends, and the probable reaction of business to these trends. Information for your report will be found in the preceding sources as well as in other materials.
3. Charles Riche is the president and principal stockholder of the United Snuff Corporation. Riche, who is 70 years old, started his career as a factory laborer at United Snuff in 1928. His grandfather founded the company in 1892 and the Riche family has continued to operate the company. With the untimely death of his father in 1935, Riche was chosen president of the company.

   Riche believes that the stable sales record of his company indicates that it is relatively free from the effects of recessions. He is proud to point out that his firm has paid the same dividend to stockholders for over 50 years. He attributes this stability to the nature of his product. Snuff is a tobacco product which is marketed in both a moist and a dry form. Individuals enjoy the biting taste and nicotine effect of moist snuff by placing it behind the lip. Dry snuff is an aromatic preparation of powdered tobacco which is often taken into the nostrils by inhaling. United Snuff specializes in moist snuff, which is the most popular kind. The biggest demand for snuff comes from blue-collar workers who cannot smoke on the job.

Since the 1930s Riche has heard critics of the small, but vigorous, snuff industry claim that snuff producers soon will be laid to rest next to the manufacturers of high button shoes, kerosene lamps, and buggy whips. Riche has not closed his ears to the utterings of these critics. Recently Riche read that some company managements were employing futurists who would identify future trends for a firm. He is seriously considering employing a futurist consultant for United Snuff.

Another of Riche's concerns is that his company is too dependent on one product line. Although other members of his family do not desire to diversify, he is actively evaluating other products which United Snuff could market. Although Riche feels that snuff is recession-proof, he has lived through enough recessions to want some additional products in his line as insurance against the collapse of the market for snuff.

a. As a futurist consultant to United Snuff, identify the future trends which will affect the operation and profitability of the company.
b. Should United Snuff diversify into other product lines? If they should diversify, what product lines should they add? Provide justification for your answers.

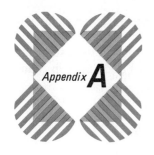

Business Career Opportunities

An opportune time for a student to establish a career objective is when he or she begins to pursue a college program. As a student approaches graduation either from an associate or bachelor's degree program, the problem of a career choice becomes critical. Prior planning and preparation will enhance a person's ability to select a career which is compatible with his or her objectives and values. Counselors, parents, professors, friends, and others can provide career guidance and direction for a student.

In recent years numerous factors have made career planning more uncertain and difficult than in previous years. Significant changes in the economic and social climate have complicated the process of selecting a career. The onset of economic recessions has halted periodically the recruiting efforts of many large companies, such as the major automobile manufacturers, and has reduced the recruiting activities of most other firms. The need for companies to increase their proportions of women and members of minority groups has frustrated the career planning of some white males. In previous years the possession of a college diploma generally assured these males of one or more job opportunities. Today, to compensate for past discriminatory actions, companies are often making job offers to women and individuals from minority groups prior to offering employment to white males.

Other factors which influence career planning include educational trends, technological advancements, and the military position of our government. The growing number of two-year associate degree programs is creating a large group of graduates who are seeking careers in mid-management positions. The availability of associate degree programs has forced many students to make a decision between enrolling in either a two-year or a four-year curriculum.

Technological advancements can change the numbers and types of occupations within an industry. For example, the emergence of the computer has created positions for systems analysts and programmers but has reduced the need for payroll and inventory control clerks. In the 1960s and the early 1970s, the draft and the prospects of military service altered the career plans of many males. Voluntary enlistments in the armed services and a reduction in international tensions may eliminate this uncertainty from future career planning.

CAREER PLANNING DECISIONS

Selecting a career involves several complex decisions on the part of the individual.

The sheer number of occupations from which one can choose causes confusion and uncertainty about his or her career prospects. It has been estimated that there are over 40,000 different occupations. Even individuals who have been employed for many years occasionally express the belief that they are still uncertain about their ultimate choice of a career.

Type of Occupation

First, a person needs to choose the type of occupation which is compatible with his or her personal goals and values. Does an individual feel strongly motivated toward a career in accounting, marketing, social work, or some other field? If a tentative career choice is made prior to starting a college or post-high school vocational program, a student can plan his or her post-high school education with a specific career objective in mind.

Kind of Industry or Organizational Setting

A second decision involves the kind of industry or organizational setting in which a person desires to work. In the accounting field one has a choice for a position among industrial firms, public accounting organizations, and government agencies. Although the body of accounting principles which is utilized by all forms of organizations is similar, the application and use of accounting procedures differ according to the type of organization. Each of the organizations provides a distinctive work environment for an accountant.

The specific requirements of a position generally vary from industry to industry. For example, a marketing researcher for U.S. Steel has different responsibilities than one for Beatrice Foods. Even within the same industry the duties of a particular job fluctuate from company to company. For example, the role of a marketing researcher is different in Beatrice Foods than in Standard Brands.

Geographic Location

Another decision which a job candidate needs to resolve concerns geographic location. Individuals tend to feel most comfortable in the area of the country in which they have spent the longest period of their lives. This, however, is not a valid reason for resisting a move to another geographic location. If job candidates restrict themselves to a particular geographic location, they also limit the number of job offers which they receive. If an individual desires employment in a company which operates nationwide, the individual should be willing to accept assignments wherever the company's plants and offices are located. A person with a strong desire to reside in the Southeast may seek and accept a job in Atlanta only to be transferred by the company several years later to Minneapolis.

Size of Company

A job candidate needs to decide upon the size of the company in which he or she wants to work. In a small company an individual frequently obtains a position which carries broader responsibilities than a similar position in a larger company with its more specialized assignments. On the other hand, the larger firm generally offers attractive advancement opportunities into many types of managerial positions. Some individuals initially desire the training program, growth prospects, and high salaries offered by the larger company. As their values change at a later period in their career, these same individuals will often seek employment in a smaller firm where they can establish a greater identity and assume more important leadership roles.

Line or Staff Position

Another decision facing the job candidate is whether to seek a line or a staff position. One may begin as a trainee or an assistant in a staff position, such as marketing research or quality control, and eventually be promoted to the head of the staff area. In many cases, however, this is as far as the individual in a staff job will rise in a firm. As indicated in Chapter 6, staff positions support the line activities. By working in these positions, a person is exposed to a variety of experiences which assist in his or her development as a future line executive. Most top management positions are held by individuals who, although exposed to some staff assignments, have moved progressively through a series of line jobs in either marketing, production, or finance.

OCCUPATIONAL SELECTION AIDS

To scan the wide spectrum of career opportunities in business requires time and patience. A student's college years should be the time to learn the relative merits of various careers. During this period a student can discover his or her own qualifications and the characteristics of a wide variety of occupations from: (1) personal evaluation, (2) college courses, (3) work experience, (4) vocational literature, (5) industry contacts, (6) biographies, business histories, and magazine articles, and (7) placement bureaus.

Personal Evaluation

Some of the following appraisals of your vocational qualifications can be measured objectively; other evaluations require a subjective treatment.

Mental Ability. Intelligence tests are available that can measure accurately your mental capacities in relationship to other college students. If you have not already taken such tests, they are available at most schools or in private counseling agencies in larger cities. Since the tests generally are prepared and validated on white middle-class Americans, the tests may contain a bias against other cultural and ethnic groups. Scores and their meanings should be obtained from persons competent to interpret them properly.

Depending upon the precision of measurement desired, there are several different types of intelligence tests available. The *Binet-Simon Test* is very accurate, but it involves a lengthy period of administration. The *Wonderlic Personnel Test*, which requires only 12 minutes, and the *Otis Self-Administering Test of Mental Ability*, which can be completed in 30 minutes, usually provide a reasonable assessment of mental ability.

Aptitudes and Interests. The extent of the ability of a person to learn how to perform certain jobs can be measured by aptitude tests. These tests measure such items as finger and manual dexterity, numerical aptitude, and eye-hand coordination. A very bright young woman who thought she would like to be a secretary found that her eye-hand coordination was so poor that she could not learn to type rapidly without making mistakes.

Two tests that measure these aptitudes are the *Differential Aptitude Tests* of the Psychological Corporation and the *General Aptitude Test Battery* of the United States Employment Service. The latter test is available to job applicants who register with the State Employment Service.

Interest tests are also available that provide an index of similarity between one's interests and those of successful men and women in a wide range of occupations. The best-known interest tests are the *Kuder Preference Record* and the *Strong Vocational Interest Blank*. These tests are usually available wherever general intelligence tests are given.

In vocational guidance centers, in state employment service offices, and at most colleges and universities, there are individuals with graduate degrees in psychology or guidance counseling, who can evaluate the mental ability, aptitudes, and potential required for achievement in a job. They are able to administer tests designed to measure intelligence, reasoning power, reading comprehension, and interest. They also know the areas of opportunities and the job requirements of applicants for these positions.

Personality. Personality traits are important in the selection of a vocation. The ability to make friends easily and to get along well with other people and a good character are a few personality elements that are necessary for success in all types of work. Other traits, such as initiative, judgment, emotional stability, and physical size and fitness, are frequently more important in one type of work than in another. Although tests and self-rating scales are available, personality traits cannot be measured with as much accuracy as can intelligence, aptitudes, and interests.

The *Minnesota Multiphasic Personality Inventory*, the *Bernreuter Inventory*, and the *California Psychological Inventory* assess personality characteristics. The latter test measures four different types of behavior. They include:

1. Self-acceptance, sociability, and sense of well-being.
2. Tolerance, responsibility, and self-control.
3. Independence, conformity, and efficiency.
4. Flexibility and perceptiveness.

Avocations. It is not at all unusual for students to gain a useful clue to their future choice of vocations through an introspective analysis of their avocations or hobbies. Many individuals have certain likes and dislikes that are shown frequently by the activities in which they engage. Students who enjoy art, writing, mathematics, working with tools, or constructing things may discover that these interests offer useful suggestions in the choice of their college majors and eventual vocational selections.

College Courses

When you complete this course and others in business subjects, you will be more familiar with the various areas of business and the activities performed in each. In most instances these activities can be translated into job opportunities. There may be some particular kind of work that, prior to learning about it during your course of instruction, was unknown to you. It may prove to be the right answer to your problem of selecting a self-fulfilling and challenging vocation. A young man studied motion and time study in a course in industrial management. Although this type of work had never occurred to him as a career opportunity, he became so interested in this technique that it became his vocational choice.

Work Experience

Some work experience, either during the school year or vacations, is desirable. If it is financially possible, a variety of jobs should be sought. Each job will provide you with a basis for evaluating the various kinds of employment. Working in a factory, an office, and a retail store, for example, will give you a firsthand contact with the requirements and responsibilities of positions in these fields. Using this procedure should help you to make some positive choices as well as to eliminate others from further consideration.

The curricula of some schools offer industrial internships and cooperative education programs which blend work experience with formal education. Through structured work assignments in a company, students are provided a realistic test of their career interests and aptitudes. As students see the relationship between their classroom assignments and their work experience, their academic studies frequently become more meaningful.

Vocational Literature

A wealth of vocational literature is available in your college library as well as in the public libraries of your home communities. The *Occupational Outlook Handbook* and the *Occupational Outlook Quarterly,* which are published by the Bureau of Labor Statistics, are particularly helpful in identifying trends and growth patterns for many different occupations.

A useful reference in investigating specific jobs is the Third Edition of the *Dictionary of Occupational Titles* and *Supplements* prepared by the U.S. Employment Service. (A 1975 supplement contains job title revisions to eliminate sex- and age-referent language from the DOT.) The DOT lists almost 22,000 occupations with more than 35,000 occupational titles and classifies them under nine headings: (a) professional, technical, and managerial occupations; (b) clerical and sales occupations; (c) service occupations; (d) farming, fishery, forestry, and related occupations; (e) processing occupations; (f) machine trades occupations; (g) bench work occupations; (h) structural work occupations; and (i) miscellaneous occupations.

Two samples from this dictionary give some idea of the type of information provided about the jobs listed.

Market-Research Analyst. Researches market conditions in local, regional, or national area to determine potential sales of a product or service: Examines and analyzes statistical data on past sales and wholesale or retail trade trends to forecast future sales trends. Gathers data on competitors and analyzes their prices, sales, and methods of operation. Collects data on buying habits and preferences of prospective customers. May specialize in advertising analysis and be designated as Advertising Analyst.

Programmer, Business. Converts symbolic statement of business problems to detailed logical flow charts for coding into computer language and solution by means of automatic data-processing equipment: Analyzes all or part of workflow chart or diagram representing business problem by applying knowledge of computer capabilities, subject matter, algebra, and symbolic logic to develop sequence of program steps. Confers with supervisor and representatives of departments affected by program to resolve questions of program intent, output requirements, input data acquisition, extent of automatic programming and coding use and modification, and inclusion of internal checks and controls. Writes detailed logical flow chart in symbolic form to represent work order of data to be processed by computer system, and to describe input, output, and arithmetic and logical operations involved. May convert detailed logical flow chart to language processable by computer. Devises sample input data to provide test of program adequacy. Prepares block diagrams to specify equipment configuration. Observes or runs tests of coded program on computer, using actual or sample input data. Corrects program errors by such methods as altering program steps and sequence. Prepares written instructions (run book) to guide operating personnel during production runs. Analyzes, reviews, and rewrites programs to increase operating efficiency or adapt to new requirements. Compiles documentation of program development and subsequent revisions. May specialize in writing programs for one make and type of computer.

Industry Contacts

Whenever the opportunity presents itself, preferably through class trips planned by the instructor, visit a factory, a store, or a bank, and see business in action. Try to imagine yourself in some of the jobs you see others filling. Also talk with employees at all levels of management about their jobs. Try to find out what they believe is important for success in their particular line of endeavor. Friends of your family and acquaintances may give you additional suggestions and ideas.

Biographies, Business Histories, and Magazine Articles

A great many books have been written about businesspersons and outstanding business firms. Many of these not only make fascinating reading but also provide a description of an industry or an individual who achieved success. Articles such as those that appear in *Fortune, Business Week, Time, Forbes,* and other magazines also provide information about companies and jobs.

Placement Bureaus

Many colleges and universities maintain placement bureaus whose primary purpose is to provide the facilities through which prospective graduates and the recruiting officers from business may meet and discuss job availabilities. These bureaus frequently place on bulletin boards and in campus newspapers notices of employment opportunities offered by firms whose personnel officers visit the campus or request help in filling vacancies. Knowledge of the types of openings that will become available to you when you approach graduation will be helpful in stimulating your thinking along vocational lines. Many of the firms that recruit college graduates have compiled brochures describing their opportunities and positions, and these are usually available in the placement bureau office.

AREAS OF EMPLOYMENT OPPORTUNITIES

As the supply of college graduates approaches the demand for graduates, a knowledge of employment opportunities becomes vitally important. Table A-1 presents the employment trends and prospects for some of the occupations which are discussed in this section. As indicated by the table, there will be wide variations in growth for the different occupations. Figure A-1 indicates the career paths in selected occupations. By examining Table A-1 and Figure A-1 and by reading the ensuing section on employment opportunities, you should be able to make more informed career decisions.

The following identification of employment opportunities generally parallels the sequence of the text material and the presentations in Table A-1 and Figure A-1: (1) establishing your own business, (2) marketing, (3) personnel, (4) production, (5) finance, (6) accounting, computer operation, and statistics, and (7) government service. The *Occupational Outlook Handbook*, 1974–1975 edition, served as a valuable resource for this section.

Establishing Your Own Business

Some of the vocational opportunities suggested by Part 2: Business Ownership,

Table A-1   **Prospects to 1985 for Selected Business Occupations**

Occupation	Estimated Employment in 1972 and Average Annual Openings[1]	Average Earnings with Experience 1973	Employment Trends and Prospects
MARKETING OCCUPATIONS			
Manufacturers' salesworkers	423,000/ 20,000	$16–32,000	Favorable job opportunities.
Wholesale trade salesworkers	688,000/ 31,000	$15,000	Moderate employment growth.
Retail trade salesworkers	2,778,000/190,000	Varies	Good employment opportunities.
Advertising workers	152,000/ (2)	$10–22,000	Employment should grow moderately.
Marketing research workers	25,000/ (2)	$15,000	Very rapid employment growth.
PERSONNEL OCCUPATIONS			
Personnel workers	240,000/ (2)	$15,000	Excellent employment opportunities.
Lawyers	303,000/ 16,500	$18–33,700	Moderate employment rise.
PRODUCTION OCCUPATIONS			
Foremen	1,400,000/ 58,000	$10,410	Moderate employment growth.
Industrial engineers	125,000/ 7,400	$19,600	Very rapid growth in job opportunities.
Industrial traffic managers	20,300/ (2)	$16–30,000	Slow employment increase.
Purchasing agents	181,000/ (2)	$10.5–15,000	Moderate employment growth.
FINANCE OCCUPATIONS			
Bank officers	219,000/ 13,600	Varies	Rapid employment gains.
Credit officials	114,000/ 7,500	$10–20,000	Rapid employment growth.
Insurance agents and brokers	385,000/ 16,000	$8–20,000	Moderate employment growth.
Underwriters	61,000/ 2,500	$10–15,000	Many opportunities as demand increases.
Actuaries	5,500/ 500	$18–25,000	Favorable job opportunities.
Securities salesworkers	220,000/ 11,900	$21,000	Moderate employment growth.
Real estate salesworkers and brokers	349,000/ 25,000	$12–20,000	Moderate employment increase.
ACCOUNTING, COMPUTER OPERATIONS, AND STATISTICS			
Accountants	714,000/ 41,900	$11.9–20,000	Good job opportunities.
FBI agents	8,600/ (2)	Start $12,776	Good job opportunities.
Programmers	186,000/ 13,000	$11–18,900	Rapid employment growth.
Systems analysts	103,000/ 8,300	$15,700	Very rapid employment growth.
Statisticians	23,000/ 1,700	Varies	Favorable employment prospects.
GOVERNMENT SERVICES			
City managers	2,500/ 150	$12–35,000	Very rapid employment growth.
Employment counselors	8,500/ 800	$9.7–15,700	Favorable employment opportunities.
Health and regulatory inspectors	25,000/ 1,700	$11.6–21,686	Very rapid employment growth.

SOURCE: "Occupational Outlook Handbook in Brief, 1974–1975 Edition," *Occupational Outlook Quarterly* (Summer, 1974), pp. 15–38.

[1]Due to growth and death, retirement, and other separations from the labor force. Does not include transfers out of the occupations.
[2]Estimate not available.

Career Paths in Selected Occupations and Industries

Approx. Annual Earnings[1]	Marketing	Retailing	Personnel	Production Management	Banking	Public Accounting	Industrial Accounting	Approx. Years of Service[1]
$40,000	Vice-President Marketing	Corporate Vice-President	Vice-President Personnel	Vice-President Production	President		Vice-President Finance	15
	National Sales or Advertising Manager	Nat'l Merchandise Manager / Nat'l Operations Manager	Corporate Personnel Staff	Division Manufacturing Manager	Senior Vice-President	Partner or Principal	Division Controller	14 – 13
	Product Group Manager	Divisional Buyer / Zone Manager		Product Group Manufacturing Staff	Vice-President		Assistant Division Controller	12 – 11
		Store Manager						10
$26,000	Marketing Staff Analyst		Plant Personnel Manager	Plant Manager	Asst. Vice-President Junior Officer	Manager	Plant Controller	9
	Regional Sales Manager	Buyer / Asst. Store Manager					Assistant Controller	8 – 7
	Branch Sales Manager	Asst. Buyer or Dept. Manager	Employment Manager	Department Manager	Branch Manager, Operations, Dept. Manager, Analyst, Trust, Commercial	Senior Accountant	Department Manager	6 – 5
$16,000	Sales Supervisor			Production Supervision				4
	Sales	Sales	Personnel Assistant	Departmental Assistant	Banker in Training	Staff Accountant	Staff Financial Analyst	3
		Trainee					General Accountant	2
$11,000 to $9,000	Marketing	Retailing	Personnel	Production Management	Banking	Public Accounting	Industrial Accounting	1

SOURCE: C. Randall Powell, *Career Planning and Placement for the College Graduate of the '70's* (Dubuque, Iowa: Kendall/Hunt Publishing Company, 1974), p. 47.

Of course, these estimates only approximate earnings and yearly progress in a purely hypothetical organization. More specific information is nearly impossible to obtain due to the wide variance between employers.

[1] Approximates a 10% increase per year (includes inflation). Based on 1974 dollars.

Figure A-1 **Career Paths in Selected Occupations and Industries**

Organization, and Management, center around going into business for yourself. Most young men and women who go into business for themselves find that the better opportunities are in their local communities and in a business that sells goods or services to the public. The operation of a motel, a fast-food service, a television and radio repair shop, and a women's apparel shop are a few examples of such enterprises. Occasionally new manufacturing operations are established to produce a good, but such enterprises are less common than the retailing of goods and services. The growth of franchising has provided a new field of self-employment for persons who have the requisite capital and abilities.

Many individuals who hope to go into business for themselves realize that they must have certain resources, both personal and financial, but they fail to consider that they should have some experience in the proposed line of endeavor or one related to it. Unless such experience has been acquired by the time the person completes college training, it may be the wisest course of action to work for someone else who is established in the same or a related business. Going into business for yourself offers opportunities for great rewards, but the risks are much higher than when working for someone else. Before deciding to operate your own business, be sure that you have the necessary personal qualities, have access to adequate capital funds, and possess the requisite experience for the type of business selected.

Marketing

The field of marketing offers numerous as well as widely varied vocational opportunities for college graduates. Salespersons are needed by manufacturers, wholesalers, retailers, and all others who produce and sell goods and services. With the exception of a very few goods that require technical training as a background for their sale, college-trained personnel with a business background are sought by many types of firms.

Because of the large number of salespersons employed, advancement possibilities are excellent. Openings such as sales supervisor, branch sales manager, regional sales manager, and national sales manager are available in industrial firms to those who have achieved outstanding sales records and possess supervisory abilities. Department stores usually promote salespersons first to the rank of assistant buyer and then to buyer for a particular department of a store. Recognizing the need for a larger number of competent and trainable personnel than is to be found in their employee ranks, many department stores have executive training programs to fill their future requirements at the managerial level.

Advertising is another area of marketing that offers a number of possibilities. Openings are available in the advertising departments of large firms and also in advertising agencies. Duties may involve copywriting and layout, or they may deal with such problems as buying or selling space. In the advertising department of a firm, one can advance to the position of an assistant advertising manager and then to advertising manager. In agencies, the first step might be to an account executive or to the managership of a department in the business.

There is an increasing demand for competent personnel in marketing research. College graduates with a background in marketing and statistics are sought after both by marketing research firms and by the marketing research departments of many companies. The initial positions might be as interviewers or in questionnaire construction, with an eventual promotion to supervisor or editor. A knowledge of statistics can lead to positions in the area of sample construction and validation.

With the expansion of international trade that has taken place during the last two decades, particularly the growth of firms with branch offices and factories in other countries, there have appeared opportunities for those who can qualify for positions in international marketing management. Multinational firms carefully select and train those individuals who will be given overseas assignments. Knowledge of a foreign language and a sensitivity to the cultural differences among countries is generally useful.

Personnel

Although the openings in the field of personnel and labor relations are limited, this area has been one of great interest to business students in recent years. Most of the larger factories maintain personnel departments; and employment possibilities in this field are greater in industry than they are in distributive, financial, and other non-manufacturing enterprises. For those who become involved in labor negotiations, a law degree is often needed. Within the personnel organization, advancement possibilities include heading a division such as employment, training, personnel services, safety and health, personnel research, wages and salaries, and labor relations. From one of these posts an outstanding individual should be able to secure a position as the personnel manager, and many firms now have a vice-president in charge of labor relations.

Production

Industries engaged in manufacturing employ approximately one fourth of all workers in the United States. Within these organizations, large and small, are numerous opportunities for college-trained students of business. Some graduates begin as machine operators and advance to such supervisory positions as line supervisor, production manager, and plant manager. Others work in industrial engineering, quality control, production control, inventory control, shipping and traffic, warehousing, and plant maintenance.

Purchasing for a manufacturing concern utilizes many of the skills and much of the knowledge acquired by a business student. Following an initial training program, a capable individual will progress from junior buyer, buyer, assistant purchasing agent, to purchasing agent. In large businesses, purchasing agents or managers of purchasing departments may become vice-presidents who are responsible for all aspects of materials management.

Finance

The field of finance offers a wealth and variety of vocational opportunities for persons with collegiate training in business. Many financial positions require an individual who has an aptitude for and an interest in working with numbers. Integrity, accuracy, and reliability are some personal traits especially necessary for success.

Commercial banking offers many exciting opportunities for those with a broad knowledge of business activities. Advancement possibilities include cashier or controller, branch manager, and trust officer. Positions are also available in governmental banking agencies, including that of a bank examiner.

In most forms of credit granting, a credit official evaluates the creditworthiness of the applicants. Positions in the credit field include credit managers, who authorize credit transactions, and loan officers, who approve cash loans by financial organizations. Credit officials examine financial reports, interview credit references, and work

598

with credit bureaus in gathering the information which is necessary for making decisions on credit granting.

One of the largest fields of endeavor for college-trained people is insurance. Life and property and liability insurance companies are continually seeking qualified individuals who desire to become agents and brokers. Other occupations, such as underwriters, actuaries, claims adjusters, and claim examiners, are also available. Since a salesperson's earnings are based on commissions from sales, some salespersons who have developed a good clientele refuse promotions. As salespersons, they can earn more than supervisors. Others move to positions as supervisors and agency managers.

The broad area of finance also includes many other types of openings. Investment banking companies and brokerage firms employ college graduates to sell stocks and bonds, to handle accounts, and to perform tasks involving the analyses of securities. If an industrial concern operates employee insurance programs and handles its own stock and bond transfers and registration, job opportunities exist in these areas as well as in the financial department of the firm.

The field of real estate properly falls in the financial category, and both selling and property management are involved. Several types of financial institutions, such as savings and loan associations, sales finance companies, and trust companies, have openings for those individuals who have the necessary experience.

Accounting, Computer Operation, and Statistics

Accounting is a large field with three major subdivisions — public, private, and governmental. Public accounting is a profession, and the usual goal is to qualify as a Certified Public Accountant. This designation is given by all states to those who pass an examination and have gained the required experience. The method of acquiring experience is to go to work as a junior accountant with a public accounting firm expecting that progress will either lead to a partnership in the firm or the establishment of one's own office.

Private accounting embraces the accounting activities of all types of firms. A major subdivision of this classification is industrial accounting, including cost accounting for manufacturing firms. Many companies also employ internal auditors whose duties are somewhat similar to those performed by public accountants. Although many starting positions are clerical, such as handling receivables or payrolls, opportunities for advancement are excellent. Many corporation treasurers and controllers have risen to their positions from routine jobs.

Governmental accounting positions are open in numerous branches of state and federal activities. Positions in the Federal Bureau of Investigation and in the Internal Revenue Service are available to graduates of collegiate schools of business who have majored in accounting. Other agencies, such as the armed services, General Accounting Office, and Department of Agriculture, employ accountants in a civil-service position.

The widespread introduction of computers and related data processing equipment has provided a growing field for college graduates with a background in business. The growth of computerization in the office has created such opportunities as director of data processing, management operations analyst, computer programmer, business-systems coordinator, program manager, and other similar managerial positions. Some of these opportunities require mathematical abilities and aptitudes in addition to a basic knowledge of business operations.

Persons qualified as statisticians are needed by industry, research organizations, and the government. Many large firms maintain their own statistical department and recruit college graduates into this field. All types of research organizations have trained statisticians on their staffs. Numerous civil-service appointments as statisticians are available to qualified men and women. A number of beginning jobs require the services of tabulating equipment operators, investigators and interviewers, and statistical clerks. Advancement to more responsible positions may lead to such managerial posts as chief statistician or director of research.

Government Service

With the increased emphasis on governmental activities in recent years, new bureaus, administrations, departments, and commissions have been created and old ones have increased in size. Government employment has surged to the point where nearly one out of every six employed persons works for the government. Many types of employment opportunities exist in government at city, state, and national levels. Jobs often carry some form of civil-service classification. Increases in salary and grade can be earned by those whose performance on the job merits recognition.

College men and women who expect to make their careers with the federal government should take the competitive Civil Service examinations that are given periodically. Individuals who score the required grade are employed as management trainees in a manner somewhat comparable to the training programs available in many industries. Starting salaries approximate those offered by business and, whereas promotion will probably be slower than in private firms, job security is very high.

CAREER PROJECT

After studying the text and reading the Appendix on Career Opportunities, you should have a better understanding of employment opportunities in business. The purpose of this project is to acquaint you with the requirements of a specific vocation. If you have not given serious consideration to a specific career, this project should assist in your career planning. The project is divided into two assignments.

1. Identify a vocational objective which you would like to attain in 10 to 15 years.
   a. Indicate the major job duties, places of employment, training, qualifications, working conditions, and employment outlook for the selected vocational objective. Library references, such as the *Dictionary of Occupational Titles,* the *Occupational Outlook Handbook*, and the *Encyclopedia of Careers and Vocational Guidance*, should be especially helpful.
   b. Relate your personal qualifications, such as education, aptitudes, skills, and personality, to the requirements of the selected vocation.
2. Interview a person who is working in the selected career. From this interview you should learn firsthand about the requirements and responsibilities of the selected career field. Friends, professors, and members of your family may provide you with suggestions concerning whom to interview.

Prepare a concise, well-organized paper on the two assignments.

Appendix B *Pleasin' Pizza*

In the fall of 1973, Dwight Plumber, an accountant who operated his own CPA firm, was talking with Jack Ponton, who owned four Pleasin' Pizza restaurants in Lima, Ohio. Dwight and Jack belonged to the same service club in Lima, and they were long-time acquaintances. Jack indicated that each of his four restaurants in Lima was quite profitable. He stated, too, that his organization was also a franchiser and had franchised 18 Pleasin' Pizza restaurants in other Ohio, Michigan, and Indiana communities. Since Dwight had some funds which he wanted to invest, the thought of owning a franchised Pleasin' Pizza restaurant suddenly intrigued him.

INVESTIGATING FRANCHISE OPPORTUNITIES

During the next several days, Dwight made inquiries concerning a Pleasin' Pizza franchise. He learned that in its tristate area of operations the Pleasin' Pizza corporation owns and operates three strategically located food commissaries which prepare the ingredients for the pizza, spaghetti, submarine sandwiches, and other Pleasin' Pizza offerings. The pizza dough and most of the other perishable food products are frozen and shipped by refrigerated trucks to the Pleasin' Pizza restaurants. Operators of the fran-

chised restaurants buy their ingredients at wholesale from the commissaries and sell the prepared items at retail to their customers. Franchisees buy their equipment and supplies directly from Pleasin' Pizza. The company has suppliers manufacture these items to Pleasin' Pizza specifications.

Dwight was informed by a Pleasin' Pizza representative that the organization supplies considerable assistance to its franchised restaurants. The company provides services such as site location assistance, standardized accounting procedures, advertising and promotional materials, training of employees, and aid in store operations. To maintain quality standards, Pleasin' Pizza personnel are permitted during regular business hours to enter the premises of any franchised restaurant and to examine any aspects of the operation such as business records, equipment, employees, routines, and products.

One aspect of the franchise which Dwight particularly liked was the flexibility of the appearance requirements for a Pleasin' Pizza restaurant. As long as the front of the building displays a Pleasin' Pizza sign, the distinctive scarlet and gray Pleasin' Pizza colors, and a unique window trim, any size or type of structure is satisfactory. Some of the most successful restaurants are renovated gasoline service stations. All of the restaurants have a small dining area of several tables in addition to a carry-out counter.

To obtain a Pleasin' Pizza franchise, a franchisee pays an initial franchise fee of $12,000. Pleasin' Pizza recommends that a franchisee be prepared to make a minimum investment of $40,000. To compensate Pleasin' Pizza for its managerial assistance to franchisees, the company is paid 2.5 percent of annual gross sales of each franchised restaurant. In the agreement between Pleasin' Pizza and a franchisee, it is generally stipulated that the franchisee should achieve and maintain gross monthly sales of $4,000. The agreement initially is for a ten-year term and is extended at the franchiser's convenience for successive five-year periods.

While talking to Jack Ponton about the possibility of obtaining a Pleasin' Pizza franchise, Dwight was informed that the franchise for the entire metropolitan Indianapolis, Indiana, market was available. Jack indicated that the Indianapolis franchisee should be willing to establish a minimum of ten Pleasin' Pizza stores in the city over the next ten years. He envisioned that the bulk of the financing for each new store in Indianapolis would come from the retained earnings accumulated from the operation of the existing stores. Dwight became excited about the earnings potential of the Indianapolis franchise. Although Dwight did not desire to invest $40,000 of his own funds in this venture, he knew several colleagues who he thought would be willing to assist in the financing.

GETTING INVESTORS TOGETHER

Dwight contacted Betty McCuen, an attorney; Fred Fulbright, assistant plant manager of a local automotive firm; and Herb Klein, vice-president of the Lima National Bank. Dwight enthusiastically explained the financial rewards of investing in a Pleasin' Pizza franchise. When he mentioned the possibility of acquiring the franchise for Indianapolis, Betty was especially eager to join the venture. She had gone to law school there, and she believed that her knowledge of the city would be an asset to the group. She expressed the belief that the success of a franchised operation depended upon a tight, clearly drawn franchise agreement which explicitly identified the rights and responsibilities of both the franchiser and the franchisee.

Fred was somewhat skeptical of the idea. He admitted that Pleasin' Pizza was successful in Lima, but Indianapolis was a larger and more competitive market. He was concerned if a small organization, such as the proposed one, could compete effectively against the large franchised chain restaurants and strongly established local operations. He offset his fears by stating that a good location would be the key to success.

Herb believed that a Pleasin' Pizza franchise in the growing Indianapolis market had a great growth potential. Since his bank serviced the financial needs of the Pleasin' Pizza corporation, he was aware of its success in the Lima market. Although two other franchised pizza restaurants and several local pizza parlors were operating in Lima, Herb knew that the Pleasin' Pizza restaurants captured the majority of the pizza market. Herb believed that the success of the enterprise would hinge upon the employment of a competent store manager. He indicated to the group that he knew a person who might be interested in managing the Indianapolis franchise.

Earlier in the week Herb had been talking with Tom Bright, who was the manager of a branch office for a large casualty and property insurance company. Tom had expressed the desire to seek a new and more challenging assignment. Prior to his promotion last year, Tom had sold insurance for three years for this company. He had been a consistently good producer for the firm. Tom had never attended college but, since high school graduation, he had worked successively as a service station attendant, stock clerk in a local factory, house-to-house salesperson, and an automobile salesperson. Although only 26, he now supervised four individuals, two of whom were in their thirties. Herb was convinced that if Tom was provided with the proper incentives, he would be a capable manager.

ORGANIZING THE PIZZACO

After several additional meetings, the four individuals agreed to invest $10,000 each and organize the Pizzaco Corporation which would obtain the Pleasin' Pizza franchise and operate under the Pleasin' Pizza name in Indianapolis. It was decided that since this was a small organization there would be only one officer in the corporation — a treasurer who would act as chairperson at company meetings. The manager of the Indianapolis franchise would report to all four investors. All major decisions would be made by a group majority vote. If a tie vote occurred, the flip of a coin would prevail.

The investors held a discussion with Tom Bright; and as a result, he agreed to move to Indianapolis and become store manager for Pizzaco. In addition to a salary of $8,000 annually, Tom would receive an incentive payment of 3 percent of gross sales. Tom was told if he was successful he would eventually become the operating manager for 10 stores in Indianapolis.

LOCATING THE SITE

After the franchise agreement for the Indianapolis market was concluded between Pizzaco and Pleasin' Pizza, the members of the Pizzaco Corporation traveled to Indianapolis to inspect tentative sites for a res-taurant. Carl Jarvis, real estate manager for Pleasin' Pizza, had spent the previous day in Indianapolis and had located three possible sites. Several years ago Carl had worked for the police department in Indianapolis, so he was familiar with the streets and the various sections of the city.

One site was a vacant building across the street from the most popular pizza restaurant in the city. Carl theorized that some of the traffic which was generated by the other restaurant would stop at Pleasin' Pizza. He believed that the superior product of Pleasin' Pizza would result in the patrons of the other restaurant becoming customers of Pleasin' Pizza.

A second location was a vacant service station located at a busy intersection close to the downtown area. On the other three corners of this junction were two other operating service stations and a church. Carl believed that the station could be remodeled inexpensively for a carry-out and small dining-room facility. This site would attract those individuals who would stop on their way home from work and order pizzas to take home.

The third site was located on a major thoroughfare which ran through an older, middle-class neighborhood. Traffic was particularly heavy on this street during the morning and evening rush hours. The area contained many trees and hills and was very scenic. A structure which presently housed a restaurant was for lease. For ten years an elderly lady had successfully operated the Hillside House at this location. She had specialized in home cooking, and her home-made pies were known throughout the city. Since she planned to close the restaurant and retire to Florida, the building would soon be available. Carl expressed the belief that if this site was selected, the favorable image which the Hillside House had developed would be passed on to Pleasin' Pizza. He confided to the investing group that sales at this location could approach $100,000 and profits could reach $20,000 annually.

After personally examining and evaluating the potential of each site, the Pizzaco investors selected the Hillside House location. Parking was adequate, and only a reasonable investment would be required to improve the leasehold and meet the standards of appearance which were required by Pleasin' Pizza. The building contained a large dining room for 60 and a convenient counter area near the door which could be used to service the carry-out trade. With the help of Carl, a five-year lease was negotiated for the property. Pizzaco would pay a fixed rent of $600 a month plus two percent of gross sales over $80,000 a year.

LAUNCHING THE BUSINESS

Tom resigned from the insurance company and moved to Indianapolis to plan for a January, 1974, opening of the Pleasin Pizza restaurant. To promote the opening of the restaurant, Tom placed ads in the morning and evening newspapers, distributed handbills in the immediate neighborhood, rented a large floodlight, and hired a young man to dress as a clown and stand on the curb to direct traffic into the parking lot. Sales were good the first week and approached $1,000. In the next few weeks, volume peaked at $1,500 and gradually dropped back to $900 a week. For several months, weekly sales fluctuated between $900 and $1,000.

INCURRING INITIAL PROBLEMS

The investing group grew quite concerned that sales were considerably less than they had anticipated. They made several trips to Indianapolis in an attempt to find ways to increase sales. During one trip, Tom indicated that rowdy teenagers were loitering in the parking area and intimidating prospective customers. As a result of this disclosure, Pizzaco hired an off-duty police officer to patrol the parking area between 4:00 P.M. and 11:00 P.M.

On another occasion, the Pizzaco investors made an unannounced visit to the restaurant at dinner time and were unable to locate Tom. An employee thought that he was probably playing golf. When questioned later about this behavior, Tom admitted that he occasionally played golf to relieve the frustrations and tensions which were caused by his job. He indicated that in his former position he was able to get out of the office frequently, but managing a pizza restaurant was an 11:00 A.M. to 11:00 P.M. job.

After a year, it was evident that additional financing was necessary to continue operations. Expenses were exceeding gross profits. Carl Jarvis optimistically indicated to the group that within the next few months sales would increase significantly. He declared that all new operations experience a breaking-in period for about a year. He stated that, as consumers learned about the excellence of the product, sales would increase. Dwight, who had been selected treasurer of Pizzaco, asked and received from each investor an additional $5,000 investment. In return each investor acquired an unsecured promissory note.

UNDERGOING PROBLEMS WITH FRANCHISER

During the next few months, sales continued at the previously disappointing levels. When the discouraged investors asked Tom about any problems which he was having, he revealed that customers were complaining about the quality of the product. The troubled investors asked if the portion control procedure was causing difficulty. The restaurant used a portion control system which insured that each pizza received a standardized amount of cheese, mushrooms, sausage, pepperoni, and other toppings. Tom stated, however, that the problem was not with portion control, but with the quality of the frozen dough which was coming from the Pleasin' Pizza commissary. Frequently the dough would not rise properly and bake evenly.

The worried investors wrote a letter to Jack Ponton and mentioned their displeasure with the quality of the frozen dough. They also stressed that the Pleasin' Pizza organization was not providing them with any managerial assistance. Carl had visited the store only four times in the last year and another Pleasin' Pizza representative had stopped in twice.

Jack replied to the letter and apologized for any lack of cooperation by the Pleasin' Pizza personnel. He admitted the commissary had experienced some quality control problems, but he believed these were resolved. Jack explained that the commissary personnel had been unable to forecast properly the demand for pizza dough from the franchised restaurants which it served. Consequently, the commissary occasionally built up an inventory of dough which became old and caused baking problems. Jack also stated that in his organization there was a young man whom he would send to Indianapolis for several days to work with Tom. The investors were relieved by the tone of the letter as well as the promise of action.

The next week, however, Tom shattered the tranquility of the investors by calling Dwight and asking him why Jack sent a young college graduate, green as grass, to help him. Tom sharply expressed the opinion that he needed an experienced person to solve Pizzaco's operating problems, not someone generalizing from textbook theory.

During the remaining months of 1975, despite a flurry of promotional activities which included an attractive luncheon menu and evening specials, Pizzaco sales averaged under $1,000 weekly. Frequent exchanges of letters took place between Pizzaco and the Pleasin' Pizza Corporation. Problems were identified by Pizzaco and tentative solutions were proposed by Pleasin' Pizza. For Pizzaco, the opening of 10 stores, or even a second store, looked like only a remote possibility.

RESOLVING A FINANCIAL DECLINE

At the end of the second year of operation, Dwight called the investors together to discuss their financial problems. Figures B-1 and B-2 are copies of the financial statements which Dwight distributed to the Pizzaco investors. He indicated to his associates that Tom was anxious to quit. In fact, an employee had told Dwight that Tom had started selling insurance on a part-time basis and using the phone at Pleasin' Pizza to contact prospects. Dwight also confided to his colleagues that the Pleasin' Pizza Corporation informally had offered to purchase the corporation for one third of their investment of $60,000.

The other investors were perplexed by this state of affairs. Herb was uncertain about selling the operation to Pleasin' Pizza since the value of Pizzaco's assets was considerably greater than the amount offered. Betty believed that if additional financing could be secured, a new manager employed, and the lease renegotiated at a lower figure, Pizzaco could still be successful. Fred suggested that Pizzaco obtain additional financing and purchase the Pleasin' Pizza commissary. He pointed out that this action would allow Pizzaco to obtain closer control over product quality, would provide the firm with an assured source of supply, and would return the wholesaler's profits to Pizzaco. Dwight listened to each comment and rubbed his thinning hair slowly, wondering what to do.

PIZZACO CORPORATION
Income Statement
For Year Ended December 31, 1975

Revenue from sales:		
Gross sales	$51,490	
Less cost of goods sold	24,715	
Gross profit on sales		$26,775
Operating expenses:		
Salaries and wages	$16,477	
Operating supplies	1,147	
Rent	7,200	
Utilities	627	
Advertising and promotion	5,140	
Taxes other than income	636	
Licenses and permits	515	
Insurance	1,305	
Franchise royalties	1,287	
Total depreciation expense	2,223	
Amortization of franchise contract	1,200	
Miscellaneous operating expense	548	
Total operating expenses		38,305
Loss from operations		(11,530)
Other expenses:		
Interest expense		1,600
Net loss		($13,130)

Figure B-1   **Income Statement for Pizzaco Corporation**

PIZZACO CORPORATION
Balance Sheet
December 31, 1975

Assets

Current assets:

Cash	$ 1,010	
Food inventory	730	
Supplies	280	
Prepaid expenses	1,220	
Total current assets		$ 3,240

Fixed assets:

Furniture and fixtures	$ 5,280		
Less accumulated depreciation	1,056	$ 4,224	
Equipment	$ 8,930		
Less accumulated depreciation	1,786	7,144	
Location sign	$ 6,110		
Less accumulated depreciation	1,222	4,888	
Leasehold improvements	$12,270		
Less accummulated depreciation	2,454	9,816	
Total fixed assets			26,072

Other assets:

Corporate organization expense		$ 617	
Franchise fee paid	$12,000		
Less amortization	2,400	9,600	
Total other assets			10,217

Total assets	$39,529

Liabilities

Current liabilities:

Accounts payable, Pleasin' Pizza	$ 4,115	
Accounts payable, other	472	
Taxes payable other than income	632	
Total current liabilities		$ 5,219

Long-term liabilities:

Notes payable, investors	20,000

Total liabilities	$25,219

Capital

Capital stock	$40,000	
Deficit (Note A)	(25,690)	
Total capital		$14,310

Total liabilities and capital	$39,529

Note A: For 1974 the net loss was $12,560, and for 1975 the net loss was $13,130.

Figure B-2   ***Balance Sheet for Pizzaco Corporation***

QUESTIONS

1. Since there are only four investors in Pizzaco, is the corporation the best form of ownership for the franchise?
2. Is a committee-type organization with only a treasurer as a corporate officer satisfactory for Pizzaco or should another form of organizational structure be used?
3. Does the lease of the Hillside House location insure that Pizzaco will have a certain volume of business? What are the differences between these two types of restaurant operations?
4. When it became necessary to raise an additional $20,000, were any sources of capital available other than the owners of the corporation?
5. What type of procedures should be initiated by Pleasin' Pizza to guarantee better quality pizza dough from its commissary?
6. What are the most important factors for success in a franchised operation?
7. What are the major causes of Pizzaco's inability to operate profitably?
8. Carefully evaluate the following alternative solutions to Pizzaco's difficulties and then recommend your solution:
   a. Should they sell out to Pleasin' Pizza for one third of their original investment of $60,000?
   b. Should they get a new manager, renegotiate the lease, and secure additional financing?
   c. Should Pizzaco obtain additional financing and purchase the Pleasin' Pizza commissary?

Index

as a social insititution, 14
commercial, 16
government regulation of, 35
industrial, 16
internationalization of, 578
large, 16
response to social environment, 44
small, 16; decline of, 29
business crimes, 495
business cycle, 31:
depression, 31
prosperity, 31
recession, 31
business decisions, and taxation,
545–547
business environment:
industrial revolution, 23
the land and people, 22
business ethics, 53
business interruption insurance,
415
business law, 491
business location, influence of
state and local taxes on, 542
business logistics, 323
business ownership, influence of
federal taxes on, 546
business paper, 198: as negotiable instrument, 499
business responsibility:
corporate and personal philanthropy, 42
pursuit of profit, 41
self-interest, 41
traditional, 41
business statistics, 480; interpretation of, 482–483
business trust, 76
buyer, 319
buying:
hand-to-mouth versus for-
ward, 311
versus manufacturing, 311
buying behavior, 156
buying cooperatives, 97
buying motive, 156
bylaws, 85

C

calculator, electronic, 458
callable bond, 359
callable preferred stock, 361
call price, 359; of stock, 361

calls, 401
capital, 10, 346:
circulating, 346
debt, 355
equity, 437
fixed, 346
rate of net income on, 446
working, 347
capital crunch, 585
capital funds, 10
capital goods, 10, 165
capitalism, 3:
basic freedoms of, 6
competition in, 11
distribution of goods in, 11
laissez-faire, 5
modified, 5
other key factors in, 10
price in, 11
production in, 10
profit in, 13
risk in, 12
role of individuals in, 7
classical theory of, 4
capitalistic ideology, 17
capital-labor ratio, 339
capital shortage, 585
capital statement, 440
carload lot (CL), 322
Carnegie, Andrew, 42
cartels, 578
case law. See common law.
cash-and-carry wholesaler, 176
cash discount, 216
cash dividend, 374
cashless society, 583
cash surrender value, 423
caveat emptor, 22, 225
Celler-Kefauver Act of 1950, 514
Center for Auto Safety, 236
Center for Study of Responsive
Law, 236
Central American Common Market (CACM), 564
central buying, 181
centralized management, 109
central processing unit (CPU),
453
certificate, trust, 76
certificate of convenience and
necessity, 524
certified public accountant, 431
chain of command, 106
chain store, 180–181
channels of distribution, 171:
decisions in selecting, 172

for consumer goods, 171
for industrial goods, 172
charge account, 348
chart:
bar, 482
circular, 482
control, 483
flow, 459
line (or curve), 482
pie diagram, 482
statistical map, 482
charter, 82; meeting requirements for, 93
Chartered Life Underwriter
(CLU), 412
Chartered Property and Casualty
Underwriter (CPCU), 412
chattel mortgage bond, 358
check, 355
checking account, 355
checkoff, 291
Chicago Board Options Ex-
change (CBOE), 401
Chicago Board of Trade, 401
chief executive officer (CEO), 86

Child Protection and Toy Safety
Act, 516
circulating capital, 346
city council, as public utility regulatory agency, 521
Civil Aeronautics Board (CAB),
527
civil law, 492
civil rights:
minority groups, 26
women, 26
Civil Rights Act of 1964, 26, 263
class-action lawsuits, 231
Clayton Act of 1914, 513–514:
amendments to, 515
unlawful practices under, 513
Clean Air Act (as amended,
1970), 48
close, 191:
assumptive, 192
choice, 192
close corporation, 95
closed-end investment company,
365
closed-loop control, 339
closed shop, 290
closed-system organization, 114
coalition bargaining, 292–293

Coalition of Black Trade Unionists (CBTU), 303

income summary. *See* income statement.

income tax:
  calculation of, 541
  corporation, 542
  federal, 540
  state and local, 535

incorporated businesses:
  cooperatives, 97
  corporations, 80–95
  credit unions, 98
  mutual companies, 99
  savings and loan associations, 99

incorporation fee, 90

indenture, 356

independents, 180

index number, 481

induction, 252

industrial businesses, 16

industrial goods, 165:
  capital goods, 165
  channels for, 172
  MRO items, 165
  unprocessed and processed materials, 165

industrial integration, 563

industrial life insurance, 424

industrial revolution, 23; laissez-faire, 23

industrial union, 292

industrial wastes, 49:
  quality of, 50
  quantity of, 49

industry (or market) forecast, 474, 476:
  expert opinion, 476
  market survey, 476
  methods of making, 475–476
  sales force opinion, 476

inelasticity of demand, 219

inflation, 31, 279:
  double-digit, 279
  features of, 31
  and unemployment, 280
  and wages, 279–280

informal organization, 115, 117

information, 452:
  competitive, 126
  environmental, 126
  internal, 126
  generation of, by computers, 465

information processing, 452

information revolution, 579

information utility, 144

informative label, 169

inheritance tax, 538

injunction, 295

inland marine insurance, 418; personal property floater, 418

innovating, 128

innovistic competition, 12

input, 454

insolvency, 383

inspection, 337; in quality control, 337

institutional advertising, 193; publicity, 193

institutional discrimination, 262

institutional management, 120

insurable risks, characteristics of, 410

insurance, 408:
  accident and sickness, 412
  automobile, 415
  business interruption, 415
  burglary, robbery and theft, 417
  credit life, 425
  depreciation, 415
  fidelity bond, 419
  fire, 413–414
  health, 412
  inland marine, 418
  liability, 419
  life, 412, 420–426
  marine, 418
  no-fault, 417
  ocean marine, 418
  on owners or executives, 425
  personal property floater, 418
  retirement and pension plans, 426
  surety bond, 419
  unemployment, 539
  workmen's compensation, 417

insurance company, 365; private, 412

insurance policy, 408

intangible assets, 439:
  copyright, 439
  goodwill, 439
  patent, 439

intangibles, 504

integrated data processing (IDP), 460

integrated wholesaling, 177

integration:
  economic, 563
  industrial, 563

interest selectivity, 194

interlocking directorate, 513

intermediate credit, 350

intermittent process, 330

Internal Revenue Service, 544

International Bank for Reconstruction and Development (IBRD), 560

International Federation of Chemical and General Workers, 304

International Metalworkers Federation, 303

International Monetary Fund (IMF), 560

international trade, 551

interpersonal communications, 135:
  barriers to, 136
  direct, 135
  feedback, 135
  one-way, 136
  two-way, 136

Interstate Commerce Act of 1887, 526

Interstate Commerce Commission (ICC), 230, 396, 526, 528

interurbia, 24

invasion of privacy, 466

inventory, 319:
  in allocation of funds, 377
  average, 318
  FIFO, 377
  LIFO, 377
  as security for loan, 353
  maximum, 318
  minimum, 318
  safety stock, 318

inventory control, 317–319

inventory cycle, 317

inventory financing, 353

inventory turnover, 445

investment banking company, 362–364

investment company, 364:
  closed-end, 365
  mutual funds, 365
  open-end, 365
  portfolio, 364

investments, 439

investor, 393

involuntary bankruptcy, 505

involuntary termination, 256:
  discharge, 256
  layoff, 256

full participation plan, 273
group incentive plan, 274
1 for 1 plan, 274
wage legislation, 277–279
wage payment:
  bonus payment, 275
  commission payment, 276
  methods of, 274–277
  piece-rate payment, 275
  shift premium plan, 275
  straight salary, 274
  time wages, 274
wages, 268:
  and inflation, 279–280
  bargaining theory of, 269
  economic theories of, 268–270
  factors determining, 270
  marginal productivity theory,
    268
  money wages and real wages,
    279
  reasons for divergent, 270–272
  standard of living theory, 269
Wagner Act, 298
wagon (or truck) distributor, 176
walkout, 293
warehouse receipt, 353
warrant, 371
warranty:
  express, 503
  implied, 503
waterways:
  fishyback freight, 323
  in materials movement, 323
welfare programs:
  Medicare plan, 27
  social, 27
what the traffic will bear, 212

Wheeler-Lea Act of 1938, 202,
  514
whole life policy, 421
Wholesale Price Index (WPI),
  221
wholesaler:
  cash-and-carry, 176
  classified by function per-
    formed, 176
  classified by line of goods han-
    dled, 175–176
  desk jobber, 176
  drop shipper, 176
  functional middleman, 176
  general line, 175
  general merchandise, 175
  limited function, 176
  merchant, 175
  rack jobber, 176
  rack merchandiser, 176
  service, 176
  services rendered to manufac-
    turers by, 174
  services rendered to retailers
    by, 175
  specialty, 176
  wagon (or truck) distributor,
    176
wholesaling, 173; integrated, 177
wildcat strike, 294
Williams-Steiger Act, 257, 258
women:
  affirmative action program re-
    quirements for, 264
  emergence in labor unions,
    303
  occupational discrimination,
    259

occupational segregation, 259
  in work force, 258–261
women's liberation movement,
  26
women unionists, 303
Wool Products Labeling Act of
  1939, 515
work environment:
  employee services, 257
  minorities in, 261–263
  as personnel function, 257–258
  safety and health, 257
  women in, 258–261
workers, role in capitalism, 8, 9
worker training at the operator
  level, 253:
  apprentice system, 254
  company school, 253
  sponsor system, 254
  vestibule school, 253
work groups, 115
work improvements, 331
working capital, 347
workmen's compensation insurance, 417
World Bank, 560
world trade, international instruments for, 559–562
world trade communities, 564–
  565

Y, Z

yellow-dog contract, 295
zero discharge, 50
zero population growth (ZPG),
  572
zoning ordinances, 518